Contents

List of Maps

About the Author

Margie Rynn has lived in France for 8 years, during which time she updated the 2002 edition of *Frommer's Paris from $80 a Day,* edited a newsletter on the ozone hole for the United Nations Environmental Program, and wrote several articles for *Budget Travel Magazine.* She has also written for *Time Out New York, Yoga Journal,* and *The Amicus Journal,* the magazine of the National Resources Defense Council. In a previous New York life, she acted in a Broadway play and performed her own one-woman show at HERE performance space. Margie is married to a kind and understanding Frenchman and they have a lovely 6-year-old son.

Acknowledgments

A heartfelt thank you to *Oliver* and *Julien* for their supreme patience during the many months it took to write this book.

An Invitation to the Reader

In researching this book, we discovered many wonderful places—hotels, restaurants, shops, and more. We're sure you'll find others. Please tell us about them, so we can share the information with your fellow travelers in upcoming editions. If you were disappointed with a recommendation, we'd love to know that, too. Please write to:

Pauline Frommer's Paris, 2nd Edition
Wiley Publishing, Inc. • 111 River St. • Hoboken, NJ 07030-5774

An Additional Note

Please be advised that travel information is subject to change at any time—and this is especially true of prices. We therefore suggest that you write or call ahead for confirmation when making your travel plans. The authors, editors, and publisher cannot be held responsible for the experiences of readers while traveling. Your safety is important to us, however, so we encourage you to stay alert and be aware of your surroundings. Keep a close eye on cameras, purses, and wallets, all favorite targets of thieves and pickpockets.

Star Ratings, Icons & Abbreviations

Every restaurant, hotel, and attraction is rated with stars ✭, indicating our opinion of that facility's desirability; this relates not to price, but to the value you receive for the price you pay. The stars mean:

No stars: Good
✭ Very good
✭✭ Great
✭✭✭ Outstanding! A must!

Accommodations within each neighborhood are listed in ascending order of cost, starting with the cheapest and increasing to the occasional "splurge." Each hotel review is preceded by one, two, three, or four dollar signs, indicating the price range per double room. Restaurants work on a similar system, with dollar signs indicating the price range per three-course meal.

Accommodations		**Dining**	
€	Up to 85€ per night	€	Main courses for 9€ or less
€€	86€ to 115€ per night	€€	Main courses for 10€ to 14€
€€€	116€ to 135€ per night	€€€	Main courses for 15€ to 22€
€€€€	Over 135€ per night	€€€€	Main courses for 23€ and over

In addition, we've included a kids icon 🧒 to denote attractions, restaurants, and lodgings that are particularly child friendly.

Frommers.com

Now that you have this guidebook to help you plan a great trip, visit our website at **www.frommers.com** for additional travel information on more than 4,000 destinations. We update features regularly to give you instant access to the most current trip-planning information available. At Frommers.com, you'll find scoops on the best airfares, lodging rates, and car rental bargains. You can even book your travel online through our reliable travel booking partners. Other popular features include:

- Online updates of our most popular guidebooks
- Vacation sweepstakes and contest giveaways
- Newsletters highlighting the hottest travel trends
- Podcasts, interactive maps, and up-to-the-minute events listings
- Opinionated blog entries by Arthur Frommer himself
- Online travel message boards with featured travel discussions

I started traveling with my guidebook-writing parents, Arthur Frommer and Hope Arthur, when I was just 4 months old. To avoid lugging around a crib, they would simply swaddle me and stick me in an open drawer for the night. For half of my childhood, my home was a succession of hotels and B&Bs throughout Europe, as we dashed around every year to update *Europe on $5 a Day* (and then $10 a day, and then $20 . . .).

We always traveled on a budget, staying at the mom-and-pop joints Dad featured in the guide, getting around by public transportation, eating where the locals ate. And that's still the way I travel today, because I learned—from the master—that these types of vacations not only save money but offer a richer, deeper experience of the culture. You spend time in local neighborhoods, meeting and talking with the people who live there. For me, making friends and having meaningful exchanges is always the highlight of my journeys—and the main reason I decided to become a travel writer and editor as well.

I've conceived these books as budget guides for a new generation. They have all the outspoken commentary and detailed pricing information of the Frommer's guides, but they take bargain hunting into the 21st century, with more information on using the Internet and air/hotel packages to save money. Most important, we stress "alternative accommodations"—apartment rentals, private B&Bs, religious retreat houses, and more—not simply to save you money, but to give you a more authentic experience in the places you visit.

A highlight of each guide is the chapter that deals with the "other" side of the destinations, the one visitors rarely see. These sections will actively immerse you in the life that residents enjoy. The result, I hope, is a valuable new addition to the world of guidebooks. Please let us know how we've done! E-mail me at editor@frommers.com.

Happy traveling!

Pauline Frommer

Pauline Frommer

THE VERY WORD "PARIS" CONJURES UP SUCH A POTENT BREW OF IMAGES and ideas that it is sometimes hard to find the meeting point between myth and reality. There is no doubt that it is a magnificent city, worthy of all the superlatives that have been heaped upon it for centuries. Its graceful streets, soaked in history, really are as elegant as they say; its monuments and museums really are extraordinary; and a slightly world-weary, *fin de siècle* grandeur really is part of day-to-day existence.

But this is also a city where flesh-and-blood people live and work, where wheels turn, and there is a palpable urban buzz. Museums are lovely, but no one wants to live in one. Paris is so much more than a beautiful assemblage of buildings and monuments; it is the pulsing heart of the French nation. This is no exaggeration: Not only is it the capital of the country, if you include the suburbs, it is the home of 19% of the population. The majority of all French jobs are to be found here; Paris is France's financial, artistic, and cultural center. In short, in terms of importance on a national scale, Paris is a little like New York, Washington, D.C., and Los Angeles all rolled into one.

Not all that long ago, Paris was not only the navel of France but the shining beacon of Europe. All the continent's greatest minds and talents clamored to come here: The city seduced Nietzsche, Chopin, Picasso, and Wilde, just to name a few. Since the end of World War II, the city has lost some of its global luster—other countries and other capitals have since stolen a lot of its thunder, and there is a certain wistfulness in the air. If you speak with Parisians, you'll hear a lot of moaning about France's place in the world and whether or not globalization is a good thing; behind the hand-wringing are some very legitimate concerns about a disappearing way of life.

> 66 *When Paris sneezes, Europe catches cold.* 99
>
> —Prince Metternich (1773–1859), Austrian statesman

But despite these concerns, or maybe because of them, Paris is still a bastion of the best of French culture. The culinary legacy alone is enough to fill several books; you can eat your way to nirvana in the city's restaurants, gourmet food stores, and bakeries (see chapter 4). The architecture ranges from the lavish opulence of **place Vendôme** (p. 149) to the contemporary madness of **Musée du Quai Branly** (p. 147). And speaking of museums, some of the world's greatest are here, including the legendary **Louvre** (p. 138). And let's not even get into the city's concert halls, nightspots, parks, gardens, and cafes—at least not just yet. In the pages to come, you'll find ample resources for the above and more. Even if you have time to see only a fraction of what you'd like to see, in the long run, it really won't matter; what counts is that you'll have been to Paris, sampled its wonders, and savored the experience—and that counts for a lot.

SIGHTS YOU'VE GOTTA SEE, THINGS YOU'VE GOTTA DO

Fortunately, the most obligatory Parisian sight, the **Eiffel Tower** (p. 128), is visible from many points in the city, so you don't really have to go out of your way to see it, though a trip to the top up to one of the observation decks really is a memorable experience. The cathedral of **Notre-Dame de Paris** (p. 129), one of Europe's most splendid examples of Gothic architecture, is a must-see, as are the exquisite stained-glass windows of the nearby **Sainte Chapelle** (p. 133), a small, jewel-like church tucked into the buildings of the Palais de Justice. The **Seine** (see Walking Tours 1, p. 229), the river that divides the city into the Right and Left Banks, is an essential reference point for your visit, and a walk along its banks, or at least across one of its more lovely bridges, like the **Pont Neuf** or the **Pont des Arts,** is one of the finest ways of really "seeing" the heart of the city. A visit to at least one of the city's majestic places, or plazas, like the **place de la Concorde** (p. 134), or the **place des Vosges** (p. 147) is not just a treat for the eyes, but a trip back in time, to the days when kings used the urban environment as a way of expressing their power.

But Paris is not all monarchs and might, as a trip to **Montmartre** (see Walking Tour 3, p. 245) illustrates: This historically working-class, villagelike neighborhood nurtured some of the finest artists and writers of the late 19th and early 20th centuries. And one shouldn't leave Paris without at least a short ramble in one of its famous gardens, such as the strictly symmetrical **Tuileries Gardens** (p. 213), a masterpiece by legendary garden designer André Le Nôtre, or the **Jardin du Luxembourg** (p. 213), a stunning ensemble of fountains and flowerbeds.

THE CITY'S BEST MUSEUMS

The density of museums per capita is one of the highest in Europe. Paris has some 130 museums, many of which are world class, including. of course, the fairest of them all: the **Louvre** (p. 138). You could probably spend your entire trip here and not have seen all there is to see, but that would be a shame, since so many other wonderful museums just wait to bewitch you. The **Musée d'Orsay** (p. 143) has the best assemblage of Impressionist art on the planet; the **Musée Rodin** (p. 145) not only has a fabulous collection of the great sculptor's works, but one of the prettiest gardens in town; and the **Musée Jacquemart-André** (p. 145) offers a chance to revel in a stunning assortment of 18th-century French art and furniture, as well as an opportunity to visit a 19th-century mansion with its original decoration. The entire history of Paris is on display at the **Musée Carnavalet** (p. 151), housed in another fabulous mansion, this time a Renaissance hôtel particulier in the Marais; nearby another stately hôtel holds the **Musée Picasso** (p. 148), perhaps the finest collection of the artist's work ever assembled. They can't seem to stop building museums here—in 2006 the oddly shaped **Musée du Quai Branly** (p. 149) opened its extraordinary collection of traditional arts from Africa, the Pacific Islands, Asia, and the Americas to the public, and in 2007 the grandiose **Cité de l'Architecture et du Patrimoine** (p. 158) burst on the scene with its stunning assortment of models, murals, plans, and plaster casts of some of France's most famous structures.

UNCOMMON LODGINGS

Many tourists feel the need to shoehorn themselves into cramped hotel rooms in the very center of town, but because Paris is a relatively small city, there is actually no harm in staying a little farther out, where you'll find higher quality lodgings at lower prices. And by "lodgings" we're not necessarily talking about hotels—some of the best places to stay in Paris are in private apartments, hundreds of which can be rented out by the week. An airy artist's loft with original artwork near the Bastille that can accommodate a family of four or more could cost you less than a couple of tiny hotel rooms near the Louvre. Your choices are many: You could camp out in a one-bedroom flat with exposed beams in the middle of the Latin Quarter, or rent an enormous room with sky-high ceilings and a private terrace in a mansion in the Marais, or cuddle up in an antique-filled bedroom in a 19th-century town house near the Grands Boulevards. You'll find resources for finding these sorts of alternative accommodations in chapter 3.

If you'd prefer to stay in a hotel, Paris has no lack of options, though I encourage you to stay away from the cookie-cutter chain hotel lodgings and opt for more original accommodations that reflect both the personality of the owners and of the city itself. At family-run hotels like the **Hôtel Vivienne** (p. 41), **Hôtel Jeanne d'Arc** (p. 43), and the **Hôtel de l'Espèrance** (p. 51), you'll enjoy a high comfort level at rates that are largely under 100€ per night. Small, off-beat hotels like **Hôtel Eldorado** (p. 67) and **Hôtel les Degrés de Notre Dame** (p. 45) offer unique decors created by local artists—lush colors, unusual mosaics, and interesting art objects are all part of the design. The owners of **New Orient Hôtel** (p. 60) and **Hôtel des Bains** (p. 64) are both inveterate flea-market browsers; the former have personally refurbished the antique furniture in the rooms, while the latter uses unique objects from the local open-air arts and crafts market to perk up the decor.

For a sense of days of old (without old-fashioned inconveniences), **Hôtel St-Jacques** (p. 49), **Hôtel Grandes Ecoles** (p. 50), and **Ermitage Hôtel** (p. 68) have all carefully and tastefully conserved historic detailing and decor. Some hotels manage to seamlessly blend the new and the old: **Hôtel Lindbergh** (p. 54), for example, has sleek, modern rooms designed by architect Jean-Philippe Nuel, with a vaguely Art Deco feel (and most doubles are only 116€).

For those looking for a clean, comfortable place to sleep that will go easy on the pocketbook, the **Tiquetonne Hôtel** (p. 41), **Hôtel du Séjour** (p. 42), **Port Royal Hôtel** (p. 50), and **Perfect Hôtel** (p. 61) are all excellent options, though you should be willing to forgo certain kinds of amenities, which may include elevators or in-room toilets. A step or two higher on the comfort scale, **Hôtel Chopin** (p. 61), **Hôtel du Champ de Mars** (p. 56), and **Hôtel Résidence Alhambra** (p. 62) are also terrific values.

DINING FOR ALL TASTES

As mentioned above, Paris is the promised land for traveling gourmets. What's more, you won't have to spend a fortune to eat well here—though you will need to know where to go. Do take advantage of the recent "neo-bistrot" trend; a bevy of top chefs, tired of the pressure of haute-cuisine, have opened dressed-down bistros where they can cook as they like (and where you can eat without getting a second mortgage). **Le Comptoir du Relais** (Yves de Camdeborde, p. 95) and

Café Constant (Christian Constant, p. 100) are two excellent examples; other good ways to eat gourmet and let your bank account live to tell the tale include the Delacourcelle brothers' **Le Pré Verre** (p. 88) and Michel Rostang's **Bistrot d'à Coté** (p. 106).

But a good restaurant doesn't have to have a famous chef's name attached to it; you can eat extremely well at some lesser known places like **La Robe et Le Palais** (p. 77), **Le Café des Musées** (p. 86), and **Chez Michel** (p. 108). Sometimes the decor is almost more of an event than the food; for the full-on Belle-Epoch experience, try **Le Grand Colbert** (p. 82), which had a supporting role in the film *Something's Gotta Give.*

Personally, I have a thing for tiny, mom-and-pop operations—there's a certain authenticity in these establishments that simply can't be found anywhere else. **Le Rendez-Vous du Marché** (p. 94), **Chez Nenesse** (p. 87), and **Le Temps des Cerises** (p. 87) are all good examples of this genre.

Finally, Paris is home to some of the best North African (Moroccan, Algerian, and Tunisian) restaurants in France, from the elegant **Mansouria** (p. 113) to the funky but fabulous **Chez Omar** (p. 85).

THE FINEST "OTHER" EXPERIENCES

Looking for ways to get off the heavily trampled tourist track? Put on a pair of in-line skates and skate through the city with 10,000 or so other Parisians when **Pari Roller** (p. 207) takes to the streets on Friday nights. Or dance to the rhythms of Argentine Tango on the banks of the Seine on a moonlit summer night during **Paris Danse en Seine** (p. 203). Learn about French wine in a nonthreatening environment (and in English, yet) at **Ô Chateau** (p. 200) with Olivier Magny, a young French sommelier. Now that you know about wine, learn about cooking at the **Atelier des Chefs** (p. 199). Don't feel like cooking? Sign up for dinner at **Jim Haynes'** (p. 208), an American expatriate who has been welcoming strangers to his Sunday dinners since the days when bell-bottoms were considered a new innovation. For a more dressy—or make that dressed-up—party, drop by the **Taverne Medievale** (p. 209), where the Knights of St-Sabin welcome anyone dressed up in medieval garb for feasting, music, and fun, in an ancient, but nicely renovated, stone cellar. Take a tour of a working tapestry factory that has been around since the days of Louis XIV, the **Manufacture des Gobelins** (p. 204), or visit artists' studios during **Portes Ouvertes** (p. 205).

These and other out-of-the-ordinary activities are detailed in chapter 6, where you'll find many opportunities to see sides of the city that outsiders rarely have a chance to see, and, most importantly, to encounter real, live Parisians.

2 Lay of the Land

The geography of Paris, the very special neighborhoods & ways of getting from place to place

ONE OF THE NICE THINGS ABOUT PARIS IS THAT IT'S RELATIVELY SMALL. IT'S not a sprawling megalopolis like Tokyo or London, in fact, Paris *intramuros,* or inside the long-gone city walls, numbers a mere 2.2 million habitants, and, excluding the large exterior parks of Bois de Vincinnes and the Bois de Boulogne, measures about 87 sq. km (34 sq. miles). (The suburbs, on the other hand, are sprawling, but chances are you won't be spending much, if any, time there.) So getting around is not difficult, provided you have a general sense of where things are.

The city is vaguely egg shaped, with the Seine cutting a wide upside-down "U" shaped arc through the middle. The northern half is known as the **Right Bank,** and the southern, the **Left Bank.** To the uninitiated, the only way to remember is to face west, or downstream, so that the Right Bank will be to your right, and the Left to your left. To add to the confusion, many guidebooks try to give each bank a particular personality, such as the Right Bank is ritzy and the Left Bank is intellectual, which doesn't really work because the neighborhoods vary radically on each side of the river.

If you can't get your banks straight, don't worry, because most Parisians don't talk in terms of Right or Left Bank, but in terms of ***arrondissements*** or districts. The city is neatly split up into 20 official arrondissements, which spiral out from the center of the city. So the lower the number, the closer you'll be to the center, and as the numbers go up, you'll head toward the outer limits. The lower numbered arrondissements also correspond to some of the oldest parts of the city, like the Louvre and the Ile de la Cité (1st arrondissement), or the Marais (3rd and 4th arrondissements). Though their borders don't always correspond to historical neighborhoods, they do chop the city up into easily digestible chunks, so if you know what arrondissement your destination is in, your chances of finding it easily go way up. Your chances will be even better if you have a good map. Even if you're only in the city for a week, it's worthwhile to invest in a purse-size map book (ask for a "Paris par Arrondissement" at bookstores or larger newsstands), which costs around 8€. The book should include a street index and a detailed set of maps by arrondissement—one of the best is called "Le Petit Parisien," which includes separate Métro, bus, and street maps for each district. To get a general sense of where the arrondissements are, see our map on p. 8.

Paris is old, so the logic of its **streets and avenues** is often as contorted as the city's history. That said, there are some major boulevards that function as reference points. On the Left Bank, boulevard St-Michel acts as a more or less north–south axis, with boulevard St-Germain cutting a vaguely east–west semicircle close to the city center, and boulevard Montparnasse cutting a larger one farther out. On the Right Bank, boulevard de Sebastopol runs north–south, with rue de Rivoli crossing east–west near the river. As rue de Rivoli heads east, it turns into rue de St-Antoine; to the west, jogs around the place de la Concorde, and becomes the Champs Elysées. Farther north, a network of wide boulevards crisscrosses the area, including boulevards Haussmann, Capuccines, and Lafayette.

There are also several enormous star-shaped traffic roundabouts, where several large avenues converge: On the Left Bank place Denfert-Rochereau and place d'Italie are major convergence points; on the Right Bank place de la Bastille and place de la République reign to the east, and place de Charles de Gaulle (also called Etoile), home of the Arc de Triomphe, commands to the west.

GETTING AROUND WITHIN THE CITY

Since the distances are not enormous in Paris, one of your main modes of transportation will probably be your feet. That said, your feet will see a lot of action, and there is no need to punish them needlessly, particularly since there is an excellent public transportation system at your disposal.

THE METRO (SUBWAY)

The city's first Métro, or subway, was at the apex of high-tech when it was inaugurated on July 19, 1900, and over a century later, it still functions very well. Its biggest problem is not actually technical but political: Subway workers are fond of strikes (*grèves*) and periodically instigate slowdowns or complete shutdowns of a few lines. Usually, strikes are merely annoying and most of the time your route will not be affected, though your trip might take a little longer than normal. If you see the euphemism "Movement Social" on the TV monitor as you enter the station, read the message carefully to see if your line is involved (low groans and cursing by ticket holders is also a good indicator of strike activity).

Strikes aside, the Métro is usually efficient and civilized, especially if you avoid rush hour (7:30–9:30am and 6–8pm). It's generally safe at night (although you might want to think twice about using it to get to more isolated parts of the city), and you don't need to worry about taking it at 2am because you can't. Alas, when people dolefully talk about "The Last Métro," they're usually not discussing a wonderful movie by François Truffaut. Instead, they're referring to a sad fact of Parisian life: Your evening out must be carefully timed so that you can run to the station before the trains shut down between midnight and 1am. To ease your pain, the transit authority has recently added an extra hour on weekends, so now the Métro closes at 2am on Friday, Saturday, and pre-holiday evenings. Each line shuts down at a slightly different time; you can get exact times either at the station or on the RATP site, www.ratp.fr. The suburban trains (the RER, see below) close down around the same time (without the weekend bonus hour).

Most Métro lines ramble across the city in anything but a straight line, connecting at strategic points where you can transfer from one to the other. A map is

Paris Arrondissements

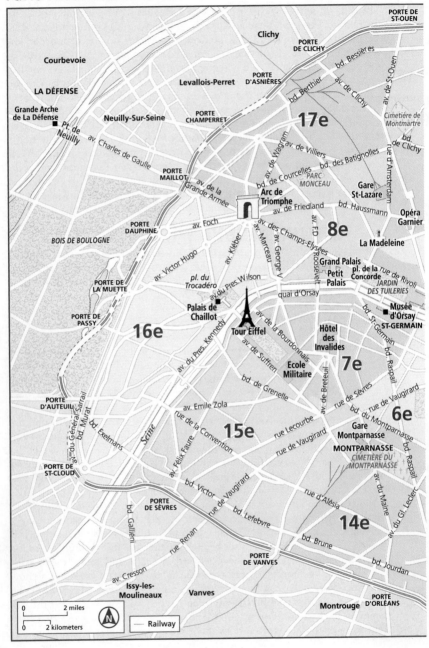

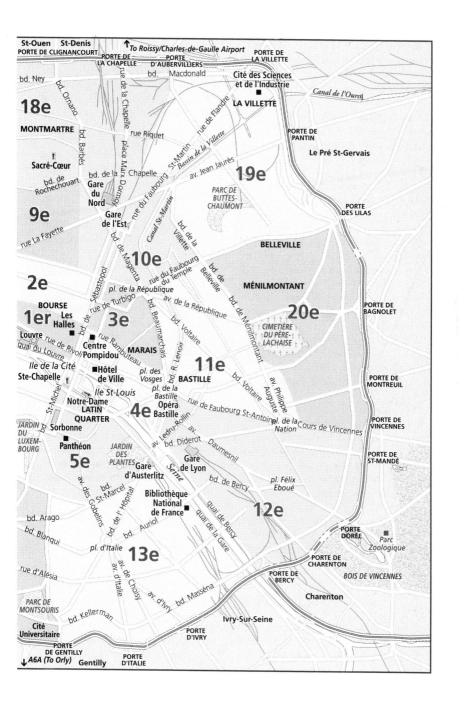

essential (pick one up at any ticket window). The key is to know both the number of the line and its final destination. So if you are on the no. 1 line (direction La Défense) and you want to transfer at the enormous Châtelet station to get to St-Michel, at Châtelet you'll need to doggedly follow the signs to the no. 4, direction Porte d'Orléans. Lines are also color coded, which helps when you're trying to figure out the signs. The train cars themselves are narrow but clean and clatter along the tracks at a good clip.

There are two more modern lines that you should know about, which are both convenient and more comfortable than others. The first is actually the oldest Métro line, the no. 1, which was completely overhauled in the 1990s and fitted with sleek, modern trains. Crossing Paris from stem to stern, east to west along the Right Bank of the Seine, this line is very handy for visiting many sites along the river. The second, no. 14, otherwise known as the Méteor, is the only express Métro line. It's one of my faves, as not only is it clean and comfortable, with space-age stations, but it can whiz you from Gare de Lyon to Gare St-Lazare in about 7 minutes.

Otherwise, your only express choice is the **RER** (pronounced "ehr-euh-ehr"), the suburban trains that dash through the city making limited stops. The three most tourist friendly lines are the A, which crosses the city east to west, the B, which crosses the city north to south (this is the line that goes to the Charles de Gaulle airport), and the C, which runs along the left bank of the Seine. The down sides are: (a) they don't run as often as the Métro, (b) they're a lot less pleasant, and (c) they're hard to figure out since they run on a different track system and the same lines can have multiple final destinations. *Important:* Make sure to hold on to your ticket as you'll need it to get out of the turnstile on the way out.

THE LOWDOWN ON PUBLIC TRANSIT FARES & PASSES

Like everything that has to do with French public administration, the fare system, to the uninitiated, looks terribly complicated. In fact, it's pretty straightforward, once you've learned the lingo. All tickets are good on the bus or Métro or RER (within Paris), or even the new tramway that's beginning to circle the perimeter of Paris. When buying your tickets, you'll need to have a basic understanding of zones. As mentioned above, Paris itself is relatively small, but the suburbs are huge. To deal with the dimensions, the transit authorities have divided the region up into zones, which spread out from the center in concentric circles; Paris within its city limits *(intramuros)* is zones 1 and 2. Most tourists will not need to worry about zones 3 through 8, unless they've got friends in the suburbs.

A Lesson in Transit Savvy

Even though you'll only need to validate your ticket on entering the Métro (or bus, or RER), make sure to hold on to it, as you can get fined if you don't have one on hand. Also, if you're transferring to the RER, you'll need to pass your ticket through more turnstiles.

INDIVIDUAL TICKETS

A regular ticket for Paris (Zones 1 and 2, now called a "t+") is 1.60€. They're also sold in bunches of 10, called a carnet (car-nay) for 11.40€, a significant reduction. Children 4 to 9 years old pay half price; children under four ride free. If you're heading out to one of the outlying regions, purchase a separate ticket. This ticket includes unlimited transfers during a one and one-half hour period between buses, or between buses and tramways, but *not* between Métro and buses or Métro and tramway. Drat.

PASSES

The weekly and monthly pass system has been overhauled and upgraded so that Parisians can now swish through turnstiles with a high-tech badge (called Navigo) that makes a melodic "bing" as it registers. You, too, can swish and bing with a special pass for visitors called **Navigo Découverte**. Ask for this pass at any Métro stop (be sure to specify "Navigo Découverte" as "Navigo" is only available for residents); you'll need an ID photo (there are photo booths in train stations and many supermarkets) and 5€ to pay for the badge (which you can use on future trips). Once you have your badge, you can line up at a machine to charge it for either weekly (16€, zones 1 and 2) or monthly (54€, zones 1 and 2) unlimited travel. This is an excellent alternative to the overpriced Paris Visite pass (see below), but there's a catch: The weekly pass always starts on a Monday (the monthly on the first of the month) so if you arrive in Paris on a Thursday, for example, you'll only be able to use it for 3 days.

If you arrive mid-week or on the weekend and you are set on an unlimited pass, you are more or less limited to the **Paris Visite** (par-*ree* vee-*seet*) tourist pass, which is not necessarily a bargain. This pass gives you 1, 2, 3, or 5 days of unlimited travel and reductions on a very limited number of museums and monuments, but unless you are going to visit all the attractions on their list, a carnet of regular tickets might very well be a less expensive option. The 1-day Paris Visite pass is 8.50€ for three zones (who needs three zones?), the 2-day pass is 14€, 3 days is 19€, and 5 days is 28€; children 4 to 11 years old pay about half these rates.

There is one other option: For heavy travel on 1 day, the **Mobilis** (moh-bee-*lees*) pass is a good buy at 5.60€ for unlimited travel within the city limits, and will cost you less than a 1-day Paris Visite, which is 8.50€. If you're under 26, you can buy a 1-day Ticket Jeune (*tee*-kay zhun) pass good on a Saturday, Sunday, or a national holiday for just 3.20€. Both passes can be bought in advance; you just write in the date you want to use it.

BUS

The Parisian bus network is relatively efficient, especially now that there are more and more dedicated bus lanes so they don't get stuck in traffic as often. Though nowhere near as fast as the Métro, buses offer the added attraction of being above ground, and in a city as pretty as Paris, that's a big plus. In fact, if you take the right line, you get a low-cost sightseeing tour of the city (see the "Do-It-Yourself Bus Tours" box in the guided tours section of the sightseeing chapter, p. 196). My advice is to take the Métro for longer trips, but if you're not pressed for time and are not going far, try the bus. If you want to get a seat, avoid rush hour (7:30–9:30am and

Velib'—A Great Way to Cycle Around Paris

"Ride a bike around Paris," you ask, "Are you nuts?" Yes and no. True, you have to have a bit of the daredevil in you to take to the streets on a bicycle in this traffic-crazed city, but since July 2007, when the City of Paris inaugurated a new system of low-cost bike rentals called Velib' (vel-*leeb*), it's really hard to resist the temptation to do so. Quite simply it's fun to check out these high-tech, sexy looking bikes and take them for a spin, dropping them off at bike stands with no fuss and no muss.

The way it works is this: You buy a 1- or 7-day subscription (1€ or 5€, respectively) from the machine at one of the futuristic-looking bike stands, which gives you the right to as many half-hour rides as you'd like for 1 or 7 days. If you want to go over a half-hour, you can either check in your bike, wait 5 minutes, and check it out again, or you can pay 1€ for your extra half-hour, and 2€ for the half-hour after that one. Everything is meticulously explained, in English, on the website, www.velib.paris.fr. There's one big catch, however—to use the machines you must have a credit or debit card with a chip in it. This can be a problem for North American tourists, *unless* they happen to have an American Express card. According to my sources, for some reason, chipless AmEx cards will work in the Velib' machines.

Once you get the machines to work, you're ready to ride. Helmets are not provided, so if you're feeling queasy about launching into traffic, bring one along. There are few bike lanes so far, but success has been such that new ones are being added, and cyclists have the right to ride in the bus lanes. **One more tip:** Before you ride, get a map of the city that shows where the bike stands are so you don't waste precious time looking for a place to check in or check out.

6–8pm). You can pick up a bus map at any Métro station (it's on the other side of the Métro map; try to get the largest size map available as they're more readable). As noted above, transit ("t+") tickets work on all modes of transport, and there are free transfers between buses or between buses and tramways for 1½ hours after you first punch the ticket. If you jump on a bus and don't have a ticket, you can buy one from the driver (have exact change; drivers can't change large bills), but these are tickets "sans correspondance," meaning, there's no transfer included. Most bus lines run from around 7am until around 9pm, but there are a few that run until 12:30am, including those that serve the major train stations, like line 63, which terminates at Gare de Lyon and line 92, which goes to Gare Montparnasse. After midnight, you'll have to take the **Noctilien** (check www.ratp.fr for lines and hours), the reduced evening bus service which uses the Gare de Lyon, Gare St-Lazare, Gare Montparnasse, Gare de l'Est, and Châtelet as hubs and operates from 12:30am to 5:30am. *Note:* Special airport buses (Orlybus, Roissybus, and so on) cost more and you'll have to buy a separate ticket to take one.

TAXI

This is the most expensive way to get around and not necessarily the most efficient. Merely hailing one can be an ordeal, as in theory you'll have to find a taxi stand (in practice, you can hail them in the street, but not all will stop). Taxi stands resemble bus stops and sport a blue "TAXI" sign; when the light on top of the car is white, the taxi is available, orange means occupied. You can also call the dispatcher at ☎ 01 45 30 30 30. Once you get inside, you'll have to pray that your driver is skilled in dodging through Parisian traffic, which is horrendous. Sooner or later you're bound to find yourself stuck in a jam, watching the meter tick and cursing yourself for not having taken the Métro.

Calculating fares is a complicated business, but here are the basic rates for Paris *intramuros:*

- ◆ Tariff A: (10am–5pm) 2.10€ as soon as you get in, then .82€ per kilometer.
- ◆ Tariff B: (5pm–10am Mon–Sat, 7am–midnight Sun and holidays) 2.10€ as soon as you get in, 1.10€ per kilometer.
- ◆ Tariff C: (midnight–7am Sun) 2.10€ once you get in, 1.33€ per kilometer.

There's a minimum fare of 5.60€; if you have more than three people in your party, you'll also be charged 2.70€ for each additional passenger. One piece of luggage per person rides for free, afterward anything that you put in the trunk that weighs more than 5 kilos (11 lb.) is .90€ each. Unless you're a math wiz, it's near impossible to calculate exactly what your fare should be, but if you feel you've been seriously overcharged, you can contact the **Préfecture de Police** (☎ 08 91 01 22 22; www.prefecture-police-paris.interieur.gouv.fr). The saving grace here is that the distances are usually not huge, and barring excessive traffic, your average cross-town fare should fall between 10€ and 14€ for two without baggage. Tipping is not obligatory, but a .50€ to 1€ tip is customary for short trips; for longer hauls a 5% to 10% tip should do.

One of the only times when taking a taxi really makes sense is after midnight when the Métro closes—alas, this too is often an exercise in frustration. Strange as it may seem, there are simply not enough taxis on the streets. In the name of protecting the cab drivers' jobs, workers' unions have insisted on limiting the number of taxis allowed on the streets, meaning that after midnight you'll have to wait in huge lines at the taxi stands. Your best strategy for late night outings: Don't stray too far from your lodgings and be prepared to walk home, or cycle on Velib' (see box), if necessary. The silver lining: Strolling around Paris late at night is not only safe in most areas but can be downright delightful—many monuments and historic buildings are beautifully lit and even more stunning than during the day.

A WORD ABOUT DRIVING IN PARIS

Don't.

Even if you are a Formula 1 racecar driver with years of experience, you'll be alternately outraged and infuriated by the aggressive tactics of your fellow drivers and the inevitable *bouchons* (literally, a bottle stopper or cork), or jams, that tie up traffic and turn a simple jaunt into a harrowing nightmare. To make matters worse, it's easy to believe that the street and direction signs were cunningly placed by a sadistic madman who gets kicks out of watching hapless drivers take wrong turns. No matter how carefully you try to follow the signs pointing toward, say, Trocadéro, you'll suddenly find yourself on an outer boulevard headed for Versailles.

Your troubles are not over once you get to your destination because then you will have to park, which is a whole other trauma. Spots are elusive, to say the least, and you'll probably find yourself touring the neighborhood for at least 20 minutes until you find one. By then you'll have figured out why it is that Parisians park on the sidewalks: Often, there's nowhere else to park.

One final hurdle: feeding the parking meter. All parking is *payant*—that is, you must pay. And you can't pay with coins anymore—you must buy a "Paris Carte" parking card at a *tabac,* or smoke shop (many bars are also *tabacs*—you'll know by the red diamond-shaped tabac sign outside). This card is inserted directly into the meter, which will print out a ticket that you must put on your dashboard; parking costs from 1€ to 3€ per hour, depending on the neighborhood, and you can't stay in the same spot for more than 2 hours. Mercifully, on Sundays and after 7pm the rest of the week, all street parking is free. A good way to avoid parking hassles is to use one of the many underground parking lots, indicated by a sign with a white "P" on a blue background; parking in one of these is around 2.50€ per hour, and you can stay all day (you don't need a card here).

If, despite my ranting, you still feel compelled to rent a car and drive around the city, or are forced to do so due to extenuating circumstances, at the very least, get your hands on a basic explanation of international street signs (this should be available at your car-rental agency), and a good street map. Try to do your driving on a Sunday, when most Parisians head for the country (but forget about Sat, when they all do their shopping). Finally, try to keep your cool, because no matter how sure you are that you are following the rules of the road, at some point, someone in another car will curse you. Good luck—you're going to need it.

THE NEIGHBORHOODS OF PARIS

As I mentioned above, Paris is a city for walkers. One lovely neighborhood after another unfolds along its sidewalks, punctuated by plazas and monuments that are best experienced at ground-level. At every turn there seems to be an intriguing area that begs to be explored. Below is a rundown on the main neighborhoods of Paris. I've placed them in order of their arrondissements so that you can easily situate the areas on your map.

1ST ARRONDISSEMENT—THE LOUVRE, ILE DE LA CITE & PLACE DU CHATELET

Best for: Museums, historic sights, architecture, transportation hubs
What you won't find: Evening entertainment, quiet streets

This is the heart of the city, and the oldest part of Paris, though you'd never know it to see it now; in the 19th century Baron Haussmann, Napoleon's energetic urban planner, tore down almost all of the medieval houses that once covered this area. The Ile de la Cité is where the city first emerged after Gallic tribes started camping out here in the 3rd century B.C. By the 1st century A.D., the Romans were building temples, and by the Middle Ages, a mighty fortress sat across the river on the Right Bank. The fortress has long since been incorporated into the majestic buildings of the Louvre, which along with the Jardin des Tuileries takes up a big chunk of the neighborhood. As you might suspect, it's a very exclusive neighborhood where only the very rich can afford to live. In fact, most of the people you'll see in the streets do not live around here, but work in the many offices that fill the gracious 19th-century buildings that line these streets.

While the major museums and sites are to the west, the people's part of this neighborhood is on its eastern edge, near Les Halles and place du Châtelet. Stuffed with stores, particularly along the bustling rue de Rivoli and around the Forum des Halles, Parisians descend on this area for their shopping needs. The western half of the Ile de la Cité comes under the domain of this arrondissement, which includes not only the lovely Sainte Chapelle church (p. 133), but also the exquisite place Dauphine (p. 235) and the Square du Vert Gallant, on the very tip of the island.

2ND ARRONDISSEMENT—THE BOURSE & THE OPERA
Best for: Good restaurants, covered passages
What you won't find: Major monuments and museums, green spaces

You'll notice lots of men and women bustling about in business suits in this area, which is the home of the Bourse, the French stock exchange. Food and finances are intricately linked in this city, and with so many business lunches and dinners in the offing, it's no wonder that there's a wide variety of restaurants to choose from around here. There's also a large Japanese population in this quarter, which will become evident as you head toward the Opéra and cross rue St-Anne, which is lined with noodle shops and sushi bars. This is the arrondissement with the greatest concentration of *passages,* covered pedestrian shopping streets that were the forefathers of today's shopping malls (but much prettier; see the "Arcadia" box, p. 254). For outdoor strolling and great window-shopping, the car-free network of streets around rue Montorgueil, just above the Les Halles area, is a delight, even if most of the shops and restaurants are overpriced.

3RD & 4TH ARRONDISSEMENTS—THE MARAIS
Best for: Restaurants, nightlife, window shopping, 17th-century mansions, museums
What you won't find: Bargain shopping, iconic sights, open spaces

What was once marshy farmland (*marais* means marsh, or swamp) quickly became a seat of power when the Knights Templar decided to built a fortress here in the Middle Ages. Other religious orders followed suit, and after King Charles V decided to build a royal residence here in the 14th century (the Hôtel St-Pol), there was a real estate boom that produced a slew of mansions and palaces. In the 17th century, King Henri IV created a magnificent square bordered by Renaissance-style town houses, today called the place des Vosges (p. 147). If the Marais was hot before, then it was positively on fire; Nobles and bourgeois pounced on the neighborhood, each one trying to outdo the other by constructing more and more resplendent *hôtels particuliers,* or private mansions.

The overstuffed quarter was already falling out of fashion by the time the Revolution flushed out all its aristocrats in the 18th century; the magnificent dwellings were abandoned, pillaged, partitioned, and turned into stores, work-shops, and even factories. The new residents were working class, with more im-mediate concerns than saving historic patrimony. The neighborhood fell into disrepair; periodic attempts on the part of the city to "clean up" resulted in the destruction of many architectural gems.

Finally, in the 1960s, a real renovation project was put in place, and today, sev-eral of the most magnificent mansions have been restored and are open to the public in the form of museums and other exposition halls. In fact, much of the area has become terribly *branché* (literally, plugged in), and you'll see some of the hippest styles in boutique windows here, as well as dozens of happening restau-rants and bars lining its narrow streets. The neighborhood is still a mix though— jewelry and clothing wholesalers bump up against stylish cafes and shops; the vibrant gay scene on rue Vielle du Temple intersects with what's left of the old Jewish quarter on rue des Rosiers. Overall, this remains a lively, interesting neigh-borhood, even if its hipness is pushing prices ever skyward.

5TH ARRONDISSEMENT—THE LATIN QUARTER

Best for: Affordable dining, student bars, art house movie theaters, museums, Jardin des Plantes

What you won't find here: Good shopping, great architecture, quiet (at least not in the environs of place St-Michel)

Since the Middle Ages, when the Sorbonne and other academic institutions were founded, this has been a student neighborhood, hence the "Latin" label—back in the old days, all classes were taught in the language of Virgil. Today the area still harbors the highest number of colleges and universities in the city. Though it's easy to over-romanticize about the intellectual life of the quarter, you'll certainly see plenty of students and professors peopling the mostly inexpensive, if not always good, restaurants and cafes around here. You'll also see plenty of tourists, who tend to swarm around the warren of tiny streets that lead off of the place St-Michel. Rue de la Huchette in particular is to be avoided (except for the great swing-dancing club, Le Caveau de la Huchette), being lined with garish restau-rants of questionable quality. Boulevard St-Michel, a legendary artery that once was lined with smoky cafes filled with thinkers and rabble-rousers, has now fallen prey to chain stores and fast food; the huge Gilbert-Joseph bookstore still holds sway, however, on the upper end of the avenue.

For a more authentic taste of this neighborhood, wander east and upward, around the windy streets on the hill that leads to the Panthéon, and around rue Monge, toward the Jardin des Plantes (p. 214). This last is a lovely place to relax; as well as the natural history museums that surround it, the park includes beauti-ful flower beds, hothouses, a zoo, and many benches for resting tired feet.

6TH ARRONDISSEMENT—ST-GERMAIN

Best for: Fine dining, historic cafes, shopping, parks (the Jardin du Luxembourg)

What you won't find here: Today's intellectuals and artists, low prices

The church of St-Germain-des-Prés, the heart of this neighborhood, got its name (St. Germain of the Fields) because at the time it was built, back in the 11th century, it was in the middle of the countryside. What a difference a millennium makes. The church became the nucleus of a huge and powerful abbey, whose grounds would eventually take up a good part of the arrondissement and would constitute an autonomous minicity, complete with a hospital and a prison. The Revolution cut the church down to its current size, and an elegant collection of apartment houses, squares, and parks grew up around it, making it one of Paris's most appealing areas to live in (as real estate prices will attest). If the neighborhood has always had aristocratic airs (it was a favorite haunt of the nobility during the 17th and 18th c.), during the last part of the 19th century up to the mid–20th century it was also a magnet for penniless artists and intellectuals, who hung out in legendary cafes like the Flore and Deux Magots.

Today few struggling creative types can afford either the rents or the price of a cup of coffee around here; young artists and thinkers have moved north and east to cheaper parts of town. Though the ambience is decidedly bourgeois these days, the neighborhood is still dynamic, and the cafes and shops along the boulevard St-Germain are crowded with a mix of politicians (there are many ministries around here), gallery owners (whose establishments line the streets around rue Dauphine), and editors (this is still the seat of French publishing). This is also a fun neighborhood for shopping—there's everything here from 500€ pumps on chic rue des St-Pères to 20€ sundresses on the more plebian rue des Rennes (see chapter 9). And when you've tired yourself out, you can stroll over to the magnificent Jardin du Luxembourg for a timeout by the fountain.

7TH ARRONDISSEMENT—THE EIFFEL TOWER & LES INVALIDES

Best for: Iconic monuments, majestic avenues, grand vistas, museums
What you won't find here: Affordable restaurants or shopping, nightlife

The Eiffel Tower reigns over this swanky arrondissement, where the streets that aren't lined with ministries and embassies are filled with elegant apartment buildings and prohibitively expensive stores and restaurants. A large portion of the neighborhood is taken up by the Champs de Mars, a park that stretches between the tower and the Ecole Militaire, and by the enormous esplanade in front of the Invalides, which sweeps down to the Seine with much pomp and circumstance. Some of the city's best museums are around here, including the Musée d'Orsay, the Musée Rodin, and the new Musée du Quai Branly, whose wacky architecture has raised some hackles in this very staid area.

While there's certainly a lot to see here, the neighborhood is a little short on human warmth—this is not the place to come to see regular Parisians in their natural habitat. A small island of affordability is the area around the pedestrian rue Cler, a market street that is home to many delightful small restaurants and food stores. Word is out about this cozy corner, however, so expect to see plenty of tourists when you go into that cute *boulangerie* for a couple of croissants.

8TH ARRONDISSEMENT—FROM THE CHAMPS ELYSEES TO PARC MONCEAU

Best for: Serious strolling (on the Champs), museums, monuments
What you won't find here: Affordable hotels or restaurants, nightlife (apart from the Champs)

The Champs Elysées cuts through this area like an asphalt river—it's the widest boulevard in Paris. Crossing the street here feels a bit like traversing a raging torrent (be sure to wait for the light). There are fans and foes of this epic roadway: Some find its lights and sparkles good clean fun; others find it crass and commercial. However you feel about the street itself, you're bound to be impressed by the Arc de Triomphe, which lords over the boulevard from its western tip. To the south of the Champs are some of the most expensive stores, restaurants, and homes in the city (particularly around Ave. Montaigne). To the north, a largely residential area extends up to the beautiful Parc Monceau, which is surrounded by some equally delightful museums, like the Jacquemart-Andrée and the Nissim de Camondo. About halfway back to the Champs Elysées is the utterly elegant rue St-Honoré, which runs parallel to the grand boulevard and is great for window shopping and dreaming of what you would do if you were rich. To the northeast, the arrondissement turns decidedly more plebian; the area around the Gare St-Lazare may not be as charming as other parts of the neighborhood, but at least here you'll find stores you can actually afford.

9TH & 10TH ARRONDISSEMENTS—FROM THE GRANDS BOULEVARDS TO THE CANAL ST-MARTIN

Best for: Affordable restaurants, nightlife, seeing a more low-key side of the city
What you won't find here: Monuments, big museums, tourists

For a long time, no one seemed to care about these arrondissements; they were too far from the center of the city, too working-class to be of interest to the trendy set, and too monument-less to appeal to tourists. Then, with real estate skyrocketing, young professionals started prospecting apartments and young artists started filling up loft spaces. Suddenly, the forgotten Canal St-Martin was blooming with cafes and restaurants, and rue des Martyrs was becoming an extension of Montmartre, with boutiques and bars cropping up between the butcher and the baker. Happily, these areas aren't gentrified (yet) and parts are infused with a certain youthful energy that's hard to come by in other areas of the city. Because there are few big-name attractions here, they're also relatively tourist free, and offer an opportunity to see a more "real" side of the city.

The 9th arrondissement's claim to fame is that it's the home of the Grand Magasins (big-name department stores), which are located on boulevard Haussmann near Gare St-Lazare. In the center, between the church of St-Georges and place Clichy, is an area known as Nouvelle Athens, or New Athens, where many artists of the 19th-century Romantic movement, like George Sand and Eugène Delacroix, lived and worked. On the western end of the arrondissement, around de Châteaudun and rue Cadet, is one of the city's largest Jewish quarters.

The 10th arrondissement is mostly known for its two huge train stations, Gare du Nord and Gare de l'Est. The area around the stations is a bit seedy, but there are some great clubs and music venues around rue des Petits Ecuries. The real draw in this neighborhood is the Canal St-Martin, which cuts through the western side of the district. The southern part of the canal is particularly scenic; leafy plane trees shade the waterway, which is crossed by unusual arched foot bridges.

> " . . . no other railroad station in the world manages so mysteriously to cloak with compassion the anguish of departure and the dubious ecstasies of return and arrival. Any waiting room in the world is filled with all this, and I have sat in many of them and accepted it, and I know from deliberate acquaintance that the whole human experience is more bearable at the Gare de Lyon in Paris than anywhere else. "
>
> —M.F.K. Fisher, *Not a Station But a Place*

11TH & 12TH ARRONDISSEMENTS— BASTILLE & THE FAUBOURG ST-ANTOINE

Best for: Nightlife, good restaurants, Revolutionary history, arty boutiques
What you won't find here: Major monuments and museums, high-end shops

These are two more arrondissements that were pretty much off the tourist radar until 1989, when the new Bastille opera house provoked an explosion of bars and restaurants in the surrounding streets. Though the shine has already worn off the nightspots of rue de Lappe and rue de la Roquette, just off the place de la Bastille, the nocturnal life of the 11th arrondissement is far from dull, as new clubs and cafes have opened further north, on rue de Charonne and rue Oberkampf. Now even Oberkampf has become thoroughly saturated, and intrepid partiers are staking out new ground in Menilmontant in the 20th.

But there's another reason to come to this area: the Faubourg St-Antoine. This historic workers quarter has been inhabited by woodworkers and furniture makers since the 13th century, when artisans in this neighborhood were given the right to ply their trades without the usual royal taxes and restrictions. At first this was a boon and industry flourished, but after a few centuries the density of underpaid, overburdened workers made St-Antoine a breeding ground for revolutionaries. The raging mob that stormed the Bastille prison in 1789 originated here, as did those of the subsequent uprisings of 1830, 1848, and the Paris commune.

Today, away from the hoopla around the opera house, St-Antoine is relatively mellow. While the architecture here is nowhere near as grand as elsewhere in Paris, the neighborhood has retained an authenticity that's rarely found in the more popular parts of the city. There are still a large number of furniture stores and *ébénistes* (woodworkers) tucked into large interior courtyards accessible by covered passages off rue du Faubourg St-Antoine. Make a point of wandering down one of these; you'll be rewarded with a look at a way of life that has survived the centuries. This quarter extends all the way past the Viaduc des Arts to the Gare de Lyon train station, a magnificent example of Belle Epoque architecture.

14TH ARRONDISSEMENT—MONTPARNASSE
Best for: Transportation hub, shopping, historic cafes, nightlife
What you won't find here: Extraordinary architecture, museums, monuments

In the early 1970s, government officials decided the time had come to make Paris a modern city. Blithely putting aside concerns for historic patrimony and architectural harmony, the old Montparnasse train station and its immediate neighborhood was torn down, and a 58-story glass tower and shopping complex was erected in its place. A new train station was constructed behind the tower, as well as a barrage of modern apartment buildings and office blocks. So much for progress. Fortunately, even ugly contemporary architecture didn't manage to kill the neighborhood—at the foot of the Tour Montparnasse, life goes on as it always has. A few steps away from the station, tiny old streets are still lined with stores, cafes, and *crêperies* (crêpe restaurants), these last being an outgrowth of the large Breton (that is, from Brittany) community that still inhabits this area. Farther down boulevard Montparnasse, you'll find legendary brasseries like La Coupole and Le Select, where Picasso, Max Jacob, and Henry Miller used to hang out in the 1920s. For a bit of calm, take a walk around the Cimetiére de Montparnasse, where artists like Charles Baudelaire and Constantin Brancusi are buried, as well as Colonel Alfred Dreyfus. In the evenings, crowds pour into the many movie theaters around the station, as well as the many restaurants in the area.

To the south, the arrondissement takes a more residential turn, with the exception of rue Daguerre, a lively market street a block south of the cemetery, and farther south, rue d'Alésia, a discount shoppers mecca (see the shopping chapter, p. 251).

16TH ARRONDISSEMENT—TROCADERO & PASSY
Best for: Gourmet restaurants, museums, architectural elegance
What you won't find here: Affordable eateries or hotels, nightlife, regular folk

The illustrious Seizième (sez-ee-*em,* sixteenth), is the most exclusive arrondissement of the city. Even dogs don't walk the streets here without a pedigree. Laying on the outer western edge of the city, this residential area is packed with magnificent 19th-century residences and apartment houses, as well as many fine parks and gardens. In fact, it shares its western border with the Bois de Boulogne, one of the city's two huge wooded parks. During the day, the streets are filled with nannies pushing strollers and well-to-do residents shopping in high-end stores; in the evening, the sidewalks roll up—with the exception of the cafes and restaurants around place du Trocadéro.

For it is Trocadéro and the surrounding area that save this neighborhood from terminal elegance. While the 16th might be pretty dull on the whole, it's also graced with a terrific array of museums. The Palais de Chaillot alone holds three

(Musée de l'Homme, Musée de la Marine, and Cité de l'Architecture), just down the street is the vast Musée Guimet, and a little farther on there are two modern art museums in the Palais de Tokyo, not to mention a half a dozen others (like the Marmottan and the Baccarat) sprinkled around the arrondissement. And a stop at the esplanade between the two pavilions of the Palais de Chaillot is a must. From there you will get a superb view of the Eiffel Tower, which you can walk to by strolling down the hill through the Jardins du Trocadéro.

18TH ARRONDISSEMENT—MONTMARTRE
Best for: Restaurants, nightlife, atmosphere
What you won't find here: Monuments (with the exception of Sacré-Coeur), major museums, grand architecture

The "Butte" (high hill) of Montmartre is such a landmark that I have put it in my list of must-sees in our sightseeing chapter (p. 124). Once a village overlooking the distant city, Montmartre is now as inseparable from Paris as the Eiffel Tower, which means it's a major target of the tour-bus crowd. And crowded it is, if you stick to the area immediately around the Basilica of Sacré-Coeur and the overdone place du Tertre. Interestingly, Montmartre is also home to an increasingly hip crowd, who stick to the more authentic area around the place des Abbesses. The narrow cobbled streets that climb past the two remaining windmills are peppered with boutiques and cute restaurants frequented by a cool combo of young professionals and budding artists.

There is another side to the 18th, the east side, to be exact, where the quaintness of the Butte gives way to a more modern dynamic—the lively immigrant quarter of Barbès. Here you'll see a different kind of Parisian: the one who wears a sari or is draped in African prints. This neighborhood is home to large communities from Africa, India, and the Magreb (north Africa), and here you'll find a jumble of inexpensive stores selling everything from long-necked teapots to pajama-like salwar trousers, as well as tiny restaurants that offer exotic delicacies.

20TH ARRONDISSEMENT—BELLEVILLE
Best for: Affordable restaurants, nightlife, atmosphere
What you won't find here: Museums, chic shops, notable architecture

This neighborhood didn't really get its fair share in this book, owing to both its location (on the outskirts of the city) and space restrictions, but it deserves better. A potent mix of ethnicities and nationalities, it's one of the preferred haunts of today's young artists and intellectuals, as well as a smattering of bourgeois bohemians who have bought apartments here. While it was once a crazy mélange of Arab, African, Jewish, and Asian residents and businesses, more recently, Chinese is the language most often heard on its streets (though the others are still all there). Young arty types, tired of the hyperactive nightlife on rue Oberkampf, have established new cafes and bars in the Ménilmontant area. The one major tourist draw here is the parklike Cimetière de Père Lachaise, which takes up about a quarter of the arrondissement.

3 Accommodations, Both Standard & Not

In which you'll discover all the options, from foldout couches in private apartments to comfy digs in boutique hotels

BRAVELY HURDLING CULTURAL BARRIERS, MORE AND MORE PARISIANS ARE renting out their apartments for the short term, a both practical and financially sound option, particularly for traveling families and groups. What's more, some fearless urbanites are actually renting out individual rooms in their own homes—a heretofore unheard of concept in this chronically introverted country. So before I get to the list of the city's best affordable hotels—and they are legion in number and wonderfully varied—I'm going to start off with several other affordable alternatives, including hosted and unhosted apartment rentals, residence hotels, youth accommodations, and a monastery or two, in the hopes of helping you find comfortable lodgings that will please both you and your wallet.

STAYING IN A PRIVATE APARTMENT

In recent years there has been a boom in short-term rentals, and there are now dozens of agencies proffering hundreds of apartments smack in the center of the City of Light. What's more, unlike hotels, prices have not risen significantly over the past couple of years. Though the rates for two people are sometimes but not always significantly less than what you'd pay at a hotel, the advantages are many, not the least of which is the fact that you can cook some of your meals at home and save yourself a wad of time and money. Even breakfast can make a big difference when it comes to adding up receipts. And there are many other, less tangible benefits like privacy, independence, and a chance to see what it's like to live like a Parisian, even if it's just for a week. If you are more than two, and especially if you are traveling *en famille,* the benefits can be huge. Family suites and/or communicating rooms are rare in Parisian hotels, and you will almost always end up paying for two doubles—that is, somewhere around 200€ to 300€ per night—whereas you could easily rent a one-bedroom apartment with a foldout couch and/or extra bed in the living room for 800€ to 1,000€ per week, or 114€ to 140€ per night. Not only that, you'll have a kitchen to prepare baby bottles or meals for finicky eaters, a door that separates you from the little ones at night, and usually, walls that block out enough sound to let your neighbors sleep in in the mornings if your children are being rowdy.

Some Definitions

Hosted apartments: Otherwise known as "bed-and-breakfasts," these are apartments that a guest shares with a Parisian who lives in another room on the premises. A 2- to 3-night minimum stay is required for this arrangement, and breakfast is always included in the price.

Unhosted apartments: Also called short-term rentals, these are furnished apartments that guests have entirely to themselves during the course of their stay. These might be part-time homes that would otherwise stay empty during several months of the year, or apartments that are maintained exclusively for tourists or business travelers. In Paris, the minimum rental is usually 7 nights; prices listed in this chapter are weekly rates.

A few examples of these types of accommodations:

- A room in an Art Deco building near the lively Bastille area decorated in bright, contemporary colors with a private access on a leafy courtyard for 75€ per night (double occupancy, Alcôve & Agapes, p. 24).
- A 52-sq.-m (560-sq.-ft.) two-bedroom apartment that sleeps four with exposed beams and a loft in the hip Montorgueuil district near Les Halles, for 953€ per week (Parisian Home, p. 27).
- A spacious loft (92 sq. m/990 sq. ft.) on an airy courtyard that sleeps six, with giant windows, sliding walls, contemporary furniture, and original artwork for 1,270€ per week. The building was once a convent (Appartement de Ville, p. 29).
- A private bedroom, living room, and bathroom in a light-filled converted artist's studio in the 6th arrondissement decorated with the host's sculptures and paintings. The price includes access to a lovely garden terrace in the quiet courtyard: 100€ per night (double occupancy, Alcôve & Agapes, p. 24).

Don't care about cooking and are working with a relatively small budget? You can pay even less for a "bed-and-breakfast," a new phenomenon on the Parisian lodging scene. For as little 69€, two people can sleep, breakfast, and enjoy a room in a historic apartment in the city center.

As you can see, there is a wide variety of great options out there for the intrepid traveler who wants to go beyond the usual hotel experience. Now it's time to get down to the nitty-gritty: how to find that special apartment rental.

HOSTED APARTMENTS

The concept of renting out a room in one's own apartment is relatively new in Paris. Though bed-and-breakfasts *(chambres d'hôtes)* are extremely common in the French countryside, in the big city, where privacy and anonymity are treasured, the idea of strangers living in one's home generally fills Parisians with horror. This is a city where despite the high rents, roommates are virtually unheard of, and poverty-stricken students would prefer to live in an attic, alone, than to share an apartment with nonfamily members.

So you won't find tons of agencies hawking these sorts of stays. That said, there are a few trusted bed-and-breakfast agencies that have been around for several years expertly matching guests and hosts. The two best known are listed below; one other, **France Lodge** (p. 28) handles both and can be found in the "Unhosted Apartments" section.

Probably the best-known B&B agency in Paris, **Alcôve & Agapes** (☎ 01 44 85 06 05; www.bed-and-breakfast-in-paris.com; MC, V) is run by the ebullient Françoise Foret, who personally inspects the 120 lodgings posted on her excellent website. Most rooms are either in Belle Epoque apartments, private houses, or artist's studios, and all adhere to strict standards. In fact, she helped write the "Authentic B&B" charter (see above) and all of her rooms live up to or surpass the label's standards. In the business for 10 years, Foret's selection criteria goes beyond good looks—she tries to choose unique lodgings that "make the guest want to ask questions" about the history of the home and the objects in it. Putting the emphasis on contact, Foret prefers to work with hosts and clients who seek cultural exchange, not just a cheap alternative to a hotel. That said, this is a cheap alternative to a hotel. Rates range from a mere 75€ per night for a nice double room with a shared bathroom, to 175€ for something truly vast and elegant, with not just a private bath, but a private breakfast nook and terrace to boot (most rooms fall in the 75€–140€ range, prices include breakfast and taxes, of course). For example, 75€ per night might get you a smallish double room in a 19th-century mansion with high ceilings, a marble fireplace, and some lovely antiques (the host's father was an auctioneer) where guests have access to a private garden and get to breakfast in an elegant, light-filled dining room. On the other end of the scale, for 175€ per night two people can sleep in an enormous room (53 sq. m/570 sq. ft.) that's larger than many Parisian apartments. It includes 4m (13-ft.) ceilings, a private terrace, flatscreen TV, and a hand-embroidered antique silk bedspread from Vietnam—not bad for accommodations in the trendy Marais. Each room is fully detailed on the website, with plenty of photos and easily readable rates, and you can reserve and confirm your stay online. Unusual for a B&B website, Foret also includes plenty of information about the hosts, including their

Two Seals of Approval

When shopping for a hosted stay, you'll see the higher-quality establishments boasting one of two different labels: the **Hôtes Qualité Paris,** a standard established by the City of Paris, and **Authentic B&B,** a charter written up by the top B&B agencies in the city (three of which happen to be those listed below). What's the difference between the two? Both labels indicate that rooms adhere to a rigorous standard, which measures everything from cleanliness, to the charm quotient, to the presence of night tables on both sides of the bed. But to get the Authentic B&B label, 100% of the rooms in the establishment must meet the standard, whereas for the Hôtes Qualité Paris only 60% of the rooms must meet these requirements.

photos, their professions, and any pet or possible allergy issues. She also works with partners, like massage therapists who make house calls, and artist hosts who give workshops. Most hosts on her list require a 3- or 4-night stay.

Though her site isn't as complete as Foret's, Christine Bokobza at **Good Morning Paris** (43 rue Lacépède, 5th arrond.; ☎ 01 47 07 28 29; www.goodmorning paris.fr; AE, MC, V) has equally lovely rooms to offer—in fact, some of them actually are the same, since the same hosts often work with more than one agency. Many of Bokobza's hosts, however, prefer to remain out of the cyber-spotlight, which accounts for the sparse information listed on her site; once contact has been made, she will send full details and additional photos.

Another difference is that Bokobza's roster, which includes some 100 rooms all over the city, favors accommodations on the lower end of the price scale: Most doubles here are either 69€ for a room without a private *salle de bain,* and 79€ to 89€ for those with private facilities. *Note:* In French, a *salle de bain,* or bathroom, doesn't necessarily include a toilet, so this could mean that you will have your own sink and tub and still have to share the john. If a private toilet is important to you, be sure to specify when you reserve. The apartments themselves might be a little smaller and a less luxurious, but the welcome will be just as warm; often retirees with an extra room now that the kids are gone, hosts generally have accumulated plenty of Parisian insider tips that they are encouraged to share with their guests. One kindly host rents out a room in her 19th-century apartment that is filled with lovely family heirlooms; breakfast is served in a large dining area whose enormous windows look out on the lush gardens of the **Arènes de Lutèce** (p. 186). Another, who lives near the Gare de Lyon, offers two spacious rooms (for members of the same family only) that are decorated with family photos and antique prints. For something with a bit more style, Bokobza also has a dozen or so more luxurious *chambres de charme* (with niceties)—like private gardens and spacious period bedrooms with potted palms; these rooms run 109€ per night for two. Even though these are less expensive apartments, they all meet Authentic B&B standards thanks to Bokobza's watchful eye.

She also offers some full apartments for rent; Bokobza lists them only if the owner lives next door and can bring over breakfast on request (apartments for two to four start at 99€ per night).

Good Morning Paris also offers packages that combine lodging and cultural events, like 3 nights in a B&B and a 3-hour cooking class for 203€ per person, or 3 nights lodging plus a 2-day Paris Museum Pass for 133€ per person. Clients receive a bimonthly newsletter with suggestions of walking tours and current expositions. Minimum stay is 2 nights.

UNHOSTED APARTMENTS

Many furnished short-term rentals in Paris are apartments that are maintained exclusively for tourists or business travelers. As such, the unscrupulous ones will try to make you believe that rents in Paris are as high as those in New York (they are not; indeed, they're much lower, but so are salaries, so they are expensive for Parisians) and charge outrageous prices. These apartments tend to fall into two categories: bland, characterless apartments meant primarily for businessmen and women; and luxurious digs meant for wealthy tourists that rent at outrageous prices. Fortunately, there is another, rapidly expanding category: private apartments whose

Pauline Frommer Says: Staying in B&Bs— Questions to Ask Your Agency

Though most in-apartment B&B stays are fun, carefree holidays, sometimes . . . well, things can go mighty wrong. It's extremely important to find out what sort of person you may be sharing your vacation with and what the apartment is like before you put down a deposit. Call your agency to go over any concerns before committing to any hosted stay.

Some questions you may want to ask:

1. **What is the host's schedule?**
   Some hosts will be in the apartment for most of the day, while others work outside the home, meaning that you'll have the apartment to yourself for large chunks of time. Find out before you leave.

2. **Where does the host sleep in relation to the room you'll be using?**
   Another privacy issue: Will your host be in the room right next door, eavesdropping, intentionally or not, on your every sigh or snore? Or will there be a room or two between your two bedrooms? In some extremely rare cases, cash-crunched hosts have been known to rent out their own bedrooms and take the living room couch for a week. If the listing is for a one-bedroom, you may want to find out if this is the case, as that can be an uncomfortable situation, especially if you have to walk through the living room to get to the bedroom or bathroom. (From what I understand, this is not a common scenario, but hey, it's better to ask.)

3. **Is the bathroom shared or private?**

4. **Are there pets in the house?**

5. **Are there any rules the host has for his or her guests?**
   Whether or not guests can smoke in the apartment is obviously a common issue, as is the guest's use of the shared space (I once met a host who only allowed the guests she liked to venture into the living room). Most hosts do not allow guests to cook, except to reheat prepared foods, so if this is an issue for you, discuss it beforehand.

6. **Will the host welcome families with children?** And if so, is there an age limit?

7. **What does the bedroom face?**
   Does the room get a lot of sun in the morning? Does it face a busy street, or a quiet back courtyard? These questions may be key if you're a light sleeper.

owners are out of town for long periods of time. These can range from lightly lived-in apartments with few personal belongings, to fully decorated homes, complete with family antiques and photos of *Maman et Papa*.

I've concentrated on this third category, focusing on seven agencies who care about content as much as context, and offer visitors not just a clean bed, but a truly Parisian experience. Though each will send you information on what to expect when you arrive, here are a few questions you should ask:

1. **Are towels and sheets provided?** They usually are, but it's smart to check.
2. **What's *not* included in the quoted rate?** Taxes, insurance, agency fees, and so forth.
3. **How large is the apartment?** This might sound silly, but let me tell you, "two rooms" can mean a lot of different things to a lot of different people. The measurement will be given to you in square meters; go to a conversion site like www.onlineconversion.com to get square feet.
4. **Will I pay for electricity used?** This too, is often included, but some agencies will bill you separately.
5. **Can I use the telephone?** In many unhosted apartments, you can call out with a calling card only.
6. **Is there a discount if I stay longer?** The answer to this one is almost always "yes." Stretching out your vacation just might turn out to be an economical choice. In any case, the minimum stay is usually 1 week.

ON TO THE AGENCIES

Parisian Home (12 rue Mandar, 2nd arrond.; ☎ 01 45 08 03 37; www.parisian home.com; Métro: Les Halles or Etienne Marcel; MC, V) has reasonably priced apartments in most of the popular parts of the city. Lodgings are clean and smart, if not particularly exciting; most apartments are furnished in a simple, modern style with lots of white walls hung with nice art prints. These apartments belong to real people, not corporations, who are generally only in town during brief periods, which explains the non-lived-in feel; owners are encouraged, however, to use their imagination, and many do make interesting choices of linens, dishes, and decorative objects. What adds to the comfort level is the fact that this agency, which has been in business for 10 years, has its act together. The website is easy to use, with plenty of pictures and a detailed list of appliances and services available for each apartment, including the presence or absence of things like washing machines, elevators, and even hair dryers and food processors. There's no contact with the owners; everything goes through the agency, which is staffed by easy-going, English-speaking professionals. Unlike some other agencies, most of their 250 apartments are in the studio/one-bedroom category, which means they have a wide range of affordable lodgings. Prices vary greatly according to the size of the apartment, for example, if you're not claustrophobic, a 15-sq.-m (160-sq.-ft.) studio near the Jardin des Plantes is 383€ per week, whereas a stylish 40-sq.-m (429-sq.-ft.) one-bedroom in the Marais will run 863€ per week. Most one-bedrooms range from around 700€ to 1,000€ per week, two-bedrooms from 900€ to 1,500€ per week, and three-bedrooms for 1,500€ to 2,000€ per week, but rates can run higher or lower, depending on your needs. Minimum stay is 1 week.

Two Ultrabudget Options on Rental Apartments

If you are willing to take a risk, or have someone in Paris who can check out the apartment for you, you'll find some of the lowest rates on short-term apartment rentals in the classified ads in *FUSAC* (France-USA-Contacts), a free biweekly magazine that can be picked up in just about any bookstore, cafe, or restaurant frequented by English speakers in Paris. They also have a website with ad postings, though there's more in the magazine: www.fusac.fr. (*Warning:* Make sure you type the right address, as there is a scam site at www.fusac.com.) Some examples: a small, sunny apartment on the Ile Saint Louis for 400€ per week; a 33 sq. m studio with a view of the Panthéon for 400€ per week; and 40 sq. m one-bedroom that sleeps four in the Marais for 780€ per week.

More good deals can be found on **Craigslist** (www.craigslist.org), the Internet classified ad phenomenon that has now gone global. On their Paris page (http://paris.craigslist.org), you can find a hip 33 sq. m one-bedroom in the Marais that sleeps four for 750€ per week, or a quaint 30 sq. m one-bedroom near the Eiffel Tower for 665€ per week. The success of this site has been such, however, that if you look carefully, prices now can be as high as those of some of the agencies we list, without the guarantees these agencies offer. While there are deals to be had on Craigslist, keep in mind that it is merely that: a list. There is no oversight and it is up to you to make sure that the renter is on the up-and-up.

The down side of side-stepping an agency is that you have no way of really knowing who or what you are dealing with until you show up at your apartment. Nothing is entirely risk free, but agencies lower the odds of unpleasant surprises considerably.

Though their website isn't as complete, **France Lodge** (2 rue Meissonier, 17th arrond.; ☎ 01 56 33 85 85; www.francelodge.fr; Métro: Wagram; MC, V) is another good agency, and it's the one that has both hosted and unhosted apartments on their roster. In the business for over 20 years, it keeps careful tabs on 100-odd apartments sprinkled around the city. After guests leave, not only do they send around a cleaning crew, but also a quality control team to check to make sure everything is in working order. Like Parisian Home, most of their unhosted apartments are owned by people who come to Paris infrequently. Though unlived in, many units have interesting architectural details and a whiff of Parisian style, and most are in great locations. For 724€ per week, you might find yourself in a quaint one-bedroom with antique armoires and oriental carpets in the Latin Quarter, or for 764€ per week, a spacious (50-sq.-m) one-bedroom with a marble bathroom in the center of pricey St-Germain. Unlike other agencies, everything is included in the price, even electricity; bed linens are provided, but you'll have to bring your own towels. And about that website: The apartments shown on the site are really just to give you an idea; the agency prefers that you fill out the form on the site with your arrival dates and needs, or contact them directly. They then will send you a selection of what's available, complete with extensive photos and details. Weekly rates for studios run from 550€ to 700€, for one bedrooms 600€ to 1,000€, and for two bedrooms 850€ to 1,100€, with a minimum stay of 1 week. *Note:* If you are planning on cooking full meals, be sure to specify that you want a real stove/oven; some apartments have only microwaves.

France Lodge has some 80 hosted options (though you'd never know it as there are even fewer photos of those apartments on their website). Rest assured that this is one of the top B&B agencies in town; in fact, they helped write the Authentic B&B charter mentioned above. They offer two types of hosted stays: The first, geared toward tourists, includes all of their Authentic B&B–labeled rooms, which means high-quality lodgings and top-class breakfasts, and run 60€ to 95€ for two. The second, which they call "chez l'habitant," are for those on a limited budget (40€–75€ double occupancy): Rooms are clean, but less classy and you'll fix your breakfast yourself.

For something with a little more pizzazz, try **Appartement de Ville** (9 rue des Trois Bornes, 11th arrond; ☎ 01 42 45 09 08; www.appartementdeville.com; MC, V). This is one of the few agencies in the city that offers apartments that owners use as a primary residence. Consequently, the lodgings have a lot more personality, especially since many of the owners are in the arts. The personable Bernard Barc—who is so friendly he often ends up having dinner with his renters—has many actors, dancers, and other artists on his roster, whose professional commitments require them to leave town for long stretches of time. Hence, you might find yourself in a huge loft in a converted convent near the place de la Bastille, with a two-person bathtub in the master bedroom and original artwork on the walls (1,270€ per week), or a small studio in a posh neighborhood near the Musée d'Orsay with hand-painted textiles dangling over the couch for 620€ per week. Barc visits all of his 200-odd apartments regularly; he is on a first-name basis with most of the proprietors and checks up on them too. The apartments are in tip-top condition (these are working artists, not the starving breed) and all over the city; prices rise as you approach the center. Some of the best deals are in the "outer" arrondissements, like the 10th, 11th, and 12th; though they might require a bit more public transportation, they are also some of the hipper, up-and-coming neighborhoods. It's hard to give a realistic range of prices with such a varied range of lodgings, but most studios range from around 450€ to 700€ per week, one bedrooms are in the 600€ to 900€ per week range, two bedrooms about 750€ to 1,200€ per week, and 1,200€ to 2,000€ per week for three bedrooms and up. Full descriptions and photos are on the website, as is a nice list of Paris links and tips. Minimum stay is 4 nights.

AGENCIES THAT ACT AS MIDDLEMEN

If you are looking for a real bargain and don't mind a more informal approach, contact **Allô Logement Temporaire** (64 rue du Temple, 3rd arrond.; ☎ 01 42 72 00 06; www.allo-logement-temporaire.asso.fr; Métro: Rambuteau; no credit cards). This is not an agency, but a nonprofit association that acts as an intermediary between apartment owners and renters. Though he mainly works with people looking for 1-month to 1-year rentals, Georg Reidiger has weekly rentals as well, though you won't have an enormous choice. The website is not slick (in fact, it won't tell you much), the apartments are not luxurious (though they are clean and well kept), but the prices are less than half what you will pay at an ordinary agency. A 24-sq.-m (258-sq.-ft) studio in a chic building in the Marais, for example, is only 300€ per week. At that price, who cares if it's a 3rd floor walk-up? Larger apartments run from around 500€ to 700€ for up to 99 sq. m (1,065 sq. ft.). Reidiger has apartments all over the city, though not surprisingly, not the sleekest neighborhoods, like the 7th and 8th arrondissements. The catch is, you have to be willing to deal with a very laid-back organizational structure. The way it works is this: You contact Allô Logement via telephone or e-mail with your dates and requirements, and you will be sent information and photos of what's available. There is no formal contract (though there is a 55€ yearly membership charge), and you must pay in cash, travelers checks, or wire transfer, as you will pay the owner directly. Reidiger is a very nice, longtime expatriate from Germany who speaks excellent English and will answer all of your questions—the only problem is, they might not be the ones you asked. If it sounds a little odd, know that Allô Logement is not only a member of the Paris Tourist Office but has also been in existence since 1988. Reidiger does next to no advertising but does a brisk business through word of mouth; he has known most of his owners and many of his clients for years. Minimum stay 1 week.

Another agency that serves as a middleman for apartment owners and clients is **Inter-Logement** (1 Villa de l'Astrolabe, 15th arrond.; ☎ 01 45 66 66 88; www. inter-logement.net; Métro: Falguière or Montparnasse; MC, V for agency fee, rentals cash only). Better organized than Allô Logement Temporaire, this agency works more or less under the same premise, and most of the time, once the connection has been made, you will pay the apartment owner directly (cash only). Unlike Mr. Reidiger, Inter-Logement has a fairly complete website where you can punch in your dates and a list of available apartments will come up, each with a detailed list of amenities and photos. Start looking about a month before your arrival date, as owners tend not to post their apartments far in advance. Rental rates are very reasonable (if not as rock-bottom as Allô-Logement); a splendid two-bedroom, 73-sq.-m (785-sq.-ft.) apartment in tip-top shape (fresh paint, tasteful antiques, designer tiles in the bathroom, full kitchen with dishwasher, washing machine and dryer) that looks out on the whimsical Stravinsky Fountain near the Pompidou Center is only 700€ per week, a far cry from what you would pay for a similar apartment at a regular agency. A cute but tiny studio (24 sq. m/258 sq. ft.) in the Marais, with exposed beams, original artwork (the owner is a painter) and an antique Chinese armoire (but no oven, and no elevator) is only 350€. For rentals of up to 2 weeks, electricity is included in the price. What is not, however, is the agency fee, which is 20% of the rental rate, plus a membership fee of 25€. Even with the fees, prices are not high, and with some 3,500 apartments on their rosters, you'll have ample choice. The down side is, with so many apartments, many of which come and go, the agency cannot personally visit all the properties. According to Inter-Logement's director, Francis Le Bars, most have been visited at least once, but not all. He also says that if the customer is really disappointed on arrival, they can ask to be relocated. The agency has been in business 11 years and is listed with the Paris Tourist Office; still, this is not as risk-free an option as the agencies I've listed above. Minimum stay 1 week.

HOME EXCHANGE

If you're willing to do a little legwork, a home exchange can be the ultimate in affordable vacation accommodations. Of course, the concept is a little scary at first glance: swapping your home with that of a stranger in another country for a week or two. But when done right, risk is at a minimum (after all, the stranger is taking the same risk, so there's leverage from the get-go) and you'll get the added benefit of staying in an apartment that is set up for daily living, and contact with natives (that is, the owners of said apartment) who can give you all sorts of tips and perks, like access to their computer or transit pass. And what's more, you won't pay a single centime (other than a membership fee). The best way to get past trust issues is to go with a trustworthy home exchange organization, like **Intervac** (www.intervac.com) or the **Home Exchange** (www.homeexchange.com), both of which have been in business for several decades and have dozens of listings for Paris apartments.

A MONASTERY

Unfortunately, the Catholic monasteries of Paris no longer take lodgers—mostly due to the advancing age and diminishing number of monks. However, there's a lovely Zen monastery that will be delighted to rent you a small apartment, provided you are willing to take off your shoes and refrain from smoking. Polish-born Zen masters Graznya and Jacob Perl run the **Centre Parisien de Zen** (35 rue de Lyon, 12th arrond.; ☎ 01 77 11 13 36; www.maisonzen.com; Métro: Gare de Lyon; no credit cards), an oasis of tranquility in the bustling neighborhood that surrounds the Gare de Lyon. Nestled in a quiet courtyard, this meditation center rents out a handful of small, spotless, simply furnished studios at reasonable weekly rates: 385€ single occupancy, and 490€ double. Larger one-bedroom apartments go for 455€ for one and 560€ for two. The tiny kitchens have two-burner stoves but no oven; dishes and cooking utensils are provided. Apartments are equipped with TVs and phone—what's more, local calls as well as calls to certain countries (like the U.S.) are free of charge. Children between 5 and 12 years old pay half price; kids under 5 stay free. Though 1 week is the usual minimum stay, you can sometimes book for just a few days, depending on availability (70€–90€ per night). Guests have access to the meditation room, but participation in the center's activities is entirely voluntary. Despite the monastic overtones, the atmosphere is very relaxed and easygoing; the Perls are very open and friendly, as well as fluent in English—in fact, Mr. Perl is a U.S. citizen. Reserve ahead, these apartments get booked up months in advance.

APARTHOTELS

Somewhere between a hotel and an apartment, "aparthotels" offer some of the benefits of both. Geared toward business travelers, these accommodations are practical and reliable, if pretty much devoid of charm. The good news is, you'll have a kitchenette, the meal-making capabilities of which should cancel out the somewhat higher rates than for a standard hotel. Rates are generally also higher than what you might pay for a short-term rental, but you get hotel-like perks like fresh towels and a reception desk to call if you need something.

The most well-known, and with 16 locations in Paris, **Citadines** (www.citadines.com; ☎ 08 25 33 33 32; AE, DC, MC, V) is popular with both tourists and business travelers. Besides being comfortable and reliable (if not particularly charm-enhanced), these aparthotels are generally very well located and near public transportation. The modern apartments are virtually identical in all locations (though Louvre, République, and Les Halles have a somewhat snazzier decor), practical, functional, with living room, bedroom, bathroom, and a full, workable kitchen that you can actually cook meals in. Studios have a similar layout (you can see both layouts on the website), but with a pull-out bed instead of a separate bedroom. There are TVs as well as stereos, and maid service is weekly. Bottle warmers, baby beds, and changing mats are also available at no extra charge. The reception desk can help arrange delivery of groceries and take-out food to your room, and there is an on-site launderette.

The one "Prestige" location, Opéra Vendôme, comes with more perks (like daily maid service) but at a substantially higher price. Rates vary according to location, size of room, and how long you stay, and when. The longer you stay, the lower the rate. Studios for two in most locations run around 115€ to 170€ per night, and from around 170€ to 250€ in the most prized locations like Louvre, Opéra, and St-Germain des Prés; add another 50% to 75% to these rates for a one-bedroom apartment that sleeps up to four. Two locations have two-bedroom apartments that sleep up to six: Trocadéro (370€–532€), and ouch, Vendôme (488€–706€), but for a big gang, renting an apartment is usually a more affordable option (p. 22).

With only four sites in Paris and a more basic comfort level, the Citéa (www.citea.com) chain comes in second in the aparthotel standings. Two locations are too far from the center for tourists, but the other two are very well located: The **Citéa Tour Eiffel** (43 rue St-Charles, 15th arrond.; ☎ 01 40 58 66 00; Métro: Charles-Michel; AE, DC, MC, V) is about a 10-minute walk from the Eiffel Tower and the **Citéa Tilsitt-Champs Elysées** (24 rue de Tilsitt, 17th arrond.; ☎ 01 55 37 80 00; Métro: Charles de Gaulle–Etoile; AE, DC, MC, V) is right behind the Arc de Triomphe. Both have simple, just-the-facts-please decor, with kitchens ranging from closet-sized to ample (ask!); the Eiffel Tower location has a more chic look. At the Champs-Elysées location, a few duplexes have great views of the upper half of the Arc de Triomphe and the Eiffel Tower (the other suites face the unexciting courtyard). All Citéas have two sets of rates, one for stays under 7 nights ("hôtelière"), with daily maid service, and one for over 7 nights ("résidentielle"), with weekly maid service. Studios at the Champs-Elysées location range from 106€ to 155€ per night for two, and suites for up to three people from 150€ to 215€ per night; at the Eiffel Tower location studios range from 109€ to 155€, and suites from 195€ to 215€ (these are high-season rates; range depends on size of lodgings and length of stay).

STUDENT HOUSING

Founded by American expatriate and heiress Grace Whitney Hoff, the **Foyer International des Etudiants** (93 blvd. St-Michel; 5th arrond.; ☎ 01 43 54 49 63; www.fie.fr; RER: Luxembourg; MC, V) offers lodgings for at least 3-night stays for tourists in the summer. Rooms are quaint and old-fashioned with wood floors, '40s-era wood furniture, and a clean, if ancient, sink (toilets and showers are in the hall). Single rooms are 34€ per night; doubles are 25€ per person, per night. Reservations can be made by telephone, e-mail, or regular mail. The building is just across the street from the Luxembourg gardens, and it is a straight shot from the Charles de Gaulle airport on the RER B line.

HOTELS

Some people prefer the traditional route, and Paris certainly does not lack for hotel possibilities. With some 75,000 rooms on offer, there's bound to be something that suits your tastes.

That said, hotels in Paris are a mixed bag. Midrange and budget hotel rates are less expensive than in some other international capitals, but most of these rooms are tiny, amenity challenged, and sometimes do not even have an elevator. Then again, the majority of the 1,500-odd Parisian hotels are small, family-run operations where friendly owners will gratefully ply you with helpful tips and personal recommendations—no small gift in a city where interacting with the natives is notoriously difficult.

WHAT TO EXPECT WHEN YOU GET THERE

Before you plunge into the list below, however, keep in mind the following: **Parisian hotel rooms tend to be small.** Why do I keep repeating this? Because inevitably, tourists who come from countries where hotel rooms are often staggeringly big (does anyone actually need two king-size beds in a double room?) are shocked when they check in to tiny, family hotels in ancient buildings. After weathering years of complaints, many Parisian hotel owners are convinced that all Americans have bedrooms the size of the Astro Dome.

Don't be too hard on the management; most historic Parisian buildings are protected by city regulations that make it difficult, if not impossible, to make structural changes. If you absolutely need room to stretch out, ask for a triple, or even a quadruple room (if they're available). Otherwise, consider an international chain hotel, where space and extra amenities are usually not a problem.

On the upside, double beds, which used to require a lot of cuddling to avoid pushing your loved one over the edge, have gotten bigger in many hotels, thanks to a new system that clips two singles together which are then covered by a thick, seamless mattress cover.

Also be prepared for **minimal amenities.** Washcloths are scarce, toiletries are basic, and many smaller hotels still don't have elevators (and when they do, they're often closet size). I will note when rooms are particularly small or spacious, otherwise, assume that they are large enough to live in comfortably, but that you'll have to do your yoga workout somewhere else. I've also mentioned when there is no elevator, or when getting to your room will be difficult if you have any mobility concerns. All of the rooms in the hotels listed below have in-room bathrooms with toilets, unless otherwise mentioned.

NOW FOR THE GOOD NEWS

Now that I've prepared you for the worst, let me tell you what Parisian hotels do have (besides charm and personality, *bien sûr*). Almost all have in-room TVs (some with cable channels), telephones, and many have hair dryers in the bathrooms. Irons, fax machines, and hair dryers (if they are not in the room) can usually be found at the reception desk. Almost all have some sort of Internet access, be it a computer in the lobby or hotel-wide Wi-Fi.

Bidding for Four-Stars & Fluffy Pillows

Always dreamed of staying in a four-star hotel in Paris, but room service alone would break your budget? If you are up to the challenge, there are amazing deals to be had on bidding sites like Priceline.com and Hotwire.com. With a little bit of informed cyber-wangling you can get discounts of 50% to 70% on rooms in luxury hotel chains like Meridian, Hilton, and Concord, which usually go for $250 to $350 per night. So that means that you might be able to stay at hotels like the Concorde Lafayette, or Le Meridien Etoile—that is, four-star, everything-you-could-ask-for lodgings—for between $125 and $175 per night for a double. To achieve deals like these, you need take a crash course on online bidding, and one of the best ways to do this is to visit www.biddingfortravel.com, a site where travelers share war stories and tell all about what price they got where through bidding on Priceline.com. They also have an excellent FAQ that explains bidding basics and best strategies for getting what you want.

Now that you're ready to bid, keep in mind the following: The hotels involved in the bidding wars, at least as far as Paris is concerned, are almost entirely big, modern, chain hotels that may have endless perks and high comfort levels, but offer up the same style of accommodations pretty much anywhere in the world. In other words, if you are looking for Parisian charm, you probably won't find it here. If you are looking for spacious rooms, fluffy pillows, and high thread counts, cyber-bidding is a good option for travelers on a budget. As an example of what I mean, the Meridian Etoile and Montparnasse hotels show up often in the bidding wars, as do the Concorde Lafayette, the Marriott Rive Gauche, the Pullman Paris Bercy and the Pullman Paris Rive Gauche.

Since the scalding heat wave of 2003, hotel owners have been scurrying to install air conditioning, but this is certainly not a citywide phenomenon. Since normal Parisian weather is anything but tropical—June and July were sweater weather in 2008—your chances of encountering sweltering heat are low; still, if you are coming in the summer months, you may want to think twice about taking a room on a non-air-conditioned top floor or facing a noisy street that makes it impossible to open the windows at night. I have mentioned air-conditioning where it is available; if it is not mentioned in the description, that means there is none.

In an effort to please hungry American and British tourists, many hotels now offer a copious "buffet" breakfast that usually includes yogurt, ham, cereal, juice, croissants, and sometimes even eggs and bacon. Should you really need to eat in the morning, and a buffet is available (around 10€–12€), go for it: You will pay a fortune for the same at a cafe, if you can even find one that serves a full breakfast. If the breakfast is "continental," which really means French, you'll get coffee or tea, a croissant, bread, and if you are lucky, juice. If you are planning on eating breakfast at the hotel, find out what it includes because you could end up paying up to 9€ for a soggy continental breakfast, when you could have paid less and had more fun munching on a croissant on a sidewalk terrace at a cafe.

WHEN TO RESERVE

Early. Paris is one of the world's top travel destinations, and hotels book up fast. Even during typical slow months, the city might be completely booked up because of a trade show or festival that you are not aware of.

Make sure you understand the cancellation policy, and try to respect it—unexpected cancellations cost family-run operations dearly. They'll cost you too: Most hotels take at least 1 night's stay as a deposit, which they will keep if you don't show up.

Though bargaining is generally frowned upon, many hotels do offer discounts for stays of over 3 nights; if they don't offer one up front, it's worth asking.

Finally, if you haven't made a reservation in advance, and you aren't having any luck with the hotels below, don't despair—the **Paris Tourist Office** (25 rue des Pyramides; ☎ 08 92 68 30 00, .34€ per minute; www.parisinfo.com; Métro: Pyramides) can help you find a room, even at the last minute.

I've organized hotels in order of price within neighborhoods, starting with the cheapest digs first. To help you find lodgings within your budget, below is a handy index by price range.

What the symbols mean:

€ Up to 90€ per night
€€ 91€ to 120€ per night
€€€ 121€ to 135€ per night
€€€€ Over 135€ per night

The Puzzling Mystery of High & Low Season

Parisian hotel rate fluctuations are a little like the weather—it's difficult to distinguish one season from the other. Everyone seems to agree that July and August are low season. That's when any Parisian with a penny to their name flees the capital, and hotels are desperate for business. The rest of the year is a free-for-all, heavily dependent on the scheduling of tradeshows. For the nitty-gritty on trade show dates, visit www.salons-online.com and click on "Paris," but in general, September and October are usually high season, November, December, and January low (except for Christmas and New Year's). Once spring arrives, prices tend to rise. The good news is that the seasonal changes seem to give owners as big of a headache as guests, and most of the hotels listed below do not change their prices during the year. I've tried to mention fluctuations when they occur—to be absolutely sure, call or check your hotel's website. It's a good idea to **check hotel websites** anyway—**hotels often offer discounts (anywhere from 10%–50%) during slow periods,** and the only way to know which period is slow is to look at the site.

Seeing Stars

French hotels are graded by a government-regulated system that hands out 0 to 4 stars, depending on the rating the lodgings receive, which the hotels then must post at the entrance to their establishment. The only problem is that the criteria used have more to do with quantity than quality. Rooms are rated on things like size, number of beds, and the presence or absence of items like hair dryers and minibars—overall atmosphere and charm are not necessarily a factor. So it's possible to end up in a darling two-star hotel that's much nicer than a three-star down the street with big rooms and a minibar with all the ambience of a rehab center. One thing is sure, the more stars it has, the more a hotel is allowed to charge. My advice: Use the French star system as a rough estimate of quality, then do some homework on your own. By the way, the stars besides the listings below are our own, and have no relation to the French star system.

In addition, many hotel listings also carry a cluster of stars ✮, indicating our opinion of the hotel's desirability (this does not have anything to do with price, but with the value you receive for the price you pay). The stars mean:

No star: Good
✮ Very good
✮✮ Great
✮✮✮ Outstanding! A must!

One other symbol: You will see 🄺 after the names of hotels that are particularly family friendly.

LOUVRE–CHÂTELET (1ST ARRONDISSEMENT)

The area surrounding the Louvre is littered with hotels, most of which are dreadfully overpriced. Even modest "budget" hotels, with no visible amenities or charm, charge high prices and get away with it because many tourists are convinced that this neighborhood is the best spot to set up camp. If you only are in town for one or two days, I'll agree, a central locale is key, since time will be of the essence. But if you have even a little more time, you'll find much more comfortable lodgings at the same or lower prices, a 10-minute walk away.

NEAR THE LOUVRE

€€   While you're not going to be bowled over by the decor at **Hôtel Louvre Richelieu** (51 rue de Richelieu, 1st arrond.; ☎ 01 42 97 46 20; www.louvre-richelieu.com; Métro: Palais Royal–Musée du Louvre or Pyramides; MC, V), you will be pleased by the friendly, helpful service, and the close proximity to the Louvre, the Palais Royal, and the Opéra Garnier. Rooms are tidy with relatively roomy bathrooms; rooms facing the street get much more light, and windows are double-paned, so noise is not a problem. The calm is reinforced by the absence of

TVs; your leg muscles will get reinforcement by the lack of an elevator. Doubles run 102€ to 122€, triples 132€, and there are two rooms with just a sink (shared facilities are in the hall): a double for 88€ and a single for 75€. All the rooms on the first floor are nonsmoking.

€€   If you simply must be right on top of the Mona Lisa, **Hôtel Louvre Forum** (25 rue du Bouloi, 1st arrond.; ☎ 01 42 36 54 19; www.paris-hotel-louvre-forum.com; Métro: Louvre-Palais Royal; AE, MC, V) is a reliable option. The air-conditioned rooms are small and style-free, buy they are in excellent shape and offer a good level of comfort for the price, 100€ to 110€ for a double. And one certainly can't complain about the location: a couple of blocks from the Louvre and the Palais Royal, and not much farther to the gardens of Les Halles. The service can be brisk but is usually attentive. Closed in August.

TOWARD LES HALLES

€€–€€€   A few streets over from the messy, but animated pedestrian area around Les Halles is a relatively quiet haven, **Hôtel du Cygne** ★ (3 rue du Cygne, 1st arrond.; ☎ 01 42 60 14 16; www.hotelducygne.fr; closed Aug; Métro: Etienne Marcel, RER: Châtelet–Les Halles; AE, MC, V). Housed in a 17th-century building, there are plenty of exposed wood beams, stone walls, and narrow staircases to admire, and rooms are decorated with a good dose of charm; old-fashioned wall paper, wooden bedsteads, and floral prints add to the ambience. Cute and cozy doubles range from 110€ to 130€ but tend to be on the small side—if you need space, or are traveling with children, ask for the "Grand Chambre," the only room large enough to accommodate an extra bed (145€–165€, depending on the season). Windows are not double-paned, but in general this is a quiet street and only a couple blocks from the food shops and cafes of rue Montorgueil.

€€–€€€   Smack in the middle of a pedestrian area, but with a little more class than the Cygne, **Hôtel Agora** ★★ (7 rue de la Cossonnerie, 1st arrond.; ☎ 01 42 33 46 02; www.hotel-paris-agora.com; Métro: Les Halles, RER: Châtelet–Les Halles; MC, V) is just a few steps away from the RER B, which will whip you directly to the Charles de Gaulle airport. The area around Les Halles may not be to everyone's liking—it's noisy and crowded and uncomfortably close to the sleaze shops on rue St-Denis—but it is centrally located, and once you get past the ugly wallpaper in the entryway this hotel is actually rather adorable. Pretty floral patterned wallpaper and a mix of antiques, modern furniture, and tasteful artwork give the rooms a dash of personality; some rooms on the fifth floor have a view of St-Eustache. Surprisingly quiet for this neighborhood, the main noise problem is not at night, but in the early morning when the garbage and delivery trucks do their rounds. As in many Parisian hotels, shower lovers get the best rates, 104€ to 120€ for a double as opposed to 156€ for those with a bath. The largest and quietest rooms are on the courtyard, but they also get the least light.

ON THE ISLANDS

€€   And now for something completely different: a hotel in a hospital. I'm serious. **Hospitel** ★★ (1 place du Parvis Notre-Dame, 1st arrond.; ☎ 01 44 32 01 00;

Accommodations on the Right Bank
(1st–4th & 9th–11th)

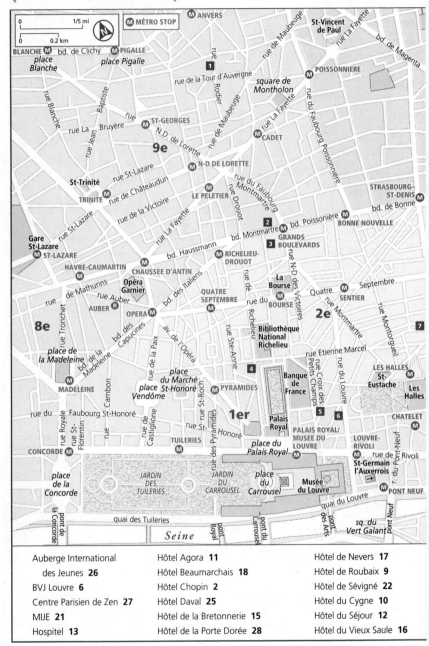

Auberge International des Jeunes **26**	Hôtel Agora **11**	Hôtel de Nevers **17**
BVJ Louvre **6**	Hôtel Beaumarchais **18**	Hôtel de Roubaix **9**
Centre Parisien de Zen **27**	Hôtel Chopin **2**	Hôtel de Sévigné **22**
MIJE **21**	Hôtel Daval **25**	Hôtel du Cygne **10**
Hospitel **13**	Hôtel de la Bretonnerie **15**	Hôtel du Séjour **12**
	Hôtel de la Porte Dorée **28**	Hôtel du Vieux Saule **16**

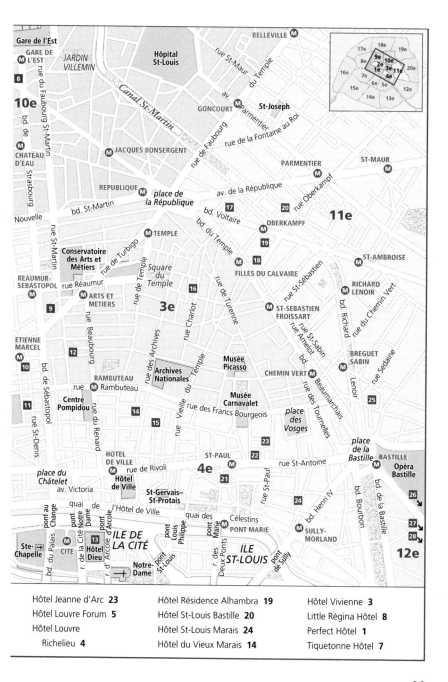

Hôtel Jeanne d'Arc **23**	Hôtel Résidence Alhambra **19**
Hôtel Louvre Forum **5**	Hôtel St-Louis Bastille **20**
Hôtel Louvre	Hôtel St-Louis Marais **24**
Richelieu **4**	Hôtel du Vieux Marais **14**

Hôtel Vivienne **3**
Little Régina Hôtel **8**
Perfect Hôtel **1**
Tiquetonne Hôtel **7**

To Surf or Not to Surf?

Countless sites on the Internet promise to save you fantastic amounts on your hotel bill, but do they really? In Paris, at least, where most of the affordable hotels are small and privately owned, you will often do better by dealing directly with the hotel, many of which have their own Internet bargains that are better than those you'll find on the big search engines. If you do decide to hunt your prey on the Web, compare and contrast some of your results with the rates on individual hotel websites. You may be surprised to find that the hotel's rates are actually cheaper than the Web "bargains." If you don't mind going corporate, and a chain is what you are after, you may very well find significant reductions on the Web, especially on "aggregator" sites that search other search engines as well as hotel websites and charge no booking fees. Here are a few suggestions:

- Mobissimo.com, HotelsCombined.com, Kayak.com, and Sidestep.com are all helpful aggregator sites, as is Travelaxe.com, which does a side-by-side comparison.
- Some French sites, like Lastminute.fr and Opodo.fr seem to have their fingers a little closer to the pulse of Parisian hotel deals; Kelkoo.fr, an aggregator, has some particularly good deals, though you should look carefully to see where the hotels are located (the cheapest are often in remote areas).
- The Paris tourist office has a good search engine on its site (www.parisinfo.com) with lots of last-minute discounts. You can also get help with reservations in person at any of the tourist office welcome centers except the Montmartre Tourist Office and Carrousel du Louvre. See the planning section for addresses.

www.hotel-hospitel.com; Métro: Cité or Hôtel de Ville; MC, V) is located on the top floor of the Hôtel Dieu, Paris's oldest public hospital. Getting there is a little unnerving—the elevators are in an operating block, and you might be sharing the ride with someone on a gurney—but once you arrive, you are charmed by the warm welcome, the cheerful decor, and the impeccably clean rooms (doubles 120€). The ceilings are *mansardé*—that is, slanted—and the exterior light source is a large skylight, a few of which reveal a corner of Notre-Dame, which is right next door. In fact, you literally can't find a hotel more centrally located than this—Point Zero, the official center of Paris, is just outside on the esplanade in front of the cathedral. Some upsides to the medical surroundings: There are two wheel-chair-friendly rooms, air-conditioning, and your orthopedist would be proud of the mattresses. If you can get beyond the fact that this is a working hospital, this is an excellent value for the location. Besides, this isn't just any hospital; it's a historic monument with a formal garden in its 19th-century inner courtyard.

OPERA–BOURSE (2ND ARRONDISSEMENT)

Though not exactly lacking for hotels, there's a dearth of affordable lodgings in this wealthy, businessy neighborhood between the lush boulevard de l'Opéra and the stock exchange *(bourse)*. If you're willing to go just a little bit off the beaten path, however, there are a couple of hidden treasures that are still only a 10 or 15 minute walk to the Louvre.

€€   It's a relief to see that the **Tiquetonne Hôtel** (6 rue Tiquetonne, 2nd arrond.; ☎ 01 42 36 94 58; fax 01 42 36 02 94; closed Aug and the week between Christmas and New Year's; Métro: Etienne Marcel; MC, V) has not succumbed to the rapid gentrification of its surrounding neighborhood. Just around the corner from the chic Passage du Grand Cerf, this bargain standby has bravely withstood the onslaught, keeping its rates way down. This is definitely a budget hotel: The doors feel a little light and the carpets are a little worn, but the paint is fresh, the ceilings are high, and the atmosphere is homey. The old-fashioned bedspreads lay over firm mattresses; if the decor isn't exactly up to date, at least it's a change from the standardized blandness of so many midrange accommodations. This is one of the few hotels left in Paris that still has cheap rooms without a toilet, singles with just a sink go for 35€. All of the doubles (55€) come with a toilet and a shower but none of the rooms have TVs and there is no Internet access. The location is excellent, steps away from Les Halles and a block or so from nifty restaurants and food shops of rue de Montorgueil.

€–€€   "We really don't charge enough," sheepishly admits the owner of **Hôtel Vivienne** ★★ 🧒 (40 rue Vivienne, 2nd arrond.; ☎ 01 42 33 13 26; www.hotel-vivienne.com; Métro: Bourse or Grands Boulevards; MC, V), with a smile. She's right—with comfortable, renovated, spotless doubles from 87€ to 114€, this place is a steal. Prices are calculated according to the size of your party, which means, space allowing, two people can stay in an extra-large triple for the price of a double. If you don't mind sharing a toilet, there are several rooms that go for 75€. The entire hotel was overhauled over the last few years; the spacious rooms are decorated with subtle floral prints, neo-deco furniture, and fresh carpets. A few rooms have small balconies; some have communicating doors, a good bet for families (other kid-friendly pluses: Children under 12 stay for free in their parents' room and cribs are available). Right next to the Passage des Panoramas and Passage Joufroy in a neighborhood filled with shops for stamp and coin collectors;

Is My Child a Full-Fledged Person?

In most Parisian hotels, if a child is sleeping in an adult-size bed, even if it is a folding one, he or she counts as an extra person. Thus, if you're traveling with a 7-year-old, for example, you will have to pay for a triple room. Children that still fit (and can sleep in) a *lit bébé* (lee bay-bay), or crib, generally do not pay—but you'll need to call ahead to see if the hotel has a crib (many do).

the location may not be exactly central, but it's a short walk to the Métro and a 10-minute stroll to the Palais Royal. If you are a light sleeper, ask for a room facing the courtyard; the street can be a little noisy.

THE MARAIS (3RD & 4TH ARRONDISSEMENTS)

Many centuries ago, this neighborhood was a swamp *(marais)*, but now it's merely swamped with stylish boutiques, restaurants, and people who seem to have just stepped out of a hair salon. Stunning 16th- and 17th-century mansions, which had fallen into disrepair, have been scrubbed down and fixed up over the past few decades, and they shine like pearls along the narrow streets of this fascinatingly mixed area where streets filled with jewelry wholesalers run up against cool bars and clubs, which are quickly closing in on what's left of Paris's historic Jewish quarter. There are many excellent museums here, including the Musée Picasso and the Musée Carnavalet. In short, this is a great area to stay in, if you don't mind being slightly out of the center of town. You can walk to Nôtre Dame in 15 to 20 minutes, otherwise buses and Metro lines will whisk you there in a snap. Surprisingly, there is a good range of affordable lodgings here.

NEAR BEAUBOURG (CENTRE POMPIDOU)

€   Mr. and Mrs. Caetano provide more than just cheap rooms at the **Hôtel du Séjour** ✹ (36 rue du Grenier St-Lazare, 3rd arrond.; ☎ 01 48 87 40 36; Métro: Rambuteau or Etienne Marcel; no credit cards); they offer a warm welcome that more than makes up for the creaky staircase and worn towels. Just a few blocks from the Centre Pompidou, but away from the annoyances of Les Halles, this budget hotel is not only a favorite with students and young people, but also with their parents, many of whom have become return clients. The clean, cheerful rooms have high ceilings and double-paned windows, through which ample sunlight streams, but that's about the extent of the amenities: There are no phones, TVs, Internet access, or elevator. Doubles with toilets and showers are 60€; if you are willing to make do with just a sink (and share toilet and shower with others), a double will cost just 50€.

€   A little further north, near the Conservatoire des Arts et Métiers, but still within walking distance of all of the sights of the Marais, is the **Hôtel de Roubaix** (6 rue Greneta, 3rd arrond.; ☎ 01 42 72 89 91; www.hotel-de-roubaix.com; Métro: Réaumur-Sébastopol or Arts et Métiers; DC, MC, V). These simple but homey lodgings are also family owned and operated, but with a slightly more upscale feel: There are TVs, telephones, an elevator (but no Internet access), and all rooms have toilets. Rooms are furnished with grandma-style floral prints on the walls and a few pseudo-antiques; mattresses, however, are on the mushy side. Another plus, the price of a double (77€–80€) includes a continental breakfast.

NEAR THE CHURCH OF ST-PAUL–ST-LOUIS

€   Brisk efficiency reigns at the **Hôtel de Sévigné** ✹ (2 rue Mahler, 4th arrond.; ☎ 01 42 72 76 17; www.le-sevigne.com; Métro: St-Paul; MC, V), a tightly run operation that offers clean, modern, air-conditioned rooms for excellent prices: 80€ to 91€ for a double room. Though the charm factor may not be particularly high here and there is no Internet access, all the rooms are in very good shape, and the location is terrific—a few minutes walk from the museums and boutiques of the Marais, and a block or two from the place des Vosges. Double-paned windows are in all the rooms, though those facing the busy rue St-Antoine do get some noise. On the other hand, they also look out on the domed church of St-Paul–St-Louis. No Wi-Fi, but you can plug your computer into the room phone for a dial up connection (at high rates).

€€   Considering its prime location—in the heart of the Marais and next to the quiet, shaded place du Marché Ste-Catherine—**Hôtel Jeanne d'Arc** ★★ (3 rue de Jarente, 4th arrond.; ☎ 01 48 87 62 11; www.hoteljeannedarc.com; Métro: St-Paul; MC, V) is an incredible deal. Yet despite the low rates (doubles range from 89€–116€), rooms are comfortable, colorful, and nicely appointed, with antique-style wooden bedsteads and furniture. So where's the catch? There isn't one, except that it books up months in advance, especially for fashion show weeks (Feb, Mar, July, and Sept), when industry insiders snap up most of the rooms. Also, prices increase dramatically for triples and quads: 146€ and 160€, respectively. Located on a quiet street, rooms get little or no noise. Unfortunately, none of them face the delightful square. The mosaic mirror in the lobby and the painted walls in the breakfast room are creations of local artists. *Note:* There is another hotel with the same name in the 13th arrondissement—make sure you are in contact with hotel in the Marais when you reserve, or you will be in for an unpleasant surprise.

€€–€€€   For something with a little more history, try the **Hôtel Saint-Louis Marais** ★ (1 rue Charles V, 4th arrond.; ☎ 01 48 87 87 04; www.saintlouis marais.com; AE, DC, MC, V). The exposed beams and narrow staircases attest to the fact that the building dates from 1720, as do the tomettes, six-sided terracotta tiles, on the floor. Not all is ancient here, however: The just-renovated rooms have new mattresses, newly tiled bathrooms, and flatscreen TVs, while the decor is a nice mix of modern and period styles. Standard doubles go for 115€; for more space, book a superior double for 140€, which can sleep three for the same price. There is no air-conditioning, but the thick stone walls and tile floors keep summer heat at bay. With only 19 rooms on four floors (there is no elevator), noise is not a problem; the adjacent streets are so calm it's hard to believe you are only a few minutes walk from the place de la Bastille, and only a short stroll from the Ile St-Louis.

NORTH OF THE HOTEL DE VILLE

€€€–€€€€   A century younger, but still busting with charm, **Hôtel de la Bretonnerie** ★★ (22 rue Sainte Croix de la Bretonnerie, 4th arrond.; ☎ 01 48 87 77 63; www.bretonnerie.com; Métro: Hôtel de Ville; MC, V) has its share of exposed beams and stone walls, but it also has canopy beds, period fabrics, and wall-to-wall carpeting. The overall feel is a little more modern, perhaps a little more plush; every room has a different color scheme and layout. There are significant reductions in August (in fact, there are periodic promotional rates throughout the year on the website). For the level of style and comfort, not to mention the excellent location, even the rack rates are very reasonable: Doubles start at

The Pros & Cons of Hotel Packages

While the recent hike in airfares has made them less attractive than they once were, if you get a good one, a package can still save you a mint. But like so many things on the Internet, and in life for that matter, you need to know where to go. This is a case where the usual suspects, Travelocity, Expedia, and Orbitz, may let you down with high-priced hotels and uninspired deals. The sites to seek out are those of package specialists, single-minded travel agencies that know the ins and outs of bundled deals.

Go-Today (www.go-today.com), considered the package king, still has good deals on Paris, like their 6-night hotel-air package for just $799 per person, about the same as the price of an air ticket alone. True, these rates are for winter, but there are good bargains for other seasons as well and with what you've saved you can buy yourself a new camelhair coat. **Gate 1 Travel** (www.gate1travel.com) is another winner, with springtime 4-night packages for as little as $799. The Paris City Break at **Europe ASAP** (www.europeasap.com) includes airfare and 6 nights in a hotel for $949.

Deciphering the nitty-gritty details of packages is an art (you'll need to add up all the fees to get the real deal). Make sure to check what is included in the package, particularly insurance, airport taxes, and fuel surcharges, which can really add up. Your choice of hotel (you'll usually pick from a list) will affect the final price tag, as will additional services like airport transfers and city tours.

Pauline Frommer Says:

"A key to deciphering packages is to remember that they're always based on double occupancy, so be sure to double the costs and then subtract the airfares to get the lowdown on what you're actually paying for the room. The one exception to this rule may be packages that you create using such sites as Travelocity, Expedia, and Orbitz. Very occasionally if you have a specific hotel in mind, you can save money this way."

125€ (there are canopy beds at this level) and go up to 160€ for the largest and most romantic *chambres de charme* (honeymooners, take note). On some floors there is a small staircase to climb after exiting the elevator.

€€€–€€€€ As the enthusiastic and gracious owner will be only too happy to explain, the **Hôtel du Vieux Marais** ★★ ✪ (8 rue du Plâtre, 4th arrond.; ☎ 01 42 78 47 22; www.vieuxmarais.com; Métro: Hôtel de Ville; MC, V) has had a complete (and in the lobby, on-going) overhaul, resulting in large, comfortable, air-conditioned modern rooms with blonde wood bedsteads and neo-Art Deco armchairs, new bathrooms with aged-marble tiles, and lots of closet space. What's more, the hotel is located smack in the middle of the Marais, and close to public transportation. The downside is the price, which varies radically according to season. When the trade shows are on, generally early fall, early spring, and early summer, doubles are 155€, which is reasonable, considering the quality of the accommodations, but not exactly a bargain. On the other hand, at all other times doubles are 115€, which is a real deal. The only way to know which price is current, aside from carefully scanning www.salons-online.com to find out when the trade shows are on, is to contact the hotel. At press time, finishing touches were being put on a new, handicap-accessible room on the ground floor.

€€–€€€€ Don't be put off by the '70s-era decor in the lobby of **Hôtel du Vieux Saule** ✮✮ (6 rue de Picardie, 3rd arrond.; ☎ 01 42 72 01 14; www. hotelvieuxsaule.com; Métro: République or Filles du Calvaire; AE, DC, MC, V)—most of the air-conditioned rooms have had a chic makeover. Wood and rattan headboards and Villeroy & Boch bathroom fixtures are de rigueur here; designer fabrics in warm colors cover beds and windows. Like the Vieux Marais, the Vieux Saule ("old willow") also suffers from seasonal price swings: During trade show season, doubles run 140€ to 180€; off season the same rooms go for 110€ to 130€. There are more amenities here—ironing boards, irons, pants presses, and flatscreen TVs are in all rooms—but the location is a bit less central, being in the northern end of the Marais. If relaxation is what you are after, take advantage of the free sauna in the cellar.

LATIN QUARTER (5TH ARRONDISSEMENT)

Central and reasonably priced, the Latin Quarter is a long-time favorite for budgeters. Unfortunately, this status has encouraged huge hoards to invade the many low-cost hotels, which have in turn raised their prices. So you might find an affordable gem, but you may just as easily end up paying midrange prices for bargain basement digs. The streets immediately surrounding the place St-Michel (especially around rue de la Huchette) are where you'll find the worst tourist traps, both hotel and restaurant-wise; better prices and quality are to be had in the quieter areas around the universities (College de France, La Sorbonne, Faculté de Sciences), a little farther from Notre-Dame but still in easy walking distance.

NEAR NOTRE–DAME

€€–€€€ On a tiny street within shouting distance of the Seine, **Hôtel les Degrés de Notre Dame** ✮✮ (10 rue des Grands Degrés, 5th arrond.; ☎ 01 55 42 88 88; www.lesdegreshotel.com; Métro: St-Michel or Maubert Mutualité, RER: St-Michel Notre-Dame; MC, V) offers a touch of class, as well as a delicious breakfast (included in the price of the room). With only ten individually decorated rooms—each with a different assortment of antiques, throw rugs, artwork, and rich fabrics—this feels more like an upscale pension than a hotel. About half of the bathrooms were just renovated with colorful tiles; the shower floors look like they're paved with pebbles. There are lots of exposed beams here; the building is centuries old, which explains the lack of an elevator or air-conditioning. On the other hand, the rooms facing the courtyard are a relatively good size for Paris, and those facing the street are downright spacious. Two rooms offer views of the towers of Notre-Dame: #47, a small double, and #510, the honeymoon suite. Complimentary breakfast is served in the cozy restaurant on the ground floor,

Accommodations on the Left Bank (5th–6th & 13th–14th)

JARDIN DES TUILERIES

JARDIN DU CARROUSEL

Musée du Louvre

1er Ⓜ PONT NEUF

Seine

pont Royal

pont du Carrousel

pont des Arts

pont Neuf

sq. du Vert Galant

Conciergerie

Sainte-Chapelle

quai des Orfèvres

quai des Grands Augustins

pont au Change

bd. du Palais

pont St-Michel

quai Voltaire

Musée d'Orsay

rue de Lille

rue de Verneuil

rue de l'Université

Ecole Nat. Sup. des Beaux-Arts

rue des Saints Pères

rue Jacob

rue Mazarine

rue de Seine

1

Ⓜ ST-MICHEL

Musée Delacroix

St-Germain-des-Prés

St-Thomas d'Aquin

bd. St-Germain

bd. St-Germain

Ⓜ RUE DU BAC

7e

ST-GERMAIN-DES-PRES Ⓜ

MABILLON Ⓜ **2**

r. de Seine

ODEON Ⓜ

3

rue Racine

rue de Grenelle

4

5 rue du Four

rue St-Sulpice

6e

place de l'Odéon

Théâtre de l'Odéon

rue de Tournon

rue de Médicis

bd. Raspail

rue de Varenne

rue du Bac

St-Sulpice

Ⓜ ST-SULPICE

rue Bonaparte

rue de Vaugirard

Palais du Luxembourg

rue de Babylone

Ⓜ SEVRES BABYLONE

rue de Sèvres

rue de Rennes

rue Madame

rue Guynemer

JARDIN DU LUXEMBOURG

rue Auguste Comte

rue Vaneau

rue du Cherche Midi

Ⓜ RENNES

Ⓜ VANEAU

Ⓜ ST-PLACIDE

Ⓜ NOTRE DAME DES CHAMPS

6

bd. Raspail

rue Notre-Dame des Champs

rue d'Assas

rue Michelet

rue de Vaugirard

rue de Rennes

Ⓜ MÉTRO STOP

Ⓡ RER STOP

0   1/5 mi

0   0.2 km

place du 18 Juin 1940

Ⓜ MONTPARNASSE BIENVENUE

Ⓜ VAVIN

14e

bd. du Montparnasse

rue Delambre

bd. Raspail

7

8 ↓

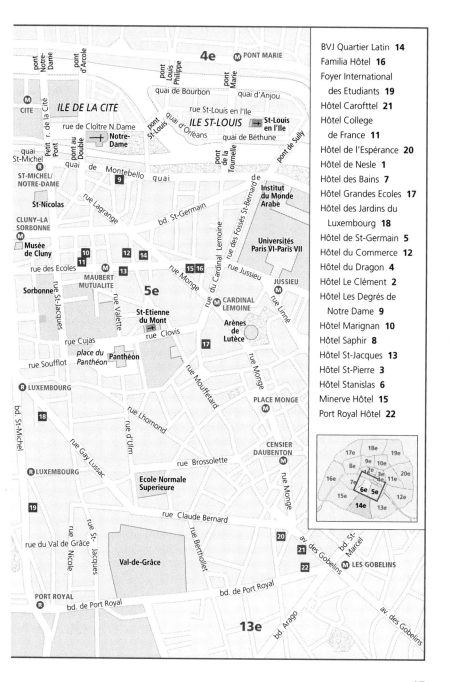

BVJ Quartier Latin **14**
Familia Hôtel **16**
Foyer International
  des Etudiants **19**
Hôtel Carofttel **21**
Hôtel College
  de France **11**
Hôtel de l'Espérance **20**
Hôtel de Nesle **1**
Hôtel des Bains **7**
Hôtel Grandes Ecoles **17**
Hôtel des Jardins du
  Luxembourg **18**
Hôtel de St-Germain **5**
Hôtel du Commerce **12**
Hôtel du Dragon **4**
Hôtel Le Clément **2**
Hôtel Les Degrés de
  Notre Dame **9**
Hôtel Marignan **10**
Hôtel Saphir **8**
Hôtel St-Jacques **13**
Hôtel St-Pierre **3**
Hôtel Stanislas **6**
Minerve Hôtel **15**
Port Royal Hôtel **22**

which serves both traditional French bistro fare and North African specialties like couscous and tajines (restaurant closed on Sun). Doubles range from 115€ to 170€; due to the small size of the hotel, babies are not accepted.

RUE DES ECOLES

€ "Cheap doesn't have to be ugly" is the motto at **Hôtel du Commerce** (14 rue de la Montagne Ste-Genviève, 5th arrond.; ☎ 01 43 54 89 69; www.commerce parishotel.com; Métro: Maubert Mutualité or Cardinal Lemoine; no credit cards), located on a small side street just off hotel-heavy rue des Ecoles. With the feel of an upscale youth hostel, these basic rooms are decorated in bright blues and yellows, with doorless closets, small desks, and either carpets or hardwood floors. There's no elevator, and some of the staircases in this ancient building are a bit tortuous, but that doesn't bother the mostly young clientele, who come for the rock bottom prices (double with sink only, 49€; double with shower and sink, 59€; double with shower and toilets, 69€). There are also triples and quads without toilets for 69€ and 99€, as well as one upscale, air-conditioned "superior" room (#8, 99€)—but if you are looking for comfort, nicer rooms for similar prices are to be had elsewhere. The shared shower is 2€. Another plus: In the dining area just next to reception, there's a communal refrigerator, coffee machine, and microwave available so that you can fix your own breakfast. Reservations can only be made online; credit cards accepted only for reservations; rooms must be paid for in cash or travelers checks.

€€–€€€   A little farther down rue des Ecoles, toward the Jardin des Plantes, are two hotels owned by the same hyperenthusiastic management. If there is a more dedicated hotel owner than Eric Gaucheron, I have yet to meet him. Every detail at the **Familia Hôtel** ✪✪ (11 rue des Ecoles, 5th arrond.; ☎ 01 43 54 55 27; www.hotel-paris-familia.com; Métro: Cardinal Lemoine; AE, DC, MC, V) has been scrupulously considered, from the carved and monogrammed cherrywood doors and headboards, to the swags of period fabrics on the windows, to the hand-painted wall murals that decorate many rooms. These air-conditioned rooms are big on charm: Some have exposed beams, others have marble bathrooms, and those on the second, fifth, and sixth floors have small balconies with nice views of the Latin Quarter. In his eternal quest to keep his clientele happy, Gaucheron has had the walls of the small interior courtyard painted with blue skies and country scenery so that those without a view don't have to suffer. He's also made sure a few rooms have tile or wood floors to accommodate guests with allergies. One thing he can't change, however, is the size of the rooms, which are decidedly on the small side. That said, so are the prices: 99€ to 129€ for a double.

€€–€€€€   For larger rooms and a little more luxe, just next door is the other Gaucheron enterprise, the **Minerve Hôtel** ✪✪ (13 rue des Ecoles, 5th arrond.; ☎ 01 43 26 26 04; www.hotel-paris-minerve.com; Métro: Cardinal Lemoine; AE, DC, MC, V). Very similar in look and feel to the Familia, but with a more refined ambience—more space, more exposed beams, more stone walls, plusher carpets, bigger bathrooms, and A/C in every room. The owner's penchant for antiques is more obvious here—vintage tapestries and prints cover the walls of the common areas. The prices are a bit higher, running from 104€ to 156€ for a double, but it is still reasonable considering the quality of the lodgings.

€€–€€€   More spacious still are the rooms at the delightful **Hôtel St-Jacques** ✪✪ (35 rue des Ecoles, 5th arrond.; ☎ 01 44 07 45 45; www.paris-hotel-stjacques.com; Métro: Maubert Mutualité, RER: Cluny-La Sorbonne; AE, DC, MC, V), which retains lots of architectural details from its Belle Epoque past. Most of the ceilings are adorned with masses of curlicues, and some have restored 18th-century murals to gaze at while you laze in bed. Like the two hotels above, there are several rooms with small balconies and Latin Quarter views, but the decor has a lighter, more feminine feel. Service is especially friendly here. Prices are reasonable, considering the comfort level and romantic decor; the roomier doubles range from 126€ to 137€, while the smaller, simpler ones on the top (sixth) floor go for 105€. (***Note:*** The elevator stops at the fifth floor; a flight of stairs leads to the sixth.) There are two very pretty wheelchair-accessible rooms on the ground floor. Movie fans take note: This hotel starred in the Audrey Hepburn/Cary Grant classic, *Charade.*

AROUND THE SORBONNE

€   The quantity of young people bounding up and down the stairs at the **Hôtel Marignan** ✪✪ (13 rue du Sommerard, 5th arrond; ☎ 01 43 54 63 81; www.hotel-marignan.com; Métro: Maubert Mutualité; MC, V) is your first clue: These lodgings cater to budget travelers looking for reasonable, centrally located lodgings, who don't mind a little noise in the hallways. (Your second clue is that there's no elevator!) Not only is the price right, but the user-friendly owner, Paul Keniger, unlike most of his colleagues, has not increased his rates in the last 2 years (65€–90€ for a double in high season, breakfast included)—a boon to travelers paying in dollars. He also offers enticing extras like free washing machines and kitchen access (after breakfast is served). Though the furnishings are pretty basic, the rooms themselves are in very good shape, with pretty carved ceiling moldings, and clean and spacious tiled bathrooms. Room sizes range from comfortable to enormous—this is one of the few hotels in Paris to offer not only triples and quads, but also rooms for five people (120€–160€). The cheapest rates involve sharing a toilet and/or shower with one other room; shared facilities are spotless. Take note that whereas summer is often low season in Paris, high season at this hotel is March through July.

€€–€€€   About a block from the imposing edifice that it is named after, **Hôtel du College de France** ✪ (7 rue Thénard, 5th arrond.; ☎ 01 43 26 78 36; www.hotel-collegedefrance.com; Métro: Maubert Mutualité; AE, DC, MC, V) has a higher comfort quotient, if perhaps a bit less personality. These are standard hotel rooms (doubles 99€–135€) with nice clean carpets, appropriate bedspreads, and a few classy photos of French movie stars. Rooms on the upper floors get significantly more light, and those on the top floor (accessible only by staircase) are larger and have high ceilings. The rooms are a little ho-hum, but the lobby is cute—the medieval theme pays homage to the 11th-century structure that once stood here, home of the commander of the knights of Saint Jean—and more importantly, the owners, the Marc family, are very welcoming.

€€€€   As its name suggests, **Hôtel des Jardins du Luxembourg** ✪✪ (5 impasse Royer Collard, 5th arrond.; ☎ 01 40 46 08 88; www.les-jardins-du-luxembourg.com; RER: Luxembourg; AE, DC, MC, V) is just around the corner from its glorious namesake. On a quiet impasse, or dead-end street, these cushy lodgings make an excellent hideaway for a romantic honeymoon or cozy retreat. The building's claim to fame is that Sigmund Freud stayed here on his first visit to Paris; perhaps this has something to do with the 1930s and 1940s touches to the decor. The Art Deco ambience of the lobby and reading lounge invites deep reflection, or at least a nice rest in one of the plush armchairs; for full relaxation, indulge in a visit to the sauna (5€). Most of your resting, of course, will be in the rooms, which are decorated with a good deal of class. While the standard rooms (142€) are quite pretty, with curly wrought-iron headboards and puffy comforters (cotton or feather), they are not nearly as nice as the superior rooms, which cost only 10€ more and have nice views, small balconies, snazzy bathrooms, and designer-fabric covered walls. All rooms are air-conditioned.

CLOSE TO THE PANTHEON

€€–€€€   Tucked into a private garden on the slope of the Montagne St-Genviève, lovely **Hôtel Grandes Ecoles** ★★★ (75 rue Cardinal Lemoine, 5th arrond.; ☎ 01 43 26 79 23; www.hotel-grandes-ecoles.fr; Métro: Cardinal Lemoine or place Monge; MC, V) gives you the impression you have just walked out of Paris and into the countryside. A path leads to a flower-bedecked interior courtyard, where birds chirp in the trees; the reception area adjoins an inviting breakfast room with potted plants and an upright piano. The spotless rooms are filled with country-style furniture and papered in old-fashioned prints; crocheted bedspreads and framed etchings of flowers complete the look. Views from most windows are of either the garden or surrounding trees. The calm is such that the hotel has nixed TVs; smoking is discouraged throughout. Incredibly, this unique ambience does not come at a high price: The least expensive rooms are only 113€, and on the high end of the scale (up to 138€) are larger rooms including several on the ground floor with French doors that open onto the garden. Speaking of the garden, in nice weather you can sip your café au lait and nibble your croissants there.

FARTHER SOUTH, NEAR RUE MOUFFTARD & GOBELINS

€   A little bit out of the way (but convenient if you need to get to the Gare d'Austerlitz train station) is the **Port Royal Hôtel** ★ (8 blvd. Port Royal, 5th arrond.; ☎ 01 43 31 70 06; www.hotelportroyal.fr; Métro: Les Gobelins; no credit cards). If it's any indication of how silly the French star system can be, there are plenty of two-star hotels in Paris that aren't as nice as this perfectly respectable and

Staying Connected

Though France isn't the most connected country in Europe, most hotels have either free Internet access in the lobby or Wi-Fi in the rooms. If your hotel doesn't, and you're in desperate need of an e-mail fix, your best bet is a cybercafe (see "Staying Wired While You're Away," p. 344). Unless otherwise mentioned, all hotels listed here have some sort of Internet access.

impeccably clean one-star. That said, do not be misled by the pretty pictures on the website; though some of the rooms have been renovated with chic fabrics and designer bathroom tiles, most have a more humble, old-fashioned decor. But considering the low prices, this place is a deal, Kenzo tiles or no. The hotel is one of the few left in Paris with lots of rooms without private toilets or showers, which means if you're willing to make do with just a lavabo (mirror and sink—spotless shared toilets and showers are in the hall), you can get a nice double for 53€. Even with private facilities, the rates are low: 79€ for a double with toilet and shower; 84€ to 89€ with toilet and bath. There are neither TVs here, nor Internet access.

€ I'm not sure why the **Hôtel de l'Espérance** ✮✮ (15 rue Pascal, 5th arrond.; ☎ 01 47 07 10 99; www.hoteldelesperance.fr; Métro: Censier Daubenton; AE, DC, MC, V) has such great rates; hotels near the Rue Moufftard with half the charm go for much more. To start with, there are the owners, the affable Mme and M. Aymard, who greet everyone like guests in their own home. Mme Aymard is responsible for the dash of flamboyance in the decor: Many of the beds are crowned with minicanopies of colorful draped fabric, a doll collection is sprinkled around the lobby, and the breakfast room is swathed in toile de jouy (printed period fabric). Beyond the canopies, the air-conditioned rooms are pretty classic, and in great shape, with fresh, clean carpets, draperies, and marble bathrooms (doubles 80€–90€). There is a small, flower-bedecked patio for eating breakfast al fresco. The hotel is located on a quiet street, about a block away from the base of rue Moufftard, where there is a lovely open-air market.

€–€€ If you need space and you don't care about looks, consider **Hotel Carofftel** **kids** (18 av. des Gobelins, 5th arrond.; ☎ 01 42 17 47 47; www.hotel carofftelgobelins.com; Métro: Les Gobelins; MC, V), right near the Métro stop on busy avenue des Gobelins. Though the decor throughout is pretty nondescript, all is clean and tidy, and some of the high-ceilinged rooms are quite large. Of particular interest to those who are looking for space are the huge triples (120€, families take note), which, depending on availability, can lodge two people for the same price as a double (84€–98€).

SAINT GERMAIN (6TH ARRONDISSEMENT)

If you look hard, you can still find affordable lodgings in this much sought after (and expensive) neighborhood. Sleek boutiques and restaurants abound; historic cafes and monuments lend plenty of atmosphere. Unlike some other chic Parisian neighborhoods, this one is still lively, even late at night; it is also centrally located and in walking distance to many top sights. The highest concentration of noise and tourist traps is around blvd. St-Germain and Carrefour de l'Odéon; once you turn down a side street things quiet down considerably.

ON THE BRINK OF MONTPARNASSE

€ In a quiet neighborhood between Montparnasse and the Jardin du Luxembourg, **Hôtel Stanislas** (5 rue Montparnasse, 6th arrond.; ☎ 01 45 48 37 05; Métro: Notre-Dame-des-Champs; MC, V) is slightly out of the center of things, but if you're strapped for cash, it's well worth the 10-minute walk to St-Germain-des-Prés.

While it certainly isn't the Ritz, rooms are clean and comfy, with old-fashioned printed wallpaper giving these spacious digs a touch of charm. There's also plenty of old-fashioned hospitality on offer from the gracious staff, as well as old-fashioned prices: just 69€ for a double, with toilet and shower—possibly the best deal on the left bank. Twin beds go for 81€, and triples are only 90€. Breakfast is served until noon in the small cafe on the ground floor, where students from the neighboring technical institute come for snacks and drinks. There's no elevator or Internet access.

NEAR THE CHURCH OF ST-GERMAIN DES PRES

€€   Another good deal that is, amazingly, right in the thick of St-Germain chic, is **Hôtel du Dragon** 🧒 (36 rue du Dragon, 6th arrond.; ☎ 01 45 48 51 05; www.hoteldudragon.com; Métro: St-Germain-des-Prés; closed in Aug; AE, DC, MC, V). All the simply furnished doubles here are 115€, which range from roomy to downright huge. Unfortunately, due to city regulations, this hotel is not allowed to add a third bed, even in the largest rooms, but folding cribs are fine (available on premises). Ceilings are very high, and some have exposed beams; rooms are painted in light colors and many have recently had a make-over. A 19th-century portrait of the hotel's founder hangs in the homey breakfast room—these lodgings have been in the same family for 120 years. There are lots of stairs here and no elevator; the owners plan to install one by 2010.

€€€–€€€€   Considerably more stylish, the **Hôtel de Saint Germain** ⭐ 🧒 (50 rue du Four, 6th arrond.; ☎ 01 45 48 91 64; www.hotel-de-saint-germain.fr; Métro: St-Germain-des-Prés; MC, V) stakes its claim on a street lined with snazzy boutiques and chic restaurants. The rooms might be small, but they are air-conditioned, and those facing the street (most do, and all have double-glazed windows) get lots of light. Colorful bedspreads and neo-country furniture add to the cheerful decor; the brand-new bathrooms all have towel-warmers. There are two corner rooms on each floor that are good for families; the hallway door can be closed off to create a small suite. Though the cost may seem high considering the small dimensions of the room, keep in mind that rates in this pricey neighborhood are generally at least double, and chances are the service won't be nearly as friendly. The price fluctuates with the seasons: In theory, doubles average 120€, but they go up to 150€ during trade shows, and down to 90€ in August and a few other slow periods. Visit the website for a month-by-month price breakdown.

€€€–€€€€   A bit more spacious and subdued, **Hôtel Le Clément** ⭐ 🧒 (6 rue Clément, 6th arrond.; ☎ 01 43 26 53 60; www.hotel-clement.fr; Métro: Mabillon; AE, MC, V) offers comfort and calm about 2 blocks away from St-Germain-des-Près. Prices are more stable here as well; spotless doubles range from 120€ to 140€ and triples go for 155€, as do "minisuites" with two communicating rooms. Facing the restaurant-lined Marché St-Germain, there's plenty going on at night; light sleepers should be advised that the least-expensive doubles all face the street. That said, all of the rooms are air-conditioned and double-paned windows keep out most noise. Walls are covered in traditional prints; beds are decked out in white quilted spreads. Service can be slightly frosty, but is generally discrete and helpful.

TOWARD PONT NEUF

€–€€   Just off the gallery-bedecked rue Dauphine is another quirky work of art, the **Hôtel de Nesle** ★★ (pronounced "nell"; 7 rue de Nesle, 6th arrond.; ☎ 01 43 54 62 41; www.hoteldenesleparis.com; Métro: Odéon; MC, V). From the moment you enter the lobby, you know that you are not in your average hotel: The entire ceiling is covered with hanging bouquets of dried flowers, country knickknacks and paintings cover the walls, and the absence of a real reception desk makes you feel like you just wandered into someone's living room. Every room is impeccably clean and has a theme reflected in the decoration, which includes interesting objects and hand-painted murals. One of the larger doubles, #5 ("Afrique," 100€), has a large bathroom, a canopy bed, African masks, a rattan armchair, and a mural portraying various explorers marching across the walls, whereas smaller #6 (85€) has twin beds, a sink and shower (toilets in the hall are spotless), mosaic tiles on the lower half of the walls, and a selection of Greek goddesses dancing above (the smallest doubles are 75€). Also good-sized with full bathroom is #13, "Moliére" (100€), which has theatre curtains in front of the bed and a small divan to recline on; like other rooms on the courtyard, this one has a lovely garden view. Many of the rooms can be seen on the website, but attempts to reserve a specific one might be met with frustration: The hotel has an equally quirky reservation policy, which involves calling 48 hours before your arrival to confirm; the management is, not surprisingly, eccentric, so bring your patience with you. There are neither TVs nor Internet access.

€–€€   **Hôtel Saint Pierre** (4 rue de l'Ecole de Médcine, 6th arrond.; ☎ 01 46 34 78 80; www.saintpierre-hotel.com; Métro: Cluny–La Sorbonne; AE, MC, V) offers more standard and predictable lodgings. The air-conditioned rooms are basic, but comfortable, and the prices are extremely reasonable for this high-demand area, on the border of the Latin Quarter and in easy walking distance to both the Luxembourg Gardens and Notre Dame. Small doubles with tiny, shower-equipped bathrooms are a mere 88€, larger versions with bath are 94€ (the larger rooms book up quickly, so reserve well in advance). While you may not be wowed by the decor here, the service is excellent; the manager is so friendly and helpful he may just end up planning your trip for you.

INVALIDES–EIFFEL TOWER (7TH ARRONDISSEMENT)

For some reason, many tourists clamor for hotels that are right near the Eiffel Tower, perhaps under the mistaken impression that this is a central location. It isn't. Not only that, the 7th arrondissement is one of the grandest in Paris, filled with government ministries and posh residences—not exactly a place where you are likely to experience a typical slice of Parisian life. That said, there's no denying it's a beautiful, if quiet, area, and that there is something magical about wandering out of your hotel in the morning and seeing the Eiffel Tower looming in the background, or the golden dome of Les Invalides shining in the sun. One thing is for sure: There are plenty of hotels in the area, many of which cater to Americans (fully English-speaking staff, larger beds, and so forth).

NEAR BON MARCHE

€–€€   The rooms are tiny, but for this terribly chic street, so are the rates at **Hôtel de Nevers** (83 rue du Bac, 7th arrond.; ☎ 01 45 44 61 30; www.hotelde nevers-saintgermain.net; Métro: Rue du Bac; MC, V). Antiques shops and pricey boutiques surround this diminutive hotel, which is just around the corner from the elegant Bon Marché department store and a short walk to the Musée d'Orsay. The cheapest double has a private toilet in the corridor (89€); other doubles are either 99€ (shower) or 115€ (bath). Two rooms have rooftop terraces that are big enough for a breakfast table (105€ and 125€).

€€–€€€   A fascination with aviation is evident at **Hôtel Lindbergh** ✪✪✪ (5 rue Chomel, 7th arrond.; ☎ 01 45 48 35 53; www.hotellindbergh.com; Métro: Sèvres-Babylone; AE, DC, MC, V), where photos of legendary pilots like Antoine de St-Exupéry and Lucky Lindy hang in the lobby. The decor goes much farther than airplanes, however; most rooms have recently had a makeover by architect Jean-Philippe Nuel, who punctuates the soft browns and beiges on the walls and floors with interesting shades of red or light green on the bedspreads. The overall effect is modern yet soft and incredibly inviting. Ceilings are high, lighting is discreet— you would think you were in a three-star boutique hotel. Yet the prices are in the realm of the doable: Doubles can go as low as 108€ in low season and won't pass 136€ during trade shows. There are also six spacious twins for 136€ to 160€ depending on the season; triples swing between 156€ to 180€. The older rooms were also done by Nuel, and are equally inviting, if perhaps a bit less chic, with off-white fabrics on the walls and deep blues on the beds. Adding to the cozy picture is the welcoming staff, headed by Zoë, an adorable Yorkshire terrier.

NEAR LES INVALIDES & THE EIFFEL TOWER

€–€€   Looking for views? If you'd like to gaze at the golden dome of Les Invalides from your bed, check in at **Hôtel de L'Empereur** ✪ (2 rue Chevert, 7th arrond; ☎ 01 45 55 88 02; www.hotelempereur.com; Métro: La Tour Maubourg; AE, DC, MC, V). The entire hotel having just had a much-needed renovation, the basic yet cute rooms are once again spotless, complete with Empire-style headboards, Napoleonic motifs and air conditioning. The Emperor's hat, laurel crown, and bee symbols abound; the color scheme includes lots of golds and greens. About half the rooms (all those facing the street) have an amazing view of Les Invalides, which you can appreciate through nice big windows (the best views are from the fifth and sixth floors). Prices for doubles range from 80€ to 105€ depending on the season; twins and triples stay at 110€ and 130€ all year. There is no extra charge for rooms with a view; simply specify your preference when you make your reservation.

€€–€€€   There may not be much of a view at **Hôtel Saint Dominique** ✪ (62 rue St-Dominique, 7th arrond.; ☎ 01 47 05 51 44; www.hotelstdominique. com; Métro: Invalides; MC, V), but so what—the minute you step outside you get an eyeful of the Eiffel Tower, which hovers over the western end of this bustling street. There are two small buildings here: The one in the front sports an elevator, while the one in the back, though quieter, has none. In any case there are only two floors. Rooms are furnished with taste and character; country style blonde wood furniture is set off by antique prints on the walls and drapes. Doubles run from 99€ to 135€ depending on the size and the season; there's a lovely, larger "superior" double that goes for 155€

€€€–€€€€   A step up on the comfort scale is **Hôtel Muguet** ✪✪ (11 rue Chevert, 7th arrond.; ☎ 01 47 05 05 93; www.hotelmuguet.com; Métro: Ecole Militaire and La Tour Maubourg; AE, MC, V). The friendly proprietors offer lovely rooms with faux-antique furniture, big wood headboards hand-painted with a lily-of-the-valley *(muguet)* motif, and pretty new bathrooms with old-fashioned wood washstands and mirror frames. Though not exactly huge, the doubles are larger than before, and the triples (180€) are downright spacious. All but 4 of the 48 rooms have queen-sized beds (a rarity in Paris), and all have air-conditioning and flatscreen TVs. Five doubles have a great view of the Eiffel Tower, three others of Les Invalides; needless to say they book up months in advance (160€–190€). But let's not forget about the other equally comfy and much less expensive rooms (135€) that look out on either the quiet street or the leafy court-yard. The entire hotel is nonsmoking; there is no elevator between the fifth and sixth floors.

€€€€   In a neighborhood chock full of government ministries housed in pala-tial mansions, the **Hôtel de Varenne** ✪✪✪ (44 rue de Bourgogne, 7th arrond.; ☎ 01 45 51 45 55; www.hoteldevarenne.com; Métro: Varenne; AE, MC, V) does its best to live up to its elegant surroundings—indeed, part of its clientele comes from the nearby National Assembly. Once the home of Nicolas-Charles Oudinot, who ended his illustrious military career as governor of the nearby Invalides, these classy accommodations provide a bit of posh at relatively reasonable prices. Since it is set back off the street, rooms are very quiet, and there is a lovely garden patio for breakfast alfresco in the warmer months. The decor is stately, without being stuffy; the furniture, which was custom-made for the hotel, is inspired by Louis XVI and Empire styles. The entire hotel has been renovated over the past few years and everything looks brand-spanking-new. Prices are not necessarily has high as they may look: Though standard doubles are 157€ with shower and 177€ with bath, the hotel regularly posts Internet promotions that drop back down to 125€ and 135€. As to be expected in this price range, amenities are plentiful and include air-conditioning, flatscreen TVs, and DVD players. Despite his suit and tie, owner Jean-Marc Pommier is very approachable and is usually to be found on the premises.

RUE CLER & ENVIRONS

€   For a good bargain basic, **Hôtel Kensington** (79 av. de la Bourdonnais, 7th arrond.; ☎ 01 47 05 74 00; www.hotel-kensington.com; Métro: Ecole Militaire; AE, DC, MC, V) fits the bill. A short walk away from the rue Cler market street and an easy jog to the Eiffel Tower, if you are on a tight budget you will appreciate the clean, efficient doubles that go for as little as 77€ and up to 92€ for one of their larger twins. Space is minimal, and the floor is a little uneven, but ceilings are nice and high, the wallpaper is fresh, and the staff is helpful and friendly. There is no Internet access.

Breaking the Chains

If you're like me, you usually steer clear of chain hotels, especially when visiting a foreign country. They tend to be a) expensive, unless you've booked them as part of a package, and b) so standardized that you are likely to wake up in the morning wondering where you are. Leaving aside megachains like Best Western and Holiday Inn (for the reasons cited above), there are a couple of decent local chains that, though not big on personality, at least are convenient and easy on the pocketbook.

The cheapest and most omnipresent chain hotel in Paris is **Ibis** (www.ibishotel.com; AE, DC, MC, V). With 45 locations dotted about the city, these modestly priced hotels provide clean, comfortable rooms (sometimes air-conditioned) with modern prints and colors on the beds and windows; you'll never have to wonder what your room will look like since all are identical to the one shown on the website. Breakfast is served until noon, and snacks and drinks are available 24/7. Doubles range from around 80€ to 115€, depending on where and when you stay.

For a bit more luxury, try **Timhotel** (www.timhotel.com; AE, DC, MC, V). Though the buildings themselves are pretty, the rooms are pretty standard (read: blah), if amply proportioned. What they do have are some brilliant locations. Timhotel Palais-Royal Louvre adjoins the beautiful Passage Vivienne; Timhotel Montmartre is just next to the Bateau Lavoir on a tiny tree-shaded square, and some rooms have an incredible view of the city. Timhotel Jardin des Plantes is just across the street from the eponymous botanical gardens, and Timhotel Louvre is about a block away from the museum on the rue St-Honoré. The rack rates are a bit lofty, in the 130€ to 175€ range for a double, but the good news is that there are often excellent reductions on the website—up to 60%, if you're lucky.

Another small, upscale chain with truly spectacular locations is **Esprit de France** (www.esprit-de-france.com; AE, DC, MC, V). Hôtel Brighton, for example, is on the rue de Rivoli; if you're willing to pay 180€, you can have a view of the Tuileries Gardens. Some rooms at Hôtel de la Place du Louvre have a view of the eastern facade of the palace; Hôtel Mansart is located right at the corner of the place Vendôme. Rooms in the more expensive locations have pretty fabrics and 19th-century architectural detailing; others like Place du Louvre are relatively modern and chainlike. Prices are high—doubles start at around 145€—but periodic discounts show up on the website, particularly in July and August.

€€   I don't know how the **Hôtel du Champ de Mars** ✪✪ (7 rue du Champ de Mars; 7th arrond.; ☎ 01 45 51 52 30; www.hotelduchampdemars.com; Métro: Ecole Militaire; MC, V) keeps its rates so low, but I'm glad it does; it's one of the cutest hotels in the neighborhood, and one of the most affordable. Recently overhauled, the rooms are still a bit small but tastefully decorated with the kind of care

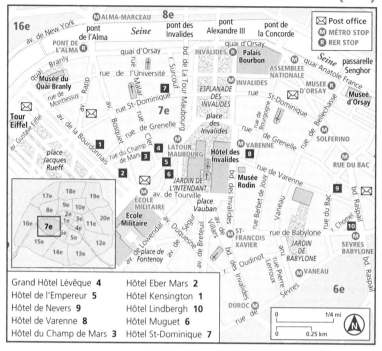

people generally reserve for their own homes: thick cotton bedspreads, framed floral prints, and designer fabrics on the beds and windows (at press time the photos on the website had not been updated). Two rooms have a tiny courtyard; those on the upper floors get lots of light. Add the fact that this quiet street is just around the corner from the shops and restaurants of rue Cler, and you have an amazing bargain: Doubles are only 90€ to 94€. Another plus, the owners, Françoise and Stéphane Gourdal, are always available, as is their adorable Cocker Spaniel, Cannelle. There's no elevator.

€€   Something of an institution, the **Grand Hôtel Lévêque** ⭐ (29 rue Cler, 7th arrond.; 01 47 05 49 15; www.hotel-leveque.com; Métro: Ecole Militaire; AE, MC, V) has recently had a makeover, thanks to its new, young owners. While the lower floors still retain much of their classic look, upstairs guests are treated to chocolate-colored textured headboards, beige carpets, purple bedspreads, and bathroom tiles that resemble leather (complete with stitching). While the designer look might not be to everyone's liking (I thought it was pretty cool), what counts is that the rooms are still clean and comfortable, the prices are still reasonable, and the hotel still is right on rue Cler, a delightful pedestrian market street lined with food stands, cafes, and cute shops. Despite the fact that all rooms have air-conditioning (available June–Sept only), the new management has kept the ceiling fans, for those who prefer old-fashioned ventilation. Prices vary according to how big they are and what they look out on: Rooms on the courtyard range from 97€ for a standard double to 110€ for a spacious "superior" twin; rooms on the street (in this case, a definite bonus) start at 102€ for a standard and go up to 125€ for a "superior" twin. Large, street-side triples run 137€ to 142€.

€€€   A block or so over is **Hôtel Eber Mars** ✪✪ (117 av. de la Bourdonnais, 7th arrond.; ☎ 01 47 05 42 30; www.hotelebermars.com; Métro: Ecole Militaire; MC, V), several notches up on the class scale. As you walk in the door, chances are you will be greeted by none other than Monsieur Eber, who keeps a careful eye on ongoing renovation of his hotel. So far, the infrastructure is up-to-date, as is the sleek, wood-paneled lobby/breakfast room (served all day), which is decorated with classy photos of 1930s movie stars. The '30s theme continues into the rooms (and even the owner's hairstyle, which is suitably slicked back), which have a streamlined period look and neutral colors. Eber is going for a specifically 1930s Parisian decor. "I like people to wake up in their room and know what country they're in," he says. At press time, the carpets, beds, wallpaper, and drapes had been done, next on the agenda is an overhaul of the bathrooms (which are actually in good shape). When all is completed, it should be terrific. Until then, you'll get a remarkably spacious, comfortable double here for 90€ to 130€; even larger triples are 130€ to 159€, and a family suite (two doubles) goes for 175€. The price range reflects the seasons (read: trade shows); for exact rates you'll have to punch in your dates on the website. Depending on availability, two can stay in a triple for double rates.

CHAMPS ELYSEES & PARK MONCEAU (8TH & 17TH ARRONDISSEMENTS)

Even grander than the 7th arrondissement, the area around the Champs Elysées is positively mythic. To the south of the boulevard, along avenues Montaigne and George V, are the most exclusive designer shops in the city; to the north, elegant buildings, shops, and restaurants stretch up to lovely Parc Monceau, which has some excellent museum neighbors, including Musée Nissim de Camondo and Musée Jacquemart-André. As you head north and east, towards the Gare St-Lazare train station, the neighborhood becomes a bit more proletarian. Needless to say, affordable lodgings are scarce around here. There are several cramped tourist hotels around the Arc de Triomphe, but not only do they tend to be overpriced, but if you stay there you will find yourself towards the outskirts of town. On the other hand, there are good bus connections to the airports from nearby Porte Maillot.

NEAR THE CHAMPS ELYSEES

€–€€   The rooms might be small, the reception can be sniffy, but there's no denying that **Hôtel Riviera** ✪ (55 rue des Acacias, 17th arrond.; ☎ 01 43 80 45 31; www.hotelriviera-paris.com; Metro and RER: Charles de Gaulle-Etoile; AE, MC, V) offers impeccable lodgings at an excellent price, particularly in this outrageously expensive neighborhood, just down the street from the Arc de Triomphe. Rooms are spick-and-span, in great shape, and decorated with imagination and style; doubles even have air-conditioning. But there's no denying they are small. If you need more space, try to reserve one of the five larger ones, though this could get tricky as they

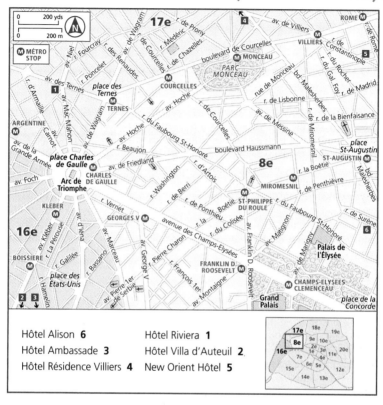

Hôtel Alison **6**

Hôtel Ambassade **3**

Hôtel Résidence Villiers **4**

Hôtel Riviera **1**

Hôtel Villa d'Auteuil **2**

New Orient Hôtel **5**

are also rented out as triples and may or may not be available/reservable, depending on the season. Doubles run 80€ to 89€, depending on size; triples are 105€ to 115€. The most recently renovated rooms are also nonsmoking. The management is stereotypically Parisian, seemingly cold and impossibly distant, but with a little work, likely to crack a wry smile or even a joke or two.

NEAR PARC MONCEAU

€   If you're willing to stay a little farther away from the madding crowd, the **Hotel Résidence Villiers** (68 av. de Villiers, 17th arrond.; ☎ 01 42 27 18 77; www.hotel-residence-villiers.com; Métro: Wagram; AE, MC, V) is one of those all-too-rare Parisian beasts: a decent budget hotel in an expensive area. This cushy residential neighborhood is calm and quiet, but not too far from the action on the Champs Elysées (about a 15-min. walk, but you can take a bus if you want to get there in a hurry). Parc Monceau and the Musée Jacquemart André are in easy walking distance, as are some nice, nontouristy restaurants—one of the perks of staying in an area like this is that you'll see Parisians in their natural habitat. Rooms are pretty basic, but clean and tidy; some have nice molded cornices on the ceilings, others have small balconies. Doubles go for 85€ to 88€; those on the street have good double-paned windows to keep the noise out.

BETWEEN PLACE DE LA CONCORDE & GARE ST-LAZARE

€€–€€€ Here's what you get if you're willing to stay just north of the Gare St-Lazare: comfortable rooms decorated with antique headboards and armoires, high ceilings with 19th-century moldings, and air-conditioning, for less than you would pay for substandard accommodations near the Arc de Triomphe. While **New Orient Hôtel** ★★ (16 rue de Constantinople, 8th arrond.; ☎ 01 45 22 21 64; www.hotel-paris-orient.com; Métro: Villiers, Europe or St-Lazare; AE, DC, MC, V) may not be on top of the Champs Elysées, it's near a good transportation hub, and is even closer to the groovy Batignolles area. The friendly owners, who are inveterate flea market browsers, have refinished and restored the antique furniture themselves. Rooms (many of which have small balconies) are in tip-top shape, bathrooms sparkle, and doubles run 106€ to 115€. Larger twins are 115€ to 140€, and a "family room" with two double beds goes for 150€. A plus (for some): The entire hotel is nonsmoking. A minus: Though there's an elevator, you'll have to negotiate stairs to get to it.

€€€–€€€€ Some hotels pay big bucks for '70s-esque interiors, but **Hotel Alison** ★★ (21 rue de Surène, 8th arrond.; ☎ 01 42 65 54 00; www.hotel-alison.com; Métro: Madeleine; AE, DC, MC, V) doesn't need to: Its spotless rooms and geometric furniture have been that way since the days of disco. There's nothing frumpy or musty about these crisp lodgings, the owners simply haven't felt the need to update the shiny white ceilings in certain rooms, or the square black headboards in most others. However you feel about beige walls and chocolate carpets, you should be pleased with the generally high level of comfort here; rooms are a good size (especially the twins), amenities are plentiful (pants presses, Roget et Gallet toiletries), and the location is excellent (around the corner from the Madeleine, a hop, skip, and a swagger from the Champs Elysées). Prices vary 10% to 20% with the season, and rooms on the leafy courtyard cost more, so doubles range from 115€ to 148€ according to when and where you're staying. If you are looking for something more up-to-date, there are some newly made-over doubles for 168€. *Families take note:* Communicating doubles cost 209€ to 296€ for the two rooms.

GRANDS BOULEVARDS TO CANAL SAINT MARTIN (9TH & 10TH ARRONDISSEMENTS)

Though there's no compelling reason to stay in this part of town—no big monuments or famous museums—there is also no reason not to: Public transportation is good, there are fewer crowds, and certain areas are actually becoming quite hip, like the area around rue des Martyrs, and more obviously, the cafe-lined Canal St-Martin. If you want to see a more low-key, regular folks part of Paris, this is a good place to find it. And while the area itself might not have any must-see sights, the

9th arrondissement is at the foot of Montmartre, and the 10th is just above the Marais.

AT THE BASE OF MONTMARTRE

€ In heated competition with the funky youth hostel across the street, **Perfect Hôtel** ✭ (39 rue Rodier, 9th arrond.; ☎ 01 42 81 18 86; www.paris-hostel.biz; Métro: Anvers or Cadet. MC, V) charges remarkably little for very decent, if not perfect, lodgings. Rooms are clean and well-maintained, ceilings are high (with original moldings), wallpaper is fresh, and the service is enthusiastically efficient—a lot more than you could say about some hotels that charge double the price. Refurbished on a regular basis, these well-kept but basic accommodations (uneven floors, doorless closet units, no TV), run just 60€ for a double, and if you are willing to make do with just a sink and share the toilet and shower in the hall, the price goes down to 50€ (tiny, toilet-free doubles that look out on a wall are only 44€). The second and fifth floor rooms facing the street have small balconies, those on the upper floors also have a nice view of the city. Rooms facing the "courtyard" (that is, the wall) are less appealing, though quieter. Though you can reserve on the Internet (and those who do get free breakfast), there is no Internet access at the hotel. Guests do have access to a small kitchen (refrigerator, microwave) though, for fixing light meals.

GRAND BOULEVARDS

€–€€ Nestled at the back of the Passage Jouffroy, **Hôtel Chopin** ✭ (46 Passage Jouffroy, entrance at 10 blvd. Montmartre, 9th arrond.; ☎ 01 47 70 58 10; www.hotelchopin.fr; Métro: Richelieu-Drouot; MC, V) has remarkably quiet rooms considering its location in the middle of the rush and bustle of the Grands Boulevards. Not a single room is on a street—the only ones that get any noise at all are next to the elevator, and those go for a lower rate. The rates are already very reasonable—doubles go from 88€ to 102€. The staircase is a little creaky (there is an elevator) and the decor is nothing to write home about, but the rooms are clean and colorful and the bathrooms are spotless. Rooms on the upper floors get more light. Just across the street from Passage Jouffroy is the entrance to a maze of other covered passages (see "Arcadia" box, p. 254), and it's about a 10-minute walk to the Palais Royal. There is no Internet access.

NEAR GARE DE L'EST

€€ If, for travel reasons (I can't think of any other), you need to stay very close to either the Gare de l'Est or the Gare du Nord train stations, **Little Régina Hôtel** (89 blvd. de Strasbourg, 10th arrond.; ☎ 01 40 37 72 30; www.paris-hotel-little-regina.com; Métro: Gare de l'Est; AE, DC, MC, V) is a good, reliable choice. Accommodations are basic, but pleasant, with standard hotel furniture and an unremarkable decor—but all is clean and fresh and well-maintained, and the management aims to please. Doubles run 100€ to 110€, and triples are 130€. Communicating doubles for families are also available for 200€. If the prices seem a little steep for what is offered, know that there are good discounts on the hotel's Internet site.

BASTILLE & FAUBOURG ST-ANTOINE (11TH & 12TH ARRONDISSEMENTS)

Another area that many people overlook when they're searching for a place to stay is the area around the place de la Bastille, and further east, towards the Gare de Lyon train station, in the Faubourg St-Antoine. This historic workers neighborhood was where revolutionary fervor came to a head on July 14, 1789 when its irate citizens stormed down the boulevard and took over the Bastille prison. Things have calmed down considerably since then, and outside of the heated nightlife scene around the rue de Charonne and rue Oberkampf, it's a pretty sleepy neighborhood. For that reason you can find some excellent rates here, particularly around the place de la République, which is a short walk from the Marais.

NEAR PLACE DE LA REPUBLIQUE

€   It may be a budget hotel, but the welcome at **Hôtel de Nevers** ★★ 🧒 (53 rue de Malte, 11th arrond.; ☎ 01 47 00 56 18; www.hoteldenevers.com; Métro: République; MC, V) merits four stars. Not only will you be greeted by the hotel's friendly and cheerful staff but also by their two cats, who are so gregarious that if you're not careful they'll sleep in your room (if you have cat allergies, this hotel may not be for you). Rooms are bright and spotless, if less than luxurious—towels are a bit frayed, beds are a bit saggy—but at prices like these, you really can't complain. A double is only 59€, a twin 64€, and if you are willing to share facilities, doubles with shower only are 55€ and those with just a sink are a mere 45€. Triples with full bathroom are 79€ and quads go for 91€, half the price of most "family rooms" in other hotels. If you've chosen a showerless option, the communal shower is 4€. Free British newspapers are available in the lobby, but the rooms don't have TVs. Don't confuse with another hotel listed in this book with the same name in the 7th arrondissement.

€   A step up on the comfort scale, but also very reasonably priced, is **Hôtel Résidence Alhambra** ★★ (13 rue de Malte, 11th arrond.; ☎ 01 47 00 35 52; www.hotelalhambra.fr; Métro: Oberkampf or Filles du Calvaire; AE, DC, MC, V). The big draw here is the lovely garden in the large courtyard, where you can eat breakfast (weather allowing). The fact that the courtyard is so big means that the rooms facing it get lots of light (not to mention a nice view); about half of the rooms face the garden, but although the friendly staff will do what they can, they cannot guarantee one when you reserve. The good news is, prices are the same no matter which side you end up on, and all rooms are nicely, if simply, decorated and in tip-top shape. Doubles and twins are only 78€ and 84€ here; good-sized triples go for 96€ to 116€. Book early; this hotel is popular with European tour groups.

OBERKAMPF

€€–€€€   Another reason to stay a little farther out of the center is **Hôtel St-Louis Bastille** ★★ (114 blvd. Richard Lenoir, 11th arrond.; ☎ 01 43 38 29 29; www.saintlouisbastille.com; Métro: Oberkampf or Parmentier; AE, DC, MC, V). Comfortable and classy, with designer fabrics in neutral, Zen colors, these smart lodgings go for the same rates as a borderline dump near the Arc de Triomphe. Here, a standard double with a shower is 115€, a slightly larger twin with bath is 135€, and there are periodic 10% discounts on the website. Though the style is more or less modern, it respects the history of the building; ceilings are high with original moldings, floors are tiled with antiqued stone, and the furniture is vaguely period. Rooms on the top floor have lower ceilings with exposed beams. A little bit of noise filters through the double-paned windows facing the busy street, but the compensation is a lovely view of boulevard Richard Lenoir, where there is an open-air market on Tuesday and Friday mornings. If you must have quiet, ask for a room on the small courtyard, preferably on a higher floor, which lets in more light. You certainly won't be in no man's land here—hip rue Oberkampf is just around the corner, the Marais a short walk, and public transport is plentiful.

€€–€€€€   Colorful and mod, the lobby of **Hôtel Beaumarchais** ✪ (3 rue Oberkampf, 11th arrond.; ☎ 01 53 36 86 86; www.hotelbeaumarchais.com; Métro: Oberkampf or Filles du Calvaire; AE, MC, V) doubles as an art gallery, with displays that rotate every 2 months. The owner is an artist himself, which explains the original styling and surprising color combinations in the air-conditioned rooms. Bright red bedspreads and drapes contrast with yellow walls and blue-gray headboards; bathroom walls are paved with tile shards and mirror pieces. Kandinsky and Miró prints complete the picture. And just up the street are the endless restaurants and bars of hip and hopping rue Oberkampf. Considering the design values, the price is not too high: Doubles and twins are 110€ to 130€, depending on the season, larger "junior suites" are 150€ to 170€, small triples are 170€ to 190€. Breakfast is served in the small garden courtyard in the warmer months.

NEAR THE PLACE DE LA BASTILLE

€   You certainly can't complain that you're in a boring neighborhood when you stay at the **Hôtel Daval** ✪ (21 rue Daval, 11th arrond.; ☎ 01 47 00 51 23; www.hoteldaval.com; Métro: Bastille; AE, DC, MC, V). Right in the thick of all the bars and restaurants on nearby rue de la Roquette and rue de Lappe, the biggest problem you'll have here is the noise from late-night revelers. If you want quiet, ask the friendly staff for a room on the enormous courtyard. The entire hotel has just had a much-needed overhaul and everything in the air-conditioned, simply furnished rooms is new, from the bedding, to the bathrooms, to the wood-paneled floors. What's more, the low rates have barely budged: Doubles are 82€, larger twins 95€, and triples 105€.

PORTE DOREE

€€   True, it's a little out of the way, but **Hôtel de la Porte Dorée** ✪✪ (273 avenue Daumesnil, 12th arrond.; ☎ 01 43 07 56 97; www.hoteldelaportedoree. com; Métro Porte Dorée; AE, DC, MC, V) is well worth the subway fare. The impeccable, air-conditioned rooms are furnished with both comfort and esthetics in mind: Period prints, antique headboards, high ceilings, and original curlicue moldings are all part of the package. You'll pay less for these charming lodgings than you will for something utterly basic in the center of town: Good-size doubles and roomier twins are only 98€ and larger triples are 110€. All floors are wood—a plus for those with allergies—and the entire hotel is non-smoking. While the location is hardly central, it is right next to the verdant Bois de Vincennes, where you can rent bikes or picnic; hardy souls can cycle to the city center via the separated bike path on Avenue Daumesnil. The Métro (there's a stop just outside the hotel) will get you to the city center in about 15 minutes. You needn't worry about a language barrier at this hotel, which is owned by a friendly Franco-American couple.

MONTPARNASSE (14TH ARRONDISSEMENT)

Montparnasse is more centrally located than it might seem—it's right on the border of St-Germain and close to the Luxembourg gardens. Also, the train station is a major transit hub for a bundle of Métro lines and bus routes. Though the utterly unaesthetic Tour Montparnasse now casts a shadow over this ancient artists haunt (Henry Miller, Man Ray, Chagall, Picasso . . .) the little streets in the surrounding area are still full of personality.

€   Rue Daguerre has everything one could need for a Parisian visit: shops, food stores, restaurants, cafes, and a reasonable place to stay, namely **Hôtel Saphir** (70 rue Daguerre, 14th arrond.; 01 43 22 07 02; www.hotel-saphir.net; Métro: Denfert-Rochereau or Montparnasse; AE, MC, V). Bright colors on the walls give warmth to these basic rooms, which are well kept and feature beds with new mattresses. The welcome is equally warm; the hotel has been in the same family for 20 years. Doubles range from 68€ to 73€; with your savings you can treat yourself to a couscous at the hotel's restaurant, La Baraka.

€–€€   With cute, comfortable rooms and excellent rates, **Hôtel des Bains** ★★(kids) (33 rue Delambre, 14th arrond.; ☎ 01 43 20 85 27; www.hotel-des-bains-montparnasse.com; Métro: Vavin or Edgar Quinet; MC, V) gets my vote as one of the best deals on the Left Bank, especially for families. In a city where family-size rooms are rare, this hotels offers several good-size, two-room suites (105€ for two people; 130€ for three; and 155€ for four), a couple of which are in a quiet annex on the large, leafy courtyard. Doubles (90€) facing the street (double-paned windows take care of most noise concerns) are somewhat smaller; if you need more space ask for one facing the pretty courtyard. The decor is simple but nicely accessorized with original objects and artwork from the art market that takes place on the nearby square every Sunday (there is also an open-air market there Wed and Sat mornings). Most rooms have wood floors (good for people with allergies), a few have tiny balconies, and all are air-conditioned. The elevator stops at a landing between floors, so you will need to be able to manage a few stairs.

TROCADERO & PASSY (16TH ARRONDISSEMENT)

Generally considered the Beverly Hills of Paris, the 16th arrondissement is very calm, very elegant, and very expensive. It is also the home of a bundle of great museums (the Musée Guimet and the Musée Marmottan, for starters) and the grandiose Palais de Chaillot on the place du Trocadéro, from which you can bask in a splendid view of the Eiffel Tower. Somewhat out of the center, and right next to the verdant Bois de Boulogne, the 16th is a nice area to stay if you need peace and quiet—and the rates don't make your hair stand on end. Below are two of the extremely rare affordable options.

€   One of the ways of getting around the outrageous prices of the 16th is to get away from Trocadéro, et al. And if you are willing to go as far as Porte d'Auteuil, you can stay at the adorable **Hôtel Villa d'Auteuil** ★ (28 rue Poussin, 16th arrond.; ☎ 01 42 88 30 37; www.cofrase.com/hotel/villauteuil; AE, MC, V) and save yourself a bundle. Many moons ago, this building was a private mansion; though the accommodations are fairly basic, the rooms still retain their high ceilings and 19th-century moldings. About half face a quiet green courtyard; the others face the street, but noise is pretty much eradicated by the double-paned windows. Rooms are well-maintained, mattresses are firm, and the decor features old-fashioned floral prints and furniture—and you'll only pay 70€ to 74€ for a double and 84€ for a triple. Management is very friendly, as is the staff: Don't be surprised if the resident parrot (an African Grey named Oscar) greets you with a high-pitched "bonjour" when you come down for breakfast. Buses and two Métro lines are very close by; Trocadéro is a 10-minute Métro ride and Notre Dame will take around a half an hour. If you're here for the Tennis open, you can walk to the stadium in a matter of minutes. There is no elevator.

€€   About half-way between the Arc de Triomphe and Trocadéro, and just around the corner from swanky Place Victor Hugo, is the nicest of the few remaining affordable hotels in the area. Besides its great location, **Hôtel Ambassade** ★ (79 rue Lauriston, 16th arrond.; ☎ 01 45 53 41 15; www.hotel-ambassade.com; AE, DC, MC, V) offers spotless, pleasant air-conditioned rooms—the entire hotel was renovated in 2006. While the odd pseudo art nouveau lobby may take you aback, do not fear, the rooms themselves are quite comfortable and the swirly motifs are kept to a minimum. The pretty dark wood furniture was custom made; the fabrics on the beds and curtains are subdued. Standard doubles go for 100€ to 114€ and larger "comfort" doubles are 122€ to 128€ depending on the season; add 10€ to the top price during trade shows.

MONTMARTRE (18TH ARRONDISSEMENT)

If you're looking for a romantic setting, you can't do much better than Montmartre. That is, unless you unwittingly pick a hotel that is smack in the middle of the tourist madness surrounding Sacré-Coeur. The hotels listed below should keep you out of harm's way; just remember to book far in advance as they're in high demand. Views are at a premium up here on the butte (a high hill), and many hotels will charge extra for rooms that have one; think twice before paying extra for what may or may not be a spectacular view, as you can easily enjoy the panorama from any number of scenic spots just outside the hotel. Another consideration: Though Montmartre is charming, it's on the northern edge of the city, so you'll need to budget extra time to get down the hill to the center of town.

NEAR PLACE DES ABBESSES

€   Located on a street that could come straight out of a scene in the film *Amelie*, **Hôtel Bonséjour Montmartre** ★ (11 rue Burq, 18th arrond.; ☎ 01 42 54 22 53; www.hotel-bonsejour-montmartre.fr; Métro: Abbesses; MC, V)—not to be confused with Hôtel Bonséjour in the Marais—belongs to that increasingly rare category of lodgings where hands-on management, a warm welcome, and rock-bottom prices largely make up for the lack of amenities. There's no question that this is a budget hotel—no elevator, no TV, and the toilets are in the hall—but with doubles going for 48€ to 55€, do you really care if the hallways are creaky and the shower stalls are strange? The enthusiastic manager goes to great lengths to keep rooms in tip-top shape; he recently installed new floors and new mattresses and pillows in all rooms, and he has put tiny showers (see above) in many so that guests don't have to use the common shower (2€) on the ground floor. On the higher end of the rate scale are rooms 23, 33, 43, and 53, which have a tiny balcony where you can nibble your croissants while you enjoy the lovely view of the cobbled streets (no breakfast is served in the hotel but bakeries are nearby). The boutiques and cafes of rue des Abbesses are just down the street; Sacré Coeur is about a 10-minute walk.

€€   A step up in terms of esthetics, **Hôtel Utrillo** (7 rue Aristide Bruant, 18th arrond.; ☎ 01 42 58 42 58; www.hotel-paris-utrillo.com; Métro: Abbesses; MC, V) has a younger, more modern look, with bright fabrics, pretty furniture, and fresh paint throughout (at press time, the photos on the website were not up-to-date). Rooms are still small, and closet space is still minimal, but the location is great (around the corner from the cute boutiques and restaurants of rue des Abbesses) and the price is right: Doubles run 85€ to 90€, the higher end being the larger rooms with bathtubs. Try to get a room on the street unless you are a light sleeper—the quieter courtyard-side rooms get less light and no view to speak of. There is a sauna in the basement (8€) for tired tourists looking for some deep relaxation.

€€   For an even better location, try **Hôtel Regyn's Montmartre** ★ (18 place des Abbesses, 18th arrond.; ☎ 01 42 54 45 21; www.paris-hotels-montmartre.com; Métro: Abbesses; AE, MC, V). Right on pretty place des Abbesses, and a stone's throw from the elegant Métro entrance, these cozy lodgings are nicely decorated with period toile de jouy fabrics on the drapes and walls and quilted cotton boutis spreads on the beds. Though the rooms are not huge here either, they are bigger than at the Utrillo; closets, however, are very small, and the bathtubs are child-sized. The trick here is to snag a south-facing room; on the lower levels you will have a picturesque view of the leafy square (doubles 99€), and on the upper levels (fourth and fifth floors) some fabulous views of the city (doubles 115€). Viewless doubles facing the courtyard run 91€.

NORTH OF SACRE-COEUR

€–€€   In a lively, cute neighborhood that has somehow escaped gentrification, **Hôtel Eden Montmartre** (90 rue Ordener, 18th arrond.; ☎ 01 42 64 61 63; www.edenhotel-montmartre.com; Métro: Jules Joffrin, MC, V) offers pleasant, if fairly basic accommodations at affordable rates. Two years ago, work began on a

Accommodations on the Right Bank (18th)

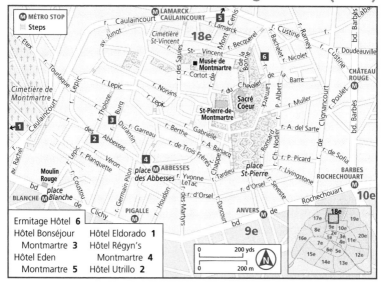

Ermitage Hôtel **6**
Hôtel Bonséjour
Montmartre **3**   Hôtel Eldorado **1**
Hôtel Eden   Hôtel Régyn's
Montmartre **5**   Montmartre **4**
                     Hôtel Utrillo **2**

hotel-wide renovation; while the furniture, bedding, and carpets are all shiny new, there are still a few nicks in the walls and an occasional crack in the bathroom tiles. Impeccable housekeeping and a warm welcome more than make up for any decor defects, as does the price: Doubles run 87€ to 92€ and triples are 97€ most of the year. If you happen to be coming during high tradeshow season, you'll pay extra—from mid-September to the end of October doubles are 108€ to 115€ and triples are 121€. Even the high season rates are reasonable when you consider that it's only a 10-minute walk to Sacré Coeur and the hotel is right next to a Métro line that leads to the center of town.

BATIGNOLLES

€   Though physically it's right outside the border of Montmartre, the soul of **Hôtel Eldorado** ★★ (18 rue des Dames, 17th arrondissement; ☎ 01 45 22 35 21; www.eldoradohotel.fr; Métro: Place de Clichy; AE, MC, V) belongs in the artistic neighborhood next door. Funky, imaginative, and downright cool is the best way to describe the decor; the owner-artist has been slowly re-doing each room over the last several years so that now each has its own personality and color scheme. No. 15, for example, has red walls, gray and white checked linoleum floors, wicker furniture and ceramic Buddha-like busts in the bedside niches. No. 22 has deep purple walls, a white ceiling, a marble mantelpiece and a tiny, sparkly chandelier. The largest and most atmospheric rooms are in the "pavilion," a small, separate house behind the main building (separated by a lovely garden patio with a restaurant—see Bistrot des Dames, p. 120—which means that there can be noise until around midnight in the warmer months); here the high ceilings and large windows, combined with the Art Deco armoires and quilted bedspreads make you feel like you are in a private home—on sunny mornings you'll hear

A Step Back in Time

€€   Behind the Sacré-Coeur, on a quiet street that winds down the north side of the hill, there is a 19th-century town house that takes lodgers: the **Ermitage Hôtel** ✦✦✦ (24 rue Lamarck, 18th arrond.; ☎ 01 42 64 79 22; www.ermitagesacrecoeur.fr; Métro: Lamarck–Caulaincourt; no credit cards). There may not be room service (although the complementary breakfast is served in your room) or much by way of amenities, but the ambience is unique. Built in 1890 by a rich gentleman for his mistress, this small mansion has been beautifully preserved, and still feels like someone's home. In fact, it virtually is: The Canipel family has run these unconventional lodgings for close to 40 years. Each of the 12 rooms has a different decor with period prints and draperies, as well as some beautiful antique bedsteads and armoires. Some of the rooms have curtained alcoves for a third bed; those facing the back on the ground floor have garden terraces, and higher up, views of the northern edge of the city (honeymooners, take note). The hallways and entry are done up in deep blues and gold leaf; the wall murals and paintings are the works of a local artist. Doubles are only 96€ to 98€, triples 120€, and quads 142€; breakfast is included in the price. There is no elevator or Internet access, and no TVs in the rooms.

birds chirping in the trees outside. Though the paint is fresh and the rooms are clean, some of the furniture is nicked and many of the bathrooms could use a makeover; closet space is minimal. But the low rates should make up for these minor imperfections: Doubles are only 73€ to 80€, an absolute steal for the quality and originality of the lodgings. Triples run 80€ to 90€ for those who are willing to share, there are a few bathroom-less triples for only 65€ (toilets and showers are in the hall).

HOSTELS

If you're willing to sacrifice things like privacy and creature comforts, hostels are a good way to get around the high cost of lodging in Paris. Though most sleeping is done dormitory style, some hostels have smaller double rooms, and a couple even have private bathrooms. Be advised that each has strict rules of behavior, and though many (including those below) are accessible 24 hours a day, you may find your room closed for a few hours in the afternoon when the cleaning crew comes through. Created with young people in mind, who make up a large part of their clientele, hostels are open to all ages. Most hostels, including those listed below, provide bed linens but not towels.

Out of the dozens of hostels in Paris, I'm listing the crème de la crème; a complete list is available on the Paris tourist office website (www.parisinfo.com). *An important point:* Though hostel rates are very appealing, it's worth your time to do some comparison shopping—in some cases hostel rates are near or the same as those of budget hotels (see below) that offer more privacy (though the location may not be as good).

€   Located in a cute neighborhood in the Faubourg St-Antoine (about a 15-min. walk from place de la Bastille), the **Auberge International des Jeunes** (10 rue Trousseau, 11th arrond.; ☎ 01 47 00 62 00; www.aijparis.com; MC, V) provides bright, modern lodgings at some of the lowest hostel rates in town. Depending on the season, a bed here costs 13€ to 17€ per person, per night, including breakfast. There are two to four beds per room; rooms for four have private toilet and shower. Reservations are by e-mail only.

€   Founded in 1948, **BVJ** (Bureau des Voyages de la Jeunesse) has two clean, pleasant hostels, both in excellent locations. As its name indicates, **BVJ Louvre** (20 rue Jean-Jacques Rousseau, 1st arrond.; ☎ 01 53 00 90 90; www.bvjhotel. com; no credit cards) is very close to the Louvre and has rooms with two to eight beds which run 28€ to 30€ per person, per night, breakfast included. Its smaller cousin, **BVJ Quartier Latin** (44 rue des Bernardins, 5th arrond.; ☎ 01 43 29 34 80; www.bvjhotel.com; Métro: Maubert Mutualité; no credit cards) is right in the heart of the Latin Quarter and also in walking distance to many of the main sights in the city center. Single rooms are available here for 42€; otherwise, rates are 28€ to 32€ per person, per night, breakfast included. Reservations for both hostels must be made no more than 15 days in advance.

€   I don't know how many hostels can boast 17th-century town houses, but **MIJE** (Maisons Internationales de la Jeunesse et des Etudiants, 6 rue de Fourcy, 4th arrond.; ☎ 01 42 74 23 45; www.mije.com; Métro: St-Paul or Pont Marie; MC, V) has three in one of the quietest neighborhoods of the Marais, just across the river from the Ile St-Louis. Though rooms are basic and modern (no private toilets, though you do get a sink and shower), you can't beat the atmosphere when you step out into the courtyard. If you don't mind sharing, a bed in a quad or bigger is 29€, and a triple 30€. Double rooms are available (two single beds) for 68€, and there are some single rooms for 47€. Breakfast is included and is served in the cafeteria in the vaulted cellar (which also serves inexpensive lunches and dinners). There's no elevator. You'll be charged 2.50€ for MIJE membership, and your stay is limited to 7 nights. The other hostels are at 11 rue de Fauconnier and 12 rue de Barres, both within a 5-minute walk. Reserve ahead (the number above is for all three sites), as these hostels are often invaded by groups.

HEUREUX CAMPERS

If all else fails, you can always pitch a tent. If you're willing to brave the frequent rain and less frequent bus service (every 15–20 min.), camping is the cheapest lodging option in town. The only campground within city limits is **Camping du Bois de Boulogne** (2 allée du Bord de l'Eau, 16th arrond.; 01 45 24 30 00; www.campingparis.fr; Bus: Line 244, "Les Moulins–Camping" stop; AE, DC, MC, V), a 7-hectare (17-acre) site with 435 pitches, a minimarket, restaurants, a Laundromat, and, in high season, a shuttle bus that will take you to the Porte Maillot Métro/RER stop. As the campground is on the western edge of the lush Bois de Boulogne, right on the edge of the Seine, you won't be in the center of town, but once you get the bus you're only 10 minutes from a Métro stop. If you don't want to bring a tent, 75 mobile homes for up to six people are available (57€–102€ per night, depending on season and type of mobile home). Rates fluctuate with the seasons: Low season is October to mid-March, mid-season is mid-March to June and September, and high season is July to August. Regular tent sites run from 11€ to 17€ for a tent-only spot with no water connection to 25€ to 36€ for a "Grand Confort" spot for tents or RVs with drinkable water, evacuation, and electricity.

4 Dining Choices

For all tastes & pocketbooks

IT OCCURRED TO ME THAT DINING SHOULD REALLY GO IN THE ACTIVITIES section of a guidebook on Paris. You come here to see the Eiffel Tower and the Louvre, of course, but you also come here to eat. Everywhere you look, someone is doing their best to ruin your waistline. *Boulangeries* (bakeries) with perfectly puffed croissants and decadent pastries seem to lurk on every street corner; *chocolateries* (chocolate stores) with tantalizing window displays abound, and cute restaurants with intriguing menus sprout up on every block.

Why this plethora of gustatory pleasures? Maybe it's because in France, eating well is more than a nice thing to do when you're out with friends, it's an integral part of a culture that celebrates the finer things in life. Food's not a pastime here, it's an art—one that's been finely honed over the centuries. Eating and drinking is a topic of serious discussion, the subject of radio shows, newspaper columns, and even feature films. The annual agricultural fair *(Salon d'Agriculture),* where the latest and finest of the country's food products and preparations are exposed, is of such importance that it's a mandatory photo-op for the nation's politicians. So it's not surprising that Paris, navel of the French universe, should boast some of the best food on Earth.

The trick is to indulge intelligently. You don't have to have a king-size budget to dine like royalty. But you do have to choose wisely. Once upon a time, you could wander into just about any restaurant in Paris and sit down to a good meal; today, this is no longer the case. Modern life is taking a heavy toll on gourmet living, and restaurant quality has suffered. France is trying desperately to keep up with the global economy, which is anything but kind to unprofitable customs like the 2-hour lunch. Try not to notice all the fast-food places that have popped up around the city, and don't even think about eating in one of the ubiquitous Chinese restaurants that serve a bland version of this marvelous Asian cuisine.

Fortunately, the guardians of good food are fighting back. Food militants like Jean-Pierre Coffe, writer and host of a popular radio show, have become media stars by challenging big-business agriculture and championing small producers and regional products. Famous chefs like Christian Constant and Yves de Camdeborde have opened dressed-down bistrots that serve modern versions of traditional worker's cuisine at prices that a worker might actually be able to afford. The search for fresh, contemporary cuisine has become a hot trend among the city's hipster crowd.

> " I said to my friends that if I was going to starve, I might as well starve where the food is good. "
>
> —Virgil Thomson, composer, on life in Paris as a young man

71

Called "le fooding," this new movement even has its own website (a good source for bar and restaurant tips, www.lefooding.com).

DEJEUNER SUR L'HERBE

Before we dive into our restaurant list, I'd like to bring up an important subject: **picnics.** Although restaurants are all very fine and good, there's a lot to be said for a quick and easy outdoor meal when you are (a) tired, (b) on a budget, and (c) a fan of Paris's many lovely parks and squares. What could be nicer (and more relaxing) than a sandwich in the Jardin du Luxembourg? Even when its lovely skyline is hemmed in by clouds, eating alfresco in a park can be a pleasant pause during an action-packed day of sightseeing. Picking up picnic ingredients is a pretty easy affair, though there's a bit of essential terminology you should be familiar with. For good take out food, look for the nearest *charcuterie* (these specialize in smoked meat, pâtés, and other yummy pork products) or *traiteur* (a store that sells prepared takeout dishes and salads). Though *traiteurs* are getting harder to find, most charcuteries do double-duty as traiteurs, as do some *boucheries* (butchers).

The easiest option, though, is on offer at almost any *boulangerie* (bakery), where you can find what may well be **the best lunch bargain in the city:** their lunch *"formule,"* or set menu. For around 6€, you can get a long sandwich (usually a half a baguette), amply filled with chicken, ham, or tuna and *crudités* (tomato, lettuce, and other saladlike items), a drink, and a yummy freshly made pastry (this is a bakery after all). Often you can substitute a slice of quiche for a sandwich. The food is generally fresh and tasty, and a heckuva lot better than what you'd get at Macdonald's. *Formules* and sandwiches are usually only available from 11am to 2pm.

For more innovative picnic fare, consider one of Paris's many upscale sandwich shops (see box, below). *Note:* Picnicking is verboten on the pristine lawns of many of the larger parks, though some, like the Jardin du Luxembourg have opened up a few select areas for legal lounging; lawns aside, you can always set up camp on a bench.

BROWSING THE BAKERIES

If you see a line outside a Parisian *boulangerie,* chances are, you're in for something good. Often doubling as a *pâtisserie* (pastry shop) these usually family-run shops are the place to pick up great bread, pastries, and sandwiches (lunchtime only). As bread is the staff of life in France, bakeries are just about everywhere, and your nose will generally tell you which are good, but here are a few ideas to get you started.

Moisan ★★ (2 rue de Bazeilles, 5th arrond.; ☎ 01 47 07 35 40; 7am–8pm, closed Thurs; Métro: Censier-Daubenton; MC, V; also at 7 rue Bourdaloue, 9th arrond; 6 blvd. Denain, 10th arrond.; 5 place d'Aligre, 12th arrond; 4 av. du Général Leclerc, 14th arrond; 59 rue Fondary, 15th arrond.; 74 rue de Lévis, 17th arrond.). Proof that organic bread doesn't have to taste excessively virtuous (heavy and bland). Some of the best bread in town (and the pastries aren't bad either).

Eric Kayser ★★ (www.maison-kayser.com). This incredibly successful young baker now has shops all over the city (11 and counting), all as good as the two originals on rue Monge (8 Monge, 5th arrond; ☎ 01 44 07 01 42; 14 rue Monge,

The Invasion of the Sandwich Snatchers

Bowing to the mounting pressure to eat fast and cheap, sandwich bars are popping up all over Paris like mushrooms after a spring rain. Many are uninspired copies of upscale New York sandwich shops, with mildly exotic pre-prepared salads and sandwiches, but one of the more interesting chains is **Cojean** (it has 10 locations, including 3 Place du Louvre, 1st arrond.; 6 rue des Mathurins, 8th arrond.; 32 rue Monceau, 8th arrond.; 16 rue Clément Marot, 8th arrond.; 6 rue de Sèze, 9th arrond; 17 blvd. Haussmann, 9th arrond.; 66 rue de Provence, 9th arrond.; and in the Bon Marché department store, 24 rue de Sèvres; www.cojean.fr; MC, V). A creation of an ex-MacDonald's executive with an almost religious fervor for fresh, healthy food, these airy, modern boutiques serve innovative salads (examples: quinoa with smoked salmon, beets, and smoked tofu), as well as quiches, sandwiches, and fresh-squeezed juices. You can eat on site at comfortable tables. Another, more conventional option for a good sandwich or bowl of soup is **Lina's** (50 rue Etienne Marcel, 2nd arrond.; ☎ 01 42 21 16 14; www.linascafe.fr; Métro: Etienne Marcel; MC, V). With branches all over Paris (not to mention Beirut and Peking), Lina's "Le Beautiful Sandwich," can be custom-constructed on your choice of bread.

5th arrond., ☎ 01 44 07 17 81; 7am–8:30pm, closed Tues; Métro: Maubert-Mutualité; MC, V). Though the main draw is the bread (in all shapes, forms, and grains), the pastries are also excellent. Some locations also serve light lunches.

Poilâne ✪✪ (8 rue du Cherche-Midi, 6th arrond.; ☎ 01 45 48 12 59; www.poilane.fr; 7:15am–8:15pm, closed Sun; Métro: St-Sulpice; ☎ 01 45 79 11 49; Métro: La Motte Picquet; AE, DC, MC, V; also at 49 blvd. de Grenelle, 15th arrond.). This legendary bread gets shipped all over the world. Chewy, firm, and dark, it's best when fresh. You can buy it by the slice or by quarters if you don't want to take an entire wheel-like loaf.

Le Boulanger de Monge ✪✪✪ (123 rue Monge, 5th arrond.; ☎ 01 43 37 54 20; www.leboulangerdemonge.com; 7am–8:30pm, closed Mon; Métro: Gobelins; MC, V). The permanent line out the door is the first tip-off—the breads and pastries here are to die for. Featuring organic and nonorganic goodies, as well as sandwiches, this bakery has a wide selection of nontraditional breads, like the excellent multi-grain fig bread, and the twisted spelt *tourte*.

Aux Désirs de Manon ✪ (129 rue St-Antoine, 4th arrond.; ☎ 01 42 72 32 91; 6am–8pm, closed Sun; Métro: St-Paul; MC, V). Not in the least bit famous, just a personal favorite that has a wonderful selection of breads and terrific sandwiches. A great place to get a picnic for the place des Vosges.

Jean Millet ✪✪ (103 rue Saint Dominique, 7th arrond.; ☎ 01 45 51 49 80; 9am–7pm Mon-Sat, 8am–1pm Sun; Métro: La Tour Maubourg; AE, MC, V). The exquisite pastries and chocolates have garnered such a reputation that they now have an outpost in Tokyo. The small shop has a few tables where you can indulge in comfort; soups and salads are on offer at lunchtime.

Gérard Mulot ✸✸ (76 rue de Seine, 6th arrond; ☎ 01 43 26 85 77; www.gerard-mulot.fr; 7am–8pm, closed Wed; Métro: Odéon; MC, V). Watch the impeccably dressed clientele try not to drool over the intoxicating pastries (say, Le Mabillon: caramel mousse with candied apricots and almond biscuits) and *macarons* (light, frothy cookies filled with cream). They have fabulous, if expensive, salads as well. They recently opened a second shop at 93 rue Glacière, 13th arrond.

Pierre Hermé ✸✸✸ (72 rue Bonaparte, 6th arrond.; ☎ 01 43 54 47 77; www.pierreherme.com; 10am–7pm; Métro: St-Germain-des-Prés; AE, DC, MC, V). The current superstar of pastry chefs thrills the crowds with his sublime pastries and tarts like the Mogador (chocolate cream, passion-fruit, pineapple and caramel) and his exotic chocolates like the Instant (filled with chocolate ganache and white Earl Grey tea jelly). They too have recently opened an impossibly hip second boutique at 185 rue de Vaugirard in the 15th arrond.

CHOOSING THE RIGHT RESTAURANT

Now, on to the main course. Below is a very selective list of restaurants, wine bars, and tearooms that serve good, honest food. But seeing as how there are thousands of restaurants in Paris, you just might wander into something wonderful and unexpected on your own. Nosing out a good restaurant is an extremely subjective affair, taking into account any number of variables and a good dose of what the French call "le feeling." That said, we recommend you take some precautions. Unfortunately, it is all too easy to waste time and money on tourist restaurants that shovel out food that is at best, unmemorable, and at worst, indigestible. Here are some things to be highly suspicious of:

◆ Restaurants with menus translated into multiple languages

◆ Restaurants with life-size statues of smiling chefs or country bumpkins holding out the menu

◆ Restaurants with tour buses parked outside

◆ Restaurants with a clientele that is mostly foreign (unless you are in a museum)

◆ Any restaurant right next to a top-ten tourist attraction. Even if the food is good, which is unlikely, the prices are bound to be exorbitant.

◆ Restaurants with front doors plastered with stickers from every guidebook on the face of the earth (except this one, of course). They could still be good, but they might just be riding on reputation. Check for the above.

THE QUEST FOR GOOD MEALS

As elsewhere in this book, I've grouped my selections geographically, starting with the center of the city center and extending outward, more or less following the numerical progression of the arrondissements, or districts, of Paris. Helpful symbols will appear next to the names the restaurants, with euro signs indicating the general cost:

Let's Do Lunch

As you may have noticed, many, if not most restaurants in Paris serve a set-price menu at lunch that is considerably cheaper than the same food served at dinnertime. It is not at all unusual to find a two- or three-course lunch prix fixe, called alternately a *formule* or a menu for 13€ to 16€, or less. If you want to eat well, and you are on a limited budget, I strongly recommend taking advantage of this lovely lunchtime tradition. Example: At the highly regarded Pré Verre, a wine bar and bistro with top-notch chefs at the helm, you can eat a three-course meal at dinner for 28€ (already quite a bargain) or a two-course meal with a glass of wine at lunch for only 13€. The only down side is that your choice of dishes will usually be limited on the *formule*. **Note:** Lunch *formules*, unless otherwise noted, are only served Monday through Friday.

€: Main courses for 10€ or less
€€: Main courses for 11€ to 15€
€€€: Main courses for 16€ to 22€
€€€€: Main courses 23€ and over

and stars for those selections deemed to have special merit:

No stars=Good
★ Very good
★★ Excellent
★★★ Not to be missed

Within each neighborhood, restaurants are listed in ascending order of cost, starting with the cheapest, so that you can quickly choose a restaurant in your price range. If all you crave is a simple meal, start with the opening selections. When you're ripe for something more elaborate, move down the text. *Note:* In the reviews below, I've often listed examples of dishes; keep in mind that menus tend to be seasonal here and change frequently, so these examples are simply to give you an idea of what kind of food is served.

LOUVRE–CHÂTELET (1ST ARRONDISSEMENT)

Dining near the Louvre can be an expensive and frustrating affair; since almost every tourist visiting the city comes to this part of town, it's rife with overpriced, mediocre tourist restaurants boasting menus in at least five languages. However, if you poke around some of the smaller streets, there are dozens of neighborhood restaurants where you can eat well without blowing a royal budget.

NEAR THE LOUVRE

€   Of the clutch of old-fashioned, Mom and Pop bar/restaurants that once thrived on this street, **Au Petit Bar** ★ (7 rue de Mont Thabor, 1st arrond; ☎ 01 42 60 62 09; noon–3pm and 7–8:30pm, closed Sun and Aug; Métro: Tuileries; no

Eating Hours

In Paris, unless you see a sign that says SERVICE NONSTOP, meals are usually restricted to a service that lasts only a few hours, which is one of the reasons it's a good idea to reserve, if you can (the other is that dining rooms tend to be small). I've noted in the reviews where reservations are necessary. Lunch is generally served between noon and 2pm (sometimes 2:30pm), and dinner is served from 7:30 to 10:30pm (sometimes 11pm). Many restaurants are closed on Sundays and/or Mondays; some have started serving brunch on Sundays, which is served from 11am to 2pm. In the following descriptions, I've listed opening hours for meal service; restaurants that have a bar tend to stay open between times for drinks and coffee.

credit cards) is the sole survivor. A testament to another era before the working class was banished to the suburbs, this tiny place proudly sticks to its proletarian roots, while its neighbors now rub shoulders with the bourgeoisie. Mom and Pop are really in the kitchen, while their son is behind the bar bantering with the customers, most of whom he knows by name. A regular wanders into the kitchen and asks what's on for lunch. "Roast veal, Henri" comes the reply. The food is simple and solid—you might start with mackerel in white wine (3.50€), followed by steak frites (10€), and finish up with a chocolate mousse (3.50€), for example. Prices are extremely reasonable, considering the close proximity to the ritzy place Vendôme; in fact, at 1.20€ it's one of the cheapest cups of coffee on the Right Bank.

€€   At the other end of the street, just behind the U.S. embassy (hence the barricade and paddy wagon) is an old family enterprise, albeit a bit more upscale. **Lescure** ✦ (7 rue de Mondovi, 1st arrond.; ☎ 01 42 60 18 91; noon–2:15pm and 7–10:15pm, closed Sat–Sun; Métro: Concorde; MC, V) has been serving generous portions of French country classics since 1919: *poule au pot* (chicken stew,13€), boeuf bourguignon (13€), and coq au vin (14€) are all on the menu, along with some Limousin (the family hails from this region around Limoge) specialties like the regional version of duck confit (16€). The homey atmosphere—braided garlic hangs from the low ceiling, straw hats decorate the walls—is enhanced by friendly service that goes against the Parisian stereotype. If you are really hungry, there is a three-course menu at lunch that includes wine or beer for 24€, but most will be happy with a main course and a drink. Come early or be prepared to wait—reservations are not accepted.

€€–€€€   Amongst the many cute restaurants with sidewalk tables on the "street of the washerwomen of Saint Opportune," **La Robe et Le Palais** ✦✦ (13 rue des Lavandières Ste-Opportune, 1st arrond.; ☎ 01 45 08 07 41; www.robe-et-palais. com; 12:30–2:30pm and 7:30–11:30pm, closed Sun; Métro: Châtelet; AE, MC, V) is one of the best. First and foremost a wine bar, with a voluminous wine list encompassing every possible region of France, it is also an excellent restaurant, serving updated bistro fare. Magret de canard, otherwise known as duck breast, is served with fresh figs (17€); a delectable slice of *sept-heure gigot* (leg of lamb that's been stewed for 7 hr.) comes in a sauce delicately flavored with Corsican figatelle sausage (18€). The chef is big on promoting regional ingredients: The smoky terrine, or pâté, is made from the black pig of Bigorre (7€), a gourmet pig that has recently been brought back from the brink of extinction. The lunch menu is a real value; two courses for 16€ or three for 19€. If you are wine-challenged, the waiters will gladly help you choose from the formidable selection. The owners have opened another establishment in the neighborhood, also playing on the double meaning of the word "robe" (both "dress" and the flavor of wine), **Le Garde-Robe** (41 rue de l'Arbre Sec, 1st arrond.; ☎ 01 49 26 90 60; Mon 3pm–12:30am, Tues–Sat 11am–3pm and 5:30pm–12:30am; Métro: Louvre-Rivoli or Pont Neuf; AE, MC, V), a wine store and cafe. Reservations are a must.

€€€   Is it a bar, a cafe, a restaurant, or a library? Whatever it is, with its high ceilings, subdued lighting, and large windows, the understatedly hip **Le Fumoir** ★ (place du Louvre, 6 rue de l'Amiral-Coligny, 1st arrond.; ☎ 01 42 92 00 24; www.lefumoir.com; noon–3pm and 7:30–11:30pm; Métro: Louvre-Rivoli; AE, MC, V) is a good place to regroup. Open from 11am to 2am, the mood changes depending on the hour. During the day, dawdling is encouraged; magazines and newspapers are available at the front entry, there's a small lending library/book exchange in the back room. At night, well-dressed 30-somethings crowd around the magnificent wood bar—which in a former life stood in a Philadelphia speakeasy—as they wait for their table. (Happy hour every night from 6–8pm features half-price drinks.) The menu changes with the season, but generally features updated classics like roasted pork loin with braised chicory and mustard sauce (19€) or sautéed scallops with parsley juice (22€). The evening three-course menu for 30€ is a good value; at lunch it's even better—two courses for 19€, or three for 22€ (available Mon–Sat). On Sundays, brunch is served from noon to 3pm for 22€. If you are hungry outside of meal hours, you can still get a light snack; ask for the "bar menu." Don't let the name fool you—since the new law went into effect, there is no smoking here.

ON THE ISLANDS

€   Finding a place to eat on the Ile de la Cité that is not (a) expensive or (b) mobbed with tourists, is a challenge, but one option for a light meal is tucked into a pretty place Dauphine. Next door to its pricey main restaurant, **Le Caveau du Palais,** is the **Bar du Caveau** (17 place Dauphine, 1st arrond.; ☎ 01 43 54 45 95; 8am–7pm, hot food 11:30am–4:30pm, closed Sun year-round, Sat Nov–Apr; Métro: Cité; no credit cards), where a handful of tables are available for nibbling on tartines (Poîlane bread and ham or dried sausage, 5.50€–6.50€), filling salads (grilled chèvre cheese and smoked ham, 9€), or perhaps a Croque Provençale (8.50€), a flavorful combination of ham, tomato, melted cheese topped with a fried egg. And let's not forget the wine, which is served by the glass (3€–5€), the "pot" (a small carafe, 15€), or the bottle (15€–25€). In the warmer months,

Where to Dine on the Right Bank (1st–4th & 9th–10th)

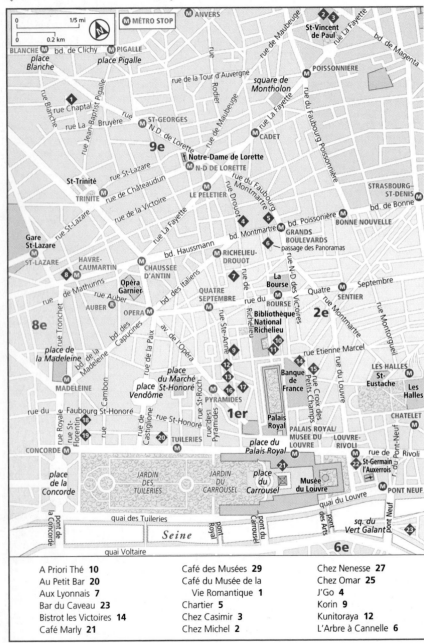

A Priori Thé **10**	Café des Musées **29**	Chez Nenesse **27**
Au Petit Bar **20**	Café du Musée de la	Chez Omar **25**
Aux Lyonnais **7**	Vie Romantique **1**	J'Go **4**
Bar du Caveau **23**	Chartier **5**	Korin **9**
Bistrot les Victoires **14**	Chez Casimir **3**	Kunitoraya **12**
Café Marly **21**	Chez Michel **2**	L'Arbre à Cannelle **6**

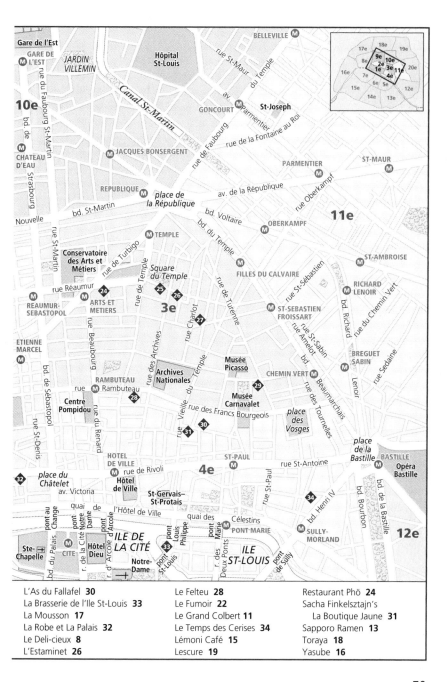

L'As du Fallafel **30**	Le Felteu **28**	Restaurant Phö **24**
La Brasserie de l'Ile St-Louis **33**	Le Fumoir **22**	Sacha Finkelsztajn's
La Mousson **17**	Le Grand Colbert **11**	La Boutique Jaune **31**
La Robe et La Palais **32**	Le Temps des Cerises **34**	Sapporo Ramen **13**
Le Deli-cieux **8**	Lémoni Café **15**	Toraya **18**
L'Estaminet **26**	Lescure **19**	Yasube **16**

Mini Food Glossary

The following terms will crop up in this section:

plat du jour—today's special

formule or *menu*—a fixed price meal, consisting of two to four courses

salade composée—a meal-size salad with a variety of vegetables and meats

tarte salée—quiche

confit de canard—a southwestern specialty: duck preserved in its own fat, then pan-sizzled to perfection (which in theory eliminates most of the fat and leaves just a crispy skin)

magret de canard—duck breast, but you would swear this lean, red meat was lamb or beef

blanquette de veau—veal stew with a mild white sauce

steak frites—steak with fries. This can come in many forms: *entrecôte, bavette, faux-filet,* and so on.

bistro—literally, a small, neighborhood restaurant and bar with a simple, common-man menu (steak-frites, roast chicken, blanquette de veau, and so on). Nowadays, it can mean many things, but it's usually small and not overly expensive.

neo-bistro—a new trend where top chefs take over a traditional bistro and freshen up both the decor and the menu, serving a smartened up version of traditional classics.

Another important distinction to make: In French, an *entrée* is an appetizer. A *plat,* or *plat principal,* is what we would call an entree, or main dish.

---

sidewalk tables offer a view of the tranquil place, a lovely spot to hide out from the crowds surrounding Notre-Dame.

€€€–€€€€   The Ile Saint Louis is even more expensive than Ile de la Cité, but it's also less crowded. Just across the Pont St-Louis, which connects the two islands, is one of the city's last independent brasseries, **La Brasserie de l'Ile Saint-Louis** ✪ (55 Quai de Bourbon, 4th arrond.; ☎ 01 43 54 02 59; noon–1am, closed Wed; Métro: Pont Marie; MC, V). Established in 1876, this brasserie does what brasseries are supposed to do: Serve healthy portions of classic Alsatian dishes, like *choucroute* garni—a small mountain of sauerkraut topped with slices of ham, sausage, and other smoked meats (18€)—in a relaxed atmosphere. If sauerkraut isn't your game, try other classic brasserie fare such as the hearty cassoulet (white bean stew, 18€) or the tender entrecôte (rib steak, 19€). The decor is rustic without being kitsch; despite the location, many of the diners are regulars. "Even the tourists are often return customers," claims the manager. Eating's not a requirement; if you want, you can just enjoy a Mutzig (Alsatian beer, 4.60€ for 25cl) on the terrace and soak up a splendid view of the buttresses of Notre-Dame. Service is "nonstop," so you can eat when you want.

OPERA–BOURSE (1ST & 2ND ARRONDISSEMENTS)

The search for a good meal gets considerably easier as you move north of rue du Rivoli. The streets behind the Palais Royal are buzzing with restaurants, many frequented by the well-dressed businessmen and women who work in this area, which also encompasses the *bourse*, or stock exchange. As you work your way towards the Opéra Garnier, you'll come across a surprisingly large Japanese neighborhood, crammed with noodle shops (see "Japantown, Parisian Style," p. 83)—a happy hunting ground for a good, cheap lunch.

NEAR THE PALAIS ROYAL

€–€€   I still can't figure out why a restaurant with a clientele as classy as this one, with a beautifully preserved bistro decor and a nice menu, is so inexpensive. The main dishes at **Bistrot les Victoires** ✪ (6 rue de la Vrillière, 1st arrond.; ☎ 01 42 61 43 78; noon–3pm and 7–11:30pm; Métro: Palais Royal–Musée du Louvre; MC, V) are only 10€ to 11€ at lunch and rise just .50€ at dinner. The food is relatively simple, but portions are extremely generous for a French restaurant. Confit de canard, steak tartare, roast chicken, are all on the blackboard, but their signature dish is a tender entrecôte (steak) with fries and burnt wild thyme. Actually, the thyme is literally on fire, either smoking or in flames on its way to the table, and the fries are hand cut, home made and delicious. There are also enormous salads (8.50€–9.50€): The Landaise, with two slices of cured ham, a small confit drumstick, a slice of foie gras and a mountain of *gesiers* (okay, they are sautéed gizzards but they are really good) is a salad for a true carnivore. Around the corner from the posh place des Victoires, the clientele here hails from both the well-heeled business crowd and the 30-something yuppie set. They don't accept reservations, so come either early or late to avoid the rush.

€–€€   If you are in the mood for something a little more heart-healthy, consider **Lémoni Café** ✪ (5 rue Hérold, 1st arrond.; ☎ 01 45 08 49 84; www. lemonicafe.fr; noon–3:30pm, closed Sat–Sun; Métro: Palais Royal–Musée du Louvre, RER: Les Halles; MC, V). Proof positive that vegetarian food doesn't have to be boring, Lémoni offers an ever changing selection of freshly made dishes inspired by the cuisine of the isle of Crete. Cretan cooking is not only delicious, but also focuses heavily on fresh vegetables, is rich in fiber, vitamins, antioxidants, and Omega-3s, and is low on fat. So there is nothing to keep you from indulging in a *risoni* pasta salad with lentils, curry, and coconut, or a leek, feta, and oregano *fondant*, or a fish *plaki* with roasted salmon and vegetables. The prices are not prohibitive, either: There are three different mix-and-match *menus* ranging from 9€ for a combination of three different salads or dishes to 14€ for the same with a drink and dessert. You can also get take-out here, which is about 10% less, but the small dining room is so fun and colorful, you might prefer to eat indoors.

€–€€   There is a large Cambodian population in the Paris area, and though the best restaurants are to be found out in the distant suburbs, **La Mousson** (9 rue Thérèse, 1st arrond.; ☎ 01 42 60 59 46; noon–2:30pm and 7–10:30pm, closed Sun; Métro: Pyramides; MC, V) offers a good opportunity to try this aromatic cuisine, which falls somewhere between Chinese and Indonesian. Large origami storks float above the 10 tables; Cambodian music clangs softly in the background. On one wall hang carvings of dancing goddesses, on the other a large framed photo of the owner with Yves Montand. The three-course lunch menu at 14€ is an excellent deal for this high-priced neighborhood; the chicken soup with bamboo shoots is both light and full of flavor, while the marinated roast pork is tender and subtly sweet. There is another more elaborate menu at 18€, while a la carte main dishes like hamok (stuffed fish with coconut milk and spices) and the cross-cultural frog-leg satay fall in the 11€ to 14€ range.

€€€   Something about the soft lighting at **Le Grand Colbert ✦** (2 rue Vivienne, 2nd arrond.; ☎ 01 42 86 87 88; www.legrandcolbert.fr; noon–1am; Métro: Bourse; MC, V, DC) makes you feel like you've just stepped into another century— the 19th, to be exact. This Belle Epoque beauty doesn't show her age—polished brass glistens, mosaic floors dazzle, antique lamps glow—you wouldn't be surprised to see Sarah Bernhardt waltz in with one of her many admirers. This is a classic brasserie, which means there's lots of expensive shellfish on offer (a half-dozen oysters, 14€–18€), but then you might neglect some of the other main dishes like roasted Landes chicken with herbs (20€), or steak tartare (20€). As the bill can add up quickly, the three-course menu (coffee included, 33€ at lunch, 40€ after 6:30pm) is a good way to go. Unlike most Parisian restaurants, service is "nonstop" from noon until 1am, so you can order a meal whenever you like. The final scene from the 2004 film *Something's Gotta Give* was filmed here.

IN THE PASSAGES

€   It's hard to pass by **L'Arbre à Cannelle** (57 Passage des Panoramas, 2nd arrond.; ☎ 01 45 08 55 87; noon–6:30pm, closed Sun; Métro: Grands Boulevards; MC, V) without gawking at its carved wood facade, which dates from 1856. What was once an elegant *chocolaterie* is now a cozy tearoom that serves quiches, salads, and baked goods—all fabricated on the premises. If you are doing a tour of the passages in the area (p. 254), this is a good place to stop for a bite. The list of *tartes salées* (quiches, 7.20€) includes a tasty mushroom, spinach and leek number, and the salades composées—meal-size salads—include the Frisée, a crispy combination of frisée lettuce, bacon, and a poached egg (7€). The *assiettes gourmands,* cold plates, range from assorted cold meats and vegetable terrine (9.80€) to a smoked salmon plate (12€). And save room for dessert (4.40€–5.80€)—those tantalizing tarts in the window are as good as they look.

€–€€   Another tearoom tucked in a passage, albeit a terribly chic one, is **A Priori Thé 🧒** (35–37 Galerie Vivienne, 2nd arrond.; ☎ 01 42 97 48 75; Mon–Fri 9am–6pm, Sat 9am–6:30pm, Sun 12:30–6:30pm; Métro: Pyramides; MC, V). The surroundings are a bit more refined, as are the prices: The quiche and salad lunch special here is 14€, as is the vegetarian chili. The atmosphere is relaxed upscale:

Japantown, Parisian Style

You are wandering around the streets near the Opéra, when you take a sharp turn onto the rue Ste-Anne. Suddenly, everything is in Japanese, and there are noodle shops everywhere! Do you ponder the existence of an alternate universe, or do you just plunge into the nearest bowl of ramen? You decide . . .

€ **Sapporo Ramen** (37 rue Ste-Anne, 1st arrond.; ☎ 01 42 60 60 98; 11:30am–3pm and 6–10pm; Métro: Pyramides; no credit cards). Here's your chance to dive in to that ramen. Enormous, steaming bowls filled with meat, fish, vegetables, and long, lovely ramen noodles for 7€ to 9€.

€–€€ **Kunitoraya** (39 rue Ste-Anne, 1st arrond.; ☎ 01 47 03 33 65; 11:30am–10:30pm; Métro: Pyramides; no credit cards). The best udon in the city—the long, fat noodles are rolled and pulled on the premises. Noodle soups 8.50€ to 15€.

€€–€€€ **Yasube** ✹ (9 rue Ste-Anne, 1st arrond.; ☎ 01 47 03 96 37; noon–2:30pm and 7–10:30pm, closed Sun; Métro: Pyramides MC, V). Succulent brochettes of grilled meat and fish are the specialty here, as well as rice bowls heaped with a variety of grilled goodies. Menus including tea, rice, and soup are 11€ to 16€ at lunch and 13€ to 25€ at dinner-time.

€€–€€€ **Korin** (58 bis rue Ste-Anne, 2nd arrond.; ☎ 01 40 20 49 93; noon–2pm and 7–10pm, closed Sun–Mon; Métro: Quatre Septembre, MC, V). This match-box-size sushi bar uses high-quality ingredients in its yummy renditions of nori-maki (sushi rolls) and nigiri sushi (the classic rice ball sushi). Sushi assortments are on offer for 13€ and 17€ at lunch, 23€ at dinner.

And for dessert (a short walk down near the place de la Concorde):

€–€€ **Toraya** ✹ (10 rue St-Florentin, 1st arrond.; ☎ 01 42 60 13 00; www.toraya-group.co.jp/paris; 10am–7pm; Métro: Concorde; closed Sun; AE, MC, V). The Parisian outpost of this traditional Japanese bakery/tea-room. Jewel-like pastries (2.90€–4.50€) and fine teas (4.20€–9€).

Here you can sip gourmet teas from the Maison Dammann with names like "Gazelle" (5.50€) and "Lea Latté" (6.50€). Quiches (13€) and salads (16€) are beautifully garnished and copious, and the deserts (6.50€–7.50€) are excellent; this is one of the few spots in Paris where you can find authentic cheesecake (the owner is American). The dining room is smoke free, but you can light up at the "outside" tables, under the lovely arches of the beautifully restored Galerie

Vivienne. Tables on the passage are also a great option for parents with strollers or kids who want to run around.

€€€–€€€€   Since Alain Ducasse took over the beautiful **Belle Epoque Aux Lyonnais** ✪✪✪ (32 rue St-Marc, 2nd arrond.; ☎ 01 42 96 65 04; www.alain-ducasse.com; 12:30–1:30pm and 7:30–10pm, closed Sat lunch, Sun–Mon all day, the last week in July, and the first 3 weeks in Aug; Métro: Italiens or Richelieu–Drouot; AE, MC, V), this once musty *bouchon* (a traditional Lyonnais bistro) has bloomed into a Parisian "must-eat." Not only do you dine in lovely surroundings (antique ceramic tiles, old bistro fixtures, floral ceiling moldings), but the young chef in charge gives a new, lighter spin on traditional Lyonnais classics such as *quenelles de brochet* (pike dumplings), and boudin noir (blood sausage). Starters include Lyonnais charcuterie and escargot (snails) in a garlicky butter sauce; as you're drifting off into nirvana, remember to order the lighter-than-air pear-liqueur soufflé. Here's the part that is truly amazing: You can experience two courses worth of gastronomic pleasure for only 30€ at lunch or dinner (main dishes run 21€–25€ a la carte). Reservations are a must (at least a week in advance).

THE MARAIS (3RD & 4TH ARRONDISSEMENT)

You should have no trouble finding good things to eat in the Marais. Between its working-class roots and its more recent makeover there is a wide range of choices, from humble falafel joints to trendy brasseries. Unlike the shops here, which have become so hip it hurts, there are still a good selection of midrange restaurants that attract both the sleek set and just regular folks. The old Jewish quarter, which has been pretty much reduced to a few blocks around rue des Rosiers, is a good bet for a quick, inexpensive meal; the tiny streets around rue Vielle du Temple are just brimming with cool cafes and slick eateries.

AROUND RUE DES ROSIERS

€   A Marais institution since it opened in 1979, **L'As du Fallafel** 🧒 (34 rue des Rosiers, 4th arrond.; ☎ 01 48 87 63 60; Sun–Thurs 11am–midnight, Fri 11am–3pm; Métro: St-Paul; DC, MC, V) has, without a doubt, the best falafel in Paris. And they're kosher, yet. True, falafel joints are scarce in this city, but that doesn't take away from the excellence of these overstuffed beauties, brimming with cucumbers, pickled turnips, shredded cabbage, tahini, fried eggplant, and those crispy balls of fried chickpeas and spices ("The Special," 6.50€). Other arrangements of similar ingredients can be found in the platters, like the "Assiette Israelienne," (9€) a generous combo of hummus, tahini, and falafel. Wash it down with an Israeli beer (5€). Service is fast and furious, but basically friendly—hoards of tourists and locals crowd in here for one of the cheapest meals in town.

€   Most people don't come to Paris for strudel, but if they knew about **Sacha Finkelsztajn's La Boutique Jaune** ✪ (27 rue des Rosiers, 4th arrond.; ☎ 01 42 72 78 91; www.laboutiquejaune.com; 10am–7pm, closed Tues; Métro: St-Paul; V), they might. The Romanian-style version is a roll of dough stuffed with a heavenly purée of raisins and almonds (3.20€) that would put your Bubbie's to shame. But let's not put the cart before the horse. Before embarking on one of their delicious desserts (Mandelbrot, poppy-seed cake, babka), you can pick out a filling (pastrami, tuna salad, smoked turkey, and so on) for a "Yiddish Sandwich," slathered with eggplant spread and served on a pretzel roll with tomatoes and cucumbers (6.90€). Other sandwiches are on offer, as well as a multitude of spreads (chicken liver, roasted peppers, hummus, and so on) and other interesting Eastern-European treats like eggplant *pirogi* or Bulgarian *böreks* (puff pastry stuffed with sheep cheese and spinach). There are just a few tables, but they do takeout—perhaps a picnic in pretty place des Vosges is in the offing?

€€–€€€   You don't expect to see Marais hipsters in an authentically funky, old-fashioned restaurant, but plenty of them pour into **Chez Omar** ✦ (47 rue de Bretagne, 3rd arrond.; ☎ 01 42 72 36 26; noon–2:30pm and 7–11:30pm, closed Sun lunch; Métro: Rambuteau; no credit cards) for a good dose of couscous. Not much has changed here in decades: not the high ceilings, the high zinc bar, nor high quality of the food. The secret to a good couscous, the most famous North African dish, is the broth—Omar's is rich and slightly tomato-scented, and filled with a variety of fresh vegetables. Once this brew is poured over a steaming plate of semoule, or couscous, and accompanied by tasty grilled meats, a delicious and filling eating experience is more or less assured. Prices start at 10€ for a vegetables only version (the broth is not vegetarian, however), rise to 13€ for chicken or merguez sausage, and go up to 24€ for the Couscous Royal, with grilled lamb, chicken, and merguez. Needless to say, you should come here with an appetite, as well as patience; reservations are not taken, so unless you get here early, be prepared to wait in line.

NEAR THE PICASSO & CARNAVALET MUSEUMS

€€   It's easy to walk right by **Le Felteu** ✦✦ (15 rue Pecquay, 4th arrond.; ☎ 01 42 72 14 51; 12:30–2:15pm and 8–10:30pm, closed Sat lunch, all day Sun and Aug; Métro: Rambuteau or Hôtel de Ville; no credit cards) without realizing that it's there, since the modest entrance and low-key signage make no attempt to draw in customers. They don't have to. Locals in-the-know crowd into this unassuming restaurant near the Hôtel de Soubise for its healthy portions of excellent food. You'll usually find either Brigitte or her husband Jerry, the long-time owners, behind the bar chatting with the regulars and escorting diners to their tables in the aging, utterly un-chic dining room. Meanwhile in the kitchen, their intense young chef will be doing magical things with grilled sea bass and fennel seeds (13€), or blood sausage and sautéed apple and potato cubes (13€) or some other traditional bistro fare. First courses (all at 7.50€) include a classic, and delicious, *soupe à l'onion,* as well as a more contemporary *salade de chèvre chaude* (goat-cheese salad). But you really don't need a starter here; the portions are copious and each dish is garnished with the vegetable du jour and/or a potato gratin. Reservations recommended.

€€–€€€   An excellent stop for weary culture vultures on museum overload is **Café des Musées** ✦✦ (49 rue de Turenne, 3rd arrond.; ☎ 01 42 72 96 17; noon–3pm and 7–11pm; closed Aug; Métro: Chemin Vert; MC, V, AE). In keeping with the "Neo-Bistro" trend, the owners have taken over an old bistrot, polished up its antique fixtures, and put a hot young chef in the kitchen. The result is classic bistrot cuisine with a dash of modern living: An appetizer of smoked salmon maison (11€) and main dishes like steak tartare (15€) and *entrecôte* (rib-steak) with béarnaise sauce and house fries (18€) are standard fixtures on the blackboard; other items change with the seasons. Noncarnivores, fear not: A vegetable casserole is also available (12€). Save room for deserts like *crème renversée* with Tahitian vanilla, or their scrumptious chocolate mousse (both 6€). The menus are true bargains: At dinner a three-course menu is 21€, and at lunchtime the *menu express*—the chef's selection of one appetizer and main course—is only 14€. Reservations recommended.

NORTHERN MARAIS

€   If you see a line outside the door of a tiny storefront in a narrow street off Rue Réaumur, you have probably found **Restaurant Phö** ✸ (3 rue Volta, 3rd arrond.; ☎ 01 42 78 31 70; 10am–4pm, closed Sun and Aug; Métro: Arts et Métiers; no credit cards). The size of an average living room, this diminutive restaurant is on the ground floor of an ancient half-timbered building that probably dates from the early Renaissance. But you don't come here for decor (there is none to speak of), you come here for excellent Vietnamese food, namely phö and bò bún. In fact, those are the only choices on the menu. The first is a bowlful of noodles, vegetables, sliced beef, and meatballs floating in a delicious, rich broth (those mint and basil leaves served on the side are meant to be mixed in to your bowl). The second is a small mountain of rice vermicelli topped with sliced beef, vegetables, crushed peanuts, and crispy imperial roll, seasoned with a flavorful sauce (be sure to stir up your bowl before you plunge in). Both come in small (7.20€) and large (8€) sizes; the "small" is really a medium. Come before 12:30 or after 2pm or you may find yourself on line outside. Closed in August.

€€   In the Marché des Enfants Rouges, hidden behind the vegetable stalls and takeout stands, is a small temple to Dionysus called **L'Estaminet** (39 rue de Bretagne, 3rd arrond.; ☎ 01 42 72 28 12; www.aromes-et-cepages.com; Tues–Sat 9am–8pm, Sun 9am–2pm; Métro: Temple or Filles du Calvaire; DC, MC, V). Intimately connected to the wine stall next door (the manager runs out to help customers), this high-ceilinged, light-filled wine bar offers gourmet nibbles and light meals to go with your glass of Côtes de Castillon. Though the atmosphere is relaxed, this is a haunt of serious wine drinkers; the house specializes in "natural" wines, not necessarily organic, but coming from vineyards that respect their *terroir* (that is, the land, soil, and general essence of the place where the grapes are grown) and reject the industrial approach to agriculture. This respect extends to the food on the menu—the cheese plates and charcuterie platters (small 6.50€, large 13€) are made up of top quality products; the ever-changing *plat du jour* (12€, the only hot food on offer other than the soupe du jour, 6.50€) is also elegantly crafted, say, stuffed veal with prunes and dried figs, for example. Sunday brunch is 20€. Reservations recommended for lunch.

€–€€   In this increasingly chic corner of the Marais, where hip boutiques and restaurants are not-so-slowly replacing local shops and cafes, **Chez Nenesse** ✸✸ (17 rue de Saintonge at the corner of rue de Poitou, 3rd arrond.; ☎ 01 42 78 46 49; noon–2:30pm and 7:45–10:30pm, closed Sat–Sun; Métro: Filles de Calvaire or

Eating Vegetarian in Paris

France is a meat-loving, carnivorous country. The most common reaction to those announcing a non-meat-eating status will be a blank stare of amazement mixed with horror. That said, there are many ways of getting around the problem. Scan menus for *salades composées,* meal-size salads that often come in meat-free versions. If you eat fish, most restaurants offer at least one or two selections. Asian restaurants usually have vegetarian offerings, but quality varies; be wary of the "traiteurs asiatiques" that are the Parisian equivalent of fast food. And there are vegetarian restaurants here. I've listed a couple (**Lémoni Café,** p. 81; **Aquarius,** p. 116) but space limitations make it hard to go in depth. For some good listings compiled by local vegetarians, try the French food sites **Où Bouffer** (www.oubouffer.com, search under the specialty "bio/vegetarienne") and **Ma Cuisine Vegetarienne** (www.cuisine-vegetarienne.com; search under the heading "Bonnes Adresses").

Oberkampf; MC, V) is a breath of fresh air. This is one of the rare places in town where you can see a roomful of happy Parisians—the smiles of the genial owners, the Leplu family, and the high quality of the food would put anyone in a good mood. At lunchtime, the chef sends out healthy portions of traditional bistro fare (like *blanquette de veau,* 10€, or rumpsteak, 11€) into the busy dining room, while dinner comes with a change in menus and ambience—the checked plastic tablecloths are traded for white linen, and *magret de canard au cassis* (duck breast with cassis liqueur, 17€) and filet *d'agneau a l'estragon* (lamb steak with tarragon, 18€) take center stage. Thursday is steak-frites day (11€); regulars crowd in at lunch for their weekly dose of the crispy house fries. Reservations strongly recommended for dinner.

VILLAGE SAINT PAUL

€–€€   I'll admit it. **Le Temps des Cerises** ★★ (31 rue de la Cerisaie, 4th arrond.; ☎ 01 42 72 08 63; 11:30am–2:30pm and 7–10:30pm (snacks only), closed Sat–Sun and Aug; Métro: St-Paul; no credit cards) is one of my favorite restaurants. It's not only friendly and unpretentious, a place where the owner behind the authentic zinc bar is on a first-name basis with a good chunk of her clientele, but it also has truly great food at equally great prices. The rump steak in pepper sauce (12€) is meltingly tender; the moist *pintade* (guinea hen, 11€) comes with an almost sweet vegetable fricassee (who knew Brussels sprouts could taste so good?). "Our chef is a trained saucier," explains the owner, meaning he studied the art of sauce-making at length in one of the city's mighty cooking schools. Come early, the tiny dining room fills to capacity at lunchtime when there is a two-course *formule* for 13€. In fact, lunch is the only meal served, though the bar is open into the evening for "tapas à la française," that is, snacks. Closed in August.

LATIN QUARTER (5TH ARRONDISSEMENT)

For over 700 years, this lively neighborhood has been overrun with students, a population that is forever on the lookout for a good cheap meal. As a result, the area is full of cheap international snack shacks, of varying quality, from souvlaki huts to Vietnamese noodle shops, to Briton crêperies. In a more recent century, tourism has made its indelible mark on Latin Quarter cuisine: Steer clear of the unbearably touristy area around rue de la Huchette, where you are bound to pay too much for mediocre product, and be wary of rue Moufftard, which was once a good bet for good food, but has since become a victim of its own success. If you want to eat well, head towards rue Monge, and the warren of streets behind the College de France. There you will find small restaurants under innovative ownership which have been cultivating a knowledgeable midrange clientele (such as, the professors and professionals who work at the university).

IN SHOUTING DISTANCE OF NOTRE DAME

€–€€   While no one could tell me why this restaurant is called "The Flying Ant," they did explain that **La Fourmi Ailée** (8 rue de Fouarre, 5th arrond.; ☎ 01 43 29 40 99; www.parisresto.com; Mon–Fri noon–2:45pm and 7–11:15pm, Sat–Sun noon–3:45pm and 7–11:15pm; Métro: St-Michel; DC, MC, V) is housed in what was once an old-fashioned bookstore, explaining the 7.5m (25-ft.) ceilings (the mezzanine has been removed), the huge windows, and the literary-themed decor. The books lining the wall are now decorative, but the atmosphere is suitably subdued, good for novel-writing or reading between meal times, when the restaurant functions as a tearoom. The menu is accordingly long on drinks (teas, wines, fruit juices) and short on meal choices, though what's on offer is of high quality. For something light, there are quiches (7.50€), salads (12€–13€) and a rather glamorous tartine of St-Pierre goat cheese on toast with figs marinated in tea and rose hips (13€); more serious eaters can opt for an old-fashioned *blanquette de veau* (sautéed veal in white sauce, 14€), or the delectable house special: half of a duck baked in a delicate salt crust, stuffed with fruit and served on a prune-cream slathered crepe (20€).

TOWARD THE SORBONNE

€€€   One of the best dining values in Paris, **Le Pré Verre** ★★★ (8 rue Thénard, 5th arrond.; ☎ 01 43 54 59 47; www.lepreverre.com; noon–2pm and 7:30–10:30pm, closed Sun–Mon; Métro: Maubert Mutualité; MC, V) manages to serve a three-course, top-grade gourmet meal for a mere 28€. How do they do it? I have no idea. The place is continually packed with fans, who range from students feeling flush, to wine aficionados (this is a wine bar, too) looking for a new thrill, to die-hard foodies aching for a taste of the Delacourcelle brothers' aromatic cuisine. Philippe Delacourcelle (his brother Marc is the wine maven) has concocted a brilliant blend of traditional French and exotic ingredients that is not particularly flashy or trendy, or even spicy, but just deliciously unexpected. Your main course could be a meltingly tender *cochon de lait* (milk-fed pork) served with a smooth cinnamon-infused sauce and a delectably crunchy mass that turns out to be cabbage. Or it might be bark-roasted cod with delicately smoked mashed potatoes. Dessert could follow with sautéed dried fruits with curry ice cream, or

Chain Restaurants

In a city where wonderful restaurants abound, why would anyone bother with a chain restaurant? Well, chains tend to keep more flexible hours than your average Parisian bistro (as in they serve nonstop until midnight or 1am), and cater to children, which is not always the case elsewhere.

The best for overall food quality and ambience is **Chez Clement** (9 place St-André-des-arts, 6th arrond.; ☎ 01 56 81 32 00; www.chezclement.com; Métro: St-Michel; AE, MC, V), which you'll recognize by its bouquet of copper pots hanging outside the door. They have 10 locations in Paris, each serving classic bistro cuisine in a faux-traditional atmosphere.

You'll see **Bistro Romain** (122 av. Champs Elysées, 8th arrond.; ☎ 01 43 59 93 31; www.bistroromain.fr; Métro: Georges V, AE, DC, MC, V) in most chain-heavy areas, which offers Italian dishes in a "Roman" decor—lots of purple and burgundy fabric and reproductions of Italian masters of the 16th to 19th century. **Hippopotamus** (29 rue Berger, 1st arrond.; ☎ 01 45 08 00 29; www.hippopotamus.fr; Métro: Châtelet, RER: Châtelet–Les Halles; AE, MC, V) serves surprisingly good French food and grilled dishes in a bright red decor. Finally, **Léon de Bruxelles** (131 blvd. St-Germain, 6th arrond.; ☎ 01 43 26 45 95; www.leon-de-bruxelles.fr; Métro: St-Germain des Prés; AE, MC, V) is a no-brainer for mussels: They have an entire menu full of variations on the moules-frites theme, as well as a nice selection of Belgian beers, and of course, Belgian waffles. All of the above have multiple locations, for specifics, visit their websites.

---

an endive tiramisu doused in coffee. It may sound weird, but I tell you, it's terrific. The menu changes with the seasons, but the prices stay the same: Appetizers are 9€, main courses are 17€, desserts are 6€, and a combination of any three is 28€. This is a joyfully noisy place, delightfully lacking in attitude (though you should dress decently, of course). The weekday lunch menu is another great deal: appetizer and main dish (chef's choice) plus a glass of wine and coffee for 13€. Reservations necessary.

€€–€€€   On a tiny medieval street creeping up the slope of the Montagne St-Geneviève, **Le Petit Prince de Paris** ★★ (12 rue Lanneau, 5th arrond.; ☎ 01 43 54 77 26; Tues–Thurs 7:30–11:30pm, Sat–Sun 7:30pm–12:30am, closed Mon; Métro: Maubert Mutualité; MC, V) is a lovely place for a romantic tête-à-tête that won't leave your wallet screaming in pain. The overall ambience is elegantly eclectic; the cozy decor includes old posters, bric-a-brac, plants and tinkling fountain. Service is kind and caring, even if it can't always keep up with the demand (don't come for a quick pretheater dinner). Though the management is openly gay (rainbow flags are in evidence) the clientele is decidedly mixed—diners of all stripes are welcome. This is a dinner-only restaurant, however, with three two-course *formules* at 16€, 22€, and 26€. Whereas the less-expensive options might include

Where to Dine on the Left Bank (5th–6th & 14th)

JARDIN DES TUILERIES

JARDIN DU CARROUSEL

Musée du Louvre

1er

PONT NEUF

pont au Change

pont du Palais

bd. du Palais

Seine

pont Royal

pont du Carrousel

pont des Arts

sq. du Vert Galant

pont Neuf

quai des Grands Augustins

Conciergerie

Sainte-Chapelle

quai des Orfèvres

pont St-Michel

quai Voltaire

Musée d'Orsay

rue de Lille

rue de Verneuil

rue de l'Université

Ecole Nat. Sup. des Beaux-Arts

rue Mazarine

rue de Seine

3

4

ST-MICHEL

5
6

rue des Saints Pères

rue Jacob

Musée Delacroix

St-Germain-des-Prés

bd. St-Germain

rue de Seine

8
9 ODEON

7

St-Thomas d'Aquin

bd. St-Germain

1 **2**

ST-GERMAIN-DES-PRES

MABILLON

6e

rue Racine

7e

RUE DU BAC

rue de Grenelle

rue du Four

12 **11**

rue de Seine

rue de Tournon

place de l'Odéon

10

Théâtre de l'Odéon

rue de Médicis

rue de Varenne

bd. Raspail

rue du Bac

13

rue St- Sulpice

St-Sulpice

ST-SULPICE

rue Bonaparte

Palais du Luxembourg

rue de Babylone

14

rue de Rennes

rue de Vaugirard

SEVRES BABYLONE

rue de Sèvres

15

rue Madame

rue Guynemer

JARDIN DU LUXEMBOURG

rue Vaneau

rue du Cherche-Midi

16

RENNES

VANEAU

ST-PLACIDE

NOTRE DAME DES CHAMPS

rue Auguste Comte

rue d'Assas

rue Notre-Dame des Champs

bd. Raspail

rue Michelet

22

place du 18 Juin 1940

VAVIN

bd. du Montparnasse

M MÉTRO STOP
R RER STOP

17

rue de Vaugirard

rue de Rennes

MONTPARNASSE BIENVENUE

20

14e

0   1/5 mi
0   0.2 km

N

18

19 rue Delambre

bd. Raspail

21

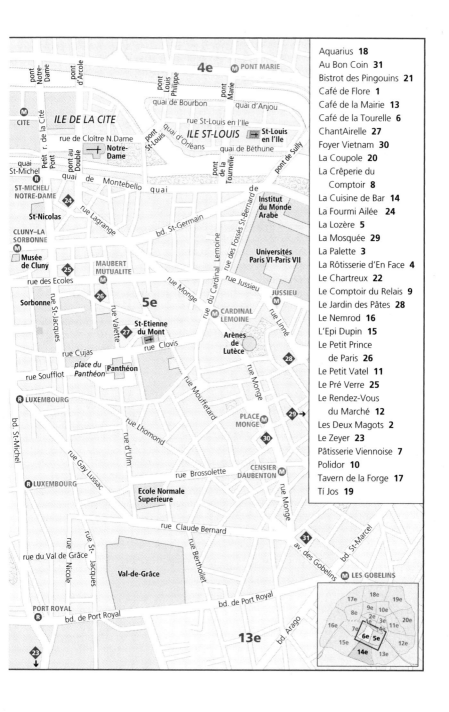

Aquarius **18**
Au Bon Coin **31**
Bistrot des Pingouins **21**
Café de Flore **1**
Café de la Mairie **13**
Café de la Tourelle **6**
ChantAirelle **27**
Foyer Vietnam **30**
La Coupole **20**
La Crêperie du
    Comptoir **8**
La Cuisine de Bar **14**
La Fourmi Ailée **24**
La Lozère **5**
La Mosquée **29**
La Palette **3**
La Rôtisserie d'En Face **4**
Le Chartreux **22**
Le Comptoir du Relais **9**
Le Jardin des Pâtes **28**
Le Nemrod **16**
L'Epi Dupin **15**
Le Petit Prince
    de Paris **26**
Le Petit Vatel **11**
Le Pré Verre **25**
Le Rendez-Vous
    du Marché **12**
Les Deux Magots **2**
Le Zeyer **23**
Pâtisserie Viennoise **7**
Polidor **10**
Tavern de la Forge **17**
Tí Jos **19**

quenelles of chèvre with fig chutney, or magret de canard with spices and mango, the higher end *formule* includes more elaborate dishes such as veal in cream sauce with stewed pineapple and carrots. Either way it's delicious. Reservations highly recommended.

€€€   Though it may look like a tourist office for the forests of Auvergne, **ChantAirelle** ✦ 🄺🄸🄳🄢 (17 rue Laplace, 5th arrond.; ☎ 01 46 33 18 59; www. chantairelle.com; noon–2pm and 7–10:30pm, closed Sat lunch, all day Sun, and the week of Aug 15; Métro: Cardinal Lemoine; MC, V) is actually a gourmet restaurant. A cow moos when you enter, on your right is a display of pamphlets for the Livradois-Forez regional park, and on the left is a small waterfall. But further on, amidst the sounds of chirping birds, are wood tables and a leafy terrace where you can sample the hearty cuisine of this mountainous region in the center of France. Start with a slice of *pounti,* a scrumptious country pâté with chard and prunes (8.80€), and move on to a *truffade,* sliced potatoes baked with Cantal cheese and served with smoked ham, or *potée* a tureen filled with pork, cabbage, potatoes, turnips, and leeks in broth. A lighter option is the sandre (a light, white fish) served with the famed green lentils of Puy and a light garlic sauce (each 17€). At lunch you can choose two courses from a more limited menu for 17€ (includes a glass of wine; same deal with three courses is 22€). If you like mineral water, ask for the "water list"—Auvergne is known for its excellent springs. Not only do you eat well here, but the kind management and relaxed ambience make it a nice place to bring the kids. Reservations recommended (you can reserve online).

TOWARD THE JARDIN DES PLANTES

€   Busy rue Monge may not be the most beautiful street in Paris, but it does have some great places to eat on a budget. One of them, **Foyer Vietnam** (80 rue Monge, 5th arrond.; ☎ 01 45 35 32 54; noon–2:30pm and 7–10:30pm, closed Sun; Métro: place Monge; no credit cards), is easy to miss because its only sign is a small one on the door (look for big windows with white curtains). Something of a local institution, this humble restaurant is usually crammed with students, professors and working stiffs who come for the generous portions of Vietnamese classics. There are several *formules,* ranging from 8.20€ to 13€ for two to three courses (beverage included), but many head straight for a big bowl of *bò bún* (6€), a heap of rice vermicelli with sliced beef and a tangy sauce. Other versions include *bún chà giò* (vermicelli and nem, Vietnamese spring rolls, 6€) and a personal favorite, *bò bún chà giò* (vermicelli, nem, and beef, 7.90€). If it's cold out, a steaming bowl of pho (meat broth with vermicelli and vegetables) might do the trick (small 4.50€, large 6€).

€€–€€€   As its name indicates, **Le Jardin des Pâtes** ✦ (4 rue Lacépède, 5th arrond.; ☎ 01 43 31 50 71; noon–2:30pm and 7–11pm; Métro: place Monge; AE, MC, V) specializes in pasta. But this is no ordinary pasta—not only are the rice, wheat, rye, and barley noodles made fresh every day, but the organic flour that goes into them is ground daily on the premises. The stress on wholesome ingredients is menu wide; even the ice cream is 100% natural. If the atmosphere is almost too healthy to be French, with lots of white walls and natural light, the food more than lives up to national standards. The rye pasta with not-too-salty,

The End of the Smoky Café

Believe it or not, in 2008 a law went into effect in France banning all smoking in public places, including restaurants, bars, and cafes. While this means that the image of world-weary Parisians lighting up in smoky cafes is now relegated to the dustbins of history, it also means that it's a lot easier to breathe in those cafes, and to taste one's food when one sits down to eat. Despite the French propensity for ignoring rules and regulations, the law is being respected, and the air quality in eating and drinking establishments has improved dramatically. So forget about doing your Alain Delon imitation with a smoldering cigarette at the bar—save it for the outdoor seating on the terrace or sidewalk.

nitrate-free ham, cream, sweet onions, white wine, and Comté cheese (12€) is surprisingly light. A less caloric choice is the barley pasta with fresh salmon, leeks, seaweed and crème fraîche (14€). The rice pasta is vegetarian, with stir-fried vegetables, tofu, and ginger (11€). Pastas are made to order, so don't be in a hurry. There are several organic choices on the wine list (of course), as well as some interesting *digestifs* like a biodynamic pear *eau-de-vie* (6€), and a delightful thyme-flavored liqueur from Provence called Farigoules (3€).

€   It might not be the first place you think of for a nosh, but the **Mosquée de Paris** (Paris Mosque, 39 rue Geoffroy St-Hilaire, 5th arrond.; ☎ 01 43 31 18 14; 9am–11pm; Métro: place Monge or Censier-Daubenton; MC, V) has a lovely tearoom, **La Mosquée,** that makes a great "time out." Suddenly you're no longer in Paris, but somewhere in the Casbah, as you walk through the arched doorways of this mosaic-bedecked cafe, just across the street from the Natural History Museum. If it's a nice day, sip your mint tea (2.50€) and nibble your *corne de gazelle* (a crescent-shaped, powdered sugar-covered pastry, 2.50€) outside on the shaded terrace while you listen to the fountain tinkle and pretend you're visiting a caliph. Meals are also served here, but better couscous can be found elsewhere. *Note:* The entry to the tearoom is not the main entrance to the mosque.

NEAR RUE MOUFFTARD

€–€€   Instead of eating an ho-hum meal at one of the overpriced tourist restaurants on rue Moufftard, wander over a block or two to **Au Bon Coin** (21 rue de la Collégiale, 5th arrond.; ☎ 01 43 31 55 57; closed Sun and 3 weeks in Aug; Métro: Gobelins; MC, V) for a more authentic eating experience. Though the decor goes a little overboard trying to be "typically Parisian," with red-checked tablecloths and hanging plastic grapes, real Parisians do eat here, as original and quirky as the artwork on the walls. If the clientele seems to be heavily male, blame it on the sly charm of Sylvie, the svelte, blonde owner, who trades barbs with the regulars with a panache only French women can muster. The menu (on the blackboard) covers all the traditional bases: *blanquette de veau, magret de canard,* and so on, and the food is correct, that is, it fulfills expectations without surpassing them. The menu is the way to go here, offering a significant reduction—the weekday two-course lunch menu is only 12€, and three courses is 14€; in the evening three courses are 18€, or 21€ for a choice of more elaborate dishes. Reservations recommended.

SAINT GERMAIN (6TH ARRONDISSEMENT)

Saint Germain is a mix of expensive eateries that only the lucky few can afford, and stalwart holdouts from the days when poverty-stricken intellectuals and artists frequented the Café de Flore. Overpriced tourist restaurants cluster around Blvd. St-Germain near the Carrefour de l'Odéon; as you head south and north of this major boulevard, your choices will expand. Though the Marché St-Germain has been transformed into a type of mall, the restaurants hugging its perimeter offer a wide range of possibilities.

AROUND THE MARCHE ST-GERMAIN

€   If you ask the owner of this tiny mom-and-pop bar and restaurant how she has survived in this *branché* ("in") neighborhood, she'll tell you: "By doing things well." And she does. **Le Rendez-Vous du Marché** ★ (9 rue Lobineau, 6th arrond.; ☎ 01 43 26 71 95; 11am–4pm for lunch, 8am–8pm for drinks, closed Sun and Aug; Métro: Mabillon; no credit cards) may not be chic, but it's honest. A true hole-in-the-wall, with just a few tables and a handful of habitués attached to the little zinc bar, meals here resemble something your aunt Thelma might have cooked up on a Sunday afternoon. You may be put off by the size of the kitchen, which consists of a couple of burners in a sort of corridor that links the two small dining areas, but Eliane manages to concoct some very tasty food there, in between refilling wine glasses and handling the cash register. The incredibly inexpensive lunch special (7€) might be a lightly seared steak with sautéed potatoes (if you don't like very rare, you'd better ask for *à point*) or *boudin* (blood sausage) with homemade mashed potatoes. A quarter liter of *vin rouge* is only 2.50€ and dessert is 2€. With what you saved on lunch, you can probably afford to have your coffee at the Café Flore down the street.

€€   Another pocket-book-friendly restaurant on the same side of the Marché is **Le Petit Vatel** ★ (5 rue Lobineau, 6th arrond.; ☎ 01 43 54 28 49; noon–2:30pm and 7–10:30pm, closed Sun–Mon; Métro: Mabillon; no credit cards). More modern in both look and menu than its neighbor, this postage-stamp of a dining room seats only 16 hungry souls, so come early to avoid the wait. The emphasis here is on healthy eating with a Mediterranean touch; ingredients are fresh and "noble," that is, of high-quality and direct from the source. The plump and delicious Diot sausage is from Savoy (as is one of the owners) and served in a light white wine sauce (all main dishes are 12€); the *pamboli* platter includes slices of Catalonian ham and cheese and a fresh tomato sauce. A nice alternative for non–meat eaters is the *assiette vegetarienne:* an assortment of roasted eggplant, lentils, rice, and vegetables. The weekday lunch *formule* includes two courses and coffee for 13€. Service can be a little curt, but very efficient.

NEAR THE ODEON

€   I'm generally not including snack shops in this section, but **La Crêperie du Comptoir** (9 Carrefour de l'Odéon, 6th arrond.; ☎ 01 44 27 07 97; 9am–1am;

Métro: Odéon; MC, V) is truly exceptional. Run by the same gang that is in charge of the gourmet Comptoir du Relais next door (see below), this tiny crêpe stand serves up some of the best in town. Sure, a crêpe is a crêpe, but these are made with copious amounts of top-quality ingredients, which you can combine as you will. Not only that but your server will ask you if you'd like to add a dash of parsley or shallots to give it that extra zing. The best deal is the 5.50€ *formule,* which includes a two-ingredient crêpe and a drink, but you can also get salads (6€–7€) and soup (4€), if you up for something lighter. There are no tables, so you'll have to find a bench somewhere nearby, like next to the fountain in front of the St-Sulpice church.

€   Squeezed between two medical schools, **Pâtisserie Viennoise** 🆔 (8 rue de l'Ecole de Médecine, 6th arrond.; ☎ 01 43 26 60 48; 8:30am–7:30pm, closed Sat–Sun and mid-July to Aug; Métro: Odéon or Cluny La Sorbonne; no credit cards) gets its share of students and professors in need of a nosh. And this is a nosher's heaven: There's a huge selection of pastries (2.70€–3.30€), including Viennese classics like Linzer torte and strudel, and the hot chocolate has got to be the best in the city (3.30€–3.80€). It's thick and dark and bitter—sugar cubes are provided so you can adjust the sweetness—and if you ask for it *à la viennoise,* it will come with a dollop of real whipped cream. The tiny dining area looks like it hasn't changed in at least 50 years: a collection of wooden booths and small tables that might have been shipped in from Vienna. Inexpensive meals are also served, including basic sandwiches, quiches, and pasta doused with a variety of sauces (7€).

€€   An unofficial historic monument, **Polidor** ✪ (41 rue Monsieur le Prince, 6th arrond.; ☎ 01 43 26 95 34; http://restaurantpolidor.info; Mon–Sat noon–2:30pm and 7pm–12:30am, Sun noon–2:30pm and 7–11pm; Métro: Odéon; no credit cards) is not so much a restaurant as a snapshot of a bygone era. The decor has not changed substantially for at least 100 years, when Verlaine and Rimbaud, the bad boys of poetry, would come here for a cheap meal. The bistro would continue to be a literary lunch room for decades: In the 1950s it was dubbed "the College of Pataphysics" by a rowdy group of young upstarts that included Max Ernst, Boris Vian, and Eugene Ionesco; André Gide and Ernest Hemingway were reputed regulars. Though the long tables are still covered with checked tablecloths, and the kitchen still cranks out *boeuf bourguignon* (11€) and *blanquette de veau* (veal in white sauce, 15€), today your tablemates will probably be other tourists, along with a dose of locals. Though the food is not particularly memorable, the ambience is unique; a good place to taste a bit of history. No reservations.

€€€–€€€€   The brainchild of super chef Yves de Camdeborde, **Le Comptoir du Relais** ✪✪✪ (9 Carrefour de l'Odéon, 6th arrond.; ☎ 01 44 27 07 97; Mon–Fri noon–6pm and dinner seats at 8:30pm, Sat–Sun noon–11pm; Métro: Odéon; AE, MC, V) has le tout Paris all a-twitter, and for good reason: The excellence of the food here will truly give you something to write home about. What's more, it's not that outrageously expensive. During the day, it's a bistro, serving relatively traditional fare that induces lots of involuntary oohs and ahhs: say, a slice of lamb with thyme sauce (19€) or maybe the *panier de cochonaille* (20€), a basket of the

Camdeborde family's own brand of sliced smoked ham, dried sausage, and other pork-based delectables. On weeknights, it's a temple to haute cuisine, with a tasting menu that might include as many as seven different dishes. This 48€ meal changes every night and is nonnegotiable, as in the chef decides what you are going to eat. But with a chef like this, you don't need to worry. Your evening might start with sautéed fresh *foie gras* with a green lentil sauce, move on to a ginger-infused seafood mousse, be followed by free-range veal with an artichoke poivrade, and finish up with a waffle with wild strawberries from Malaga. Despite the hype, the atmosphere is refreshingly relaxed; the decor is simple and non-threatening. There are no reservations at lunch, or on the weekends when the bistro menu is served from noon to 11pm, so arrive early or be prepared to wait. Reservations for weeknights should be made at least 2 months in advance, but don't despair; you can always try calling to see if there are any cancellations.

QUAI DES GRANDS AUGUSTINS

€–€€   Housed on the ground floor of one of the oldest residences in Paris (dating from the 13th c.), **Café de La Tourelle** (5 rue Hautefeuille, 6th arrond.; ☎ 01 46 33 12 47; Mon–Fri noon–2pm and 7–10pm, Sat 7–10pm, closed Sun and Aug; Métro: St-Michel; MC, V) gets its name from the small tower hanging off of one side of the building. Cute and cozy, with low ceilings and wood wainscoting, this friendly place draws lots of editors and graphic artists from nearby publishing houses at lunchtime, and young urban types at night. The menu is about half classic French (steak tartare, steak frites, and andouillette) and half modern (cumin-flavored lamb brochettes, scallops with basil), all well-executed and sometimes quite good, like the fish and vegetable loaf with aioli. The three-course lunch *formule* is only 15€, at dinner it's 21€, and main courses a la carte are 10€ to 12€.

€€–€€€   Travel to another region of France at **La Lozère** ★ (4 rue Hautefeuille, 6th arrond.; ☎ 01 43 54 26 64; www.lozere-a-paris.com; Tues–Sat noon–2pm and 7:30–10pm, closed Mon; Métro: St-Michel; MC, V). Owned and operated by the Maison de la Lozère, a regional tourist office (you can pick up brochures at their office across the street), here you will take a culinary journey to a part of France that most French people have trouble finding on the map. Not really Provence, and not quite in the Southwest, the Lozère is a sparsely populated, rugged terrain where the air is clear and the food is of the rustic, stick-to-your-ribs variety. The most famous dish is Aligot d'Aubrac, a deliciously smooth combination of whipped mashed potatoes, tomme fraîche (a white, soft cheese), and crème fraîche, which is served along side a filet of trout, or hand-made sausage, or a nice pork chop in garlic cream sauce, depending on your stomach's limits. You can get the full experience on Thursday nights, otherwise known as "soirée aligot," when the dish takes precedence on the menu. At all other times, you can choose some thing a little lighter from the regular menu, like salmon trout with chives (12€) or the excellent Gévaudan lamb with roasted garlic (17€). Evenings, there is a three-course *formule* for 22€; at lunchtime you can get three courses plus a glass of wine for 17€, or, for more prudent appetites, two courses plus wine for 16€.

€€€€   Just a couple of blocks away, but in another culinary galaxy, is **La Rôtisserie d'en Face** ★★ (2 rue Christine, 6th arrond.; ☎ 01 43 26 40 98; www.jacques-cagna.com; noon–2pm and 7–11pm, closed Sun; Métro: Odéon; MC, V). En face, or across the street, is Jacques Cagna's hugely famous restaurant, here is his dressed-down rotisserie where those with earth-bound pocketbooks can still enjoy some of the stardust that falls off of the magician's magic wand. At lunchtime, you can indulge in three scrumptious courses from a short list of choices for 31€; at dinner, you can choose whatever you like and three courses will come to 45€. Naturally, at these prices the cuisine is less haute than across the street, but there's nothing shameful in appreciating a fine roast Scottish salmon rolled in sesame and hazelnuts, or lamb *Parmentier* with dried apricots and spiced bulgur wheat. If you'd prefer to order a la carte, main dishes are all 19€ at lunch and 22€ at dinner. Reserve a day ahead—this place is a favorite of knowing Left Bank gourmets.

AROUND RUE DU CHERCHE-MIDI

€–€€   Making the most of its next door neighbor, the legendary Poilâne bakery, **La Cuisine de Bar** (8 rue du Cherche-Midi, 6th arrond.; ☎ 01 45 48 45 69; noon–7pm, closed Sun–Mon; Métro: Sèvres-Babylone or St-Sulpice; MC, V) serves delicious open-faced sandwiches (tartines) on their famous bread. Get here early for a light lunch as the sleek dining room fills up quickly with impeccably dressed locals lusting after the tartine of sardines with olive oil and sea salt, or chicken with garlic mayonnaise and capers (both 11€). A *formule* including a tartine, a small salad, a glass of wine, and coffee is 13€.

€–€€   When you just can't take any more shopping in the discount stores on rue St-Placide, **Le Nemrod** ★ 🧒 (51 rue du Cherche-Midi, 6th arrond.; ☎ 01 45 48 17 05; Mon–Sat noon–11pm, Sun 10am–2pm; Métro: Sèvres-Babylone; MC, V) is the perfect place to sit down and have a bite. At the intersection of rue du Cherche-Midi, in warm weather it has wraparound sidewalk seating (great for strollers) and for once, there's not a lot of traffic to stink up your lunch. This place is always packed, and for good reason: The food is good, portions are generous, and the service is excellent (if not particularly smiley). The owners are from Auvergne and regional specialties figure prominently on the menu, like *pounti* (country pâté with prunes, 9.50€) and *truffade* (a mix of gratin potatoes and smoked ham, 17€). Lots of other dishes are on offer, including a *plat du jour*, often fish, for 15€ to 19€ and if you're looking for a good salad, look no further. They are big, fresh, and delicious. The Perigourdienne is a personal favorite, heaped with duck confit, smoked *maigret* (duck breast), chicken livers, and green beans (14€). They also make a killer croque-monsieur on Polâine bread that comes with a small salad (7.20€). If you still have room, indulge in the *tarte tatin*, it's worth the 6€. Brunch is served on Sundays.

€€–€€€   Here is another opportunity to eat inventive, gourmet food in a relaxed atmosphere. On a small street near the Bon Marché department store lies **L'Epi Dupin** ★★ (11 rue Dupin, 6th arrond.; ☎ 01 42 22 64 56; www.epidupin.com; Mon 7–10:30pm, Tues–Fri noon–2:30pm and 7–10:30pm, closed

Sat–Sun and Aug; Métro: Sèvres-Babylone; MC, V). It's clear that the food is what counts here—there's no fancy decor, nor model wannabe waiters. For a worthwhile splurge, come in the evening for the three-course, 34€ menu (yes, you have to take all three courses). For something a little lighter on both the pocketbook and the waistline, come at lunch, when two courses with a glass of wine is 25€). If the size of your meal is inflexible, the contents aren't: You have a choice of five superb appetizers, main courses, and desserts, each lovingly created by Chef François Pasteau (even the bread is made in house here). How about sautéed scallops with orange and mascarpone risotto? Or Tandoori pork with crispy polenta? The menu changes with the seasons, so this is just to give you an idea; but who knows, you might have a chance at the filet mignon with rosemary—it's to swoon over. Reservations recommended.

PORT ROYAL

€€–€€€   Around the corner from the Luxembourg gardens, in a quiet neighborhood near the University of Paris, is a restaurant that looks like a setting for a 1960s Truffaut movie. You almost expect to see a young Jeanne Moreau sitting at the Formica-topped bar of **Le Chartreux** ✪ (8 rue de Chartreux, 6th arrond.; ☎ 01 43 26 66 34; RER: Port Royal; Mon–Sat noon–3pm and 7–10:30pm [drinks 7:30am–midnight], the first 3 weeks of Aug Sat noon–3pm; MC, V), gazing at the tiles painted with pictures of kids doing the twist. There are photos of French film stars of the era, as well as a real vinyl banquette. This isn't a theme restaurant, the decor is authentic, as is the food, which is fresh and simply served in copious portions. Classics like duck *confit* are on the menu, as well as a very French (and delicious) version of a cheeseburger (both 13€). The salads are nice here too (the chicken and arugula is delicious, 12€). Though you won't see Moreau, you may see some contemporary French film stars who live in the neighborhood, like Jean-Pierre Bacri, munching their croissants in the morning.

INVALIDES–EIFFEL TOWER (7TH ARRONDISSEMENT)

Crowded with ministries and important people, this neighborhood is so grand, you half expect to hear trumpets blowing each time you turn a corner. Eating here on a budget takes some skill, or at least a bit of insider knowledge. Though there aren't exactly oodles of dining choices, there are a few streets that are fairly lively, namely rue Cler, a pretty market street, and rue St-Dominique, home to some of the best restaurants on this side of the Seine. You're likely to get fleeced if you insist on eating right next to the Eiffel Tower—that is, if you can find a restaurant, as the pickings are pretty slim in the Iron Lady's immediate vicinity.

NEAR BON MARCHE

€   Once you've visited the plush department store Bon Marché, you will be bound to be feeling a bit peckish. Now is the moment to visit the store's equally smart cousin next door: **La Grande Epicerie de Paris** (38 rue de Sèvres, 7th arrond.; ☎ 01 44 39 81 00; www.lagrandeepicerie.fr; Mon–Sat 8:30am–9pm, closed Sun; Métro: Sèvres-Babylone; AE, MC, V). It is most certainly grand, in both the French and English senses of the word. Dean & Delucca could only dream of the heights this gourmet supermarket has reached, both in size and content: The bottled water selection alone includes an astounding variety of international brands. If you have had enough of trying to decipher the difference between Fijian mineral water and Sparkletts, skip over the designer mangos and the Japanese tea crackers and head straight for a table at **Le Comptoir Picnic** (next to the amazing takeout delicatessen). For no particular reason, drinks are significantly cheaper than the same bottles on the shelves (juices around 2.15€; waters 1.35€–1.65€); custom-made sandwiches are a bargain too, at 5.40€ a pop. Hot dishes are made in a wok, on a grill, or in a steamer and range from 8.05€ to 13€, using the same high-quality ingredients as on display nearby.

NEAR LES INVALIDES

€–€€   Hipsters looking for a cheap lunch fix descend on **Le Café du Marché** ★ (38 rue Cler, 7th arrond.; ☎ 01 47 05 51 27; Mon–Sat 11am–11pm, Sun 11am–3:30pm; Métro: Ecole Militaire; MC, V), and for good reason: The portions are large and the food is great. Taking up the corner of rue du Champ de Mars and rue Cler (a pedestrian market street), this busy place has one of the nicest sidewalk terraces in the area. If you want to eat there, arrive early, otherwise you might be relegated to one of the crowded back rooms, which are nonsmoking in theory only. A mixed crowd, including sleek office workers, trendy go-getters, and tourists come here to partake of the simple, but well executed bistro dishes like crispy duck *confit* and thick slabs of grilled lamb, as well as more modern turns like salmon brochettes with balsamic vinegar and ginger. All the main dishes, as well as the ever-changing *plat du jour* are 10€, all the huge salads are 9€ (add .50€ to these prices at dinnertime), and if you have room for dessert, it's 5.50€.

€–€€   Tiny and old-fashioned with a large dose of French ambience, **Au Pied de Fouet** (45 rue de Babylone, 7th arrond.; ☎ 01 47 05 12 27; Mon–Sat noon–2:30pm and 7–11pm, closed Sun; Métro: St-François Xavier or Vaneau; MC, V) has been in operation for 150 years, and has lovingly conserved every historic detail, down to the menu, which though tasty, would certainly not win a "heart healthy" label. Main dishes are limited to sautéed chicken livers (7.90€), steak and mashed potatoes (11€), duck *confit* (11€), and a *plat du jour,* but at these prices, in this expensive neighborhood, a little cholesterol should be allowed for authenticity's sake. There's a wider selection of appetizers (including various salads, 3€–5€, and desserts, 3€–4€), and if nothing else, the cheerful atmosphere will suit everyone's diet. Reservations aren't accepted so get here early.

ON OR NEAR RUE ST-DOMINIQUE

€€   Like its name, which means simply "The Bistro of the 7th Arrondissement," **Le Bistrot du 7eme** ★ (56 blvd. de la Tour Maubourg, 8th arrond.; ☎ 01 45 51 93 08; Mon–Fri noon–2:30pm and 7–11pm, Sat–Sun 7–11pm; Métro: La Tour Maubourg; MC, V) is a straightforward place. Elegant, but not trendy, this is the type of eatery you would feel comfortable bringing your parents. In fact, judging from the older clientele, this is where people bring their parents. And why not? The food is simply, but beautifully executed and presented; basic bistro dishes like grilled

Where to Dine on the Left Bank (7th)

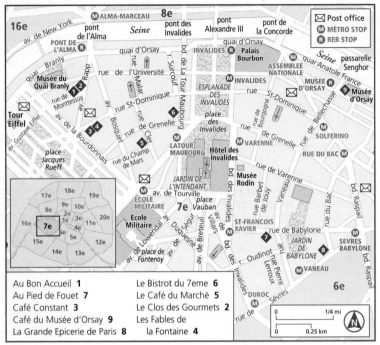

Au Bon Accueil **1**
Au Pied de Fouet **7**
Café Constant **3**
Café du Musée d'Orsay **9**
La Grande Epicerie de Paris **8**

Le Bistrot du 7eme **6**
Le Café du Marché **5**
Le Clos des Gourmets **2**
Les Fables de
  la Fontaine **4**

lamb chops (12€) and poached salmon with olive oil (12€) take on a whole new meaning when made with high quality ingredients and care. The small dining room has a glassed-in terrace area that opens out onto the street in warm weather, when tables spill onto the sidewalk. The service is remarkably friendly for this fussy neighborhood, and the prices are reasonable, particularly if you go for the menu. I doubt if you can find a better three-course lunch menu around here for only 16€; there's a more elaborate range of choices on the 21€ menu, which is also available at dinner. Save room for dessert—if the homemade apple tart is on the menu, grab it, it is terrific. Reservations recommended.

€€   After making a huge splash with his gourmet upscale Violon d'Ingres down the street, super-chef Christian Constant did what every French chef seems to dream of doing: He opened a little corner cafe where he could cook what he felt like cooking. **Café Constant** ✪✪✪ (139 rue St-Dominique, 7th arrond.; ☎ 01 47 53 73 34; noon–2:30 and 7–10:30pm, closed Sun and Mon; Métro: Ecole Militaire, RER: Pont d'Alma; MC, V) is the result, and it is really and truly a relaxed kind of place, where you are quite likely to find the master himself at the bar smoking a cigar during his off hours. The decor is blissfully unpretentious, as is the service. The menu features an upscale version of French comfort food: starting with appetizers like homemade terrine de foie gras or pumpkin soup with gruyere, main dishes like delicate sautéed scallops in butter with salad, or tender roasted milk-fed lamb with thyme, and desserts like rice pudding or crème caramel. All appetizers are 11€, all mains 15€, and desserts are 7€, and there is a lunch *formule* (Tues–Fri only) that includes the chef's choice of two courses for 16€ or three courses for 23€—a phenomenal deal for this level of quality. Reservations are not accepted, so get here early to avoid a wait.

€€€€   In a small square dominated by an enormous fountain of the Roman god of war (the surrounding buildings were once military barracks) is yet another Constant enterprise, **Les Fables de La Fontaine** ✪✪ (131 rue St-Dominique, 7th arrond.; ☎ 01 44 18 37 55; noon–2:30pm and 7:15–10:30pm, closed Sun and Mon; Métro: Ecole Militaire, RER: Pont d'Alma; MC, V). This small restaurant is a temple to fish, in all its many forms. In fact, outside of desserts, that is all you find on the menu, which changes daily. The decor here is decidedly more stylish, as are the prices: Here all appetizers are 15€, all main dishes 25€, and all desserts 8€. The dishes are more elaborate, though still relatively uncomplicated, and always exquisite—you might start with a "cappuccino" of crab with wasabi served with a foamy sprout bouillon, followed by sea bass grilled a la plancha with eggplant caviar, artichoke mousse, and wild mushrooms. This place has gotten a lot of good press, making reservations essential.

IN THE SHADOW OF THE EIFFEL TOWER

€€€   For a romantic gourmet meal, you can't really go wrong at **Le Clos des Gourmets** ✪✪ (10 av. Rapp, 7th arrond.; ☎ 01 45 51 75 61; www.closdes gourmets.com; Métro: Alma Marceau, RER: Pont d'Alma; 12:15–2:30pm and 7:15–10:30pm, closed Sun–Mon; MC, V). High ceilings, creamy yellow paneling, and white linen tablecloths set the stage for the carefully crafted cuisine of Arnaud Pitrois, a talented up-and-coming chef. Dazzle your companion by ordering the Bouchot mussels with chorizo-scented fish bouillon and spiced bread to start, and then slay them with your savoir-faire by ordering seared Scottish salmon served with Jerusalem artichokes and grated green apples. If he or she hasn't swooned by the time you've finished your mango and lime tiramisu, you can saunter out and take a stroll down the moonlit street to the foot of the twinkling Eiffel Tower. While the evening version of this extravaganza, a three-course dinner menu for 35€ is a fun splurge, keep in mind that the same three courses are 29€, at lunchtime, when there is also a two-course option for 25€). The only catch is that you must take the menu (which offers a good range of choices); you can't order just one dish. Reservations indispensable.

€€€–€€€€   Subdued elegance reigns at **Au Bon Accueil** ✪✪ (14 rue de Monttessuy, 7th arrond.; ☎ 01 47 05 46 11; closed Sat–Sun; Métro: Alma Marceau, RER: Pont d'Alma; AE, MC, V), whose solemn beige upholstery, dark wood tables, and off-white walls are relieved by a large Impressionist-style painting of an outdoor scene. If the atmosphere is a little less hospitable than its name would make one expect ("The Warm Welcome"), the food does not disappoint: Chef Jacques Lacipière knows his stuff. There are two different menus here, one where

Dining Out on Art

Though too many museum cafes are overpriced and tasteless (in both the design and gustatory sense), a few have restaurants that are almost worth the visit in themselves:

* €€   Peer up at the Tiepolo ceiling as you sip your coffee at the **Café Jacquemart-André** ★ (Musée Jacquemart-André, 158 blvd Haussmann, 8th arrond.; ☎ 01 45 62 11 59; Métro: Miromesnil; AE, MC, V). Set in the dining room of the former private home of Edouard André and Nélie Jacquemart, this must be one of the most beautiful tearooms in the city. Light lunches are served from 11:45am to 3pm and tea and pastries from 3 to 5:30pm. Though it's not exactly a bargain—the 17€ lunch *formule* includes quiche and a pastry, 9€ will buy you tea and a pastry at tea time—what better way to finish off a visit to this 19th-century marvel. Access to the tearoom is independent of the museum; in summer there are tables outside in the lovely courtyard (but then you'll miss the Belgian tapestries and the Tiepolo).

* €   When it's nice out, the vast terrace bridging the two wings of the Palais de Tokyo are filled with tables, but in fact there are two cafes here: On one side, **Tokyo Idem** (13 av. du President Wilson, 16th arrond.; ☎ 01 47 20 00 29; noon–midnight, closed Mon; Métro: Iéna; MC, V), the cafeteria for the wacky contemporary art space, Palais de Tokyo, stakes out its territory with hard tables, square chairs and artistic fusion food (quiches 4€–5€, salads 5.50€, *plat du jour* 9.50€). On the other side is the **Café du Musée d'Art Moderne de la Ville de Paris** (11 av. du Président Wilson, 16th arrond.; ☎ 01 53 67 40 47; noon–3pm for lunch, 9am–6pm for drinks, closed Mon; MC, V), a little more cushy, a little less innovative, with a choice of four salads going for 8.90€, two salads 5.90€, and the *plat du jour* 9.80€. What they both have is a delightful outdoor ambience with a view of trees, the Seine, and off to one side, the Eiffel Tower.

all starters are 8.50€, all mains 17€, and all desserts 8.50€, and all three for 27€ at lunch, and 31€ at dinner. The other, a la carte menu is more elaborate, and considerably more expensive, with main dishes running from 28€ (roast Bresse pigeon and baby vegetables with foie gras) to 38€ (filet of sole with champagne butter). Main dishes on the first menu are nothing to sniff at however: The thyme-roasted duck with celery root is delectable, as is the tender veal with sautéed leeks. If it looks like the weather is going to be nice, ask for an outdoor sidewalk table when you reserve (essential), and you'll have a lovely view of the Eiffel tower.

♦ €-€€   The interior courtyard of the Petit Palais is endowed with one of the loveliest little gardens in Paris. Fountains burble, pools reflect, lush greenery soothes, and the majestic dome of the main building serves as a backdrop. What's more, you can admire all this beauty while sipping your drink at **Le Jardin du Petit Palais** (av. Winston Churchill, 8th arrond.; ☎ 01 53 43 40 00; 10am–6pm, closed Mon; Métro: Champs Elysées–Clemenceau; AE, MC, V). Soft green velour upholsters the chairs, dark wood covers the walls, bringing the garden ambience indoors (tables are set outside in warm weather). Since the hours are the same as the museum, breakfast and lunch are the only mealtime possibilities; there is a 14€ *formule* at lunch that includes the *plat du jour* and a dessert, as well as one at 10€ featuring a salad or quiche and dessert.

♦ €€   Starting in mid-April, the tables come out in the rustic garden of the **Musée de la Vie Romantique** ★ (16 rue Chaptal, 9th arrond.; ☎ 01 40 16 16 28; mid-Apr to mid-Oct 11:30am–5:30pm, closed Mon; Métro: Blanche; MC, V). Admire the foliage and listen to the birds chirp as you sip your tea and nibble on quiches and cakes— you'll forget you're in the city and imagine you've suddenly been dropped into a country setting from one of George Sand's novels. In case of rain, you can take cover at a table in the greenhouse.

♦ €-€€   When it was still a train station, the **Musée d'Orsay** (62 rue de Lille, 7th arrond.; ☎ 01 45 49 47 03; 11:45am–2:45pm, closed Mon; Métro: Solférino, RER: Musée d'Orsay; AE, MC, V) contained a beautiful Belle Epoque hotel with a gorgeous, high-ceilinged, chandelier-bedecked restaurant. Guess what? The hotel is gone, but the restaurant is still there, providing refreshment and relief to tired museum-goers. Come here for lunch (two-course *formule*, 15€), or simply take tea (3:30–5:30pm, Tues, Wed, Fri–Sun). Dinner is served on Thursday nights (7–9:30pm), when the museum stays open late.

CHAMPS ELYSEES–PARC MONCEAU (8TH & 17TH ARRONDISSEMENTS)

Mobbed with tourists, oozing with opulence, the Champs-Elysées is a difficult place to find a good meal. Mediocre chain restaurants abound on the grand avenue itself, kebob joints mingle with frighteningly expensive gourmet palaces on the surrounding side streets. If you have no strings attached to your wallet, you can explore dinners in the many two- and three-Michelin star restaurants in the area; if you are like the rest of us, consider splurging on lunch in one of these same eateries for half the price. As you head further away from the Champs, restaurants return to normal proportions, both physically and financially.

NEAR THE CHAMPS ELYSEES

€–€€ Strange as it may seem, right behind the opulent Palais de l'Elysées (where the French president lives and works) is an unassuming little restaurant with a great two-course menu for only 13€. At the **Taverne de l'Elysées** (3 rue Duras, 8th arrond.; ☎ 01 42 65 00 69; Mon–Fri noon–2:30pm, closed Aug; Métro: Champs Elysées–Clemenceau or Miromesnil; MC, V), you will share your meal with a odd combination of three-piece-suited ministerial types, office staff, and maybe a couple of construction workers stopping in for a quick bite. All seem to agree that the laid back ambience is just the thing for letting off steam at lunch (the only meal served), and the nonthreatening menu (changes weekly, main dishes like risotto with haddock, pork roast with sage are all 11€) satisfies all parties.

€€–€€€ Say you're strolling down the Champs Elysées and you are feeling a little peckish. Provided you're dressed appropriately, why not indulge in an utterly Parisian experience at **Ladurée** ★ (75 av. des Champs Elysées, 8th arrond.; ☎ 01 40 75 08 75; www.laduree.fr; 7:30am–12:30am; Métro: Franklin Delano Roosevelt; AE, DC, MC, V). Surely, you will find no better opportunity to bask in the glamorous glow of this over-hyped avenue without spending your children's inheritance. Instead of dining on an overpriced sandwich (16€–26€) or *plat du jour* (29€), simply sip demurely on a cup of their legendary hot chocolate (6.10€), or one of their exquisite teas (6.30€–7.30€) while noshing on one of their delectable pastries or their heavenly *marcarons* (light, puffed cookies). The atmosphere is sublime; chandeliers and 19th-century elegance abound. Other Paris locations: 16 rue Royale, 8th arrond.; ☎ 01 42 60 21 79, and 21 rue Bonaparte, 6th arrond.; ☎ 01 44 07 64 87.

NEAR PLACE DES TERNES

€–€€ If the pomp of Champs Elysées has left you feeling meek and downtrodden, treat yourself to a laid-back meal at **Dada** (12 av. des Ternes, 17th arrond.; ☎ 01 43 80 60 12; Mon–Sat noon–11pm, Sun noon–7pm, drinks start at 8am; Métro: Ternes; AE, MC, V). With its wide terrace and relaxed menu, you'll know you are in a place where you can let down your hair without being judged on the state of your coiffure. While the wacky tiles on the floor and the bar are definitely artistic, there is nothing particularly surreal here that harkens back to the bizarre Dada movement of the early 20th century, but no matter, by now your mind is fixing on more earth-bound subjects, like the blanquette d'agneau or the free-range chicken (both 12€). Lighter options include crêpes (6.70€–8.50€) and salads (10€), as well as a range of omelets (6.50€–8.80€). After your meal you can stroll down adjacent rue Poncelet and check out the open-air market.

€€–€€€ For reasons that escape me, the area around the Champs Elysées is heavy with Lebanese restaurants of varying quality. For a sure shot at some excellent hummus, baba ghanouj, and grilled meats, as well as many other less well-known delicacies, tuck in at **Naï** ★ (229 rue du Faubourg Saint-Honoré, 9th arrond.; ☎ 01 40 68 90 70; Mon–Sat noon–2:30pm and 7–11pm; Métro: Ternes; AE, DC, MC, V). Once you've been seated at a comfy table by your gracious hosts, you could launch into a two-course menu express with coffee for 21€, but you'll

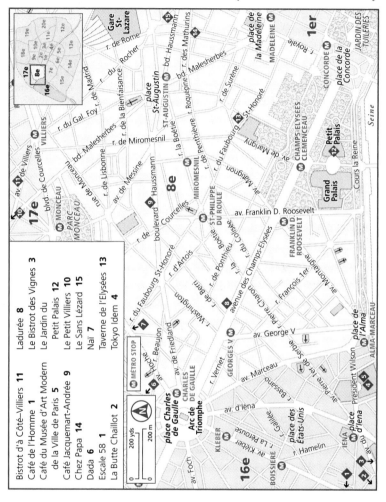

Bistrot d'à Côté-Villiers **11**
Café de l'Homme **1**
Café du Musée d'Art Modern
  de la Ville de Paris **5**
Café Jacquemart-Andrée **9**
Chez Papa **14**
Dada **6**
Escale 58 **1**
La Butte Chaillot **2**
Ladurée **8**
Le Bistrot des Vignes **3**
Le Jardin du
  Petit Palais **12**
Le Petit Villiers **10**
Le Sans Lézard **15**
Naï **7**
Taverne de l'Elysées **13**
Tokyo Idem **4**

probably be more than satisfied with one of their regular platters, like the one that offers eight mezzes, or small dishes (hummus, baba, tabbouleh, kebbe, and so on), for 16€. The same platter comes in a vegetarian version for the same price; other tasty options include *chiche Taouk* (marinated chicken brochettes served with salad and fries, 16€), or mixed grill with hummus and tabbouleh (19€). There are dozens of mezzes a la carte (6€–8.50€); once you're done stuffing yourself, you'll be ready for *mouhalabieh,* a creamy orange-flower-flavored flan garnished with pistachio nuts.

A Word About Kids in Restaurants

Many foreigners wonder how French people manage to make their kids behave so well in restaurants. While the ritual of long Sunday family lunches probably trains them to sit still at an early age, there's also the fact that childhood rowdiness is not well tolerated in eating establishments. If the kids can't sit still, the parents simply don't eat out with them. It's rare to find crayons, puzzles and other kid-friendly items in Parisian restaurants, though they usually have high-chairs (*chaise-haute*, shehz-*oht*), if not booster seats (*réhausseur*, ray-hoh-sur*). Chain restaurants tend to be better prepared to handle toddlers. That said, by and large French people are kid-friendly, so small, family-owned restaurants will usually be pretty understanding, as long as you don't let your kids run wild. Ask if there's a child menu (menu enfant). While not particularly nutritious, they'll usually keep small ones busy with plenty of french fries. Below is a short list of some restaurants that are particularly amenable to the kid contingent:

◆ **Le Nemrod** (p. 97), with its wide outdoor sidewalk terrace, is a good bet for the stroller set; even inside it's so noisy that no one will notice when the kids start to fight over dessert.

◆ **A Priori Thé** (p. 82) is a tearoom located in a covered pedestrian passage with "outside" tables where kids can run free without risk to life and limb.

NEAR PARC MONCEAU

€–€€   Elegant and residential, the 17th is not exactly rife with affordable restaurants—which is why **Le Petit Villiers** 🛝 (75 av. de Villiers, 17th arrond.; ☎ 01 48 88 96 59; noon–2:30pm, 7–11pm; Métro: Wagram; AE, MC, V) is such a welcome haven. The atmosphere is relaxed and inviting and in the warmer months tables are laid on the wide sidewalk. The menu is as down-to-earth as the atmosphere; steak *frites* and grilled salmon are the main attractions at lunch—and the weekday lunchtime *formule* is a steal: 13€ for two courses and 16€ for three. The 21€ *formule,* available both lunch and dinner, comes with more expansive choice (veal with sauce Normand, duck confit); main dishes a la carte run 12€ to 18€. Though the food will not knock you off your feet, the overall experience is a very pleasant one.

€€€   To heck with smiling waiters, you say, I want to get knocked off my feet. In that case, take a stroll down the avenue to **Bistrot d'à Côté–Villiers** ★★ (16 av. de Villiers, 17th arrond.; ☎ 01 47 63 25 61; www.bistrovilliers.com; Mon–Fri noon–2:15pm and 7:30–10:30pm; Métro: Villiers; AE, MC, V). Yet another bistro created by a superchef, here's an opportunity to see how the mighty Michel Rostang interprets humble bistro cuisine. As to be expected, he does it with panache: You could stick to the basics, like a heavenly 300g rib steak with béarnaise, but why would you when you could try veal stuffed with olives and braised lemons? In keeping with the neo-bistro trend, prices have been streamlined here—all appetizers are 12€, all mains 22€, and all desserts 12€. Or you could spring for the menu at 39€ for three courses, 34€ for two. Though the decor is homey, the staff will not let you forget that you are in the presence of a Michelin-starred chef. Reservations are necessary.

BETWEEN PLACE DE LA CONCORDE & GARE ST-LAZARE

€–€€   One thing is for sure, you will not be hungry when you leave **Chez Papa**
★ (29 rue de l'Arcade, 8th arrond.; ☎ 01 42 65 43 68; www.chez-papa.info; Mon–Sat noon–midnight, Sun 7pm–midnight; Métro: Madeleine; AE, DC, MC, V). Not only is southwestern French cooking particularly rib-sticking, but also the size of the portions here are, well . . . manly. Even the salads are hard to finish; the Boyard, which includes lettuce, sautéed potatoes, cantal and bleu de brebis cheese, and dried ham (8.20€) will send you waddling out the door. Food here is not just cheap and filling—it is also quite good. The *piperade* (15€)—a Basque specialty combining tomatoes, red bell peppers, eggs, and onions—is a mouthful of flavor, and actually, not at all heavy. If you've got an appetite, a burbling pot of *cassoulet*—a scrumptious stew of white beans, sausage, and duck meat (18€)—will set you up for a long afternoon of site-seeing, if not a good hike in the Pyrenees. There are several *formules* here, from the "Papamule," a limited choice of two courses and coffee (9.55€), to a three-course-plus-coffee number (24€) with pricier dishes like rump steak and *magret de canard* (duck breast). Given the dearth of affordable dining in the area, this place is almost always jam-packed, so come early. There are seven other Papa outposts: 153 rue Montmartre, 2nd arrond., ☎ 01 40 13 07 31; 127 rue de la Colonie, 13th arrond.; ☎ 01 45 88 30 98; 185 rue Marcadet, 18th arrond., ☎ 01 42 57 41 75; 101 rue de la Croix Nivert, 15th arrond., ☎ 01 48 28 31 88; 6 rue Gassendi, 14th arrond., ☎ 01 43 22 41 19; 206 rue Lafayette, 10th arrond., ☎ 01 42 09 53 87; and 125 av. Gambetta, 20th arrond., ☎ 01 40 31 63 48.

€€–€€€   About a block from the Gare St-Lazare train station, **Le Sans Lézard** (58 rue de l'Arcade, 8th arrond.; ☎ 01 55 06 10 75; Mon–Fri noon–10pm; Métro: Gare St-Lazare; MC, V) is crammed with young professionals at lunchtime who appreciate laid back atmosphere and straightforward menu. None of that fancy-pantsy vanilla infused monkfish carpaccio stuff here, thank you very much. The emphasis here is on meat—large, tender chunks of it, served the way Parisian bistros have done since time immemorial, with sauce. Your *pavé de boeuf* (thick beef steak) comes with a choice of *beurre maitre d'hôtel* (butter, parsley, and a dash of lemon, 14€), Roquefort, green peppercorn, or béarnaise sauce (all 15€), and a healthy mound of home-made frites, or fries. Gluttons for punishment can order a 350g *entrecôte* (17€), and adventurous souls can try the chopped, not ground, raw steak tartare (15€). Nonbeef options include roast chicken (14€) and duck confit (15€), and a range of hearty salads (12€). Wine is served *à la ficelle* here, which means that a full bottle is set on your table and you pay according to how much of it you drink (most cost between 13€–22€ if you drink the whole thing). If you have room for dessert, the chocolate mousse (5.50€) is excellent.

GRANDS BOULEVARDS TO CANAL SAINT MARTIN (9TH & 10TH ARRONDISSEMENTS)

There are no big tourist attractions to speak of in this area, which is probably why it harbors so many low-cost/high-quality eateries. Despite the popularity of the delightful Canal St-Martin, the restaurants lining this humble waterway have, for the most part, stayed true to the working-class roots of the neighborhood. Young artistic-types as well as bobos (bourgeois bohemians) live around here, and restaurants tend to reflect the youth and creative spirit of the area's inhabitants.

NEAR THE OPERA

€–€€   At the top of the escalator that leads to the ninth floor of Printemps de la Maison (part of the clutch of buildings that makes up the Printemps department store) you'll see the sky. That's because the restaurant on the top floor, **Le Deli-cieux** 🧒 (9th floor, Printemps de la Maison, 64 blvd. Haussman, 9th arrond.; ☎ 01 42 82 58 84; www.printemps.com; Mon–Wed and Fri–Sat 11am–3pm, Thurs 11am–3pm and 6–9:15pm; Métro: Havre–Caumartin, RER: Auber; MC, V) has entirely glass walls, the better to see the amazing 360 degree view of the city. An even better view can be had from the huge rooftop terrace (great for families), where you can also nibble on healthy salads, soups, and generally lean cuisine. Service is cafeteria-style: You can choose your salad components (3€ or 7€ for the leafy base, then .50€–2€ per ingredient), then move on to the grill, where roast free-range chicken (13€) and steak (17€), among other things, are available for heartier appetites.

NEAR GARE DU NORD

€€–€€€   Two lovely restaurants, both the offspring of top chef Thierry Breton, are tucked behind the church of St-Vincent-de-Paul. The first is **Chez Casimir** ★ (6 rue de Belzunce, 10th arrond.; ☎ 01 48 78 28 80; 11:45am–2:30pm and 6:45–10:30pm, closed Sat–Sun and 3 weeks in Aug; Métro: Gare du Nord; MC, V), a relaxed, old-fashioned bistro, complete with zinc bar, serves up traditional, savory dishes like *pot au feu* (boiled meat with herbs and vegetables) and *cochon de lait* (suckling pig). There is no a la carte ordering, but at lunch you have a choice of three formulas: two courses for 22€, two courses with cheese plate for 26€, or, the grand slam—three courses with cheese plate for 29€. At dinner, you must take the 29€ *formule*. Reservations recommended.

€€€   Just next door, **Chez Michel** ★★ (10 rue Belzunce, 10th arrond; ☎ 01 44 53 06 20; Métro: Gare du Nord; Tues–Fri 11:45am–2pm and 6:45pm–midnight, Mon 6:45pm–midnight; MC, V) offers haute cuisine at a petit prix (good price). In an unassuming dining room, whose only hint of the chef's Brittany roots is a little lighthouse on the door, simple but succulent culinary wonders like tender, white-fleshed *rascasse* (fish) with eggplant caviar, are set down before grateful customers, who happily wolf down the entire 30€ three-course menu (there's no a la carte ordering here either) without a second thought. The menu is seasonal, but not particularly Breton, with the exception of the occasional appearance of Breton lobster, and the permanent presence of Kouign Amann (an intensely buttery cake) on the dessert list. If you come in autumn there's bound to be a good dose of game on the menu, like the baby wild boar with cèpes (much-cherished wild mushrooms). This restaurant has valiantly refused to raise prices since 2000; with food like this at these prices, tables fill quickly. Reservations are recommended.

GRANDS BOULEVARDS

€–€€   A historic monument, **Chartier** ✹ (7 rue du Faubourg Montmartre, 9th arrond.; ☎ 01 47 70 86 29; www.restaurant-chartier.com; 11:30am–10pm; Métro: Grands Boulevards; MC, V) claims to have served some 50 million meals since it opened in 1896, and though I haven't done the math, considering the fact that the vast dinning room can seat over 300 people and that the restaurant is open every day of the year, it seems entirely possible. This gargantuan establishment is one of the last of the bouillons, or workers' restaurants, that used to be found all over Paris back in the 19th century. The idea was to serve good food at modest prices, an idea that has still speaks to working Parisians over 100 years later, if the line out the door is any indication. You come here for the experience, more than for the food, which is tasty, but certainly won't win any Michelin stars. The menu covers a wide variety of traditional dishes like roast free-range chicken with fries (8.70€) or rump steak with pepper sauce (11€). Service is fast and furious (how could it not be with this many tables?) but it's all part of the atmosphere, which is something that belongs to another time and place. There are no reservations, so be prepared to wait.

€€–€€€   Something's wrong here. The waiters, for example. They're . . . smiling! They're joking around! Are we really in Paris? Well, not entirely. Just about the entire staff of **J'Go** ✹✹ (4 rue Drouot, 9th arrond.; ☎ 01 40 22 09 09; www.lejgo.com; Mon–Sat noon–3pm and 7pm–midnight; Métro: Richelieu Drouot or Le Peletier; AE, MC, V) pronounced *zhee-go*, as in *gigot*, as in leg of lamb) as well as the cuisine, have been imported from southwest France, land of the bon-vivant. But don't let the light-hearted ambience at this casual-chic restaurant make you think that they are not serious about their food: Not only is it delicious, but it is also made with the finest ingredients, like free-range Quercy lamb, and *porc noir* (black pig) from Bigorre. Even the vegetables are brought in from the southwest—almost all come from the same carefully tended farm. The resulting dishes are simple but succulent. A *plat du jour* might be sautéed lamb with parsnips, or homemade sausage with mashed potatoes (both 12€); the grilled sliced duck breast in Madiran wine (18€) is one of the stars of the regular menu. The lunch *formule* "bistr'O" (served Mon–Fri) is a good value at 16€ for two courses and 21€ for three courses.

BASTILLE & FAUBOURG ST-ANTOINE (11TH & 12TH ARRONDISSEMENTS)

Delightfully free of must-see tourist sights, this is a nice area for pottering around and experiencing a more low-key side of Paris. Bastille, which was really hot in the late '90s, has lost some of its cachet; the hip crowd now wanders up rue de Charonne and rue Oberkampf towards Menilmontant. A multitude of cute restaurants have sprouted up in the wake of this migration. Further east, towards the Gare de Lyon, is a mostly residential area with neighborhood cafes packed with locals who know where to go to find *la bonne bouffe* (the good grub).

A Stroll Along the Canal St-Martin

Only recently "discovered" by young artistic types and their bobo (that is, bourgeois bohemian) contemporaries, the quays of the Canal St-Martin are now blooming with lovely little restaurants, cafes, and bars. While there's nothing particularly historic or spectacular about the architecture in this proletarian (at least, up until now) neighborhood, the canal's arching bridges and leafy plane trees give a delightful touch of country charm to this otherwise urban scene. Here are a few quayside restaurant options (that is, if you don't decide to picnic under the trees):

€€   A local hang-out with an artistic flair, the green and yellow walls of **Poêle Deux Carrottes** (177 quai de Valmy, 10th arrond.; ☎ 01 46 07 69 40; Mon–Sat noon–3pm and 7:30–11pm; Métro: Louis Blanc; MC, V) harbor a cozy cafe where you can dine on simple, reliable fare like steak-frites or toasted goat-cheese salad, or just have a beer at the red linoleum bar. At lunch, all main dishes are 11€ and all salads 9.50€; prices go up 1.50€ at dinner.

€€   Slightly more upscale, at least where the cuisine is concerned, is **La Chaland** ★ (163 quai de Valmy, 10th arrond.; ☎ 01 40 05 18 68; Tues–Sun noon–3pm and 6:45–10:30pm; Métro: Louis Blanc or Château Landon; MC, V). On nice days, this lovely cafe with a wood bar and mosaic-tile floor opens out onto the sidewalk. The always-interesting *plat du jour*, which might be a shark lasagna or sautéed duck with honey, is only 9.50€, the weekday lunch *formule* for 12€ includes the above plus dessert.

NEAR THE PLACE DE LA BASTILLE

€   At last, a place to get just a bowl of soup. A new concept in France, where soup is regarded as either a first course or something you eat at home late at night, **Le Bar à Soupes** ★ (33 rue de Charonne, 11th arrond.; ☎ 01 43 57 53 79; www.lebarasoupes.com; Mon–Sat noon–3pm and 6:30–11pm; Métro: Bastille or Ledru-Rollin; MC, V) is just what it sounds like, a soup bar where you can get a big bowl of soup, a fresh roll, and a small salad, if need be. And this being France, these are no ordinary soups. The owner, Anne-Catherine Bley, has published her own cookbook (now available in English), revealing the ingredients of the luscious concoctions listed on the blackboard (which changes daily). If it's hot out, cold carrot soup with coconut milk or fresh green pea with mint might be on offer; for cold days Portuguese haddock soup or Indian yellow lentil soup might hit the spot. A naked, but plentiful bowlful runs 5€ to 5.60€; the lunchtime *formule* includes a bowl of soup, either a salad, or a cheese plate, or a dessert, plus a glass of wine or a cup of coffee for 9.50€.

€   If you're looking for a full meal in the same minimalist price range, head on to **Le Dallery** (6 passage Charles Dallery, 11th arrond.; ☎ 01 47 00 11 72;

Otherwise, main courses like Tandoori chicken brochettes run around 13€, and salads are 9.50€.

€€-€€€ Despite its name, **Le Poisson Rouge** ✸ (112 quai de Jemmapes, 10th arrond.; ☎ 01 40 40 07 11; www.le-poisson-rouge.com; Sun–Thurs noon–2:30pm and 7:30–11pm and Fri–Sat noon–3pm and 7:30–11pm; Métro: Château Landon or Jacques Bonsergent; MC, V) is not a fish restaurant, though they do have some nice selections on the menu (seared tuna in a sesame crust, 17€). "Our specialty is not to have a specialty," declares the owner, whose ever-changing menu includes plenty of meat, like the thick steak sautéed with mushrooms and zucchini (17€). The food is a tad more gourmet here; the wine list is particularly fine, with many selections coming from small, quality vineyards. At lunch, the *plat du jour* is only 10€, a two-course *formule* is 13€, and three-course one is 18€.

€€-€€€ One of the first cafes to open on the canal, and the most well-known, **Chez Prune** (21 quai de Valmy, 10th arrond.; ☎ 01 42 41 30 47; noon–3pm and 7–10:30pm; Métro: Jacques Bonsergent or République; MC, V) has become a victim of its own success. Though this is still a fun place to come for lunch (main courses around 13€) or a drink in the afternoon when things are calm, it is to be avoided in the evenings when the testy servers become even more so and the trendy crowd is impossibly noisy. For hot food come at lunch; cold plates and salads are served in the evening. Brunch served Sunday noon to 4pm.

Mon–Sat noon–3pm, closed in Aug; Métro: Ledru Rollin; MC, V). This tiny, old-fashioned restaurant has gotten a fresh coat of paint and some new modern art from its most recent owners, who hail from Algeria. That's about all that has changed, however—aside from the excellent couscous served on Fridays, the menu is typically French, featuring grilled lamb chops, roast chicken, and the ever-popular steak-*frites*. Even the prices hail from another era: Main dishes (with fries or veggies) are only 8.50€, and the three-course-plus-drink *formule* is a mere 11€. If that's too much for you, a main course, dessert, and coffee combo is only 10€. The only down side is that these tasty meals are only served at lunchtime, in the evenings the ancient zinc bar serves drinks only. The ambience is relaxed and blissfully nonhip; the place is crowded with happy locals who are on a first name basis with the owner/waiter/barman.

€ Farther down rue de Charonne is a little Vietnamese restaurant with a seemingly permanent line outside (at least at dinnertime), **Paris-Hanoi** ✸ (74 rue de Charonne, 11th arrond.; ☎ 01 47 00 47 59; noon–2:30pm and 7–10:30pm; Métro: Charonne or Ledru Rollin; no credit cards). Hungry Parisians young and old (but mostly young) crowd in here to partake in large portions of yummy food at ridiculously low prices. The majority of the main dishes run 8.50€ to 11€, including heaps of lemon grass chicken, steaming bowls of *pho* (noodle soup with meat and vegetables), and healthy servings of *bò bun* (cold noodles with sautéed beef) as well as a variety of meal-size salads. A nice place to start an evening of bar-hopping. Success has been such that the restaurant has opened a second branch at 9 rue Mont-Louis (11th arrond.; ☎ 01 46 59 01 40; Mon–Sat noon–2:30pm and 7–10:30pm; Métro: Philippe Auguste). Reservations accepted at both locations and strongly recommended.

€€–€€€   Around the corner you can take another gastronomic voyage, this time to Africa. **Waly Fay** ✿ (6 rue Godefroy Cavalgnac, 11th arrond.; ☎ 01 40 24 17 79; 8pm–2am; Métro: Charonne; MC, V) offers a delicious combination of Sub-Saharan African and Creole cuisine. Cool music and candlelight set the scene for some of the best *poulet yassa* (12€, chicken marinated in lime and onions) in Paris; *n'dolé mixte* (15€, smoked fish with shrimp) is another star attraction. Less adventurous eaters might like the marinated brochettes (15€), which are grilled over a wood fire. Fill out the meal with a side order of fried plantains or *atéké* (granulated manioc, both 2€). Reservations recommended.

FAUBOURG ST-ANTOINE

€   Several small mountains of exquisite Algerian pastries are lined up on the long counter as you enter **La Bague de Kenza** (173 rue du Faubourg St-Antoine, 12th arrond; ☎ 01 43 41 47 02; Sat–Thurs 9am–8pm, Fri 2–9pm; Métro: Faideherbe–Chaligny; MC, V), a lovely tearoom east of Bastille and close to one of the city's largest outdoor markets, the Marché d'Aligre. The way it works is this: You choose your pastries downstairs (you can simply sigh and point) and then you head upstairs to where you will be served at your table. You can then choose your tea—there's quite a variety, including the traditional pot of mint tea, which goes so well with these delicacies. Light lunches are also served; there is a range of *for-mules,* each including tea and pastry, for 7.80€ to 12€. There are two other tea-room locations, 84 rue Jean-Pierre Timbaud (11th arrond.) and 233 rue de la Convention (15th arrond.), as well as the original bakery at 106 rue St-Maur (11th arrond.).

€€–€€€   In a quiet neighborhood off the busy blvd. St-Antoine, tiny **Le Temps au Temps** ✿✿ (13 rue Paul Bert, 11th arrond.; ☎ 01 43 79 63 40; Tues–Sat noon–2pm and 8–10pm; Métro: Faideherbe–Chaligny; MC, V) offers upscale cuisine at affordable prices, with virtually no attitude. A smiling waitress takes your order as the restaurant fills up with locals from this up-and-coming neighborhood. Portions are small but delectable and exquisitely presented. A con-struction of caramelized endives and balsamic vinegar sits atop a luscious cut of pollack (a white fish), an appetizer of eggplant caviar and smoked salmon is crowned with a curly mass of glistening alfalfa sprouts. The limited-choice lunch *formule* is priced according to your appetite, a main dish is 12€, a main dish with either an appetizer and dessert is 15€ and all three courses is 18€. If you're will-ing to spend 30€ you'll have a choice of three courses from the other chalkboard (which changes daily) honey-glazed lamb with wild mushrooms, or ray stew with curry, wild black mushrooms, and zucchini might be a couple of your options. Reservations recommended.

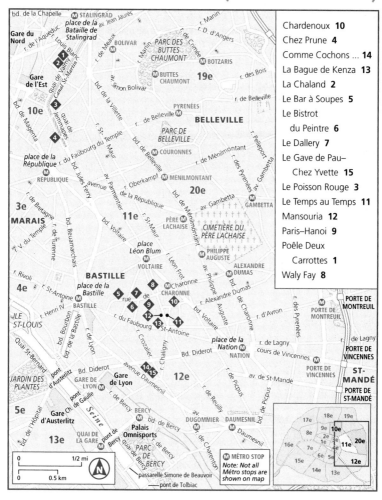

Chardenoux **10**
Chez Prune **4**
Comme Cochons ... **14**
La Bague de Kenza **13**
La Chaland **2**
Le Bar à Soupes **5**
Le Bistrot
   du Peintre **6**
Le Dallery **7**
Le Gave de Pau–
   Chez Yvette **15**
Le Poisson Rouge **3**
Le Temps au Temps **11**
Mansouria **12**
Paris–Hanoi **9**
Poêle Deux
   Carrottes **1**
Waly Fay **8**

€€€   Yet another fabulous cuisine from an ex-French colony is that of Morocco, and there are few places north of Fez where you will find as excellent an example as **Mansouria** ✪✪✪ (11 rue Faidherbe, 11th arrond.; ☎ 01 43 71 00 16; Mon–Thurs 7–10:30pm, Fri–Sat 7–11pm, Wed–Sat 12:30–2:30pm, closed week of Aug 15; Métro: Faideherbe-Chaligny; MC, V). Generally accepted as the queen of Moroccan cooking (she's published six cookbooks), Fatéma Hal rules supreme in the kitchen of this elegant restaurant, which sends out platters of perfumed dishes such as *kmama,* a chicken *tagine,* or stew, cooked with tomato jam and rose petals. Hal goes to the roots of this illustrious cuisine: One dish, La Mourouzia, is a 12th-century recipe featuring lamb seared in real *ras al hanout*—an intense mixture of

A Different Kind of French Restaurant

You may have noticed: Many Parisians do not look very French. This is because large communities from former French colonies in Southeast Asia and Africa have flourished in recent years, bringing a whole new dimension to local culture, not to mention local cuisine. If you've had enough of France in your dinner plate, take a quick side trip to Algeria, Africa, or Vietnam, and feast on couscous, poulet yassa, pho, or any number of dishes that put a whole new spin on the idea of "French cuisine." While the best ethnic restaurants are in some of the more far-flung arrondissements (the 13th, 18th, and 20th, for example), the 11th and 12th have probably the best selection of choices closer to the center of town.

27 spices—and stewed in honey, raisins, and almonds. Both of these are 19€; the terrific couscous variations are in the same range. Reservations are a must.

€€€   Getting back to France . . . you'll feel like you've walked into the 19th century when you pass through the doors of **Chardenoux** ✸✸ (1 rue Jules Vallés, 11th arrond; ☎ 01 43 71 49 52; Mon–Sat noon–2:30pm and 7–10:30pm Métro: Faidherbe-Chaligny; MC, V), possibly the quintessential Parisian bistro. It's not just the swirling floral decorations on the ceiling, the old wooden tables and chairs, or the dozens of bottles lined up behind polished zinc bar, but also the waiters, with their white starched shirts and black pants covered by the archetypal long white apron. The menu, however, does not restrict itself to Paris; you're liable to find a southern *aioli* (garlic mayonnaise) of fresh cod, or tuna steak with *ratatouille* (sautéed vegetable stew), both 19€ alongside a roasted slice of lamb with potatoes gratin Dauphinoise (22€). Reservations strongly recommended.

NEAR THE GARE DE LYON

€–€€   One of the last of a dying breed, **Le Gave de Pau–Chez Yvette** ✸✸ (147 rue de Charenton, 12th arrond.; ☎ 01 43 44 74 11; Mon–Sat 7am–midnight; Métro: Gare de Lyon or Reuilly-Diderotl; MC, V) is one of those one-man-show (or in this case, one-woman) bar-cafes where patrons come as much for the personality of the owner as the food. Hailing from the region around Pau (pronounced *po*) in the French Southwest, Yvette serves up regional specialties with a large helping of southern hospitality and general good cheer. Regulars crowd in to the tiny dining room to partake in the savory *magret de canard* and duck *confit* (both 11€), or other items (like a *piperade,* a luscious mix of egg, red bell peppers and ham, 8€) appearing on the ever-changing blackboard menu. Whatever it is, it's bound to be good, especially if it's washed down with a glass of Madiran or one of the other featured regional wines. A three-course *formule* is 13€ at lunch and 15€ at dinner. For something lighter, there is a good selection of meal-size salads as well (8€–9€). Yvette cooks everything herself in between waiting tables and manning the bar (where her daughter helps out when she can). Come here soon—Yvette is building herself a house in the Pyrenees, where she plans to retire.

€€–€€€   Not even a block away (and still only 10 min. max to the station) is another welcoming place, **Comme Cochons . . .** ★ (135 rue de Charenton, 12th arrond.; ☎ 01 43 42 43 36; noon–3pm and 8–11pm; Métro: Gare de Lyon or Reuilly-Diderot; MC, V). Contrary to what you might gather from the name, which translates literally as "like pigs," this is not a pork-based restaurant, nor a place where you can eat like a slob; the name actually comes from a proverb and refers to having loads of friends. Which says something about the atmosphere—this is a relaxed place that is low on attitude and high on culinary values. More modern than its neighbor, the cozy room greets locals who come for the traditional dishes with a contemporary touch, like the roast bass with fennel (16€) or the *faux-filet bordelaise* (steak in wine sauce, 17€). Though dinner is more fun (and on alternate Thursday nights there's live jazz), lunch is easier on the budget; a three-course *formule* is only 15€, and two courses is 12€. The honey-almond mousse makes a great finish.

MONTPARNASSE (14TH ARRONDISSEMENT)

The famous cafes (Le Dôme, Le Select, La Coupole, and so on) where struggling writers and artists like Picasso, Hemingway, and Chagall, once hung out are now much too expensive for most ordinary mortals, much less struggling artists, and having a drink and soaking up the atmosphere is probably the most affordable way to enjoy them. But the history of this quarter is not just about art—it is also the most Breton (that is, from Brittany) section of Paris. The trains from Brittany arrive and depart from Montparnasse, and the story goes that between the Wars, fresh-off-the-train Bretons, not knowing where else to go, settled in the immediate vicinity. Hence the high density of crêperies (the crepe having its origins in Brittany).

NEAR THE GARE MONTPARNASSE

€   One of the oldest crêperies in Paris, **Tí Jos** ★ 🧒 (30 rue Delambre, 14th arrond.; ☎ 01 43 22 57 69; www.restaurant-tijos.com; Mon–Sat 11:30am–2:30pm and Wed–Mon 7–11:30pm, closed last week in Aug; Métro: Edgar Quinet or Vavin; AE, MC, V) serves excellent *galettes* (made with a slightly salty, buckwheat batter and used for meal-type crêpes) and crêpes (a sweeter wheat-based batter, used for dessert crêpes), ranging from a simple cheese crêpe (5.30€) to a *super-complète* with egg, ham, cheese, and mushrooms (8.30€). The menu sticks close to the traditional line; no guacamole-goat cheese concoctions here and includes a good list of mildly alcoholic ciders (the traditional accompaniment) as well as a few hot dishes. Should you show up on a Thursday night in wintertime, you can try a plate of *kig ha farz* (17€) a Breton specialty involving a crumbled buckwheat dumpling and a hearty slice of smoked bacon (reserve ahead). The *far* is on the dessert menu year-long, a creamy, custardy slice of tart, sometimes made with prunes. Informal Celtic music concerts have been known to happen on Friday nights.

€–€€   Just across the street is an opportunity to visit another French province, this time Alsace. Decked out with a traditional wooden interior and a wood-burning oven, **Tavern de la Forge** ★ 🧒 (63 blvd. de Vaugirard, 15th arrond.; ☎ 01 43 20 87 10; Mon–Sat noon–3pm and 7–11pm; Métro: Montparnasse-Bienvenüe; MC, V) serves up delicious *flammekueches,* the Alsatian version of pizza. The delicate, thin crust is spread with a sinful mix of *crème fraîche* (a kinder, gentler sour cream) and *fromage blanc* (another mild and creamy dairy product) and then dotted with sautéed onions, smoked ham, mushrooms, or a variety of other goodies like potatoes, or smoked salmon. Strange as it sounds, *flammenkueches* are not unbearably heavy, due to prudent dosing of fatty ingredients. Prices range from 7.90€ for simple versions to 12€ for the full monty. Other Alsatian specialties include variations on the melted-Munster-cheese-on-potatoes theme, as well as *choucroute,* smoked meats on a heap of cooked and shredded cabbage.

RUE DAGUERRE

€–€€   The atmosphere is laid back and easygoing at **Bistrot des Pingouins** (79 rue Daguerre, 14th arrond.; ☎ 01 43 21 92 29; Mon–Fri 11:45am–3pm and Mon–Sat 7pm–12:45am; Métro: Gaité or Denfert-Rochereau; MC, V), which is one of the primary reasons it is packed most nights. That, and the fact that there is very reasonable three-course *formule* available at both lunch (14€) and dinner (15€)—a rarity in these parts. While the food does not usually surpass what the French call "correct" (that is, good, but not great), it is generous and tasty. The regular menu includes standards like confit de canard (14€), while the *formule* offers choices like gratin of salmon and chicken brochettes. The *mascarpone du jour* (6€), a creamy dairy confection, is an excellent way to finish your meal. Reservations recommended.

OFF RUE D'ALESIA

€€   One of the best vegetarian restaurants in Paris, **Aquarius** ✮ (40 rue de Gergovie, 14th arrond.; ☎ 01 45 41 36 88; Mon–Sat noon–2:15pm and 7–10:30pm; Métro: Pernety; AE, DC, MC, V) is nestled in a pretty neighborhood with nothing much to say for itself aside from the fact that it's charming. Using as many organic ingredients as possible, this brightly colored, slightly hippyesque restaurant cooks up tasty meat-free dishes such as a hearty vegetarian lasagna and a divine *roti aux noix* (nut roast) with cassis jelly (both 12€). The three-course weekday lunch menu is only 12€ and includes a choice from the ever-changing blackboard menu; a two-course menu in the evenings is 16€. There is a nice selection of generously portioned salads (all between 10€–11€), like the *salade orientale,* which comes with tabbouleh, veggie pâté, eggplant caviar, hummus, Greek-style mushrooms, seaweed, and vinaigrette. The wine list includes lots of organic options, and there is a selection of fresh squeezed fruit and vegetable juices. Reservations recommended.

TROCADERO & PASSY (16TH ARRONDISSEMENT)

The 16th arrondissement is generally considered the Beverly Hills of Paris. Stately mansions abound, tony shops beckon, and restaurant prices make one's eyes roll back in their sockets. For a romantic evening or a special event, however, you can't beat dinner and a stroll to the place du Trocadéro: The view of the glittering Eiffel Tower from esplanade of the Palais de Chaillot is simply unforgettable.

AROUND TROCADERO

€ You'll know you've found **Escale 58** ★ (58 rue de Longchamp, in the Galerie Longchamp arcade, 16th arrond.; ☎ 01 47 27 25 08; Mon–Fri 11:30am–3:30pm, Métro: Trocadéro, no credit cards) when you see the line out the door—this is one of the rare places in this neighborhood where you can find tasty, well-prepared food at low prices. There are actually two lines, one for take-out and one to wedge yourself into the restaurant, where space is so limited that you might find yourself sitting across from a stranger if you arrive during the rush. The homey dinning room is abuzz with jovial office workers; the biggest crowd is on Thursday, when they serve a succulent couscous, in addition to the regular blackboard menu, which might feature salmon in dill sauce, or roast chicken. The food is simple, but made with fresh ingredients and loving care, which is probably why the place is packed with people who look like they can afford to eat elsewhere. All main dishes, which are garnished with a generous portion of fries or rice, are 9€, salads are 6.50€ to 7.50€ and their homemade soup is 3.50€. There is a *formule* that includes soup, a small salad, and dessert or a drink for 8.50€; knock 1€ off all of these prices for takeout.

€€€–€€€€ Underplayed elegance is on the menu at **La Butte Chaillot** ★★ (110 bis av. Kléber, 16th arrond.; ☎ 01 47 27 88 88; www.guysavoy.com; closed Sat lunch; Métro: Trocadéro; AE, DC, MC, V), which serves simply, but beautifully executed gourmet fare in a classy, modern environment. Waiters flutter gracefully around the tables like butterflies; the atmosphere is calm and quiet. The lunch crowd is mainly upscale professionals in suits—dinner brings a dressier clientele. The signature dish is the thyme-roasted free-range chicken with mashed potatoes (19€), filets of redfish with eggplant caviar (26€) makes an excellent second choice. The 33€, three-course menu, available at both lunch and dinner, is a sensible splurge. A great place for a classy dinner before a night at the theater at the Palais Chaillot.

PASSY

€€–€€€ After quenching your literary thirsts at the Maison de Balzac, a quick stroll to **Le Bistrot des Vignes** ★ (1 rue Jean Boulogne, 16th arrond.; ☎ 01 45 27 76 64; 12:30–2:30pm and 7–10:30pm, closed first 3 weeks in Aug; Métro: Passy or La Muette; AE, MC, V) will satisfy your hunger for more basic needs—lunch, perhaps. A pleasant corner "neo-bistro" with mustard-colored walls and a Mediterranean air, this is a relaxed environment for enjoying refined bistro fare, like an appetizer of foie-gras with green lentils (all starters 6€), or a main dish such as *magret de canard* (duck breast) with honey and roasted sesame oil (all mains 15€). There's a hint of the south in the menu; tomatoes, eggplant, and olives tend to show up in many dishes. Around here, the 21€ two-course lunch menu is a deal; three courses go for 28€, and a single main dish is 15€. Add 2.50€ to these prices for the same menu at dinner. They are known for their wine list; many offerings are available by the glass.

MONTMARTRE (18TH ARRONDISSEMENT)

The great thing about Montmartre: You need only walk in the opposite direction of the tourist traps (which are concentrated around the Sacré Coeur and the place du Tertre) to find yourself in some lovely little neighborhood that looks like it belongs in a painting by Utrillo. To the north and west of the basilica is where you will find the villagey atmosphere you've heard so much about; to the east and south Montmartre gives way to Barbès, a lively immigrant neighborhood where you are just as likely to see women in Indian saris and African prints as in smart Parisian apparel. Either way, you're bound to come across good food.

NEAR PLACE DES ABBESSES

€€–€€€   Montmartre—like all the best parts of Paris—has been discovered by the hip crowd, as will become obvious as you stroll down rue des Abbesses on a Saturday night and observe the flora and fauna spilling out the bars and cafes onto the sidewalks. A good way to partake in the joys and avoid the nuisances is to treat yourself to a meal at **Café Burq** ★ (6 rue Burq, 18th arrond.; ☎ 01 42 52 81 27; Mon–Fri noon–2:30pm and 6pm–2am, Sat 6pm–2am; Métro: Abbesses; MC, V), where you can both party and eat excellent food. Flirt at the bar while you wait for your table (reservations—a must—are only for the first seating, after 9pm it's first-come, first-served), then saunter into the dining area to contemplate the blackboard menu, which might include a tender rumpsteak with shallots, or braised pork with mangos and red bell pepper. Finish it all off with dessert (perhaps a pear gazpacho with almond milk?) and then move back to the bar for an after-dinner drink. At dinnertime, main dishes are around 18€; a two-course *formule* is 28€, and three courses is 32€. At lunch, a mellower mood prevails, both in terms of atmosphere and finances: Main courses are 13€, two courses are 15€ and three courses are 19€. For a "light" lunch, try the baked Camembert with honey (served with salad, 10€)—it's delish.

€€€   Just a short walk from the tourist hoards hovering around Sacré Coeur is a remarkably authentic restaurant called **A La Pomponnette** ★★ (42 rue Lepic, 18th arrond.; ☎ 01 46 06 08 36; Tues–Sat noon–2:30pm and 7–11pm, Mon 7–11pm, closed Aug; Métro: Abbesses; AE, DC, MC, V). In the same family for several generations, this gracefully aging bistro dates from around 1900, attested to by the gently yellowing photos and etchings on the walls, which also frame several beautiful canvases by local artists. Red-checked linens cover the tables, polished fixtures gleam on the beautiful old wood bar. On the menu, superb renditions of French classics like duck *confit* with potatoes sautéed in garlic, *daube* (a rich beef stew), or *lapin chasseur* (hunter-style rabbit) with fresh pasta (all 23€), all served in generous portions and beautifully presented. At lunch there is a two-course menu for 20€, otherwise, the three-course menu at 32€ is available at both lunch and dinner. On the third Saturday of every month there is a "soirée chanson" after 10:30pm where guests are invited to sing along to French cabaret standards. Reservations essential.

NEAR SACRE COEUR

€–€€   If you wander down the east side of the hill from Sacré Coeur, in a matter of minutes you are in relatively quiet neighborhood with outdoor cafes, the

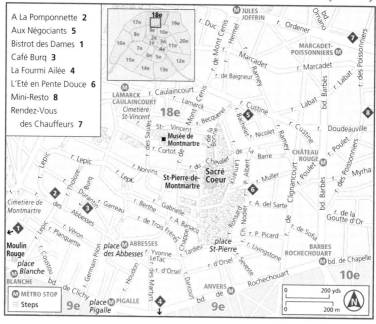

A La Pomponnette **2**
Aux Négociants **5**
Bistrot des Dames **1**
Café Burq **3**
La Fourmi Ailée **4**
L'Eté en Pente Douce **6**
Mini-Resto **8**
Rendez-Vous
   des Chauffeurs **7**

nicest of which is **L'Eté en Pente Douce** ✮ (23 rue Muller, 18th arrond.; ☎ 01 42 64 02 67; www.parisresto.com; Mon–Fri noon–2:45pm and 7–11:15pm, Sat–Sun noon–3:45pm and 7–11:15pm; Métro: Anvers or Château Rouge; MC, V). The outdoor terrace is one of the prettiest in town; a lovely place to have a salad (niçoise, or goat cheese with figs, 12€) or a quiche (vegetable or mushroom, all served with small salad, 7.50€) on a hot day. They serve excellent hot food as well, like the *blanquette de veau* with mushroom rice (14€), or if you really want to go all out, the house specialty is a half of a duck in a salt crust stuffed with vegetables and fruits (20€), if the menu sounds familiar, it might be because this is the sister restaurant of **La Fourmi Ailée** (p. 88). If the weather refuses to cooperate (when doesn't it?) don't despair, original mosaics and huge windows make indoors as pleasant as out.

€–€€   On the other side of the hill is a mixed neighborhood where regular folks live and eat or drink at places like **Aux Négociants** ✮ (27 rue Lambert, 18th arrond.; ☎ 01 46 06 15 11; Métro: Lamarck-Caulaincourt or Château Rouge; noon–2:30pm and 8–10:30pm, closed Aug; AE, MC, V). Well, I guess I shouldn't say just anyone—famed photographer Robert Doisneau used to hang out here way back when—but for the most part, this tiny, traditional wine bar has kept its neighborhood clientele, even if more and more *bobos* (bourgeois bohemians) keep dropping in. If you're here to sample the wine, you'll find terrific homemade *terrine* and *rilletes* (both variations on the pâté theme, both 6.80€ for a generous serving) to accompany your glass of pinot d'Aunis. The owner is an ex-charcutier, which is another way of saying he knows his pâtés and sausages. If you want something more substantial, a selection of traditional French comfort food is proffered. Main courses run 12€ to 14€, and might include a *parmentier de morue* (a sort of shepherd's pie with cod) or andouillette sausage.

AT FOOT OF THE HILL—BATIGNOLLES

€€   One of the rare Parisian restaurants with a plant-filled patio for alfresco dining, **Bistrot des Dames** ✪ (18 rue des Dames, 17th arrond.; ☎ 01 45 22 13 42; www.eldoradohotel.fr; Mon–Fri noon–2pm and 7–10:30pm [bar until 2am], Sat–Sun 12:30–10:30pm [bar until 2am]; Métro: place de Clichy; AE, MC, V) is a pleasant oasis for bobos (bourgeois bohemians), artists, and just plain folks. In theory, this is a wine bar, which explains the emphasis on cheese and *charcuterie* platters—the classic accompaniment for the fruit of the vine—as well as an excellent, if sparse, wine list featuring the house favorites. But most come here to linger over a meal outdoors, under the trees. If you're not up for one of the platters (7€–14€), there are some other perfectly acceptable main dishes, like a veal hamburger (14€) or roast chicken breast with giant prawns doused with coconut milk and a dash of Espelette pepper (20€). Salads are a good way to go here; their copious chicken Caesar (14€) is an excellent choice on a hot summer night.

OUT OF AFRICA—BARBES

€€   Be prepared to be stared at when you enter **Mini-Resto** ✪ (rue des Poissoniers, 18th arrond.; ☎ 01 42 54 97 11; 11am–1am; Métro: Château Rouge or Marcadet-Poissoniers; MC, V), one of the best places in town to eat *n'dole*, a delicious African stew made with a spinachlike vegetable, peanuts, spices and either meat or fish. Don't worry, once the initial questioning looks have passed, you will be very welcome in this homey restaurant, known for its excellent Cameroon cuisine. Located in a primarily African neighborhood, and frequented by locals, you can be sure that you are getting the real thing. Aside from the variations on n'dole (11€–15€), there is also a range of *gombos* (10€–12€, an okra stew with chicken or fish, the ancestor of gumbo), as well as braised fish (15€).

€–€€   If you're not up to the challenge, regular old French food can be found down the street at **Rendez-vous des Chauffeurs** ✪ (11 rue des Portes Blanches, 18th arrond.; ☎ 01 42 64 04 17; Tues–Sat noon–2:30pm and 7:30–10:30pm; Métro: Marcadet-Poissoniers; MC, V). In fact, it doesn't get much more typical than this adorable old bistro, with its mustard colored walls, yellow-checked tablecloths, red leatherette banquettes and enameled metal advertisements on the walls. Older regulars kid with the owner behind the bar; a mix of ages gathers around the scattered tables to savor the classics on the menu, like blood sausage with apples and potatoes, duck with pears, sautéed veal Marengo, and *bavette* with fries. At lunch, a two-course *formule* is only 11€ and three-courses 16€. The same holds true in the evening up until 8:30pm, after which it's a la carte only from the somewhat sexier main menu (rump steak 15€, medallions of monkfish "à l'americaine," that is, in a lobster bisque sauce, 14€). Reservations strongly recommended—the word has gotten out about this hidden gem, and the small dining room fills up fast.

CAFE CULTURE

It would be a crime to come to Paris and not stop to have a coffee (or other drink) in a cafe. Cafe life is an integral part of the Parisian scene, and it simply won't do to visit the capital without at least participating once. ***Important note:*** Cafes are not bars, in the North American sense—though they generally serve alcohol, they are not places where people come to get smashed. They are places where people come to just "be," to sip a drink, to take a break, to read a book, or to simply watch the world go by. Perhaps that's why the great Existentialist himself, Jean-Paul Sartre, spent so many of his waking hours in cafes. If you have any interest in discovering what real Parisians are like, cafes are a great place to watch them in their natural habitat. Naturally, for authenticity's sake, you should stay away from those right next to tourist hotspots (the high prices and the multilanguage menu should be your first tip-off); cafes in "uninteresting" residential neighborhoods are best. By the way, most cafes (and all those listed) are open until around 2am.

There must be thousands of cafes in Paris, and a thorough run down would easily fill a book. Though you could probably have a primal cafe experience in just about any corner operation, here are a few ideas for your own personal cafe tour.

CAFES WITH HISTORY

A monument to the St-Germain quarter's intellectual past, **Café de Flore** ✪✪ (172 blvd. St-Germain, 6th arrond.; ☎ 01 45 48 55 26; www.cafe-de-flore.com; 7:30am–1am; Métro: St-Germain-des-Prés; AE, DC, MC, V) is a must-sip on the cafe tour circuit. Seemingly every great French intellectual and artist seems to had their moment here: Poets Apollinaire and André Breton cooked up Dadaism; Zadkine, Picasso and Giacometti came to take refuge from Montparnasse; literary and theatrical stars came to preen; and of course, philosophers gathered to figure out the meaning (or nonmeaning) of life. During the war, Simone de Beauvoir and Jean-Paul Sartre more or less moved in, and Sartre is said to have written his trilogy *Les Chemins de la Liberté (The Roads to Freedom)* here. The atmosphere now is less thoughtful and more showbiz, but it still may be worth an overpriced cup of coffee just to come in and soak it up.

After the war, de Beauvoir and Sartre picked up and moved to **Les Deux Magots** ✪✪ (6 place St-Germain-des-Prés, 6th arrond.; ☎ 01 45 48 55 25; www.lesdeuxmagots.com; 7:30am–1am; Métro: St-Germain-des-Prés; AE, DC, MC, V), where they continued to write and think and entertain their friends for a good chunk of the rest of their lives. The literary pedigree here is at least as impressive as that of its neighbor: Poets Verlaine and Rimbaud camped out here, as did François Mauriac, André Gide, Paul Eluard, Albert Camus, and Ernest Hemingway. Since 1933, Les Deux Magots has been handing out a literary prize (in 1994 the Flore came up with its own). The outdoor terrace is particularly pleasant early in the morning before the crowds wake up.

The artistic legacy of **La Coupole** ✪ (102 blvd. Montparnasse, 14th arrond.; ☎ 01 43 20 14 20; www.lacoupoleparis.com; 8:30am–1am; Métro: Vavin; MC, V) is almost as vast as this enormous brasserie's square footage: Soutine, Chagal, Josephine Baker, Henry Miller, Salvador Dalí, and Ernest Hemingway are just some of the stars that lit up this converted charcoal depot. One of the largest

Coffee Talk

Ordering a cup of coffee in Paris is not quite as simple as it sounds. There is a multitude of delightful caffeinated (and decaffeinated) java possibilities at most any cafe. Here is a miniglossary to help you navigate once your waiter makes it over to your table.

Café (ka-*fay*)—coffee. This is pure, black espresso, albeit lighter than the Italian version, served in a small demi-tasse cup. Always served with sugar on the side.

Décaf (*day*-ka)—decaf, or decaffeinated coffee. An unleaded version of the above.

Café serré (ka-*fay* sehr-*ay*)—smaller in volume, but packs a bigger punch. Resembles an Italian espresso.

Noisette (nwa-zet)—a café with a dash of steamed milk (my favorite).

Café crème (crem)—a café with an equal amount of steamed milk, served in a larger cup.

Café au lait (ka-*fay* oh lay)—virtually identical to the above, sometimes with a bit more milk. The biggest difference is the time of day; in the morning they call it a café au lait, in the afternoon a crème.

Cappuccinos, by the way, are rare in Parisian cafes, and when you do get one, chances are it won't resemble anything you'd get in Italy. ***Important tip:*** Drinks at the bar (coffee or otherwise) can cost half what you will pay sitting down at a table.

---

restaurants in France, this Art Deco mastodon first opened in 1927, and has been hopping ever since. Thirty-three immense painted pillars hold up the ceiling; huge murals and paintings cover the walls. Though the food is good (the lamb curry is the signature dish), you can also just come here for a drink, grab a table by the windows, and watch the world go by.

CAFES WITH A VIEW

Few experiences are as delicious as having a drink on the terrace of the **Café Marly** ☆ (93 rue de Rivoli, 1st arrond.; ☎ 01 49 26 06 60; 8am–2am; Métro: Palais Royale–Musée du Louvre; AE, DC, MC, V) after a long day at the Louvre. Tucked into the Richelieu wing, you can sip your pricey espresso while gazing out on I.M. Pei's glass pyramid and the Denon wing on the opposite side of the vast courtyard. Don't be in a hurry; though the tall, perfect waiters bustle about with great purpose, they seem to ignore all but the most glamorous customers.

Surely one of the best views of the Eiffel Tower is to be had from the terrace of the **Café de l'Homme** (Palais de Chaillot, 17 place du Trocadero, 16th arrond.; ☎ 01 44 05 30 15; open for drinks 4–6pm and 11pm–2am; Métro: Trocadero; AE, DC, MC, V). If you can stomach the price of a cocktail (12€), this is the place to come to see and be seen, lesser mortals can sip a cup of coffee (4€) and enjoy the same view. Service is distinctly snobby; be prepared to be ejected at mealtimes when the restaurant takes precedence.

CAFES WITH DECOR

Artists, hipsters, and other fauna from the bustling rue de Charonne area crowd in to **Le Bistrot du Peintre** ✭ (116 av. edru-Rollin, 11th arrond.; ☎ 01 47 00 34 39; 7am–2am; Métro: Ledru-Rollin; MC, V), which sports an authentic Art Nouveau interior with the original peeling paint. Lean up against the zinc bar and admire yourself and others in the vast mirror behind the barman, or simply slouch at one of the tiny tables that tumble out onto the sidewalk.

After a hard day of shopping in the discount stores on rue d'Alesia, nothing could be nicer than a steaming café crème at **Le Zeyer** ✭ (62 rue d'Alesia, 14th arrond.; ☎ 01 45 40 43 88; 8am–midnight; Métro: Alésia; AE, MC, V). This gorgeous Art Deco brasserie, one of the last of its kind that hasn't been turned into a tourist trap, happens to have a spacious covered terrace—the perfect spot for a rainy afternoon.

CAFES FOR PEOPLE-WATCHING

An old cafe that's had a modern makeover, **La Fourmi** ✭ (74 rue des Martyrs, 18th arrond.; ☎ 01 42 64 70 35; Mon–Sat 8am–2am and Sun 10am–2am; Métro: Abbesses or Pigalle; MC, V) is now a neighborhood nerve-center in lower Montmartre and is generally bubbling with bobos (bourgeois bohemians) and other customers from the cool crowd. Not only does the clientele make good people-watching, but the cafe's proximity to place Pigalle means you're bound to see something interesting through the floor-to-ceiling windows as well.

A neighborhood cafe with antique ceiling cornices and a huge mirror behind the bar, **La Palette** ✭ (43 rue de Seine, 6th arrond.; ☎ 01 43 26 68 15; Mon–Sat 9am–2am; Métro: Mabillon; MC, V) attracts a heavy art-world clientele—it's that kind of a neighborhood. Gallery owners, would-be artists, and more or less regular folk come here to chat and look at each other; in nice weather tables clutter the entire corner—a great place to hang on a summer's evening.

What could be nicer than sitting in a wicker chair at a sidewalk table at the **Café de la Mairie** ✭ (8 place St-Sulpice, 6th arrond.; ☎ 01 43 26 67 82; 7am–2am; Métro: Mabillon or St-Sulpice; no credit cards) on the place St-Sulpice? Relatively car-exhaust free (there is one lane of traffic between you and the place), in good weather tables on the wide sidewalk are much in demand; you may have to hover a while to get one. Indoors, it's a 1970s archetype: Formica bar, boxy chairs, too much smoke, and an odd assortment of pensioners, fashion victims, students, and would-be novelists. In short, it's perfect.

5 Remarkable Sights & Attractions

Let's rank the ones you definitely should see

THERE IS SO MUCH TO SEE IN THIS CITY THAT YOU COULD EASILY SPEND several months touring nonstop and still wonder if you haven't missed something. With over 130 world-class museums and just as many nonmuseum attractions to discover, not to mention extraordinary architecture to gape at and wonderful neighborhoods to wander, Paris is an endless series of delights. But where do you start? What do you leave out?

To begin with, a very good case can be made for allocating some of your time to just plain roaming without a plan. Lolling on a park bench, dreaming over a drink at a sidewalk cafe, or noodling around an unknown neighborhood, can be the stuff of some of your best travel memories.

That being said, there are 10 must-see attractions, 10 iconic places (like the Eiffel Tower, like Notre Dame, the Louvre, and Musée d'Orsay) that I'll list at the start of this chapter. I'll then list a secondary set of 12 extraordinary museums and monuments that may not be household words, but are well worth your time. Depending on your own personal tastes, these "secondary" ten may be more important than the "top" 10 (who's to say that smaller museums like the Musée Carnavalet and Musée Jacquemart-André are any less enjoyable than the Louvre?).

I've then grouped everything else into separate sections by subject matter. You'll find their location on the maps included with this chapter.

In later chapters, you'll find discussions of Paris's outdoor spaces and activities (p. 212), nightlife (p. 276), and historic walks (p. 229). Finally, don't forget to look at our "Other Paris" chapter (p. 198) for sights and activities that should help you get "under the skin" of the city and allow you to actually meet Parisians and see how they work, play, and learn. From philosophy discussion groups to rollerblade rallies, from shopping in open-air markets to visiting artists' studios, these are the types of experiences I'll detail that will help give your vacation depth and flair.

A final note for younger travelers—while many of the sights and museums below are appropriate for kids (we've marked them with our 🧒 symbol to help you find them), there are many other kid-friendly activities hiding out in Paris's parks and green spaces, like zoos, amusement parks, and puppet shows, which you'll find in chapter 7.

MAKING THE MOST OF YOUR TIME

If you have just 1 day in Paris Your biggest challenge will be trying not to spend the whole day wishing you had more time. First, put on a good pair of walking shoes and make a beeline for the **Eiffel Tower.** Hopefully you've gotten there early on a weekday and it won't take too long to go up and take a gander at the splendid view of the city from the second floor. If lines are long, skip the view and cross the bridge (Pont d'Iéna), heading up to the esplanade at the **Palais de Chaillot,** where you can admire the Iron Lady in all her splendor. Now hop on the no. 63 bus at the place du Trocadéro (direction Gare de Lyon), which will cruise past **Les Invalides,** and bring you straight into the center of the **St-Germain** quarter. Get off at the church of **St-Germain des Prés** and find a nice spot for lunch, then mosey down rue Dauphine to the **Pont Neuf,** which will lead you to the **Ile de la Cité.** Follow the quays around the southern edge of the island until you find yourself before the towers of **Notre Dame.** After visiting the cathedral, take a bus or a Métro to the **Louvre** (you could walk, but by this point you'll be losing steam) and spend what's left of the afternoon admiring the outsides of the buildings (save the museum for the next trip) and wandering through the **Tuileries Garden.** At the western edge, you'll find yourself on the **place de la Concorde,** where you see the **Arc de Triomphe** in the distance at the end of the **Champs Elysées.** If you still have energy in the evening, finish your visit with an **evening cruise** along the river; from which you can admire just about all of the above gussied up in elegant lighting effects.

If you have 2 days Start the itinerary off the same way, but this time wait in line to go up the **Eiffel Tower.** This should take at least a couple of hours, so by the time you've come back down you'll be ready to eat. Take the RER directly to St-Michel and look for lunch in the **Latin Quarter.** Now you can easily cross over one of several bridges to **Notre Dame.** If you are feeling ambitious, you could follow up the cathedral with the **Sainte Chapelle,** also on the Ile de la Cité; otherwise, you could immediately cross over to the Right Bank and spend the afternoon shopping and strolling around the **Marais.** Around sunset, stop by **place des Vosges** for a pre-dinner *aperitif* before you hunt down a restaurant, after which, feet willing, you could put on your cool duds and head towards the bars and clubs on rue de Charonne, near the **place de la Bastille.**

Day two should start with the **Louvre,** which will keep you going until at least lunch, when you can either call it quits or simply take a nice long break and eat at one of the restaurants around the **Palais Royal.** After lunch, if you aren't returning to the museum, you can relax in **Tuileries Gardens,** ambling down to the western end to admire the **place de la Concorde** and the view of the **Arc de Triomphe** down the **Champs Elysées.** Cross over the bridge and end your day in the **St-Germain** quarter, where you can easily find dinner and maybe even take in an evening of theater at the Théâtre de l'Odéon (p. 280).

If you have 3 days Now you can afford to take a bit more time to savor the city. Devote each day to a different section. Day one is for the Left Bank, starting with the **Eiffel Tower** and either the **Musée d'Orsay** or the **Musée du Quai Branly.** Lunch at a restaurant in **St-Germain,** after which a leisurely ramble in the **Jardin**

Top Paris Attractions

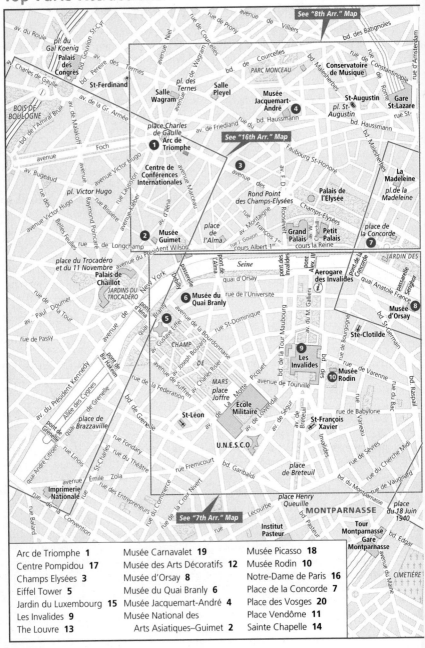

Arc de Triomphe **1**

Centre Pompidou **17**

Champs Elysées **3**

Eiffel Tower **5**

Jardin du Luxembourg **15**

Les Invalides **9**

The Louvre **13**

Musée Carnavalet **19**

Musée des Arts Décoratifs **12**

Musée d'Orsay **8**

Musée du Quai Branly **6**

Musée Jacquemart-André **4**

Musée National des
   Arts Asiatiques–Guimet **2**

Musée Picasso **18**

Musée Rodin **10**

Notre-Dame de Paris **16**

Place de la Concorde **7**

Place des Vosges **20**

Place Vendôme **11**

Sainte Chapelle **14**

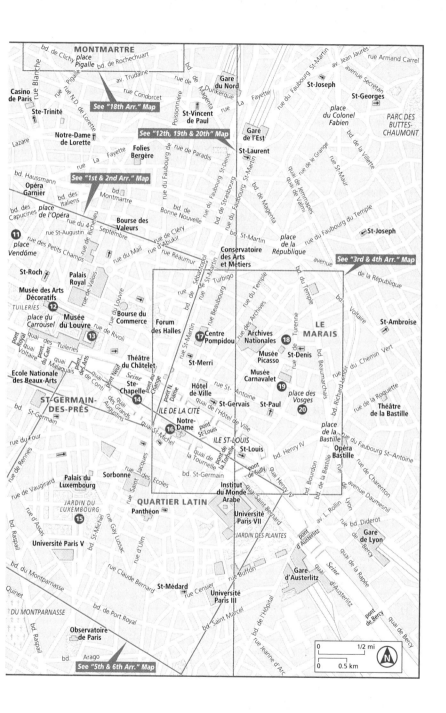

MONTMARTRE
place Pigalle
bd. de Clichy
bd. de Rochechouart
Casino de Paris
Ste-Trinité
av. Trudaine
rue Condorcet
Gare du Nord
St-Joseph
St-Georges
place du Colonel Fabien
PARC DES BUTTES-CHAUMONT
av. Jean Jaurès
rue Armand Carrel
avenue Secrétan

See "18th Arr." Map

St-Vincent de Paul

Notre-Dame de Lorette

See "12th, 19th & 20th" Map

Folies Bergère

Gare de l'Est

St-Laurent

rue du Faubourg St-Martin

See "1st & 2nd Arr." Map

Opéra Garnier

place de l'Opéra

bd. des Capucines

11 place Vendôme

Bourse des Valeurs

rue de Cléry

rue d'Aboukir

rue du Mail

rue Réaumur

Conservatoire des Arts et Métiers

place de la République

See "3rd & 4th Arr." Map

de la République

St-Roch

Palais Royal

Musée des Arts Décoratifs

TUILERIES

12

place du Carrousel

Musée du Louvre

13

Bourse du Commerce

Forum des Halles

17 Centre Pompidou

Archives Nationales

18

LE MARAIS

St-Ambroise

St-Denis

St-Merri

Musée Picasso

Musée Carnavalet

19

place des Vosges

20

Ecole Nationale des Beaux-Arts

Théâtre du Châtelet

Seine

Ste-Chapelle

14

ST-GERMAIN-DES-PRÉS

Hôtel de Ville

St-Gervais

St-Paul

ILE DE LA CITÉ

Notre-Dame

16

ILE ST-LOUIS

St-Louis

place de la Bastille

Opéra Bastille

Théâtre de la Bastille

rue du Faubourg St-Antoine

Palais du Luxembourg

Sorbonne

Institut du Monde Arabe

JARDIN DU LUXEMBOURG

15

Panthéon

QUARTIER LATIN

Université Paris VII

Gare de Lyon

Université Paris V

St-Médard

Université Paris III

JARDIN DES PLANTES

Gare d'Austerlitz

DU MONTPARNASSE

Observatoire de Paris

bd. Arago

See "5th & 6th Arr." Map

0   1/2 mi
0   0.5 km

N

127

du Luxembourg will probably be in order. Finish the day exploring and dining in the **Latin Quarter,** ending the evening with a stroll along the Seine on the quai **St-Bernard.**

Day two could start on the **Ile de la Cité,** with visits to **Notre Dame** and **Sainte Chapelle.** Then amble over to the **Ile St-Louis,** from which you can cross the Pont Marie for lunch in the **Marais.** Spend the afternoon alternating window shopping with museum hopping, choosing between **Musée Carnavalet, Musée Picasso,** and the **Musée de l'Art et de l'Histoire de Judaisme.** Around sundown, head up to **Montmartre** for the view in front of **Sacré Coeur,** and dinner. Spend the evening lounging in the bars and cafes around **place des Abbesses.**

By day three, it will be time to get serious, so you could devote most of the daylight hours to the **Louvre,** leaving time for a look at the **place de la Concorde** and **place Vendôme.** After finding a good place to eat dinner, you could end your visit with a long stroll up the **Champs Elysées** to the **Arc de Triomphe,** where you can say goodbye to Paris from the panoramic terrace on the top.

If you have 4, 5, 6, or 7 days   Follow our itinerary for 3 days, and work in more museums and sites that appeal to you, as well as a stroll in one of the lesser-known neighborhoods, like **Nouvelle Athens** in the 9th arrondissement or the **Canal St-Martin** in the 10th (see "Lay of the Land," p. 6, for descriptions). You might want to commit a good part of 1 day visiting one of the grand châteaux outside the city limits, like **Versailles** or **Fontainbleau,** or the magnificent cathedral in **Chartres.** Set aside an evening or two for theater, or dancing, or a long nocturnal stroll, and don't forget to scan chapter 6, "The Other Paris," for ideas on more idiosyncratic ways to fill your time.

PARIS'S 10 ICONIC SIGHTS

Of all the sights in Paris, here are 10 that are must-sees:

THE IRON LADY   In his wildest dreams, Gustave Eiffel probably never imagined that the tower he built for the 1889 World's fair would become the ultimate symbol of Paris, and for many, of France. Originally slated for demolition after its first 20 years, the **Eiffel Tower** ★★★ (Champs de Mars, 7th arrond.; ☎ 01 44 11 23 23; www.tour-eiffel.fr; first level 4.80€ 12 and over, 2.50€ ages 3–11; second level 7.80€ 12 and over, 4.30€ ages 3–11; third level 12€ 12 and over, 6.70€ ages 3–11; stairs to the first and second levels 4€ over 25, 3.10€ under 25; Jan–June 12 and Sept–Dec elevator 9:30am–11pm, stairs close at 6pm; June 13–Aug elevator and stairs 9am–midnight; Métro: Ecole Militaire or Trocadéro, RER: Champs de Mars) has survived over a century and is one of the most visited sites in the nation. No less than 50 engineers and designers worked on the plans, which resulted in a remarkably solid structure that despite its height (324m/1,063 ft., including the antenna) does not sway in the wind.

But while the engineers rejoiced, others howled. When the project for the tower was announced, a group of artists and writers, including Guy de Maupassant and Alexandre Dumas fils, published a manifesto that referred to it as an "odious column of bolted metal." Others were less diplomatic: Novelist Joris-Karl Huysmans called it a "hole-riddled suppository." Despite the objections, the tower was built— over 18,000 pieces of iron, held together with some 2.5 million rivets. In this low-tech era, building techniques involved a lot of elbow grease: The foundations, for example, were dug entirely by shovel, and the debris was hauled away in horse-drawn carts. Construction dragged on for 2 years, but finally, on March 31, 1889, Gustave Eiffel proudly led a group of dignitaries up the 1,710 steps to the top, where he unfurled the French flag for the inauguration.

Over 100 years later, the tower has become such an integral piece of the Parisian landscape that it's impossible to think of the city without it. Over time, even the artists came around—the tower's silhouette can be found in the paintings of Seurat, Bonnard, Duffy, Chagall, and especially those of Robert Delaunay, who devoted an entire series of canvases to the subject. It has also inspired a whole range of stunts, from Pierre Labric riding a bicycle down the stairs from the first level in 1923, to Philippe Petit walking a 700m-long (2,296-ft.) tightrope from the Palais de Chaillot to the tower during the centennial celebration in 1989. Eiffel performed his own "stunts" towards the end of his career, using the tower as a laboratory for scientific experiments. By convincing the authorities of the tower's usefulness in studying meteorology, aerodynamics, and other subjects, Eiffel saved it from being torn down.

The most dramatic view of the tower itself is from the wide esplanade at the Palais de Chaillot (Métro: Trocadéro) across the Seine. From there it's a short walk down through the gardens and across the Pont d'Alma to the base. Though several elevators whisk visitors skyward, they do take time to come back down, so be prepared for a wait. Personally, I think the view from the second level is the best; you're far enough up to see the entire city, yet still close enough to clearly pick out the various monuments. But if you are aching to get to the top (and unlike me, don't get vertigo), an airplanelike view awaits. The third level is, mercifully, enclosed, but thrill-seekers can climb up a few more stairs to the outside balcony (entirely protected with a grill). On the way back down to Earth, consider stopping on the first floor to visit the exhibits about the tower and its history, including a short film. Now your only problem will be squeezing into the crowded elevator when you are ready to go down. (*Tip:* Climb the short flight of stairs to the two-tiered elevator's upper waiting deck, where fewer people wait.)

QUASIMODO SLEPT HERE   Crowning the Ile de la Cité is one of France's most brilliant expressions of medieval architecture—the **Cathedral of Notre-Dame de Paris** ✪✪✪ (Parvis Notre-Dame, 4th arrond.; ☎ 01 42 34 56 10; www.cathedraledeparis.com; cathedral free admission; treasury 3€ adults, 2€ students, 1€ under 12; cathedral 8am–6:45pm; treasury: Mon–Fri 9:30am–6pm, Sat 9:30am–6:30pm, Sun and religious holidays 1:30–6:30pm; Métro: Cité or Saint-Michel, RER: Saint-Michel Notre-Dame). This remarkably harmonious ensemble of carved portals, huge towers, and flying buttresses has survived close to a millennium's worth of French history and has served as a setting for some of the country's most solemn moments. Napoleon crowned himself and Empress Josephine here, Napoleon III was married here, and some of France's greatest generals (Foch, Joffre, Leclerc) had their funerals here. In August 1944, the liberation of Paris from the Nazis was commemorated in the cathedral, as was the death of General de Gaulle in 1970.

The story of Notre Dame begins in 1163, when Bishop Maurice de Sully initiated construction, which lasted over 200 years. (The identity of the architect who envisioned this masterpiece is a mystery.) The integrity of the building was relatively untouched up until the end of the 17th century, when Louis XIII, who had sworn to build a new altar if he would ever have a son, finally got his wish (the future Louis XIV) and implanted vast changes to the medieval chancel. More unfortunate changes were made in the 18th century when the stained glass windows were replaced with clear glass, and the walls whitewashed. By the time the Revolutionaries decided to convert it into a "Temple of Reason," the cathedral was already in a sorry condition—the pillaging that ensued didn't help. The interior was ravaged, statues were smashed, and the cathedral was a shadow of its former glorious self.

We can thank the famous "Hunchback" himself for saving Notre Dame. Victor Hugo's novel, *The Hunchback of Notre Dame,* drew attention to the state of disrepair, and other artists and writers began to call for the restoration of the edifice. In 1844, Louis-Phillipe hired Jean-Baptiste Lassus and especially architect/archeologist/writer/painter Viollet-le-Duc to restore the cathedral, which they finished in 1864. Though many criticized Viollet-le-Duc for what they considered to be overly romantic and unauthentic excesses, he actually took extreme care to remain faithful to the historic gothic architecture. His addition of a 45m (148-ft.) spire, for example, was in fact a re-creation of one that existed in the 13th century. Made out of lead-covered oak *(chene),* it weighs 750 metric tons (827 U.S. tons).

Begin your visit at **Point Zéro,** just in front of the building on the parvis (the esplanade). It is literally the epicenter of French life, the official center of Paris and the point from which all distances relative to other French cities are calculated. Before you are three enormous **carved portals** depicting (from left to right) the Coronation of the Virgin, the Last Judgment, and scenes from the lives of the Virgin and St-Anne. Above is the **Gallery of the Kings of Judah and Israel—** thought to be portraits of the kings of France, the original statues were chopped out of the facade during the Revolution; some of the heads were eventually found in the 1970s and now are in the Musée National du Moyen Age/Thermes de Cluny. Above this is the superb **rose window,** which you will better appreciate from the inside, over which soar the two bell **towers** of Quasimodo fame.

Upon entering the cathedral, you'll be immediately struck by two things: the throngs of tourists clogging the aisles, and then, when you look up, the heavenly dimensions of the pillars holding up the ceiling. Soaring upward, these delicate archways give the impression that the entire edifice is about to take off into the sky. Up there in the upper atmosphere are the three remarkable stained-glass **rose windows,** one for each of the west, north, and south ends of the church. The north window retains almost all of its 13th-century stained glass; the other two have been heavily restored. There is an impressive **treasury** filled with relics of various saints including the elaborate cases for the **Crown of Thorns,** brought back from Constantinople by Saint Louis in the 13th century. The crown itself is not on display; however, it can be viewed, along with a nail and some pieces of the Holy Cross, on the first Friday of the month (3pm), every Friday during Lent (3pm) and Good Friday (10am–5pm). For a detailed look at the cathedral, take advantage of the **free guided tours in English** (Wed–Thurs 2pm, Sat 2:30pm) or rent an **audioguide** for 5€.

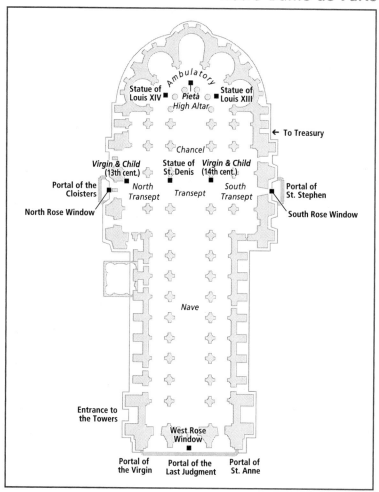

When you leave, be sure to take a stroll around the outside of the cathedral to admire the other portals and the famous flying buttresses.

AN EMPEROR'S LEGACY   If there is one monument that symbolizes "La Gloire," or the glory of France, it is the **Arc de Triomphe** ✪✪✪ (Place Charles de Gaulle, 8th arrond.; ☎ 01 55 37 73 77; www.monum.fr; 8€ adults, 5€ 18–25, free under 18 when accompanied by adult; Apr–Sept 10am–11pm; Oct–Mar 10am–10:30pm; Métro and RER: Charles de Gaulle-Etoile). This mighty archway that crowns the Champs-Elysée both celebrates the military victories of the French army and memorializes the sacrifices of its soldiers. Over time, it has become an icon of the Republic and a setting for some if its most emotional

Avoiding Lines

Though long lines at major monuments are an unfortunate fact of Parisian life, there are a few things you can do to ease the pain.

- ◆ Visit the most popular sights on weekdays. You'll still have plenty of company, but at least the locals won't be as abundant (French tourists generally swarm on the weekends, particularly on Sun).
- ◆ If you can, get there early, before 11am, when even the late sleepers are up and in line. The only problem with this strategy is that you might run into tour groups, who tend to rise at dawn. Your other option is to visit around 5 or 6pm, when the buses are gone and the monuments and museums empty out. Double-check hours to make sure you have enough time left for your visit.
- ◆ Buy or reserve your ticket in advance. You may have to pay a small reservation fee, you'll usually have the right to a *coup fil* (to go through a special entrance where you won't have to wait in line). Check to make sure you get this benefit when reserving.

moments: the laying in state of the coffin of Victor Hugo in 1885, the burial in 1921 of the ashes of an unknown soldier who fought in World War I, and General de Gaulle's pregnant pause under the arch before striding down the Champs Elysées before the cheering crowds after the Liberation in 1944.

It took a certain amount of chutzpah to come up with the idea to build such a shrine, and sure enough, it was Napoleon who instigated it. In 1806, still glowing after his stunning victory at Austerlitz, the Emperor decided to erect a monument to the Imperial Army, along the lines of a Roman triumphal arch. He handed this project to architect Jean-François Chalgrin, who promptly began building an arch measuring 50m (163 ft.) high and 45m (147 ft.) wide, the largest of its type on the planet. Unfortunately, the defeat at Waterloo put an end to the Empire before the arch was finished and construction came to an abrupt halt. It wasn't until 1823, when Louis XVIII wanted to celebrate his army's victory in Spain, that building got going again. The arch was finally finished in 1836 by Louis-Philippe.

The arch is covered with bas-reliefs and sculptures, the most famous of which is the enormous *Depart of the Volunteers* of 1792, better known as the Marseillaise, by François Rude, showing winged, female Liberty leading the charge of Revolutionary soldiers. Just above is one of the many smaller panels detailing Napoleonic battles—in this case, Aboukir—wherein the Emperor trods victoriously over the Ottomans. At the base of the arch is the Tomb of the Unknown Soldier, over which a flame is relit every evening. The inscription reads ICI REPOSE UN SOLDATE FRANÇAIS MORT POUR LA PATRIE, 1914–1918 ("Here lies a French soldier who died for his country").

Don't even think about crossing the traffic circle—the busiest in Paris—to get to the arch, instead take the underpass near the Métro entrances. Though not as heart-stopping as the view from the Eiffel Tower, the panorama from the roof-top terrace is quite impressive. Directly below you will see the 12 boulevards that radiate from the star-shaped intersection (hence the moniker "Etoile"), most of which are named after Napoleonic battles. Out front is the long sweep of the Champs-Elysées, ending at the obelisk of the place de la Concorde, behind which lurks the pyramid of the Louvre. In the other direction you will get a good gander at the modern Grande Arche de la Défense, a huge, hollow cubelike building that could fit Notre-Dame under its arch.

THE JEWEL IN THE CROWN   A wall of color greets the visitor at **Sainte Chapelle** ★★★ (4 blvd. du Palais, 1st arrond.; ☎ 01 53 40 60 80; www. monum.fr; 7.50€ adults, 4.80€ students under 26, free under 18 accompanied by an adult; or use the combined ticket with Conciergerie: 10€ adults, 7.50€ students under 26; Mar–Oct 9:30am–6pm; Nov–Feb 9am–5pm; Métro: Cité or St-Michel, RER: St-Michel). Stained-glass windows make up a large part of the walls of the upper level of the church, giving worshippers the impression of standing inside a jewel-encrusted crystal goblet. What isn't glass is elaborately carved and painted in gold leaf and rich colors: vaulting arches, delicate window casings, and an almost oriental wainscoting of arches and medallions. The 15 windows recount the story of the Bible, from Genesis to the Apocalypse, as well as the story of St-Louis, who was responsible for the chapel's construction. Back in the early 13th century, Louis IX (who was later canonized) spent 2 years bargaining with

The Two Towers

The lines are long and the climb is longer, but the view from the **rooftop balcony** (☎ 01 53 10 07 00; www.monum.fr; 7.50€ adults, 4.80€ under 26, free under 18 and the first Sun of month; no credit cards; Apr–June and Sept 10am–5:45pm, July–Aug Mon–Fri 10am–5:45pm, Sat–Sun 10am–10:15pm, Oct–Mar 10am–4:45pm) at the base of the cathedral's towers is possibly the most Parisian of all views. After trudging up some 255 steps (a narrow winding staircase with a handrail—not for small children or anyone with mobility concerns) you'll be rewarded with a panorama that not only encompasses the Ile de la Cité, the Eiffel Tower, and Sacré-Coeur, but is also framed by a collection of photogenic **gargoyles.** These fantastic monsters, composed of various portions of apes, birds, and even elephants, came directly from the imagination of Viollet-le-Duc, who placed them during the restoration of the cathedral. One of the most famous is the **Stryga,** a horned and winged beasty holding his head in his hands, pensively sticking his tongue out at the city below. Squeeze around the narrow first balcony to the entrance to the belfry, Quasimodo's old haunt; its massive wood beams hold up a 14-ton bell. Another 147 steps up another narrow stairway lead up to the summit of the **south tower,** from which there is an endless view of Paris. To minimize the wait, come in the morning before the crowds get thick, and avoid weekends.

Emperor Badouin II of Constantinople for some of the holiest relics in Christendom: the crown of thorns and a piece of the Holy Cross. The relics were finally purchased for a princely sum, and Louis decided that they should be housed in an appropriately splendid chapel in the royal palace (the relics are now in the treasury of Notre-Dame). The record is not clear, but the architect may have been the illustrious Pierre de Montreuil, who worked on the cathedrals of St-Dennis and Notre-Dame. Whoever it was was a speed-demon; the chapel was built in record time for the Middle Ages, from 1241 to 1248. He was also quite brilliant, as he managed to support the structure with arches and buttresses in such a way that the walls of the upper chapel are almost entirely glass.

The lower chapel, which was meant for the servants, has a low, vaulted ceiling painted in blue and red and gold and covered with fleur-de-lys motifs. Up a small staircase is the upper chapel, clearly meant for the royals. This masterpiece suffered both fire and floods in the 17th century and was pillaged by zealous Revolutionaries in the 18th. By the mid–19th century, the chapel was being used to store archives—2m (6½ ft.) of the bottom of each window was removed to install shelves. Fortunately, renewed interest in medieval art staved off plans for Ste-Chapelle's demolition, and eventually led to a conscientious restoration by a team that was advised by master restorer Viollet-le-Duc. The quality of the work on the windows is such that it is almost impossible to detect the difference between the original and the reconstructed stained glass (which makes up about one third of what you see). There are free guided tours daily in French (and occasionally English) at 11am and 3pm; or pick up a free English brochure at the entrance.

GUILLOTINES AND GLORY   Like an exclamation point at the end of the Champs-Elysées, the **place de la Concorde** ✹✹✹ (8th arrond.; Métro: Concorde) is a magnificent arrangement of fountains and statues, held together in the center by a 3,000 year-old **Egyptian obelisk** (a gift to France from Egypt in 1829). When it was inaugurated in 1763 during the reign of Louis XV, this vast plaza was on the outer edges of the city, and its gardens and fountains opened out onto the countryside. Today, though it's part of an urban landscape, it still gives the impression of open space, as it's bordered by the gardens of the Tuileries and the Champs Elysées on two sides, and the Seine on the third. If it wasn't for the cars hurtling around the obelisk like racers in the Grand Prix, this would be a delightful spot for a breath of fresh air (if you feel compelled to cross to the obelisk and you value your life, find the stoplight and cross there). Regardless, the place de la Concorde is a splendid sight: The best **view** is from the Tuileries Gardens, from which you can see not only the plaza but also the long view down the Champs Elysées all the way to the Arc de Triomphe, with the Grande Arche de la Défense hovering in the distance.

It's hard to believe that this magnificent square was once bathed in blood, but during the Revolution, it was a grisly stage for public executions: King Louis XVI and his wife, Marie-Antoinette, both bowed down to the guillotine here, as did many prominent figures of the Revolution, including Danton, Camille Desmoulins, and Robespierre. Once the blood stopped flowing, and the monarchy was back in place, the plaza hosted less lethal public events like festivals and trade expositions. In 1835 the *place* was given its current look: Two immense fountains, copies of those in St-Peter's Square in Rome, play on either side of the obelisk; 18 sumptuous columns decorated with shells, mermaids, sea horses, and other sea creatures each hold two lamps; and eight statues representing the country's largest cities survey the scene from the edges of the action. On the side facing the Champs Elysées are the famous **Marly Horses,** actually copies of the originals, which were suffering from erosion and have since been restored and housed in the Marly Court at the Louvre. On the north side of the square are two palatial buildings that date from the square's 18th-century origins: On the east side is the **Palais de Gabriel,** now the home of the Naval Ministry, and on the west side is the **Hôtel Crillon,** where on February 6, 1778, a treaty was signed by Louis XVI and Benjamin Franklin, among others, wherein France officially recognized the United States as an independent country and became its ally. Speaking of the United States, that building surrounded by barricades next to the Crillon is the American Embassy.

TILTING AT WINDMILLS   There are few places in this city that will fill you with the urge to belt out sappy show tunes like the **Butte Montmartre** ✮✮✮ (18th arrond.; Métro: Abbesses). Admiring the view from the esplanade in front of the oddly Byzantine **Basilique du Sacré-Coeur,** you'll feel like you have finally arrived in Paris, and that you now understand what all the fuss is about. High on a hill overlooking the city, Montmartre has always stood a little bit apart from the rest of Paris—and vestiges of the villagelike atmosphere are still to be found, if you know where to look. Try to ignore the tour buses and crowds mobbing the church behind you and wander off into the warren of streets towards the **place des Abbesses,** or up **rue Lepic** where you'll eventually stumble across the **Moulin de la Galette** and **Moulin du Radet,** the two surviving windmills (there were once 30 on this hill). As you move away from Sacré-Coeur and the hideously touristy **place du Tertre,** the crowds thin dramatically, and before you know it you'll feel like you are in a scene from Jean-Pierre Jeunet's film Amélie. Cobbled streets, corner cafes, and arty boutiques beckon; historic apartments and studios of artists and writers pepper the streets.

What started out as a sacred hill, dedicated to the Roman god Mercury, became the home of Benedictine monks in the Middle Ages. According to legend, St-Denis was martyred here, and in the 9th century the hill was dubbed *Mons martyrium,* which time transformed into Montmartre. The usually peaceful activities of its inhabitants did not take away from its strategic value, however, and several decisive battles were played out on these heights from the Renaissance up to the 19th century, when the hill was annexed to the city of Paris. In 1871, Montmartre was a stronghold of the Paris Commune—a ground-breaking socialist movement that ruled Paris for a few short months before it was brutally crushed by the French government. Towards the end of the century, artisans and workers, chased out of the center of Paris by the urban renewal schemes of Baron Haussmann, moved up here to take advantage of the low rents, good wine (there are two remaining vineyards) and country atmosphere, which created a unique village ambience. In time, artists and poets, always in search of cheap lodgings and a convivial atmosphere, would follow, and the legendary Montmartre art scene was born. Renoir and Utrillo painted street life, and the **Bateau Lavoir** (13 place Emile Goudeau), an old wash-house converted into artists' studios, overflowed with talent: Max Jacob, Matisse, Apollinaire, and Braque all worked here, as did Picasso, who created *Les Demoiselles d'Avignon* on the premises in 1907. The best way to visit this area is by foot; see "Walkabouts," p. 229.

And what about that church? Poised at the apex of the hill like a *grande dame* in crinolines is **Sacré-Coeur** ★★ (35 rue du Chevalier-de-la-Barre, 18th arrond.; ☎ 01 53 41 89 00; www.sacre-coeur-montmartre.fr; cathedral: admission free, dome: 5€; cathedral: daily 6am–11pm; dome and crypt: daily 9am–6:30pm; Métro: Anvers or Abbesses, at street level follow signs to the funiculaire, which will bring you all the way up to the church for an extra Métro ticket; no credit cards). After France's defeat in the Franco-Prussian War, prominent Catholics vowed to build a church consecrated to the Sacred Heart of Christ as a way of making up for whatever sins the French may have committed that had made God so angry at them. Since 1885, prayers for humanity have been continually chanted here (the church is a pilgrimage site, so dress and behave accordingly). Inspired by the Byzantine churches of Turkey and Italy, construction of this multidomed confection began in 1875. It was completed in 1914, though it wasn't consecrated until 1919 due to World War I. The white stone was chosen for its self-cleaning capabilities: When it rains, it secretes a chalky substance that acts as a fresh coat of paint. The interior of the church includes a somewhat garish mosaic ceiling, installed in the 1920s. Most visitors climb the 237 stairs to the **dome,** where the splendid view of the city extends over 48km (30 miles).

FOUNTAINS AND FANTASY   Out of the many parks and gardens in Paris, the **Jardin du Luxembourg** ★★★ 🄺 (6th arrond.; ☎ 01 42 34 23 62; free admission; 8am–dusk; Métro: Odéon, RER: Luxembourg) is one that shouldn't be missed. Rolling out like an exotic oriental carpet before the Italianate Palais du Luxembourg (the seat of the French Senate since 1958, not open to the public), this vast expanse of fountains, flowers, lush lawns, and shaded glens is the perfect setting for a leisurely stroll, a relaxed picnic, or a serious make-out session, depending on who you're with. At the center of everything is a fountain with a huge basin, where kids can sail toy wooden sailboats (2€ for a half-hour) and adults can sun themselves in the green metal chairs at the pond's edge. Sculptures abound: At every turn there is a god, goddess, artist, or monarch peering down at you from their pedestal—Vulcan, Venus, George Sand, or Anne de Bretagne, to name but a few. The most splendid waterwork is probably the Medici Fountain (most easily reached via the entrance at place Paul Claudel behind the Odéon), draped with lithe Roman gods sculptured by Auguste Ottin, and topped with the Medici coat of arms, in honor of the palace's first resident, Marie de Medicis.

In 1621, the Italian-born French queen, homesick for the Pitti Palace of her youth, bought up the grounds and existing buildings and had a Pitti-inspired palace built for herself as well as a smaller version of the sumptuous gardens. She moved in in 1625, only to be banished in 1630 for taking the wrong side against powerful Cardinal Richelieu. The palace passed on to various royals until the Revolution, when it was turned into a prison. American writer Thomas Paine was incarcerated there in 1793 after he fell out of favor with Robespierre; he narrowly escaped execution. On the plus side, the Revolutionaries increased the size of the

Attention Bored Kids & Tired Parents

Frazzled parents take note: There are lots of activities in the Jardin de Luxembourg for kids who need to blow off steam. First off, there is the extra-large **playground** (1.60€ adults, 2.60€ under 12) filled with all kinds of things to climb on and play in. Then there are the wonderful wooden **sailboats** (2.50€ per half-hour) to float in the main fountain, as well as an ancient **carousel** (1.80€, next to the playground). At the **marionette theater** (in French only, 4.60€ each for parents and children; Wed, Sat, Sun, and public holidays, as well as school vacations; show times vary but usually start after 3pm, Sat–Sun additional shows at 11am), you can see Guignol himself (the French version of Punch) in a variety of puppet shows. If that doesn't do it and you really need a break, there is a **daycare center** for tots (near the marionette theater; ☎ 01 43 25 55 87; Mon–Sat), which takes kids 18 months to 6 years old. Rest assured, this is a municipal *garderie* that must live up to the same high standards as all other French public day care centers, to which I have entrusted my own son and give a solid thumbs up. The way it works is this: You show up at 2pm with something official indicating your child's vaccination history and you can leave him or her there to play and have a snack until 6pm for a mere 9€ per child (let's hear it for subsidized child care). There are no reservations in advance, so come early (around 1:45pm), and there is a 9€ inscription fee that is good for the entire season the garderie is open, which is May 1 through September 15.

garden and made it a public institution. The orchards of the neighboring charterhouse were annexed, the remnants of which can still be visited at the southwest corner of the gardens. There, visitors can visit a horticulture school where pear trees have been trained into formal, geometric shapes, as well as beehives (yes, beehives) that are maintained by a local apiculture association. After the Revolution, the palace and grounds stayed in government hands up until today, with the exception of the Orangerie, which now houses the **Musée du Luxembourg** (19 rue de Vaugirard, 6th arrond.; ☎ 01 42 34 25 95; www.museeduluxembourg.fr; hours vary with expositions, check listings guides; Métro: Odéon, RER: Luxembourg), which is only open for its excellent temporary exhibits.

THE ELYSIAN FIELDS   Once considered "the most beautiful avenue in the world," the **Champs Elysées** ★★ 🧒 (8th arrond.; Métro: Champs Elysées-Clémenceau or Franklin Delano Roosevelt, RER: Charles de Gaulle–Etoile) is still a looker, even if it has suffered the slings and arrows of rampant commercialization in recent years. An odd combination of flashy megastores and high-end boutiques line the upper reaches of the avenue, as if the street can't decide if it's in Paris or Las Vegas. Mid-way down the tone changes as you slide by the opulent Grand Palais and elegant Avenue to Montaigne. Down towards the place de la Concorde, grandeur gives way to greenery as lush gardens unfold on both sides of the boulevards; there is a small **playground**, a **merry-go-round**, and a **marionette theater** on the north side of the street.

As its name suggests, the *champs,* or fields, was once open countryside on the outskirts of the city. In the 17th century, an avenue was laid down whose primary purpose was to extend the perspective of the Tuileries Gardens. For decades, there were barely any houses along the road; in 1777 a colonel in the Swiss Guard noted in his report that the cows grazing in the middle of the avenue were blocking pedestrian traffic. It wasn't until the Second Empire (mid- to late 1800s) that elegant apartment buildings sprung up and the wide boulevard became the height of elegance. In the late 20th century, the avenue was invaded with movie theaters and fast food joints, prompting cries of outrage and finally, a major renovation that was finished in 1994. Crass commercialism has been reigned in, and the avenue has regained a bit of its elegant aura, but the many huge stores flaunting brand names (Renault, Disney, Vuitton, Virgin) and shopping complexes give at least the western end of the boulevard a bit of a theme-park ambience. Some find it appealing, others find it appalling, but in any event the Champs Elysées is worth a stroll, even if it won't be the most authentically Parisian experience.

ICONIC MUSEUMS

As noted above, there are scores of museums in Paris. But two are so grand in scope and ambition, and so profound in their impact on visitors that they deserve to be counted as iconic experiences.

CULTURE & KINGS   The best way to thoroughly visit **The Louvre** ★★★ (34 quai du Louvre, 1st arrond.; ☎ 01 40 20 50 50; www.louvre.fr; permanent collection: 9€ adults, after 6pm 6€; temporary exhibits: adults 9€; combined ticket 13€, after 6pm 11€; free under 18; tickets to the permanent collection also include entrance to the Musée National Eugène Delacroix; Mon, Thurs, Sat–Sun 9am–6pm, Wed and Fri 9am–9:45pm; Métro: Palais Royal–Musée du Louvre) would be to move in for a month. Not only is it one of the largest museums in the world, with over 35,000 works of art displayed over 60,000 sq. m (645,835 sq. ft.), but it's packed with enough artistic masterpieces to make the Mona Lisa weep. Rembrandt, Reubens, Botticelli, Ingres, and Michelangelo are all represented here; subjects range from the grandiose (Antoine-Jean Gros's gigantic *Napoleon Bonaparte Visiting the Plague-Stricken in Jaffa*) to the mundane (Vermeer's tiny, exquisite *Lacemaker*). You can gape at a diamond the size of a golf ball in the royal treasury, or marvel over exquisite bronze figurines in the vast Egyptian section. There's something for everyone here, even the crankiest member of your party who insists he or she "doesn't like art."

Today, the building is divided into three wings, Sully, Denon, and Richelieu, each one with its own clearly marked entrance, found under I.M. Pei's glass pyramid. Get your hands on a museum map (there's an excellent interactive map on the museum's website), choose your personal "must-sees," and plan ahead. There's no way to see it all, and you'll be an instant candidate for early retirement if you try. Mercifully, the museum is well organized and has been very reasonably arranged into color-coded sections. If you're really in a rush, or you just want to get an overall sense of the place, you can take the introductory guided tour in

The Museum as Work of Art

Few buildings have had as turbulent a history as the one that houses the Louvre museum. "Born" in the 12th century as a gloomy fortress on the outskirts of the city, it was reborn during the Renaissance when a succession of monarchs turned it into a fabulous pleasure palace, each adding a new element over several centuries. That came to an end when Louis XIV decided to move the court to Versailles, ending all work on the Louvre and leaving the buildings of the Cour Carrée roofless and exposed to the elements. They stayed that way for over a century; in the 18th century squatters moved in, building fires in the middle of galleries to stay warm and draping the walls with drying laundry. In 1793, in the aftermath of the Revolution (which did away with the monarchy altogether . . . at least temporarily), the Louvre became one of the world's first public museums. When the royals came back to power, they didn't move back in—but they did finally finish building the palace, and in 1857, Napoleon III oversaw the finishing touches to the enormous central courtyard. Not long after, in 1871, the nearby and connected Tuileries palace burned down—the surviving Pavilion de Flore and the Pavilion de Marsan are the only remnants of that building. The finance ministry moved into what's now the Richelieu wing (it became part of the museum in 1993), and slowly the nascent museum filled the endless rooms of this mighty structure.

English (1½ hr.; 11am, 2, and 3:45pm daily; 5€). You won't see as much as you would on your own, but at least you'll know what you are seeing.

The museum's three biggest stars are all located in the Denon wing. La Joconde, otherwise known as the *Mona Lisa* (see the "Men Have Named You . . ." box, below), now has an entire wall to herself, making it easier to contemplate her enigmatic smile. Another inscrutable female in this wing is the *Venus de Milo,* who was found on a Greek Island in 1820. Possibly the most photographed woman in the world, this armless marble goddess gives no hint of the original position of her limbs or her exact identity. The *Winged Victory of Samothrace,* another magnificent Greek sculpture, is the easiest to locate. Standing at the top of a majestic flight of stairs, her powerful body pushing forward as if about to take flight, it's easy to imagine this headless deity in her original location: overlooking the Sanctuary of the Great Gods on the island of Samothrace.

Because a complete listing of the Louvre's highlights would fill a book, below is a decidedly biased selection of favorite areas:

13th- to 18th-century Italian Painting   The immense Italian collection is conveniently arranged in chronological order so that you walk from the iconic, two-dimensional art of the early Renaissance into the ever increasing realism and perspective of later artists. A few standouts include the delicate fresco by Botticelli *Venus and the Three Graces Presenting Gifts to a Young Woman,* Veronese's enormous

The Louvre

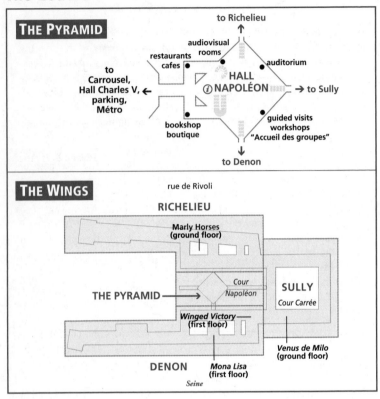

Wedding Feast at Cana, and of course, the *Mona Lisa.* The Divine Miss M is in a room packed with wonders, including several Titians and Tintorettos. Once you've digested this rich meal, stroll down the endless Grande Galerie, past more da Vincis (*Saint John the Baptist, The Virgin of the Rock*), as well as works by Raphael, Caravaggio, and Gentileschi.

Greek & Roman Sculpture   While the *Winged Victory of Samothrace* and the Venus de Milo are not to be missed, the Salle des Caryatides (the room itself is a work of art) boasts marble masterworks like *Artemis* hunting with her stag and the troubling *Sleeping Hermaphrodite,* an alluring female figure from behind—and something entirely different from the front.

The Galerie d'Apollon   Recently restored, this gold-encrusted room is an excellent example of the excesses of 17th-century French royalty. Commissioned by Louis XIV, aka "The Sun King," every inch of this gallery is covered with gilt stucco sculptures and flamboyant murals invoking the journey of the Roman sun god Apollo (ceiling paintings are by Charles Le Brun). The main draw here is the collection of crown jewels. Amongst necklaces bedecked with quarter-sized sapphires and tiaras

Scaling the Pyramid & Nocturnes

There are several ways to avoid the lines that often snake around the glass pyramid that serves as the primary entrance to the Louvre:

- **Enter** directly from the Palais Royal–Musée du Louvre Métro stop. If you are above ground, there are two staircases on either side of the Arc du Carrousel that lead downstairs to the ticketing area.
- The access at 99 rue du **Rivoli.**
- The entrance at Porte des Lions (in the Denon Wing), which includes elevators for wheelchairs and strollers.

The addition of **ticketing machines** (cash only) and **advanced ticket sales** online or by phone at **Fnac** (☎ 08 92 68 36 22; www.fnac.com; in person in any Virgin Megastore; and on the Louvre website, www.louvre.fr) has diminished the lines at the ticket windows, and even at the Pyramid entrance. So you might end up passing easily through I.M. Pei's intriguing geometry after all.

Even better, you might consider an evening visit to the Louvre on a Wednesday or Friday. Not only are tickets 2€ to 3€ cheaper after 6pm, but the tour buses have all left and the crowds thin dramatically. On Friday nights, the museum is free if you are under 26 and there are a number of thematic tours and workshops (4.50€–8.50€; see website or ask for a brochure; all activities in French only) for young people. You'll also get to see one of most magical sights in Paris when you leave the building: the Louvre lit at night. Be sure to pass through the Cour Carrée—the eerie, yet elegant lighting makes you half expect to see gilded carriages with ethereal footmen passing under the archways.

dripping with diamonds and rubies are the jewel-studded crown of Louis XV and The Regent, a 140-carat diamond that he used to decorate his hat.

The Egyptians The largest collection outside of Cairo, thanks in large part to Jean-François Champollion, the 19th-century French scientist and scholar who first decoded Egyptian hieroglyphs. Sculptures, figurines, papyrus documents, steles, musical instruments, and of course, mummies, fill numerous rooms in the Sully wing, including the colossal statue of Ramses II, and the strangely moving Seated Scribe. He gazes intently out of intricately crafted inlaid eyes: A combination of copper, magnesite, and polished rock crystal create a startlingly lifelike stare.

Large-Format French Paintings There's an entire floor full of French paintings in the Sully wing, but these three rooms (rooms 75, 76, and 77) pack the biggest punch. Enormous floor to ceiling (and these are high ceilings) paintings of monumental moments in history cover the walls. The overcrowded and legendary *Coronation of Napoléon* by Jacques-Louis David depicts the newly minted Emperor crowning Josephine, while the disconcerted pope and a host of notables

Men Have Named You . . .

Everything about the Mona Lisa is mysterious—the identity of the sitter, how long it took to paint, and how it got into the French royal collection, among other things. Most scholars agree that it is a portrait of Lisa Gheradini, the wife of one Francesco del Giocondo, but Ms. Lisa could also be Isabella of Aragon (as suggested by the patterning of her dress) or simply be an embodiment of beauty and happiness (hence the smile), as suggested by the Italian word, *gioconda.*

Recently, researchers did a three-dimensional scan of the painting, and discovered evidence of a fine, translucent veil around the subject's shoulders, a garment women in Renaissance Italy wore when they were expecting, provoking an onslaught of speculation that her secret smile had to do with her being pregnant.

What's certain is that the painting created a sensation. The overall harmony of the composition, the use of a distant landscape in the background, the lifelike quality of the subject (enhanced by Leonardo's use of *sfumato,* a technique that replaces distinct outlines with blurred transitions from light to dark) had a huge impact on early-16th-century Florentine art. As Giorgio Vasari, a Renaissance painter and biographer lamented, "it may be said that it was painted in such a manner as to make every valiant craftsman, be he who he may, tremble and lose heart."

The painting's fascinating history doesn't stop there. One morning in 1911, a Parisian artist name Louis Béroud came in to the museum to sketch a copy of the famous portrait. What he found was a bare spot with four hooks in the wall where the Mona Lisa usually hung. When he alerted the guard, the latter replied that it was probably just upstairs being photographed and took no further action. After a few hours, Béroud finally bribed the guard to go up to the photo studio to find out what happened. It wasn't until the guard found out that the painting wasn't upstairs that anyone realized it had been stolen. The thief had entered the museum posing as a visitor, hid in the building overnight, and in the morning

look on. On the facing wall, *Madame Récamier* (also by David), one of Napoleon's loudest critics, reclines fetchingly on a divan. Farther on are several tumultuous canvases by Eugène Delacroix, including *Liberty Guiding the People,* which might just be the ultimate expression of French patriotism. In the painting, which evokes the events of the revolution of 1830, Liberty—breast exposed, a rifle in one hand, the French flag in the other—leads the crowd over a sea of dead bodies. High ideals and gore sort of sums up the French revolutionary spirit.

NEXT STOP—IMPRESSIONISM　What better setting for a world-class museum of 19th-century art than a beautiful example of Belle Epoque architecture? The magnificent Gare d'Orsay train station, built to coincide with the 1900 disguised himself as a workman and made off with the painting while the guard went out to smoke a cigarette. Needless to say, panic ensued. Not only was there a nationwide investigation, but the borders were sealed. What the police didn't realize is that the painting was at first hidden only a mile from the Louvre. Conspiracy theories spread through the newspapers—some thought it was merely a publicity stunt on the part of the museum. There was a lot of criticism about the Louvre's lax security, in particular from poet Apollinaire. He soon found himself arrested as a suspect, and his friend Pablo Picasso was also brought in for questioning after they were caught in possession of some other art objects of dubious origins. After they both broke down in tears before the bench, the judge let them go with a slap on the wrist.

After 2 years of false leads and bungled investigations, the Mona Lisa was finally found when the thief, Vincenzo Perugia, tried to sell it to an art dealer in Florence. What was the motive for the crime? It seems that Perugia, an Italian patriot who had once worked at the museum, simply felt that the Mona Lisa belonged in her country of birth, Italy. During his trial, Perugia claimed to have been bewitched by the painting—and indeed, who hasn't been?

The life of a superstar certainly isn't easy. With millions of admirers around the world (and even more since the publication of *The Da Vinci Code*), at least a couple are bound to have a few screws loose. Once she was back at the museum (under increased security, of course), things calmed down until 1956, when a deranged visitor threw acid on the painting, severely damaging its lower half (restoration would take several years). A few months later, someone threw a rock at her. The painting is now covered with bullet-proof glass, and a full time guard stands at the ready. So try to be patient with the lines and the velvet ropes—if the Mona Lisa gets the kind of security usually reserved for rock stars or heads of state, she has certainly earned it.

World's Fair, has been brilliantly transformed into the **Musée d'Orsay** ✮✮✮ (62 rue de Lille, 7th arrond.; ☎ 01 40 49 48 14; www.musee-orsay.fr; 8€ adults, 5.50€ 18–30, free under 18, combination ticket with Musée Rodin 12€; Tues–Wed, Fri–Sun 9:30am–6pm; Thurs 9:30am–9:45pm; Métro: Solférino, RER: Musée d'Orsay), a true pleasure to visit. The huge, airy central hall lets in lots of natural light, which has been artfully combined with artificial lighting to illuminate a collection of treasures that were once scattered among the Louvre, the Jeu de Paume, and the Musée National d'Art Moderne. The collection spans the years 1848 to 1914, a period that saw the birth of many artistic movements, such as the Barbizon School and Symbolism, but today it is best known for the emergence of

Impressionism. Seeing them all together in one place makes it instantly obvious what a fertile time this was. All the superstars of the epoch are here, including Monet, Manet, Degas, and Renoir, not to mention Cézanne, and Van Gogh.

Paintings are organized both chronologically and according to artistic trends. The ground floor is devoted to the era leading up to 1870, when artists like Ingres, Delacroix, and Millet set the stage for the first steps of Impressionism, like Edouard Manet's masterpiece, *Le Déjeuner sur l'Herbe*. Though Manet's composition of bathers and friends picnicking on the grass draws freely from those of Italian Renaissance masters, the painting shocked its 19th-century audience, which was horrified to see a naked lady lunching with two fully clothed men. Manet got into trouble again with his magnificent *Olympia*, a seductive odalisque stretched out on a divan. There was nothing new about the subject; viewers were rattled by the unapologetic look in her eye—this is not an idealized nude, but a real woman, and a tough cookie, to boot.

The upper floors get into the major Impressionist period. There are so many highlights here that you might feel the need to put on sunglasses. A few standouts:

◆ Renoir's *Dance at Le Moulin de la Galette, Montmartre*—the dappled light and the movement of the crowd in this joyous painting are such that you wonder if it's not going to suddenly waltz out of its frame. The blurred brushstrokes that created this effect rankled contemporary critics.

◆ Monet's *La Gare St-Lazare*—here is another train station when steam engines were still pulling in on a regular basis. The metallic roof of the station frames an almost abstract mix of clouds and smoke; rather than a description of machines and mechanics, this painting is a modern study of light and color.

◆ Van Gogh's *Church at Auvers-sur-Oise*—after spending time in an asylum in Provence, the artist moved to this small town north of Paris, where he painted this ominous vision of the town church—one of some 70 paintings he produced in the 2 months leading up to his suicide.

There are also sculptures and decorative arts on display here, including a remarkable collection of Art Nouveau furniture and objects. Photo fans will appreciate the fine examples of early photography, including Félix Nadar's portrait of Charles Baudelaire; there are also some interesting works by nonphotographers like Edward Dégas and Emile Zola.

Touring the Station

Confronted with so many famous paintings, even the most stalwart museum-goer is likely to feel a little overwhelmed. Fortunately, there are a variety of **guided tours** (7.50€ adults, 5.70€ 13–17) in English. For a good overview, try "The Masterpieces of the Musée d'Orsay", and for a closer look at the Impressionists pick "In-Depth Tours: 19th Century Art" (tours usually last 1½ hr.; pick up a brochure at the entrance or scan the website for program and hours). If you want to go it on your own, but with a bit of help, multilingual **audioguides** rent for 5€.

TWELVE RUNNERS-UP TO THE ICONIC SIGHTS

The following 12 museums and sights might not be considered iconic, but they could make just as big an impact on your visit as the 10 listed above. If you have the time, try to supplement the "iconic" sights with these "runners-up."

A LEGEND IN SCULPTURE   There are not many museums that draw visitors who never even go inside. The grounds of the **Musée Rodin** ✸✸✸ (79 rue de Varenne, 7th arrond.; ☎ 01 44 18 61 10; www.musee-rodin.fr; 6€ adults, 4€ students over 18, free under 18, families (2 adults and 2 children) 10€; park only: 1€; audioguides 4€; museum: Oct–Mar Tues–Sun 9:30am–4:45pm; Apr–Sept Tues–Sun 9:30am–5:45pm; park: Oct–Mar Tues–Sun 9:30am–5pm; Apr–Sept Tues–Sun 9:30am–6:45pm; Métro: Varenne, RER: Invalides) are so lovely that many are willing to pay 1€ just to stroll around. Behind the Hôtel Biron, which houses the museum, is a formal garden with benches, fountains and even a little cafe (no picnics allowed, unfortunately). Of course, it would be foolish not to go inside and drink in the some of the 6,600 sculptures of this excellent collection (don't worry, not all are on display), but it would be equally silly not to take the time to admire the large bronzes in the garden, which include some of Rodin's most famous works. Take for example, *The Thinker*. Erected in front of the Panthéon in 1906 during an intense political crisis, Rodin's first public sculpture soon became a Socialist symbol and was quickly transferred to the Hôtel Biron by the authorities, under the pretense that it blocked pedestrian traffic. Other important sculptures in the garden include the *Burghers of Calais, Balzac,* and the *Gates of Hell,* a monumental composition that the sculptor worked on throughout his career.

Indoors, marble compositions prevail, although there are also works in terracotta, plaster, and bronze, as well as sketches and paintings on display. The most famous of the marble works is *The Kiss,* which was originally meant to appear in the *Gates of Hell.* In time, Rodin decided that the lovers were too happy for this grim composition, and he explored it as an independent work. The sculpture was inspired by the tragic story of Paolo and Francesca, in which a young woman falls in love with her husband's brother. Upon their first kiss, the husband discovers them and stabs them both. As usual with Rodin's works, the critics were shocked by the couple's overt sensuality, but not as shocked as they were by the large, impressionistic rendition of *Balzac,* exhibited at the same salon, which critic Georges Rodenbach described as "less a statue than a strange monolith, a thousand-year-old menhir." There are hundreds of works here, many of them legendary, so don't be surprised if after a while your vision starts to blur. That'll be your cue to head outside and enjoy the garden.

AN ART-FILLED MANSION   The love-child of a couple of passionate art collectors, the **Musée Jacquemart-André** ✸✸✸ (158 blvd. Haussmann, 8th arrond.; ☎ 01 45 62 11 59; www.musee-jacquemart-andre.com; 10€ adults, 7.30€ students under 26 and children 7–17, free under 7; 10am–6pm; Métro: Miromesnil) is a gem—a 19th-century mansion filled with fine art and decorative objects. One of the best things about this museum is that it is of a blissfully reasonable size—

The Man of Stone

Rodin's life was anything but conventional. Born in 1840, Auguste Rodin was 17 when he applied for admission to the renown Ecole des Beaux Arts; he was rejected three times (which should comfort anyone who's ever applied to art school!). To make a living, he did decorative stonework and eventually went to study and collaborate with sculptor Carrier-Belleuse. About this time he met Rose Beuret, who became a life-long companion and a model for many of his works. Together they took a trip to Italy, which inspired his *The Age of Bronze,* which caused a scandal because of the naked figure's realism—the first of many scandals sparked by Rodin's originality, sensuality, and stubborn disregard for what other people thought. These qualities came up in his personal life: At age 43, he started a relationship with sculptor Camille Claudel, who at the time was only 19 years old. The long-suffering Rose dutifully ignored their affair (which lasted over a decade), during which Rodin refused to break with his devoted helpmate. In the end, Rose's staying power paid off. Claudel, however, did not fare so well—she slowly went insane after the breakup (it's all chronicled in the film *Camille Claudel*). Despite his unconventional ways, his talent was such that it couldn't go unrecognized—over the years he collected as many honors as criticisms, and towards the end of his life he was named a grand officer of the Legion of Honor. The year of his death, at 77 years old, he finally married Rose Beuret. She died a month later, and he not long after.

you can see a wide range of beautiful things without wearing yourself to a frazzle in about an hour and a half.

The house itself is a work of art: At its inauguration in 1875, the marble Winter Garden with its spectacular double staircase was the talk of the town. Nélie Jacquemart and Edouard André devoted their lives to filling this splendid dwelling with primarily 18th-century French art and furniture. The paintings of Fragonard, Boucher, and Chardin are in evidence, as is an impressive assortment of Louis XV- and Louis XVI-era decorative objects. There are many superb portraits, including that of an officious-looking *Comte Français de Nantes* by David. To honor the artists that influenced these French painters, the couple also amassed a number of 17th-century Dutch paintings, including Rembrandt's *Pilgrims at Emmaus*. The play of light in this enigmatic tableau is incredibly evocative; Christ is shown only in silhouette, while his dining companion, at the center of the composition, provides the "reaction shot." Is he afraid? Has he recognized his tablemate? Rembrandt lets the viewer decide.

The peripatetic couple, who traveled frequently in search of new items for their collection, also took an interest in Renaissance Italian art; though at the time considered "primitive" by most art fans, that didn't stop Jacquemart and André from snapping up Quattrocento masterpieces like Botticelli's *Virgin and Child*.

Personally, I think the Italian collection (on the second floor) is the most awe-inspiring part of the museum—not only are there works by masters like Bellini, Uccello, and Mantegna, but they are presented in an intimate space with excellent lighting. You feel like you are walking into a felt-lined jewel-box. Leave time to eat a light lunch or have tea in the lovely restaurant here—see box, "Dining Out on Art," p. 102), and don't neglect to pick up a **free audioguide** when you enter the museum—you'll find it helpful in a home packed with this much history.

A ROYAL RETREAT   Possibly the prettiest square in the city, the **place des Vosges** ★★★ (4th arrond.; Métro: St-Paul or Bastille) combines elegance, greenery, and quiet. Nowhere in Paris will you find such a unity of Renaissance-style architecture; the entire square is bordered by 17th-century brick town houses, each conforming to rules set down by Henri IV himself, under which runs arched arcades. In the center is a garden with a geometric arrangement of lush lawns, fountains, and trees. At the epicenter is a huge equestrian statue of Louis XIII, during whose reign (1610–1643) the square enjoyed a golden age of festivals and tournaments. But it was a tournament in a previous century that proved pivotal to the creation of this square. In the 16th century, a royal palace called the Hôtel des Tournelles stood on this site. In 1559, an organized combat was held there, during which the current monarch, feisty Henri II, defeated several opponents. Feeling pleased with himself, he decided to fight Montgomery, the captain of his guard. A badly aimed lance resulted in Henri's untimely death; his wife, Catherine de Medicis, was so distraught she decided to have the palace demolished. His descendant, Henri IV, took advantage of the free space to construct a royal square. Over the centuries, a number of celebrities lived in the 36 houses, including Mme de Sévigny and Victor Hugo (whose house is now a museum, the Maison de Victor Hugo; see p. 169). By the early 20th century, the square had fallen into disrepair, as had most of the Marais, and like the rest of the neighborhood, has had a splendid rebirth. Now the homes are for the rich, as are many of the chic boutiques under the arcades, but the park, the fountains, and the children's playground are for everyone.

AGELESS ART IN MODERN WRAPPINGS   In the shadow of the Eiffel Tower, a new museum has emerged that will forever change the architectural landscape of this rigidly elegant neighborhood. The enormous central structure of the new **Musée du Quai Branly** ★★★ (37 quai Branly, 7th arrond.; ☎ 01 56 61 70 00; www.quaibranly.fr; 8.50€ adults, 6€ students, free under 18; combined ticket including permanent and temporary exhibits: 13€ adults, 9.50€ students; Tues–Wed and Sun 11am–7pm, Thurs–Sat 11am–9pm; Métro: Alma-Marceau or Bir Hakeim, RER: Pont d'Alma), floats on a series of pillars, under which lays a lush garden, which is separated from the noisy boulevard out front by a huge glass wall. Looking up from the garden level, the museum looks a little like the hull of a container ship, with its rust colored body and oddly stacked "boxes" sticking out from its sides. However you feel about the outside, you cannot help but be impressed by the inside: a vast space filled with exquisite examples of the traditional arts of **Africa, the Pacific Islands, Asia, and the Americas.** Designed by veteran museum-maker Jean Nouvel (Fondation Cartier, Institute du Monde Arabe), this intriguing space makes an ideal showcase for a category of artwork that has too often been relegated to the sidelines of the museum world.

Quai Branly assembles 5 centuries' worth of collecting, including many objects from the Musée de l'Homme and the now-defunct Musée des Arts d'Afrique et d'Océanie. Delicately carved head rests from Papua New Guinea in the form of birds and crocodiles vie for your attention with intricately woven and painted masks from Melanesia. You can not only look at, but listen to giant wooden flutes from Papua New Guinea, which are displayed with an on-going recording. A selection of "magic stones" from the island nation of Vanuatu includes smooth abstract busts reminiscent of Brancusi sculptures. Farther on, a fascinating collection of Australian aboriginal paintings segues into the Asian art section and the journey continues into Africa, starting with embroidered silks from Morocco and heading south through magnificent geometric marriage cloths from Mali and wooden masks from the Ivory Coast. The Americas collection includes rare Nazca pottery and Inca textiles, as well as an intriguing assortment of North American works, like Haitian voodoo objects, Sioux beaded tunics, and a huge totem pole from British Columbia. Though some documentation is translated in English, **audioguides** (5€ for one, 7€ for two) are a big help for non-French speakers.

PICASSO—ALL HIS PERIODS   When Picasso died in 1973, his heirs were allowed to donate the artist's works in exchange for the taxes owed on his estate. The result was the creation of the **Musée National Picasso Paris** ✮✮ (Hôtel Salé, 5 rue de Thorigny, 3rd arrond.; ☎ 01 42 71 25 21; www.musee-picasso.fr; 6.50€ adults, 4.50€ 18–25, free under 18; Apr–Sept Wed–Mon 9:30am–6pm, Oct–Mar Wed–Mon 9:30am–5:30pm; Métro: St-Paul or St-Sébastien Froissart), an immense cache of 203 paintings, 158 sculptures, 29 bas reliefs, 88 ceramics, 1,500 drawings and collages, and 1,600 engravings, not to mention some 50 paintings from Picasso's personal collection (Braque, Matisse, Cézanne, Degas, and others) left by his wife after her death in 1990. The collection is housed in a magnificent 17th-century mansion called the Hôtel Salé, which owes its name (the Salty Mansion) to the fact that it was built by a seigneur who was the salt tax collector.

With so much in the inventory, it isn't surprising that the collection is exhibited in rotation; chances are, each time you visit Paris you'll see something new here. Works are displayed chronologically, starting with the artist's early years and his "Blue Period," which includes a rather melancholy *Self-Portrait* painted at 20 years old, when Picasso was recovering from the shock of his friend and fellow painter Casagemas's suicide. His cubist phase is documented with paintings like *Homme à la Guitare,* a shimmering study of light and dark with just the barest hints of the actual subject matter (a man with his guitar). Further on, the artist returns to representative painting and more classic themes, like bathers and circus figures, including a sweet portrait of his son Paul *(Paul en Arlequin)* dressed up like Harlequin. The visit continues to wind through Picasso's life and obsessions (bullfights, war, women), passing through a series of large rooms and sculpture atriums and ending in a tranquil garden. *Note:* At press time, the museum was planning on closing for renovations sometime after mid-2009.

A SENSE OF DECORUM   Can history be told through furniture? If the **Musée des Arts Décoratifs** ✮✮✮ (107 rue de Rivoli, 1st arrond.; ☎ 01 44 55 57 50; www.lesartsdecoratifs.fr; 8€ adults, 6.50€ 18–25, free under 18; combined ticket with Musée Nissim de Camondo: 11€ adults, 8€ 18–25, free under

18; Tues–Wed, Fri 11am–6pm, Thurs 11am–9pm, Sat–Sun 10am–6pm; Métro: Palais Royal–Musée du Louvre) is any indication, the answer is a wholehearted "yes." Possessing some 150,000 items in its rich collection, this fascinating museum offers a spectrum of objects that range from medieval traveling trunks to Philippe Starck stools. The collection is organized in more or less chronological order and, more importantly, by theme. So once you've passed into the Renaissance, for example, you will find displays of paintings from the First Italian Renaissance, cases of delicate Venetian glassware, and a separate room filled with exquisite 15th-century intarsia, "paintings" made out of intricately inlaid wood that include landscapes, still lives, and even portraits. Another standout in this section is a 15th-century bedroom that was largely lifted from a castle in central France. The walls are hung with tapestries showing scenes of courtly love, the four-poster bed is covered in plush green velvet, and the furniture—yes, despite all the empty castles you see today, they did once have furniture—is delicately carved with Gothic motifs.

As you continue through time, you'll learn the difference between *marqueterie* and *parqueterie,* gape at huge 17th-century German armoires carved with architectural elements so they resemble buildings, and marvel at a tiny room covered in gilded woodwork from an 18th-century mansion in Avignon. The 18th-century rooms are organized according to the various styles and fashions that blew through that century, like rococo, neo-classicism, and *chinoiserie.* While the objects themselves are beautiful, the link between style and historic context is illuminating; the endless curlicues of the rococo style, which perfectly reflected the excesses of Louis XV's court, for example, gives way to more puritanical neo-classicism, which developed during the Enlightenment, when unrestrained frivolity began to look degenerate.

Even if you can't read the French descriptions, you can still share in the wealth here: an infamous 19th-century courtesan's bedroom, which apparently served as a model for a setting in Zola's *Nana,* and a stunning Art Nouveau dining room are just a few of the gems that you'll drool over here. The collection weakens after 1930; it's hard to tell if this is due to a lack of imagination on the part of the museum or on the part of 20th-century designers. The chronological sequence can be hard to follow; note that the visit starts on the third floor.

If you still have the strength, on the first floor there is a gallery with rotating themed exhibits, as well as a Toy Gallery with expos on novel playthings. There are also two other museums in the building: the **Musée de la Publicité** (same hours as above, entry included in price of ticket to Arts Décoratifs), which takes on the history of advertising, and the **Musée de la Mode et du Textile** (ditto), which hosts temporary exhibits on the many facets of clothing, including the works of famous couture houses like Christian Lacroix and Dior.

HAIL TO THE SUN KING   In 1686, Louis XIV decided the time had come to design a magnificent square, at the center of which would stand a statue of His Royal Highness. Though the statue is long gone, the **place Vendôme** ✮✮✮ (rue de Castiglione, 1st arrond.; Métro: Tuileries or Concorde) is still one of the classiest squares in the city. It doesn't get much more elegant than this octagonal ensemble of 17th-century buildings—in fact, the original Ritz Hôtel, as well as the world's most glitzy jewelry makers (Cartier, Van Cleef and Arpels, and

Boucheron, for example) can all be found here. The work of Jules Hardouin-Mansart, this opulent enclosure was designed to function as a sort of giant ballroom; indeed, glamorous balls were held here during its early years. The famous statue, Giradon's representation of Louis in Roman garb on horseback, reigned over the square up until the Revolution, when it was sent off to the foundry to be melted down for scrap. When Napoleon took over, he decided it was the perfect place for a huge Roman-style column honoring his glorious army (yes, once again), this time documenting its victory at Austerlitz. A long spiral of bas-reliefs recounting the campaign of 1805, march up the **Colonne de la Grande Armée** which was crowned by a statue of the Emperor himself. The original statue did not survive the regime; a few decades later, Napoleon III replaced it with the existing copy. The fabulous apartments in the square have been inhabited by a wide spectrum of the rich and famous: Chopin died in number 12 in 1849.

MODERN MASTERS & OTHER MADNESS   The bizarre architecture of the **Centre Pompidou** ★★ (Place George Pompidou, 4th arrond.; ☎ 01 44 78 12 33; www.centrepompidou.fr; museum and temporary exhibits: 10€ adults, 8€ 18–25, free under 18; Atelier Brancusi free admission; Wed–Mon 11am–10pm [museum until 9pm], Atelier Brancusi 2–6pm; Métro: Rambuteau, RER: Châtelet-Les Halles) provokes such strong emotions, it's easy to forget that there is something inside the building. Believe it or not, President Pompidou searched far and wide to find an architect. In 1971, an international design competition was held, attracting 681 entrants from 49 different countries, the winners being the Italo-British design team of Renzo Piano and Richard Rogers. Their concept was to put the support structure and transport systems on the outside of the building, thereby liberating space on the inside for a museum and cultural center. The result was a gridlike exoskeleton with a tubular escalator inching up one side, and huge multicolored pipes and shafts covering the other. To some, it's a milestone in contemporary architecture, to others, it's simply a horror. Either way, it's one of the most visited structures in France. Some six million people visit each year, and that's not counting the patrons of the chic restaurant Georges on the top floor.

The Pompidou is much more than an art museum. Its over 100,000 sq. m (1,076,390 sq. ft.) of floor space includes a vast reference library, a cinema, bookshops, and a music institute, as well as a performance hall and areas for educational activities (not many museums can boast as many electronic music fests or underground film series). This might be one of the reasons why the center has an entirely different feel than your standard museum. It's striking how many young people frequent the center—quite a change from the staid atmosphere at the Louvre. In addition to events inside, a nonstop circus of comics, mimes, and other performances goes on outside on the vast esplanade that slopes down towards the building.

The actual museum, the **Musée National d'Art Moderne,** is on the fourth and fifth floors. Getting there is half the fun as you glide up the exterior escalators. As the collection is in constant rotation, it's impossible to say what you are likely to see on your visit, but the emphasis is generally on works from the second half of the 20th century, with a good dose of surrealism, Dada, and other modern movements from the first half. This is not "pretty" art, but art that is designed to make you think. It might make you think about heading straight for the exit, but if nothing else, there are things here that will surprise you, and get your juices flowing. Works range from relatively tame abstracts by **Picasso** and **Kandinsky,** to **Andy Warhol**'s multiheaded portrait of Elizabeth Taylor, to a felt-wrapped piano by **Joseph Beuys.** Video-installations are often highlighted, as well as expositions of new artists. Possibly the biggest draws at the center are the **temporary exhibitions,** which can be quite wonderful. In 2008, exhibits included a Giacometti retrospective and a survey of the work of Richard Rogers + Architects, responsible for, among other things, the Pompidou Center. Just outside of the front of the center is the **Atelier Brancusi,** where the sculptor's workshop has been reconstituted in its entirety; in his will, Brancusi left the workshop's contents to the museum on the condition that every sculpture and object be displayed exactly as it was found in his studio on the day of his death.

HISTORY TOLD THROUGH ART   Paris has served as a backdrop to centuries' worth of dramatic events, from Roman takeovers to barbarian invasions, from coronations to decapitations to the birth of the modern French republic. These fascinating stories and others are told using objects, paintings, and interiors at the **Musée Carnavalet** ✸✸✸ (23 rue de Sévigné, 3rd arrond.; ☎ 01 44 59 58 58; www.carnavalet.paris.fr; free admission except temporary exhibitions; Tues–Sun 10am–6pm; Métro: St-Paul). The collection is displayed in over 140 rooms in two extraordinary 17th-century mansions—works of art in their own right. Starting with prehistory and continuing into the 20th century, the history of Paris is illustrated with items as diverse as a Neolithic terracotta female figurine, Ragunet's 18th-century depiction of the Pont-Neuf, and a detailed re-creation of Marcel Proust's bedroom.

Built in 1548 for the president of the French parliament, the main building, the Hôtel de Carnavalet, is a Renaissance mansion that had a makeover by François Mansart (of rooftop fame) in 1660. Finding it much to her liking, the prodigious letter-writer and woman of the world Madame de Sévigné rented the mansion in 1677 and lived there until her death in 1696. The other half of the museum is in the adjoining Hotel Le Peletier de St-Fargeau built in 1688, for an aristocrat whose claim to fame is that he voted for the execution of Louis XVI and was subsequently assassinated by a royalist. Little of the original interior decoration remains in either building, but this is made up for by the importation of entire rooms, including wall paneling and furniture, from various private mansions of different epochs. Highlights include the Louis XV–style **Salon des Philosophes,** with its beautiful *boiseries* (carved wood paneling) and historical objects like the inkwell of Jean-Jacques Rousseau; and the Louis XVI–era **Salon of Graveur Demarteau,** painted by the likes of Boucher, Fragonard and Jean-Baptiste Huet to give the impression of stepping into an idyllic pastoral scene.

The luxury and expense of the salons of the aristocracy make a fitting prelude to the excellent section on the French Revolution. Along with portraits of key figures like Marat, Danton, and even Dr. Guillotin (who didn't actually invent the dastardly execution machine, but did advocate its use as a means of capital punishment), are several fascinating mementos, such as the keys to the Bastille prison and a copy of the Declaration of the Rights of Man that once hung behind the president of the Convention. Particularly moving are the personal objects of the royal family from their last days in prison—a lock of Marie Antoinette's hair,

Long Live the Lizard King

Though the grave itself is unexceptional, the tomb of '60s rock star **Jim Morrison** is possibly the most visited, or at least the most hyped, in the cemetery. For years, fans made pilgrimages, leaving behind so much graffiti, litter, and mind-altering substances that families of those buried nearby began to complain, and the tomb was surrounded by a fence. More recently, a cleaning company has been hired to periodically clean the grave, and a security guard posted to ward off the overenthusiastic. But nothing can dispel the enduring attraction of the Morrison legend. In 1971, battling a variety of drug, alcohol, and legal problems, the singer/musician came to Paris, ostensibly with the goal of taking a break from performing and getting his life back on track. Four months later, he was found dead in a Parisian bathtub, at age 27. Since no autopsy was performed, the exact cause of his death was never known (though there was good reason to suspect a drug overdose), which has lead to wild speculation on the part of his fans. Rumors still circulate that he was a target of the CIA, murdered by a witch, committed suicide, or that he faked his own death and is currently residing in India, Africa, or New Jersey under the name "Mr. Mojo Risin'." The inscription on his grave, in ancient Greek, has been imaginatively interpreted by some as meaning "burnt by his demons," but the phrase, selected by his family, actually translates as "True to His Own Spirit." Can't argue with that.

Louis XVI's razor and water glass, the young Dauphin's writing exercises—reminders that these iconic figures were in fact made of flesh and blood.

Although all the labels and descriptions are in French, you can purchase an English-language guidebook of the museum in the bookstore; even without translations, most of the art and objects speak for themselves.

DEATH BECOMES THEM   Cemeteries are not usually on anyone's list of top tourist attractions, but **Cimetière Père Lachaise** ✪✪✪ (blvd. de Ménilmontant, 20th arrond.; ☎ 01 55 25 82 10; www.pere-lachaise.com; free admission; mid-Mar to Oct Mon–Fri 8am–6pm, Sat 8:30am–6pm, Sun 9am–6pm; Nov to mid-Mar Mon–Fri 8am–5:30pm, Sat 8:30am–5:30pm, Sun 9am–5:30pm; Métro: Père Lachaise or Philippe Auguste) is no ordinary cemetery. Romantic and rambling as a 19th-century English garden, this hillside resting-place is wonderfully green, with huge leafy trees and narrow paths winding around the graves, which just about every French literary or artistic giant you can imagine, plus several international stars. Proust, Apollonaire, Collette, Delacroix, Seurat, Modigliani, Bizet, Rossini, are all here, as well as Sarah Bernhardt, Isadora Duncan, Simone Signoret and Yves Montand (buried side by side, of course). Though some are simple tombstones, many are miniature architectural marvels, embellished with

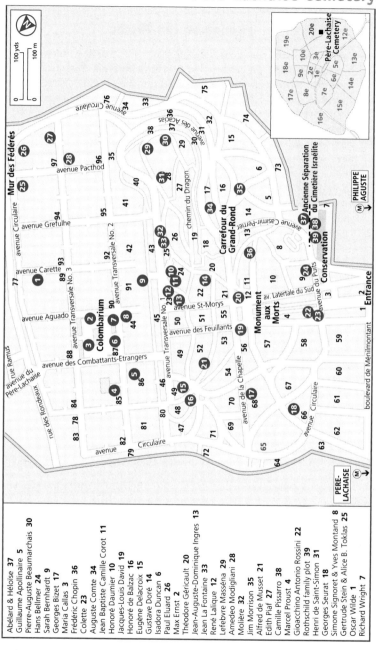

Abélard & Héloïse **37**
Guillaume Apollinaire **5**
Pierre-Auguste Beaumarchais **30**
Hans Bellmer **24**
Sarah Bernhardt **9**
Georges Bizet **17**
Maria Callas **3**
Frédéric Chopin **36**
Colette **23**
Auguste Comte **34**
Jean Baptiste Camille Corot **11**
Honoré Daumier **10**
Jacques-Louis David **19**
Honoré de Balzac **16**
Eugène Delacroix **15**
Gustave Doré **14**
Isadora Duncan **6**
Paul Eluard **26**
Max Ernst **2**
Théodore Géricault **20**
Jean-Auguste-Dominique Ingres **13**
Jean La Fontaine **33**
René Lalique **12**
Lefebvre Masséna **29**
Amedeo Modigliani **28**
Molière **32**
Jim Morrison **35**
Alfred de Musset **21**
Edith Piaf **27**
Camille Pissarro **38**
Marcel Proust **4**
Gioacchino Antonio Rossini **22**
Rothschild family plot **39**
Henri de Saint-Simon **31**
Georges Seurat **18**
Simone Signoret & Yves Montand **8**
Gertrude Stein & Alice B. Toklas **25**
Oscar Wilde **1**
Richard Wright **7**

153

Passing on the Passes

During your stay, or perhaps before, you will doubtless come across brochures touting the wonders of the **Paris Museum Pass** (www.paris museumpass.fr), which offers direct access to more than 60 museums and monuments in Paris and the surrounding region. You can buy a pass that is good for 2, 4, or 6 consecutive days, for 30€, 45€, or 60€, respectively. The pass can be bought in advance; the meter starts running the first day you decide to use the pass, which allows you to skip the long lines at the ticket counter.

But before you rush to pull out your wallet, do some quick calculations to see if the pass will really be worth your while. Yes, you will have free entry to 60 top attractions (permanent exhibits only), but how many of those are you going to see in 2 days? For example, if you are going to the Louvre on one day (9€) and the Musée Rodin (6€) and the Arc de Triomphe (8€) the next, that still doesn't add up to the 30€ you paid for the pass. On the other hand, if you are going to the Musée Rodin, the Conciergerie (6.50€) and the Arc de Triomphe on one day (total 21€) and Versailles (up to 20€ to see the entire chateau) the next, you'd be saving a fair amount of money (about 10€). Of course, you'd also be exhausted, but that's another issue.

Since I subscribe to the one-or-two-museums-per-day philosophy, I personally don't see the value here, but for those who want to cram in all they can it's an interesting option. If you do decide to buy a pass, make sure your days don't fall on a holiday or a Sunday or Monday, when many museums are closed. Passes are sold at any participating museum or monument, any branch of the Paris Tourist Office, and any Fnac store.

exquisite marble and stone figures, or even phone-booth-size chapels, complete with stain glass windows. Some of the standouts include:

Héloïse and Abélard   These two legendary lovers actually existed, and their 12th-century remains were brought here in 1817, when the city built them this monument which is covered by an openwork chapel taken from an abbey in southwestern France.

Molière and La Fontaine   Though there was no romantic link, the celebrated playwright and noted fablewriter were also brought here in 1817 and placed in nearby sarcophagi, both of which stand appropriately high on pillars. If the authenticity of the remains is in doubt, they still make a fitting memorial to these two brilliant talents.

Oscar Wilde   Usually covered with lipstick kisses, this huge stone monument is topped with a winged figure that resembles an Aztec deity. An elegant homage to this brilliant writer, who died a pauper in Paris in 1900.

To find your way around, pick up a free map at the main entrance on boulevard de Ménilmontant; there is also a good interactive map on the website. The city sponsors many **guided tours,** and in July and August, you can take one in English (☎ 01 40 71 75 60; 6€ adult, 3€ student; Sat at 3pm).

BONAPARTE'S BONES   Military history rules at the appropriately grandiose **Les Invalides** ✦✦ (place des Invalides, 7th arrond.; ☎ 01 44 42 38 77; www.invalides.org; 8€ adults, 6€ students under 26, free under 18; tickets include entry to the museum, the church, and Napoleon's Tomb; Oct–Mar Wed–Mon 10am–5pm, Tues 10am–9pm; Apr–Sept Wed–Mon 10am–6pm, Tues 10am–9pm; June 15–Sept 15 Napoleon's tomb open until 7pm, Oct–June closed first Mon of each month; Métro: Invalides or Varenne, RER: Invalides), which houses a military museum, church, tomb, hospital, and military ministries, among other things. Over the entryway, Ludovicus Magnus is inscribed in huge letters, in homage to the builder of this vast edifice, otherwise known as Louis XIV. Determined to create a home for soldiers wounded in the line of duty, Louis ordered his Secretary of War, Louvois, to head the project, who in turn chose Libéral Bruant as architect. He designed a structure of monumental scale with formal gardens on what was then the outskirts of the city. The first war veterans arrived in 1674—between 4,000 and 5,000 soldiers would eventually move in, creating a minicity with its own governor. An on-site hospital was constructed for the severely wounded, which is still in service today.

As you cross the main gate, you'll find yourself in a huge courtyard (102×207m, 335×207 ft.), the *cour d'honneur,* which was once the site of military parades. At the far end on the second story is a statue of *The Little Corporal* (otherwise known as Napoleon I) that once stood on top of the column in place Vendôme. The surrounding buildings house military administration offices and the **Musée de l'Armée** a world-class military museum, which is undergoing extensive renovations. Several sections are closed until 2009, including everything from Louis XIV to Napoleon III, a vast chunk of French history. Fortunately, the World War I, World War II, and the excellent Arms and Armor section have reopened (the latter's a collection of 13th- to 17th-c. weaponry that will thrill anyone who ever dreamed of knights in shining armor). Just under Napoleon is the entrance to the **Eglise des Soldats,** actually the front half of the **Eglise du Dome,** which was split in two when Napoleon's tomb was installed under the dome. The "Soldier's Church" is lovely and light-filled, decorated with magnificent chandeliers and a collection of flags of defeated enemies.

On the other side of the glass partition rests the Little Corporal himself. The **Tomb of Napoléon** lies under one of the most splendid domes in France. Designed by Hardouin-Mansart and constructed from 1679 to 1706 the interior soars 107m (351 ft.) up to a skylight, which illuminates a brilliantly colored cupola fresco by Charles de la Fosse. Ethereal light filters down to an opening in the center of the room, where you can look down on the huge porphyry sarcophagus, which holds the emperor's remains, encased in five successive coffins (one tin, one mahogany, two lead, and one ebony). Surrounding the sarcophagus are the tombs of two of Napoleon's brothers, his son, and several French military heroes. Don't blame the over-the-top setting on Napoleon; the decision to transfer his remains to Paris was made in 1840, almost 20 years after his death. Tens of thousands crowded the streets to pay their respects as the coffin was carried under the

Arc de Triomphe and down the Champs Elysées to Les Invalides, where it waited another 20 years until the spectacular tomb was finished.

AN ASIAN TEMPLE OF ART   The airy halls of the **Musée National des Arts Asiatiques–Guimet** ✪✪ (6 place d'Iéna, 16th arrond.; ☎ 01 56 52 53 00; www.museeguimet.fr; 6.50€ adults, 4.50€ 18–25, free under 18; Wed–Mon 10am–6pm; Métro: Iéna) harbor a superb collection of Asian art, originally set up by 19th-century industrialist Emile Guimet. A passionate collector, whose dream was to create a museum of Asian, classical Greek, and Egyptian religious art, Guimet toured the world in search of remarkable pieces and found many. His museum was a huge success, and over the decades it grew and evolved into one of the largest Asian art collections in Europe. The focus is now more on culture than religion, and the art is specifically Asian—hundreds of works from Afghanistan, India, Tibet, Nepal, China, Vietnam, Korea, Japan, and other Asian nations. You could spend an entire day here, or you could pick and choose regions of interest (displays are arranged geographically); the free audioguide is a good bet for finding standouts and providing cultural context. Highlights include a marvelous Tibetan bronze sculpture *(Hevajra and Nairâtmya)* of a multiheaded god embracing a ferocious goddess with eight faces and 16 arms; a blissfully serene stone figure of a Cambodian king *(Jayavarman VII)* that makes you wonder if life was easier in the 12th century; and Chinese carved-lacquer screens in the cupola on the top floor. A few minutes' walk from the museum is the **Panthéon Bouddhique** (19 ave. d'Iéna; ☎ 01 40 73 88 00; free admission; Wed–Mon 10am–5:45pm), an old mansion where Guimet's collection of Buddhist art from China and Japan is displayed. Digest this artistic cornucopia in the adjoining Japanese garden, a peaceful haven for tired tourists and other serenity-seekers.

MUSEUMS FOR VISITORS WITH SPECIALIZED INTERESTS

The number of museums in Paris is staggering: At last count there were 130, and more open (and reopen) every year. Below are some of the choicest of the bunch (other than those listed above), separated into categories and then listed in order of importance. Entry fees are given for permanent collections only; payment by credit cards is usually only allowed for purchases above 15€ or 20€.

ARAB HISTORY & ART

In an age when Islam is all over the headlines, the **Institute du Monde Arabe** ✪ (1 rue Fossés St-Bernard; 5th arrond.; ☎ 01 40 51 38 38; www.imarabe.org; 5€ adults, 4€ under 26, free under 12; Tues–Sun 10am–6pm; Métro: Jussieu or Cardinal Lemoine) is a good place to come to find out what the word actually means. The building alone is almost worth the price of admission; designed by architect Jean Nouvel (who designed the newly opened Musée du Quai Branly, p. 147) in 1987, the south facade, which has a metallic latticework echoing traditional Arab designs, includes 30,000 light-sensitive diaphragms which regulate the penetration of light by opening and closing according to how bright it is outside. Dedicated to the art and culture of Arab and Islamic civilizations from their origins to the present day, the collection includes beautiful examples of traditional

Seeing Museums for Free

Since Mayor Bertrand Delanoë took office, with one or two exceptions, all city museums are free (permanent collections only), all the time. That includes the following cultural cornucopias:

Musée Carnavalet (p. 151)
Musée d'Art Moderne de la Ville de Paris (p. 160)
Maison de Balzac (p. 170)
Musée Bourdelle (p. 167)
Musée Cernuschi (p. 159)
Musée Cognacq-Jay (p. 162)
Petit Palais (p. 168)
Maison de Victor Hugo (p. 169)
Musée Zadkine (p. 166)

You can also get into all national museums free of charge on the first Sunday of every month. Expect even bigger crowds than usual—Sundays tend to be a busy museum day anyway, and the free entry makes them even busier. National museums include:

Musée du Louvre (p. 138)
Musée National des Arts Asiatique–Guimet (p. 156)
Musée National Eugène Delacroix (p. 166)
Musée National Gustave Moreau (p. 166)
Musée National du Moyen Age/Thermes et Hôtel de Cluny (p. 172)
Musée de l'Orangerie (p. 164)
Musée d'Orsay (p. 143)
Musée National Picasso Paris (p. 148)
Musée Rodin (p. 145)

calligraphy, miniatures, ceramics, woodwork, and carpets, as well as contemporary art from the Arab world. Though the permanent collection is interesting, the temporary exhibitions are truly excellent—recent shows examined the wonders of Phoenician civilization and Napoleon's forays in Egypt.

ARCHAEOLOGY

In 1965, archeologists were brought in when excavations for a parking lot under the Notre-Dame esplanade uncovered a vast network of ruins, now protected in the **Crypte Archéologique de Parvis de Notre-Dame** (1 place du Parvis Notre-Dame, 4th arrond.; ☎ 01 55 42 50 10; 3.30€ adults, 2.20€ seniors over 60,

1.60€ 14–26, free under 14; Tues–Sun 10am–6pm; www.carnavalet.paris.fr; Métro: Cité). A big chunk of the history of Paris is on display here, from Gallo-Roman ramparts, to Medieval streets, to the 17th-century foundations of a city orphanage. Over the centuries, new constructions were built over the old, raising the level of the Ile de la Cité some 6.9m (23 ft.). There are scale models of how Paris grew from a tribal settlement to a Roman city, as well as a few displays of ancient objects found during the dig. It's pretty dark down there, despite the clever lighting, and you'll need to use a lot of imagination to be able to re-create the buildings out of this tangle of ruins. Still, it's an impressive site.

ARCHITECTURE

Feel like seeing some of the great architectural monuments of France, but don't have the time to travel? At the **Cité de l'Architecture et du Patrimoine** ★ (1 place du Trocadéro, 16th arrond.; ☎ 01 58 51 52 00; www.citechaillot.fr; 8€ adults, 5€ 18–25, free under 18; Wed, Fri–Sun 11am–7pm, Thurs 11am–9pm; Métro: Trocadéro) you can gape in front of life-sized plaster casts of portions of magnificent cathedral facades, palace decorations and decorative sculptures all over France without ever leaving the building. Opened (or reopened) in 2007, after several years of remodeling and reconstruction, this vast institution takes up most of one of the wings of the monumental Palais de Chaillot, and includes a museum, research facility, and a top-notch school of architecture. The enormous *Galerie des Moulages*, with its vaulting skylights that bathe the displays in natural light, exhibits casts of the gems of French architecture from the 12th to the 18th centuries, which were commissioned starting in the late 19th century as a way of documenting France's architectural heritage. The project turned out to be an invaluable tool when it came to restoring the ravages of two world wars. The cast of the beautiful Queen of Sheba, for example—the original of which graced the facade of the Reims Cathedral—made it possible to create a faithful reproduction after the original was seriously damaged during the First World War. Other highlights of this section include the entryway of the 12th-century Abby of St-Pierre in Moissac, a stunning example of Roman-Languedocian art depicting the Evangels of St-John. Farther on, the Gallery of Paintings presents copies of wall paintings and frescos from various chapels, apses, castles, and crypts that are not only works of art in their own right (they were commissioned for the 1937 International Exposition, housed in this building) but are presented in architectural context; that is, a room that re-creates the original chapel, dome, crypt, and so on.

When you've had enough of the past, head for the 2nd floor, where you'll dip into the cool waters of 20th- and 21st-century architecture, primarily represented by intricate architectural models of structures as diverse as Piano and Rogers' Pompidou Center (p. 150) and Rem Koolhaus' Maison Lemoine, a three-layer home built in Floriac, France, for a paralyzed man and his family. Don't miss clambering through a reconstruction of an apartment from Le Corbusier's Cité Radieuse, a shockingly (for the time, late 1940s) modern approach to urban housing. This well-placed museum offers lots of opportunities to ogle the Eiffel Tower; be sure to take a moment to have a drink on the cafe's outdoor terrace, which offers a stellar view of the Iron Lady.

ASIAN ART

Though nowhere near as comprehensive as the Musée National des Arts Asiatiques–Guimet (p. 156), the **Musée Cernuschi** ✪ (7 ave. Vélasquez, 8th arrond.; ☎ 01 53 96 21 50; www.cernuschi.paris.fr; free admission; Tues–Sun 10am–6pm; Métro: Monceau or Villiers) offers a chance to contemplate exquisite examples of mostly **Chinese art** in a handsome mansion facing the Parc Monceau. This is a museum on a human scale; within an hour you can see most of it and still have plenty of energy to do a tour of the park next door. The displays are streamlined; a limited number of objects are on offer, making it easier to concentrate and appreciate their beauty. The collection rotates, but a couple of permanent highlights include a Tang Dynasty (11th-c. B.C.) bronze vase in the shape of a tigress who seems to be about to swallow a man who is clinging to her, and an enormous 18th-century bronze Buddha. There's a fine collection of terracotta funerary figures, including a delightful orchestra of eight young girls playing instruments on horseback. Unfortunately, there's very little documentation (although there are some panels in English), and what there is is overly pedantic. In general, however, the beauty of the objects speaks for itself.

COINS, MEDALS & OTHER TREASURES

The **Musée des Monaies, Medailles et Antiques** ✪ (58 rue de Richelieu, 2nd arrond.; ☎ 01 53 79 59 59; www.bnf.fr; free admission; Mon–Fri 1–5:45pm, Sat 1–4:45pm, Sun noon–6pm; Métro: Palais-Royal or Pyramides) presents treasures from the Bibliothèque Nationale de France's (the French National Library) special collections. Trinkets and baubles that once belonged to the kings and queens of yesteryear include an emerald that once sat on the crown of Catherine de Medicis and Diane de Poitier's fan—one of the oldest in France. A splendid, multicolored cameo that was transferred here from Saint-Chapelle by none other than Louis XVI dates from the 1st century and shows Emperor Tiberius receiving Germanicus is also on display. Other standouts include the silver cup of the Ptolémées and the Treasure of Childéric, some of the oldest souvenirs of the French monarchy.

CONTEMPORARY ART

If you're traveling with cranky teenagers who've had enough of La Vieille France, or if you're also sick of endless rendezvous with history, the **Palais de Tokyo** ✪ (13 ave. du Président Wilson, 16th arrond.; ☎ 01 47 23 54 01; www.palais detokyo.com; 6€ adults, 4.50€ over 60 and under 26, 1€ artists, art teachers, and art students [with card to prove it], free under 18; Tues–Sun noon–midnight; Métro: Iéna or Alma-Marceau) is the place to come for a blast of contemporary madness. This new contemporary art space not only offers a rotating bundle of expositions, events, and other happenings but is also one of the only museums in Paris that stays open until midnight. While some might quibble about whether or not the works on display are really art, there's no denying that this place is a lot more fun than its stodgy neighbor across the terrace (see below). You'll find a completely different crowd here: generally young and intense, and often sporting gravity-defying hairdos. There's no permanent collection, just continuous temporary exhibits and events, some of which feel more like a visit to a fun house than a museum. In 2008, for example, a Swiss artist installed a modular hotel room ("Hotel Everland") on the top of the building where those who could afford to pay for a night got a killer view of the city. A survey of the French contemporary art scene revealed a watermelon on a pedestal, an obese Batman sculpture, and a flattened airplane rolled up like the lid of a sardine can. The center, whose mission includes nurturing, promoting, and even providing studio space for emerging artists, has a very complete website with a long list of current programs and events. In warm weather, you can eat on the splendid terrace, see the box "Dining out on Art" in the restaurant section (p. 102).

Though not as well-known, there's another modern art museum lurking in the massive Palais de Tokyo, built for the Paris Exposition of 1937. The **Musée d'Art Moderne de la Ville de Paris** (11 ave. du Président Wilson, 16th arrond.; ☎ 01 53 67 40 00; www.mam.paris.fr; free admission; Tues–Sun 10am–6pm, Thurs until 10pm during temporary expositions; Métro: Alma-Marceau or Iéna) is the municipal modern art collection, spanning about the same timeframe as the Pompidou but on a smaller scale, and with a stronger emphasis on the first half of the 20th century. The works are presented chronologically, with each section representing a different artistic movement. Though several big names are represented (Picasso, Rouault, and Picaba, to name a few), these are not their well-known works; highlights include a room dedicated to surrealism (the personal collection of André Breton) and a series of paintings by Delaunay and Léger. The contemporary section, from 1960 on, covers seriously abstract movements like Fluxus and Figuration. There's also a huge room entirely covered with brilliant wall murals by Raoul Dufy (*La Fée Electricité)*, as well as another huge room with two enormous versions of *La Danse* by Matisse. Commissioned by Albert Barnes for his foundation near Philadelphia (where the final version hangs), these two "failed" versions offer a chance to see how the artist's projects evolved. If the permanent collection isn't particularly exciting, the temporary exhibitions often are so check the website for current listings.

DECORATIVE ARTS

Having made a fortune in his business ventures, in 1914 Count Moïse de Camondo built a mansion in the style of the Petit Trianon at Versailles and furnished it with 18th-century furniture, paintings, and art objects (like a magnificent tapestry screen made by the famous Savonnerie workshop, and two remarkable vases made out of bronze and petrified wood that once belonged to Marie Antoinette). After the count's death in 1935, the house and everything in it was left to the state as a museum, the **Musée Nissim de Camondo** ★★ (63 rue Monceau, 8th arrond.; ☎ 01 53 89 06 40; www.ucad.fr; 6€ adults, 4.50€ 18–25, free under 18; Wed–Sun 10am–5:30pm; Métro: Monceau or Villiers), named after the count's son, who was killed fighting in World War I. The family's troubles did not stop there—in 1945, the count's daughter and her family were deported and died at Auschwitz. This little-visited museum is a delight—the sense of a real home has been scrupulously preserved, and you can wander through not only sun-filled salons filled with gilded mirrors, inlaid tables and Beauvais tapestries, but also the fully equipped kitchen and the gigantic tiled bathroom. A special room displays the Buffon service, a remarkable set of Sèvres china decorated with

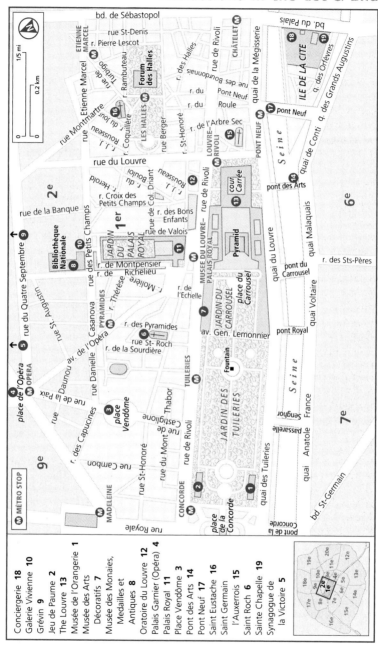

bd. de Sébastopol
rue St-Denis
r. Pierre Lescot
ETIENNE MARCEL
rue Montmartre
rue Etienne Marcel
rue Tiquetonne
r. Rambuteau
Forum des Halles
r. des Halles
rue de Rivoli
CHÂTELET
bd. du Palais
ILE DE LA CITE
q. des Orfèvres
q. des Grands Augustins
quai de la Mégisserie
rue des Bourdonnais
LES HALLES
r. du Jour
r. Coquillière
r. Berger
r. St-Honoré
Pont Neuf
r. du Roule
LOUVRE RIVOLI
pont Neuf
PONT NEUF
r. de l'Arbre Sec
Seine
rue du Louvre
r. Hérold
r. du Bouloi
rue Rousseau
r. J. J. Rousseau
2e
rue de Rivoli
cour Carrée
pont des Arts
quai de Conti
6e
rue de la Banque
r. Croix des Petits Champs
r. de Col Driant
r. des Bons Enfants
Bibliothèque Nationale
1er
JARDIN DU PALAIS ROYAL
rue de Valois
MUSÉE DU LOUVRE-PALAIS ROYAL
Pyramid
quai du Louvre
quai Malaquais
r. des Sts-Pères
r. des Petits Champs
r. de Montpensier
r. de Richelieu
r. de Montpensier
r. de l'Echelle
place du Carrousel
pont du Carrousel
rue du Quatre Septembre
rue St. Augustin
r. Molière
r. Thérèse
JARDIN DU CARROUSEL
av. Gen. Lemonnier
pont Royal
PYRAMIDES
r. des Pyramides
rue St-Roch
r. de la Sourdière
quai Voltaire
rue de l'Opéra
av. de l'Opéra
rue Danielle Casanova
OPERA
place de l'Opéra
rue de la Paix
rue Daunou
TUILERIES
Fountain
Seine
7e
rue de Mont Thabor
r. des Capucines
place Vendôme
rue de Castiglione
JARDIN DES TUILERIES
passerelle Senghor
quai Anatole France
rue Cambon
rue St-Honoré
rue du Mont Thabor
rue de Rivoli
MADELEINE
CONCORDE
rue Royale
place de la Concorde
Pont de la Concorde
quai des Tuileries
bd. St-Germain

N
1/5 mi
0.2 km
0

M MÉTRO STOP
9e
8e

Seeing Museums on Wheels

Most Parisian museums now have some degree of accessibility regarding handicapped visitors, the details of which can usually be found on the website. What's more, the majority of museums offer free entry for handicapped visitors and the person accompanying them.

a myriad of bird species, reproductions of drawings by the renowned naturalist, the Count of Buffon. Be sure to pick up a free English audioguide.

The founder of La Samaritaine department store, Ernest Cognacq, led a rags-to-riches life: At 12 years old, he was selling odds and ends as an itinerant merchant, by the end of his life he was the owner of a fabulously successful department store with a prodigious private art collection. His fine assortment of 18th-century art and furniture now make up the contents of the **Musée Cognacq-Jay** ✸ (8 rue Elzévir; 3rd arrond.; ☎ 01 40 27 07 21; www.cognacq-jay.paris.fr; free admission; Tues–Sun 10am–6pm; Métro: St-Paul or Rambuteau), a small museum housed in one of the Marais' lovely *hôtels particuliers* (mansions). Leaning heavily towards the romantic side of the century, with many lesser works by famous artists like Chardin and Fragonard, what's most impressive in this museum is the furniture, like the bed *"à la polonaise"* draped in blue damask and framed in gilt and curlicues, or the exquisite Louis XVI-era writing table with its geometric wood inlay. Many of the rooms are paneled with *boisserie:* delicately carved wainscotings sometimes of floral motifs.

Since 1794, Baccarat crystal has been hand-crafted in a village of the same name in eastern France, but you don't have to go there to get a glimpse of some of their most spectacular works. The company headquarters, as well as the **Galerie-Musée Baccarat** ✸ (11 place des Etats Unis, 16th arrond.; ☎ 01 40 22 12 11; www.baccarat.fr; 5€ adults, 3.50€ 18–26, free under 18; Mon, Wed–Sat 10am–6pm; Métro: Iéna or Boissière) have recently been transferred to what used be the mansion of Marie-Laure de Noailles, an early-20th-century patron of the arts, and completely done over by Philippe Starck. He has confected several "spaces" to display the many Baccarat marvels created over the centuries from the massive Czar Nicolas II candelabra to crystal furniture that once belonged to Maharajas to classics like the Simon vases.

HUNTING

If you can get over the fact that it's a museum dedicated to hunting, **Musée de la Chasse et de la Nature** ✸ (62 rue des Archives, 3rd arrond.; ☎ 01 53 01 92 40; www.chassenature.org; 6€ adults, 4.50€ students 18–25, free under 18; Tues–Sun 11am–6pm; Métro: Hôtel de Ville or Rambuteau) makes for a rather pleasant outing. After a 2-year renovation, the museum reopened in 2006 with a new look and more importantly, a new way of looking at the subject matter. There are still stuffed animals (that is, taxidermy), but they are now discretely presented amongst an elegant collection of paintings, tapestries, sculptures, and even contemporary art. Housed in two 17th- and 18th-century mansions, the museum has been arranged

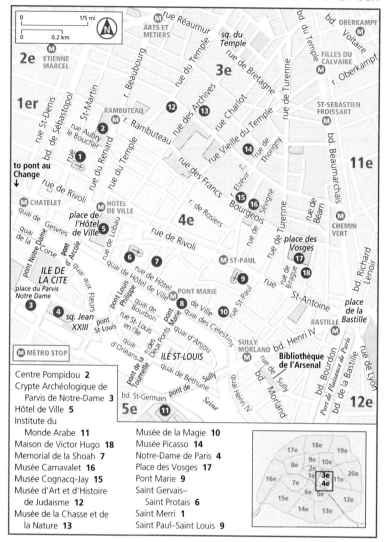

Centre Pompidou **2**
Crypte Archéologique de
    Parvis de Notre-Dame **3**
Hôtel de Ville **5**
Institute du
    Monde Arabe **11**
Maison de Victor Hugo **18**
Memorial de la Shoah **7**
Musée Carnavalet **16**
Musée Cognacq-Jay **15**
Musée d'Art et d'Histoire
    de Judaisme **12**
Musée de la Chasse et de
    la Nature **13**

Musée de la Magie **10**
Musée Picasso **14**
Notre-Dame de Paris **4**
Place des Vosges **17**
Pont Marie **9**
Saint Gervais–
    Saint Protais **6**
Saint Merri **1**
Saint Paul–Saint Louis **9**

to suggest a private home stocked with an incredible collection of artwork. Each room has a theme: For example, the blond wood-paneled Salle Cerf et Loup takes on the imagery of the stag and the wolf, illustrated in paintings by artists as disparate as Renaissance-era Lucas Cranach and 20th-century fauvist André Derain. The emphasis is not so much on the kill, as the symbolism behind the images: In the Middle Ages, the stag, which represented Christ, and the wolf, which represented the Devil, could coexist, a theme that is echoed in the 16th- and 17th-century tapestries that cover the walls. Once you've sauntered through rooms dedicated to dogs, birds, horses, and even unicorns, however, you will walk smack into the trophy room, where discretion is abandoned and hunting is blatantly celebrated in all its gory glory. Intricately inlaid rifles and the heads of various exotic animals bring you back from the celestial spheres of the intellect. Still, there is something intriguing about this place; it reminds you that the relationship between humans and animals dates to way before there were naturalists and environmentalists, and if that relationship was filled with animosity and fear, it was also tinged with a sort of mystical respect.

IMPRESSIONISM

The world can once again enjoy Monet's stunning **water lilies** as they were meant to be enjoyed at the **Musée de l'Orangerie** ★★ (Jardin des Tuileries, 1st arrond.; ☎ 01 44 77 80 07; www.musee-orangerie.fr; 7.50€ adults, 5.50€ students under 26, free under 18; 12:30–7pm Wed, Thurs, Sat–Mon, 12:30–9pm Fri; Métro: Concorde) thanks to a 6-year-long renovation of this historic building. Two large oval rooms are dedicated to these masterpieces, in which Monet tried to replicate the feeling and atmosphere of his garden at Giverny. He worked on these enormous canvases for 12 years, with the idea of creating a peaceful haven where men and women could contemplate and reconnect with nature—in what we would now call an art installation.

The other highlight here is the Guillaume collection, an impressive assortment of late-19th- and early-20th-century paintings. It's now been relegated to the basement, but with a difference—a huge trench was dug on the side of the building during a recent renovation to allow sunlight to reach underground. Renoir and Cezanne profit the most from this arrangement; their paintings, mostly portraits (like Renoir's glowing, idyllic *Femme Nu dans un Paysage* and Cézanne's rather dour looking *Madame Cézanne*) and still lifes (including a vase with flowers by Cézanne that was cut in two and sold as two separate paintings) are illuminated by the sun. The rest of the collection is under artificial lights: Slightly sinister landscapes by Rousseau, enigmatic portraits by Modigliani, abstracts by Marie Laurencin, as well as some kinder, gentler Picassos (*Les Adolescents* bathed in pink and rust tones). This collection has a history as stormy as that of the museum—after Guillaume's death, his rather flamboyant wife rearranged the collection to her own taste, selling off some of the more "difficult" paintings. The result is a lovely collection that lacks a certain bite—truly impressive works by these masters can be seen elsewhere.

More water lilies can be seen at the **Musée Marmottan Monet** ★★ (2 rue Louis Boilly, 16th arrond.; ☎ 01 44 96 50 33; www.marmottan.com; 8€ adults, 4.50€ students under 25, free under 8; 10am–6pm Tues–Sun; Métro: La Muette, RER: Boulainvilliers), which houses the most Monets of any collection in the world. In the first roomful of Monets is the canvas that is held responsible for the name of an entire artistic movement. Pressed to give a name to this misty play of light on the water for the catalogue for the 1874 exposition that included Cézanne, Pissarro, Renoir, and Degas, Monet apparently said, "put 'impression.'" The painting, Impression, Sunrise, certainly made one, as did the show—thereafter the group was referred to as the Impressionists. Monet never stopped being fascinated with the interaction of light and water, be it in a relatively traditional portrait of his wife and daughter against the stormy sea in *On the Beach at Trouville,* or in an almost abstract blend of blues and grays in *Charring Cross Bridge.* It wasn't just the quality of light that interested Monet, but also its transformation; he

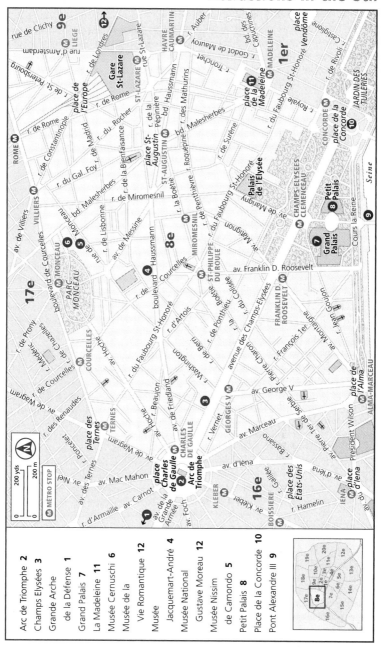

Arc de Triomphe **2**
Champs Elysées **3**
Grande Arche
  de la Défense **1**
Grand Palais **7**
La Madeleine **11**
Musée Cernuschi **6**
Musée de la
  Vie Romantique **12**
Musée
  Jacquemart-André **4**
Musée National
  Gustave Moreau **12**
Musée Nissim
  de Camondo **5**
Petit Palais **8**
Place de la Concorde **10**
Pont Alexandre III **9**

One Man, One Museum

Paris has provided a home for many artists and now provides a home for the museums that celebrate these artists. Beyond the famed Picasso and Rodin museums, the following smaller institutions give visitors an opportunity to commune one on one with some of the top painters and sculptors of the last 2 centuries:

◆ **Musée National Eugène Delacroix** (6 rue de Furstenberg, 6th arrond.; ☎ 01 44 41 86 50; www.musee-delacroix.fr; 5€ adults, free under 18. Wed–Mon 9:30am–5pm; Métro: St-Germain-des-Prés) is housed in part of what was once the painter's apartment and studio. Old and sick, Delacroix moved here in 1857 to be closer to the church of St-Sulpice, where he was decorating a chapel. He managed to finish the paintings, 3 years before he died here, in 1863. "It takes great fortitude to be yourself," he once said, and he certainly had it: At his death he left behind some 8,000 paintings, drawings, and pastels. Though none of his major works are in the museum, several of his smaller paintings decorate the walls, including the mysterious *Mary Magdalene in the Wilderness*. Furniture, mementos, and other personal items are on display, including the artist's palate and paint box.

◆ **Musée National Gustave Moreau** (14 rue de La Rochefoucauld, 9th arrond.; ☎ 01 48 74 38 50; www.musee-moreau.fr; 5€ adults, 3€ students under 26 and for all on Sun, free under 18; Wed–Mon 10am–12:45pm and 2–5:15pm; Métro: Trinité or St-Georges). In 1896, Gustave Moreau opened a museum dedicated to works by . . . himself. It was constructed on top of the artist's family home, preserving his personal apartments on the first floor and creating an airy gallery upstairs for his eerie paintings, both of which are open to the public. A leading figure in the 19th-century Symbolist movement, Moreau painted mystical, mysterious landscapes that evoke legend and myth. Simultaneously pretty and disconcerting, these dreamlike canvases will thrill some, perturb others, but leave none indifferent.

◆ **Musée Zadkine** ✷ (100 bis rue d'Assas, 6th arrond.; ☎ 01 55 42 77 20; www.zadkine.paris.fr; free admission; 10am–6pm Tues–Sun; Métro: Notre-Dame des Champs or Vanvin). A contemporary and neighbor of artists such as Brancusi, Lipchitz, Modigliani, and

often painted the same subject at different times of the day. One of his famous series on the Cathedral of Rouen is here: *Effect of the Sun at the End of the Day.*

Paintings of the likes of Renoir, Sisley, Degas, and Gaugin can be seen in the light-filled rooms on the upper floor, as well as one of the only female members of the group, Berthe Morisot, who gets an entire room devoted to her intimate portraits and interiors.

Picasso, sculptor Ossip Zadkine lived and worked here from 1928 to his death in 1967. Closely associated with the Cubist movement, his sober, elegant, "primitive" sculptures combine abstract geometry with deep humanity. Zadkine volunteered during the World War I and was forced to spend World War II in exile in America; his wartime experiences made a strong impression. One of the museum's most moving pieces is a bronze study for his monumental sculpture *To a Destroyed City,* which was designed as a war memorial commemorating the destruction of the center of Rotterdam during World War II. The original stands some 5.4m (18 ft.) tall in that city.

- **Musée Bourdelle** ✪ (18 rue Antoine Bourdelle, 15th arrond.; ☎ 01 49 54 73 73; www.bourdelle.paris.fr; free admission; Tues–Sun 10am–6pm; Métro: Montparnasse) is a testament to the sculptor Antoine Bourdelle, whose work went far beyond the 10 years he spent as Rodin's assistant. A renowned teacher who influenced an entire generation of sculptors, including Alberto Giacometti and Aristide Maillol, Bourdelle was one of the pioneers of 20th-century monumental sculpture. Proud, muscular centaurs, gods, and goddesses stride across these rooms, as well as monuments to famous people.

- **Musée Maillol** (61 rue de Grenelle, 7th arrond.; ☎ 01 42 22 59 58; www.museemaillol.com; 8€ adults, 6€ students, free under 16; Wed–Sun 11am–6pm; Métro: Rue du Bac). You've probably seen the art of Aristide Maillol, a prolific painter and sculptor, whose works are a celebration of the female form (several of his bronzes are in the Tuilleries Gardens). In search of the perfect model for his well-rounded, smooth bodies, he came across 15-year-old Dina Vierny, who became his source of inspiration for the rest of his life. Vierny was such a find that she posed for some of Maillol's closest friends, like Matisse, Bonnard, and Dufy. After Maillol's death, she became an important art collector and gallery owner, and in time, opened this museum to celebrate his oeuvre. Along with Maillol's work, there are drawings by Matisse, Cezanne, and Picasso; and excellent temporary exhibitions on other artists (see the website for current offerings).

JEWISH HISTORY & ART

It took a while, but the French government is finally coming to terms with some of the less palatable aspects of its World War II past. Inaugurated in 2005, the **Mémorial de la Shoah** ✪ (17 rue Geoffroy-l'Asnier, 4th arrond; ☎ 01 42 77 44 72; www.memorialdelashoah.org; free admission; Sun–Wed, Fri 10am–6pm, Thurs

An Artistic Smorgasbord in One Bite-Sized Museum

Though you won't see any legendary masterpieces at the **Petit Palais** ✦✦ (ave. Winston Churchill, 8th arrond.; ☎ 01 53 43 40 00; www.petitpalais. paris.fr; free admission to permanent collection; Tues–Sun 10am–6pm; Métro: Champs-Elysées Clemenceau), you will see an impressive array of paintings and sculptures by well-known geniuses. The collection's chronology stretches from the ancient Greeks to World War I and the paintings of famous masters like Monet, Ingres, and Rubens are displayed here, as well as the Art Nouveau dining room of Hector Guimard, and the exquisite multilayered glass vases of Emile Gallé. Those interested in earlier works will find Greek vases (including some unusual wine pitchers with animal heads that would spit the wine into the goblet), Italian Renaissance majolica, and a small collection of 16th-century astrolabes and gold-and-crystal traveling clocks. Intricately carved ivory panels and delicately sculpted wood sculptures (including a grinning, long-locked Saint Barbara who looks like she is about to burst out in a fit of the giggles) stand out in the small Medieval section, and a series of rooms dedicated to 17th-century Dutch painters like Steen and Van Ostade is considered one of the best collections of its kind in France (after the Louvre). There's even a small Rembrandt here, one of his numerous self-portraits, this time done up in "oriental" attire. X-rays of the painting revealed that the artist, unhappy with the position of his legs in the painting, shortened them, and when that didn't work, finally covered them up entirely with a dog. It's heartening to know that even geniuses make mistakes.

Best of all, the size of the place is not overwhelming; works from each era and artistic movement have been carefully chosen and displayed, though the sequence of exhibitions can be a little hard to figure out. After musing over large-scale 19th-century Naturalist paintings by Alfred Roll, you might wander into an adjoining room dedicated to 18th-century art under Louis XV. The coy, hard-to-find signage will not help, either. In fact, it's a little hard to say exactly what this museum is altogether. It's not entirely paintings and sculptures, and it's not entirely decorative arts either—it's more like a bridge between the two.

10am–10pm; Métro: St-Paul or Pont Marie) is a **Holocaust memorial, museum, and documentation center.** The memorial includes a wall listing the names and birthdates of some 76,000 Jewish men, women, and children who were deported to Nazi camps from France between 1942 and 1944—of which only 2,500 survived. Equally moving is the **Memorial to the Unknown Jewish Martyr,** an existing memorial created in 1957. Lying beneath the documentation center in the crypt, this huge somber sculpture, which contains ashes from the extermination camps and the Warsaw Ghetto, is illuminated by a perpetual flame.

Housed in the magnificent Hôtel de Saint Aignan, one of the many palatial 17th-century mansions that dot the Marais, the **Musée d'Art et d'Histoire de Judaïsme** ✮ (71 rue de Temple, 3rd arrond; ☎ 01 53 01 86 60; www.mahj.org; 6.80€ adults, 4.50€ 18–26, free under 18; Mon–Fri 11am–6pm, Sun 10am–6pm; Métro: Rambuteau or Hôtel de Ville) chronicles the art and history of the Jewish people in France and in Europe. This relatively new museum (1999) has a superb collection of objects of both artistic and cultural significance (a splendid Italian Renaissance torah ark, a German gold and silver Hanukka menora, a 17th-c. Dutch illustrated torah scroll, documents from the Dreyfus trial), which is interspersed with texts, drawings, and photos telling the story of the Jews, and explaining the basics of both Ashkenazi and Sephardic traditions. You'll do a lot of reading here; documentation is translated in English, but if you're feeling lazy there's also an informative audioguide. The final rooms include a collection of works by Jewish artists, including Modigliani, Soutine, Lipchitz, and Chagall.

LITERARY HISTORY

I know it sounds ho-hum, a museum that contains nothing but letters and manuscripts, but the new **Musée des Lettres et Manuscrits** ✮✮ (8 rue de Nesle, 6th arrond.; ☎ 01 40 51 02 25; www.museedeslettres.fr; 6€ adults, 4.50€ under 25, students, and over 60, free under 12; Tues–Fri 10am–8pm; Sat–Sun 10am–6pm) is utterly fascinating. The sheer volume of famous historical figures represented is staggering—letters from René Descartes, Vincent Van Gogh, and Marcel Proust are all on display, not to mention Catherine de Medici, Napoleon, and Charles de Gaulle. There's something about seeing the actual handwriting of these legendary figures that makes you feel like you're listening in on their private conversations. (It also makes you wonder what we will leave to posterity, now that e-mail has replaced the art of letter-writing.) And these are not mere handwriting samples—content counts in this museum. A brief memo from General Eisenhower, marked "Top Secret" announces the end of the World War II in a single sentence "The mission of this Allied Force was fulfilled at 0245, local time, May 7th, 1945." Calculations by Albert Einstein and Michele Besso that led to the theory of relativity are scrawled across dozens of pages. There's a short note from Louis XIV to his son, an unpublished manuscript by George Sand, a ribald poem by Verlaine and Rimbaud *(The Asshole Sonnet),* and a letter from Sarah Bernhardt to Montesquieu complaining about her arch-rival Eleanor Duse. Original scores handwritten by Mozart, Beethoven, and Berlioz, among dozens of other composers are on display. The only down side is that all documentation is in French; at press time the museum was working on a multi-media language solution for this rotating collection.

The life of Victor Hugo was as turbulent as some of his novels. Regularly visited by both tragedy and triumph, the author of The Hunchback of Notre Dame lived in several apartments in Paris, including one on the second floor of a corner house on the sumptuous place des Vosges, now known as the **Maison de Victor Hugo** ✮ (6 place des Vosges, 4th arrond.; ☎ 01 42 72 10 16; Métro: St-Paul; www.musee-hugo.paris.fr; free admission; Tues–Sun 10am–6pm). He lived there with his wife and four children from 1832 to 1848, during which time he wrote Ruy Blas, part of Les Miserables, met his lifelong mistress and muse, Juliette

A Temporary Exhibition Space Worth Checking Out

After being closed for 12 years of renovations, the beautiful glass roof of the **Grand Palais** ✪ (3 ave. du Général Eisenhower, 8th arrond.; ☎ 01 44 13 17 17; www.rmn.fr; 10€ adults, 8€ under 25, free under 13; hours vary with exhibits, check website for current information; Métro: Champs Elysées–Clemenceau or Franklin Delano Roosevelt) has been completely replaced, and if you get a chance to go inside, it's a magnificent site. Originally constructed for the Universal Exposition of 1900 under the direction of Charles Girault, this enormous edifice was meant to be a "monument consecrated by the Republic to the glory of French art." The "grand palace" has kept its promise; since its inception, it has been a premier site for major art expositions. The only catch is that everyone seems to come, and the lines at the entrance can be atrocious. By all means, reserve ahead if you can at www.rmn.fr, www.fnac.com, or www.ticketnet.fr; by phone through FNAC (☎ 08 92 68 36 22, .34€ per minute) or Ticketnet (☎ 08 92 39 01 00, .34€ per minute); or at any FNAC or Virgin Megastore.

Drouet, was elected to the Academie Française, lost his 19-year-old daughter in a boating accident on the Seine, and entered the political arena. When Napoleon III seized power in 1851, this passionate advocate of free speech, universal suffrage, and social justice was made distinctly unwelcome, particularly after he declared the new king a traitor of France. Fearing for his life, Hugo left the country and lived in exile until 1870 when he triumphantly returned to France and was elected to the senate. By the time he died in 1885 he was a national hero; his funeral cortege through the streets of Paris is the stuff of legend, and his body was one of the first to be buried in the Panthéon. The museum's collection charts this dramatic existence through the author's drawings, original manuscripts, notes (including some scrawled on scrap paper and the backs of envelopes), furniture, and personal objects, like his inkwell.

The home of another famous author with a tempestuous, if less grandiose, life story can be found on a quiet hillside in the villagelike neighborhood of Passy. Fleeing his creditors, in 1840, writer Honoré de Balzac rented a small house, now called the **Maison de Balzac** ✪ (47 rue Raynouard, 16th arrond.; ☎ 01 55 74 41 80; www.balzac.paris.fr; free admission; Tues–Sun 10am–6pm; Métro: Passy or La Muette), and lived there for 7 years under an assumed name. He also worked like a demon: He was capable of writing for up to 20 hours a day for weeks at a time. Though there is much less on display in this quiet little dwelling than in Victor Hugo's action-packed museum, for some reason one feels the author's presence much more. The five rooms of Balzac's apartments are hung with paintings and portraits of his family and friends, including several of Madame Hanska, whom he finally married after 18 years of passionate correspondence. There are also a few manuscripts and personal objects, including his turquoise-incrusted cane, which

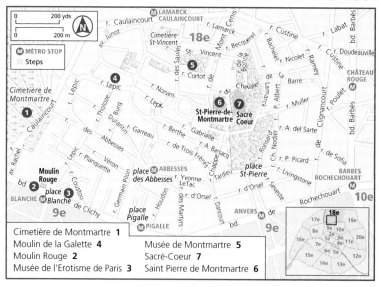

Cimetière de Montmartre **1**	
Moulin de la Galette **4**	Musée de Montmartre **5**
Moulin Rouge **2**	Sacré-Coeur **7**
Musée de l'Erotisme de Paris **3**	Saint Pierre de Montmartre **6**

was the talk of Paris, and his monogrammed coffee pot, which kept him going through his marathon work sessions. In his office is the little table where he wrote *The Human Comedy,* "a witness," he wrote to Madame Hanska, "to my worries, my miseries, my distress, my joys, everything . . . my arm almost wore out its surface from taking the same path over and over again."

Though perhaps now best known for wearing men's clothes and being the lover of artists like Chopin, in her time, George Sand was a respected figure in the Romantic movement, as well as an outspoken political activist, and her writing was lauded by the likes of Dostoyevsky and Flaubert. But even if you are not (like me) a George Sand fan, you might be tempted to make a visit to the **Musée de la Vie Romantique** (16 rue Chaptal, 9th arrond.; ☎ 01 55 31 95 67; www.vie-romantique.paris.fr; 7€ adults, 5.50€ 60 and over, 3.50€ 14–26, free under 14; Tues–Sun 10am–6pm). This light-filled Restoration-epoch house was not actually Sand's home; it belonged to Dutch painter Ary Scheffer, friend and neighbor of George Sand. But it now houses a museum dedicated to Sand's life and works, including a re-creation of her salon, letters, portraits, personal objects, and even watercolors that she painted when she wasn't writing one of her dozens of novels, plays or articles. And all in a very homelike setting. Some of Scheffer's paintings, as well has his personal memorabilia is on display in the artist's studio, in a separate out-building.

MARITIME HISTORY

Awe-inspiring model ships are on display at the **Musée de la Marine** (Palais de Chaillot, 17 place du Trocadéro, 16th arrond.; ☎ 01 53 65 69 69; www.musee-marine.fr; 8€ adults, 6€ students under 25, 4€ 6–18 years old, free under 6; Wed–Mon 10am–6pm; Métro: Trocadero), many of which come from the private collection of Louis XV. The intricately crafted scale models, which must have taken an eternity to make, are near to exact replicas of some of the finest sailing vessels of the 17th to 20th centuries. Highlights include La Ville de Dieppe, a three-masted sailing ship entirely sculpted in ivory, including threadlike ropes and paper-thin sails, presented as a gift from the town of Dieppe to Napoleon on the birth of his son. There are more than just models here: Napoleon's elaborately sculpted imperial boat is on display, as are a variety of figureheads, navigational instruments, and an ample collection of paintings on maritime themes. Temporary exhibitions cover historic journeys, as well as current scientific exploration. By the way, the museum is part of the Palais de Chaillot, an ensemble of buildings constructed for the International Exhibit of 1937. Be sure to check out the view of the Eiffel Tower (one of the best in the city) along with the monumental pavilions crowning each wing and inscribed with quotations by poet Paul Verlaine.

MEDIEVAL ART

Ancient Roman baths and a 15th-century mansion set the stage for the **Musée National du Moyen Age/Thermes et Hôtel de Cluny** ✮✮ (6 place Paul Painlevé, 5th arrond.; ☎ 01 53 73 78 00; www.musee-moyenage.fr; 7.50€ adults, 5.50€ 18–25, free under 18. Wed–Mon 9:15am–5:45pm; Métro: Cluny-La Sorbonne, RER: St-Michel-Notre-Dame), a terrific collection of Medieval art and objects. Built somewhere between the 1st and 3rd centuries, the baths (visible from blvd. St-Michel) are some of the best existing examples of Gallo-Roman architecture. They are attached to what was once the palatial home of a 15th-century abbot, whose last owner, a certain Alexandre du Sommerard, amassed a vast array of Medieval masterworks. When he died in 1842, his home was turned into a museum and his collection put on display. Sculptures, textiles, furniture, and ceramics are shown, as wells as gold, ivory, and enamel work. There are several magnificent tapestries, but the biggest draw is the *Lady and the Unicorn* series, one of only two sets of complete unicorn tapestries in the world (the other is in New York City). In five of these late-15th-century tapestries, the lady, her unicorn, a lion, and various other symbolic representations of the animal and vegetable kingdoms illustrate the five senses, while in the sixth she stands before a tent bearing the inscription "To My Only Desire" while placing a necklace in a case held by her servant. The meaning of this last tapestry remains an enigma—but the mystery merely adds to its beauty.

Among the many sculptures are the famous severed heads from the facade of Notre-Dame. Knocked off of their bodies during the furor of the Revolution, 21 of the heads of the Kings of Judah were found by chance in 1977 during repair work in the basement of a bank. Though damaged, the delicately carved stonework retains traces of the original paint. In a room lined with precious objects, a 7th-century votive crown is a standout. Found in Guarrazar, Spain, this gold crown, studded with gems, once dangled above an altar—a gift from a wealthy lord intended to demonstrate his submission to the Church. Leave time to visit the beautiful medieval garden, added in 2000, inspired by the works in the museum.

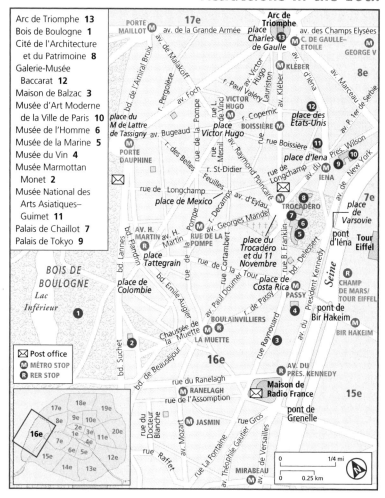

Arc de Triomphe **13**
Bois de Boulogne **1**
Cité de l'Architecture
  et du Patrimoine **8**
Galerie-Musée
  Baccarat **12**
Maison de Balzac **3**
Musée d'Art Moderne
  de la Ville de Paris **10**
Musée de l'Homme **6**
Musée de la Marine **5**
Musée du Vin **4**
Musée Marmottan
  Monet **2**
Musée National des
  Arts Asiatiques–
  Guimet **11**
Palais de Chaillot **7**
Palais de Tokyo **9**

Post office
MÉTRO STOP
RER STOP

PARISIAN HISTORY

A relic of the darker side of the Revolution, the **Conciergerie** ✦✦ (blvd. du Palais, 1st arrond.; ☎ 01 53 40 60 80; www.monuments-nationaux.fr; 7.50€ adults, 4.80€ students under 26, free under 18 accompanied by an adult, combined ticket with Sainte Chapelle: 10€ adults, 7€ students under 26; Mar–Oct 9am–6pm, Nov–Feb 9am–5pm; Métro: Cité or St-Michel, RER: St-Michel) was where some of its most famous participants spent their final days before making their way to the guillotine. Danton, Desmoulins, Saint-Just, and Charlotte Corday passed through these doors, but perhaps its most famous guest was Marie Antoinette, who spent her time here in a dismal cell, reading and praying while she awaited her fate. After doing away with the monarchy, the Revolution began to eat itself alive; during the particularly bloody period known as the Terror, murderous infighting between the various revolutionary factions engendered panic and paranoia that led to tens of thousands of people throughout the country being arrested and executed. Twenty-two of the leaders of one of the leading factions, the Girondins, were condemned to death; legend has it that on the eve of their execution they drank and sang until dawn in their cell (now called the Chapelle des Girondins). Eventually Robespierre, the main force behind the Terror, and perhaps the most ardent advocate for Marie-Antoinette's execution, found himself in the cell next door to the one she stayed in.

Though it's been a prison since the 15th century, the building itself is actually what remains of a 14th-century royal palace built by Philippe le Bel. When the kings abandoned the castle for the Louvre, it was turned over to the Parliament and other administrative powers, including the "Concierge," or guardian, who reigned over the judicial matters. The Concierge turned part of the building into a prison, which retained the name of its master. Even before the Revolution, the Conciergerie was notorious: Henry IV's murderer, Ravaillac, was imprisoned here before an angry crowd tore him apart alive. The enormous Salle des Gens d'Arms, with its 8.4m-high (28-ft.) vaulted ceiling, is an impressive reminder of the building's palatial past. As for the prison itself, though the cells have been outfitted with displays and re-creations of daily life (including wax figures), it's a far cry from the dank hell it once was. Fresh paint and lighting make it a little difficult to imagine what it was like in the bad old days, but a few areas stand out, like the Cours des Femmes (the women's courtyard), which virtually hasn't changed since the days when female prisoners did their washing in the fountain. Marie Antoinette's cell was converted into a memorial chapel during the Restoration; a re-creation of her cell, containing some original objects, is on display. There are some fascinating historical exhibits, including a list of the names of all those guillotined during the Revolution, 2,780 in Paris alone.

The history of Montmartre has served as fodder for countless films, books, and song lyrics, but what was the real story? Find out at the **Musée de Montmartre** ★ (12 rue Cortot, 18th arrond.; ☎ 01 49 25 89 37; www.museedemontmartre.fr; 7€ adults, 3.50€ over 60 and under 26, free under 10; Tues–Sun 11am–6pm; Métro: Abbesses or Lamarck–Caulaincourt), where a local historical society has carefully preserved paintings, photos, posters, and other articles that document the history of this famous butte (hill) from the days when its importance was mainly religious, to the growth of village life, to the gory days of the Paris Commune, and finally to the artistic boom in the 19th and 20th centuries. The building itself is fraught with history: Originally owned by Rosimond, a famous 17th-century actor who was a member of Molière's troupe, the house (which is surrounded by a garden) later served as a studio for Renoir, who painted "Le Bal du Moulin de la Galette" here, among other legendary canvases. Other famous lodgers included a turbulent trio: Suzanne Valadon, her lover André Utter, and her son, painter Maurice Utrillo. Along with conventional museum displays, there is also a re-creation of a bistro, complete with a zinc bar, an engraving studio, and a scale model of what the village Montmartre looked like, back in the day.

About Those Museum Hours . . .

The museum hours listed in this chapter are the official opening and closing times; be advised that most museums sell their last ticket anywhere from one half-hour to an hour before closing.

MUSIC

In the vast, modern, and somewhat kooky Parc de la Villette (see "Paris Outdoors," p. 212), at the edge of the city limits, lies the Cité de la Musique, a complex of concert halls, studios, and a lovely museum, the **Musée de la Musique** ✪ (221 ave. Jean Jaurès, 19th arrond.; ☎ 01 44 84 45 00; www.cite-musique.fr; 7€ adults, 6.40€ 18–26, free under 18; Tues–Sat noon–6pm, Sun 10am–6pm). The permanent collection includes over a thousand instruments, sculptures, paintings, and other objects that recount the history of music in Europe from the 16th to 20th centuries. Pore over a beautiful and rare 17th-century guitar with ivory inlay, a clutch of Stradivarius violins, or a concert piano that Franz Liszt once played on. A separate section on music from around the world includes another 700 objects, mostly from Africa and Asia. There are a variety of **guided tours** (all in French, 10€), including tours given by musicians, who play examples of the music discussed. Free **audioguides** play excerpts from major works and provide commentary (in English) that places the instruments in historical context. The museum closed in 2008 for an overhaul; it is scheduled to reopen in spring 2009 with a new layout for the same impressive collection.

PHOTOGRAPHY

Originally built by Napoleon III as an indoor court for playing a game that was the ancestor of tennis, by the early 1900s the **Jeu de Paume** (1 place de la Concorde, 1st arrond. [entrance in the **Tuileries Gardens**]; ☎ 01 47 03 12 50; www.jeudepaume.org; 6€ adults, 4€ over 60 and under 25, free under 10; Tues noon–9pm, Wed–Fri noon–7pm, Sat–Sun 10am–7pm; Métro: Concorde) had become a prime exhibition space. Since 2002, its focus has been on photography, and the museum has a second location at the magnificent **Hôtel de Sully** ✪ (62 rue St-Antoine, 4th arrond.; ☎ 01 42 74 47 75; 5€ adults, 2.50€ over 60 and under 25, free under 10; Tues–Fri noon–7pm, Sat–Sun 10am–7pm; Métro: St-Paul or Bastille). There is a combined ticket for the two museums: adults 8€, over 60 and under 25 4€. Expositions in 2008 included a survey of early-20th-century photographic postcards, and a retrospective of the works of Richard Avedon.

SCIENCE

The **Muséum National d'Histoire Naturelle** ✪ 🅚 (57 rue Cuvier, 5th arrond.; ☎ 01 40 79 30 00; www.mnhn.fr; admission to one site grants reduced admission at others; Métro: Gare d'Austerlitz or Censier Daubenton, RER: Gare d'Austerlitz) was established in 1793, under the supervision of two celebrated naturalists, George Louis Lerclerc, Count of Buffon, and Louis Jean-Marie Daubenton.

Originally (and still) an academic research institution, this temple to the natural sciences contains a series of separate museums, each with a different specialty. The biggest draw is no doubt the **Grande Galerie de la Evolution** (36 rue Geoffroy Saint Hilaire, 5th arrond.; 8€ adults, 6€ children 4–13, free under 4; Wed–Mon 10am–6pm), where a sort of Noah's ark of animals snakes its way around a huge hall filled with displays that trace the evolution of life and man's relationship with nature. The dim lighting and eerie soundtrack might be a bit much for the under-7 crowd, so plan accordingly. Particularly moving is the large section devoted to extinct species—seeing the actual animals in the flesh, if not blood, makes you want to run out and join the Audubon Society to save what's left. Another interesting hall, the **Galerie de Minérologie et de Géologie** (36 rue Geoffroy Saint Hilaire, 5th arrond.; 7€ adults, 5€ children 4–13, free under 4; Wed–Mon 10am–5pm), includes a room full of giant crystals, and another with eye-popping precious stones from the Royal Treasury, as well as various minerals and even meteorites. For dinosaurs, sabre-toothed tigers, ancient humans, and thousands of other fossilized skeletons, repair to the **Galeries de Paléontologie et d'Anatomie Comparée** (2 rue Buffon, 5th arrond.; 6€ adults, 4€ children 4–13, free under 4; Wed–Mon 10am–5pm).

Even bigger is the **Cité des Sciences et de l'Industrie** ★ 🅺🅸🅳🆂 (30 ave. Corentin-Cariou, 19th arrond. in the Parc de la Villette; ☎ 01 40 05 70 00; www.cite-sciences.fr; admission for the Explora expositions: 11€ adults, 8€ under 25, free under 7; Tues–Sat 10am–6pm, Sun 10am–7pm; Métro: Porte de la Villette), which includes a planetarium, a 3-D movie theater, and a multimedia library. The heart of the museum is **Explora,** an entire floor (in a building this size, that means a lot), of interactive exhibits and displays, as well as excellent temporary exhibits. Some of the highlights of 2008 included expositions on genetically modified organisms (very controversial in France), the Citroën "deux cheveux" (the French equivalent of the VW Bug), and the opening of a permanent exhibit on the creation of the universe. On the ground floor, parents will be delighted to find the **Cité des Enfants** (separate admission, 6€ per person for a 1½-hr. session; see website for hours, reservations recommended, particularly during French school vacations), which has separate programs for 2- to 7-year-olds and 7- to 12-year-olds. Kids get to explore their own sensations and the world around them in a series of hands-on activities and displays. If all this isn't enough, outside you can clamber into the **Argonaut** (3€, free under 7), a real submarine that was one of the stars of the French navy in the 1950s, or dip inside the gigantic metal sphere, called the **Geode** (adults 11€, under 25 9€, pregnant women or children under 3 prohibited), an IMAX-type movie theater showing large screen films.

SEWERS

Ever wanted to pretend you were Jean Valjean in Les Miserables? Take a trip through the sewers of Paris at the **Musée des Egouts** (Pont de l'Alma, in front of 93 quai d'Orsay, 7th arrond.; ☎ 01 53 68 27 81; www.paris.fr; 4.20€ adults, 3.40€ students and children 6–16, free under 6; Oct–Apr Sat–Wed 11am–4pm, May–Sept Sat–Wed 11am–5pm; RER: Pont de l'Alma). Though you won't actually get on a boat, you will be able to walk through 500m (about a third of a mile) of sewers (don't worry, you'll be on a raised sidewalk on the side of the, uh, water),

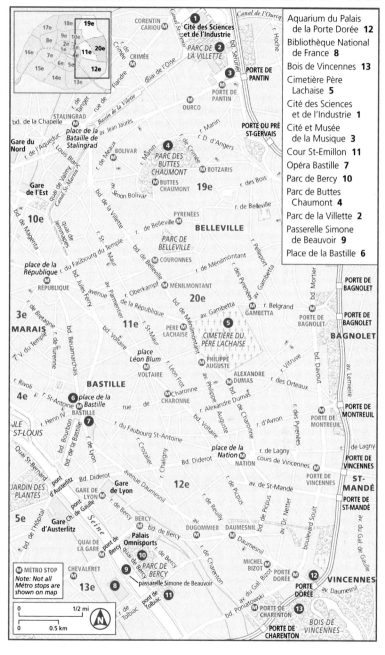

Aquarium du Palais de la Porte Dorée **12**

Bibliothèque National de France **8**

Bois de Vincennes **13**

Cimetière Père Lachaise **5**

Cité des Sciences et de l'Industrie **1**

Cité et Musée de la Musique **3**

Cour St-Emillon **11**

Opéra Bastille **7**

Parc de Bercy **10**

Parc de Buttes Chaumont **4**

Parc de la Villette **2**

Passerelle Simone de Beauvoir **9**

Place de la Bastille **6**

which should give you a pretty good idea of the different types of passageways and equipment that exist in this underground domain. There's also a museum that explains the history and technical aspects of this stinky world. Because it is indeed stinky—delicate noses should think twice before entering.

SEX, YES SEX

Located in the city's most famous red light district, the **Musée de l'Erotisme de Paris** (72 blvd. de Clichy, 18th arrond.; ☎ 01 42 58 28 73; www.musee-erotisme. com; 8€ adults, 5€ students and over 60 [you must be at least 18 to be admitted], 3€ reduction coupon on website; 10am–2am daily; Métro: Blanche) attempts to take a serious look at erotic art, from Peruvian pottery to R. Crumb. Lower floors are devoted to traditional and popular works from various cultures—Japanese prints, Persian miniatures, and Indian statues depicting bodies in a multitude of gymnastic poses. As you work your way up the stairs (there are seven floors here), you'll see antique collections of naughty postcards, modern art, and temporary exhibits on subjects such as Japanese erotica or contemporary erotic photography. Although most of the displays are merely titillating, the exhibit on the bordellos of Paris and Marseilles is actually interesting. Covering the period from the end of the 19th century to 1946 (when bordellos were declared illegal and closed down in France), these poignant photos and prints document a hazy subculture that, for better or worse, has ceased to exist. There's no English language text, but this is one place where the subject matter is pretty universal.

WINE

Everything you ever wanted to know about wine is explained at the **Musée du Vin** (Rue des Eaux, 16th arrond.; ☎ 01 45 25 63 26; www.museeduvinparis.com; 8.90€ adults, 7€ seniors, 7€ students, free under 15, audioguide in English 2€; Tues–Sun 10am–6pm; Métro: Passy). Housed in a series of underground tunnels that are carved out of ancient limestone quarries, this series of displays covers everything from vine cultivation, to barrel construction, to fermentation, tasting, and bottling, with a good dose of wine history to boot. If you can't read the

---

The Light at the End of the Tunnel

As mentioned above, the Musée du Vin takes up part of a vast network of tunnels that are what's left of ancient limestone quarries. At the end of the 15th century, a monastery was erected nearby, and the monks used the tunnels to stock the wine they made: a claret that was so good that it is said King Louis XIII would stop off for a glass on his way back to the chateau after a day's hunting in the Bois de Boulogne. In the early 19th century, the tunnels served yet another purpose: They made a convenient escape route for nearby resident **Honoré de Balzac.** When he heard his creditors banging at the door, he opened a trapdoor in his basement that led down into the tunnel, where he would skitter all the way down to the river and take a boat into town.

French explanations, ask for a free English guidebook at the entrance. For the uninitiated, the endless cases filled with wine tools and paraphernalia may not seem terribly exciting, however, at the end you will be rewarded with a glass of wine served by a member of the staff who will unveil the mysteries (in English or in French) of the substance you are about to drink. You can lunch or have another glass of wine in the restaurant in the vaulted cellars at the entry, which were used by 16th-century monks to store their wine barrels (three-course menu 25€). The museum also offers wine tasting classes (see "The 'Other' Paris," p. 198).

ESPECIALLY FOR CHILDREN

Along with those sights marked with a 🧒, the little ones will get a kick out of the next two museums:

The **Musée de la Magie** 🧒 (11 rue St-Paul, 4th arrond.; ☎ 01 42 72 13 26; www.museedelamagie.com; 7€ adults, 5€ children under 13; Wed and Sat–Sun 2–7pm; Métro: St-Paul) where real magicians lead the tours, explaining some (but not all) of the tricks of the trade. Trick mirrors, animated paintings, and talking genies will thrill the little ones. Live magic shows are performed in French on a small stage in the museum throughout the day. The museum recently unveiled a second set of exhibits, the Musée des Automates (6€ adults, 5€ children 3–12; combined ticket for both museums 12€ adults, 9€ children 3–12) where you can marvel at the antics of 100 different antique mechanized toys.

Children will also enjoy **Grévin** 🧒 (10 blvd. Montmartre, 9th arrond.; ☎ 01 47 70 85 05; www.grevin.com; 19€ adults, 16€ students, 11€ 6–14; Mon–Fri 10am–6:30pm, Sat–Sun and French school holidays 10am–7pm, closed first week of Jan; Métro: Grands Boulevards), a vast cavern of wax figures including movie stars, historical figures, and rock and rollers, as well as notables from the current political scene. If you're not up on French history or pop culture, you might not recognize some of the faces, but don't worry, Elvis Presley, Arnold Schwartzenegger, Spiderman, and Madonna are here, too. Stars appear in their natural habitats: chic brasseries, cocktail parties, and fashion shows. You'll also get to partake of Grevin's famous historical tableaus, which feature scenes like Joan of Arc being burned at the stake, and Louis XIV holding court at Versailles. If you've had enough wax, take a peek at the light show in the just-renovated Palais des Mirages, a leftover from the Universal Exposition of 1900.

ARCHITECTURAL MASTERPIECES & MONUMENTS

Paris is a city that is incredibly easy on the eyes. The lack of glass towers (for the most part) and hard edges makes this a graceful urban landscape, thanks in part to Baron Haussmann (see the "Baron Haussmann," box below) whose ruthless urban renewal plan in the 19th century gave the city an architectural unity and harmony that is rare in big cities, let alone major capitals like Paris. Below are the major highlights, including historic buildings, plazas, bridges, and even cemeteries. At the end of this section, I list churches and other houses of worship by geographical area. Even if you don't go out of your way to visit them, you'll surely pass by, over, or through some of the following during your visit.

Baron Haussmann: A Man with a Plan

The Paris you see before you was radically transformed in the late 19th century by a pugnacious urban planner named Georges-Eugène Haussmann. Before Haussmann got his hands on it, Paris was a mostly medieval city of tiny streets and narrow alleyways, and major sanitation problems. Everyone agreed that something needed to be done to facilitate traffic and clean up the city, but no one managed to come up with a solution. Enter Baron Haussmann. Named prefect of the Seine by Napoleon III, Haussmann pushed through wide boulevards (Malsherbes, Haussmann, and Sebastapol, among others), demolished dozens of old neighborhoods, and encouraged promoters to build new buildings, following, of course, his strict rules on the style of the facades and the height of the structures. The result was the elegant "Haussmannian" architecture that lines most of the city's streets, as well as the system of central arteries that collect in star-shaped intersections at various strategic points. In fact, the boulevards were indeed strategic—one of the reasons for their creation was to make it easier to crush rebellions in the worker's quarters, and garrisons were set up at crucial intersections. Streets were also now too wide in most areas to be easily barricaded. Haussmann also accessorized his new neighborhoods and streets; the famous kiosks, benches, and lampposts you'll see around the city also date from this epoch. While there's no denying his projects improved traffic, sanitation, and security, and gave a pleasing architectural unity to the cityscape, Haussmann's take-no-prisoners approach has been criticized for having neutered the personality of entire neighborhoods (the Ile de la Cité, for example, was almost entirely razed) and destroying important historical buildings.

HISTORIC SQUARES, ARCADES & BUILDINGS

The gardens and long arcades of the **Palais Royal** ★★ (rue St-Honoré, 1st arrond.; gardens open 7:30am–dusk; Métro: Palais Royal–Musée du Louvre) are a not only a delight to stroll through, but were also witnesses to one of the most important moments in French history. But first the backstory: Built by Cardinal Richelieu, the lavish palace was left to the King upon his prime minister's death. It was subsequently occupied by a number of royal family members (including Louis XIV as a child) until it came into the hands of a certain Duke Louis Phillippe d'Orleans at the end of the 18th century. An inveterate spendthrift, the young lord soon found himself up to his ears in debt. To earn enough money to pay off his creditors, he came up with the shockingly modern idea of opening the palace gardens to development, building apartments on the grounds. The bottom floor of these lodgings, which make up three sides of the enclosure you see today, were let out as shops, cafes, and boutiques. Though the neighbors screamed, their cries were drowned out by the success of the new project, which made the area

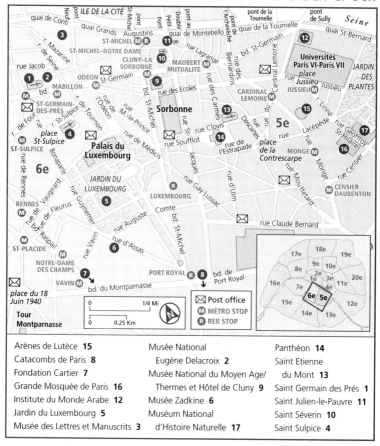

Arènes de Lutèce **15**	Musée National	Panthéon **14**
Catacombs de Paris **8**	Eugène Delacroix **2**	Saint Etienne
Fondation Cartier **7**	Musée National du Moyen Age/	du Mont **13**
Grande Mosquée de Paris **16**	Thermes et Hôtel de Cluny **9**	Saint Germain des Prés **1**
Institute du Monde Arabe **12**	Musée Zadkine **6**	Saint Julien-le-Pauvre **11**
Jardin du Luxembourg **5**	Muséum National	Saint Séverin **10**
Musée des Lettres et Manuscrits **3**	d'Histoire Naturelle **17**	Saint Sulpice **4**

into a commercial hub. What's more, since the police had no power over these royal grounds, all sorts of usually illegal activities were given free reign here. Gambling houses and bordellos sprang up between the shops and cafes, and the gardens became the central meeting place for revolutionaries. Things came to a head on July 12, 1789, when Camille Desmoulins stood up on a table in front of the Café de Foy and called the people to arms—2 days later, the mob would storm the Bastille, igniting the French Revolution. The glory days of the Palais Royal would come to an abrupt end in 1815, when a new Louis-Philippe showed up, decided this was not the way to treat the home of his ancestors, and kicked everyone out. Once the royals finally left in the 19th century, the palace was taken over by various government ministries, and the apartments in the galleries were let out to artists and writers, including Collette and Jean Cocteau.

Today the shops in the arcades are very subdued, and very expensive—mostly antique toy and stamp dealers, a smattering of high-end designer clothes, and a couple of pricey restaurants, including the legendary Grand Véfour. The cour

Journées Européens du Patrimoine

Wouldn't you love to actually go inside the sumptuous Hôtel de Sully, or see the famous chapel at the Sorbonne? Well, for 2 days in September, you can. During the **Journées Européens du Patrimoine** (www.journeesdu patrimoine.culture.fr) dozens of mansions and monuments that are usually off-limits to the general public open their doors for guided tours. For a full program and this year's dates, look at the website listed above. Otherwise, keep an eye on listings magazines like *Pariscope* and *l'Officiel du Spectacle* for details.

d'honneur on the south end is filled with black and white striped columns by Daniel Buren; though most Parisians have now gotten used to this unusual instal-lation, when it was unveiled in 1987 it caused almost as much of a stir as Camille Desmoulins.

The most notable thing about the **place de la Bastille** ✫ (12th arrond.; Métro: Bastille) is the building that's no longer there: the Bastille prison. What's now an enormous traffic circle where cars careen around at warp speed, was once the site of an ancient stone fortress that became a symbol for all that was wrong with the French monarchy. Over the centuries, kings and queens condemned rebellious citizens to stay inside these cold walls, sometimes with good reason, other times on a mere whim. By the time the Revolution started to boil, though, the prison was barely in use; when the angry mobs stormed the walls on July 14, 1789, there were only seven prisoners left to set free. Be that as it may, the destruc-tion of the Bastille came to be seen as the ultimate revolutionary moment; July 14 is still celebrated as the birth of the Republic. Logic notwithstanding, the giant bronze column in the center of the plaza honors the victims of a different revolu-tion, that of 1830.

No, it's not a hotel. The enormous Neo-Renaissance wedding cake that is the **Hôtel de Ville** ✫ (place du Hôtel de Ville, 4th arrond.; ☎ 01 42 76 40 40; Métro: Hôtel de Ville) is Paris's city hall, and is not open to the public, except by appoint-ment (☎ 01 42 76 54 04). Though you probably won't be able to see the sump-tuous halls and chandeliers (you can sometimes get a peek through the windows), you will be able to feast on the lavish exterior, which includes 136 statues repre-senting historic VIPs of Parisian history. Since the 14th century, this spot has been an administrative seat for the municipality; the building you see before you dates from 1873, but it is a copy of an earlier Renaissance version that stood in its place up until 1870, when it was burned down during the Paris Commune. The vast square in front of the building, which used to be called the place du Grève, was used for municipal festivals and executions, and it was also the stage for several important moments in the city's history, particularly during the Revolution: Louis XVI was forced to kiss the new French flag here, and Robespierre was shot in the jaw and arrested here during an attempted coup. Today the square is host to more peaceful activities: There's usually a merry-go-round or two to captivate the little ones, and in winter an **ice-skating rink** is set up.

MODERN PARIS

That immense cube on the other side of the Arc de Triomphe is the **Grande Arche de la Défense** ✪ (1 parvis de la Défense, La Défense, ✪ 01 49 07 27 16; www.grandearche.com; 9€ adults, 7.50€ students and children 6–12, free under 6; Apr–Sept 10am–8pm, Oct–Mar 10am–7pm; Métro: La Défense–Grande Arche), designed by Danish architect Johan Otto von Spreckelsen, who unfortunately died in 1987, 2 years before the building was finished. Situated on the same axis that runs from the obelisk on the place de la Concorde, up the Champs Elysées and through the Arc de Triomphe, this massive structure takes the form of a hollowed-out cube, the inside of which could fit the Cathedral of Notre-Dame. Made out of concrete, the entire building is covered in white marble and glass, giving it a lightness that's completely out of keeping with the reality of its 300,000-metric-ton (330,693-U.S.-ton) weight. Lit at night, it takes on a surreal appearance that's at once futuristic and dreamlike. If you don't mind heights, there's an **observation platform** on the roof, 110m (361 ft.) up where you have an equally otherworldly view of the city.

In 1988, then president François Mitterrand announced the creation of a new megabuilding to house the gigantic collection of the **Bibliothèque National de France** (Site François Mitterand 11 quai François Mauriac, 13th arrond.; ☎ 01 53 79 59 59; www.bnf.fr; Métro: Bibliothèque François Mitterrand). Ten years, and who knows how many millions of euros later, the four towering L-shaped buildings (conceived to resemble open books) opened to the public. Though many have questioned the logic in putting books in glass towers (wooden screens had to be installed throughout to avoid sun damage to the books), it's turned out to be an excellent research facility. Unless you are an architecture fan (the building was designed by Dominique Perrault), or you are going to a temporary exposition (the library occasionally offers a peek at the wonders of its massive collection, see site for details) you can probably get a good enough gander from the Parc de Bercy on the other side of the Seine.

FAMOUS BURIAL GROUNDS

High atop the "montagne" (though the word means mountain, it's actually a medium-sized hill) of St-Geneviève, the dome of the **Panthéon** ✪ (place du Panthéon, 5th arrond.; ☎ 01 44 32 18 00; www.monuments-nationaux.fr; 7.50€ adults, 4.80€ 18–25, free under 18; Oct–Mar 10am–5:15pm, Apr–Sept 10am–5:45pm; Métro: Cardinale Lemoine, RER: Luxembourg) is one of the city's most visible landmarks. This erstwhile royal church has been transformed into a sort of national mausoleum—the final resting place of luminaries such as Voltaire, Rousseau, Hugo, and Zola. Initially dedicated to St-Geneviève, the church was commissioned by a grateful Louis XV, who attributed his recovery from a serious illness to the saint. The architect Jacques-Germain Soufflot took on the project, taking his inspiration from the Pantheon in Rome. It must have been magnificent—the vast interior was clearly created with a higher power in mind. However, during the Revolution its sacred mission was diverted towards a new god—the Nation—and it was converted into a memorial and burial ground for Great Men of the Republic. This meant taking down the bells, walling up most of the windows, doing away with religious statuary and replacing it with works promoting

Home of the Phantom

Flamboyant, extravagant, and baroque, the **Palais Garnier** ★★ (place de l'Opéra, 9th arrond.; ☎ 08 92 89 90 90; http://visites.operadeparis.fr; 8€ adults, 4€ students and 10–19, free under 10; daily 10am–5pm; Métro: Opéra) is a splendid example of Second Empire architectural excess. Corinthian columns, loggias, busts, and friezes cover the **facade** of the building, which is topped by a semiflattened gold dome. 73 sculptors worked on the decoration, which includes portraits of composers, Greek gods, and symbolic representations of Music (by Guillaume), Lyric Poetry (by Jouffroy), Lyric Drama (by Perraud), and Dance (by Carpeaux). The interior of the building is no less dramatic. The vast **lobby,** built in a spectrum of different colored marble, holds a spectacular double staircase that sweeps up to the different levels of the auditorium, as well as an array of glamorous antechambers, galleries, and ballrooms that make you wonder how the opera scenery could possibly compete. Mosaics, mirrors, gilt, and marble line these grand spaces, whose painted ceilings dance with fauns, gods, and nymphs. The largest room, called the **grand foyer,** is drenched in gold leaf and hung with gigantic chandeliers, looking something like a real palace, which was in fact, the effect Garnier was going for. The main event, of course, is the **auditorium,** which might seem a bit small, considering the size of the building. In fact, it holds not even 2,000 seats. The horseshoe shape of the seating area assures that viewers see both the stage and each other—19th century operagoers were equally concerned with what was on the stage and who was in the house. The beautiful

patriotic virtues. The desired effect was achieved—the enormous empty space, lined with huge paintings of great moments in French history, resembles a cavernous tomb. Though the building is of architectural interest, unless you're a fan of one of the men (or women) who are buried under the building (a staircase leads down to the actual crypt), it's probably best admired from the outside. Other than the massive paintings, the only object of note in the sanctuary is **Foucault's Pendulum,** hanging down from the center of the dome, whose changing direction demonstrates the rotation of the Earth.

Definitely not for the faint of heart, the **Catacombs de Paris** (1 ave. du Colonel Henri Roi-Tanguy, 14th arrond.; ☎ 01 43 22 47 63; www.carnavalet.paris.fr; 7€ adults, 5.50€ over 60, 3.50€ 14–26, free under 14, bring proof of age for older children; Tues–Sun 10am–5pm; Métro and RER: Denfert-Rochereau) are filled with the remains of millions of ex-Parisians, whose bones line the narrow passages of this mazelike series of tunnels. In the 18th century, the Cimetière des Innocents, a centuries-old, overpacked cemetery near Les Halles, had become so foul and disease-ridden that it was finally declared a health hazard and closed. The bones of its occupants were transferred to this former quarry, which were later joined by those of other similarly pestilential Parisian cemeteries. The quarry, part of a vast

ceiling was painted with colorful images from various operas and ballets by Marc Chagall in 1964.

All of this (with the exception of the Chagall ceiling) sprang from the mind of a young, unknown architect named Charles Garnier, who won a competition launched when Napoleon III decided the time had come to build himself an opera house. Though the first stone was laid in 1862, work was held up by war, civil unrest, and a change in regime; the Palais Garnier was not inaugurated until 1875. Some contemporary critics found it a bit much (one called it "an overloaded sideboard"), but today it is generally acknowledged as a masterpiece of the architecture of the epoch.

And what about that phantom? Gaston Leroux's 1911 novel, *The Phantom of the Opera,* clearly was inspired by the building's **underground lake,** which was constructed to help stabilize the building.

You can visit the building on your own (for a fee, see ticket prices above), but there's so much history here, and so many good stories, you might want to take advantage of the **guided visits in English** (☎ 01 41 10 08 10; 1¹/₂-hr. tours 12€ adults, 10€ over 60, 9€ students, 6€ under 10; Sept–June Wed, Sat–Sun 11:30am and 2:30pm, July–Aug daily 11:30am and 2:30pm). Either way, your visit will be limited to the lobby, the surrounding foyers, the museum, and the auditorium—this is not a backstage tour (sorry, you won't get to see the lake). Be sure to ask before you buy your tickets if the auditorium is open; depending on rehearsal schedules it could be closed to the public.

network of tunnels that honeycomb the city's entrails, was consecrated after an official benediction in 1786 and accepted new lodgers up until 1814. Stacks and stacks of carefully lined up bones line the passages, which are topped with skulls at regular intervals. Plaques are carved with poetic inscriptions, starting with the one at the entrance, which reads stop: Here is the empire of death. The visit will be fascinating for some, terrifying for others; definitely not a good idea for claustrophobics or small children. The Catacombs were renovated in 2005, new lighting (appropriately eerie, bring a flashlight if you really want to see) and trilingual explanations (English, French, Spanish) should make your visit if not exactly pleasant, at least a little more comfortable. The ceiling still drips however, so a hooded jacket or sweatshirt and rubber-soled shoes are indispensable. You'll want to bring a sweater of some sort anyway, as it's cool down here (around 54°F/12°C).

ROMAN RUINS

As you noodle around the streets near the Jardin des Plantes, you may be surprised to discover a small Roman arena hidden in a leafy garden near place Monge. Although ancient documents long indicated its existence, no one could find the

Arènes de Lutèce (rue des Arènes, 5th arrond.; Métro: Place Monge), until 1869, when workers forcing rue Monge through this Left Bank neighborhood ran into its ruins. While parts of rue Monge still cover parts of the amphitheater, and an overenthusiastic restoration distorted its original form, this is still a lovely spot for a pause or a picnic. Children cavort, old men play *petanque* (a French version of lawn bowling)—a little slice of low-key Parisian life can be observed here amongst blocks of stone dating from the 1st century A.D.

CHURCHES & OTHER HOUSES OF WORSHIP

Only God knows how many churches exist in this city (there are 110 parishes, not counting the dozens of chapels), but many of them are exquisite and most can be visited 7 days a week during daylight hours. If you can, try to get your hands on a booklet called **Patrimoine Sacré de Paris–Guide de Visites d'Eglises,** which is available in many Parisian churches and has a complete listing of all the major Catholic churches in Paris, contact numbers, and information on guided visits. I've organized these edifices by area; though all the famous churches in Paris are Catholic ones, at the end of this section I've also listed a few singular representatives of other religions.

NEAR THE LOUVRE

The destruction of the old Halles (the city's wholesale covered market) in the late 1960s may have been considered heresy by some, but it did expose one of the most beautiful churches in Paris to the light of day. **Saint Eustache** ✪✪ (place du Jour, 1st arrond.; ☎ 01 42 36 31 05; www.saint-eustache.org; Métro: Les Halles, RER: Chatelet-Les Halles), a Gothic church with a Renaissance decor, is one of the largest in the city, over 105m long (344 ft.) and 43m wide (141 ft.). It was built from 1532 to 1640 along the plan of Notre-Dame; the intertwined arches of the ceiling give a similar sense of exalted elevation. These dimensions result in excellent acoustics for the church's huge 8,000-pipe organ, which was recently restored and is considered one of the finest in the city. The church's musical reputation stretches back centuries; Berlioz and Liszt both conducted their works here, among others. Before the Revolution, Saint Eustache was a parish where both the nobility and working class came to worship—Cardinal Richelieu and Madame de Pompadour were both baptized here, as was the playwright Molière. After the Revolution it was turned into a temple to agriculture, and like many Parisian churches, its interior suffered mightily. It was subsequently restored and is currently undergoing another go-round. Work is progressing at a slow pace, and many chapels are still very gloomy, but you can still admire the soaring nave and the overall effect of this graceful edifice.

Recently restored, and with very little stained glass, the interior of **Saint Roch** ✪ (296 rue Saint Honoré, 1st arrond.; ☎ 01 42 44 13 20; www.saintroch. esqualite.com; Métro: Tuileries or Palais Royal–Musée du Louvre) is bright and airy, making it easy, for once, to see the artwork in the chapels. And what artwork—this church has enough **18th and 19th-century paintings and sculptures** to be a museum in its own right. The first thing that strikes you is the brilliantly painted ceiling; the bright colors of the freshly restored Assumption by Jean-Baptiste Pierre illuminate the interior of the dome. Below is the impressive

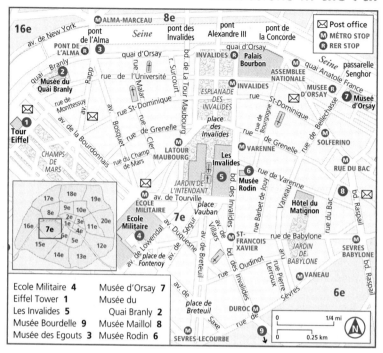

Ecole Militaire **4**	Musée d'Orsay **7**
Eiffel Tower **1**	Musée du
Les Invalides **5**	Quai Branly **2**
Musée Bourdelle **9**	Musée Maillol **8**
Musée des Egouts **3**	Musée Rodin **6**

Chapel of the Virgin, bedecked with sculpted clouds bursting with rays of light. Other sculptural highlights include the bust of Maréchal François de Créqui by Antoine Coysevox, and *Christ in the Garden of the Olive Trees* by Etienne Falconet. In the eastern "arm" of the church is the massive *Miracle des Ardents,* by Doyen, which commemorates the end of a nasty plague in Paris in 1130, thanks to the divine intervention of Saint Genevieve. Not to be overlooked is the magnificent 18th-century **organ,** an official historic monument, with some 2,832 pipes linked to four different keyboards.

Saint Germain l'Auxerrois (2 place du Louvre, 1st arrond.; ☎ 01 42 60 13 96; www.saintgermainauxerrois.cef.fr; Métro: Louvre–Rivoli) is a church with a check-ered past. Designated the royal church when the Valois moved in across the street at the Louvre in the 14th century, kings, queens, and their entourages often attended mass here. Many of the artists who worked on the Louvre are buried here, including architects Le Vau and Soufflot. But its most infamous moment came at dawn on August 24, 1572, when the church's bells sounded the signal that began the Saint Bartholomew's Day massacre. Despite her erstwhile toler-ance, Catherine de Medicis and her son Charles IX gave their blessing to a plot to slaughter the Huguenot (Protestant) leaders. The crowd murdered every Protes-tant in sight—between 2,000 and 4,000 were killed over the following 5 days.

The church has been rebuilt several times over the centuries, resulting in a mix of architectural styles. The 12th-century Romanesque tower hovers over a 15th-century Flamboyant Gothic porch embellished with human and animal figures.

The Bridges of Paris

The **Pont Neuf** ✪✪ (Ile de la Cité, 1st and 6th arrond.; Métro: Cité) has had a makeover and indeed it looks brand spanking *neuf* (new) even if it is in fact, the oldest bridge in Paris. Built to make it easier for the king to get from the Louvre to the abbey of Saint-Germain-des-Prés on the other side of the Seine, the first stone was laid by King Henri III in 1578. The bridge was an instant hit when it was inaugurated by Henri IV in 1607(its ample sidewalks, punctuated by semicircular outcroppings with benches, combined with the fact that it was the first bridge sans houses, made it a delight for pedestrians). It still is, especially if you can ignore the cars and just take in the lovely views. For a quieter experience, take the stairs by the statue of Henri IV (in the center of the span) down to the **Square du Vert Galant** (Henri's untranslatable nickname, which refers to both his gallantry and his love of wine, women, and song), one of my favorite picnic spots. Christo wrapped this bridge in 1985.

The **Pont des Arts** ✪✪ (1st and 6th arrond.; Métro: Louvre–Rivoli) was Paris's first iron bridge, originally constructed at the beginning of the 19th century. Delicately arching over the river, the bridge was deemed overly fragile during a survey in 1976, a fact that was confirmed when it was hit by a barge and collapsed in 1979. After much debate, it was reconstructed (albeit with a few less arches), much to the relief of Parisian pedestrians. This is probably the most romantic bridge in the city—with its splendid view of the Ile de la Cité and its itinerant artists sketching along the railing—and an absolute must at sunset.

The newest way to get from the Left to the Right bank is the **Passerelle Simone de Beauvoir** ✪ (Parc de Bercy to quai François Mariac, 12th and

The vaulted interior is relatively simple and shelters some interesting works of art, amongst which are a monumental **sculpted wooden pew,** designed for the royal family in 1684 by Le Brun, and a 16th-century carved wood **retable** depicting scenes from the life of Christ.

MARAIS

Though you would never know from its grimy outside, the inside of **Saint Paul-Saint Louis** ✪ (99 rue St-Antoine, 4th arrond.; ☎ 01 42 72 30 32; www.saint paulsaintlouis.com; Métro: St-Paul) is an airy delight. One of the few churches in Paris built by Jesuits, the sanctuary is a paradigm of baroque architecture. The lofty ceiling is dominated by an enormous **dome,** the first of its kind in the city and precursor of those on the Sorbonne and Les Invalides. Inaugurated in 1641 with a mass by Cardinal Richelieu, it became the parish of choice for some of the Marais's more illustrious residents, such as Madame de Sévigné. The mausoleum of Henri II was here for many years, along with the hearts of Louis XIII and Louis XIV. Though most of the art works were pillaged during the revolution, there are

13th arrond.; Métro: Bercy or Bibliothèque François Mitterand). A graceful pedestrian passage, the bridge consists of two arching bands of oak and steel, which somehow intertwine and cross the river without the support of a central pillar. The central lens-shaped structure was constructed by the Eiffel factory, which was founded by Gustave.

With its enormous pillars topped by gilded statuary, it's hard to miss the **Pont Alexandre III** ★ (7th and 8th arrond.; Métro: Champs-Elysées Clemenceau or Invalides). Linking the vast esplanade of the Invalides with the glass-domed Grand Palais, this elegant bridge fits right in with its grand surroundings. The span was named after Czar Alexander III of Russia, and his son, the unfortunate Nicolas II, laid the first stone in 1896. Inaugurated at the opening of the Paris Exposition of 1900 (as were the Grand and Petit Palais), each of its four stone pillars holds a different configuration of winged horses, each created by a top sculptor of the era.

One of the older bridges in Paris, construction of the **Pont Marie** (4th arrond.; Métro: Pont Marie) was both built and financed by 17th-century architect Christophe Marie. Incredibly, this small and lovely bridge, composed of three gentle arches, was once loaded down by some 50 houses. The structure could not hold its charge, and during a flood in 1658, the Seine washed away two of its arches and 20 houses fell into the water. The tragedy, which claimed 60 lives, got city officials to thinking, and finally, in 1769, homesteading on bridges was outlawed.

still some important paintings on display, including Delacroix's Christ in the Garden of Olives. The two holy water fonts, in the form of giant shells, were gifts of another famous parishioner, Victor Hugo.

LATIN QUARTER

One of the prettiest churches in the city, **Saint Etienne du Mont** ★★ (place St-Geneviève, 5th arrond.; ☎ 01 43 54 11 79; Métro: Cardinal Lemoine, RER: Luxembourg) is a joyous mix of late Gothic and Renaissance styles. The 17th-century facade combines Gothic tradition with a dash of classical Rome; inside, the 16th-century chancel sports a magnificent **rood screen** (an intricately carved partition separating the nave from the chancel) with decorations inspired by the Italian Renaissance. Bookended by twin spiraling marble staircases, this rood screen is the only one left in the city. The entire church has been cleaned, making it easy to appreciate its riches, which include 16th- and 17th-century stained glass. A pilgrimage site, the empty **sarcophagus of Saint Geneviève** lies in an ornate shrine—her bones were burned during the Revolution, and their ashes were thrown in the Seine. The remains of two other great minds, Racine and Pascal are buried here.

Built and rebuilt since the 14th century, what you see today at **Saint Séverin** ★ (1 rue des Prêtres St-Séverin, 5th arrond.; ☎ 01 42 34 93 50; www.saint-severin.com; Métro: St-Michel) is literally a pastiche. The portal on the west side of the building comes from another church: St-Pierre-aux-Boeufs on the Ile de la Cité, which was torn down in 1837. Generally Gothic in design, the church harbors a grand 18th-century organ (which unfortunately hides part of the rose window), and has a unique double ambulatory (sort of a chancel behind the chancel) with palm-tree style columns that unfold into the arches of the ceiling. The center column is of particular note with its multiple, spiraling "palm fronds." Also of note are the **stained-glass windows;** the traditional 15th- and 19th-century depictions of saints and religious events blend harmoniously with colorful 20th-century windows by Jean Bazine.

SAINT GERMAIN

Equally ancient, but with a much larger role in the city's history, **Saint Germain des Prés** ★★ (place St-Germain des Prés, 6th arrond.; ☎ 01 55 42 81 33; www.eglise-sgp.org; Métro: St-Germain des Prés) was first established by King Childebert in 543, who constructed a basilica and monastery on the site. Built, destroyed, and rebuilt several times over the centuries, nothing remains of the original buildings (although the foundations of the basilica were recently uncovered), but the bell tower dates from the 10th century and is one of the oldest in France. Most of the rest of the church was built in the 11th and 12th centuries and is Romanesque in style. The church and its abbey became a major center of learning and power during the Middle Ages, remaining a force to be reckoned with up until the eve of the French Revolution. Once the monarchy toppled, however, all hell broke loose: The abbey was destroyed, the famous library burned, and the church vandalized. Restored in the 19th century, the buildings have regained some of their former glory, though the complex is a fraction of its original size.

The first thing you'll notice on entering is that much of the interior is painted in a range of greens, and golds—one of the few Parisian churches to retain a sense of its original decor. There are several murals by 19th-century artist Hippolyte Flandrin over the archways in the nave. The heart of King Jean Casimir of Poland is buried here, as are the ashes of the body of René Descartes (his skull is in the collections of the Musée de l'Homme). On the left as you exit is the entrance to the **chapel of St-Symphorien,** where during the Revolution over 100 clergymen were imprisoned before being sent outside to be executed on the square in front of the church. The chapel was restored in the 1970s and decorated by contemporary artist Pierre Buraglio in 1992; it can be visited on Tuesdays and Thursdays from 3pm to 6pm (Tues only during July and Aug).

The hulking majesty of **Saint Sulpice** ★ (place St-Sulpice, 6th arrond.; ☎ 01 42 34 59 98; www.paroisse-saint-sulpice-paris.org; Métro: St-Sulpice or Sèvres–Babylone) looms over an entire neighborhood; this is one of the largest churches in Paris, and one of the richest. Construction started in the 17th century over the remains of a medieval church; it took over a hundred years to build, and one of the towers was never finished. Inside, the cavernous interior seems to command you to be silent; several important works of art are tucked into the chapels that line the church. The most famous of them are three masterpieces by Eugène Delacroix, *Jacob Wrestling with the Angel, Heliodorus Driven from the Temple,* and *St-Michael Vanquishing the Devil* (on the right just after you enter the church). Jean-Baptiste Pigalle's statue of the *Virgin and Child* lights up the Chapelle de la Vierge at the farthest most point from the entrance. A bronze line runs north–south along the floor; during the equinoxes and the winter solstice, sunlight runs up this meridian, climbs an obelisk to a globe and lights up the cross. The organ is a work of art in itself; its case was designed by Chalgrin, and the instrument, which dates from 1781, was made by Cliquot.

NEAR THE OPERA

As you peer up the rue Royale from the place de la Concorde, you'll see something that very closely resembles a Roman temple. **La Madeleine** (place de la Madeleine, 8th arrond.; ☎ 01 44 51 69 00; www.eglise-lamadeleine.com; Métro: Madeleine) is in fact a church that owes its unusual form to its equally singular history. In 1763, architect Pierre Constant d'Ivry laid the first stone of a church that would include a neoclassical facade with multiple columns. He didn't get very far. First the architect died, and then the Revolution broke out, during which construction ground to a halt. Then no one could figure out what to do with the building. A church was out of the question for the new anticlerical government, but surely they could find some use for the structure? France's greatest architects debated the question for years until finally Napoleon strode onto the scene and declared that it would become the Temple de La Gloire, to honor the glorious victories of his army. He designated an architect, Pierre Vignon, and gave him strict orders as to how the work should be carried out. He wanted something "solid" because he was sure that the monument would last "thousands of years." Unfortunately for him, his army didn't last nearly that long. Military defeats and mounting debt would again delay construction until Napoleon decided that maybe it wouldn't be such a bad idea to make it a church after all—that way Rome would foot the bill. Once Napoleon was out of the picture for good, inertia took over the project again, and it wasn't until 1842, under the Restoration, that La Madeleine was finally consecrated.

The inside of the church is pretty dark, owing to a lack of windows, but there are actually some interesting works of art here, if you can make them out in the gloom. On the left as you enter is François Rude's *Baptism of Christ,* further on is James Pradier's sculpture *La Marriage de la Vierge.* Sculptor Charles Marochetti designed the enormous statue on the altar, which portrays Mary Magdalene being carried off to heaven by two enormous angels.

MONTMARTRE

Just behind the hullabaloo of place du Tertre lies a small church that has been in operation for nearly a millennium. **Saint Pierre de Montmartre** ✪ (2 rue du Mont Cenis, 18th arrond.; ☎ 01 46 06 57 63; Métro: Anvers) is the last remnant of an important Benedictine abbey that held sway in Montmartre up until the Revolution. Erected on the site of an ancient sanctuary dedicated to Saint Denis, the church was consecrated in 1147 by Pope Eugene III. The columns in the chancel most probably were taken from the original gallo-roman temple that preceded the sanctuary.

What's nice about this church, aside from its ancient roots, is its human scale. The architecture is partly Romanesque, partly early Gothic; the lovely stained glass windows date from 1954 and replace the originals, which were destroyed during World War II. The tombstone of the abbey's founder, Adelaide of Savoy, is in the left aisle.

OTHER HOUSES OF WORSHIP

France is home to the largest Jewish community in Europe (approximately 700,000 strong), so it's not surprising that it also boasts the largest synagogue on the Continent. Built in the late 19th century by Alfred-Philibert Aldrophe, the **Synagogue de la Victoire** (44 rue de la Victoire, 9th arrond.; ☎ 01 40 82 26 26; www.lavictoire.org; Métro: Le Peletier or Notre-Dame de Lorette) is a joyous mix of neoclassical and Byzantine architecture. Arches, mosaics, and columns abound; 12 stained glass windows represent the 12 tribes of Judea. The synagogue had its share of trauma during the war years—a bombing in 1941, vandalism in 1942, and a round-up in the middle of Rosh Hashana services in 1943. Perhaps this, along with terrorism and other depressing recent world events, explains the intense security procedures one must go through to enter the structure, which is only open for services, held at 6:30pm Friday night, and 9:30am Saturday morning.

The Muslim community, which numbers some 5 million, is the largest non-Christian group in France, with many small mosques in different parts of the city. The most splendid is the **Grande Mosquée de Paris** (2 bis place du Puits de l'Ermite, 5th arrond.; ☎ 01 45 35 97 33; www.mosquee-de-paris.org; visits Mon–Thurs and Sat–Sun 9am–noon and 2–6pm; 3€ entry fee; Métro: Place Monge or Censier–Daubenton), which sports not only a religious sanctuary, but also a tearoom, restaurant, hamman (traditional baths), and boutique. Inspired by the great Moorish mosques of pre-Renaissance Spain, the arcades and patios were built in the early 1920s; the minaret stands 33m (108 ft.) tall. Intricate mosaics cover some walls and ceilings; Andalusian-style fountains tinkle in the gardens.

Historically, Protestants have not had it easy in France. Subject to multiple "ethnic cleansings" over the centuries by overzealous Catholics, today they represent only about 2% of the French population (about 1,100,000). There are several Protestant churches in Paris (called "temples"), one of the loveliest being the **Oratoire du Louvre** (1 rue de l'Oratoire, 1st arrond.; ☎ 01 42 60 21 64; www.oratoiredulouvre.fr; Métro: Louvre-Rivoli). Originally a Catholic chapel used by the Royals at the Louvre, this 17th-century church saw the funerals of Cardinal Richelieu and Louis XIII. Relieved of its religious functions during the Revolution, it was subsequently used as a conference hall, a stock exchange, and finally, a warehouse for theater scenery. In 1811, Napoleon offered the chapel to the Reform Church, which has made itself a home here ever since. The church is only open Sundays, when it hosts services at 10:30am.

TOURING THE CITY OF LIGHT

There are any number of different kinds of guided tours of the city available, from the classic bus route to boat cruises to bicycle tours. Below are of some of my favorites, in a range of styles and sizes.

WALKING TOURS

To really get down to the nitty gritty in Paris, you need to walk—there's no other way to really appreciate the finer details. While there are dozens of books outlining walking tours (including this one; see chapter 8), there are not that many group walking tours guided by a real person, and even fewer in English. Below is a short list of some of the better ones; I've stuck to those that are low-cost and easy to hook up with, staying away from the pricier private guided tours (though all besides the first company offer them). Schedules and meeting points are detailed on each organization's website.

Comité Départemental de la Randonée Pédestre de Paris (35 rue Piat, 20th arrond.; ☎ 01 46 36 95 70; www.rando-paris.org). The name is complicated but the concept is simple: This is a volunteer-based hiking association (there are branches all over the country) that organizes walks in Paris. There is no "guide" on, but you'll be walking with real live Parisians who know the territory, and what's more, there's no charge. Visit the site for a calendar and rendezvous points.

Paris Walks ✪✪ (12 passage Meunier, St-Denis; 01 48 09 21 40; www.paris-walks.com; 10€ adults, 8€ students under 21 (with I.D.), 5€ children under 15). "We try to make our tours as lively and as fun as possible," says Peter Caine, who has been organizing these excellent tours with his wife Oriel since 1994. This is the only company that specializes in English-language walks; all of their certified guides are long-term expats or English-speaking locals, whose thorough, well-researched commentaries are peppered with a large dose of humor and good gossip. The regularly scheduled tours shed new light on the most famous neighborhoods. Paris Walks also offers in-depth, theme-oriented tours, like the French Revolution, Hemingway's Paris, and of course, the Da Vinci Code. (Caine has written a book on this last subject.) The 2-hour tours are offered every day of the year, rain or shine; no reservations are necessary.

Soundwalk (www.soundwalk.com). There are dozens of mp3 audio tours available these days on the Web, but this one enters an entirely different dimension. These are not simply walking tours describing interesting tourist sites; these are soundtracks for an independent film. Best known for their quirky and fascinating tours of New York City, Soundwalk now has five audio tours of Paris, each one narrated by a different up-and-coming young French actress. Each tour has a premise, ranging from a fairly straightforward tour through the shops and history of the Palais Royal district by Hélène Fillières, to a skitter through the Marais with Isild Le Besco, who is on her way to an audition and has left her demo tape somewhere in the neighborhood. Follow an enticing young man through St-Germain with Virginie Ledoyen, or get your jollies in the Pigalle red-light district with the impossibly pouty Lou Doillon. Each tour is scored with appropriately atmospheric music and sound effects, and each is guaranteed to nourish the fantasy that Paris is crawling with sexy women with alluring accents. Aside from the entertainment value, these tours are punctuated with intriguing facts, anecdotes, and interviews, as well an assortment of tiny details that you would probably miss if you were on your own. Each download comes with a French and English version, as well a map, and costs $12.

BOAT TOURS

Since the Seine neatly divides this egg-shaped city in two lengthwise, and because many of its most famous monuments are located on its banks, a boat cruise along the river is a great way to see the city, particularly if you're strapped for time. The downside: You won't be alone. Not only do the tours tend to be crowded and noisy, but the recorded information that is barked at you from speakers in several languages is not particularly informative. If you can manage to concentrate on the beauty before you, and come armed with a good guidebook, you'll still get something out of these floats; if you can't handle the crowds try the Batobus (see below), or opt for a walk down the quays on your own (see "Walkabouts," p. 229).

On the Seine

Compagnie des Bateaux Mouches ✪ (Port de la Conférence, Pont de l'Alma, 8th arrond.; ☎ 01 42 25 96 10; www.bateaux-mouches.fr; 10€ adults, 5€ over 65 and children 4–12, free under 4; Métro: Alma-Marceau). The biggest of the boat tours, these are the classic Bateaux Mouches you've probably heard about: enormous glass-topped affairs that blast multilingual commentary at passengers as they float down the Seine. Don't worry about reserving: Boats leave every 20 minutes from 10:15am to 3:15pm and 4–11pm in high season (Apr–Sept), every 45 minutes the rest of the year. Though they are extremely touristy and crowded (the boats can hold around 1,000), it must be said that the view from the outdoor seating area is splendid and the price is right.

Bateaux Parisiens (Port de la Bourdonnais, at the foot of the Eiffel Tower, 7th arrond.; ☎ 01 76 64 14 45; www.bateauxparisiens.com; sightseeing cruises 11€ adults, 6€ children 3–12, free under 3; lunch cruises 52€–72€ adults, 31€ children under 12; dinner cruises 95€–150€ adults [no children's menu]; Métro: Bir-Hakeim, RER: Champ de Mars–Tour Eiffel). The same idea, but on a smaller scale (boats hold 350–500), these cruises take off from a port at the foot of the Eiffel Tower, and in high season (Apr–Oct) there is a second embarkation point below Notre-Dame. Less noisy and more civilized, these boats broadcast their commentary on individual handsets that let you choose your language. Many choose this line for its lunch or dinner cruises, which come with live music and dancing.

Les Vedettes du Pont Neuf ✪ (square du Vert-Galant, 1st arrond.; ☎ 01 46 33 98 38; www.vedettesdupontneuf.com; 11€ adults, 6€ 4–12, free under 4; Métro: Pont Neuf; no credit cards). With boats around the same size as the Bateaux Parisiens, the big difference here is that there is a real live person guiding the cruise, who not only offers commentary in both French and English, but will actually answer questions. Unlike all the other cruises, which depart from the Eiffel Tower, this one leaves from the lovely square du Vert Galant at the tip of the Ile de la Cité, which means you'll have fewer crowds to deal with. Boats leave every 30 to 45 minutes in high season (mid-Mar to Oct) and every 45 to 60 minutes the rest of the year; there is a 2€ to 4€ reduction if you buy your ticket on their website.

Batobus ✪ (Port de la Bourdonnais, 7th arrond.; ☎ 08 25 05 01 01; www.batobus. com). A floating version of the hop-on, hop-off bus tours, Batobus is not only a low-key way to cruise the river but is also a way of getting around town. There's no commentary, recorded or otherwise; the boat stops at eight points on the river (including Notre-Dame, the Eiffel Tower, the Musée d'Orsay, and the Champs Elysées) every 15 to 30 minutes. For 12€ (6€ for children under 16) you can hop on and off the boat all day, for 14€ (child 7€) you can do the same for 2 consecutive days, and for 17€ (child 8€) you can float through Paris for 5 days. There's a slight reduction if you buy your ticket in conjunction with l'Open Tour (p. 196). You can buy your ticket at the tourist office, the airport, or any of the stops.

Canal St-Martin

If you're looking for a different kind of boat tour, the arched bridges and locks of the Canal St-Martin are a good choice, particularly in the spring and summer, when the plane trees that line the canal provide a leafy canopy over the water. These cruises float through little-known neighborhoods where regular working folk live and offer another look at the city. Part of the canal has been paved over, so a portion of the cruise will go underground.

Canauxrama (Bassin de la Villette, 13 quai de la Loire, 19th arrond.; ☎ 01 42 39 15 00; www.canauxrama.com; 15€ adults, 11€ students and seniors, 4–12 8€, free under 4, except weekend and holiday afternoons, when everyone, even the tiny tots, pay 15€) offers a 2½-hour cruise from Port de l'Arsenal next to the place de la Bastille to the Bassin de la Villette in the 19th arrondissement, next to the Parc de la Villette. Live guides offer commentary in both French and English; reservations are mandatory from Oct–Mar. They also offer an evening Bistrot Cruise on the Seine with bar service, as well as a day-long cruise from the Seine to the Marne, known for the old-fashioned "guinguettes," or open-air dance halls, on its banks.

Paris Canal (Bassin de la Villette, 19-21 quai de la Loire, 19th arrond.; ☎ 01 42 40 96 97; www.pariscanal.com; 17€ adults, 14€ 12–25 and over 60, 9€ 4–11, free under 4) costs a little bit more, but your cruise will include a jaunt on the Seine, from the Musée d'Orsay to the Port de l'Arsenal, where you'll head up the canal and follow the same route as Canauxrama. You can take the cruise in either direction, but it runs from mid-March to mid-November only. The ride, which takes around 2½ hours, includes live commentary in both French and English. Reservations required. They also offer a day-long tour to the Marne.

BUS TOURS

I'm not a fan of Parisian bus tours; at best they're superficial, and at worst, a waste of time. Remember: Parisian traffic is dreadful and the buses are not immune to its caprices. Plus the "hop-on, hop-off" bus companies start their service at 9:30am, ending between 6 and 8pm (varying by season), so in reality your day is quite limited. And commentary (when you can hear it; the headphones are notoriously spotty) tends to be poorly done. In recent years, hop-on, hop-off tours (where you can get on and off the bus at designated points around the city) have become popular—though the advantages might seem to be many, be forewarned that this is a very expensive way to get around town, and you likely won't learning anything new about the city (commentary tends to be poorly done). Be that as it may, I have listed the two most popular companies below.

Do-It-Yourself Bus Tours

Hop off that expensive bus tour and get yourself a Paris Visite pass (see "Lay of the Land," p. 6); for about half the price (14€), you can hop on and off comfortable city buses (and use the subway system) for 2 days (including evenings). Outside of the rush hour crush (8–9:30am and 5:30–8pm), you'll usually get a seat, and now that there are more and more bus lanes, you shouldn't get stuck in traffic. Ask for a Métro-bus map at your nearest Métro stop, which should have a good map of the bus routes on one side. Some lines are merely practical, but others are truly scenic. A few favorites: **Line 63,** which starts at Porte de la Muette and passes by the Eiffel Tower, through St-Germain and the Latin Quarter and back over the Seine to the Gare de Lyon; **Line 87,** which starts at the Champs de Mars, scoots through St-Germain and the Latin Quarter and crosses the Seine to the Bastille; **Lines 21 and 27,** which run from the Opéra to the Ile de la Cité and on the Jardin du Luxembourg; and **Line 73,** which runs down the Champs Elysées and ends at the Musée d'Orsay.

If none of this dampens your enthusiasm for the hop-on, hop-off experience (and these buses do have their fans), read on: Below you will find pertinent information for the two existing Parisian bus companies of this type.

L'Open Tour (13 rue Auber, 9th arrond.; ☎ 01 42 66 56 56; www.paris-opentour. com; Métro: Opéra or Havre-Caumartin). The most omnipresent of the bus tours, this hop-on, hop-off operation is the result of a partnership between Cityrama tours and the RATP (the Parisian rapid transit system). While the four different lines certainly cover a lot of territory (you can transfer from one to another free of charge), you will pay a high price for this convenience: 29€ for a 1-day pass and 32€ for a 2-day pass (children 4–11 pay 15€ for 1 or 2 days). Tickets can be bought on the bus, at any of the branches of the Paris Tourist Office, or at many hotels and travel agencies.

Les Cars Rouges (17 quai de Grenelle, 15th arrond.; ☎ 01 53 95 39 53; www.carsrouges.com; Métro: Bir Hakeim). These red double-decker buses (car in French means tour bus) run on the same concept as L'Open Tour, with a more limited circuit (one line with 10 stops) and a cheaper ticket (24€ adults, 12€ children 4–12, for a 2-day pass). Tickets are purchased on board.

By the way, the city of Paris has its own public transportation versions of bus tours (see www.ratp.fr for route maps): In Montmartre, you can ride the **Montmartrobus,** which does a nice circuit of the neighborhood and costs one regular bus ticket, and in the center of town the **Balabus** hits the main tourist highlights between the Gare de Lyon and La Défense. The advantages of this second line are questionable, however, as you must pay several tickets if you are crossing town, and you can do the same trip on regular public buses for fewer tickets (see the "Do-It-Yourself Bus Tours," box above).

BIKE TOURS

Paris is steadily becoming more and more bike-friendly, particularly since Velib', the city's almost-free rent-a-bike program came into being in 2007 (for details on how it works see the box on p. 12 in "Lay of the Land," or visit www.velib.fr). More and more bike lanes are appearing, as well as more and more cyclists. Even if you aren't ready to brave Parisian traffic on two wheels, a group rides can be a lot of fun, and cars will rarely try to intimidate bicycle riders en masse. A good tour offers a great way to see Paris at eye-level without wearing out your best walking shoes, as well as an opportunity to work off some of those croissants you've been gorging on. All of the tour companies listed below also rent bikes by the hour or by the day.

Paris à Vélo C'est Sympa (22 rue Alphonse Baudin, 11th arrond.; ☎ 01 48 87 60 01; www.parisvelosympa.com; Métro: Richard Lenoir; 34€ adults, 26€ 12–26, 18€ under 12, minimum height 135cm or 4'5"; reservations are mandatory). The name roughly translates as "It's fun to ride around Paris on a bike," and I certainly couldn't argue with that. This company was the first to launch bike tours of the city, and in high season (Apr–Oct) runs 3-hour tours almost every day (Nov–Mar weekends only). In addition to a good tour of the city's highlights, they also offer an evening tour, as well as tours that cover less well-known parts of the city and its parks. Tours are conducted in English and French.

Bike About Tours (☎ 06 18 80 84 92; www.bikeabouttours.com; Métro: Cité or St-Michel; 25€ adults, 23€ students with ID; minimum age: 10). For a good tour that hits all the major highlights, this friendly, English-only bike tour company does a 3½-hour tour of the city every day, with a break for lunch or a snack. You'll meet up at 10am (from May–Oct there is a second tour that leaves at 3pm, evening tours leave from the same spot at 7pm) at the statue of Charlemagne in front of Notre Dame and take off on an inventive circuit that includes tantalizing details like a stray cannonball that dates from the Revolution, a 1,000-year old wall, and the tour guides' favorite bakeries. Tours run from April through October, rain or shine (rain ponchos available); reservations are not obligatory (except for the evening tour), but highly recommended. This caring company, which offers helmets to riders, donates a percentage of its profits to charities that work with the homeless.

Paris Bike Tour (38 rue Saintonge, 3rd arrond.; ☎ 01 53 39 13 14; www. parisbiketour.net; Métro: République or Filles de Calvaire; 29€, minimum age: 12). Another outfit that believes in small groups (10–15 riders) and helmets, this well-established company offers two different tours, one focusing on the Right Bank and another on the Left. You must reserve at least 24 hours in advance; the 3-hour tours are conducted in French, English, and a handful of other languages if need be (specify when reserving). The company recently inaugurated an evening tour that covers both sides of the Seine.

6 The "Other" Paris

In which we reveal aspects of the city that are usually hidden to outsiders & how to experience them the way the locals do

PARIS IS A CITY THAT PROUDLY DISPLAYS ITS OBVIOUS CHARMS: BEAUTIFUL architecture, marvelous monuments, gorgeous gardens, and atmospheric streets. But when it comes to getting up close and personal, it balks. It's not for nothing that Parisians have been pinned with a stereotype of being cold and distant, or even downright rude to outsiders. Some of it is cultural: In France, friendships are something to be nurtured over time, and superficial alliances are viewed with suspicion. Parisians, in particular, are accused even by their own countrymen of being overly aloof, a quality that is exacerbated by their fast-paced lives which seem to keep them from noticing the world around them, much less interacting with it. Needless to say, this attitude does not exactly heighten a tourist's cross-cultural experience. In fact, it is no doubt at the root of the much-repeated sentiment: "I love Paris; it's the Parisians I can't stand."

But is this really fair? Or even accurate? Believe it or not, in recent years, the city government has been behind a campaign of sorts to get its citizens to loosen up, and to a certain degree, it has worked. Overall, there is a lot more tolerance for foreigners, and many Parisians actually enjoy showing off their English these days (although you still should *not* assume that everyone can speak English). Instead of calling them cold, it might be more instructive to call Parisians introverted. While it is true that chances are, you won't be invited out to dinner through a casual encounter with a group of natives, if you approach them gently and don't scare them off, you might at least have a conversation, which could develop into a discussion, and then who knows? They might invite you to dinner after all (it can happen—I met my husband that way). In my experience, Parisians can be friendly . . . but they will rarely make the first move (unless we're talking about seduction, which is an entirely different discussion). The key is to get into a situation that is conducive to communication, or get involved in an activity where you'll see the locals in a relaxed or even open frame of mind. Even if you don't end up bonding with François or Françoise, you'll get a peek at another side of the city, and it will add another dimension to your trip—and a better understanding of what Paris is really all about.

Below are a number of things you can do to experience an insider's view of Paris. I've divided these up by category: learning, working, and playing. Even if your time here is limited, I urge you to try at least one or two of these activities as a way of filling out the socio-cultural gaps in your itinerary—and of having a great time in the process.

HOW PARISIANS LEARN

Despite their busy work schedules (or perhaps because of them), Parisians flock to various types of courses and classes for *la détente* (relaxation) and to *changer les idées* (literally, to change one's ideas, or to think about other things than work, for example). Here are a few where language should not be a barrier to learning and anyone can join in for a session.

COOKING CLASSES

If there's one thing that you can take home that will both last a lifetime and not take up any space in your suitcase, it's a little French culinary savoir-faire. You may not have time to do any in-depth study, but the tips that you'll pick up can be mighty useful back home, and heaven knows, you'll have fun eating the results of your coursework.

Amaze your friends and wow your family with the tricks you learned at **L'Atelier de Fred** (6 rue des Vertus, 3rd arrond.; ☎ 01 40 29 46 04; www.latelierdefred.com; 60€ adults, 35€ children 9–12; Métro: Arts et Métiers), a small-scale cooking class taught in someone's actual apartment. In the space of 3 hours, Fred Chesneau, a self-taught chef with a gift for inventive, contemporary cuisine, will teach five students how to make a mouth-watering three-course meal for company without going crazy or spending a fortune. The first 2 hours focus on preparation; the last is for eating the meal you created with your new friends, accompanied by a good bottle of wine, *bien sûr*. Fred also offers courses for children 9 to 12, which mostly revolve around baking and sweet things; he's also created a "Cook Dating" evening, which consists of a regular adult atelier for singles. Fred speaks excellent English—should you be so inclined and have four friends with you, he will conduct a class in your mother tongue. Even if you take a regular class in French, he will be happy to help you through any linguistic snarls. Owing to the small class size, you should reserve well in advance. There are regular adult classes both morning and evening Tuesday through Friday with the exception of Wednesday morning (reserved for children's workshops) and Thursday evenings (which is Cook Dating night).

> "Paris: a city of pleasures and amusements where four-fifths of the people die of grief."
>
> —Sébastien-Roch Nicolas de Chamfort, 18th-century French writer, *Maxims and Considerations*

For a taste of the big time, without signing up for a year's worth of courses at the Cordon Bleu, try a class at **L'Atelier des Chefs** (10 rue de Penthièvre, 8th arrond.; ☎ 01 53 30 05 82 (all locations); www.atelierdeschefs.com; Métro: Miromesnil). In this modern, glass-roofed workshop you'll work with young chefs whose resumes include stints at top restaurants like Lassere and the Ritz. There is a long menu of class options here to choose from: You could try to absorb a recipe for salmon tartare with baby spinach (17€, half-hour class), or you could plunge into "molecular cuisine" and learn how to make virtual yogurt raviolis and mussels in spheres of parsley juice (72€, 2-hr. class). Though there is a lot more variety here and the chefs are real professionals, the classes are generally shorter and more crowded than Fred's; class size varies from 8–20 students. You'll get to eat what you've cooked in the dining area after the class is over (except for a few cases where your results will be takeout); the recipes are sent to you via e-mail. Classes are in French, but that doesn't stop their international students from learning; seeing and tasting is at least as important as listening here. There are special themed classes on particular wines, cheeses, or ingredients, as well as children's ateliers and weekend events. Reserve well in advance, particularly for the shorter class that takes place at lunchtime, which is extremely popular with the office crowd. There are two other smaller sites in department stores, one at **Galeries Lafayette** (Lafayette Maison, 35 blvd. Haussmann, 9th arrond.; Métro: Chausée d'Antin–Layfayette) and the other at a branch of **Printemps** on the eastern end of the city (Printemps Nation, 21–15 Cours Vincennes, 20th arrond.; Métro: Nation); a new atelier/boutique has recently opened at 27 rue Peclet, 15th arrond.; ☎ 01 56 08 33 50; Métro: Cambronne or Commerce).

WINE-TASTING CLASSES

Instead of being intimidated by the seemingly impenetrable mysteries of French wine, why not learn what it's all about? Believe me, even French people aren't always sure about the difference between a Côtes de Blaye and a Côtes du Rhône, which explains the proliferation of wine courses with *dégustations* (tastings) across the city. Although classes are open to everyone, reservations are a must for the first two listed below.

"Bonum vinum laetificat cor hominum" is the motto of the Echansons de France, which loosely translates as "good wine makes you strong." They should know—this association of wine connoisseurs and vendors was created to defend and promote the best wines of France. Back in the old days, an *echanson* was the King's personal wine-taster, whose job was to make sure that the wine was good enough for His lips . . . and not poisoned. Today, poisonings are few and far between (as are kings), so the Echansons devote themselves to less risky activities, like spreading the good word about the pleasures of the vine. This is why they sponsor wine-tastings and oenology classes three or four times a month at the **Musée du Vin** (Rue des Eaux, 16th arrond.; ☎ 01 45 25 70 89; www.museedu vinparis.com; Métro: Passy), which they own. You'll taste at least five wines during the 2-hour classes, which are taught by experts like Monique Josse, who digs deep into both theory and practice. Though classes are usually taught in French (most teachers are bilingual and can translate when necessary), from time to time there are classes in English (check website for schedule). The tasting courses usually take place on Saturday mornings from 10am to noon; you must reserve ahead of time. The price is a bit high (45€), but you'll be learning from real pros, who are serious about their subject—to assure an unpolluted tasting atmosphere, they ask that you do not use perfume or aftershave on the day of the class.

For wine tasting in a more relaxed atmosphere, try **Ô Chateau** (The Wine Loft, 100 rue de la Folie Méricourt, 11th arrond.; ☎ 08 00 80 11 48, toll-free in France, 01 44 73 97 80 for overseas calls; www.o-chateau.com; Métro: République). Olivier Magny, a young French sommelier, has created a mini–wine school for English-speaking enthusiasts. His mission: to demystify French wines and offer a nonintimidating approach to this grand tradition. In large part, he succeeds—his

English-only classes are fun and easygoing, and he passes on a good chunk of interesting and helpful information (you'll go home with a cheat sheet of useful tips). Magny sticks to affordable wines that truly represent a region, so you'll get a better handle on the style; after the class you'll have a chance to purchase a bottle or two (or three). Although his school is definitely geared towards a non-French clientele, and it may be a bit less serious than other courses, this is a great way to learn about this heady subject without having to hurdle language barriers, or endure hours of boring wine minutia. A 1-hour introductory class including three wines is 20€ (Mon and Wed at 3pm); a 2-hour, more in-depth 7-wine class runs 50€ (Mon, Wed, Fri, and Sat at 5pm); and a 1¹/₂-hour wine and cheese tasting (five wines) costs 65€ (Fri–Sat at noon). You can reserve by phone or on the website.

Another great place to learn about wine is the biannual **Salon des Vignerons Indépendants** (Espace Champerret, porte de Champerret, 17th arrond.; ☎ 01 53 02 05 18; 6€ adults, 3€ students, free under 12; Métro: Porte de Champerret). Usually held in April and November, this huge trade show features small, independent wineries that not only grow their own grapes but also carefully oversee the fermentation, processing, and bottling of the exquisite final product (unlike larger cooperative operations). There is nothing corporate about this gathering; 9 times out of 10, the vintner him/herself will be at the helm of the stand, volunteering information about and samples of their treasured elixir. Yes, you can taste yourself into a stupor here, as everyone (and there are hundreds of stands) will gladly proffer you a glass of their wares. What's more, there are free tasting classes given three times a day by wine experts (in French only), so you'll know how to appreciate what you are being offered. *A word of warning:* Unless you're prepared for a big headache and/or a long nap, make use of the spittoons at the stands—true, it's a shame to waste good wine, but it's really a shame to be so whacked that you can't distinguish between Châteauneuf-du-Pape and Ripple. *Another note:* Before you get all excited and start buying cases of wine, check to see what your home country will let you take home. Usually, the November show is held at the Paris Expo convention center at Porte de Versailles (15th arrond.; Métro: Porte de Versailles), and the spring show (held in Mar or Apr), is at the Espace Champerret (see address above). For exact dates and more details, see their website.

DANCE CLASSES

Being the center of French culture, Paris is home to the country's top dance companies and schools, and students trek in from around the nation to study here. While tomorrow's prima ballerinas are generally found in the national conservatories, other aspiring dancers and people who just like to dance head towards the many dance studios sprinkled around the city. Aside from any physical benefits you might get from a class (especially after a long stint in a cramped airplane), this is a great opportunity to see what life is like on the other side of the orchestra pit. Even if you didn't bring your tights, you can take part in one of the many partner-dance classes on offer—after which, you can trot out to one of the swing or salsa clubs listed in our nightlife chapter (p. 276).

Getting to your class is half the fun at the **Centre de Danse du Marais** (41 rue du Temple, 4th arrond.; ☎ 01 42 77 58 19; www.paris-dance.com; Métro: Hôtel de Ville or Rambuteau), which is hidden in an ancient cobbled courtyard down a covered lane in the Marais. This multistudio complex, which takes up most of the building, offers dozens of different kinds of dance forms, from hip-hop to ballet to tap-dance to tango, with a good dose of yoga, martial arts, and theater to boot. You can take most dance classes on a per-class basis; beginning level partner-dance courses (salsa, swing, ballroom, and so on) are particularly easy to pop into without being a regular student. After class, you can cool off with a drink at the cafe-restaurant in the courtyard, while you watch students haul their cumbersome dance bags in and out of the studios. Visitors will find a little bit of everything here, from enthusiastic amateurs to hard-core professionals. There is one price grid for all classes: 18€ for one class, 61€ for four, 102€ for eight, and 143€ for 12. You'll also get a slight reduction if you take the "Pass 5 Cours," which gives you access to five different classes for 70€. *Note:* If you take more than one or two classes, you'll be asked to pay an 11€ annual insurance fee.

I don't know if the movie *Last Tango in Paris*, had anything to do with it, but Paris and tango seem to have a thing for each other. Maybe there's something about this elegant, enigmatic dance form that strikes a chord amongst Parisians; this is a dance where you can commune with your most passionate impulses without ever mussing your hair. There are classes all over town, but one of the easiest to drop into for beginners (believe me, Argentine tango is not as easy as it looks) is **Espace Oxygene** (4 Impasse Cordon Broussard, just off 247 rue des Pyrénées, 20th arrond.; ☎ 01 49 29 06 77; www.espaceoxygene.com; Métro: Gambetta). Several excellent teachers hold classes here; Imed Chemam's débutant level on Saturday nights (7:30pm) is a good one for absolute beginners. Though your lessons will not be in English, that shouldn't keep you from learning—the language of dance is pretty universal. Once you've gotten a taste for tango, you can continue your explorations at clubs like La Latina, or stop by the on-going milonga on the Seine on summer nights (see box "Paris Danse en Seine," p. 203).

READINGS IN ENGLISH

Though the Lost Generation is long lost, and Hemingway and Fitzgerald no longer scribble in fabled cafes, that doesn't stop boatloads of English-language writers from coming here to try to recapture that magical epoch. Maybe it's the literary legacy, or maybe it's just the abundance of cafes to hang out and write in, but Paris continues to draw writers, which becomes evident when you frequent the city's English-language bookstores. Beyond selling books, these stores serve as mini–cultural centers for wayward English-speakers, and they often sponsor readings and other literary events that are free to one and all.

Courting the literary crème de la crème, the **Village Voice** (6 rue Princesse, 6th arrond.; ☎ 01 46 33 36 47; www.villagevoicebookshop.com; Métro: Mabillon or St-Germain des Prés) gets the most prestigious authors (Edmund White, Mavis Gallant, and Russell Banks are just a few of the names on their list of past events) and offer one or two readings per month. Though you may not immediately recognize the names of the authors reading at **Red Wheelbarrow Bookstore** (22 rue St-Paul, 4th arrond.; ☎ 01 48 04 75 08; www.theredwheelbarrow.com; Métro: St-Paul), most have been widely published; readings by novelists, poets, and children's authors are scheduled once or twice a month. Some of the authors that have presented their works here include novelist Amy Bloom, and mystery writer

Paris Danse en Seine

It's been going on for years—every summer a dozen or so different groups of dance fans stake out a spot on the Quai St-Bernard (along which runs the **Jardins Tino Rossi**), set up a boom box, and start dancing. With Notre-Dame and the Seine in the moon-lit background, this has got to be one of the most romantic spots in Paris for dancing cheek to cheek. There's no charge, no sign up, just show up on a summer evening and pick your poison: Argentine tango, salsa, swing, capoeira, samba—each group takes over a separate concrete inlet in the park. Anyone can join in, but you should know your moves; a lot of die-hard dance fanatics come here and if you're an absolute beginner you'll soon find yourself on the edges of the action. But there is hope for daring debutants: Several groups offer on-site initiation classes an hour or so before the dancing starts. A couple of years ago, the groups formed an association which now has the official stamp of approval from city hall: **Paris Danses en Seine.** In general, dancing starts around 9pm Monday to Saturday and 7:30pm Sunday. Initiation classes around 7pm Monday to Saturday and 6pm Sunday.

Cara Black, who uses Paris as a backdrop in her novels. **Brentano's** (37 av. de l'Opéra; 2nd arrond.; ☎ 01 42 61 52 50; www.brentanos.fr; Métro: Pyramides) not only has readings but also has a reading club that meets once a month, and a "cafe tricot"—a club where you can come by and talk books while you knit (see website for dates and times). Canadian authors are highlighted at the **Abbey Bookshop** (29 rue de la Parcheminerie, 5th arrond.; ☎ 01 46 33 16 24; www. abbeybookshop.net; Métro: St-Michel), but the appeal here goes beyond books— this friendly place also organizes hikes in nearby forests, and offers customers a free cup of "Canadian Coffee," sweetened with real maple syrup.

Though the ambience at **WHSmith** (248 rue de Rivoli, 1st arrond.; ☎ 01 44 77 88 99; www.whsmith.fr; Métro: Concorde), an English chain store, might be less compelling than elsewhere, they also have interesting readings, as well as a "Kids' Club" where the latest children's books are presented. On the other end of the spectrum, the militantly offbeat **Shakespeare & Company** (37 rue de la Bucherie, 5th arrond.; ☎ 01 43 25 40 93; www.shakespeareco.org; Métro: St-Michel) presents readings by mostly local writers and poets, as well as play-readings of works in progress. An informal writer's group also meets here on Saturdays at 3pm to exchange ideas and discuss their latest work.

For an up-to-date listing of all current literary events, visit Paris Readings & Events Monthly at http://parisreadingsmonthlylisting.blogspot.com.

HOW PARISIANS WORK

True, you can't visit the offices and workshops where millions of Parisians earn their daily bread, but there are a few places you can go where you can see them in action. Want to sit in on an art auction? Spy on skilled weavers creating gorgeous tapestries? Watch fruit and vegetable vendors try to outdo each other hawking their wares at an open-air market? Read on . . .

AUCTIONS

You can see some of Brassaï's best photography, Lalique glassware, or Louis XIV–epoch cabinetry for free—if you dare to enter the mysterious world of art auctions. Though the buyers are generally outrageously wealthy and the objects are exquisite and rare, in fact, every sale in Paris is open to the public, which means you too can go. If you don't feel like going to the sale, you can come the day before for the presentation—a miniart exhibit that is absolutely free. Drouot is the name to remember in Paris auctions—you can't miss it as there is an entire quarter and a Métro stop that shares the same name. Paintings, furniture, and art objects go on auction in the 16 rooms of the **Hôtel Drouot** (9 rue Drouot, 9th arrond.; ☎ 01 48 00 20 20; www.drouot.fr; Métro: Richelieu-Drouot), where the goods go on display the day before the auction from 11am to 6pm and the day of the auction from 11am to noon, usually on Tuesday, Thursday, and Saturday. You can also watch the sale (no bidding or fur coats needed); simply check the website of the Gazette de l'Hôtel Drouot (www.gazette-drouot.com) for the program and show up at the appointed hour. Jewelry and very high-end merchandise require more exclusive surroundings—these auctions go on at **Drouot Montaigne** (15 av. Montaigne, 8th arrond.; ☎ 01 48 00 20 80; Métro: Alma-Marceau), in the ultrachic area just south of the Champs Elysées.

A TAPESTRY FACTORY TOUR

Back in the 17th century, Louis XIV purchased the **Manufacture des Gobelins** (42 av. des Gobelins, 13th arrond.; ☎ 01 44 08 52 00; www.mobiliernational.culture.gouv.fr; guided visits only: 10€ adults, 7.50€ 13–25; free under 12; guided tours Tues–Thurs 2 and 3pm, reserve at least a day ahead at ☎ 08 92 68 36 22, or at www.fnac.fr, or in person at any Fnac store; Métro: Gobelins) with the aim of furnishing his new chateau (Versailles) with the most splendid tapestries around. France's most skilled workers created sumptuous carpets and wall-coverings using designs sketched by the top artists of the era (Le Brun and Boucher, to name just two). The workshop's reputation has survived the centuries, and the factory is still active, using the same materials used in the time of Louis XIV (wool, cotton, silk). Still state-owned, today the factory operates under the auspices of the French Ministry of Culture, and produces modern tapestries to hang in some of France's most grand public spaces. This is definitely not a mass-market operation—these tapestries take several years to finish. Highly skilled workers (they study for 4 years at the on-site school) work from paintings by contemporary artists to create enormous works of art; during the tour you'll see the weavers in action at their giant looms. It is humbling to see how carefully and patiently the weavers work, tying tiny individual knots and/or passing shuttles of wool through a forest of warp and weft, all the while following an intricate design scheme. To visit the ateliers, you must take a guided, 1^1/$_2$-hour tour (which are in limited supply—see hours above); there is also a newly re-opened exposition space that offers temporary shows on design themes (Tues–Sun 12:30–6:30pm).

STUDIO VISITS

You can walk right into an artist's studio during **Portes Ouvertes** (various sites around the city), when artists' associations "open their doors" to art fans, buyers, and anyone interested in seeing what's cooking in the Paris art world. During a period of 3 or 4 days in spring and fall, the public is invited to visit studios, apartments, and lofts where up-and-coming artists show their wares in the place they were created. Since each association is defined by a geographic neighborhood, on these art walks you'll not only see paintings and sculptures, but also parts of the city that you might not otherwise venture into. You might even bring home a unique souvenir. In November 2007, for example, a group of artists living in the 18th and 9th arrondissements, "Anvers aux Abbesses," opened 118 different studios and living spaces to the public. In the 20th, the unofficial capital of young Parisian art, three different associations open their doors: the smallish Les Ateliers du Père Lachaise, a collective of 50 artists; the medium-sized Ateliers de Ménilmontant, which counts 150 members; and the mammoth Ateliers des Artistes de Belleville, a consortium of 250 painters, sculptors, video artists, and photographers. Generally, these events are well organized, and you can download detailed maps with pertinent information from the associations' websites. The only problem is finding out exactly when they are happening. You can look on the following websites for details on the four described above: **Anvers aux Abbesses** (www.anversauxabbesses.free.fr); **Les Ateliers du Père Lachaise** (www.apla.fr); Les Ateliers des Artistes de Belleville (www.ateliers-artistes-belleville.org); and **Les Ateliers de Ménilmontant** (www.ateliersdemenilmontant.org). Otherwise, ask at the Paris tourist office (www.parisinfo.com) and/or keep an eye out in the listings magazines.

OPEN-AIR MARKETS

For direct access to the heart of French tradition, you need only visit one of the city's many open-air markets, or *marchés* (mar-*shay*). *Marchés* are small universes unto themselves where nothing substantial has really changed for centuries. The fishmonger trumpeting the wonders of this morning's catch probably doesn't sound a whole lot different than his ancestor in the Middle Ages (though their dress has changed), and I'm sure housewives assessed the fruits and vegetables in the stalls with the same pitiless stares that they do today. Certainly the hygiene and organization have improved and there are no more jugglers or bear baiters to entertain the crowds, but the essence of the experience remains the same—a noisy, bustling, joyous chaos where you can buy fresh, honest food.

Does food taste better when you buy it from a smiling farmer, whose cucumbers were just picked that morning and still bear little white flowers? You bet it does. And even if many sellers are middlemen who buy their products at the central market at Rungis, you're still a lot closer to the source than you would be at a shop or a supermarket. Quality aside, you'll find one thing at a *marché* that you will never find at a supermarket: character. The people who work here are anything but citified, suit-wearing office types; they are salt of the earth, hard-working personalities who will not hesitate to tell you what they think, or make a joke, or give you tips and recipes, for that matter. Even if you don't have access to cooking facilities, *marchés* are great places to pick up picnic goodies or just a mid-morning nosh; along with fruit and vegetable vendors, you'll find bakeries, charcuteries (sort of

Paris Greeter: Proof That Parisians *Can* Be Friendly

While it's basically a walking tour, **Paris Greeter** (www.parisgreeter.org) has something that no other tour group outfit does: volunteer guides with an urgent need to share their love of the city with visitors. A nonprofit association that has received the blessing of city hall, this volunteer network offers not only in-depth visits of Parisian neighborhoods, it also gives tourists a chance to get to know at least one real, live Parisian, namely the person conducting the tour. What's more, it's free. You simply sign up on the website at least a week in advance and Paris Greeter will let you know when and if a group is meeting up during your stay (even with over 100 volunteers, availability is not guaranteed). If the answer is affirmative, you'll meet up with your Paris Greeter and four or five other like-minded visitors at a given site, and off you go on a 2- or 3-hour journey discovering parts of the city that you may have never even heard of, let alone explored. Guides share their favorite haunts, as well as historical details that you won't find in guidebooks (except this one, of course). Like the reason for the vast, empty esplanade in the middle of the two wings of the Palais de Chaillot (plans to build an actual palace were scrapped when financing fell through) or that lines 6 and 2 of the Paris metro follow the outline of the old city walls (once the walls were knocked down there was a convenient corridor for a metro line). Though it's up to the guide to choose the itinerary, it's not fixed in stone; before the tour gets started, the Greeter will generally canvas the group to find out where they've already been and what interests them in particular. The unusual set-up makes for a wonderfully relaxed atmosphere; both the guides (who are at least bi-lingual) and the tour-ees are eager to interact with each other. Questions and answers fly back and forth; tours often end up at a café where addresses and e-mails are exchanged.

like a deli, but better), and other small stands selling homemade jams, honey, or desserts.

If you're in the mood for people-watching, you'll get a wonderful show at a *marché*. All types of shoppers come here, from grannies pushing shopping carts, to earnest young professionals, to noisy families looking for fixings for Sunday lunch. Some of the covered markets have small cafes inside—these are ideal for sitting down and soaking up the atmosphere. Some markets, like the Marché Raspail, are entirely outdoor affairs that stretch down the median of a large avenue; others, like the enormous Marché d'Aligre, have both indoor and outdoor sections that take up almost an entire neighborhood. Outdoor markets tend to be open only in the morning; covered (indoor) markets are usually open all day with a break for lunch.

A few marché rules: Unless you see evidence to the contrary, don't pick up your own fruits and vegetables with your hands. Wait until the vendor serves you and point. Also, don't be surprised if the line in front of the stand is an amorphous blob of people; this is the French way. Surprisingly, fist-fights are rare; somehow everyone seems to be aware of who came before them, and if they aren't, no one seems to care.

There are *marchés* in every arrondissement in the city. Below is a selective list; you can search the municipal website (www.paris.fr, search for "marchés parisiens") for a complete listing, or ask at your hotel for the one closest to where you're staying.

Marché d'Alésia (rues de la Glacière et de la Santé, 13th arrond.; Wed and Sat 7am–2:30pm; Métro: Glacière)

Marché d'Aligre (also called Marché Beauveau, place d'Aligre, 12th arrond.; outdoor market Tues–Sun 9am–1pm, covered market Tues–Sat 9am–1pm and 4–7:30pm, Sun 9am–1:30pm; Métro: Ledru Rollin or Gare de Lyon)

Marché Barbès (blvd. de la Chapelle in front of Hospital Lariboisière, 18th arrond; Wed and Sat 7am–2:30pm; Métro: Barbès-Rochechouart)

Marché Bastille (blvd. Richard Lenoir between rue Amelot and rue St-Sabin, 11th arrond.; Thurs and Sun 7am–2:30pm; Métro: Bastille)

Marché Batignolles (organic; blvd. Batignolles, 17th arrond.; Sat 9am–2pm; Métro: Rome)

Marché Grenelle (blvd. Grenelle, between rue Lourmel and rue du Commerce, 15th arrond.; Wed and Sun 7am–2:30pm; Métro: La Motte Picquet–Grenelle)

Marché Monge (place Monge, 5th arrond; Wed, Fri, and Sun 7am–2:30pm; Métro: place Monge)

Marché Raspail (blvd. Raspail between rue de Cherche-Midi and rue de Rennes, 6th arrond.; Tues and Fri, 7am–2:30pm; Métro: Rennes)

Marché Saxe-Breteuil (ave. du Saxe, 7th arrond.; Thurs Sat 7am–2:30pm; Métro: Ségur)

HOW PARISIANS PLAY

Despite complaints that their lives consist of nothing but "boulot, Métro, dodo" (work, subway, sleep), Parisians do, in fact, get out and party whenever they can. For a rundown of the many nightlife possibilities on offer, take a look at our nightlife chapter (p. 276). For a short survey of some more unusual versions of Parisian playtime, scan the next section for philosophy discussion groups, medieval balls, roller-skating parties, and other urban activities.

ROLLERBLADING MADNESS

Imagine—it is late at night and you are walking near the church of St-Germain des Prés, admiring the lights dancing on the rooftops, when suddenly you hear a noise. Out of the blue, a seemingly endless hoard of in-line skaters come streaming down the boulevard, in every size, shape, and color, rocketing through space like some sort of urban TGV. No, you didn't drink too much Bordeaux at dinner, you are simply witnessing **"Friday Night Fever,"** a weekly phenomena that has been hitting the streets of the city since 1994. Every Friday night, some 15,000 skaters gather at the foot of the Tour Montparnasse and take off for a 3-hour circuit through the streets of Paris. A nonprofit group, **Pari Roller** (16 blvd. St-Germain, 5th arrond.; no phone; www.pari-roller.com) supplies an organizational structure, and most importantly, experienced volunteers who ride with the crowd and help maintain the security and safety of the riders. Now that the rides have taken on gargantuan proportions, the police are also involved—they now have their own roller brigade that skates along with the crowd.

"Friday Night Fever" starts at place Raoul Dautry (that's the big plaza between the Tour Montparnasse and the entrance to the train station) every Friday night at 10pm unless it rains or the streets are wet. The circuit is for experienced skaters, as the pace is swift and the road is not always smooth and flat. Don't feel discouraged if your skating is less than expert—there is a kinder, gentler ride on Sunday at 2:30pm that leaves from 37 blvd. Bourdon next to place de la Bastille. Organized by another rollerblading group called **Rollers & Coquillages** (23–25 rue Jean-Jacques Rousseau, 1st arrond.; ☎ 01 44 54 94 42; www.rollers-coquillages. org), the only requirement here is that you have a minimum of experience (that is, this is not your first skate). If you didn't bring skates, don't worry, there are plenty of places to rent listed on both websites, like **Nomades Roller Shop** (37 blvd. Bourdon, 4th arrond.; ☎ 01 44 54 07 44; www.nomadeshop.com; Métro: Bastille).

OPEN PARTIES

For some, bars and clubbing are not enough. Craving contact and conversation, intrepid Parisians are now turning to "private" parties where you don't have to put up with high cover charges, irksome attitude, and ear-splitting noise. Situated in unusual locations, or just private homes, these alternative get-togethers can be a great way to mingle with the natives, if you can find out where they are. Interestingly, some of the oldest of these soirées are those that were started by expatriates, whose long-standing weekly gatherings have become an essential stop for new arrivals to the Parisian scene.

If there ever was an institution on the Parisian ex-pat scene, it is **Jim Haynes' Sunday dinners** (83 rue de la Tombe Issoire, 14th arrond.; ☎ 01 43 27 17 67; www.jim-haynes.com; Métro: Denfert-Rochereau). A Louisiana native, Haynes has led a fascinating life that includes founding a theater company (the Traverse Theatre) in Edinburgh, starting a countercultural magazine with Germain Greer in Amsterdam, and hanging out with just about every icon of the '60s you can imagine. Sometime in the 1970s, Haynes got into the habit of inviting strangers to his home for food, talk, and fellowship. You'll meet anywhere from 30 to 40 people at these free-form fiestas, which are frequented by a intriguing mix of long-time residents, hangers-on, and people passing through town for one reason or another. Nationalities are mixed, too: Though most are native English-speakers, diners can hail from all parts of Europe, as well as further flung continents. The emphasis here is on meeting people: Visitors are not allowed to stand on the sidelines. If you try, Haynes will be at your side in a minute, introducing you to someone. A good number of the people who come here have been here before, which is why the chat is so lively. Now you can come too; just call or write a week ahead (you can also reserve on the website), and call again on Sunday morning to confirm. Dinner starts at 8pm sharp, a contribution is politely requested (from each according to his or her means, but many give around 20€).

If the atmosphere at **Patricia Laplante-Collins' dinners** (Paris Soirées, 13 rue Mulhouse, 2nd arrond.; ☎ 01 43 26 12 88; www.parissoirees.com; Métro: Sentier) is a little more subdued, the offerings aren't any less interesting. Held in a small, but lovely apartment, Patricia's parties are also frequented by both residents and visitors, though here almost everyone speaks English, even the French people who pop in. The soirées, which are held on Wednesdays and Sundays, start at 6:45pm, and chatting and introductions continue for about an hour until a buffet is served. After dessert, everyone settles down to listen to the guest speaker, who could be anyone from an actress reciting Oscar Wilde's *Salomé*, to a famous movie director talking about his films and his life as an expat. One of the nice things here is the ethnic diversity of not only the speakers, but also the people attending. Reserve at least a few days in advance by phone or e-mail; have a 20€ contribution ready at the door. Wednesday nights are often about networking, while Sundays are strictly social (see the website for a schedule of speakers and an e-mail address).

For 9 years, Michael Muszlak has opened the doors of his Latin Quarter apartment to visitors looking for a cup of tea and some chat. Called **Teatime** (☎ 01 43 25 86 55; michael@muszlak.com), this low-key event takes place just about every Saturday between 5 and 8pm, when a stream of friendly faces fills up Muszlak's living room and starts exchanging names. As it's still early evening, the atmosphere is laid back and casual—sometimes newfound companions will hook up to continue the party elsewhere. Tea, of course, is served, as are cakes and finger-food; a small contribution (I'm not supposed to tell you how much, but I can say that it's about half what you'll pay at the two above) is requested as compensation. A French/British polyglot (he speaks five languages), Muszlak started these events to keep his linguistic muscles flexed; both languages are in evidence here, though you are asked to stick to one at a time. You must call ahead and chat a bit before Muszlak will give you the address and directions; this is his home after all, and he needs to sift out any potential crazies.

On Thursdays, from 8pm to 2am, the Confrèrie des Chevaliers de St-Sabin (that's the Confederacy of the Knights of St-Sabin, to you) invite you to join them at **La Taverne Medievale** (Les Caves, 50 rue St-Sabin, 11th arrond.; ☎ 01 40 21 00 13; Métro: Breguet-Sabin or Chemin Vert) for an evening of feasting, music, and good fun in their ancient vaulted cellar. This huge underground space (350 sq. m/3,767 sq. ft.), which dates from at least the 17th century, has been completely restored and subtly beautified with wood carvings, lanterns, and the occasional antique column or statue. First there is the food, which involves appropriately medieval-inspired dishes like spiced beef and chicken with dates (main dishes 10€–15€). Then there are the drinks: Care for a glass of mead (a fermented honey concoction) or rosé wine? Finally, there is the entertainment: Wonderful live medieval music (these are not amateurs but professional groups that come in from all over France, Europe, and even overseas) is on offer, as are strolling troubadours, sorcerers, storytellers, jugglers, and the occasional marionette artist. If you don't feel like socializing, you can play chess or watch a duel, or both. Or you could dance—if you get there at 7pm, you can take a medieval dance class (5€, reserve ahead, these fill up quickly).

There is no cover if you are in costume, otherwise, you'll be asked to rent one for (15€). It may sound silly, but the costumes are important; there's something about being in one that seems to level the playing field and allows people to open up. The crowd, which spans an age range from mid-twenties to retirement, is eclectic, to say the least. Though there are a lot of "medievalists" who take their

Middle Ages pretty seriously, there are plenty of others who simply come to have a good time in extraordinary surroundings. Some don't even bother to find a medieval costume, just a historic one: Louis XVI occasionally shows up, as does Napoleon and a samurai or two.

PHILOSOPHY DEBATES

Believe it or not, in Paris, people sit around and talk philosophy for fun. Remember, this is a country where living, breathing philosophers can make a living, and it is not unusual for one of them to print an article on the front page of *Le Monde,* the nation's leading newspaper. There's a long tradition of philosophical reverence here: Some of the pillars of Western philosophy, like Descartes and Rousseau, were French, and it is still a required subject in school from an early age.

But even if you don't know Sartre from the Simpsons, **cafés philos** (ka-*fey fee*-lo) can still be a fun way to see the French mind (and mouth) in action. For one thing, you are usually not discussing deconstructionist theory at these weekly get-togethers. Subject matter tends towards more universal puzzlements, like: "Is hope a violent thing?" "How far is too far?" or a general theme, like sacrifice, narcissism, or even Santa Claus.

Here's how it works: The group assembles at the appointed hour, usually in an appropriately atmospheric cafe. Then the moderator (there is always a moderator) will choose a topic from the participant's suggestions, and then the assembled great minds are off and running. The moderator sees to it that no one hogs the spotlight and that everyone gets a chance to talk (though it's not required, you can just come and watch the proceedings if you prefer). Academic discourses and posturing are frowned upon, as is chatty "coffee-talk." Cafés philos have become so popular that you can now find them all over the world (if you look hard); in Paris, there are even a few in English. Participation is usually free, though you'll have to pay for your own drinks. Below, I've listed the best known philosophical meeting points, but for a more complete list, visit the Café des Phares website (see below).

Surely the ghosts of Sartre and de Beauvoir, among other former philosophical regulars, watch over the English-only café philo at the **Café de Flore** (172 blvd. St-Germain, 6th arrond.; ☎ 01 45 48 55 26; www.cafe-de-flore.com; Métro: St-Germain-des-Prés) on the first Wednesday of every month at 7pm. Ask for the "café philo" when you come in; the waiter will point you up the staircase where you'll find a crowd of like-minded thinkers sitting on the plush red banquettes. Come early, as this is a popular activity for both long-term residents and visitors swinging through town for a few days; anywhere from 20 to 70 people can show up. The group has a Web page with a calendar and comments at http://philosophy.meetup.com/274.

If you feel your French is good enough, you're ready for the mother of all cafés philos, which takes place at **Le Café des Phares** (7 place de la Bastille, 4th arrond.; ☎ 01 42 72 04 70; www.cafe-philo-des-phares.info; Métro: Bastille) every Sunday at 11am. It was here that the first café philo started, back in 1992, when Marc Sautet and his friends got together for a good yak fest. They decided it was so much fun, they'd do it on a regular basis, and *voilà,* an institution was born. Naturally, there is a website (see above) with explanations and a code of conduct, as well as a good list of other cafes in France and abroad. The broad sidewalk and comfortable outdoor seating make this a particularly good choice when the weather is nice.

STEAM BATHS

One of the best ways to melt away stress is to visit a **hammam.** An import from the ex-French colonies in North Africa, these are traditional steam baths with both hot and cold pools, usually decorated with intricate arabesque tiles and motifs. Exclusively single-sex operations (usually certain days are for men, others for women), there is nothing unseemly going on here, other than a lot of healthy sweating. The most culturally accessible is the **Hammam de la Grande Mosquée de Paris** (39 rue Geoffroy St-Hilaire, 5th arrond.; ☎ 01 43 31 38 20; www.la mosquee.com; women Mon, Wed, Thurs, Sat 10am–9pm, Fri 2–9pm; men Tues 2–9pm, Sun 10am–9pm. Swimsuit obligatory; bring a towel, or rent one for 4€; Métro: Censier-Daubenton), which is in the complex that houses the Mosque of Paris, and caters to a both Arab and non-Arab clientele. Beautiful mosaics and tinkling fountains decorate the rooms; billows of steam waft from pools of hot water (there's a cold plunge pool, too, for when you've had enough). A number of *"formules,"* or packages, including baths, exfoliation, massage, and mint tea are available, starting at 38€, but massages here are pretty lightweight and you might be just as happy with simply lounging in the baths for a mere 15€ entry fee.

7

Paris Outdoors

Where to go for a little R&R after a hard day at the Louvre

Though Parisians might not seem like a very outdoorsy bunch, they actually do appreciate green spaces, as demonstrated by the quantity of urbanites that prostrate themselves on any chair, bench, or lawn available the minute the sun comes out. Despite its density, Paris has a large number of parks and gardens to choose from. There are tiny squares tucked into tranquil neighborhoods, as well as magnificent gardens "à la française," like the Tuileries, not to mention the city's two huge parks attached to its east and west borders: the Bois de Boulogne and the Bois de Vincennes. These last two are particularly attractive to parents with kids, for their zoos, amusement zones, and so on, and *sportifs,* or athletic types, who want to do some running, rollerblading, or just plain hiking. Even Parisians are getting serious about sports and exercise these days. Though gyms and health clubs are still rare, there are a number of places where even folks who are just passing through can go to swim, bike ride, or go for a run.

Armchair athletes won't feel left out either. Though you won't see baseball or football here, there's a gigantic stadium, just north of Paris, for soccer, a national passion. There are also several hippodromes for racing fans, and the fabled Roland-Garros Stadium for the Paris Open. And if you are in Paris in July, watching the last stage of the Tour de France cycling race as it whizzes up and down the Champs Elysées is an unforgettable sight. So here's to the great Parisian outdoors—it's a lot more than a sidewalk table at a cafe.

PARIS'S GREAT PARKS & GARDENS

There are hundreds of green spaces in the city, but most of them are small to postage-stamp size. Below I've focused on the largest and most easily accessible. A note about the words "park" and "garden": In Paris the two are virtually interchangeable, gardens are often found in parks and visa versa. For the purposes of this guide, I'm calling "parks" the larger green spaces that are mostly lawns, trees, and natural areas, "gardens" are primarily known for their flowers and intense, often geometric landscaping. For a complete rundown on Parisian greenery, visit the city's website at www.jardins.paris.fr.

THE BEST PARKS & GARDENS IN THE CITY CENTER

The city center doesn't have the largest parks, or those with the most facilities (see Bois de Vincennes and Bois de Boulogne, later in this chapter), but they're the most historic and several include beautiful gardens. The most delightful combination of park, gardens, and children's activities can be found at the **Jardin du**

Luxembourg ✪✪✪. In fact, this is such a lovely place that I've included it in my top 10 list of sights to see in the city—please refer to p. 136 for a description of the park and its facilities.

After Luxembourg, the star of Parisian green spaces is the **Tuileries Gardens** ✪✪✪ (rue de Rivoli, 1st arrond.; ☎ 01 40 20 90 43; www.louvre.fr; free admission; Oct–Mar 7:30am–7:30pm, Apr–Sept 7am–9pm; Métro: Tuileries), an exquisite park that spreads from the Louvre to the place de la Concorde. One of the oldest gardens in the city—and the first to be opened to the public—it's also one of the largest; the entire area (including the garden around the Arc du Carousel) measures over 26 hectares (64 acres). In the Middle Ages, there was a factory here that made clay tiles *(tuiles),* a word that was incorporated into the name of the palace that Catherine de Medicis built at the far end of the Louvre in 1564. Such a grand palace needed equally splendid Italian gardens; later in the mid-1600s, Louis XIV gave master landscape artist André Le Nôtre—the man behind the gardens of Versailles—the job of giving them a more French look. Le Nôtre's elegant geometry of flowerbeds, parterres, and groves of trees made the Tuileries Gardens the ultimate stroll for well-to-do Parisians.

Though the Tuileries Palace burned down during the Paris Commune in 1871, the landscaping lived on. During World War II, furious fighting went on here, and many statues were damaged. Little by little in the post-War years the garden put itself back together. Seventeenth- and 18th-century representations of various gods and goddesses were repaired, and the city added new works by modern masters such as Max Ernst, Alberto Giocometti, Jean Dubuffet, and Henry Moore. Rodin's "The Kiss" and "Eve" are here, as well as a series of 18 of Maillol's curvaceous women, hidden in the green **labyrinth** ✪ of hedges in the Carousel Gardens near the museum. In the early 1990s, when I.M. Pei's pyramid changed the face of the Louvre, the gardens were also given a major overhaul: The essential elements of Le Nôtre's design were preserved, while adding a few modern touches, like the somewhat bizarre **playground** on the north side of the park with modern structures that are nice to look at but difficult to play on. Over a thousand trees were planted during the restoration; today 125,000 plants and flowers are set in the garden each year by a battalion of gardeners.

The far end of the garden near the place de la Concorde, with its large **octagonal basin,** is the most faithful to Le Nôtre's vision. On a wide terrace, next to the rue de Rivoli, a **fun fair** takes place in July and August with a variety of vertiginous rides and merry-go-rounds. Back in the garden's interior, you'll follow a wide pathway down the center to the **Grand Carée** ✪✪ a huge square area with brilliant flower beds and a large **fountain** ✪ where in the warmer months, you can sail miniature sail boats (2.50€ per half-hour). You'll see snack bars and restaurants under the trees—these are nice for a drink but prohibitively expensive for an actual meal (even the drinks add up here).

Marcel Proust used to laze under the trees in the beautiful **Parc Monceau** ✪✪ (blvd. de Courcelles, 8th arrond.; ☎ 01 42 27 39 56; free admission; Nov–Mar 7am–8pm, Apr–Oct 7am–10pm; Métro: Monceau), and who could blame him? The lush lawns and leafy trees of this verdant haven would brighten the spirits of even the most melancholy writer. Located in a posh residential neighborhood and

The Playgrounds of Paris

I'll admit, Paris is not a paradise for kids—but it does have a remarkable number of small playgrounds for tiny and not-so-tiny tots. These *jardins d'enfants* or *aires de jeux* can be a lifesaver when you're wandering around Paris and your child has reached the boiling point. All of the larger parks and gardens have playgrounds, and several are sprinkled around each arrondissement, usually in the small squares in residential neighborhoods. For precise locations, visit www.jardins.paris.fr (part of the municipal website), ask at your hotel, or just follow the strollers—you're bound to find one, if you keep an eye out. There are also merry-go-rounds in many of the larger gardens and squares.

Sitting on a bench in front of the delightful flowerbeds of the **Jardin des Plantes** ✿✿ 🧒 (rue Geoffroy-St-Hilaire, 5th arrond.; ☎ 01 40 79 56 01; www.mnhn.fr; free admission; 7:30am–7:30pm; Métro: Gare d'Austerlitz or Censier–Daubenton), it's hard to believe that, in theory at least, you're in the Latin Quarter, a neighborhood known more for bustle than botany. But in fact, this historic botanical garden is right next to the Faculté des Sciences, a major university, and a short walk from the Panthéon.

While it may not be a typical university, this place is indeed a place of learning. Created in 1626 as a medicinal plant garden for King Louis XIII, by the time Louis XIV was on the throne, the garden and the surrounding buildings had become a center for the study of botany. Enter Georges-Louis Leclerc, Count of Buffon. This 18th-century naturalist, mathematician, and biologist, with the help of fellow-naturalist Louis-Jean-Marie Daubenton, turned the complex into an internationally famed scientific institution. Not only did Buffon establish the museums and the menagerie, which took in refugees from the royal zoo at Versailles, he also helped create the botanical gardens that you see before you. Today the museums are still part academic institutions, but you certainly don't need to be a student to appreciate these lush grounds.

Often overlooked by tourists (but certainly not by locals, who swarm in on the weekends), this huge park and garden is not only a lovely spot for

ringed by stately mansions, this small park has a certain aristocratic charm, which may be due to its origins. It was the duke of Chartres (the future Philippe Egalité) who hired a playwright-gardener by the name of Carmontelle back in 1769 to create a fanciful garden filled with **"folies,"** faux romantic ruins, temples, and antiquities inspired by exotic far-away places. Don't be surprised to stumble upon a minaret, a windmill, or a mini-Egyptian pyramid here; one of the more unusual structures is an arcade from the ruins of the Hôtel de Ville that burned down during the Paris Commune and added by a 19th-century landscape artist. In fact, this park has had several makeovers, but it is still essentially an English-style garden, complete with wooded glens and hillocks. The park went public in 1861, and a walk or a rest but also a repository of all sorts of fascinating creatures, plant or otherwise. Framed on two sides by the mighty **Muséum National d'Histoire Naturelle** (p. 175), this park also harbors:

* A small, but well-kempt zoo (**Ménagerie du Jardin des Plants** ⭐ 🧒; ☎ 01 40 79 37 94; 7€ adults, 5€ children 4–13, free under 4; 9am–6pm; Métro: Gare d'Austerlitz). Created in 1794, this is the oldest zoo in the world. Because of its small size, the zoo focuses on the conservation of smaller species, in particular birds, which make up almost half of the inventory, and reptiles. But there's also a healthy selection of mammals (240 to be exact), including rare species like red pandas, Przewalski horses, and even Florida pumas (you'll get an up-close view of these magnificent creatures if you go in the late afternoon when they are up and about). The one downside, particularly for the animals, is that the cages are on the small side; on the other hand, it makes it easy to see the animals in action. This is a great break for both you and your kids; the zoo is small enough to be seen in a couple of hours and right in the middle of town so you won't up your exhaustion level getting there.

* Two enormous **greenhouses,** one filled with desert plants from Mexico **(La Serre Mexicaine)** and the other with tropical trees and plants **(Le Jardin d'Hiver).** At press time, both greenhouses were closed for renovations, but scheduled to re-open in 2009.

* An Alpine garden (**Le Jardin Alpin;** Mon–Fri free admission, Sat–Sun 1€ adults, .50€ 4–13, free under 4; Mon–Fri 8am–5pm, Sat 1:30–6pm, Sun 1:30–6:30pm), where astute gardeners have managed to grow delicate flowers and plants from mountainous regions around the world in the middle of Paris.

* A botany school (**Ecole Botanique;** daily 8am–7:30pm), whose exotic gardens and koi pond are open to the public.

ever since has received the more or less genteel inhabitants of the surrounding neighborhood.

On all four sides of the park, the entrances are framed by monumental **grillwork** trimmed with gold that give you the impression you are entering a royal domain. The most famous *folie* is the **Naumachie** ⭐, a large oval pond surrounded in part by Corinthian columns. There is a sizeable **playground** in the southwest corner, as well as a **merry-go-round** near the north entrance, where there is a **round pavilion** surrounded by columns; the Duke of Chartres used to keep a small apartment on the second floor from which he could see the entire park. Today the pavilion serves a more practical purpose: Inside you'll find clean public toilets. The grounds contain the **city's oldest tree:** an Oriental plane tree whose circumference measures 7m (23 ft.).

That vast patch of greenery between the Ecole Militaire and the Eiffel Tower is the **Champ de Mars** ★ 🄺🄸🄳🅂 (place Joffre, 7th arrond.; Métro: Ecole Militaire, RER: Champ de Mars–Tour Eiffel). Originally created as a parade ground and practice battlefield for the military school during the Revolution, the field *(champ)* was used to stage giant patriotic festivals like the Fête de la Fédération and the Féte de l'Etre Supreme (literally, the feast of the Supreme Being). In the 19th century, it became the setting for a series of Expositions Universelles (World's Fairs), including the one in 1889, which left an enormous souvenir at the northern end of the field, namely, the Eiffel Tower. In the early 20th century it was transformed into a verdant park, with gardens, playgrounds (parents take note), and a huge green lawn that's now used for outdoor concerts and public events (in 2007 the Bastille Day fireworks blasted off from this spot).

One of city's most unusual garden strolls is the **Promenade Planté** ★ (ave. Daumesnil, 12th arrond.; www.viaduc-des-arts.com; Mon–Fri 8am–dusk, Sat–Sun 9am–dusk; Métro: Bastille, Ledru-Rollin, or Gare de Lyon). Stretched out along 4.5 km (2¾ miles) of a converted train viaduct, this is a rare chance to stop and smell the roses high above the hustle and bustle of the Bastille area. You'll find the entrance just behind the Bastille opera house on avenue Daumesnil where a staircase leads up to this very long and narrow garden. Here you can stroll, sans cars, down the viaduct, taking in the myriad flowers, trellises, ponds, and plant life, all the way to the Bois de Vincennes, should you feel so inclined (at ground level, under the arches, are a series of high-end crafts ateliers and galleries). The viaduct actually runs out at the Parc de Reuilly, an installation of grassy lawns and playgrounds in a modern section of the arrondissement; you'll then cross a bridge, and a stretch of pavement, until you come to a tunnel that will spit you out on another long section of verdant pathway, this time at ground level. Once you get to the Péripherique, the ring road that circles Paris, you'll have to duck into another tunnel, and then you'll be in the Bois de Vincennes. This is also an excellent place for a run.

Another garden-promenade is the delightful **Jardin Tino-Rossi** ★ (Quai St-Bernard, 5th arrond., access via staircase on the quay in front of the Institute du Monde Arabe; Métro: Gare d'Austerlitz or Jussieu). The stars of this "garden" are not begonias or peonies, but modern sculpture: Some 29 artists are represented in this **Musée des Sculptures en Plein Air,** including Brancusi, Zadkine, Ipoustéguy, Rougemont, and César. Not only that, but this contemporary park is actually a promenade that runs down the Quai St-Bernard along the Seine (if you want, you walk all the way to place St-Michel in about 15 min.). Along the bank, the sculptures punctuate a long stretch of greenery shaded by ancient plane trees, weeping willows, and Austrian black pine. This is wonderful picnic country; not only can you pitch your tablecloth wherever you feel like, but you'll have a splendid view of the Seine and the Right Bank before you, with the flying buttresses of Nôtre-Dame fanning out to the west. On summer evenings, this is where **Paris Danses en Seine** takes place; in each semi-circular concrete inlet by the river, there's a different style dance party (see "The 'Other' Paris," p. 198 for info). By the way, in case you are wondering who Tino Rossi was, he had nothing to do with sculpture—he was a wildly popular singer who wowed France in the 1930s and '40s.

MORE GREAT PARKS & GARDENS IN
THE OUTER ARRONDISSEMENTS

These lovely open spaces are often unjustly ignored by tourists just because they are a few stops further out on the Métro. It's too bad because 1) they are some of the larger parks and have some of the most unusual and original landscaping, and 2) they are less crowded than the ones in the center.

Up until 1860, **Buttes Chaumont** ★★ 🌟 (rue Botzaris, 19th arrond.; 7am–dusk; Métro: Buttes Chaumont) was a 45m (147-ft.) deep limestone quarry, but thanks to Napoleon III, this gaping hole was turned into an unusual park, full of hills and dales, rocky bluffs and cliffs. It took 3 years to make this romantic garden; over a thousand workers and a hundred horses dug, heaped, and blasted through the walls of the quarry to create green lawns, a cool grotto, cascades, streams, and even a small lake. By the opening of the 1867 World's Fair, the garden was ready for visitors. The surrounding area was, and still is, working-class; the Emperor built it to give this industrious neighborhood a green haven and a bit of fresh air.

The **lake** ★ is the central feature of the park; in the center of this 5-acre body of water, a pile of boulders has been artistically arranged to create a picturesque **island** ★ topped by a small faux Roman temple, which you can access either by bridge or by boat, several of which are available for rental at the lake's edge. An impressive staircase, called the **Chemin des Aiguilles,** has been carved into a rocky escarpment; it leads down to the lakeside, where there is a **cafe, merry-go-round,** and a **puppet theater** (Guignol Anatole 1836; ☎ 01 40 30 97 60; www.petits-bouffons.com; 3€ adults and children; Apr–Oct Wed, Sat, Sun at 3:30 and 4:40pm) featuring the enduring hero of traditional shows, Guignol. One of

---

Floating on Air over Paris

You may have seen it from a distance while walking around the city: a huge hot-air balloon floating peacefully above the 15th arrondissement. But you probably didn't know that you can climb aboard. The **Air de Paris Balloon** ★ (Parc André Citroën, 15th arrond.; ☎ 01 44 26 20 00; www.aeroparis.com; Mon–Fri 10€ adults, 9€ 12–17, 5€ under 12, free under 3; Sat–Sun 12€ adults, 10€ 12–17, 6€ under 12; scheduled every 10 min.; Métro: Balard) takes off every 10 minutes or so from the Parc André Citroën (see above), weather permitting. This enormous orb, which stands 32m (105-ft.) tall, is the largest hot air balloon in the world. It also serves as an ecological indicator: The balloon changes color according to current air quality conditions. You won't go far in distance, as the balloon is tethered firmly to the ground, but you will rise 150m (492 ft.) high for a view that rivals that of the Eiffel Tower. Beyond the view, the experience itself is memorable, slowly floating seemingly into the outer atmosphere without noise or vibration or the other usual annoyances of modern transport. Any kind of excess in weather or wind cancels flights; call ahead to be sure the balloon is running on the day you are coming.

the oldest Guignol companies in Paris (founded in 1836), the theater is a particularly lovely outdoor setting; bad weather cancels performances (shows are in the afternoons, see website for exact times). Two artificial streams curl through the park cascading over a waterfall as they empty into the lake and falling over a **grotto** with artificial stalactites hanging from its 20m (65-ft.) ceiling.

Tired of romantic gardens that look like something out of a centuries-old painting? See what modern landscaping can do at the contemporary **Parc André Citroën** ★★ (Quai André Citroën, 15th arrond.; Mon–Fri 8am–dusk, Sat–Sun 9am–dusk; Métro: Balard). When the Citroën automotive factory closed down and moved out of town, it freed up 24 hectares (about 60 acres) of land next to the Seine. In 1992, 14 of those (35 acres) were transformed into a unique park that combines vast open lawns with small garden enclosures and greenhouses. The result is an inviting space where kids can run around and play ball to their hearts content, and adults can poke around hidden gardens and find quiet nooks to read or lounge about.

Two gigantic transparent **greenhouses** frame a large, ground-level **fountain,** whose evenly-spaced jets shoot directly skyward; a summer favorite for overheated kids, who love to run around and through the jets. From here, an enormous lawn spreads down to the banks of the river, interrupted only by the presence of a huge **hot-air balloon** that takes visitors 150m (492-ft.) up for a superb view of the city (see the "Floating on Air over Paris," box). On the north side of the lawn are six **small greenhouses,** surrounded by six **small gardens,** each with a different botanical theme. Off to the southwest, there are two other gardens, the tiny **Jardin Blanc,** which has a small **playground** and **Ping-Pong tables,** and the larger **Jardin Noir,** a square-shaped configuration of small playgrounds, sandboxes, trees and plants centered around a fountain.

For truly contemporary garden design, it doesn't get much wackier than **La Villette** ★★ (211 av. Jean Jaurès, 19th arrond.; ☎ 01 40 03 75 75; www.villette.com; 6am–1am; Métro: Porte de Pantin). This vast complex, which includes a park, museums, concert halls, and other cultural institutions, was built on the site of the city's slaughterhouses, abandoned since the mid-1970s. Construction began in 1980, when Bernard Tschumi, a French-Swiss architect, was chosen to create an urban cultural park accessible to one and all. The park is certainly a success on the cultural end: It harbors **Cité de la Musique** and **Cité des Sciences et de l'Industrie**—two excellent museums (p. 277 and 176), as well as the **Zénith** and **Cabaret Sauvage** concert halls (p. 287 and 288), and other assorted theaters and cultural spaces. As far as the park—well, let me put it this way: If it is possible for a park to have a sense of humor, this one definitely has one. There are 11 themed gardens, around which are dotted 25 red "folies"—oddball contemporary structures that sometimes house a drink stand or an information booth, and sometimes are just there for the heck of it. The gardens range from the sublime to the silly; a few are strictly reserved for children (who can bring along their parents). Here are a few highlights:

⬩ The **Jardin des Miroirs** (Mirror Garden) seems to be an odd collection of concrete monoliths and woodland pines, until you get to the center and turn around and see that on the other side of the concrete are giant mirrors, which reflect the trees and the other mirrors, creating gardens inside gardens.

❦ The **Jardin des Dunes** (Dune Garden, 12 and under and their parents only), has a seaside theme—walls made out of sails flop in the wind, bamboo bridges and boats beckon, and small pedal-powered windmills turn in the breeze.

❦ The **Jardin de la Treille** (Trellis Garden) is draped with grape vines and climbing plants; 90 tiny fountains bubble next to the pathways.

❦ The **Jardin des Frayeurs Enfantines** (The Garden of Childhood Fears) is a mysterious forest of blue spruce and silver birch where eerie music plays from an unknown source.

There are also grassy lawns and open spaces. From mid-July to mid-August the **Cinéma en Plein Air** takes place Tues–Sun at sundown, presenting classic movies for free.

Proof that contemporary landscaping can be beautiful, the **Parc de Bercy** ✿ (rue François Truffaut, 12th arrond.; Mon–Fri 8am–dusk, Sat–Sun 9am–dusk; Métro: Bercy or Court St-Emillon) covers an area that was once a commercial mecca. In the 19th century, this choice spot, right on the Seine where the barges could easily unload their cargo, was the largest wine trading center in the world. By the 1950s, this prosperous epoch had come to a close, and the area became a sort of industrial wasteland until the early 1990s, when an extensive renovation project was launched, which included the creation of this modern green space, inaugurated in 1997.

The park is split up into three parts. The **parterres,** at the center of the park, are divided up into nine different thematic gardens, including a **rose garden,** a **small vineyard,** and a "**scent garden,**" where you can inhale the delightful odors of a variety of herbs and flowers. The second part is the **Grande Prairie,** to the west, a series of shaded lawns meant for lounging about; the new **Passerelle Simone de Beauvoir,** a futuristic pedestrian bridge (p. 188), crosses the Seine from here. Finally, to the east of the parterres are the **Romantic Gardens,** laced with gently curving pathways, hillocks, and duck ponds, in the center of one of which is a startling modern sculpture, Demeure X by Etienne Martin. There's a small lake here, with an island, upon which sits the **Maison du Lac,** a relic from the days of the wine trade, which hosts temporary exhibits. Two other older buildings are the **Chai de Bercy,** an old warehouse that now is used as an exhibition space, and the **Maison du Jardinage,** where you can pick up loads of gardening tips, as well as sign up for gardening classes (all in French, call ☎ 01 53 46 19 19 for more information). To the west of the park is **Bercy Village** (www.bercy village.com; Métro: Cour St-Emillon), also called the Cour St-Emillon, a pleasant pedestrian zone where converted *chais* or wine warehouses now house shops and restaurants.

TWO HUGE PARKS ON THE OUTSKIRTS OF TOWN (BUT WORTH THE SCHLEP)

In the 7th century, Dagobert, King of the Francs, used to go a-hunting in the woods that we now know as the **Bois de Boulogne** ✿✿✿ 🅚🅘🅓🅢 (16th arrond.; www.jardins.paris.fr; Métro: Sablons, Porte Dauphine, or Porte Maillot); it remained a hunting domain for the kings of France up until Louis XVI, who finally opened it up to the public. That was mighty grand of him, and we thank him for it—this lovely natural haven is just what stressed-out Parisians need. Thick stands of trees, broken up by **grassy knolls, manicured gardens,** and even a **lake or two** plus several posh restaurants are tucked into this verdant spread. There is even a nice spot for tiny urbanites to unwind: the **Jardin d'Acclimatation,** a large children's garden/amusement park is a delight for kids of all ages.

What you see today, however, is not what Dagobert saw. Once Louis XVI was beheaded, and the Revolution got underway, the park was ravaged. What was left of it was completely demolished during subsequent military campaigns: In 1814 it was occupied and pillaged by some 40,000 English and Russian soldiers. It wasn't until Napoleon III decided to remodel the entire city in the mid-1800s that the Bois de Boulogne was attended to. Inspired by the English public parks that he had visited during his years of exile, the Emperor gave the command to rebuild the park. Over 400,000 trees were planted, and dozens of chalets, pavilions, snack stands, and restaurants were built. A network of roads and trails was laid down totaling 95km (59 miles). Finally, the park was ready for the public, and the public was definitely ready for the park. Here are a few of its most popular areas:

◆ The **Parc de Bagatelle** ✸✸ is a park-within-a-park, a lush **garden,** a small **château** (where in the summer there are concerts, check listing magazines for details), and a **rose garden** with over 1,000 varieties. New varieties are introduced every year in June, during an international rose competition. The version of the garden you see today was designed by Forestier, a friend of Monet, who was inspired by Impressionist art, which is evident in the artfully placed clusters of flowers and plants.

◆ The **Pré Catelan** ✸ is most famous for its elegant and extremely pricey restaurant, but there are plenty of other reasons to come here. This green enclave includes lush lawns, playgrounds, and flowerbeds, as well as the **Jardin Shakespeare,** which attempts to re-create settings from the Bard's plays. Here you'll find the heaths of Macbeth, the Forest of Arden, and the pond where Ophelia meets her watery death in Hamlet.

◆ The **Jardin d'Acclimatation** ✸ (☎ 01 40 67 90 82; www.jardindacclimatation. fr; May–Sept 10am–7pm, Oct–April 10am–6pm; Métro: Sablons) was created by Napoleon III to "acclimatize" city folk to the wonders of Nature. The 19th-century idea of Nature, however, was a bit um . . . different. Along with plants and animals, at the end of the century, humans were exhibited here—peoples from far away places that Europeans found "exotic." Unfortunate Eskimos, Pigmies, and North American Indians were put on display; this abominable practice finally stopped in 1914. Today, the park serves a much more healthy purpose—providing fun and games for children (and their parents). There are still animals on view, particularly at the **farm,** but the main attraction is the **amusement park,** which is filled with rides, merry-go-rounds, and other attractions. The Enchanted River boat ride is the oldest attraction, but there are also mini–roller coasters, auto circuits, and dozens of other noisy ways to have a good time. It will cost you though—if you are over 3, you'll pay 2.70€ just to enter the park, and an additional 2.70€ per ride (you can buy a book of 15 tickets for 32€). This is a nice alternative to Disneyland, but if you aren't careful, it will cost you as much. Fortunately,

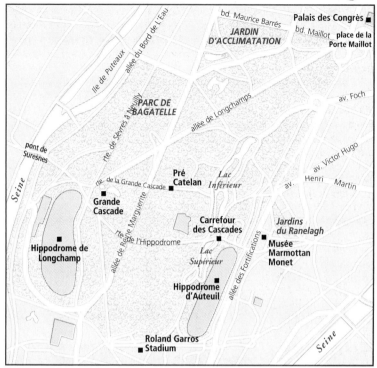

there are lots of other things you can do here besides rides; if you carefully circumvent the area with all the rides *(manèges),* you'll find a great **playground** with fun stuff to play on for free, including an area where kids can run around under giant sprinklers in the hot weather. In the same area, you'll find a **puppet theater** (☎ 01 45 01 53 52; www.guignol.fr; Wed, Sat, Sun, and holidays 3 and 4pm); Guignol's adventures are presented free of charge.

In addition to walking, rollerblading, and cycling (**bike rentals** at the edge of the Lac Inferieur, and at the Jardin d'Acclimatation), you can **rent a boat** on the lake or even **go fishing** in some of the ponds.

There aren't as many gardens and restaurants at the **Bois de Vincennes** ✹✹✹ (12th arrond.; www.jardins.paris.fr; Métro: Château de Vincennes or Porte Dorée), but there is more of a sense of wilderness in this vast patch of greenery on the eastern end of Paris. Endless paths and alleys wind through woods and open fields; this is a great place for a long bike ride or a hike. Not that there are just trees here—if rambling isn't your game, there are plenty of other things to do as well. For starters, there are the remains of a medieval castle and a large garden in the park, as well as theaters and a hippodrome for those who prefer to sit back and watch the action. In short, there are almost as many pleasures here as in the Bois de Boulogne, if not as much elegance.

Like its western counterpart, the Bois de Vincennes was once a royal hunting ground with a lodge built by Louis VII back in the 12th century. By the 13th century, it had grown into a castle, which Louis IX (St-Louis) became very fond of; it is said that he dispensed justice under one of the nearby oak trees. It wasn't until the 18th century, under Louis XV, that these woods were turned into a public park; unfortunately, after the Revolution, the army decided to use it as a training ground, and the castle became a prison (some of its more famous lodgers included the Marquis de Sade and the philosopher Denis Diderot). Needless to say, this did not do wonders for the landscaping. Finally, in the 19th century, Napoleon III made the park part of his urban renewal scheme, and it got the same thorough makeover as the Bois de Boulogne. Its troubles were not completely over however. In 1944, the retreating German army left the château in ruins, but it has since been almost completely restored.

A few of the park's high points:

The **Parc Floral** ★★ 🧒 (route du Champ de Manoeuvre, just behind the esplanade of the château; ☎ 01 43 28 41 59; www.parcfloraldeparis.com; during summer concert season 5€ adults 3€ 7–25, free under 7, the rest of the year: free for everyone; 9:30am–dusk; Métro: Château de Vincennes) is just that, a park filled with flowers. Created in 1969, this modern mix of **flowerbeds, ponds, picnic areas,** and **playgrounds** (including a few rides) is a very pleasant place to spend the afternoon, particularly between May and September when there are music and theater performances at the open-air theater. In July, the Paris Jazz Festival takes off for 3 weeks, and in most of August and September, the Festival Classique au Vert cooks up a great program of classical music (for both, see "Paris's Visit-Worthy Annual Events," p. 323). For the kids, **Guignol puppet shows** (☎ 01 49 23 94 37; www.guignol-parcfloral.com; 2.60€ adults and children) play most Wednesdays, Saturdays, and Sundays at 3pm, 4pm, and 5pm, and every day during school holidays.

The **Parc Zoologique de Vincennes** is closed for extensive renovations; estimated re-opening in 2012.

Guignol, the Puppet Show Hero

Created by an itinerant merchant and tooth-puller in Lyon about 200 years ago, **Guignol,** the sly hero of traditional French puppet shows, is still packing houses all over the country. This valiant valet, who often finds himself in difficult situations due his master's mischief, has an amazing way with children, who scream, hoot, and holler according to how Guignol's adventures unfold. There's lots of audience participation: The wide-eyed puppet will ask the children to help him find the robber/wolf/bad guy, and then will promptly head in the wrong direction as the kids desperately try to get him back on track. It's noisy, but good fun—even if you don't understand French, the stories are pretty easy to figure out. This is a great way to take part in an authentically French experience—though it might be a little overwhelming for sensitive souls under 3.

La Tempête—The Storm of the Century

On December 26, 1999, France was lashed by one of the worst storms to ever hit the continent, killing 88 people in France, and dozens more in nearby countries. Entire forests were flattened in the Vosges; millions of homes were left without electricity or running water. The Paris area was not spared, particularly its forests—in less than 2 hours, over a million trees where blown down; the gardens of Versailles, the Bois de Boulogne and the Bois de Vincennes took direct hits. It took a couple of years just to remove all the fallen trunks, but since then, thousands of trees have been replanted and a massive restoration project has been put in place. So don't be surprised if the wooded areas of these large parks seem a little thin—the trees are growing back as fast as they can.

The ongoing restoration of the **Château de Vincennes** ✸ (ave de Paris, main entrance to the Bois de Vincennes, 12th arrond.; ☎ 01 48 08 31 20; www.chateau-vincennes.fr; 7.50€ adults, 4.80€ 18–25, free under 18; 10am–5pm; Métro: Château de Vincennes) resulted in the reopening of the medieval donjon, or keep, in 2008; visitors now have access to two floors of this mighty structure. While the rooms are bare, the architecture is impressive: The vaulted ceilings and stone walls make it easy to imagine kings and courtiers and hard to imagine how anyone kept warm living here. The lovely chapel, which was modeled after Ste-Chapelle on the Ile de la Cité, was closed for a makeover at press time, but you can still take a stroll around the ramparts and pretend you are a knight on the lookout for enemy invaders. The grounds are shared by the ministry of culture and the military, which means that parts are used for storing military archives and administrative offices, and thus closed to the public.

Like the Bois de Boulogne, there are plenty of other outdoor activities here. You can **rent bikes** in front of either of the two large lakes, or on the esplanade by the château, or **boats** for rowing around the lake. There are several **playgrounds,** as well as a **farm** (La Ferme de Paris) where children can watch cows being milked and sheep being shorn. There is also a **hippodrome** here for thoroughbred racing fans; see "Spectator Sports," below, for details.

SPORTS & RECREATION OPPORTUNITIES

"Working out" is still a somewhat foreign concept in France, but that doesn't mean that you can't exercise. Though gyms are few and far between, pools are everywhere, and any enterprising sports enthusiast can easily find places to bike, rollerblade, or run. Here are a few ways of working off all those croissants.

PUBLIC POOLS

There are 37 public pools (*piscines,* pee-*seen*) in Paris, and they are accessible to one and all, even tourists passing through town. They are generally quite clean and always have lockers and dressing areas. The size of the pools varies—most are 25m (82 ft.), and a few, like the one at Les Halles, are 50m (164 ft.). The best way to find addresses and hours, and even photos of the pools, is to **visit the city hall website: www.sport.paris.fr**. Entry to almost all municipal pools is 2.60€; you can buy a card for 10 entries for 21.50€.

But before you put on your suit, a word of advice: Public pools are one place where the Latin side of the French character comes out. Don't expect people to necessarily swim in a straight line, or pay too much attention to where they are going; though there are usually at least a couple of lanes reserved for serious swim weenies, other pool areas can be a little free-form. On the upside, it's nice to see people actually enjoying themselves in a sports environment; grown-ups and kids alike splash around, swim, and generally have a good time. Below is a short list of municipal pools; see the website above for locations near your lodgings.

Suzanne Berlioux ✪✪ (10 place de la Rotonde, Forum des Halles, level 3, 1st arrond.; ☎ 01 42 36 98 44; Métro: Les Halles). Vast, modern, 50m (164-ft.) pool in the underground Forum des Halles (there's a wall of windows so there's natural light). Serious swimmers come here. This is one of the few pools with "special" fees: 4€ adults, 36€ for 10 entries.

Georges Vallerey ✪ (148 ave Gambetta, 20th arrond.; ☎ 01 40 31 15 20; Métro: Porte des Lilas). A huge modern facility with sliding roof that turns the 50m (164-ft.) indoor pool into an outdoor one in nice weather.

St-Germain ✪ (12 rue Lobineau, 6th arrond.; ☎ 01 56 81 25 40; Métro: Mabillon) is a 25m (82-ft.) pool in a slick modern underground space (under the Marché St-Germain).

Reuilly (13 rue Hénard, 12th arrond.; ☎ 01 40 02 08 08; Métro: Montgallet) is a 25m (82-ft.) pool with large windows that look out on nearby park.

Josephine Baker ✪✪ (quai François Mauriac, 13th arrond.; ☎ 01 56 61 96 50; Métro: Bibliothèque François Mitterand). This floating pool, which cost some 17 million euros to construct, opened with much ado in 2006. Much vaunted by the city for its chic look and facilities (there's a gym here), it's been much criticized by the public for the relatively small size of the pool (25m/82 ft.) and the high cost of all the accoutrements, like the sauna, fitness room, and restaurant. Not only that, but due to "technical difficulties" the pool is periodically closed for repairs. Controversy aside, there's no denying that this is a unique environment for taking a swim, and 10€ for a workout on the machines is actually less than you'll pay elsewhere.

Now private, **Piscine Pontoise** ✪ (18 rue de Pontoise, 5th arrond.; ☎ 01 55 42 77 88; www.clubquartierlatin.com; Métro: Maubert–Mutualité) is still open to one and all, for a reasonable entry fee of 3.70€ (30.20€ for 10 entries), which includes a chance to swim in a lovely 33m (108-ft.) pool with 1930s-era tiles setting. There is also a gym here (19€ for one entry, 151€ for 10) which offers classes, machines, and sauna.

ICE SKATING RINKS

Every year, **two large outdoor rinks** are set up from December through February that are free of charge—you'll just have to pay 5€ for skate rental. By far the most scenic is the one in front of the **Hôtel de Ville** (4th arrond.; Mon–Thurs noon–10pm, Fri noon–midnight, Sat–Sun 9am–midnight; Métro: Hôtel de Ville); the over-the-top neo-Renaissance building provides a splendid backdrop for this 1,050 sq. m (11,300 sq. ft.) oval. There's also a small beginners' rink here for little

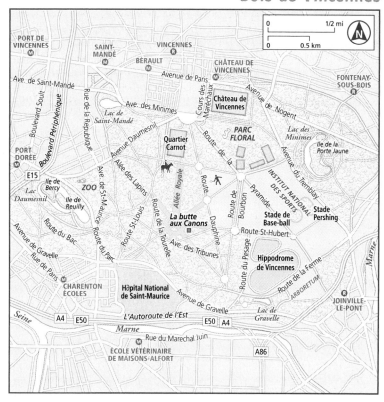

ones. The one on the esplanade in front of the homely **Gare Montparnasse** (14th arrond.; Mon–Fri noon–8pm, Sat–Sun 9am–8pm; Métro: Montparnasse) is smaller (770 sq. m/8,288 sq. ft.) and is not open as late.

CYCLING

You can ride a bike in the Bois de Vincennes and the Bois de Boulogne, or if you don't mind battling horrendous traffic, around town. If you've got the right kind of credit card, you can check out Velib', the new, high-tech, rent-a-bike program sponsored by the city (see box in chapter 2, p. 12). If you'd prefer the old-fashioned route, or you'd like to rent for a longer stretch of time, one of the best deals for bike rental is the **Roue Libre** (1 passage Mondétour, 1st arrond.; ☎ 01 44 76 86 43; Thurs–Mon 10am–6pm) service run by the transit authority. Since the arrival of Velib' on the scene, Roue Libre has reduced their services, but they still rent bikes (with helmets) by the hour (4€), the day (10€–15€), or the weekend (28€) from the address listed above. Ask for a free map that shows the city's bike paths. If Roue Libre isn't convenient, try any of the bike tour companies listed at the end of chapter 5 (p. 197), all of which rent bikes as well.

RUNNING

When I went running in the Jardin du Luxembourg in the mid-1990s, people found it so extraordinary that they actually applauded as I ran by. Today, le footing, as it is called, is considered pretty commonplace, though nowhere near as omnipresent as in London or New York. You can run anywhere, of course, but a few favored places are around the lakes in the **Bois de Boulogne** and the **Bois de Vincennes,** the **Promenade Planté** (p. 216), and along the quays of the Seine. You could also try the Jardin du Luxembourg, but there won't be any more clapping, I'm afraid.

SPECTATOR SPORTS

They may not be the ones you are used to, but there are some championship events that take place here—mainly horse races, soccer matches, and tennis opens.

HORSE RACING

Given the high concentration of hippodromes here (3 within the city limits), there are numerous opportunities to see professional thoroughbred racing. And it's not expensive: You can get into most races for a few euros. Of course, if you decide to bet on a race, your financial fortunes might take a more radical turn. There are races all year long; to find out where and when, call the **France Galop** information line at ☎ 08 21 21 32 13, or visit the websites listed below.

Some 150 races happen each year at the **Hippodrome de Vincennes** (Bois de Vincennes, 2 route de la Ferme, 12th arrond.; ☎ 01 49 77 17 17; www.cheval-francais.com; RER: Joinville le Pont; 3€ adults, 1.50€ 18–25 and over 60, free under 18), including the Prix d'Amérique, the Prix de France and the Prix de Paris. This enormous structure, which can hold up to 35,000 spectators, has two tracks, one for day races and the other for "nocturnes." The specialty here is harness racing.

The event of the year at the swanky **Hippodrome de Longchamps** (Bois de Boulogne, route de Tribunes, 16th arrond.; ☎ 01 44 30 75 00; www.france-galop.fr; weekdays: 3€ adults, 1.50€ students and over 60, free under 18, weekends: 4€ adults, 2€ students and over 60, free under 18; Métro: Porte d'Auteuil then shuttle bus) is the Grand Prix Arc de Triomphe (8€ adults, 4€ students and over 60, free under 18), when the ladies arrive in their frou frou hats and the gents knot their cravats just so. There are free guided visits of the track's "backstage" areas race days at 2:30, 3:30, and 4:30pm, as well as free pony rides for little ones (Sun when there are races, 1:30–6pm).

The **Hippodrome d'Auteuil** (Route des Lacs, Bois de Boulogne, 16th arrond.; ☎ 01 40 71 47 47; www.france-galop.fr; weekdays: 3€ adults, 1.50€ students and over 60, free under 18, weekends: 4€ adults, 2€ students and over 60, free under 18; Métro: Porte d'Auteuil–Hippodrome) is known for its obstacle races like the Grand Steeple-Chase de Paris, where horses must leap over barriers for 5,800m (19,024 ft.). If you like to watch horses jump over hedges and splash through ponds, this is the place for you. There are free pony rides for children ages 3 to 10 here too on Sunday race days, as well as free guided visits at 2:30, 3:30, and 4:30pm.

SOCCER

Even the catastrophic 2006 World Cup has not dampened French enthusiasm for this sport, which is called "football" on this side of the Atlantic. Zidane may be gone, but "le foot" lives on.

Built for the 1998 World Cup, the **Stade de France** (ZAC Cornillon Nord, St-Denis; ☎ 08 92 70 09 00, .34€ per minute; www.stadefrance.fr; Métro: St-Denis–Porte de Paris, RER: La Plaine–Stade de France) is an 80,000-seat behemoth where you can see major soccer and rugby matches as well as the occasional mega-concert. Prices for sports matches range from 60€ to 80€ for seats up by the action, to 5€ to 10€ for those in the outer atmosphere (of course, tickets for big events like the World or European cup go for more). Tickets are sold at all the major ticketing outlets, like **Fnac** (☎ 08 92 68 36 22, .34€ per minute; www.fnac.fr) and **Ticketnet** (☎ 08 92 39 01 00, .34€ per minute; www.ticketnet.fr). Both rugby and soccer matches go on all year long.

TENNIS

Probably the most famous sporting event in Paris is the French Open at the **Roland-Garros Stadium** (2 av. Gordon Bennet, 16th arrond.; ☎ 01 47 43 45 55; www.rolandgarros.com; Métro: Porte d'Auteuil; MC, V, AE, DC). One of the four tennis events in what is known as the Grand Slam, this tournament takes place every year during the last week of May and the first week of June. Ticket demand is such that they have started a lottery system. You can download a reservation request on the website, which provides detailed instructions in English; the lottery entry period is usually between November and March. If you don't make the lottery, there are a couple of last minute options for getting tickets: You can either go to the ticket office right before the Open opens (the third week in May; check site for the exact date the box office starts selling leftovers), or try to get a "Les Visiteurs du Soir" (Night Visitors) ticket during the first week of play. The way it works is this—starting at 5pm, depending on how many seats are available, you can buy a low-price ticket (10€–28€) for the rest of the evening's matches. Don't try buying any tickets at an unofficial outlet, however, as you might not be allowed in the stadium.

If you're not in town in June, but you'd like to pretend you were, visit the **Tenniseum** (Roland-Garros Stadium, 2 av. Gordon Bennett, 16th arrond.; ☎ 01 47 43 48 48; www.fft.fr/site-tenniseum; 10€ adults, 8€ students and under 18, 20€ families (2 adults, 1 child); Wed, Fri, Sat, Sun 10am–6pm, museum closed during the French Open, 3rd week of May to mid-June; Métro: Porte d'Auteuil), a new multimedia museum dedicated to the art of tennis. Tucked into the stadium complex, this slick facility offers the opportunity to view over 4,000 hours worth of tennis archives and interviews, as well as displays of historic tennis equipment and photography. True tennis fans will appreciate the guided backstage tours of the stadium (in both French and English; reserve ahead at the number listed above).

CYCLING

Despite the doping scandals, the **Tour de France** (www.letour.fr) is still one of the world's top athletic events, and there are few sites that can compare with seeing the *peleton* (the group of riders) zooming up and down the Champs Elysées for the final stage of the race. The Tour stretches over 3 weeks in July; check the website for a detailed rundown on each day's itinerary. If you can't (or don't want to) beat the crowds around the Champs (get here early in the morning, around 9am, to get a good spot), visit the website or watch the local newspapers, to see where else in Paris the race is passing—in past years you could also see the fun at place de la Bastille, place de la Concorde, and on the Pont d'Alma in front of the Eiffel Tower.

8 Walkabouts

A curbside view of the best show in town: the streets of Paris

PARIS IS A WALKING CITY. YOU SIMPLY WON'T BE ABLE TO FULLY APPRECIATE the flavor of the place if you don't get out, stroll through the streets and absorb the sights, sounds, and even smells that make up its sensory identity. And the identity of Paris runs deep: A mere city block can encompass several centuries' worth of history and happenings. Even if most of the elegant Belle Epoque buildings you will pass date from the late 19th century—when über-urban planner Baron Haussmann remade what was essentially a medieval city—if you look closely, you'll find ample evidence of its glorious past. Renaissance squares, 17th-century palaces, and medieval ramparts are tucked in and around more recent structures; Gallo Roman baths and 10th-century towers bump up against swank boulevards and legendary cafes where Sartre and de Beauvoir held court in the '30s and '40s. While wandering aimlessly can be a delightful way to get to know a place, a loosely structured itinerary can help make sure that you don't miss something wonderful. Below are three walking tours of three of the city's best areas for ambling about.

Walking Tour 1: The Quays of the Seine

Start:	Quai St-Bernard (Métro: Austerlitz; a ramp opposite the entrance to the Jardin des Plantes on the riverside leads down to the quay)
Finish:	Place de la Concorde
Time:	About 2 hours, not including snack breaks or dawdling on benches
Best times:	Almost any time is good. Long stretches of the quays are closed to traffic on Sundays (see the "Car Free Sundays" box below)
Worst times:	Some of the quays, particularly on the islands, may be more crowded on weekends

If you only have time for one walk, make it this one. The Seine is the city's widest and most beautiful boulevard, running through Paris in a graceful arc, and passing by almost all of its most famous monuments. By all means, bring your camera on this walk; the city neatly composes itself around the river, just about begging you to take a picture. The only sour note is the traffic; in the '60s, the authorities had the brilliant idea of running an expressway along some parts of the river, particularly on the Right Bank. This may have eased traffic congestion, but it stole away a good chunk of what was historically a vital part of the Parisian landscape. Slowly, the city is reclaiming the quays—the reinforced banks that serve as docking areas for boats but also promenades for walkers—and pushing cars away from the river's edge. While you cannot walk on one side from one end of the city to the other, more and more quays are being overhauled for pedestrians. Once you take the stairs down by the water, the urban noise fades and the atmosphere is surprisingly tranquil; you almost forget you are literally in the middle of the city.

Back in the day, a century or so ago, this river was the primary transport link between Paris and the outer world. The Seine was clogged with boats and barges, and its muddy banks were dotted with ports. A frenzy of mercantile activity buzzed around the river's edge, which drew workers, wanderers, and even some Very Important People. In fact, place de la Grève (today's place de l'Hôtel de Ville), which sloped down to the water, was the town center, where everything from national celebrations to public executions took place. Since the advent of planes, trains, and automobiles, the river has lost some of its clout, but none of its appeal; over the centuries various monarchs and mayors have gone out of their way to accentuate its natural beauty with elegant quays and bridges.

① Quai St-Bernard

The first thing you'll notice when you come down the ramp is a floating police station: The River Brigade is equipped with both boats and skin diving suits. On the other side of the river, you'll see the lock that is the entrance to the Canal St-Martin, which glides north through the 10th arrondissement.

Soon you will be walking through a lovely green sculpture garden, the **Musée des Sculptures en Plein Air,** which is part of the **Jardin Tino Rossi,** a modern park created in 1985 (see "Paris Outdoors," p. 212). At the end of the garden is a nice **playground** for the smaller travelers in your party. Though you'll have to look up to see it, at street level you are passing by the **Faculté de Sciences,** an unfortunate foray into Stalinist architecture that houses the city university's science division, after which is the much more lovely and more modern **Institute du Monde Arabe,** designed by Jean Nouvel (see the museum section in

chapter 5). On the river side, you will see the tip of **Ile St-Louis,** the next stop on our tour.

Go up the stairs and cross the Pont de Sully to the Ile St-Louis. Continue a few paces along the blvd. Henri IV and turn left on the quai d'Anjou (don't continue on the bridge or you'll end up on the Right Bank). Stay on the street level this time, instead of taking the stairs down to the water's edge.

② Quai d'Anjou

This is probably the prettiest spot on this delicious island, which is home to some of the most exquisite dwellings in the city. Up until 1614, there were actually two islets here: the Ile aux Vaches (Cow Island), and the Ile Notre-Dame, which belonged to the parish on the Ile de la Cité. Then an energetic contractor/developer named Christophe Marie came up with the idea of uniting the islands and building a town. He got a 60-year lease on the

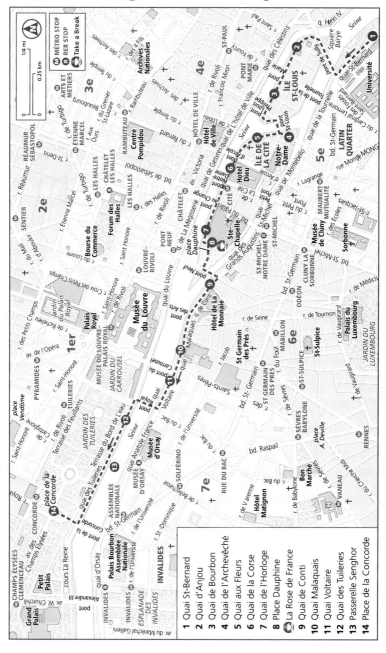

1 Quai St-Bernard
2 Quai d'Anjou
3 Quai de Bourbon
4 Quai de l'Archevêché
5 Quai aux Fleurs
6 Quai de la Corse
7 Quai de l'Horloge
8 Place Dauphine
9 La Rose de France
10 Quai de Conti
11 Quai Malaquais
12 Quai Voltaire
13 Passerelle Senghor
14 Place de la Concorde

Barging on the Seine

You'll see many barges tied up on the banks of the river; some a little on the scruffy side, others, beautifully redone. Despite the decline of river traffic, many people still live on barges—an interesting alternative to apartment dwelling in a city where real estate prices have skyrocketed. Though it looks ever so romantic and is certainly a unique approach to urban living, the upkeep on these floating homes is labor intensive and can be costly. Most barges are old, if not antique, and just finding the parts to patch them up can be a challenge; once you've finally managed to fix up your aging beauty, it may sprout holes and leaks all over again the next time a nasty storm comes along. For a fascinating look at life on a barge and a good history of the river, pick up a copy of *The Secret Life of the Seine,* by journalist Mort Rosenblum. On your walk, you may notice odd banks of mailboxes on the quays: This is how the river residents get their daily mail.

land from Louis XIII, and set to work—but the project took so long (a dike had to be built around the islands and they wouldn't be completely united for 37 years) that Marie went bankrupt and was replaced, and it was legendary architect Louis Le Vau (of Versailles fame), who finished off the job and got the glory. (Marie got a bridge named after him, but that was about it.) The elegant ensemble of streets, neatly divided in two by the shop-lined rue St-Louis-en-Ile, drew the attention of upper crust Parisians, who soon built beautiful homes along the quays. The quai d'Anjou is the most splendid; almost every building on it boasts a plaque announcing that some famous person or another lived there. At **No. 9** lived artist and caricaturist Honoré Daumier; and at **No. 17,** lived the Duke of Lauzun, a favorite of Louis XIV. While a variety of nobles lived at the Hôtel de Lauzun over the years, it was the bibliophile and Baron Jérôme Pichon who put it on

the literary map: He rented rooms to Charles Baudelaire and Théophile Gautier, among others. Note the gilded drainpipes, which are each adorned with a fantastical fish.

Cross the rue des Deux Ponts and admire tiny Pont Marie before heading down the

❸ Quai de Bourbon

At No. 1 you'll see the Franc Pinot, once a sailors' haunt and today a great jazz club. More plaques decorate the buildings further on: The very stately **No. 11** was the home of Philippe de Champagne, official painter to Marie de Médicis, the capricious second wife of Henri IV and mother of Louis XIII, who so relentlessly conspired against her own son that he eventually had her exiled. Champagne's paintings decorate Marie's palace in the Luxembourg Gardens; he also painted religious works for Cardinal Richelieu, her son's powerful Chief Minister. At **No. 15** lived Emile Bernard, a painter who is considered one of the founders of Symbolism, and at **No. 19** lived sculptor and Rodin protégé Camile Claudel, who spent her last creative years working here in the ground-floor studio, before being shipped off to an insane asylum in 1913. Her turbulent love affair with Rodin and her fight for recognition as an artist was the subject of a 1988 film, *Camile Claudel,* starring Isabel Adjani.

Walk all the way to the end of the quay. Cross the bridge to the Ile de la Cité, taking in the dome of the Panthéon in the distance to the left, and the Hôtel de Ville on the right. At the end of the bridge, you'll be right behind Notre Dame, on

4 Quai de l'Archevêché

Take a minute to enjoy a view of the glorious flying buttresses fanning out from the back of Notre Dame in the tiny but tranquil **Square Jean XXIII** behind the cathedral. These double-span buttresses were some of the first used on a cathedral; designed to support the high walls of the choir and the nave, for many years critics said they resembled scaffolding that someone had forgotten to take down. Exit the square and enter the **Square de l'Ile de France** on the other side of the street. Down a somber staircase is the **Memorial des Martyrs de la Déportation** a spare, but moving memorial to French citizens deported to Nazi concentration camps, including some 76,000 Jews. The underground memorial, which was inaugurated in 1962, is a series of narrow passageways and chambers with the names of the camps inscribed on the walls. At one point you will be in front of a long, square shaft that disappears into the darkness; its walls are lined with thousands of tiny lights representing the deportees.

Backtrack to the Pont St-Louis, but don't cross it; continue to

5 Quai aux Fleurs

Though you wouldn't know it from looking at the buildings, this is one of the more ancient parts of the city. This was the site of the oldest and largest port: Port St-Landry (the current quay was built in the 18th century, after the port was closed down). Legendary lovers Heloise and Abelard lived at **No. 9** in 1118; the building you see today was rebuilt in 1849. When Abelard, a famed 12th-century philosopher and scholar, fell for the much younger Heloise, his student, scandal ensued—particularly after Heloise got pregnant. They eventually married and lived in this house for a time, but they most certainly didn't live happily ever after; the new bride's furious uncle hacked off Abelard's manhood with a knife, after which Heloise retreated to a convent. The letters they wrote to each other in the aftermath of these events survived and have since been published. A rare medieval house (restored in 1960) is visible from the quay on the adjacent rue des Ursins.

Cross rue d'Arcole (which continues over Pont d'Arcole) and continue down

6 Quai de la Corse

At the beginning of this stretch of quay, you'll be presented with the back end of the **Hôtel Dieu,** Paris's oldest hospital. The original structure (which was on the other side of the Parvis Notre Dame, where Square Charlemagne is now), built in the 7th century, suffered

Bateaux Lavoirs—Life Before the Washing Machine

At the foot of quai de la Corse was once an impressive sight: the so-called Arche de Marion, a stretch of 12 linked barges—measuring over 200m (656 ft.)—that served as a giant floating laundry. At water level, the washing went on; upstairs it was hung out to dry. For centuries, *bateaux lavoirs*, boats where washerwomen did their work, were fixtures on the Seine; on the eve of the Revolution there were 80 or so on the river. Needless to say, this was an impediment to navigation, and so they were abolished in 1805, only to come back in greater numbers during the Restoration, when the Arche de Marion stretched from the Pont d'Arcole to the Pont Notre Dame. There was room for some 250 *lavandières*, or washerwomen, on the decks. Whether the clothes actually got clean is anyone's guess, considering the quality of the water in the Seine; aside from the many boats muddying up the waters, tanneries and factories regularly dumped their wastes in the river.

several fires and was built and rebuilt many times. It was then razed by Baron Haussmann (as was much of the Ile de la Cité) in the 19th century; the building you see before you dates from 1877. Enter from the front (on the Parvis Notre Dame) and admire the French gardens in the courtyard.

Farther down, at the place Louis Lepine, is a **flower market** (Mon–Sat 8am–7:30pm), where you can pick up a bouquet, as well as potted plants and ceramic gifts. On Sundays, it's a bird market (8am–7pm) filled with hundreds of twittering finches, parakeets, and other feathered friends. When you get to Pont du Change, you'll get a good look at the **place du Châtelet** across the river on the Right Bank. Sitting on top of a gargantuan métro station, this grand plaza was the site of a huge 12th-century fortress that, during the Middle Ages, served as a kind of city hall and later became an infamous

prison. It was knocked down at the beginning of the 19th century, and the new plaza was bookended by two enormous and still existing theaters: The **Théâtre du Châtelet** and the **Théâtre de la Ville.** This last was once owned by the great actress Sarah Bernhardt, and is where she played in *l'Aiglon* by Edmond Rostand, considered the high point in her career. At 76, after a leg amputation, she was still strutting (well, maybe hopping) her stuff on stage here.

Continue, crossing Blvd du Palais (Ste-Chapelle is to your left) to

⑦ Quai de l'Horloge

Those towers and turrets before you are what is left of the royal palace that housed the Capetian kings back in the Middle Ages. The first one, the Tour de l'Horloge, dates from the reign of John the Good (14th century), and sports the city's first public clock, which first ticked in 1371. The clock no longer works (even life-time warranties don't last over 7 centuries), but the tower still proudly looms, as do three others from the same era: the Tour César, the Tour d'Argent, and the Tour Bonbec. By the Renaissance, the kings had more or less moved over to the new castle on the Right Bank (the Louvre). The palace then became the seat of Parliament, and ever since has served a judicial function. Its most infamous days were under the Revolution; it was here that the Revolutionary tribunal was set up; it was so efficient that between April 1793 and July 1794 it had ordered the execution of some 2,600 citizens. The Tribunal's victims included some of the Revolution's leaders, notably Danton and Robespierre, as well as the royal family. Marie Antoinette spent her last days in the prison here, the infamous Conciergerie, before being carted off to the guillotine. After that grisly interlude, the palace remained a courthouse, though judicial procedures were much altered and improved. Today the vast building, which has suffered many fires and been reconstructed and enlarged over the centuries, is still the home of the **Palais de Justice.** The neighborhood is overrun with as many lawyers and judges as tourists; you'll see the former striding about in their long, black robes, and the latter queuing up to visit the **Ste-Chapelle** (p. 133), which is tucked into the maze of buildings.

Turn left after the Palais de Justice on rue de Harlay, where you will come upon

⑧ Place Dauphine

This lovely triangular "square" is an oasis of calm that you could easily overlook, if you didn't know it was there.

Built by Henri IV, who conceived the similarly symmetrical and harmonious place des Vosges, it originally had identical town houses and arcades like its sister in the Marais, but time has not been as kind to this *place.* The eastern side, which was once another wall of pretty Renaissance buildings, was knocked down in the 19th century, the better to admire the grandiose facade of the Palais de Justice. Even if the architectural unity of place Dauphine has been roughed up a bit, it is still delightful and blissfully undercrowded. Tall trees shade the center; small restaurants and galleries line its edges.

Take a Break

One of the cafes on the place Dauphine is tiny **La Rose de France** (24 place Dauphine, 1st arrond.; ☎ 01 43 54 10 12; www.larosedefrance.com), which offers gourmet meals as well as drinks either outside on its sidewalk tables, or indoors in the rustic dining area. For a light meal, try **Le Bar du Caveau,** on the other side of the square (p. 77).

Leave place Dauphine through the narrow opening that leads to Pont Neuf and turn left and cross over the bridge to the Left Bank and

⑨ Quai de Conti

You'll get your first glimpse of *bouquinistes* on this stretch; those famous booksellers that have permanent stalls on the river's edge. A lot of their wares are now overpriced and geared towards tourists, but if you're a good browser, you can still pick up some great used and/or antique books here. Soon you'll see an imposing

18th-century building on your left: the **Hôtel de la Monnaie,** or the National Mint. Though French euros are actually minted at a factory in the southwest, medals are made here, and you can tour the workshops or visit the museum (**Musée de la Monnaie,** 11 quai de Conti, 6th arrond.; ☎ 01 40 46 56 66; www.monnaiedeparis.com; 5€ adults, free under 16; Tues–Fri 11am–5:30pm, Sat–Sun noon–5:30pm). Opposite the entrance, on the river side, is a staircase that will lead you away from the dreadful street traffic, down to a tranquil quay on the water's edge where a bevy of restored barges are moored. Don't give in to the temptation to go sit on one of the cute patios on the decks (they are private property, after all). Above and to the left is the **Pont des Arts** (see box in chapter 5, "The Bridges of Paris," p. 188), a pretty pedestrian bridge from which there is another fabulous view of the island.

Stroll under the bridge and take the stairs back up to street level

⑩ Quai Malaquais

The dusty looking building in front of you is the **Ecole Nationale Superieure des Beaux Arts** (14 rue Bonaparte, 6th arrond.; ☎ 01 47 03 50 00; www.ensba.fr), a prestigious art school that refused the likes of Rodin, but accepted Degas, Matisse, Monet, and Renoir. Taking up a major chunk of real estate that stretches from rue Jacob down to the Seine, this elegant ensemble of 17th-, 18th-, and 19th-century buildings must be a constant source of inspiration for its students. Though the studios are off-limits, you are welcome to investigate the grounds (entrance at 14 rue Bonaparte), including the **Cour du Mûrier,** a beautiful cloister in a building that was once a convent.

Car-Free Sundays

Bike riders, joggers, and rollerbladers take note: Big chunks of the roads along the quays are closed to vehicular traffic on Sundays between 9am and 5pm. On the Right Bank, that includes from the quai des Tuileries to the Port de l'Arsenal, and on the Left Bank from the quai Branly through the quai Anatole France.

Continue down the quai to

⑪ Quai Voltaire

This quay gets its name from its most illustrious inhabitant: François Marie Arouet, otherwise known as Voltaire. A key figure of the Enlightenment, this writer/essayist/philosopher was known for his bracing wit and his defense of civil liberties. His willingness to criticize both the government and the Catholic Church got him into trouble throughout his life, starting in his early 20s when he was thrown into the Bastille prison for 11 months for writing satiric verses about the aristocracy. He made good use of his time: He wrote his first play, *Oedipe,* which was a huge success and brought him fame and followers. After a turbulent life, which included several imprisonments and exiles, in 1778 he died at No. 27, the comfortable home of the Marquis de Villette. During his last days at the Marquis' he received the likes of Condorcet, and Benjamin Franklin. His death, like his life, created controversy—a loud critic of the Church, Voltaire, though never officially excommunicated, refused to recant or receive last rites, and died as firmly attached to his ideals as ever. Through the finagling of his priest nephew, however, the philosopher did manage to get a decent burial in a graveyard, as opposed to a nameless ditch, where nonbelievers were usually interred. In 1791 his remains were transferred to the Panthéon.

Plenty of other great minds lived on this quay, including the painter Ingres, who died at No. 11, and Delacroix, who worked in a studio at No. 13; when he moved out, Corot took his place. No. 19 was a residence hotel that saw a gaggle of great writers and musicians, including Oscar Wilde, Jean Sibélius, and Charles Baudelaire. Marie d'Agoult, a countess who wrote books under the pen name of Daniel Stern and was Franz Liszt's companion, lived in the Hôtel de Mailly-Nesle at No. 29. On the other side of the Seine, that splendid building is the **Louvre** (p. 138).

At the end of the quay, turn right on the Pont Royal, and cross the Seine and take the stairs down to the

⑫ Quai des Tuileries

From this side of the river you can take a nice long look at the Left Bank, which at this juncture includes the **Musée d'Orsay** (p. 143). This erstwhile train station, like the Gare de Lyon, was built for the 1900 World's Fair and is a model of Belle-Epoque splendor. At the time, it was the pinnacle of high-tech, with ramps and lifts for luggage, elevators for passengers, and 16 underground tracks. Its glory days only lasted until 1939, however, when the electrification of the railway made the station obsolete. At first it was used for suburban trains, later it was converted into a postal center and then a receiving station for soldiers returning from World War II prison camps. Its state of genteel decay made it an ideal movie set: Orson Welles' adaptation of Kafka's *The Trial* was filmed there. It was about to be torn down to make way for a modern hotel complex in the 1970s, when it was snatched from the jaws of fate by

the commission for historic monuments. We all know the happy ending: To the joy of culture mavens the world over, in 1986 it opened as a stunning museum featuring 19th-century art.

That beautiful small building to the right of the museum is an 18th-century mansion called the Hôtel de Salm-Kyrburg that today houses the **Palais de la Légion d'Honneur.**

Continue down the quay to the

⑬ Passerelle Senghor

Recently renamed (it used to be called the Passerelle Solférino) after the Senegalese poet-president Sédar Senghor, this unusual footbridge was inaugurated in 2000. Its modern design allows pedestrians to access the bridge from either the water level, or the street level, yet rises high enough not to impede boat traffic.

Walk to the end of the quai des Tuileries, under the Pont de la Concorde, and up the ramp that leads to street level, where you will be face to face with the

⑭ Place de la Concorde

Try to ignore the traffic (not easy) and just admire the geometry of this 19th-century configuration of fountains, lampposts, and statuary, centered around a giant Egyptian obelisk (for a detailed description, p. 134); if you can get yourself to the center (there is a traffic light and a crosswalk, believe it or not), you can stand in a spot where the obelisk lines up with the Champs Elysées and the Arc de Triomphe to the west, and the Tuileries Garden, the Arc du Carousel, and the Louvre to the east. Speaking of the Tuileries Garden, those chairs around the fountain near the entrance are probably looking very appealing right about now.

Walking Tour 2: The Marais

> **Start:** Village St-Paul (23–27 rue St-Paul, Métro: St-Paul)
> **Finish:** place des Vosges
> **Time:** About 1½ hours, not including time spent in shops, restaurants, or museums
> **Best times:** During the week, when the streets are full of life, and Sundays, when unlike other parts of the city, many shops and restaurants are open
> **Worst times:** Saturdays, when most of the neighborhood is flooded with shoppers, and the Jewish quarter is completely shut down (the Sabbath starts on Fri night, so many shops will be closed late Fri afternoon as well)

The Marais is one of the few areas that Baron Haussmann largely ignored when he was tearing up the rest of the city; for that reason it still retains a medieval feel. Though very few buildings actually date from the Middle Ages, this warren of narrow streets and picturesque squares is layered with a rich history, which is apparent in the pleasing hodgepodge of architectural styles. The neighborhood's glory days date from the 16th and 17th centuries when anyone who was anyone simply had to build a mansion or a palace here. Though the area fell from grace in the 18th and 19th, many of the grand *hôtels particuliers* (private mansions) survived the slings and arrows of time and were reborn as museums and public archives when the neighborhood was restored in the later half of the 20th century. Today, the Marais is a fascinating mix of hip gentrification and the remnants of a working class neighborhood. It is at once the center of the city's gay life, as well as the oldest Jewish quarter, with a heavily traditionalist bent. Some of the city's best museums are here, and the best boutiques for browsing, so depending on your interests, you could spend a few hours or an entire day here.

❶ Village St-Paul

Many centuries ago, when the area was still mostly marshland (*marais* means swamp), a church was built down near the Seine and a small village grew up beside it. While the neighborhood has been transformed many times since, a small reminder of this village lives on, hidden behind an ordinary row of buildings on rue St-Paul. Pass through the entryway, and you'll come into a kind of large interior courtyard, whose dimensions and floral squares are left over from the 14th century, when it was part of the gardens of Charles V's royal residence. At one point the houses and buildings that were built over and around the gardens were slated for demolition; a neighborhood committee saved them and in the 1970s the village was restored and turned into a sort of antiques center, with dozens of stores. The village hosts seasonal *déballages,* or outdoor arts and antiques fairs. Today the commercial emphasis has shifted from antiquities to design; though there are still antiques, other storefronts feature cutting edge furniture, tableware, and decorative objects.

Exit the village on rue des Jardins St-Paul. On one side of this street is a playground that runs along a huge stone wall, the

❷ Rampart of Philippe Auguste

Before you is the best-preserved stretch of the city walls built by Philippe

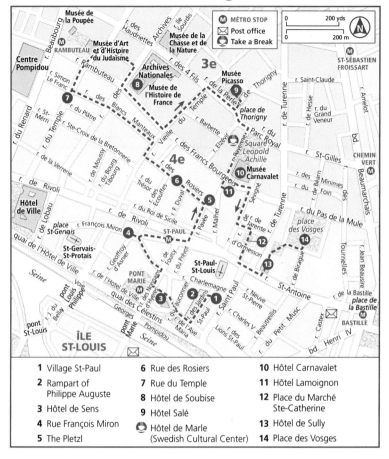

1 Village St-Paul	**6** Rue des Rosiers	**10** Hôtel Carnavalet
2 Rampart of Philippe Auguste	**7** Rue du Temple	**11** Hôtel Lamoignon
3 Hôtel de Sens	**8** Hôtel de Soubise	**12** Place du Marché Ste-Catherine
4 Rue François Miron	**9** Hôtel Salé	**13** Hôtel de Sully
5 The Pletzl	Hôtel de Marle (Swedish Cultural Center)	**14** Place des Vosges

Auguste. Before leaving town on a crusade in 1190, Philippe decided the time had come to beef up security. The result was a mighty rampart that defined what was then the city limits. The wall in front of you once ran in a semicircle from the Seine, up to around rue Etienne Marcel and curved over to protect the Louvre and back down to the Seine (a similar semicircle was built twenty years later on the Left Bank). Aside from this stretch, there are only small fragments here and there on both banks so you'll have to imagine the rest; you'll also have to imagine the towers

and the six massive portals that once were the only land access into the city.

Turn left down rue des Jardins St-Paul and right on rue de l'Avé Maria. Just where it branches off to the right on rue du Figuier is

3 Hôtel de Sens

Built between 1475 and 1519, this splendid fortress/mansion is a rare example of medieval urban architecture. When Paris came under the jurisdiction of the Bishop of Sens back in the 15th century, he promptly built himself a suitably fabulous home in the city. His successors only came into town periodically, so the building was often uninhabited; Henri IV briefly used it to house his strong-minded wife, Queen Margot, whose many love affairs were causing him no end of headaches. The marriage, which was arranged for purely political reasons, was eventually dissolved in 1599; by then Margot had spent several decades under virtual house arrest. The bishops stopped coming to the Hôtel de Sens altogether in 1622, preferring to rent it out; after the Revolution it was at one time or another a laundry operation, a jam factory, and a glass warehouse. By the time it was bought by the city in 1911 it was in a pitiful state; the building's restoration—which started in 1929—wouldn't be completed until 1961. The Hôtel now houses the Bibliothèque Forney, a library dedicated to the decorative arts and techniques. Take a minute to contemplate the turrets and towers in the courtyard (visible from the street).

Follow the side of the building down rue du Figuier and turn left onto the path that leads around to the back of the hôtel, where there are pretty French gardens. The path leads to rue des Nonnains d'Hyères, where you'll turn right, then walk left on rue de Jouey to where it intersects with

❹ Rue François Miron

In front of you, on the other side of the street, is a lovely Belle Epoque bakery, **Le Petit Versailles du Marais** (1 rue Tiron, 4th arrond.; ☎ 01 42 72 19 50; Mon–Sat 7am–8pm), which has a nice tearoom where you can fortify yourself with a coffee and croissant before taking on the rest of the quarter (be sure to look up at the pretty painted tile ceiling). Now turn left and walk down rue

François Miron to the corner of rue Cloche Perce. You will notice two multistoried half-timbered houses: the **Maison à l'Enseigne du Faucheur** (No. 11) and the **Maison à l'Enseigne du Mouton** (No. 13). Pre-Haussmann, there were houses like these all over the city; now they are extremely rare. These two date from the 14th century, though after 1607 the crisscrossed wood facades of all such houses were covered with a layer of plaster in accordance with a law that aimed to reduce the risk of fire. When these houses were restored in the 1960s, the plaster was removed, and the wood was once again revealed.

Return to the bakery and continue down rue François Miron until it ends at the St-Paul Métro station. Cross the rue de Rivoli and continue up rue Pavée.

❺ The Pletzl

You are now entering the city's oldest Jewish quarter, once called the *Pletzl* ("little place" in Yiddish), where there has been a Jewish presence since the 13th century. This community swelled and shrank over the centuries, in line with various edicts and expulsions, but the largest influx was in the 1880s, when tens of thousands of Eastern European Jews, fleeing poverty and persecution back home, settled in France. The Pletzl was hit hard during the infamous roundups of 1942, when police came and emptied apartment buildings and even schools of their Jewish occupants and sent them off to Nazi concentration camps. Though the neighborhood is slowly being eaten up by the advancing gentrification in the area, and chic shops butt up against kosher butchers, there's still a strong community here, and a fairly traditional one at that. At No. 10, you'll see an unusual synagogue, known as the **Synagogue de la rue Pavée** (10 rue Pavée 6th Arrond., ☎ 01 48 87 21 54), which was designed by Hector Guimard, the Art Nouveau master who created the famous Métro entrances. This is the only existing religious edifice by Guimard, whose wife was Jewish (they fled to the U.S. during World War II). In 1940, on Yom Kippur, the Germans dynamited the synagogue; it was eventually restored and is now a national monument (open for religious services only).

Continue up rue Pavée to where it crosses

6 Rue des Rosiers

Rumor has it that this street got its name from the rose bushes that once lined its edges, back in the days when it ran along the exterior of the city walls. Today it's the main artery of the Jewish quarter, and is filled with kosher butchers, bakers, and candlestick makers, as well as a number of kosher restaurants. There's great falafel to be found here (see L'As du Fallafel, p. 84); if you're lucky and happen to be in the area around lunchtime, you might get handed a free sample from one of the competing restaurants.

Turn left on rue des Rosiers and continue to the end, where you'll turn right on rue Vieille du Temple. You are now in the thick of the trendier (and gay) part of the neighborhood, which is filled with fun restaurants and boutiques. Take the first left at rue des Blancs Manteaux and follow this pretty street all the way to where it ends at

7 Rue du Temple

By the time you hit this street you'll notice that the neighborhood has changed from trendy to workaday; rue du Temple is lined with jewelry and clothing wholesalers. But this street—which back in medieval times led to the stalwart fortress of the Knights Templar—also harbors some lovely examples of 17th-century *hôtels particuliers* (private mansions). Start at **No. 41** (about a half a block to the left), which has a sign that reads "Café de la Gare" over the entryway. You can go into the courtyard and admire the handsome exterior of what was once the snazzy digs of a certain Nicolas Faure, lord of Berlize, a chief of protocol during the reign of Louis XIV. Today this building houses one of the city's major dance schools, the **Centre de Danse du Marais** (p. 201). Now move on north, to No. 71, the **Hôtel de St-Aignan,** otherwise known as the **Musée d'Art et d'Histoire du Judaïsme** (p. 169). Even if you don't visit the museum, you can peek into the courtyard during opening hours, which is definitely worth seeing. This exercise in 17th-century grandeur includes a sneaky architectural lie: One of the three facades facing the courtyard, which seems to be the front of an enormous building, is really just a facade. Despite the presence of carefully curtained windows, on the other side of the wall is merely another wall, yet another chunk of Philippe Auguste's ramparts. The false front not only makes for an elegant symmetry, but it makes the entire ensemble look much bigger than it really is.

A little farther up the street, at No. 79, is another splendidly restored hôtel, but unfortunately, you generally can't get past the giant doors that close off the courtyard. Still, the beautiful exterior of the **Hôtel de Montmor** is worth a quick look; built in 1623, the erstwhile owner of this luxurious palace, Henri Louis de Montmor, who was a great patron of literature and science, used to entertain brilliant minds like René Descartes and Pierre Gassendi. When Molière's play, *Tartuffe*, was banned by the authorities, he gave a private reading of it here.

Backtrack and turn left on rue de Braque. Walk down to the end, where the street intersects with rue des Archives.

⑧ Hôtel de Soubise

The vaulted archway before you is what is left of the **Hôtel de Clisson,** a magnificent mansion that was built in 1380 and for centuries housed some of the grandest of the grand, including dukes of Guise, who hung out there for 135 years. Well, it may have been good enough for them, but by 1700, when the François de Rohan, the Prince of Soubise got his hands on it, he decided the time had come for a change. Turn right and walk down rue des Archives to rue des Francs Bourgeois and turn left to see how the Prince transformed the medieval edifice.

The first gateway on your left opens out onto the enormous *cour d'honneur* of the **Hôtel de Soubise.** A huge horseshoe-shaped courtyard, edged with open galleries holding 56 pairs of double columns closes in a largely 17th-century palace, which now holds the National Archives. This jaw-dropping sight was the creation of architect Pierre Alexis Delamair, who was hired by the Prince build to the courtyard and overhaul the building. Later the prince's son, the future Cardinal de Rohan, asked Delamair to build him his own palace next door, the adjoining **Hôtel de Rohan-Strasbourg** (more archives are stashed here, not open to the public). A part of the Hôtel de Soubise currently houses the **Musée de l'Histoire de France** (60 rue des Francs-Bourgeois, 3rd arrond.; ☎ 01 40 27 60 96; www.archivesnationales.culture.gouv.fr/chan; 3€ adults, 2.30€ students and over 60, free under 18; Mon, Wed–Fri 10am–12:30pm and 2–5:30pm, Sat–Sun 2–5:30pm), which displays tantalizing items from the vast National Archives in a continually rotating series of temporary expositions. In 2008, you could see the Serment de Jeu de Paume, a document that signaled the birth of the French republic, and Marie Antoinette's last letter. You can also visit the apartments of the Prince and Princess of Soubise, though you would never know, since there is virtually no signage indicating their existence. Though just a few rooms, they retain the sumptuous decor of the period and give a sense of how the other half lived in the 18th century. You will most likely have the rooms to yourself—giving the odd impression that you have somehow stumbled into a private château.

Continue down rue des Francs Bourgeois to the next intersection and turn left on rue Vieille du Temple. You will pass by the entrance of the Hôtel de Rohan on your left. Turn right on rue de la Perle and left on rue Thorigny.

⑨ Hôtel Salé

Since Picasso's tastes in lodgings tended towards the old and splendiferous—castles in Provence, Belle-Epoch apartments—one can't imagine that he would complain about the building that houses the Musée Picasso, one of the world's greatest museums devoted to his works (p. 148). The 17th-century Hôtel Salé, with its sculpted ceilings and sumptuous central staircase would fit right into the artist's real estate preferences; built for a rich financier and salt tax collector (hence the nickname, Hôtel Salé, or Salty Mansion), this is one of the most exquisite hôtels in the Marais. The mansion took four years to build, but our poor salt man, Pierre Aubert de Fontenay, only got to enjoy it for one: Implicated in the financial scandals surrounding Nicolas Fouquet (see Vaux le Vicomte, p. 310), he could no longer pay his creditors and ended up losing his home. The mansion was subsequently purchased by various wealthy Parisians, and later served as the Embassy of the Republic of Venice. It was then transformed into various schools of arts and manufacturing, which wreaked havoc on the original decor. Finally, it was bought by the city in 1964, and in 1974 a 10-year restoration project was commenced. The museum opened its doors in 1985. Those doors remain open during opening hours, so you can look into the courtyard if you don't have time to visit the museum.

Walk back down rue de Thorigny to rue de la Perle and turn left. The street takes a short jog to the left and the name changes to rue du Parc Royal. Turn right on rue Payenne and walk about halfway down to No. 11.

Take a Break

The **Hôtel de Marle** is presently the home of the **Swedish Cultural Center** (11 rue Payenne, 3rd arrond.; ☎ 01 44 78 80 20; Tues–Sun noon–6pm), which has a lovely cafe with tables in the courtyard. Nibble a vanilla-scented *kanelbulle* while you take in the exterior of this 16th-century mansion, which at one point was the home of Yolande de Polastron, a close friend of Marie Antoinette. If you still need a rest, sprawl out on a bench in the **Square Georges Cain,** a small, but leafy park just across the street.

Continue down the street and turn left on rue des Francs Bourgeois.

⑩ Hôtel Carnavalet

One of the great things about the Musée Carnavalet (p. 151) is that it's free, so even if you don't feel like doing the museum, there is nothing to stop you from lounging in its beautiful gardens. Take a rest on a bench while you admire the exterior of this magnificent mansion, which dates from the Renaissance. Originally built in 1548, the hôtel got its name from its second owner, the widow of a Breton nobleman named François Kernevenoy, whose surname no one could pronounce. The mangled Parisian pronunciation, "Carnavalet," stuck. In 1660, a new owner gave François Mansart the job of enlarging and modernizing his lodgings—the result was so pleasing that in 1677, Madame de Sévigné, famed letter-writer and woman of the world, rented the building and lived there until her death. When it was made into a museum, in 1866, more improvements and enlargements were made, including the creation of two garden courtyards, the Cour de la Victoire (which you can enter directly from rue des Francs Bourgeois in good weather), and the Cour Henri IV. There are superb sculptures in the various courtyards, including *L'Imortalité* by Boizot, in the Cour de la Victoire, which once stood in the place du Châtelet, and the bronze statue of Louis XIV in the Cour d'Honneur at the main entrance. This last, by Coysevox, once stood in the courtyard of the Hôtel de Ville and is one of the rare surviving bronzes of a French king—almost all the others were melted down during the Revolution.

From rue des Francs Bourgeois, back-track to the intersection with rue Payenne and take a short detour about a half a block down rue Pavée

⑪ Hôtel de Lamoignon

Built in 1584 for Diane de France, the legitimized daughter of one of Henri II's extramarital encounters, the Hôtel de Lamoignon was acquired by a famous family of magistrates (the Lamoignons) in the 17th century. The enormous entryway sports two nude cherubs, one holding a mirror, one holding a snake, symbols of Truth and Prudence—essential bywords amongst the Lamoignon clan. You'll have no problem getting into the courtyard here (the building now houses the Library of the History of the City of Paris), where you can get a good look at the facade. The dog's heads, arrows, quivers and other hunting imagery carved into the stonework are references to the first owner's namesake, Diana, goddess of the hunt. A later Lamoignon, Guillaume, who was the first president of the Parisian Parliament, turned his home into a meeting place for the leading lights of the epoch—Madame de Sévigné, Racine, and Bourdaloue were regulars at his parties. The building became a library in the 1960s.

Go back up to rue des Francs Bourgeois and turn right. Turn right again on rue de Sévigné and left on rue de Jarente to

⑫ place du Marché Ste-Catherine

Though there's no longer an open-air market here, as the name suggests, this shaded plaza is still an absolutely lovely oasis of green and quiet in this busy neighborhood. There are, for once, no cars allowed on the square, and the cafes on its edges all have outdoor seating in nice weather.

Continue to rue St-Antoine and turn left without crossing the street to No. 62.

⑬ Hôtel de Sully

The most splendiferous of the many splendiferous mansions in Marais, the **Hôtel de Sully** (62 rue St-Antoine, 4th arrond.; ☎ 01 42 74 47 75; www.jeudepaume.org; Métro: St-Paul) was built by a rich 17th-century business-man, a certain Mesme-Gallet. While his version was quite sumptuous, the mansion really came to life when it was bought by the Duc de Sully, who hired architect François Le Vau to give it a makeover. After his death, like so many mansions in the Marais, the palace-like edifice was sold, divided, and built upon; in 1827 it was a boarding house for young girls, and up until the end of World War II it was still disfigured by shops and outbuildings. Using the origi-nal plans and contemporary drawings and etchings, the building was com-pletely restored in the 1970s to Le Vau's version; you can now stroll through the courtyard and admire the sculpted ex-terior in its virtually pristine state. Though the building is closed to the public, there's a wonderful **bookstore** in a nook between the front and rear courtyards, and an **exposition space** (see Jeu de Paume, p. 175) that presents periodic photography exhibits. The rear courtyard opens up on a peaceful gar-den and orangerie (a hothouse for orange trees).

Go out the archway to the

⑭ place des Vosges

This exquisite Renaissance plaza is so beautiful that I've devoted space to it in chapter 5 (p. 124). Officially inaugu-rated in 1612, the square, bordered by 36 virtually identical stone and brick town houses, was the idea of King

Henri IV, who unfortunately didn't live to see it finished. After a stroll under the arcades, which run below the town houses, have a seat on a bench in the square and admire the tall trees and the elegant symmetry of the landscaping, as well as the huge statue in the middle of Louis XIII astride his horse. This statue is a 19th-century replacement for the original, which was melted down during the Revolution.

The square has seen a number of illustrious tenants over the centuries: Madame de Sévigné was born at No. 1 *bis,* the 19th-century actress Rachel lived at No. 9, poet Théophile Gautier and novelist Alphonse Daudet both lived at No. 10. The most famous inhabitant, no doubt, was Victor Hugo, who lived at No. 6 from 1832 to 1848; his house is now a museum (p. 169).

Walking Tour 3: Montmartre

Start:	Place des Abbesses (Métro: Abbesses)
Finish:	Place du Parvis du Sacré Coeur
Time:	About 1 hour, not including time spent in shops and restaurants
Best times:	Weekdays, when you'll see signs of life in the quiet residential areas, and the shops will be open but not crowded
Worst times:	Weekends, when the crowds around Sacré Coeur resemble the Métro at rush hour (other parts of the Butte are less crowded, though)

Montmartre is an area that has become forever linked with a certain mythic image of Paris: quaint cobblestone streets, accordion serenades, and the Sacré-Coeur hovering in the background. Or maybe it's the Moulin Rouge and Can Can girls whooping it up on the place Blanche. Although the area just around the Sacré-Coeur is probably the most tourist-clogged in the capital, and the Moulin Rouge is a tour-bus trap, there's still magic on the Butte, and it's not hard to find. If legendary artists like Picasso and Utrillo are gone, new ones have taken their place, and they aren't the ones hawking portraits in the place du Tertre. In fact, within a couple blocks from the mobs on the *place,* there actually *are* quiet cobbled streets, lined with lovely vine-trimmed houses, and punctuated by cute cafes and shops. Away from the more obvious tourist attractions, Montmartre is considered one of the coolest places to live in the city, and a young, hip crowd has been steadily filling up apartments once inhabited by poets and painters like Max Jacob and Modigliani. Basically, if you walk in the opposite direction of the crowds, you are bound to stumble onto something lovely—here is an itinerary that will lead you in the right direction.

Note: The actual distance on this walk is not long, but the terrain will make it seem a lot longer. A good deal of Montmartre's charm is linked to the fact that it is up on a high hill (a *butte*) overlooking the city, so be prepared for some steep ups and downs, as well as a few flights of stairs. Visitors with reduced mobility might replace parts of this walk with the **Montmartrobus,** a bus that is part of the city bus system and makes a circuit of the Butte. The bus, which costs a regular Métro ticket, leaves place Pigalle every 12 minutes. For more information and a map, visit www.ratp.info/tourists and click "tourist excursions" on the "Discover Paris" menu.

① place des Abbesses

The first thing you'll notice when you are coming out of the Métro is the exit itself: This lovely Art Nouveau confection of smoked glass and metal is one of two surviving Métro entrances by Hector Guimard with a glass roof. Next you'll notice the leafy trees and benches and get the feeling that you're not in Kansas, er, I mean Paris, anymore. Montmartre was once an outlying village, and though it's considerably built up, the small size of the buildings and the presence of greenery gives it a less urban feel. That strange-looking brick church on the south side of the square, **St-Jean l'Evangeliste,** was built at the end of the 19th century by Anatole de Baudot, an architect who was very much taken with the spirit of the Industrial Revolution and believed that gritty materials like reinforced concrete were beautiful. Opposite the church is a pretty green enclosure called **Square Jehan Rictus,** which harbors a small **playground.**

Walk west on rue des Abbesses to rue Ravignan, where you will make a right uphill. At the top of the short street is place Emile Goudeau.

② The Bateau Lavoir

No. 13 started out as a piano factory but later was a home to a virtual "hall of fame" of artists, actors, and poets, when they were all young and struggling. In 1889, this odd edifice—constructed on different levels to accommodate the steep slope it was built on—was split up into artists' studios. By 1904, a young man named Pablo Picasso was living and working there, as well as Kees Van Dongen, Juan Gris, and Amadeo Modigliani, not to mention the poets Max Jacob and Guillaume Apollinaire, and a whole palate-full of others. It was here

that Picasso painted *Les Demoiselles d'Avignon* (even though he was nowhere near Provence), a painting that signaled the birth of Cubism. Unfortunately, this fertile artistic breeding ground, which was dubbed the **Bateau Lavoir,** or the Floating Laundry, by Jacob, burned down in 1970. All that's left of the original structure is one facade on the small plaza, the rest was rebuilt in 1978 and today still houses artists' studios. You can see a few vine-covered studios when you round the corner.

Turn left on tiny rue d'Orchampt, a quiet cobbled street, which curves up to an intersection with rue Lepic.

③ The Moulin de la Galette & the Moulin du Radet

There were once over 30 windmills on Montmartre's slopes, which were covered in vineyards. Before you is one of the last two that still exist, the Moulin du Radet, which is now a swank restaurant called the Moulin de la Galette. What is even more confusing is that the "real" Moulin de la Galette, of Renoir painting fame, is down the street at No. 75, and is also known as the Moulin Blute-Fin. Whatever its name, this old mill, which was owned by the same family of millers since the 17th century, was a witness to tragedy. In 1814, it had the misfortune of being attacked by a garrison of Cossacks, who were in town because the Allies (Germany, Prussia, and Russia, among a host of others) had come to Paris to stop French attacks on the rest of Europe and put Napoleon in his place. The miller tried valiantly to defend his property but ended up hacked to pieces and nailed to the blades of his windmill. Years later, the miller's son, perhaps trying to harken back to gayer times, turned the farm into an outdoor

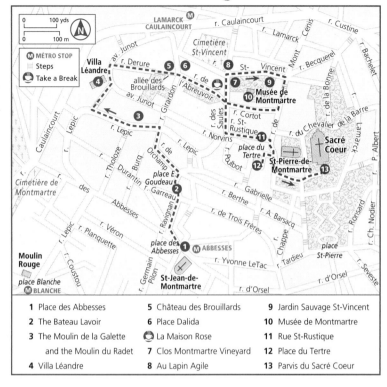

1 Place des Abbesses	**5** Château des Brouillards	**9** Jardin Sauvage St-Vincent
2 The Bateau Lavoir	**6** Place Dalida	**10** Musée de Montmartre
3 The Moulin de la Galette	La Maison Rose	**11** Rue St-Rustique
and the Moulin du Radet	**7** Clos Montmartre Vineyard	**12** Place du Tertre
4 Villa Léandre	**8** Au Lapin Agile	**13** Parvis du Sacré Coeur

music hall, the famous Moulin de la Galette depicted in a legendary painting by Renoir (you can see the painting at the Musée d'Orsay, p. 141). Other painters that frequented these bucolic dance parties included Toulouse-Lautrec, Van Gogh, and Utrillo. Today you won't get to dance here—the mill is private property and a prim little sign outside informs you that it is under electronic surveillance and protected by radars and guard dogs.

Walk down rue Lepic to No. 65 and turn right and go up the stairs past big old houses and quiet gardens. The path ends at the elegant Avenue Junot. Turn left and left again on

④ Villa Léandre

Named after painter and humorist Charles Léandre, this tiny, pristine lane is lined with quaint cottages that look like they belong in the English countryside. Max Ernst once lived on this street, and he was no fool—this is some of the most desirable real estate in Paris. The houses at the end of the lane have marvelous views of the city. Back out on Avenue Junot, are some of Montmartre's most elegant homes, including No. 13, which was inhabited and decorated by the artist Francique Poulbot, and No. 15, which was built for Dadaist writer Tristan Tzara, by the Austrian architect Adolf Loos.

From the intersection of Villa Léandre and Avenue Junot turn left and immediately right on rue Simon Dereure. The street ends at place Casadesus; climb the stairs to the footpath called Allée des Brouillards.

5 Château des Brouillards

This tranquil path leads past a number of massive houses, set back in large gardens, most of which are at least partially shielded from prying eyes by tall fences. The largest garden surrounds a white country manor known as the **Château des Brouillards,** or Fog Castle. Built in 1772 for a lawyer in the Parisian Parliament, this romantic dwelling most likely got its name from the mist that crept up from a nearby spring when the water contacted the cold morning air (real fog is a rare thing up here). Gérard de Nerval lived here in 1854, and surely this was the ideal writer's haven for this quintessential Romantic-era poet. The painter Pierre-Auguste Renoir lived and worked in one of the houses behind the Château; his son, filmmaker Jean Renoir, was born there.

Continue down the path to its end, at

6 place Dalida

Out in front of the mansion is place Dalida, which is graced with a bust of one of Montmartre's most beloved residents, Yolanda Gigliotti, aka Dalida. This Egyptian-born singer, of Italian ancestry, was one of France's biggest stars, recording hundreds of hits and winning 70 gold records. The blond bombshell moved to the Butte in 1962, where she lived out the rest of her stormy life in a four-story mansion that her fans dubbed "Sleeping Beauty's Castle." After a series of unfortunate love affairs, two of which ended with her partners' suicides, she took her own life in 1987. Her statue looks out on one of the most prototypical views of

Montmartre, down rue de l'Abreuvoir: a cobbled lane leading up a hill with the Sacré-Coeur in the background.

Walk down rue de l'Abreuvoir and turn left on rue des Saules.

> **Take a Break**
>
> Your last chance for refreshment before you hit the tourist madness is a charming little cafe that happens to be in **La Maison Rose** (2 rue de l'Abreuvoir, 18th arrond.; ☎ 01 42 57 66 75), the house that Utrillo made famous in one of his first successful paintings.

7 Clos Montmartre Vineyard

As you make your way down rue des Saules, you will notice an unlikely vineyard on the right hand side of the street. This is in fact the last of Montmartre's vineyards—for centuries the Butte was covered with them. Back in the 16th century, winemaking was the primary industry in the area—though nobody ever bragged about the high quality of the product, which was mainly known for its diuretic virtues. A ditty about Montmartre's wine went thus: "The wine of Montmartre—whoever drinks a pint, pisses a quarte." By the way, in those days, a "quarte" equaled 67 liters (70 quarts). Whatever its merits, this tiny vineyard still produces; rare bottles of Clos Montmartre are auctioned off every year by the district and the proceeds benefit local public projects.

Continue down rue des Saules to the intersection with rue St-Vincent

8 Au Lapin Agile

Now we're getting into serious tourist territory—you'll know by the marauding bands of camera-wielding sightseers converging on an innocuous-looking inn called **Au Lapin Agile.** The story goes that a habitué of this rowdy corner cabaret—which was then called the Cabaret des Assassins—a certain André Gill, painted a sign for the place showing a rabbit *(lapin)* jumping out of a stock pot. The cabaret became known as the Lapin à Gill (Gill's rabbit), which in time mutated into Au Lapin Agile (the Agile Rabbit). The singer Aristide Bruant (immortalized in a poster by Toulouse-Lautrec) bought the inn in 1902, and asked Frédé, a local guitar legend, to run it. Under Frédé's guidance, the cabaret thrived, and the best and the brightest of the Montmartre scene was drawn to its doors; Picasso, Verlaine, Renoir, Utrillo, and Apollinaire, were just some of the young upstarts that used to show up for wine, women, and song. Not everyone who came was a fan of modern art, however. The writer Roland Dorgelès had had enough of "Picasso's band" from the Bateau Lavoir and decided to play a trick on them: He tied a paintbrush to the end of Frédé's donkey, Lolo, and let him slop paint over a canvas. Dorgelès then entered the painting, which he entitled: *And the Sun Set Over the Adriatic,* in the Salon des Independants, a major art show in Paris. The critics loved it—until they found out who really painted it and a scandal ensued.

Today's **Au Lapin Agile** (22 rue des Saules, 18th arrond.; ☎ 01 46 06 85 87; www.au-lapin-agile.com) still considers itself a cabaret, and indeed it has become a showcase for many new talents in the world of chanson française (traditional French song; see the "Chanson" box on p. 289). Though a little heavy on nostalgia, the Lapin does its best to remain authentic, and you can see a show Tuesday through Sunday nights for 24€, 17€ students under 26 with ID (one drink included).

Turn left on rue St-Vincent

⑨ Jardin Sauvage St-Vincent

At the end of this pretty street, on the right-hand side, is a barely noticeable entrance into an unusual park. The Jardin Sauvage St-Vincent is 1,500 sq. m (16,145 sq. ft.) worth of wilderness right in the middle of Montmartre. The idea is simple: What would happen if you just let a piece of urban land grow wild? The answer is in this incredibly lush patch of green, which has been left more or less on its own since 1987. A well-marked path leads through this delightful miniecosystem; a haven of peace only minutes from Sacré-Coeur. The garden is only open on Saturdays from April 1 to October 31.

Turn right on rue du Mont Cenis and climb the stairs to rue Cortot, where you will turn right again.

⑩ Musée de Montmartre

You might be so absorbed in looking around pretty rue Cortot that you walk right by the **Musée de Montmartre** at No. 12 (p. 174), but that would be a shame, as not only does the museum provide an overview of the history of the neighborhood, but it is housed it what was once the residence of Rosimond, a famous 17th-century actor who was in Molière's troupe. In another century, Renoir painted here (this is where he created the "Bal du Moulin de la Galette"), as did Utrillo, who lived here with his mother, the model and painter Susan Valadon, and her lover André Utter.

Continue to the end of rue Cortot and turn left on rue des Saules; walk up to rue St-Rustique and turn left.

⑪ Rue St-Rustique

By now you'll have noticed the crowds thickening, and a change in the atmosphere towards the Disneyesque. Trinket shops appear on every corner, and "artists" badger you to draw your portrait. Dive quickly into rue St-Rustique, a narrow channel of calm. Not only does the noise die down, but you'll be rewarded with an excellent photo-op of the bulb-like tops of Sacré Coeur sprouting above the end of the street. This is one of the oldest streets in Montmartre; it has no sidewalks and a medieval-style gutter runs down its center.

Walk to the end of rue St-Rustique and turn right. On your right is the entrance to

⑫ Place du Tertre

Now there's no avoiding it. It's there, in your face, the most tourist-drenched, mob-swamped spot in Paris. If you squint hard enough and use a tremendous amount of imagination, you'll see the lovely village square as it once was—but most likely you'll just be trampled by the crowds who are wandering around trying to figure out what all the fuss is about. Do not eat here, even if you are starving—you will be taken for a ride. A quick walk down the hill towards the place des Abbesses will lead you to plenty of nice restaurants and cafes. You will probably be approached by people begging to do your portrait—these "artists" may do nice caricatures, but if you think you're looking at the next Picasso, you're kidding yourself. Our advice: Take a quick peek and continue on the tour.

Duck back out of place du Tertre and continue down rue du Mont Cenis until it curls around to the left and becomes rue Azaïs. Keep walking until you're in front of

⑬ Parvis du Sacré Coeur

After you've looked up at the gleaming white basilica and its odd, pseudo-Byzantine domes, turn around and admire the stunning view from the esplanade, or parvis, in front of the church; on a clear day you can see as far as 50 km (31 miles). No matter how many people are standing around snapping pictures, or how many would-be rock singers are crooning John Lennon tunes, it just won't ruin the beauty of this sight. Though you won't be able to see the Eiffel Tower (it's too far over on the right, though you can see it if you climb up the dome) you will take in a majestic panorama that includes the Pompidou Center, St-Eustache, the Opéra, and the Louvre, not to mention distant hills and vales beyond the city. What you are mainly looking at here is eastern Paris, the more plebian side—an entirely appropriate view from this historically working-class, low-rent neighborhood. The view actually gets better as you walk down to the bottommost level of the esplanade; from here you can also take in the lovely gardens below, which had a starring role in the ultimate Montmartre movie, Amélie, by Jean-Pierre Jeunet.

Le Shopping

From the practical to the posh

LET'S FACE IT: NO ONE COMES TO PARIS FOR BARGAIN SHOPPING. AS EARLY as the 16th century, the city was known as the place to go for luxury goods, and over the centuries an entire industry grew up around the whims and whimsies of the French aristocracy. To keep up appearances, nobles spent outrageous amounts of money on sumptuous clothing, opulent homes, and lavish dinner parties for dozens of similarly well-heeled aristocrats. By the 18th century, thousands of merchants and artisans were working full-time to fill the voluminous orders of some 150 grand families, not to mention Louis XIV and his court in Versailles. So it's no wonder that even today, the high and mighty, or just plain rich, come here to deck themselves out in the best of the best.

So where does that leave those of us who don't have money to burn? Rest assured that the vast majority of Parisians are in the same boat as you, and are on the constant lookout for ways of staying stylish without going broke. Because some of what you have heard is true: Parisians, both male and female, like to dress and live well, and will jump through a number of hoops to do that on their limited budgets. Though social services may be plentiful here, salaries are quite low in comparison with those in some English-speaking countries. Yet your average Parisian looks remarkably well put together. What's their secret? Read on as we shed some new light on this puzzling mystery; the shops and services listed below will give you a good point of departure for your Parisian shopping adventure.

> ❝ When I shop it's not so much about buying. Whether you get something or not when you go in a store, you see what Paris is like. ❞
>
> —Sofia Coppola, in an interview with the *New York Times*

Before we begin, a word on taxes: Most items purchased in stores (aside from certain categories like food and tickets to performances) are subject to a 19.6% Value Added Tax (VAT) which is included in the price you pay (and not tacked on at the end like in the U.S.), and which explains why everything seems so expensive here. The good news is that non-European Union residents (sorry, that excludes U.K. citizens) who are over 15 and stay in France less than 6 months can get a refund of VAT (TVA in French) if they spend over 175€ in a single shop on the same day. Ask the retailer for the two-page form, which will be signed by the retailer and yourself. When you leave the EU (no longer than 3 months after you made the purchase), present the form

---

In-Store Etiquette

You know the stereotype: The Parisian store clerk who is cold, unhelpful, and downright nasty. But did you know that to them, often it's us who are rude? French storekeepers, particularly in smaller operations, work like devils to present the best products they possibly can in the most attractive displays. They take incredible pride in their work and expect others to respect this—so try to imagine how they might perceive loud, bossy tourists wandering in and demanding this and that without so much as a polite *bonjour*. France is a formal country: What may seem like trivial niceties, like saying hello, goodbye, and thank you *(bonjour, au revoir, merci)*, are matters of great importance here, and ignoring their existence is likely to result in a cultural collision. I'm not saying that there aren't store clerks here who are just plain grumpy—heaven knows, they are legion—but I guarantee that a bit of respect and politesse will go a long way towards soothing frayed nerves on both sides of the counter.

---

and the goods to customs. At the airport, look for the *comptoire détaxe* (you'll find them in all three terminals at Charles De Gaulle), where you can get your forms stamped by customs. Then, if you want to get an immediate cash refund, go to an American Express exchange counter and present your form (American Express will take a small fee for this service). If you're leaving the European Union by train to go to, let's say, Switzerland, you will get your form stamped either on the train or at the station in Geneva, where you will have to pass through customs. Once you get back home, send the pink sheet to the retailer and keep the green one in case of a dispute. The retailer must get his sheet within 6 months of the sale of the goods. Some shops are willing to give you the refund at the time of purchase, but you'll still have to sign forms and get your sheet stamped at customs. This refund scheme applies to most, but not all goods; for details, visit the French Customs website (www.douane.gouv.fr) and click the English language box.

SHOPPING NEIGHBORHOODS & STREETS

Shopping is not a precise art; it takes some studied wandering around to find what you want. Fortunately, Paris is a great place to wander around for any reason, and if you're shopping, you'll have a ball in the areas and streets listed below.

THE MAIN MIDRANGE SHOPPING NEIGHBORHOODS

Fortunately, Paris is virtually mall free, with lovely shops all over the city. That said, there are several areas with high concentrations of chain and other midrange stores that serve a mall-like purpose, in that you can get a lot of shopping done in a small geographic area (and you will most certainly have a better choice of places to take a coffee break than you would in a mall!). They are:

- ◆ **Rue St-Antoine** (11th and 12th arrond.; just off place de la Bastille)
- ◆ **Rue de Rennes** (6th arrond.; especially near the Tour Montparnasse)
- ◆ **Champs Elysées** (8th arrond.; oh yes, there are chain stores here)
- ◆ **Les Halles** (1st arrond.; try to avoid the dreadful underground mall, Forum des Halles, with its cold florescent lighting and its industrial escalators that make you feel as if you're descending into the bowels of the Earth; plenty of good stores are above ground here)
- ◆ **Boulevard Haussmann** (9th arrond.; and the little streets that weave around the Printemps and Galeries Lafayette department stores)
- ◆ **Avenue du Général Leclerc** (14th arrond.; between Métro stop Alésia and Porte d'Orléans)

DISCOUNT STREETS

Though boutiques throughout the city might seem uniformly expensive, there are a few discount-packed streets where those in the know go to stock their wardrobes and apartments with clothes and knickknacks at significantly reduced prices.

On the **rue d'Alésia** ★★ (14th arrond.; Métro: Alésia), for example, everywhere you look, you'll see signs for stock and de-stock, which is the French way of saying overstock or outlet stores. Many feature designer overstock, including:

- ◆ **SR store** (64 rue de Alésia, 14th arrond.; ☎ 01 43 95 06 13; Métro: Alésia, also at 110-112 rue d'Alésia; ☎ 01 45 43 80 86). That's SR as in Sonia Rykiel—deep discounts bring these pricey items out of the stratosphere and closer to Earth.
- ◆ **Cacharel Boutique Outlet** (114 rue d'Alésia, 14th arrond.; ☎ 01 45 42 53 04; Métro: Alésia). A voluminous selection of last season's offerings at significant reductions—men's shirts start at 39€, women's dresses start around 90€.
- ◆ **Stock Jeans Ober** ★ (111 bis rue Alesia, 14th arrond.; ☎ 01 45 41 21 10; Métro: Alésia). This closet-size store is stuffed with a wide range of body-hugging jeans and pants by the one and only French jeans label, Ober. You'll pay half what you would pay at Printemps (jeans here start at 49€); a great pair of jeans with a matching jacket can be had for fewer than 100€.

Another great street for bargain hunters is just around the corner from the Bon Marché department store: **rue St-Placide** ★ (6th arrond). Here you'll find great discounts on women's apparel, children's clothes, and linens, as well as some of the less expensive chain stores. The obligatory stop here is:

- ◆ **Mouton à Cinq Pattes** ★ (8 and 18 rue St-Placide, 6th arrond.; ☎ 01 45 48 86 26; www.mouton-a-cinq-pattes.info; Métro: St-Placide or Sèvres–Babylone). Sift through the packed racks of designer markdowns and you just might find Moschino slacks or a Gaultier dress at a fabulous price. If you do, grab it fast—it might not be there tomorrow. These are some of the best designer discounts in town, but you really have to look. The store at No. 8 is women's apparel only; No. 18 serves both sexes, as does their other equally overstuffed store at 138 blvd. St-Germain also in the 6th arrondissement.

Arcadia

One of the major challenges in visiting Paris is trying to figure out how to wander around and enjoy the city without getting rained on. An umbrella is imperative, of course, but you might also consider a stroll through one or several of the city's many covered arcades, primarily in the 2nd arrondissement. These lovely iron and glass galleries are 19th-century-antecedents of today's shopping malls—each one is lined with shops, tea-rooms, and even the occasional hotel—and range in ambience from slightly seedy to ultra hip.

The longest, and in the worst shape (of those listed here) is the **Passage Choiseul** (40 rue des Petits Champs, 2nd arrond.; Métro: Pyramides), which runs from rue des Petits Champs all the way to rue de Saint Augustin. Built in 1825, its elegant, peeling arches shelter various shoe shops, used book stores and, of all things, a bagel cafe. French writer Louis-Ferdinand Céline grew up here and wrote about it in his novel, *Death on the Installment Plan*.

The **Passage des Panoramas** (11 blvd. Montmartre, 2nd arrond.; Métro: Grands Boulevards) intersects with several other short arcades (**Feydeau, Montmartre, Saint-Marc,** and **Variétés**), making an interesting warren of bookshops, collectors' shops (stamps, coins, postcards, engravings), and restaurants. One of the first arcades (dating from 1800), it was an unqualified hit with Parisians. Though the glory days are clearly long gone, this is still a lively place. Look into the window at No. 47, **Graveur Stern** for a glimpse into another century—the decoration hasn't changed one iota since 1840. Nearby is the extraordinary woodwork facade of **L'Arbre à Cannelle** tearoom (p. 82) as well as the stage entrance to the Théâtre des Varietés, which Zola described in his novel Nana.

Across the street is the entrance to **Passage Jouffroy** 10 Blvd. Montmartre (9th arrond.; Métro: Grands Boulevards), lined with more

Also, look out for **Caroll Stock** (30 and 51 rue St-Placide, 6th arrond.; ☎ 01 45 48 83 66; www.caroll.com; Métro: Sèvres–Babylone or St-Placide), which is the outlet shop for the elegant Caroll brand (p. 263).

And don't forget **rue de la Chaussée d'Antin** ✪ (9th arrond.), which bisects the Galeries Lafayette department store. Laden with small shops and good prices, this street excels at moderately priced shoe stores, such as:

♦ **La Chausseria** ✪ (39 rue de la Chaussée d'Antin, 9th arrond.; ☎ 01 48 74 90 28; Métro: Chaussée d'Antin-La Fayette). An excellent array of real leather shoes and boots at affordable prices. There are three other locations: 68 rue de Passy, 16th arrond.; 13 rue du Vieux Colombier, 6th arrond.; and 20 rue de Buci, 6th arrond.

shops for collectors, this time figurines and dollhouses. Pricier gifts are to be found at **Passage Verdeau** (across the street from the back end of Jouffroy, 31 bis rue du Faubourg Montmartre, 9th arrond.; Métro: Grands Boulevards) a particularly atmospheric arcade that doesn't seem to have changed for at least 50 years. The stores are a little classier here, selling rare books, antique engravings, and vintage photos.

Farther south, near the Palais Royale, is the terribly chic **Galerie Vivienne** ⭐ (4 rue des Petits Champs, 2nd arrond.; Métro: Bourse), a beautifully restored arcade with a mosaic tile floor, classical arches and its own website (www.galerie-vivienne.com). High-rent clothes, handbags, textiles and objets d'art are sold here—even if the merchandise is out of your price range, the window shopping here is excellent. There are several restaurants including the Belle Epoque wonder, **Le Grand Colbert,** as well as the **A Priori Thé** tearoom (p. 82 and 82). Wine fans should pop into the amazing **Legrand Filles et Fils,** which has heaven knows how many fine bottles of wine, as well as bookshop, wine school, and cafe.

Toward Les Halles is the slightly more intimidating **Passage du Grand Cerf** (10 rue Dussoubs, 2nd arrond.; www.passagedugrandcerf.com; Métro: Etienne Marcel), which is filled with flashy designer jewelry, clothing stores, and interior design agencies—it's hard to imagine shopping here without being dressed in the latest hipster fashions. The **Galerie Véro-Dodat** (2 rue du Bouloi, 1st arrond. near the Bourse du Commerce; Métro: Palais Royale-Musée du Louvre) is mostly interesting for its decor: Dark wood paneling and bronze detailing give this arcade a serious and somber air. Composed of mostly high-end furniture and antiques shops, there is an old-fashioned luthier, or guitar maker, at No. 17.

BOUTIQUE STREETS

Unless you come during sale season (p. 259), you won't find many fantastic bargains on these streets, but at the very least you will enjoy some excellent window shopping and browsing in darling clothes, jewelry, home design, and other boutiques (streets listed in ascending order, price-wise):

Rue des Abbesses (18th arrond.; Métro: Abbesses) affordable chic, lots of hip, young start-up designers have shops here.

Rue de Charonne ⭐ (11th arrond.; Métro: Bastille) midrange prices, youth-oriented fare.

Rue du Four (6th arrond.; Métro: St-Germain-des-Prés) chic and trendy, a mix price-wise.

Shopping Hours

Before you head out to the stores take note: For shoppers, Paris is most definitely not a 24-hour city. In general, shops are open from 9 or 10am to 7pm; many are closed on Monday, and almost all are closed on Sunday, which is still considered a day of rest in this country. This is great for family get-togethers, but hard on working shoppers, who have only Saturday to get to the stores. Which leads to my next point—don't shop on Saturday if you can avoid it; the crowds are annoying, to say the least.

The French tradition of closing for lunch is quickly vanishing in Paris (though it is still very common elsewhere in France); almost all larger and chain stores stay open, as well as many mid-sized boutiques. Smaller, family-run operations often still close between noon and 2pm.

Another new trend: many larger stores and most department stores stay open late (that is, 9pm) one night during the week (called a nocturne) and most supermarkets are open until at least 8pm, often 9 or even 10pm. Very slowly, stores are starting to open on Sunday (you can almost always find a *boulangerie* open on the Sabbath), but this development is hotly contested by the unions, so don't get your hopes up. Fortunately, for food and toiletry emergencies, there are tiny minimarkets (called alimentations), usually run by Arab immigrants, that are open late into the night 7 days a week.

Final note: Many shops close down for 2 or 3 weeks during July or August, when a mass vacation exodus empties out major portions of the city.

Rue des Francs Bourgeois ✖ (4th arrond.; Métro: St-Paul) pricey hip boutiques.

Avenue Montaigne (8th arrond.; Métro: Franklin Delano Roosevelt) breathtakingly expensive designer goods.

DEPARTMENT STORES

Though the larger department stores (see "Les Grands Magasins", below) are definitely more chic; some smaller, cheaper versions do exist (see "The Less Grand Magasins," below). Both types are filled with goodies, of course. Where you go will depend largely on what you already have in your pocketbook.

LES GRANDS MAGASINS

Known as the *Grands Magasins* (that is, Big Stores), the great Parisian department stores were born in the late 19th century and have become landmarks in their own right. Though not exactly cheap, they often have mini-sales lasting a few days or a week. You'll see giant posters advertising these sales in the Métro and around town, as well as in various newspapers; you can also check the stores' websites. Of course, the time to find fabulous markdowns is during the sale season. Printemps and Galeries Lafayette offer a 10% discount coupon to tourists; if you didn't pick one up at your hotel, ask at the welcome desk (you'll need to show a passport or national identity card).

The most stylish, and expensive, department store is **Le Bon Marché** ✹✹ (24 rue de Sèvres, 7th arrond.; ☎ 01 44 39 80 00; www.lebonmarche.fr; Métro: Sèvres–Babylone) with beautiful displays and fabulous clothes. Its humongous designer supermarket, **La Grande Epicerie** (38 rue de Sèvres, 7th arrond.; ☎ 01 44 39 81 00; www.lagrandeepicerie.fr) stocks every imaginable gourmet substance and has a welcoming cafe (p. 98).

The glistening domes of **Printemps** ✹ (64 blvd. Haussman, 9th arrond.; ☎ 01 42 82 50 00; www.printemps.com; Métro: Havre Caumartin) bring to mind a grand hotel on the French Riviera—its three buildings are filled with fashion, beauty, and home products. Free fashion shows every Tuesday morning at 10am on the 7th floor of Printemps de la Mode.

A tiny bit less expensive than its next door neighbor Printemps, and even more vast, **Galeries Lafayette** ✹ (40 blvd. Haussman, 9th arrond; ☎ 01 42 82 34 56; www.galerieslafayette.com; Métro: Havre–Caumartin) is often jam-packed—come weekdays before 4pm to avoid the crowds. Beautiful housewares are available at Lafayette Maison (across the street).

Finally, a department store that even men will love. Sure, **BHV** (52–64 rue de Rivoli, 4th arrond; ☎ 01 42 74 90 00; www.bhv.fr; Métro: Hôtel de Ville) has acres of clothes and perfumes, but it also has a huge selection of hardware, electronics, gadgets, and other items for *bricoleurs* (do-it-yourselfers) of all nationalities. Be sure to visit its housewares and decoration department.

Sad, but true, in 2005 **La Samaritaine** (67 rue de Rivoli, 1st arrond.; ☎ 08 00 01 00 15; www.lasamaritaine.com; Métro: Pont Neuf or Châtelet–Les Halles) was closed for urgent repairs after the 1906 landmark building was declared a fire hazard. The store is not scheduled to reopen for at least 5 or 6 years.

THE LESS GRAND MAGASINS (BARGAIN DEPARTMENT STORES)

It isn't cool, hip, or even happening, but **Tati** (4 blvd. Rochechouart, 18th arrond.; ☎ 01 55 29 50 20; www.tati.fr; Métro: Barbès Rochechouart) has everything you'll ever need to complete your wardrobe for ridiculously low prices (polo shirts for 3.95€, slacks for 18€). Just around the corner, at 5 rue Belhomme, is **Tati Mariage,** where you can find a lovely assortment of wedding gowns starting at as low as 39€ (!) and going up to 399€. Okay, the quality might not be top-notch, but hey, you're only going to wear it once! Five more branches at: 76 avenue de Clichy, 17th arrond., ☎ 01 58 22 28 90, Métro: La Fourche; Galerie Gaîté Montparnasse, 68 ave. du Maine, 14th arrond., ☎ 01 56 80 06 80, Métro: Gaîté; Centre Commercial Italie 2, 30 ave. d'Italie, 13th arrond., ☎ 01 53 80 97 70, Métro: Place d'Italie; and 172 rue du Temple, 3rd arrond., ☎ 01 42 71 41 77, Métro: République, and 106 Faubourg du Temple, 11th arrond., Métro: Goncourt.

And what would we do without **Monoprix** (21 ave. de l'Opéra, 1st arrond.; ☎ 01 42 61 78 08; www.monoprix.fr; Métro: Pyramides)? When push comes to shove, and you simply must find a sundress/T-shirt/pullover, duck into one of

Sale Mania

In the name of fair competition, the French government has slapped strict controls on sales. Two times a year, around the second week in January and the second week in July (official dates are pasted a couple of weeks in advance on advertisements all over the city), retailers are allowed to go hog wild and slash prices as far as they want. The rest of the year sale prices don't usually dip down below 30% when they happen, which is rarely (usually only in the big department stores). Naturally, everyone breathlessly awaits the two big seasonal sales, and when the opening day finally arrives, chaos ensues. Don't feel you have to get there the first day—not only are the crowds horrific, but many stores are coy about their initial reductions and you may not turn up any really good bargains. Personally, I think the best time to go is the second or third week, when the crowds have thinned and the stores start really cutting their prices (sales go on for at least 5 weeks). Whatever you do, unless you are a dedicated masochist, don't try to shop on a weekend during sale season. You'll be trampled on, sneered at, and will probably be so sick and tired of the whole thing you won't even end up buying anything. If you must shop on the weekend, go early in the morning when the stores open.

these "everything stores" (which are everywhere), and you're bound to come up with something. In fact, many Parisians stock up on remarkably stylish duds here, though they would never admit it to anyone. You can usually find affordable housewares and toiletries, too, and sometimes groceries.

SECONDHAND & OTHER DISCOUNTED CLOTHING TREASURES

I'll be discussing two different types of stores in this section. The first is *dépôt vente* (*day*-po vahnt). These are consignment stores, where some Parisians go to sell used goods, and others go to buy them (the store owner, of course, chooses what he or she wants to sell and takes a cut of the profit). In Paris, most of these stores sell lightly-used, high-end items, designer sportswear and the like, which means even if the price is a fraction of what you would have paid for it new, chances are, those Moschino slacks are still going to cost over 50€. (For truly inexpensive clothing and household items, your best bet is the flea markets, see below.) The other type of store listed below is the *dégriffe* (*day*-greef). Unlike the secondhand stores, these discount boutiques sell new goods (albeit often last year's styles) that are significantly marked down.

THE BEST OF DEPOT VENTE

The stores listed below sell both men's and women's clothing and accessories but as usual in apparel stores; there tends to be a lot more women's stuff.

The largest *dépôt vente* in the city is **Reciproque** ✄ (95 rue de la Pompe, 16th arrond.; ☎ 01 47 04 30 28; www.reciproque.fr; Métro: Rue de la Pompe) which takes up almost an entire street in the posh 16th arrondissement. Each of the eight different boutiques specializes in a particular category (evening wear, handbags, mens' clothing, and so on) of lightly used designer items. This is the place to come if you've always dreamed of owning a Chanel suit, though even used Chanels cost money; they start here at around 500€ (but that's still a smashing bargain when you consider a new one costs anywhere from 3,000€–5,000€).

Another store in the same neighborhood that's worth scoping out is **Nip'shop** (6 rue Edmond About, 16th arrond.; ☎ 01 45 04 66 19; Métro: Rue de la Pompe). Stock rotates quickly here; labels like Dior, Yves St-Laurent, and Sonia Rykiel show up frequently on the racks. They have bags and jewelry, too.

The five stores that make up **Chercheminippes** ✄ (102, 109, 110, 111, and 124 rue du Cherche-Midi, 6th arrond.; ☎ 01 45 44 97 96; www.chercheminippes. com; Métro: Vaneau) present an entire universe of almost-new men's, women's, and children's clothing, as well as decorative items, toys, and baby stuff. Conveniently laid out with easily scannable displays and racks, it's a stylish assortment with reductions of up to 50% off major name brands. Not the cheapest of the cheap, but it's a wide selection of high-quality goods.

Typically tiny and overstuffed, **Au Gré du Vent** (10 rue des Quatre Vents, 6th arrond; ☎ 01 44 07 28 73; Métro: Odéon) specializes in designer labels with a nice selection of costume jewelry.

You wouldn't expect to find a secondhand clothes store in this chi-chi neighborhood, but **Griff'troc** (119 blvd. Malesherbes, 8th arrond; ☎ 01 45 61 19 47; Métro: Monceau) has a great selection of, you guessed it, haute couture.

CHILDREN'S DEPOT VENTE

Clothes as well as toys and books fill the shelves at **La Reserve des Sioux** (25 ave. de Tourville, 7th arrond.; ☎ 01 53 59 94 50; Métro: Ecole Militaire). Not enormous quantity, but high quality offerings.

There's nothing like looking in the chic neighborhoods for chic castoffs. **Baby Troc** (16 rue de Magdebourg, 16th arrond.; ☎ 01 47 27 37 28; Métro: Trocadéro) is a gold mine of barely-used designer baby and children's clothes at substantial reductions.

DEPOT VENTE FOR HOUSEWARES

People who are trying to unload an entire apartment full of stuff often turn to consignment shops—an excellent source of buried treasure, though you'll have to do a lot of digging. Try **La Salle des Ventes du Particulier** (117 rue d'Alesia, 14th arrond.; ☎ 01 45 42 42 42; Métro: Alésia), a huge space filed to the brim with furniture, china, and other goodies where you might turn up Art Deco objects or 1950s kitchen sets. If this isn't enough for you, they have a second location: **Dépôt Flandres** (63 quai de Seine, 19th arrond.; ☎ 01 40 35 40 29; Métro: Riquet de Paris). A much smaller operation with a good selection of reasonably priced items is **Antiquités de Paris** (157 blvd. Brune, 14th arrond.; ☎ 01 45 41 00 13; Métro: Port d'Orléans).

DISCOUNT STORES (DEGRIFFES)

Owned and operated by an American fashion victim, **Anna Lowe** (104 rue du Faubourg St-Honoré, 8th arrond., next to the Bristol Hôtel; ☎ 01 42 66 11 32; www.annalowe.com; Métro: Miromesnil or St-Philippe de Roule) specializes in top-end designer wear (Chanel, Armani, Yves St-Laurent) at 40% to 60% percent off. Though shopping here is more relaxed than at the sleek boutiques down the street, these relative bargains (a 900€ Armani blazer marked down to 420€, a 4,000€ Chanel jacket for 1,800€) will still take a big bite out of your pocketbook.

Closer to Earth, **La Clef des Marques** ☆ (122/126 blvd. Raspail, 6th arrond.; ☎ 01 45 49 31 00; www.laclefdesmarques.com; Métro: Notre Dame des Champs) offers 30% to 70% discounts on men's, women's, and children's clothing. Brands tend towards the medium-upscale; coats start at 79€, dresses 29€, and skimpy tops at only 19€.

Mountains of sweaters and other knitted clothing for as much as 50% off are on offer at **Smart Stock** (94 avenue du Général Leclerc, 14th arrond.; ☎ 01 45 39 60 90; Métro: Alésia). They have two other stores at 3 blvd. De Charrone in the 11th and 11 blvd. Davout in the 20th.

Younger, more modern designer clothes can be found at **L'Habilleur** (44 rue de Poitou, 3rd arrond.; ☎ 01 48 87 77 12; www.habilleur.fr; Métro: Filles du Calvaire), which stocks hip brands like: Michel Klein, Nuur, and Paul & Joe, for example. Discounts here can easily go over 50%.

ANTIQUES & BROCANTES

You've probably heard of the famous *marché aux puces,* or **flea market** at Clignancourt (see below), and if you are an inveterate browser, it's probably worth the visit. But the better deals are to be had at the ***brocantes,*** antiques or jumble sales, held periodically around the city. Though most of what you will find at these sales is sold by professional *brocanteurs,* who scout estate sales and other insider sources, your selection will be much wider and the chances of your finding a post-war ceramic pastis pitcher, or heirloom lace curtains at affordable prices are much higher than at some of the more overpopulated flea markets. Your first place to look for what's on when you're in town is in the **special supplements** of the following Parisian newspapers: *Le Journal du Dimanche* (Sun), *Le Parisien* (Sun), or *Le Figaro* (Wed, the supplement is called *Figaroscope*). There are also specialized magazines (found at larger kiosques) like *Collectionneur et Chineur, Antiquités-Brocantes,* and *Aladin.* You can also try your luck on the Web at www.la-brocante.com and http://vide-greniers.org, but these websites are in French only and not always easy to navigate.

FLEA MARKETS

Engulfing the Porte de Clignancourt at the northern edge of the city, the **Marché aux Puces de Paris St-Ouen** ☆ (Porte de Clignancourt, 18th arrond.; www.parispuces.com; Métro: Porte de Clignancourt) claims to be the largest antiques market in the world. Thousands of visitors descend on this sprawling minicity each weekend, which is split up into 15 *marchés,* each with its own specialty. Once a bargain-hunter's dream, prices now often rival those of regular antiques dealers. Still, hard-core browsers will get a big kick wandering through the serpentine alleyways of this Parisian medina.

Less well-known, the **Marché aux Puces de la Porte de Vanves** ★ (ave. Marc Sangnier and ave. Georges Lafenestre, 14th arrond.; http://pucesdevanves.typepad. com; Sat–Sun 7am–1pm on ave. Marc Sangnier, Sat–Sun 7am–3pm on ave. Georges Lafenestre; Métro: Porte de Vanves) is a happy hunting ground for treasure-seekers who don't mind getting up at the crack of dawn—the best stuff goes fast. Everything from classy antiques to piles of old clothes.

INDIVIDUAL STORES YOU'LL WANT TO VISIT

APPAREL

As anyone can tell you, Paris is a capital of style. But what's truly puzzling is how Parisians, the majority of whom don't make a lot of money, manage to look so chic, even if they're just wearing jeans and a T-shirt. Some of it's genetic (I'm convinced), but a lot of it has to do with knowing where to go to buy great jeans and a hip T-shirt at a good price. Here's to knowing—below are some *bonnes adresses* (literally, "good addresses") to get you going on your style search.

CHILDREN'S CLOTHES

Like so many things in Paris, if you've got the money, you can get the most fabulous children's clothes you've ever seen. Fortunately, even if you don't, there are still some French chains that have inexpensive clothes for kids with a big dose of style. Some of the stores mentioned below, like Monoprix and H&M also have a good range. All of the following have multiple locations; see websites for additional addresses.

I'll readily admit, after 8 years in France, I still can't figure out what **Du Pareil au Même** ★★ (1 rue St-Denis, 1st arrond.; ☎ 01 42 36 07 57; www.dpam.com; Métro: Les Halles) means, but one thing I do know is that they have adorable kids clothes at great prices. Covering everything from baby needs to early adolescence, DPAM is a good place to find inexpensive gifts or last minute necessities. The style here is fun and original, with lots of bright colors, cute logos and appliqués. Quality varies—knees tend to give out on pants, but shirts and dresses are fine.

Offering a little better quality at slightly higher prices, **Sergent Major** ★ (109 ave. Victor Hugo, 16th arrond.; ☎ 01 53 65 12 18; www.sergent-major.com; Métro: Victor Hugo) is another source of excruciatingly cute baby through adolescent wear, though here the style is a little more classic and the colors more subdued than at DPAM. By the way, that's pronounced "Sehr-zhan Ma-zhor" around these parts . . .

Thinking of moving to the 16th arrondissement? You'll need to stock up at **Jacadi** (89 ave. Paul Doumer, 16th arrond.; ☎ 01 45 24 70 77; www.jacadi.fr; Métro: La Muette) if you want your kids to look as cute and refined as your neighbors'. Clothes are more frou-frou here than at the stores mentioned above—a good place to pick up high-end gifts for the babies waiting back home.

What's up with the strange names of French children's stores? Whatever the reason, **Catimini** ★ (10 rue Vavin, 6th arrond.; ☎ 01 44 41 02 33; www.catimini. com; Métro: Vavin) has some of the most gorgeous and stylish kiddie togs you can imagine—it will be hard to pass up the exquisite sweaters, dresses, and outfits here, even if the prices are high. Clothes here are particularly well-suited to the under-5 crowd.

MEN'S CLOTHES

French men dress well and rarely worry about whether or not being well-dressed makes them look like a sissy. In addition to the stores listed below, some of the women's chains below also sell men's clothing; in particular, Zara has a good selection of the latest male fashions.

For casual wear, the best of the men's chain stores is **Celio** ★ (134 blvd. St-Germain, 6th arrond.; ☎ 01 55 42 93 63; www.celio.com; Métro: Odéon), which stocks a wide range of inexpensive, youthful, classics. In the market for polo shirts, casual slacks, jackets, and so on? Look no further.

Designer discounts by the bushel are the order of the day at **Mi-Prix** (27 blvd. Victor, 15th arrond.; ☎ 01 48 28 42 48; Métro: Ballard or Porte de Versailles), where top names like Karl Lagerfeld and Missoni are on sale for a fraction of their usual price. You'll have to do some hunting here, as the store is a little unorganized.

Tired of *dépôt ventes* that cater to women? **Fabienne** (77 bis rue Boileau, 16th arrond.; ☎ 01 45 25 64 26; www.depotventehomme.com; Métro: Exelmans) stocks a wide range of strictly masculine, somewhat used fashions, including designer suits by Smalto and Hermès that go as low as 100€. They even have ties and cufflinks, just in case you plan on eating at the Tour d'Argent.

Now here's an idea: Instead of buying international designer togs that you could get back home, why not have a custom suit made in Paris? True, it won't be free, but it will be memorable and long-lasting. Founded in 1948, **Teddy's Fashion** (7 bis rue de Monceau, 8th arrond.; ☎ 01 42 89 22 17; Métro: Courcelles or St-Philippe de Roule) is a Parisian institution, where you can have a suit made from the best Italian and English fabrics without needing to take out a second mortgage. Suits are 390€, shirts 60€, and pants 110€. The service is as professional and discreet as the clothing is elegant.

WOMEN'S CLOTHES

A "women's clothing store" can mean a lot of things in a city where fashion models, punked-out teenagers, and sultry secretaries each have a clear idea of exactly what their "look" is about. Here is a brief survey of a variety of different types of shopping haunts.

BOUTIQUES

Paris seems to specialize in adorable boutiques with pricey, to-die-for clothing, with possibly the highest concentrations in the Marais (rue des Francs Bourgeois). I'm not going to give an extensive list here (that would fill an entire book), but here are a few ideas for where to start your *leche-vitrine* (window shopping, literally "window licking").

You'll only find tops at **Des Petits Hauts** ★ (24 rue de Sévigne, 4th arrond.; ☎ 01 48 04 77 25; www.despetitshauts.com; Métro: St-Paul), but what tops they are: all original designs, and depending on the season they could be fuzzy grape-colored mohair sweaters, or skimpy cream-colored camisoles—all of which are positively delicious. They have four other stores: 5 rue Keller, 11th arrond.; 70 rue Bonaparte, 6th arrond.; 21 Rue Beaurepaire, 10th arrond.; and 8-10 rue Montmartre, 1st arrond.

Cute boutiques like **Vicxite.A** ★ (47 rue des Abbesses, 18th arrond.; ☎ 01 42 55 31 68; Métro: Abbesses) are popping up all over the streets surrounding

Montmartre's place des Abbesses, where new, young designers are selling their wares. You'll find fun, contemporary wear here in bright patterns and unusual combinations, what's more, prices are actually affordable.

Hot pink is the signature color at **Antoine et Lili** ✦✦ (87 rue de Seine, 6th arrond.; ☎ 01 56 24 35 81; www.altribu.com; Métro: Odéon), where the gaily painted walls are hung with oodles of colorful objects from around the world. Clothes are innovative and fresh, yet wearable, and come in a range of colors. Six other branches are sprinkled around town, check the wacky website for addresses.

A store that smells as good as it looks, **Des Filles à la Vanille** ✦✦ (56 rue St-Antoine, 4th arrond.; ☎ 01 48 87 90 02; Métro: St-Paul) has a great selection of big, fuzzy, funky sweaters, unusual long slit skirts, and gauzy dresses, as well as its own line of perfumes, including a vanilla-scented number, *bien sur*. There is another branch at 79 rue Mouffetard in the 5th arrondisement.

CHAIN STORES

Several European chain stores sell fashionable clothing at remarkably low prices. Fresh and fun, these stores have loads of colorful, mod clothing—but don't expect high quality. Best for lighter clothes in warmer seasons, here is a good way to save some money so you can buy those good wool slacks in the winter. The following stores have branches throughout the city—though I've listed only one address, several others are listed on the stores' websites.

My personal favorite is the French chain **Promod** ✦ (142 rue de Rennes, 6th arrond.; ☎ 01 45 49 05 49; www.promod.com; Métro: Montparnasse). Even in the midst of the most appalling fashion trends, this store manages to produce great clothes in wearable colors. The look is young, but not adolescent; shoppers here include both working 20-somethings and their mothers.

More fun clothing and good styling is to be found at **Mango** (82 rue de Rivoli, 4th arrond.; ☎ 01 44 59 80 37; www.mango.com; Métro: Hôtel de Ville). Colors at this Spanish chain tend to favor a Mediterranean complexion, a big relief for those of us who can't quite hack the Nordic hues at stores like H&M.

Another Spanish outfit, **Zara** ✦ (39–41 blvd. Haussmann, 9th arrond.; ☎ 01 40 98 01 46; www.zara.com; Métro: Havre–Caumartin or Auber) stocks clothes for the young and trendy, as well as dressier attire for working women. It's a good place to find basics like bright, mono-colored turtlenecks, cardigans, and T-shirts.

You can continue your European tour of chain stores at Swedish **H&M** ✦ (120 rue de Rivoli; 1st arrond.; ☎ 01 55 34 96 86; www.hm.com; Métro: Châtelet, RER: Châtelet-Les Halles), which hit North American shores a few years back and has altered the shopping habits of many of its inhabitants. Fashionable and extremely affordable, H&M stocks everything from evening wear to bare-bones basics, and collaborates from time to time with high end design houses, or pop stars like Madonna.

A little more upscale and a tad more conservative, **Caroll** (156 blvd. St-Germain, 6th arrond.; ☎ 01 44 07 39 00; www.caroll.com; Métro: St-Germain-des-Prés) has a great selection of moderately priced, classy basics, suits, and separates for working women who want something more feminine than a power suit (remember, in France it's okay to look sexy at work). It's also good for low-key "going-out" clothes.

Somewhat jazzier than Caroll and with an equally interesting men's department, **Alain Manoukian** ✮ (14–16 rue Halevy, 9th arrond.; ☎ 01 44 79 92 36; www.alain-manoukian.fr; Métro: Chausée d'Antin–Lafayette) offers distinctive design at moderate prices. Colors tend towards the bright and punchy; clothes are well tailored and democratically suited to the young and not-so-young of both sexes.

LINGERIE

Judging from the sheer number of lingerie stores in even the smallest towns in France, French women must put aside a large portion of their budgets for underwear purchases. And for good reason—French lingerie is exquisite and worth the splurge. If your budget is tight, and you've missed the seasonal sales, here are a few discount options:

Deep discounts on major brands (Léjaby, Simone Pérèle) can be found at **Tab Lingerie** (55 rue de la Chausée d'Antin, 9th arrond.; ☎ 01 48 74 41 11; Métro: Chausée d'Antin-La Fayette), which tempts passersby with a rack stuffed with lacy things at 30% to 70% off—the actual store entrance is at the end of the narrow corridor. They have a second store at 31 rue d'Avron, 20th arrond.; ☎ 01 43 73 93 63; Metro: Avron.

You'll have to do some serious searching through the racks at **Comptoir de la Lingerie** ✮ (175 rue du Faubourg St-Antoine, 12th arrond.; ☎ 01 43 07 32 63; Métro: Faidherbe–Chaligny), but it will be worth it: Discounts on major brands of both underwear and bathing suits can go as low as 50%. This place has a large size range too; cups go up to G.

Younger women descend on the popular chain store **Etam** (67/73 rue de Rivoli, 1st arrond.; ☎ 01 44 76 73 73; www.etam.com; Métro: Châtelet–Les Halles) in droves for its inexpensive, stylish underclothes. In addition to lacey lingerie and swimsuits, this is a good place to come for pajamas, bathrobes, and more practical items (they also have a nice ready-to-wear section). Locations are all over the city; see website for addresses.

Orcanta ✮ (60 rue St-Placide, 6th arrond.; ☎ 01 45 44 94 44; www.orcanta.fr; Métro: St-Placide), is another chain, albeit a smaller one, with seven locations in the city center (see website for addresses) and good discounts on name brands (such as Lise Charmel, Chantal Thomas, and Huit).

MATERNITY CLOTHES

Even pregnant women look stylish in France. I swear, even waddling into their eighth month, French women somehow manage to put together a look, that while in no way hiding their condition, manages to make them look both radiant and hip. I don't know how they do it, but I'm sure shopping at these specialty stores helps:

For classic casuals suited to well-rounded bellies, **Natalys** (74 rue de Rivoli, 4th arrond.; ☎ 01 40 29 46 35; www.natalys.com, Métro: Hôtel de Ville), a French chain, has a nice selection. They have about a dozen locations in Paris; see website for addresses. They also have pricey but adorable baby and toddler togs.

Neuf Lune ✮✮ (42 rue du Cherche-Midi, 6th arrond.; ☎ 01 45 48 33 63; Métro: Sèvres-Babylone; also at 43 rue Caumartin in the 9th) is a pregnant woman's dream: clothes that are both stylish and comfortable. They even have evening wear (true confessions: I bought my wedding dress here).

Buying Beauty in a Jar

Beauty products are something the French excel in, and they won't take up too much space in your suitcase. The huge selection of creams, lotions, powders, and oils ranges from deluxe brands like **Darphin** and **Clarins,** to lesser-known, less expensive names that never make it overseas. Among these, there are a number of great products that use ingredients from various thermal springs, like **Avene, Uriage,** and **La Roche Posay.** Often recommended by dermatologists, they are usually hypoallergenic, and only sold by pharmacies, or their cheaper cousins, *parapharmacies.* (These look and act like pharmacies but don't sell medicine, and often offer reductions on cosmetics.) If you don't know the brands, the staff is usually highly informed. Excellent hair products can also be found; keep an eye out for **Klorane, Phyto,** and **René Furterer** brands.

BOOKS

English language bookshops tend to double as cultural meeting places. Good for browsing (prices for new books in English tend to be high), picking up the English language newsletters, and readings (sometimes by famous authors), these bookstores draw expats from all over the city.

The most literary bookstore is probably the **Village Voice** ✮ (6 rue Princesse, 6th arrond.; ☎ 01 46 33 36 47; www.villagevoicebookshop.com; Métro: Mabillon or St-Germain des Prés). Writers like Adrienne Rich and David Sedaris have been known to have readings here, and the crème de la crème of the English-language literary scene is represented on its shelves. The staff is extremely knowledgeable, if a little stuffy. See website for upcoming events.

For a similarly top-notch selection in a friendlier atmosphere, visit **Red Wheelbarrow Bookstore** ✮✮ (22 rue St-Paul, 4th arrond.; ☎ 01 48 04 75 08; www.theredwheelbarrow.com; Métro: St-Paul). There are readings here as well, and they also have a good stock of children's books.

If a big bookstore is what you're after, a visit to the Paris branch of the English chain **WHSmith** (248 rue de Rivoli, 1st arrond.; ☎ 01 44 77 88 99; www.whsmith.fr; Métro: Concorde) might be in order. They have the largest selection of English-language books in the city, as well as a huge range of magazines.

One of the most historic English-language bookshops is **Brentano's** ✮ (37 ave. de l'Opéra; 2nd arrond.; www.brentanos.fr; ☎ 01 42 61 52 50; Métro: Pyramides; MC, V, AE). They have an excellent stock that ranges from art books to business primers, and their special events include a readers' club as well as a "Café Tricot" for knitting and chatting about books.

Canadians will be happy to find **The Abbey Bookshop** (29 rue de la Parcheminerie, 5th arrond.; ☎ 01 46 33 16 24; www.abbeybookshop.net; Métro: St-Michel), a cozy store that specializes in Canadian authors, as well as other English-language literature. Books are piled everywhere; the readings here are relaxed and fun.

Sylvia Beach—Mother of the Lost Generation

Born in Baltimore in 1887, **Sylvia Beach** fell in love with Paris early in life and moved there for good at the end of World War I. A few years later, with the encouragement of her companion, bookshop owner Adrienne Monier, Beach opened **Shakespeare & Company**, a bookstore and lending library specializing in English and American books. For the next 20 years, the shop at 8 rue Dupuytren served as an unofficial welcome center for American and English visitors, particularly literary ones, and specifically those who would later come to be known as members of **"The Lost Generation."** T.S. Eliot, Ezra Pound, F. Scott Fitzgerald, Gertrude Stein, and Ernest Hemingway were all regular visitors to the shop and friends of its owner, but the one who made the biggest impression, literally, was James Joyce. After his novel *Ulysses* was banned in both the U.S. and England and no publisher would touch the manuscript, Beach courageously volunteered to publish it herself. In February 1922, after endless proofs and corrections by the author, the 1,000 copies arrived in the store, almost all of which were snapped up instantaneously. Later, the book became a modern classic, making a mint for its publisher, Random House. Beach never saw a penny but claimed that she didn't mind because she would have done anything for Joyce and his art. In 1941, during the Nazi occupation of Paris, the contents of the entire bookstore "vanished" overnight (hidden in a vacant apartment in the same building) to avoid confiscation by the Germans. The books were saved, but Beach spent 6 months in an internment camp. After the war, she returned to Paris, but the bookshop's doors never reopened. The store's memory lives on, however, in its more recent incarnation at 37 rue de la Bucherie (see Shakespeare & Company, above).

No rundown on English-language Parisian bookstores would be complete without **Shakespeare & Company** ✪✪ (37 rue de la Bucherie, 5th arrond.; ☎ 01 43 25 40 93; www.shakespeareco.org; Métro: St-Michel). Though George Whitman, who opened this store in 1951, may not have the literary pedigree of Sylvia Beach, who founded the original Shakespeare and Company in 1919 (see box, above), he's a remarkable character in his own right with a personal history that includes friends like Lawrence Ferlenghetti and hiking solo across South America. Many a legendary writer (Alan Ginsberg, Henry Miller) have stopped in over the decades for a cup of tea; many an aspiring author has camped out here in one of the back rooms (Whitman likes to think of his store as a "writer's sanctuary"). At 90-something years old, George has finally passed on the reins and retired, but his presence is still felt at this historic bookshop, which sells used and new books.

Since new books in English are very expensive in Paris, there's a steady traffic in used books in the expatriate community, with a couple of bookstores devoted to the task. **San Francisco Book Company** (17 rue Monsieur Le Prince, 6th arrond.; ☎ 01 43 29 15 70; www.sanfranciscobooksparis.com; Métro: Odéon) is centrally located and has a good stock of used books as well some that are rare and out of print. It's a good place to unload those books you lugged along for airplane reading.

More disorganized, and a little more fun, **Tea & Tattered Pages** ✸ (24 rue Mayet, 6th arrond.; ☎ 01 40 65 94 35; www.teaandtatteredpages.com; Métro: Duroc or Falguière) offers up thousands of used books as well as a tiny tearoom where you can sip a cup of tea and munch on cupcakes while you read.

FRENCH BOOKS

To give you an idea of the importance of literature in this country, one of the only products with strict price controls are books. Stores are not allowed to discount more than 5%, which has kept many small shops alive in these times of megastores. Sprinkled around most of the city's neighborhoods, you'll find the heaviest concentration in, not surprisingly, the Latin Quarter, where the mother of all French bookstores, **Gibert Joseph,** reigns supreme over blvd. St-Michel.

Even if you don't speak French, it would be a shame not to wander the endless aisles of **Gibert Joseph** ✸ (26–34 blvd. St-Michel, 6th arrond.; ☎ 01 44 41 88 88; www.gibertjoseph.com; Métro: Cluny–La Sorbonne). There are six stores to choose from (all right next to each other), selling used books, new books, as well as CDs, DVDs, art supplies, and stationery (see stationery stores, below). Sometime back in the 1970s the Gibert family split and another store, Gibert Jeune now takes up several other buildings in the area. Like its ancestor, Gibert Jeune specializes in new and used books, but also branches out into stationery.

Sandwiched between Café Flore and Les Deux Magots, **Librairie La Hune** (170 blvd. St-Germain, 6th arrond.; ☎ 01 45 48 35 85; Métro: St-Germain des Près), has been catering to existentialists and other intellectuals since 1945. Excellent selection, mostly in French.

CHOCOLATES

Now here's something that the folks back home are guaranteed to love—provided it doesn't melt in your suitcase. A favorite standby for a gift to bring Tati Odile or Papi Jean-Pierre, French people give chocolates year-round, which accounts for the vast number of *chocolatiers* in Paris. Below are just a few ideas . . .

My vote for the chocolatier with the best sense of humor is **Michel Chaudun** ✸✸ (149 rue de l'Université, 7th arrond; ☎ 01 47 53 74 40; Métro: Invalides). Where else would you find a chocolate Prada purse or a chocolate power drill? This is also the place to find a chocolate Eiffel Tower that actually tastes good, as well as Arc de Triomphes, musical notes, and mini soccer balls. The "regular chocolates" are sensational, too: Be sure to try the paves—little squares of chocolate ganache made to resemble the cobblestones thrown at the police during the legendary student uprising of 1968.

Not to be confused with the above, **Michel Cluizel** ✸ (201 rue St-Honoré, 1st arrond.; ☎ 01 42 44 11 66; www.cluizel.com; Métro: Tuileries) is the name you've seen on dark tablets of designer chocolate at just about every gourmet grocer worth his or her salt. Here at the mothership, you can ogle these and other chocolates (containing "noble" ingredients and no artificial anything), from grand boxed assortments to humble lollipops.

Do-It-Yourself Dining

Does one really have to eat at a restaurant to eat well in Paris? If you have access to a kitchen, a microwave, or even just a picnic table, the answer is: No, one doesn't. Do-it-yourself dining is a wonderful alternative to eating out, and there are a multitude of shops where you can fulfill your deepest food fantasies for a fraction of what you'd pay in a restaurant. Not only will you pay less, but you will also be able to participate in one of the nation's favorite sports—food shopping and preparation. What better way to get to know a country than via its stomach? Watch that icy cheese seller melt when you show an interest in the difference between this and that goat cheese. Pick up a new recipe from the grocer hawking a batch of spring artichokes.

For basics, like napkins, nonalcoholic drinks, dairy products (experiment with the many yummy variations on the yogurt theme), **small supermarkets** like Petit Casino, Franprix, and Monoprix are sprinkled throughout the city. *Boulangeries* or bakeries, are everywhere, and crispy, long baguettes will generally cost around 1€. *Charcuteries,* which sell cured meats, pâtés, and other sinful pork products, as well as prepared salads and some main dishes, are getting harder to find, but nowadays, most *boucheries* (butchers) also serve this function. Speaking of which, be prepared to find a lot of cuts you've never seen or heard of; if you stick to steaks *(steack)* or roasts *(roti)* you won't go too far wrong. By the way, you'll never have to worry about hormones or antibiotics in the meat in France—they are prohibited by government regulations. *Traiteurs* specialize in prepared dishes; if you don't want to cook, but feel like eating at home, this is an excellent option. *Fromageries* (cheese stores) are also becoming rare. When you do find one, the selection is so excessive that your best bet is to close your eyes and point. Fruits and vegetables are best bought at one of the city's many **open-air markets.** Not only are the products fresher and cheaper here than in a supermarket, but it's also much more fun to choose them. Everyone yells: The vegetable seller hawking his potatoes, the fishmonger telling jokes, the customer screaming his order over the din; it's a boisterous mix of smells, sights, and sounds, the most recent version of a way of life that dates back centuries. In fact, shopping in open-air markets is such an excellent adventure that I've written it up in detail, along with a list of markets, in "The 'Other' Paris," p. 198.

It's worth a visit to the original **A La Mère de Famille** ✸ (35 rue du Faubourg Montmartre, 9th arrond.; ☎ 01 47 70 83 69; www.lameredefamille.com; Métro: Grands Boulevards) just to admire the ancient exterior and the windows filled with every imaginable chocolate and bonbon *gourmandise.* Founded in 1761, this piece of Parisian history (rumor has it the original owner hid the mother superior of the nearby convent from raging revolutionaries during the Terror) has committed its soul to candies and chocolates *à l'ancienne*. The addresses of the four other branches are on the website.

With five shops in Paris, and a few others in London, New York, and Tokyo, I guess you could call it a chain, but **La Maison du Chocolat** (225 rue du Faubourg St-Honoré, 8th arrond.; ☎ 01 42 27 39 44; www.lamaisonduchocolat.com; Métro: Ternes) is still one of the better places to buy chocolate. You'll find everything here, from exquisite basics, to modern fantasies, like chocolates infused with apricot and lavender, or port wine and melon.

For cutting edge chocolate in a boutique that could easily be mistaken for a jewelry shop, **Patrick Roger** (108 blvd. St-Germain, 6th arrond.; ☎ 01 43 29 38 42; www.patrickroger.com; Métro: Cluny-La Sorbonne) is a good bet; here you can sample chocolates with names like "Instinct" (almond praline) and "Jacarepagua" (spicy mint and lemon grass), as well as candied fruits, nougat, and other delicacies. Sister store at 45 avenue Victor Hugo in the 16th arrondisement.

FOOD

The following are some of the most easily accessible of the umpteen thousand food shops in this gourmet city; you're bound to find many more gems on your own as you stroll around town. Before you load up with gifts, however, check with your customs office to make sure that you'll be allowed to bring them home, as there are many restrictions on taking food items across borders. See chapter 12 for more information on this subject.

With its incredible volume of gourmet treats, **La Grande Epicerie** ★★ (Au Bon Marché, 38 rue de Sèvres, 7th arrond.; ☎ 01; www.lagrandeepicerie.fr; Métro: Sèvres–Babylone), the immense supermarket attached to the Au Bon Marché department store is a foodie's wet dream—some 5,000 different products from around the world beckon from its stylish shelves. There's a great takeout prepared foods section, as well as a nice cafe.

Not one to be outdone by its posh competitor, **Lafayette Gourmet** ★ (97 rue de Provence, 9th arrond.; ☎ 01 42 82 34 56; www.galerieslafayette.com; Métro: Havre–Caumartin), the gourmet section of Galeries Lafayette offers a similarly decadent lineup, at somewhat less caustic prices. A great place to come for picnic goodies.

You can't walk by **Davoli–La Maison du Jambon** ★ (34 rue Cler, 7th arrond.; ☎ 01 45 51 23 41; Métro: Ecole Militaire) without emitting at least a small gasp: The window is a magnificent homage to everything that a real charcuterie should be: pâtés, salads, sausages, salamis, and of course ham, in all its many forms and fashions.

The French take their tea seriously, as demonstrated by the presence of **Le Palais des Thés** ★ (64 rue Vieille du Temple, 3rd arrond.; ☎ 01 48 87 80 60; www.palaisdesthes.com; Métro: St-Paul or Rambuteau), which was created by an association of tea aficionados. Aside from a stunning range of teas, this shop also sells teapots, tea measures, and even tea-scented candles. Loose teas start at 2.70€ for 100g of St-James black breakfast tea, and go up to 135€ per 100g for a rare Taiwanese tea called "Oriental Beauty." Visit the website for addresses of the four other shops.

Making the Most of Market Streets

In addition to the many open-air markets that pop up around the city on certain mornings of the week, there are also several market streets which offer up delectable goodies all day and all week long. These streets are almost always pedestrian areas and offer the duel pleasure of outdoor stalls (mostly in the morning) and permanent boutiques (all day long). While there are lots of food-themed boutiques, there are also often other interesting shops, as well as cafes and restaurants where you can stop for refreshment. In short, these streets offer the ideal conditions for an all-out food orgy. The following is a short list of the more well-known market streets; you are bound to find others in less frequented parts of the city. *Note:* Most streets pretty much close down on Sundays, though some are open in the a.m.

- **Rue Cler** (6th arrond.)
- **Rue Daguerre** (14th arrond.)
- **Rue Poncelet** (17th arrond.)
- **Rue Lévis** (17th arrond.)
- **Rue Mouffetard** (only on the bottom third of the street, 5th arrond.)

GIFTS

Dollhouse fanatics shouldn't miss **La Boite à Joujoux** (41 Passage Jouffroy, 9th arrond.; ☎ 01 48 24 58 37; www.joujoux.com; Métro: Grands Boulevards). Everything from magnificent houses to miniature violins to electrical equipment can be found in this overstuffed store, hiding in a corner of the Passage Jouffroy. These are miniatures, not toys—they aren't suitable for children. The sister store, **La Boite à Doudou,** (same address) sells hundreds of figurines from mostly French-language comic strips (such as Asterix and Tintin).

In the same passage is a small gold mine for movie fans called **Cinedoc** (45–53 passage Jouffroy, 9th arrond.; ☎ 01 48 24 71 36; www.cine-doc.fr; Métro: Grands Boulevards), where there is a terrific assortment of film posters, as well as stills, books, DVDs, and other movie-themed items.

What can you say about a store that sells both hypercool jewelry and stuffed animals? **Colette** ✪ (213 rue St-Honoré, 1st arrond.; ☎ 01 55 35 33 90; www.colette.fr; Métro: Tuileries or Pyramides) is both high style and high concept—basically, if its utterly cool and happening, they sell it. Longchamps bags shaped like gold cards, rainbow-colored Alan wrenches, "Pick Your Nose" paper cups (each cup has a different nose on it), hip CDs and art prints, and Marc Jacobs "Stinky Rat" brooches that goes for a mere 395€. Though not everything is that expensive, nothing's a bargain—many of their offerings are limited-series collector's items—but if you don't buy anything, you could spend hours just looking around.

KITCHENWARE

It's only natural that in a country as food-obsessed as France, you'll find some of the finest cooking equipment on Earth. Some of the most famous are the professional cooking outfitters that sell to amateurs in the Les Halles area (see E. Dehillerien and Verrerie des Halles, below), but there are plenty of others. Though most stores specialize in one domain, they usually cover other cooking bases as well, so a glassware store will also stock cutlery, and a porcelain outfit will often also carry cooking utensils.

A culinary presence for some 200 years, **E. Dehillerin** ✖✖ (18 and 20 rue Coquillière and 51 rue Jean-Jacques Rousseau, 1st arrond.; ☎ 01 42 36 53 13; www.e-dehillerin.fr; Métro: Les Halles) offers a phenomenal range of cooking products, everything from cake-molds to cutlery, in every size, shape, and material. You can download a catalogue from the website.

As the name indicates, **Verrerie des Halles** ✖ (15 rue du Louvre, 1st arrond.; ☎ 01 42 36 80 60; www.verreriedeshalles.com; Métro: Louvre-Rivoli) is primarily known for its vast stock of stemware, but its inventory doesn't stop there: Porcelain and cutlery are also in evidence, and prices are reasonable, too.

With five locations in the city center, **La Vaissellerie** ✖✖ (332 rue St-Honoré, 1st arrond.; ☎ 01 42 60 64 50; www.lavaissellerie.fr; Métro: Tuilleries) is the most convenient choice for discount china and ceramics. These small stores are so chock-full of cute gift items that their wares generally spill out onto the sidewalk. In addition to china, they have piles of pepper grinders, butter knives, and all sorts of utensils you never knew you needed (like foie gras cutters) as well as kitchen magnets, aprons, dish towels, and so on. Other locations are listed on the website.

Of the multiple stores selling discounted china on rue de Paradis, **La Maison de la Porcelaine** ✖ (21 rue de Paradis, 10th arrond.; ☎ 01 47 70 22 80; www.maisonporcelaine.com; Métro: Poissonieres or Gare du Nord) is the best for *porcelaine blanche,* the famous white porcelain that is a staple in French kitchens. They also stock reproductions of historic china patterns, as well as glassware and gift items.

JEWELRY

Just down the street from the Hôtel de Cluny, **Le Parthenon** ✖ (54 rue des Ecoles, 5th arrond.; ☎ 01 43 54 26 04; Métro: Cluny–La Sorbonne) offers a small but lovely selection of mildly abstract original creations for those who are fond of the uncluttered look. Subtly modern dangly earrings and understated silver rings are the strong points here.

"Jewelry by the Pound" is the motto at **Gudule** (3 rue de la Roquette, 11th arrond.; ☎ 01 47 00 82 83; www.gudule.com; Métro: Odéon), which sells heaps of bracelets, rings, earrings, and other objects from mostly India, Tibet, and Central Asia. Prices are calculated according to weight and are exceedingly reasonable. Addresses of other branches can be found on the website.

Crammed to the rafters with glorious baubles, trinkets, and costume jewelry **Monic** ✖ (5 rue des Francs Bourgeois, 4th arrond.; ☎ 01 42 72 39 15; Métro: St-Paul) is one of the few affordable stores left on this utterly hip street. Sparkly earrings, clear plastic rings, and flamboyant medallions and necklaces all clamor for attention on the walls and in the display cases of this small enterprise, which is almost always full of in-the-know local shoppers.

A distant cousin of the Tati department store family, **Verlor** (19 rue de la Paix, 2nd arrond.; ☎ 01 40 07 06 76; www.verlor.com), offers similarly wild designs—this store sells 18-carat gold jewelry at up to 40% less than traditional jewelers. See website for other branches around town.

PERFUME

At the airport, you'll be assaulted with **duty-free shops** carrying loads of tax-free perfume, and another colony of similar shops is near the Opéra. If you don't want to hassle with the crowds and the cranky staff at these virtually identical operations, don't be afraid to go elsewhere because the chances are you will get the same tax rebate no matter where you go (as long as you spend over 175€, see taxes, earlier in this chapter). Discounts can also be found at two huge perfume chains: the ubiquitous **Marionaud** and the user-friendly **Sephora.** If you're willing to spend a little more, you might also consider some of the custom fragrance boutiques listed in this section—you'll probably spend more than you would for the known brands, but you'll bring home something unique.

One of the most affordable independently owned operations (a rare breed since the advent of chain stores) is tiny **Catherine** ✭ (7 rue de Castiglione, 1st arrond.; ☎ 01 42 61 02 89; Métro: Tuileries), which has excellent prices on a variety of well-known heavenly scents. Not only are the discounts attractive, but the service is also excellent.

Founded by the Countess of Presle in 1905, **Detaille 1905** ✭ (10 rue St-Lazare, 9th arrond.; ☎ 01 48 78 68 50; www.detaille.com; Métro: Notre Dame de Lorette) has its own elegant line of eau de toilette for both men and women, as well as other beauty products, such as its signature *Baume Automobile,* developed by the Countess when she realized (even back then) what pollution can do to your skin. These unique products are not available in department stores or perfume shops; you can only purchase them at the boutique or order them online through the shop's website or by phone.

The creations of master perfumer Patricia de Nicolaï are on offer at **Nicolaï** (69 ave. Raymond Poincaré; 16th arrond.; ☎ 01 44 55 02 00; www.pnicolai.com; Métro: Trocadéro or Victor Hugo), the only place where you can pick up one of these unique fragrances. Created with both body and home in mind, the inventory includes perfumes, bath products and "household fragrances," as well as diffuser lamps. There are two other locations at 80 rue de Grenelle in the 7th and 28 rue de Richelieu in the 1st.

For those who are ready to invest, a trip to **Editions de Parfums Frédéric Malle** ✭✭ (37 rue de Grenelle, 7th arrond.; ☎ 01 42 22 76 40; www.editionsde parfums.com; Métro: Rue du Bac) is in order. Fifteen original fragrances have been developed in this temple to the nose, which you sample in special "smelling columns," round, phone-booth-like tubes where you can experience aromas like the newest addition, French Lover. Two other stores are at 140 avenue Victor Hugo in the 16th arrondissement, and 21 rue du Mont Thabor in the 1st.

SHOES

How **Kevin Dorfer** ✭ (80 rue du Bac, 7th arrond.; ☎ 01 42 22 71 00; Métro: Rue du Bac) manages to keep his prices so low on this high-end street is anyone's guess,

Treating Yourself to a Beauty Treatment

While you may have seen their beauty products displayed in various para-pharmacies around town, you may not have known that Nuxe has its own spa. **Spa Nuxe** (32 rue Montorgueil, 1st arrond.; ☎ 01 55 80 71 40; www. nuxe.com; Métro: Etienne Marcel) pampers both men and women in a modern salon in a converted 17th-century wine cellar with stone walls and exposed beams, where clients are slathered with loads of fruit and/or vegetable-infused treatments. Facials run 55€ to 100€, and massages 77€ to 120€. Second location at **Printemps** (64 blvd. Haussmann, 9th arrond., Printemps Beauté Maison, 1st Floor; ☎ 01 42 82 52 52; Métro: Havre–Caumartin).

but here you will find elegant, Italian-made pumps and sandals for anywhere from 55€ to 140€.

Everything from snappy sandals to designer pumps are on display at **Moda di Andréa** (79 rue de la Victoire, 9th arrond.; ☎ 01 48 74 48 89; Métro: Chausée d'Antin), a small store hidden behind the Grands Magazins that specializes in designer markdowns on both men's and women's shoes.

STATIONERY

Sadly, there are fewer and fewer papeteries, those wonderful French stationery stores with sublime selections of pens, papers, notebooks, and other necessities. A hardy few have managed to hang on through the Office Depot onslaught (yes, they're here too).

One of the largest selections of everything from elegant fountain pens to creamy pastels is to be found at **Gibert Joseph** ✖ (26–34 blvd. St-Michel, 6th arrond.; ☎ 01 44 41 88 88; www.gibertjoseph.com; Métro: Cluny–La Sorbonne). Mostly geared toward student needs, this is a good place to find both the practical and the pretty at reasonable prices.

A little more modern, a little more do-it-yourself, **L'Art du Papier** (48 rue Vavin, 6th arrond.; ☎ 01 43 26 10 12; www.art-du-papier.fr; Métro: Vavin) has a fabulous selection of papers and envelopes (including the fixings for custom invitations), as well as ink-stamps, sealing wax, and the essentials for the latest Parisian fad: "le scrapbooking." There are two other locations, one at 16 rue Daunou in the 2nd arrondissement, and one at 197 blvd. Voltaire in the 11th (see website for details and product line).

TOYS

Baby intellectuals and kids looking for fun will all be happy at **Fnac Eveil & Jeux** ✖✖ (19 rue Vavin, 6th arrond.; ☎ 08 92 35 06 66, .34€ per min.; www. eveiletjeux.com; Métro: Vavin), which has a lovely selection of toys and games for children from 0 to 12. Educational toys are in evidence, as are danger-free bath buddies, great dress-up costumes, and wooden knight's castles. The accent is on imagination here; along with fun playthings, you can find books, card games, and art materials for little ones. There are five other locations in the city: Printemps de la Maison, 64 blvd. Haussmann, 9th arrond., Métro: Havre Caumartin; Bercy Village, Cour St-Emillon, 12th arrond., Métro: Cour St-Emillon; 148 ave. Victor Hugo, 16th arrond., Métro: Rue de la Pompe; 155 rue de Courcelles, 17th arrond.; Métro: Perèire, and Printemps Nation, 21 cours de Vincennes, 20th arrond. (all stores have the same phone number).

Wooden toys are the order of the day at **Le Bonhomme de Bois** ★ (43 blvd. Malesherbes, 8th arrond.; ☎ 01 40 17 03 33; www.bonhommedebois.com; Métro: St-Augustin). This small chain has human-sized stores where you can wander freely through a world of wooden trains, puzzles, pull-toys, and mobiles, as well as small stuffed animals, card games, small-scale plastic animals, and mini-knights in shining armor. This is a wonderful place to find an unusual gift for a small person back home. There are three other branches in Paris: 141 rue d'Alésia, 14th arrond., ☎ 01 40 44 58 20, Métro: Alésia; 56 rue de la Convention, 15th arrond., ☎ 01 45 78 66 30, Métro: Javel; and 46 ave Niel, 17th arrond, ☎ 01 40 54 79 88, Métro: Pereire.

WINE

Wine in France is stunningly cheap. Whereas you will need to pay at least $15 for a barely drinkable French wine in New York, in Paris you can sip on something extremely pleasant for as little as 5€ or 6€, and let's not even mention those 2€ to 3€ glasses of wine at cafes (cheaper than a Coca-Cola). Unless you are a serious connoisseur, who must have the best vintage bottles, a good bottle of Bordeaux won't usually cost much more than 10€. But before you start planning to stock your wine cellar back home, consider this sad truth: most non-EU countries won't let you bring back much more than a bottle or two (see chapter 12 for details), in an effort to protect their own wine industries. Your best bet is to choose your take-home bottle(s) carefully, and drink up while you're here. Wine stores abound—try to avoid the chains and stick to the independent operations. They are generally staffed by knowledgeable wine-lovers and will be glad to help you find the perfect accompaniment to that *roti de boeuf* you've got in mind for tonight's dinner.

More than just a wine store, **Legrand Filles et Fils** ★★ (1 rue de la Banque, 2nd arrond.; ☎ 01 42 60 07 12; www.caves-legrand.com; Métro: Bourse) is a place where you can learn everything there is to know about the sacred grape. Not only do they have a dedicated, knowledgeable staff and a huge stock of wines, but they also host wine tastings, wine classes, and have a bookshop filled with tomes on the subject (as well as wine paraphernalia and glasses). Both shops are in the glamorous Passage Vivienne (the cafe/wine store on one side, the bookshop on the other).

Every French wine-drinker knows that you'll get the best prices when you by direct at a vineyard. In an attempt to make these prices available to urbanites, **Les Domaines Qui Montent** ★ (22 rue Cardinet, 17th arrond.; ☎ 01 42 27 63 96; Métro: Courcelles or Wagram), an association of some 250 wine producers, offers a vast selection of *vins du producteur*, wines that come from small, independent vineyards where the emphasis is on quality and *terroir*, not quantity. Prices are almost the same as they would be if you schlepped out to the country (although you won't have the same scenery). If you'd like to sample the goods, head to the on-site wine bar that also serves light meals. A second location is at 136 blvd. Voltaire in the 11th arrondissement.

Crammed in a corner of the festive Marché d'Aligre is **Aux Caves d'Aligre** (3 place d'Aligre, 12th arrond.; ☎ 01 43 43 34 26; Métro: Ledru–Rollin), a tiny place where you need only stick your head in and cry "Help! I'm having oysters tonight!" and the kind staff will quickly hand you a fine bottle of Muscadet from the Loire Valley. They also host periodic unannounced wine tastings.

Hipsters like wine, too, as proved by the success of **Cave des Abbesses** (43 rue des Abbesses, 18th arrond.; ☎ 01 42 52 81 54; Métro: Abbesses), a small bottle-filled shop in Montmartre that doubles as a wine bar where you can sample some excellent vintages and nibble on cheese and charcuterie.

Another small but hip wine find is **La Cave des Papilles** (35 rue Daguerre, 14th arrond.; ☎ 01 43 20 05 74; Métro: Denfert Rochereau), which is staffed by knowing experts who will steer you in the right direction.

10 Nightlife in the City of Light

A wide range of delights tempt the evening adventurer

PARIS BLOOMS AT NIGHT. ITS MAGNIFICENT MONUMENTS AND BUILDINGS become even more beautiful when they're cloaked in their evening illuminations. Since New Year's Eve 2000, the already glowing Eiffel Tower even bursts out in twinkling lights; the thousands of tiny strobe lights that are attached to the monument make it literally sparkle for the first 10 minutes of every evening hour. While simply walking around town can be an excellent night out, it would be a shame not to take advantage of the city's rich evening offerings. True, this isn't a 24-hour town like some international capitals, and many neighborhoods may seem pretty quiet after sundown, but fear not, there are plenty of places to go if you are ready to shake your booty. Bars and clubs abound in a variety of styles, from the chic to the shaggy; you never know what may lurk on a seemingly quiet street. Culture vultures will find all sorts of marvelous ways to fill their evenings; being the nation's capital, Paris is home to France's most prestigious theater and dance companies as well as several top-class orchestras. Film fans will also be in heaven; this cinephile city has literally hundreds of movie theaters, and dozens of art houses where great movie classics are shown in their original (nondubbed) versions.

> **Outside of Paris, there is no hope for the cultured.**
>
> —Molière, *Les Précieuses Ridicules*

So whether you're determined to spend the bucks to go to the Moulin Rouge, or happy with a 2€ beer in a student bar in the Latin Quarter, I'm here to help you find your way. Gay or straight, rich or poor, young or old, you're bound to find a club/bar/theater/hangout that suits your purposes. Below is a biased selection of some of the better ways to spend your Parisian evenings; you'll find the different options grouped according to entertainment category.

CLASSICAL MUSIC

Sporting splendid friezes by Antoine Bourdelle, the elegant **Théâtre des Champs-Elysées** ✪✪ (15 av. Montaigne, 8th arrond.; ☎ 01 49 52 50 50; www.theatre champselysees.fr; Métro: Alma–Marceau or Franklin Delano Roosevelt) is considered one of the best classical music venues in Paris. Stravinsky's *Sacré de Printemps* created a scandal when it premiered at the theatre's inauguration in 1913; Debussy's *Les Jeux* had its debut here as well. Stars continue to light up this stage, supernovas like Juan Diego Florez and Anne Sofie von Otter are on the roster for the 2008 to 2009 season. Four major orchestras play here on a regular basis:

Finding Out What's On

For up-to-the-minute dates and schedules for what's happening in music, theater, dance, and film, pick up the **weekly listing magazines** *Pariscope* (.40€) or *l'Officiel des Spectacles* (.35€), the Parisian bibles for weekly events. While it is mostly a television guide, *Télérama* (2€) also has a weekly pull out listings guide, complete with reviews and articles (unlike the two listed above). All of the above come out on Wednesdays and are available at any newsstand.

The city's two free English-language magazines have both closed down their paper versions, but they survive on the Internet and are a good source for English-language events around town. The long-established *Paris Voice* can now be found at www.parisvoice.com, and the newer *Paris Times* is at www.theparistimes.com.

Orchestre de France, directed by Kurt Masur; Ensemble Orchestral de Paris, directed by John Nelson; Orchestre Lamoureux, directed by Yutaka Sato; and Orchestre Français des Jeunes, directed by Dennis Russell Davis, not to mention visiting orchestras and soloists. Opera is also on the menu, as are a few world and pop music concerts. Ticket prices vary according to performances, ranging from around 150€ for orchestra seats for star attractions, to 25€ to 30€ seats in the peanut gallery. If you don't mind a restricted (or even nonexistent) view, you can enjoy the music for 5€ to 12€. If the concert is not sold out, 1 hour before curtain remaining seats are sometimes sold to those under 25 or over 60 for 50% off; contact the theater beforehand to make sure the reduction is available.

The mythic **Salle Pleyel** ★★ (252 rue du Faubourg St-Honoré, 8th arrond.; ☎ 01 42 56 13 13; www.sallepleyel.com; Métro: Ternes or Charles de Gaulle–Etoile) has hosted the likes of Otto Klemperer and Daniel Barenboïm, not to mention Louis Armstrong and Ravi Shankar. Thanks to a 2006 renovation it now has more comfortable seating and cutting edge acoustics. The Orchestre de Paris, directed by Christoph Eschenbach, makes its home here, and the Radio France Philharmonic also makes numerous appearances. Orchestra seats range from 30€ to 85€, though "exceptional" concerts go up to 160€. The back of the second balcony is always 10€. There is a last-minute deal here, too: If you are under 27 or over 65, 1 hour before curtain you can buy a ticket for between 10€ and 30€ (depending on availability).

A little more out of the way, but a lot less expensive, the ultramodern **Cité de la Musique** ★ (221 av. Jean Jaurès, 19th arrond.; ☎ 01 44 84 44 84; www.cite-musique.fr; Métro: Porte de Patin) offers a wide range of music options, from classical to contemporary to jazz. Along with impressive classical offerings by visiting orchestras and soloists, there's also a good dose of traditional and nontraditional music from around the world, say the Istanbul Tekno Roman Project (Turkish Gypsy music) or French accordionist Yvette Horner. Young musicians and rising stars are highlighted; small orchestras and chamber musicians also show up on the

Heaven-Sent Music Venues: Concerts in Churches

Many of Paris's most beautiful churches and cathedrals, including Notre Dame, St-Eustache, and Sainte-Chapelle, host organ and other classical music concerts. Not only is the setting delightful, but the acoustics are generally otherworldly as well. While there is no ticket central for these artistic houses of God, concerts are usually listed in the weekly listings magazines *(Pariscope, l'Officiel des Spectacles)* under classical music. The churches generally print monthly music schedules, which they display near the entrance to the sanctuary (and sometimes post on their websites); be sure to look down from the stained glass and vaulting arches from time to time to see if you spy a copy. Ticket prices are very reasonable; you shouldn't pay more than 25€ and usually much less.

program. The Jazz à La Villette festival in August/September is not to be missed. Ticket prices are very democratic: Top names (some of the same as you'll find at the two venues listed above) rarely run over 35€, and many concerts have a one-price ticket for around 15€ to 20€.

OPERA & DANCE

If the architecture of the **Opéra Bastille** ✰✰ (Place de la Bastille, 130 rue de Lyon, 12th arrond.; ☎ 0 892 89 90 90, .34€ per min. (in France only), 01 72 29 35 35 (from overseas); www.operadeparis.fr; Métro: Bastille) might not be to everyone's taste, the quality of the performances should more than make up for it. This slate-colored behemoth has been looming over the place de la Bastille since 1989, when the national opera company decided it needed a new home. Not wanting to abandon the Palais Garnier, the company decided to split its energies between the two venues. In theory, more operas are performed at the Bastille, which has more space and top-notch acoustics, and the Garnier now focuses more on dance performances, but the reality is you can see either at both. Opera tickets the Bastille run up to around 170€ for orchestra seats; seats in the upper atmosphere can drop to as little as 5€. Dance performances top out at 85€, and music concerts will generally not cost more than 47€. There are often reductions for those under 28 or over 60 for unsold tickets on the day of performance; arrive 1 hour before to get in line. Take advantage of the Thursday lunchtime "Casse-Croûte," a free miniconcert from 1 to 2pm by musicians of the Orchestre de l'Opéra (held in the Studio Bastille).

It's worth it to get tickets to a show at the **Palais Garnier** ✰✰✰ (place de l'Opéra, 9th arrond.; ☎ 0 892 89 90 90 (.34€ per min., in France only), 01 72 29 35 35 (from overseas); www.operadeparis.fr; Métro: Opéra) just to gaze up at the Chagall ceiling from your box seat. And all the seats are boxes in this Second Empire extravaganza; it's easy to imagine them filled ladies and gentlemen in sumptuous attire discretely assessing the competition. Though the boxes are fun, be careful when buying your tickets that you don't get stuck in the back of one—you'll have trouble seeing the stage if you're neighbor's hair is too poofy. The home of the Ballet de l'Opéra de Paris, this is the place to see great ballet classics, as well as new works by world class choreographers like William Forsythe and Maurice Béjart. Opera prices are comparable with those at the Opéra Bastille; ballets are divided into two price categories, with orchestra seats ranging from 45€ to 85€. The same reductions apply here for last minute tickets as at the Bastille Opera. If you are really on a budget, but you'd like to see a show here, there are chamber music concerts here one Sunday each month for 21€. Be sure to take a stroll through the opulent "Grand Foyer" during intermission.

Empress Eugénie attended the inauguration of the **Théâtre du Châtelet** ★ (1 place du Châtelet, 1st arrond.; ☎ 01 40 28 28 40; www.chatelet-theatre.com; Métro: Châtelet) back in 1862; the "Théâtre Musical de Paris," as it is now subtitled, has boasted packed houses ever since. Modern musicals and operas hog most of the spotlight here, though orchestral works and dance concerts are also on the program. The 2008 to 2009 season included an operatic version of Cyrano de Bergerac staring Placido Domingo and Mathew Bourne's ballet Edward Scissorhands (based on the Tim Burton film). Tickets are all over the map: Orchestra seats for A-class opera tickets go as high as 200€ but down to 30€ for more humble offerings; the Sunday morning concert series is 23€.

For a lighter take on opera, try the **Opéra Comique/Salle Favart** (5 rue Favart, 2nd arrond.; ☎ 08 25 01 01 23, .15€ per min.; www.opera-comique.com; Métro: Richelieu–Drouot or Quatre-Septembre). Created in 1714 for staging theatrical performances that included songs, the Opéra Comique endured several fires before finally settling down in a beautiful 19th-century theatre complete with huge chandeliers and endless gold curlicues. Operettas and musical comedies are the main course here—everything from *The Merry Widow* to a modern homage to Josephine Baker, with an adaptation of Apollonaire's *Breasts of Tiresias* thrown in for good measure. Prices vary dramatically, depending on the production; new contemporary shows can run as high as 100€ for orchestra seats, old standards do not go past 60€ for the front of the house.

THEATER

There are hundreds of theaters in Paris, most of which have something going on almost every night. The obvious catch here is, almost all of it is in French. If your language skills are good enough to follow what's happening on stage, by all means, take advantage of the cultural cornucopias listed below. If you can't spit out much more than *bonjour* and *merci,* take heart, there are some alternatives for the language-challenged (see the box "But I Don't Speak French!" on p. 281).

In 1680, Louis XIV announced the birth of a company of actors, chosen by Himself, with the aim of "making theater productions more perfect." You can decide for yourself how perfect they are, but some 300 years later, the **Comédie-Française** ★★ (place Colette, at the corner of the Palais Royal, 1st arrond.; ☎ 01 44 58 15 15; www.comedie-francaise.fr; Métro: Palais Royal–Musée du Louvre) is still considered by many the crème de la crème of the French theater scene. Keepers of the flame of classic French theater (Corneille, Racine, Molière), in the 1960s, the troupe branched out into more modern territory (Chekov, Strindberg, Genet), and more recently, started presenting works by contemporary, and even living, authors. Two new theaters were added in the 1990s to accommodate this voluminous repertoire, the medium-size **Théâtre du Vieux Colombier**

Where to Get That Theater, Dance, or Concert Ticket

Many hotels will help you get tickets, and most venues have a reservation link on their websites, but if you want to get a ticket in your hands quick, the easiest thing might be to wander into the nearest **Fnac,** the giant bookstore/music chain that has one of the most comprehensive box offices in the city (follow the signs to the "Billeterie"). It's worth the extra euro or so you'll pay for your ticket for the convenience. You can also order your tickets online at www.fnac.fr (many venue sites will send you directly here) or by phone at ☎ 08 92 68 36 22 (.34€ per min.). **Ticketnet.fr** offers a similar service, though their roster of events isn't as extensive; you can buy tickets either online (www.ticketnet.fr), by phone (☎ 08 92 39 01 00, .34€ per min.), or in any Virgin Megastore. For tickets to events as well as reviews and descriptions, visit Evene.com, an excellent website (in French only) that offers reduced prices through a discount site (ticketac.com).

Discount hunters can stand in line at one of the city's three **half-price ticket booths,** both run by **Le Kiosque Théâtre** (www.kiosquetheatre.com; Tues–Sat 12:30–8pm, Sun 12:30–4pm). There's one in front of the Montparnasse train station, the other is on the west side of the Madeleine (facing 15 place de la Madeleine, exit rue Tronchet from the Madeleine Métro stop), and a third in the center of Place des Ternes (17th arrond., near the Arc de Triomphe). Half-price tickets for same-day performances go on sale here at 12:30pm. Don't dawdle—by noon the line is usually already long. Not up to the challenge? If you can get yourself to a computer, you can find plenty of ticket discounts (although usually not as good as the ones at the Kiosque) at **BilletRéduc,** www.billetreduc.com (in French).

(21 rue du Vieux Colombier, 6th arrond.; ☎ 01 44 39 87 00; www.comedie-francaise.fr; Métro: St-Sulpice or Sèvres–Babylone) and the smaller **Studio-Théâtre** (Galerie du Carrousel du Louvre, under the Pyramid, 99 rue de Rivoli, 1st arrond.; ☎ 01 44 58 98 58; www.comedie-francaise.fr; Métro: Palais Royal–Musée du Louvre). Though something of a dinosaur, there is no denying the high quality of the acting and the magnificent decors, and despite the prestige, ticket prices are quite reasonable, ranging from 11€ to 44€, with a variety of discounts for the under 27 set.

Less musty and more modern, the **Odéon–Théâtre de l'Europe** ★★ (place de l'Odéon, 6th arrond.; ☎ 01 44 85 40 40; www.theatre-odeon.com; Métro: Odéon), which recently had a 30-million-euro makeover, presents both new plays and old classics, but even the classics usually get a modern twist. The 2008 to 2009 season included new versions of *Othello, Midsummer Night's Dream,* and *Tartuffe,* as well as *Gertrude (The Cry)* by contemporary author Howard Barker. The season usually includes at least a few productions from other European countries (hence the moniker "Théâtre de l'Europe." If the productions here aren't exactly light

But I Don't Speak French!

Let's face it—if your French isn't good, traditional theater performances will leave you pretty limp. So what's a traveling theater junkie to do? Never fear, there are several English-language theater companies in Paris, and while none of them has a permanent home, many make regular appearances at **Théâtre de Nesle** (8 rue de Nesle, 6th arrond.; ☎ 01 46 34 61 04; www.galeriedenesle.com; Métro: Odéon); Théâtre Les Dechargeurs (3 rue des Déchargeurs, 1st arrond.; ☎ 01 42 36 00 02; Métro: Châtelet), and **Sudden Théâtre** (14 bis rue Ste-Isaure, 18th arrond.; ☎ 01 42 62 35 00; www.suddentheatre.fr; Métro: Simplon), so keep an eye on listing magazines, and visit the *Paris Voice* and *Paris Times* websites (see box, p. 277). If all else fails, consider an evening of avant-garde theater, where visual language can be as important as spoken, and literal comprehension isn't really necessary. Two world-famous avant-garde companies have their headquarters in Paris, Les **Bouffes du Nord** (37 bis, blvd. de la Chapelle, 10th arrond.; ☎ 01 46 07 34 50; www.bouffesdunord.com; Métro: La Chapelle), run by legendary director Peter Brook, and **Le Théâtre du Soleil** (La Cartoucherie, Bois de Vincennes, 12th arrond.; ☎ 01 43 74 24 08; www.theatre-du-soleil.fr; Métro: Château de Vincennes, shuttle bus at performance times), helmed by Ariane Mnouchkine, but there are dozens of others to choose from.

comedy, at least you can be reasonably sure they are interesting; ticket prices range from 7.50€ to 30€, and there are 30% to 50% discounts for those under 30. The Odéon's second space, **Ateliers Berthier** (1 rue André Suarès, 17th arrond.; ☎ 01 44 85 40 40; www.theatre-odeon.fr; Métro: Porte de Clichy) presents smaller scale productions, as well as theater for young actors.

For truly contemporary theater, head to **Théâtre National de la Colline 5** (15 rue Malte-Brun, 20th arrond.; ☎ 01 44 62 52 52; www.colline.fr; Métro: Gambetta). Somewhat off the beaten track (on place Gambetta near the Père Lachaise cemetery), the season here is usually peppered with premieres and unusual productions. That said, the 2008 season included several older, though still modern works like Paul Claudel's *L'Echange,* Marguerite Duras' *The Lover,* and Samuel Beckett's *The Lost Ones.*

If you are having trouble deciding what you want to see, the **Lucernaire** ★ (53 rue Notre Dame des Champs, 6th arrond.; ☎ 01 45 44 57 34; www.lucernaire.fr; Métro: Notre Dame des Champs) is an excellent option: With three theaters, an arthouse movie theater, an art gallery, and a book store, as well as a nice bar-restaurant, you are bound to find something to your liking. Not only that, but the shows generally last only an hour or so, which gives you plenty of time to eat, drink, and browse. The theatres are small but the production level is high; showtimes range from 6:30 to 9:30pm and prices are 15€ to 30€.

CROSS-PLATFORM CONCERT HALLS

It's hard to say which lineup is the most impressive at the **Théâtre de la Ville** ✦✦ (2 place du Châtelet; 1st arrond.; ☎ 01 42 74 22 77; www.theatre delaville.com; Métro: Châtelet): theater (new and recent authors), dance (modern dance companies like Anne Teresa De Keersmaeker and Pina Bausch), or music (mostly young stars of the classical music scene). And if that doesn't get you going, there's a separate World Music series featuring groups from all over Europe, Asia, and Africa. What's more, tickets are not expensive: The priciest seats are only 23.50€ with the cheapest at 12€. The trick is to reserve early enough to get a good seat.

Dance and theater are on equal footing at the **Théâtre National de Chaillot** ✦ (1 place du Trocadéro, 16th arrond; ☎ 01 53 65 30 00; www.theatre-chaillot.fr; Métro: Trocadéro), where contemporary choreographers and theater directors share a jam-packed program. Theater offerings are high quality, but entirely in French; nonfrancophones will get more out of the excellent dance schedule. There are also a few music recitals on the schedule. The 2008/2009 season included William Forsythe, Ute Lemperer, and a dance homage to George Gershwin. Tickets run 18.50€ to 33€, with substantial reductions for under 26 and over 60.

One of the largest cinemas in Europe, **Le Grand Rex** ✦ (1 blvd. Poissionière, 2nd arrond.; ☎ 08 92 68 05 96, .34€ per min.; www.legrandrex.com; movie tickets Grand Rex theater: 11.50€, other theaters 7€; Métro: Bonne Nouvelle) is the last remaining movie palace in Paris. Built in the 1930s, this Art Deco wonder hosts not only film festival and first run movies, but also jazz, rock, and classical concerts. The **main theater,** Le Grand Rex, is huge, with 2,750 seats, about half of which are on the enormous balcony. Three smaller **screening rooms** were added in the 1970s; downstairs is one of Paris's hottest clubs, **Le Rex Club** (see "Clubbing," later in this chapter). For an extra 9.80€ you can take an interactive tour called "Les Etoiles du Rex," which combines a backstage tour with theme-park-style special effects that try to make you feel you've stepped into a film.

MOVIES

With 376 movie theaters and between 450 and 500 films on offer every week, Paris merits its title as cinephile capital of the world. Close to 90 of its theaters have been officially dubbed "Arts et Essai," or art house cinemas, which specialize in rare films and old classics, as well as new independent works. These theaters often host film series on a particular auteur (Woody Allen, John Huston, and others), and they always show films in v.o. (version *originale*), the original, non-dubbed version. Most mainstream movies are shown in the big chain movie theaters dubbed in French (v.f., or version *française*); if you want to see a mainstream English-language film, make sure you find one in v.o. (this will be marked in the listing guides, see above). Serious cinema fans can get a good overview of what's on this week at www.seances.org, a local cinephile group.

Some of the most famous art houses include **Le Champo, Reflet Medecis, Action Ecoles,** and **Accatone,** all in the 5th arrondissement (Latin Quarter, you'll find schedules and addresses in listing magazines). One of the prettiest, though, is over in the 7th near Les Invalides: **La Pagode** (57 bis rue de Babylone, 7th arrond.; ☎ 01 45 55 48 48; Métro: Sèvres–Babylone or St-François-Xavier). This incredible oriental pagoda was a gift from a 19th-century Bon Marché department store manager to his wife—unfortunately, the wife ran off with a colleague's son a year after the pagoda was finished. Her loss—the building became a cinema in 1931, and today the exquisite sculpted woodwork, brocaded fabrics, and lacquered tiles (all recently restored) decorate a small temple to film. In spring and summer, tea and drinks are served in the lovely garden during opening hours.

In addition to regular movie theatres, there are three giant cinema archives that have their own theaters and programs:

Designed by Frank Gehry, the wacky building that houses the **Cinémathèque Française** ✪ (51 rue de Bercy, 12th arrond.; ☎ 01 71 19 33 33; www.cinematheque. fr; Métro: Bercy) was originally the home of the now defunct American Center, a much-mourned cultural meeting place for expats and artists. Nowhere near as exuberant as other Gehry creations, this odd white stone edifice, which is sort of like a cross between a traditional office building and a freeform construction is now the home of a cinema library, museum, and research center. The entire history of cinema can be found between these walls, and programming includes comprehensive retrospectives of great cineastes and themed series on the evolution of film.

In the mighty monster that is the **Centre Pompidou** ✪ (Place Georges Pompidou, 4th arrond.; ☎ 01 44 78 12 33; www.centrepompidou.fr; Métro: Rambuteau, RER: Châtelet–Les Halles), there are two movie theaters, both of which show selections from the center's huge collection. The Pompidou often presents themed series; in fall 2008, for example, they hosted a survey of contemporary experimental cinema.

Funded by the City of Paris, the **Forum des Images** (Forum des Halles, Porte St-Eustache, 1st arrond; ☎ 01 44 76 63 00; www.forumdesimages.net; Métro: Châtelet–Les Halles) has a collection of over 6,600 films that feature Paris as either the subject or the setting. But the agenda is not limited to the French capital; features and documentaries from all over the world are shown here. At press time, the center was undergoing renovations, and the Forums' films were being shown in other art house theatres around town. The shiny new Forum is scheduled to open in December 2008; check the website for schedule and offerings.

Summer Rhythm & Blues

With few exceptions, the major concert halls and theaters are in action between September and June, taking off the summer months. Not only that, but since the city virtually empties out as Parisians storm the beaches during the annual vacation exodus, many smaller venues and dance clubs also close their doors. On the upside, there are several wonderful summer music festivals, including the Festival Chopin and Jazz à La Villette (p. 325), many of which take place in Paris's lovely parks and gardens. But if you have your heart set on opera or theater, you're better off visiting during the colder weather.

CAN YOU DO THE CANCAN?

At the end of the 19th century, cabarets and music halls opened in Montmartre, frequented by oddballs and artists, as well as bourgeois, aristocrats and demi-mondaines looking for a good time. At the time, these nightclubs offered an off-beat reflection of the times, where singers like Aristide Bruand would sing about the life of the destitute and sharp political satire would share the stage with cheeky dancing girls dancing that new step, the cancan. Those days are long gone. Although some visitors feel they simply haven't enjoyed the true Paris experience without seeing a show at the Moulin Rouge or the Lido, these days there is nothing particularly Parisian, or even French about them. Maybe they still were a few decades ago, when performers like Edith Piaf and Yves Montand were on the bill and the crowds included the crème de la crème of Parisian society, but today's audiences are more likely to arrive in tour buses than touring cars, and today's shows are more Vegas than Paris. In fact, if feathers and fantasy are what you're after, you will probably see better in Vegas. What you will see here is a lot of scenic razzmatazz and many sublime female bodies, mostly *torse nue* (topless). If you still want to see one of these shows, do yourself a favor and have dinner somewhere else. The food in these establishments is generally mediocre, at best, and with the extra 40€ to 50€ you save, you can have a wonderful meal at one of the restaurants I've listed in the dining chapter.

(All of the following theaters have strict dress codes, so be sure to inquire about them when making reservations.)

When it opened in 1889, the **Moulin Rouge** (82 blvd Clichy, 18th arrond.; ☎ 01 53 09 82 82; www.moulinrouge.fr; show only 89€–99€, dinner show 145€–175€; Métro: Blanche) was the talk of the town, and its huge dance floor, multiple mirrors, and floral garden inspired painters like Toulouse-Lautrec. In 1907, Mistinguett made her debut here; in later decades legendary French singers like Charles Trenet and Charles Aznavour regularly wowed the crowds. Times have changed—today's Moulin Rouge relies heavily on lip-synching and prere-corded music, backed up by dozens of be-feathered Doriss Girls, long-legged ladies that prance about the stage. Be prepared for lots of glitz and not a whole lot else; this tired operation is definitely geared to the tour bus crowd.

For the full-on glamour gala, head for the **Lido** (116 bis av. du Champs Elysées, 8th arrond.; ☎ 01 40 76 56 10; www.lido.fr; show only 90€–100€, dinner show 140€–195€; Métro: George V). The costumes here are truly amazing—many a bird must have sacrificed its feathers for the greater good of the Blue Bell Girls. Headdresses and high heels are of such dimensions that the dancers can't really do much dancing, but you're probably not coming here for prima ballerina turns. Unlike the Moulin Rouge, the music is live, and the singers sing, so the overall talent level is higher.

Less feathers but more fun, the **Paradis Latin** (28 rue du Cardinal Lemoine, 5th arrond.; ☎ 01 43 25 28 28; www.paradis-latin.com; show only 82€, dinner show 117€–170€; Métro: Cardinal Lemoine) may offer less in terms of spectacle, but more in terms of talent. As in, the performers here seem to actually have some. There is a fair amount of interaction with the audience, and a good portion of the show is translated in English. The metallic armature holding up the roof here was designed by Gustave Eiffel.

Don't come to the **Crazy Horse Paris** (12 av. George V, 8th arrond.; ☎ 01 47 23 32 32; www.lecrazyhorseparis.com; Métro: Alma Marceau or Champs Elysées–Clemenceau) expecting to see cancan. This temple to "The Art of the Nude" presents an erotic dance show with artistic aspirations; unlike the other shows, this one is known for what the girls aren't wearing. Lighting effects are plentiful, music is mostly modern, and the performers, who slither, swagger, and lip-synch with panache, have names like Zula Zazou and Misty Flashbag. The stage is small, and there are only a dozen or so dancers; people come here for the relatively classy sensual content more than sparkle and spangles. Dinner is not an option, tickets are 100€ to 120€ depending on where you are sitting, and a seat at the bar is 70€ (no reservations, first come, first served) for adults and 50€ for students.

LIVE MUSIC CLUBS

There's a wide range of places to go to hear live music in Paris, ranging from tiny medieval basements to huge, modern concert venues. Wherever your musical tastes lead you, you are bound to enjoy your outing: Not only do many of the world's greatest musicians swing through the city on a regular basis, but you can't beat the walk to the nighclub/bar/theater with the lights of Paris twinkling in the background. Below is a sampling of some from the city's vast musical menu.

JAZZ

Paris has been a fan of jazz from its beginnings, and many legendary performers like Sidney Bechet and Kenny Clark made the city their home. Still a haven for jazz musicians and fans of all stripes, there are dozens of places around town to duck in and listen to a good set or two. Here are a few of the best:

If you're looking for big names and hot acts, look no further. **New Morning** ★★★ (7 and 9 rue des Petites Ecuries, 10th arrond.; ☎ 01 45 23 51 41; www.new morning.com; Métro: Château d'Eau) has incredible lineups, including both jazz giants like Ravi Coltrane Quartet (son of John and Alice), Take 6, and violinist Regina Carter, as well as international world music masters like Hugh Masekela and Elza Soares. This relatively large club (the room holds 300), fills up quick and it's no wonder: This truly is one of the best jazz venues in town, and tickets range from only 18€ to 24€.

Much smaller, but more famous, **Le Duc des Lombards** ★★ (42 rue des Lombards, 1st arrond.; ☎ 01 42 33 22 88; www.ducdeslombards.com; Métro: Châtelet) is an obligatory stop for touring European jazz stars, though greats from the other side of the pond like Brandford Marsalis and Jon Hendricks have also been known to come through. Tickets range from 19€ to 25€; Monday through Thursday the under-25 set can get in for 12€ or 18€, depending on the concert. Recently, Le Duc has hooked up with three other clubs on this jazz-rich street, namely, the Sunside, the Sunset, and the Baiser Salé, to create the Paris Jazz Club, which offers discounts and exclusive themed events where for 20€ you can get into all four clubs (check website for dates and times).

Like their famous neighbor, the dual clubs **Sunset/Sunside** ★★ (60 rue des Lombards, 1st arrond.; ☎ 01 40 26 46 60; www.sunset-sunside.com; Métro: Châtelet) are major players on the Parisian jazz scene. Big names like Kenny Barron and Kurt Elling make appearances, as well as young innovative musicians from around the world. A few years ago, the older venue, the Sunset, bought up the restaurant next door and turned it into a second club, called the Sunside. Whereas the Sunset is now dedicated to electric jazz and world music; the Sunside features primarily acoustic jazz. Concerts at the Sunset take place in a vaulted cellar with white tiles like you might see in a Métro tunnel; at the Sunside you'll sit above-ground in a cozy space with brick walls. Tickets are in the 15€ to 22€ range; discount promotions of up to 50% are offered on the website.

Another Paris jazz institution is **Le Petit Journal Montparnasse** ★ (13 rue du Commandant Mouchotte, 14th arrond.; ☎ 01 43 21 56 70; www.petitjournal-montparnasse.com; Métro: Montparnasse–Bienvenue). Roomier, and with a smart restaurant, this class act has an elegant glassed-in dining terrace as well as a plush wood-paneled area where you can sup closer to the stage. The headliners here are mostly French jazz artists like Claude Bolling and Manu di Bango. Show plus dinner (three courses plus wine and coffee) runs 60€ to 85€, depending on who's playing; if you are coming just for music, the 25€ entry (15€ for students) includes a drink, but you'll usually have to sit at the bar. Its sister club, **Le Petit Journal Saint-Michel** ★ (71 blvd. St-Michel, 5th arrond.; ☎ 01 43 26 28 59; http://perso.orange.fr/claude.philips; closed Sun and Aug; RER: Luxembourg) is a temple to New Orleans jazz; the ambience here is more cozy and low-key, and the action takes place underground in yet another old cellar. The cover includes one drink (17€ nonalcoholic, 20€ for a cocktail, students get 30% discount); a dinner concert with wine runs 45€ to 50€.

IT'S ALL IN THE MIX

Many of the city's most interesting live music clubs offer a wide range of styles and sounds. It's hard to really categorize these places in terms of music, so I'm listing them according to the type of venue and general ambience.

Mythic Venues

Every city has its share of concert halls that are THE places to hear the most happening singers and the hippest bands. The following are some of Paris's best-known venues where stars shine and bodies rock.

Legends like Georges Brassens, Edith Piaf, Louis Armstrong, and Aretha Franklin have all appeared at the **Olympia** ★ (28 blvd. des Capucines, 9th arrond.; ☎ 08 92 68 33 68, .34€ per min.; www.olympiahall.com; Métro: Madeleine or Opéra), an iconic music venue that continues to attract international stars like Chic Corea and Percy Sledge as well as French superstars like Bernard Lavilliers and Hélène Segara. Arrive early to get a good seat; often tickets are not numbered, which means first-come, first-serve for the best vantage point.

Another famous cabaret theater that has gotten a second lease on life is **La Cigale** (120 blvd. Rochechouart, 18th arrond.; ☎ 01 49 25 81 75; www.lacigale.fr; Métro: Anvers or Pigale). Mistinguett and Maurice Chevalier once crooned at this theater, which has been declared a historic monument; today, after a chic makeover by Philippe Stark, it is known as the place to go to see the best singers and new groups, from artists like Ani di Franco to Willy De Ville, with a ton of fascinating new names in between.

Remember the poster by Toulouse-Lautrec for the Divan Japonais? This celebrated cabaret lives on, believe it or not, though there's been a slight change in the interior decoration. Now encompassing three performance spaces/dance floors, **Le Divan du Monde** (75 rue des Martyrs, 18th arrond.; ☎ 01 40 05 06 99; www.divandumonde.com; Métro: Pigalle or Anvers) hosts everything from rock to electro to world music, not to mention the occasional "apéro tzigane" (gypsy cocktail hour) or "music for toys" festival. Entrance fees range from free to around 15€; dance parties generally cost 10€.

Located in the Parc de la Villette, on the outer edge of the 19th arrondissement, the **Zenith** (211 av. Jean Jaurès, 19th arrond.; ☎ 01 42 08 60 00; www.le-zenith.com; Métro: Porte de Pantin) is a mega-concert hall holding close to 6,000 spectators. French pop idols like Lara Fabian and Corneille play here, as well as international stars like Mary J. Blige and Lenny Kravitz.

Music Afloat

Once upon a time, on the banks of the Seine you could find *guinguettes,* outdoor cabarets where musicians play and couples dance on the decks of converted barges—those long, low boats that are used to shuttle heavy loads up and down the river. Although few *guinguettes* have survived (and those that have are east of Paris), today the younger generation has transformed some recently retired vessels into a new sort of music venue—floating bar/cafe/dance clubs, three of which have lowered their anchor next to Quai François Mauriac, across the river from the Parc de Bercy and just in front of the Bibliothèque François Mitterand.

There are no exotic trinkets in the cargo of the Chinese junk docked on Quai François Mauriac, just music. Though it recently changed its name, the **Dame de Canton** ★★ (Quai François Mauriac, 13th arrond.; ☎ 01 44 06 96 45; www.damedecanton.com; Métro: Bibliothèque François Mitterand or Quai de la Gare) is still the same uniquely wacky place to enjoy an eclectic range of music styles: Depending on the day of the week, you might find Django-style jazz, slam dancing, or French chanson in the bowels of this red wooden boat. Weekend evenings are generally dedicated to Afro-Cuban music or other festive world beats, and after the concert the DJs come out and the boat turns into a nightclub. Cover is anywhere from free to 10€; there's a restaurant if you are feeling peckish. Believe it or not, there are also children's activities here (during the day of course), like storytelling (in French) and music. For a schedule, consult the website.

For serious drinking and dancing, stroll over to **Batofar** ★ (quai François Mauriac, 13th arrond.; ☎ 01 53 60 17 30; www.batofar.org; Métro: Bibliothèque François Mitterand or Quai de la Gare). This bright-red boat is topped by an old-fashioned searchlight (or *phare*) that sends out a signal to electronic music fans all over the city. Electro, techno, jungle, take the helm; reggae, ragga, and funk are also in the mix. Great DJs from all over Europe come here, as well as live bands; the look is dressed down and casually cool. The cover ranges from nonexistent to around 10€.

Tucked in between Batofar and Guinguette Pirate is an actual barge, the **Peniche El Alamein** (quai François Mauriac, 13th arrond.; ☎ 06 82 04 82 46; http://elalamein.free.fr; Métro: Bibliothèque François Mitterand or Quai de la Gare). Though there is a good music lineup here (primarily French chanson and vocal groups), many come to have a drink on the delightful garden terrace on the deck. All concerts are 8€.

Culture Clubs

There are some music venues out there that truly defy categories, like the following young and happening club/cafe/gallery/cultural center/screening room/poetry lounge/and so on . . . *Note:* Performances in these venues book up quick; if possible, buy your ticket ahead of time at Fnac (p. 280).

Is it a club or a circus tent? The answer is not clear at **Cabaret Sauvage** ★★ (Parc de la Villette, entrance at 59 blvd. Mac Donald, 19th arrond.; ☎ 01 42 09 01 09; www.cabaretsauvage.com; Métro: Porte de la Villette), where you are just as likely to encounter Brazilian samba, electro funk, or trapeze artists. Blues bands from the Balkans and Vietnamese jazz musicians share the calendar with avant-garde circus acts and Algerian acrobats. Although this **big-top cabaret** is essentially a performance space with an accent on **world music and dance,** it also hosts **themed dance parties,** where you can boogie to jungle and techno, as well as raï, mambo, samba, and so forth. There is a bar, *bien sur,* as well as a restaurant that serves light meals (depending on the event). Tickets cost 15€ to 25€.

Describing itself as a "center for artistic dynamics," **Point Ephemere** ★ (200 quai Valmy, 10th arrond.; ☎ 01 40 34 02 48; www.pointephemere.org; Métro: Jean Jaurès), a converted warehouse on the banks of the Canal St-Martin, prides itself on nurturing up-and-coming artists, musicians, dancers, and filmmakers, and offers residencies to a chosen few who work in studios on the premises. Cultural mission aside (this is a nonprofit organization that was set up with the blessing of both neighborhood and municipal leaders), this is an extremely happening spot. The packed program includes lots of "soirées," or dance parties, with an emphasis on **electronic music,** in all its usual (electro, techno), and unusual (hip-hop neo-klezmer, anyone?) forms, though plain old **experimental rock** is represented as well. Dance concerts, art expositions, and discussion forums are also on the agenda. Tickets for most events are in the 10€ to 15€ range. There is a suitably downscale-hip quay-side bar and restaurant, with an outdoor terrace in nice weather.

A relic from the aftermath of the Paris Commune, when it was the home of the first workers' cooperative, **La Bellevilloise** ★★ (19–21 rue Boyer, 20th arrond.; ☎ 01 53 27 35 77; www.labellevilleoise.com; Métro: Gambetta) has been rescued from clutches of real estate developers and transformed into a space dedicated to "light, night, and creativity." In regular language, that means over 2,000 square meters divvied up into art galleries, performance spaces, a concert hall, a club, and a restaurant with a lovely outdoor terrace where you can have a drink. The program ranges from film festivals to fashion shows, with a good dose of contemporary music on the roster. The building, which used to offer meeting rooms and cultural activities to downtrodden workers, has conserved its high ceilings and loft-like spaces, giving the place an airy, open feeling that is a welcome change from the usual dank nightspots.

LET'S GO DANCING

Though they may not be the most rhythmic of peoples, that doesn't keep the French from filling up dance clubs all over the city. The good news is, you don't have to worry about looking uncoordinated—you'll have plenty of company. The bad news is you might get your toes stepped on. If you are willing to take that

Chanson

When I first moved here, I too thought that chanson—that peculiarly melody-challenged style of French singing that (at least in the old days) involved a lot of tremulous vibrato—was pretty sappy stuff. That was before I really understood French. Now I've realized that it's the words that count in chanson, and that in fact it's probably best to think of chanson as poems set to music. In fact, some of the more famous singers, like Léo Ferré, have literally set French poetry (Aragon, Apollonaire) to music. Which partially explains why so many French people get all misty-eyed when they start listening to Jacques Brel and Georges Brassens. Not only did they grow up with the music, but the lyrics often cover subject matter that is near and dear to the French psyche, like war, injustice, love, and sex. Songs can be funny or tragic, or just plain morose, but they usually are trying to say something that you will remember. In recent years, chanson has made a comeback. Young singers and writers are coming up with their own poetic versions of the trials and tribulations of life, and their heroes are not so much Piaf and Aznavour as Leonard Cohen and Bob Dylan. As you may have noticed, chanson pops up in live music club programming all over the city, but here are a few venues that specialize in this quintessentially French style:

Au Limonaire ✯ (18 Cité Bergère, 9th arrond.; ☎ 01 45 23 33 33; http://limonaire.free.fr; Métro: Grands Bouvlevards). Here you not only can listen to the freshest crop of chanson talent, but you also can sing along. There is no cover; they pass the hat (as management puts it "It's worth at least the price of a movie"). Doubles as a restaurant/wine bar; reserve ahead if you want to eat here.

Café de la Dance (5 passage Louis Phillipe, 11th arrond.; ☎ 01 47 00 57 59; www.chez.com/cafedeladanse; Métro: Bastille). Though you might also hear rock and roll or Portuguese fado at this eclectic cabaret, there is a very strong chanson streak in the programming here. Pick up tickets (15€–25€) at any Fnac outlet (www.fnac.fr).

Peniche El Alamein (see "Music Afloat" above).

risk, there are plenty of options out there. Be it tango or hip-hop, salsa or slam dancing, there is a toe-tapping activity out there to suit your purposes.

PARTNER DANCING?

Though it might not be particularly hip or trendy, partner dancing is very popular in Paris, and practitioners can pick from a wide range of styles, from Argentine tango to Cuban salsa, passing by ballroom and swing. *Note:* What the French call "le Rock," is what most English-speakers would consider jitterbug or swing dancing.

Since 1946, **Caveau de la Huchette** ✦✦ (5 rue de la Huchette, 5th arrond.; ☎ 01 43 26 65 05; www.caveaudelahuchette.fr; Métro: St-Michel, RER: St-Michel–Notre-Dame; cover: Mon–Thurs 11€, Fri–Sat 13€) has been a temple of swing. Count Basie and Lionel Hampton once played here; though today's program is considerably less illustrious, some excellent jazz musicians still play here, setting the groove for the dance floor. Swing and Lindy Hop are the watchwords in this ancient cellar; though there are some serious dance weenies here, you'll have a good time, no matter what your level of expertise.

Even older and more historic, **Le Balajo** ✦ (9 rue de Lappe, 11th arrond.; ☎ 01 47 00 07 87; www.balajo.fr; cover 10€ Mon–Thurs, 20€ Fri–Sat [includes 1 drink], Sun afternoon tea dances 8€; Métro: Bastille) is one of the last of the great 1930s dance halls. When it opened, in 1936, it was a huge success, frequented by stars like Arletty and Marlene Dietrich. Today the mood is eclectic: Tuesday and Thursday nights is salsa; Wednesday, rock and swing; and Friday and Saturday are a catch-all of R&B, disco, funk, and groove. In short, there is something for everyone, and no need to worry about being snubbed by the doorman.

Argentine tango fans gather at **Bistrot Latin** ✦ (41 rue Beaubourg, 3rd arrond.; ☎ 01 48 04 80 74; www.bistrolatin.fr; Métro: Rambuteau), a restaurant and bar that hosts milongas, or tango dances, Monday through Saturday starting at 9pm and last until 2am; beginners should come with a partner as the level is fairly advanced. Tango-challenged dancers should come early: There are tango classes at 7pm. Cover is 8€. For more information on other Parisian milongas, visit www.tango-argentin.net.

Latin Salsa and then some is on the program at **Barrio Latino** (46/48 rue du Faubourg St-Antoine, 12th arrond.; ☎ 01 55 78 84 75; Thurs–Sat 20€ cover (one drink included), other nights no cover; Métro: Bastille), a multileveled restaurant/bar/dance palace with Latin/Caribbean theme. The spacious main floor of this former furniture showroom is ringed by pretty wrought-iron balconies (think Galeries Lafayette goes to the Tropics); the atmosphere is festive, fun, and relatively unpretentious. Though Latin rhythms get priority here, the musical menu can also feature African, R&B, and pop, depending on the DJ.

CLUBBING

If a "real" club is what you are after, Paris has plenty to keep you busy. While new, hot clubs cool off quickly, even older clubs can still draw a hot crowd, depending on the night, because a lot of what counts here is not the club, but the party. Just about every club hosts themed "soirées" on different days of the week, each with its own DJ and style of music; sometimes the soirées are a bigger hit than the actual club. For a detailed rundown on where the soirées are this week, visit the club websites below, or general websites like www.tilllate.com, or www.parisbouge.com, which also has a good list of clubs with reader reviews (in French).

ULTRAHOT

Le Baron ✦ (6 av. Marceau, 8th arrond.; ☎ 01 47 20 04 01; Métro: Alma–Marceau) is one of the hottest clubs in town, and subsequently, one of the hardest to get into.

Club & Bar Hours

Clubs open at varying times, but the crowd doesn't usually show up until at least midnight. Once you've made it in, you can dance literally 'til dawn, as most clubs don't close until around 6am.

Parisian **bars** can open as early as noon, or even earlier, depending on where they stand on the bar/cafe scale (see below), but they almost always close between 1:30 to 2am.

If you are Sofia Coppola or Björk, there's no problem; if you are a lesser mortal, you'd better know how to dress, be blessed with stunning physical attributes, or know someone on the guest list. There's no cover, but drinks will cost you dearly. The decor is inspired by the club's former life as high-end brothel; soft red couches, velvet curtains, and tasseled lamps create a plush backdrop for the Beautiful People. The DJ spins a mix of styles, including lots of retro from the '70s and '80s.

Perhaps harkening back to the days (a couple of centuries ago) when this historic site was full of bordellos, cafes, and gambling houses, **Cab** (short for "Cabaret" 2 place du Palais Royal, 1st arrond.; ☎ 01 58 62 56 25; www.cabaret.fr; Métro: Palais Royal–Musée du Louvre) has taken up residence just next to the Palais Royal. A very modern bar/restaurant/club, with intimate alcoves and low lighting for chatting and chatting up, Cab does not neglect its dance floor where DJs spin deep house and hip-hop, among other styles. While the concept is low-stress, the entry process isn't: Be prepared (that is, dressed), for a rigorous selection process at the door. No cover but the drink prices will make up for it.

The beacon of Paris's electronic music scene, **Rex Club** ★ (5 blvd. Poissonnière, 2nd arrond.; ☎ 01 42 36 10 96; www.rexclub.com; Métro: Bonne Nouvelle) churns up the dance floor with **electro, techno, dub,** and **house.** Brooding under the Grand Rex movie theater (see above), this dark, gray, and very high-tech haunt draws a primarily young and intense crowd. Rex's claim to fame is that it helped launch French mega-DJ Laurent Garnier, who still comes by to spin tunes. Though this is a very popular club, they have a refreshingly democratic entry policy, and the cover is reasonable: between 7€ and 13€. Music blasts; bring earplugs if your ears are delicate.

Recently overhauled, **La Fleche d'Or** (102 bis rue de Bagnolet, 20th arrond.; ☎ 01 44 64 01 02; www.flechedor.fr; Métro: Gambetta or Alexandre Dumas), has a seemingly inexhaustible supply of young talent that excels at whipping up a groove on the dance floor. Groups with names like "The Queen of Yogurt" and "Moon Engineer" play at this indie-rock and electro club, which lives in what was once a train station for a now defunct line. There is nothing defunct about the ambience, which is young and wired, with a downtown, disheveled edge; what's more, there is no cover except for a few rare extra special concerts, when the bill is 10€.

WORLDLY

If you are allergic to the hipster club scene, try **Le Canal Opus** ✖ (167 quai de Valmy, 10th arrond.; ☎ 01 40 34 70 00; http://opusclub.free.fr; Métro: Louis Blanc), on the Canal St-Martin. There's no bouncer here to judge your outfit, just lots of great music and dancing. The evenings start with **live jazz and world music** concerts (6€–10€); after, **eclectic dance parties** (cover 10€) rock until dawn to the beat of **house, funk,** and **R&B** as well as **Latino, Zouk, and Caribbean** rhythms. The decor includes polished wood and cozy corners; there is an in-house restaurant if you want to eat before you dance. Open only Fridays and Saturdays (parties only, no concerts) in August.

The sounds of Brazil are what fuels the party at **Favela Chic** ✖ (18 rue du Faubourg du Temple, 11th arrond.; ☎ 01 40 21 38 14; www.favelachic.com; Métro: République), a bar/restaurant where the clientele just can't seem to stay in their seats. Maybe it's the great caipirinhas and mojitos, or maybe it's just the fab music, which goes on until 4am. This is an incredibly popular place, and there are major crowds on the weekends; get here early if you want to get in at all. Success has been such that they recently opened a branch in London. Though the main-stay here is **Brazilian music,** which branches out in some surprising directions (bossa jazz, samba rap), a variety of DJs come through here, so **funk, reggae, and house** are also on the menu. If you make it in Tuesday to Thursday, there's no cover; Friday to Saturday the 10€ cover includes one drink.

GAY, BUT OPEN-MINDED

Though it mostly draws a gay crowd, anyone is welcome at the latest version of **Les Bains Douches** ✖ (7 rue du Bourg l'Abbé, 3rd arrond.; ☎ 01 48 87 01 80; www.lesbainsdouches.net; Métro: Etienne Marcel), which serves up an eclectic mix of **hip-hop, R&B, and electro,** depending on the night. Wednesday is hip-hop, Thursday is 80s and 90s retro-kitch, Friday and Saturday features house, trance, and electro. Cover 10€ to 20€ depending on the evening's offerings.

Another gay club that opens its doors to heteros is **Le Queen** (102 ave. des Champs Elysées, 8th arrond.; ☎ 01 53 89 08 90; www.queen.fr; Métro: George V), in fact, word is that this mythic nightspot has become seriously mixed, with a high youth contingent, both gay and straight. One of the biggest draws here is the Disco Queen party on Monday nights where you can shake your bootie to disco, funk, and pop hits of the '70s and '80s. Tuesday is "Saved by the Queen" night (house and electro), Wednesday is Ladies Night, and Thursday through Sunday varies according to which DJ is hosting what party (see website for this week's program). Cover 15€ to 20€ depending on the night's offerings. For gay bars, see p. 297.

BARS & LOUNGES

I feel the need to make a distinction here between cafes and bars. Though both serve alcoholic beverages, cafes offer a laid-back, hang out atmosphere at any time of day or night, whereas anything that actually calls itself a bar usually has an edgier feel and only really gets going after the sun goes down. While it's difficult to draw a definitive line between one type of establishment and another (in fact, many have a little bit of both kinds of ambiences), the bars and lounges listed below lean towards the latter category, that is, nighttime places where adults collect to meet, drink, and be merry. (For a good sample of cafes, see the "Dining Choices" chapter) Many of the bars listed below also offer music, live or recorded, but this is their secondary function. For a selected list of live music venues and dance clubs, see the headings above.

NEAR THE LOUVRE–PALAIS ROYAL

The birthplace of the Bloody Mary, **Harry's New York Bar** ✸ (5 rue Daunou, 2nd arrond.; ☎ 01 42 61 71 14; www.harrysbar.fr; Métro: Opéra or Pyramides) hasn't changed significantly since it first opened in 1911. Literally transplanted piece by piece from a bar in New York City, this American outpost was a favorite of Ernest Hemingway, who held court here in the post–World War II years. Today's regulars are well-heeled expats, tourists, and others who enjoy the polished wood ambience and the piano bar in the cellar.

Just across the street from the Théâtre du Palais Royal, tiny **Bar de l'Entracte** (47 rue de Montpensier, 1st arrond.; ☎ 01 42 97 57 76; Métro: Musée du Louvre–Palais Royal) spills out onto the sidewalk, tempting passersby with food, drink, and old-fashioned ambience. Though frequented by a relatively hip crowd, this postage-stamp-size bar is about as typically Parisian as it gets (it even made it into a tourist poster by George Bates).

Perched on the top floor of the Kenzo building, **Kong** (1 rue du Pont Neuf, 1st arrond.; ☎ 01 40 39 09 00; www.kong.fr; Métro: Pont Neuf) is designer Philippe Starck's latest hallucination: a glowing red bar, steely gray banquettes, transparent Louis XVI chairs, and bizarre Japanese manga imagery backed up by a fabulous view of the city. Be prepared to dress the part—and pay the price—for an evening at this sleek and trendy bar-restaurant.

MARAIS

A twist on the name of a famous pop-artist, **Andy Waloo** ✸✸ (69 rue des Gravilliers, 3rd arrond.; ☎ 01 42 71 20 38; Métro: Arts et Métiers), which means *I have nothing* in Arabic, is a tiny temple to North African culture and kitsch. Smoke a hookah beneath a silk-screened Moroccan coffee ad and listen to some of the best Algerian raï around. Come early before the fashionable crowd snatches up all the upturned paint cans that serve as seating.

Sip your drink while taking in the wacky architecture of the Centre Pompidou on the terrace of the **Café Beaubourg** (100 rue St-Martin, 4th arrond.; ☎ 01 48 87 63 96; Métro: Rambuteau or Hôtel de Ville). The Costes brothers' first Parisian enterprise is still a happening spot: Between the excellent view and the sleek decor, this is a perennial on the hipster bar scene. Despite the heady pedigree, the atmosphere here is relatively low-key.

The horseshoe-shaped bar at **Au Petit Fer à Cheval** (30 rue Vieille du Temple, 4th arrond.; ☎ 01 42 72 47 47; Métro: Hôtel de Ville or St-Paul) is the original; when this cafe first opened in 1903 coffee and chocolate sellers negotiated deals over this curved countertop. The current owner, who has opened a spate of similarly adorable cafes in this neighborhood, has kept the original detailing and spirit of the place, with a few modern touches—like the frighteningly modern steel bathrooms. If you're hungry, the menu is fresh and contemporary.

LATIN QUARTER

Though it's also known as a jazz club, I'm putting **Caveau des Oubliettes** ✦ (52 rue Galande, 5th arrond.; ☎ 01 46 34 23 09; Métro: Maubert–Mutualité) in the bar section because this is a truly unique place to come for a drink. Located on one of the oldest streets in Paris, this ancient building harbors a wacky bar where real grass grows on the floor beneath your feet, and a genuine Guillotine from the French Revolution hovers in the background. The crowd is a good mix of students and low-key hipsters; a narrow winding staircase leads to a 12th-century vaulted stone cellar, where local jazz groups jam. If you ask, you can visit the medieval "oubliettes," dank cells where prisoners were more or less forgotten about (the moniker comes from the French verb "to forget," *oublier*).

A Latin Quarter institution, **Le Piano Vache** ✦ (8 rue Laplace, 5th arrond.; ☎ 01 46 33 75 03; www.lepianovache.com; Métro: Maubert Mutualité) has been welcoming the young and young at heart since its beginnings in 1969, in the wake of the student uproar that started the year before. Layers of posters and handbills for concerts and events paper the walls; a broken-down piano broods in a corner. If you are looking for an escape from the slick and trendy, this wonderfully grungy student hangout should fill the bill. Music starts up most nights after 8pm; DJs favor '80s music, Goth, punk, and rock.

ST-GERMAIN

Despite appearances, you do need to be over 18 to get into **Zéro de Conduite** ✦ (14 rue Jacob, 6th arrond.; ☎ 01 46 34 26 35; www.zerodeconduite.fr; Métro: St-Germain-des-Près or Mabillon), where your drink will be served in a baby bottle, and you can watch cartoons on wide-screen TVs. Once you've ordered your "Peter Pan" (coconut punch, banana, and blue curaçao) or "Snoopy" (white rum and raspberry juice), you can play games (Sun night is Monopoly night, reserve ahead), or answer Trivial Pursuit questions, or just regress in the company of like-minded drinkers.

It's 4am and you're still not ready to go home? Have a drink at **Le Pré** (4 rue du Four, 6th arrond.; ☎ 01 40 46 93 22; Métro: Mabillon) one of the few bars around town that is open almost 24 hours a day (they close only between 5am–7am to freshen up). Even during daylight hours, this cool cafe-bar is a nice place to hang out; the entire bar is open out on to the street, great for people-watching—and for being watched, as well.

It might be best to just have a drink at the bar at the **Closerie des Lilas** ✦ (171 Blvd du Montparnasse, 6th arrond.; ☎ 01 40 51 34 50; www.closerie deslilas.fr RER: Port Royal), that way you can pretend you're Hemingway without going broke in the process. In fact, he wrote a large chunk of *The Sun Also Rises* while standing at the bar, so you wouldn't be too far off. Actually, few of the artists and writers (Gertrude Stein, Picasso, Henry James . . .) who frequented this hallowed ground would be able to afford it today; it is defiantly elegant and not for the jeans and sneakers crowd.

CHAMPS ELYSEES

In a neighborhood where stores and restaurants continually try to out-do each other in matters of decor, **Le Music Hall** (63 ave. de Franklin D. Roosevelt, 8th arrond.; ☎ 01 45 61 03 63; www.music-hallparis.com; Métro: Franklin D.

Roosevelt) is a standout. Six hundred computer-controlled projectors, capable of making 16 million different colors (who knew there were so many?), create a non-stop light show on the white diamond-shaped pattered walls. The effect is relatively subtle; the luminous ambience changes slowly enough to avoid headaches. A low-key DJ spins in the lounge, where you can sip original cocktails by the gourmet bartenders.

For a fabulous view of the Arc de Triomphe and the Champs, stop for a drink at the massive, glass-enclosed **Drugstore Publicis** (133 ave. des Champs Elysées, 8th arrond.; ☎ 01 44 43 79 00; www.publicisdrugstore.com; Métro: Charles de Gaulle–Etoile). In case you are wondering, a "drugstore" on the Champs Elysées is not a place to pick up dental floss (although there is a pharmacy here). Rather, it's a mini-shopping center catering to luxurious tastes that includes cinemas, restaurants, shops, and a sleek bar with glass plate walls that offer the aforementioned view. The glass theme extends to the bar itself, which is translucent.

GRANDS BOULEVARDS

Within convenient walking distance to some of the more happening clubs (Rex Club, Pulp), the lofty ceilings of the **Delaville Café** ✪✪ (34–36 blvd. Bonne Nouvelle, 10th arrond.; ☎ 01 48 24 48 09; www.delavillecafe.com; Métro: Bonne Nouvelle) shelter a decor that successfully blends modern styling with 19th-century grandeur. Splendid mosaics frame the bar, red columns line the staircase, and sleek neo-fifties chairs surround the tables. There's a classy restaurant, a not-too-trendy bar, a huge, if noisy, sidewalk terrace, and a bevy of DJs that spin dance music into the wee hours. By day, young and not-so-young bobos (bourgeois bohemians) bring their laptops; at night, they bring their dates.

CANAL ST-MARTIN

The setting for the legendary film by Marcel Carné, **Hôtel du Nord** (102 quai de Jemmapes, 10th arrond.; ☎ 01 40 40 78 78; www.hoteldunord.org; Métro: République or Jacques Bonsergent) has recently been transformed into a sleek, *branché* (literally, "plugged in") bar-restaurant where stars dine and high-style hipsters lean over the bar. Probably not what Marcel had in mind, but that doesn't seem to stop the crowds. A nice place to start your evening stroll along the Canal St-Martin.

Farther up the canal, on the Bassin de la Villette, is a lovely little bar that better reflects the personality of the neighborhood, **La Bastringue** (67 quai de Seine, 19th arrond.; ☎ 01 41 09 89 27; Métro: Riquet). An old cafe that has been given a good freshening up, a young crowd of friendly 30-somethings, and some well-placed tables on the sidewalk equals a low-key night out in a fun, up-and-coming Parisian neighborhood.

PLACE ST-MARTHE

Decked out in bright colors, with a decidedly counter-culture feel, **Le Panier** ✪ (Place St-Marthe, 10th arrond.; ☎ 01 42 01 38 18; Métro: Belleville) sports a delightful, exhaust-free terrace on the laid-back place St-Marthe. The ambience is so relaxed, you almost forget you're in Paris; in fact, the name of the bar refers to a neighborhood in Marseilles. The *rhum arrangé* (rum with tropical fruit) is delicious. Whatever you do, don't dress up to come here.

Irish Bars & Other English-Speaking Watering Holes

Had enough of trying to speak French? Looking for a place to unwind in semifamiliar surroundings? There are a few dozen Irish bars in Paris (where aren't there?), where you can appreciate the joys of a good pint of Guinness. Americans and Canadians have set up shop here as well—see below for details.

Tucked into an ancient building on the quai des Grands Augustins (shouting distance from place St-Michel), **Galway's** ★ (13 quai des Grands Augustins, ☎ 01 43 29 64 50; Métro: St-Michel) might be a little dark and a little cramped, but it's almost always filled to the brim with happy customers sipping a pint and swapping war stories. Live music Thursday to Monday; Guinness, Murphy's, and Kilkenny on tap.

You can stretch out at **Carr's Restaurant & Pub** ★ (1 rue du Mont-Thabor, 1st arrond.; ☎ 01 42 60 60 26; www.carrsparis.com; Métro: Tuileries), where several spacious rooms cater to the drinking and eating needs of expats, tourists, and a varied assortment of Parisians. Known for its live music, Celtic and otherwise, as well as its Irish stew. One of the older Irish bars in the city, with lots of dark wood and old photos.

A lively, expatriate gang gathers at the **Lizard Lounge** ★★ (18 rue du Bourg-Tibourg, 4th arrond.; ☎ 01 42 72 81 34; www.cheapblonde.com/lizard; Métro: Hôtel de Ville), where drinks and chat give way to live DJs and dancing in the "Underground" dance cellar, below bar-level. Owned by an American-Irish-British trio, this roomy bar, graced by a chic metallic mezzanine, has become a fixture of the Marais bar scene.

Homesick Canadians will appreciate **The Moose** ★ (16 rue des Quatre Vents, 6th arrond.; ☎ 01 46 33 77 00; www.canadianbarsparis.com; Métro: Odéon), where the walls are decorated with ice hockey paraphernalia and the beer is, not surprisingly, Moosehead. Sports is a major item on the agenda here; you can see one of their six plasma TV screens from anywhere in the bar. French, Canadian, American, and British fans gather here to cheer their teams and each other, pint in hand.

BASTILLE—RUE DE CHARONNE

The original **Café de l'Industrie** ★ (16 rue St-Sabin, 11th arrond.; ☎ 01 47 00 13 53; Métro: Bastille or Bréguet Sabin) was so successful (and crowded) that the owners decided to open a second restaurant across the street (it's now called Cafés de l'Industrie), and have recently added a third enterprise: a lingerie shop called L'Industrie Lingerie. Aside from being a lovely place to eat, this is great spot for a drink, during an evening's ramble. The decor is subdued eclectic: Black-and-white movie star portraits share the walls with contemporary paintings and colonial knick-knacks. In the annex, there's a piano-bar. And in the lingerie store, well, use your imagination . . .

Right in the thick of the madness on rue de Lappe is **Sister May** (25 rue du Lappe, 11th arrond.; ☎ 01 48 05 99 41; www.sistermay.com; Métro: Bastille), a cozy bar with minimal attitude. Exposed stone walls, low velvet-covered benches, neo-Victorian settees and throw pillows set the tone in this popular spot, where you might happen in on a theme night, like a Brazilian party, or a Soirée Japonaise.

RUE OBERKAMPF

One of the first bars to take over rue Oberkampf in the 1990s, **Café Charbon** ★★ (109 rue Oberkampf, 11th arrond.; ☎ 01 43 57 55 13; Métro: Oberkampf) is still an excellent choice for an evening out. This turn-of-the-20th-century beauty (it was once a dance hall) welcomes hoards of happy night-birds under its arched ceilings; the door in the back leads to the nightclub, La Nouvelle Casino, where live bands and DJs shake it up until the wee hours. You can enjoy the atmosphere here any time of day, for coffee, a drink, or a good meal.

MONTMARTRE

Aside from a small mirror ball and a mermaid hanging from the ceiling, there's nothing particularly notable about the decor at **Le Sancerre** ★ (35 rue des Abbesses, 18th arrond.; ☎ 01 42 58 08 20; Métro: Abbesses), but no matter: This is one of the most happening bars in Montmartre. During the day, 20-somethings attached to their iPods nurse hangovers at the sidewalk tables; at night, beautiful bobos (bourgeois bohemians) and authentic artists jostle for a place at the bar. Service can be a bit lax, but then, you don't come here for a quick drink.

GAY PAREE

Gay travelers will be pleased to find that Paris is a delightfully "live and let live" kind of place when it comes to one's personal life; the mayor, for example is openly gay and it was *not* an issue during his campaign (what a concept). Hence the gay scene is low-key and open, with a good realm of choices. Though the Marais is by far the main gay area, clubs and events are also sprinkled throughout the city. For listings, pick up *2X* or *Illico,* both distributed free in gay bars and bookstores; the monthly magazine **Têtu** (www.tetu.com) is another good source, as is their website. On the Web, www.paris-gay.com offers a rundown of current events. For recommended gay dance clubs, see p. 292. Below are a few of the better-known bars.

BOYS WHO LIKE BOYS

Terribly hip, **Le Carré** (18 rue du Temple, 4th arrond.; ☎ 01 44 59 38 57; www.lecarre.fr; Métro: Hôtel de Ville) offers sleek, modern furnishings, a glowing bar, and Chagal-esque stained glass on the walls. Listen to cutting-edge electro while sipping your Pink Flamingo (that's a kind of wine, here) and watching the cool crowd saunter past the bar.

More relaxed, and more diverse, the **Open Café** (17 rue des Archives, 4th arrond.; ☎ 01 42 72 26 18; Métro: Hôtel de Ville) is a cafe-bar with a busy sidewalk terrace that is usually full both day and night. Everyone from humble tourists, to sharp-looking businessmen, to TV stars hangs out here.

Considerably cozier, **Amnesia Café** (42 rue Vieille du Temple, 4th arrond.; ☎ 01 42 72 16 94; Métro: Hôtel de Ville or St-Paul) is an oasis of relative calm on the rugged Marais nightlife scene. Comfortable armchairs beckon, amber walls and soft lighting set the tone. Even when the crowd pushes in the evening, there's less cruising here, and more talking. Small dance floor and live DJs fill the basement.

Looking for a something a little more wild? **Raidd Bar** ★ (23 rue du Temple, 4th arrond.; ☎ 01 47 27 80 25; www.raiddbar.com; Métro: Hôtel de Ville or Rambuteau) offers hunky bartenders, a spacious dance floor, go-go dancers, and strippers who take it all off under an open shower. Very trendy, on weekends you'll have to get past the *selectionneur* at the door who decides who's cool enough to enter.

GIRLS WHO LIKE GIRLS

The oldest lesbian bar in the city, **La Champmeslé** ★ (pronounced shamp-mel-*ay*; 4 rue Chabanais, 2nd arrond.; ☎ 01 42 96 85 20; www.lachampmesle.com; Métro: Pyramides) is a classic: ancient stone walls, exposed beams, '50s furniture, and a cabaret every Thursday. The openings for the monthly art expos are a good bet for meeting new faces.

Les Scandaleuses, the Marais' most famous lesbian bar, has closed, and **Le 3W Kafé** (8 rue des Ecouffes, 4th arrond.; ☎ 01 48 87 39 26; Métro: Hôtel de Ville) has taken its place; freshening up the decor and opening up their door policy: Now boys can enter this womanly realm, provided they are accompanied by a girl. DJs and dancing downstairs on the weekends.

11 Get Out of Town

Round out your trip with a visit to a nearby marvel

MANY VISITORS (AND PARISIANS, FOR THAT MATTER) MAKE THE MISTAKE OF thinking that Paris is France, but this couldn't be farther from the truth. The minute you disentangle yourself from Paris and its suburbs, another country appears—a gentle rural landscape dotted with small towns, not-so-small castles and other fascinating sites. With so much to see in Paris, you probably won't have time to travel far into the provinces, but that doesn't mean you can't get out and see nearby treasures—especially since it's pretty easy to get out of town without a car (in fact, it's generally easier than if you had one, given the traffic jams on the outer arteries).

Paris has no lack of interesting day-trip destinations. Your main problem will be deciding which one(s) to go to. My two cents: If you've never been there, your first choice should be the château and gardens of Versailles. They're close by, easily accessible by train, and truly not to be missed. Aside from its historical significance (this is where the French monarchy spent its final hours of glory before the Revolution), there's the sheer magnificence of the building itself—this is the largest castle in France, and the most impressive. Chartres would be my second choice, even though it's an hour away by train, because its Gothic cathedral contains some of the most stunning stained-glass windows on the planet, and the winding streets and half-timbered houses of the town will give you a taste of something completely different from Paris. After that, it's a toss-up. If castles are your game, Vaux le Vicomte and Fontainebleau should be high on your list; if you want to get out in the country, Monet's garden at Giverney is a good choice (get there early before the crowds pour in). Lastly, if you're yearning for Mickey and Minnie (or your kids are), there is Disneyland Paris, a European version of the American theme park. I'm listing these destinations according to my own biased priorities, taking into consideration both cultural value and accessibility.

VERSAILLES

It's hard not to feel infinitely small and humble before the grandeur of the **Château de Versailles** ✪✪✪ (Versailles; ☎ 01 30 83 78 00; www.chateau versailles.fr; château Nov–Mar Tues–Sun 9am–5:30pm, Apr–Oct Tues–Sun 9am–6:30pm; Domaine de Marie Antoinette Nov–Mar noon–5:30pm, Apr–Oct noon–7pm; gardens daily 8am–dusk), which is exactly the effect Louis XIV was going for when he dreamed up this gargantuan palace in the 17th century. Having been badly burned by a nasty uprising called Le Fronde, wherein attempts were made by petty nobles to restrict royal power, Louis decided to move his court from Paris to Versailles, a safe distance from the intrigues of the capital. He also decided to have the court move in with him, where he could keep a close eye on

Ile de France

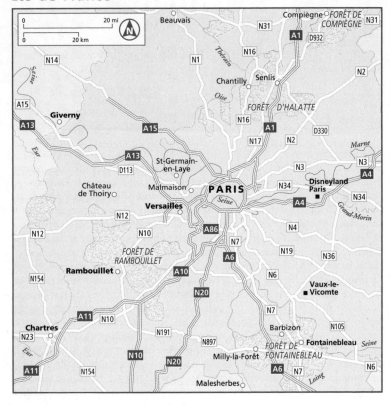

them and nip any new plots or conspiracies in the bud. This required a new abode that was not only big enough to house his court (anywhere from 3,000 to 10,000 people would be palace guests on any given day), but also one that would be grand enough to let the world know who was in charge.

As you gape at the grandiose entryway, I think you'll agree that he achieved his objective—this massive palace simply dwarfs the rest of the town, let alone any mere mortals strolling before it. The three enormous boulevards leading up to it should be a dead giveaway (the central one, the Avenue de Paris, is wider than the Champs Elysées); this castle was meant to be the focus of not just the town, but the French universe—and Louis, in bronze, perched atop a mighty stallion in the courtyard, was the lord and master.

There was already a château on the site when Louis came to town; his father, Louis XIII, had built a small castle, "a hunting lodge," there in 1623. This humble dwelling simply would not do for the so-called "Sun King," who brought in a flotilla of architects, artists, and gardeners to enlarge the castle and give it a new look. In 1668, the King's architect, Louis Le Vau, began work on the enormous "envelope," which literally wrapped the old castle in a second building; this magnificent limestone facade, and its two huge wings are best seen from the gardens.

Seasons in Versailles

At Versailles, high season refers to the period of April through October, and low season is November through March.

From the front, you can see the remnants of the old castle; the buildings that surround the recessed central courtyard (called the Marble Court) are what's left of that structure.

Meanwhile, legendary garden designer André Le Notre was carving out formal gardens and a huge park out of what had been marshy countryside. Thousands of trees were planted; harmonious geometric designs were achieved with flower beds, hedges, canals, and pebbled pathways dotted with sculptures and fountains.

Construction, which involved as many as 36,000 workers, ground on for years; Le Vau died, François d'Orbay took over, and eventually Jules Hardouin Mansart joined the project. In 1682 the King and his court moved in, but construction went on right through the rest of his reign and into that of Louis XV. Louis XVI and his wife, Marie Antoinette, made few changes, but history made a gigantic one for them: On October 6, 1789, an angry mob of hungry Parisians marched on the palace and the royal couple was eventually forced to return to Paris. Versailles would never again be a royal residence.

Life at Versailles was a series of heavily orchestrated rituals that started with getting out of bed. In fact, the King's awakening and morning ablutions were a kind of daily ceremony involving a battalion of servants, doctors, and a few honored guests. At 8:30am sharp, the King would be awakened by his valet, who would then let in the crowd to assist and watch His Highness be washed and shaved. Then the Officers of the Chamber and Wardrobe would arrive to dress the King, after which he would breakfast on a bowl of bouillon. Around 100 people, all told, would be present each morning for this absurd spectacle, many of them high ranking officials. But this was not the worst of it; there was a strict code of conduct for everything that one did at the castle, from addressing a superior, to sitting down on a sofa. Failure to follow the incredibly complex etiquette could mean a serious downshift in one's place in the palace's rigid hierarchy of power and influence; backbiting and betrayal were common currency. Needless to say, all this could be extremely wearying, especially on young, impressionable queens. Louis XVI's bride, a certain Marie Antoinette, decided she simply couldn't take it anymore and fled to the **Petit Trianon** (a small manor house deep in the gardens), where she constructed a kinder, gentler fantasy world.

The upside of all this refined living was that Versailles soon became a repository of great art. Starting with Louis XIV—a devoted patron of the arts—thousands of exquisite paintings, sculptures, and furniture pieces were commissioned to decorate the 700 rooms of this oversized palace. Subsequent monarchs made their mark with new purchases and interiors. Not only did this keep an army of artists and craftsman in business, it established Versailles as a sort of living museum of culture. Today there are 6,400 paintings, 2,000 sculptures, and 17

Versailles

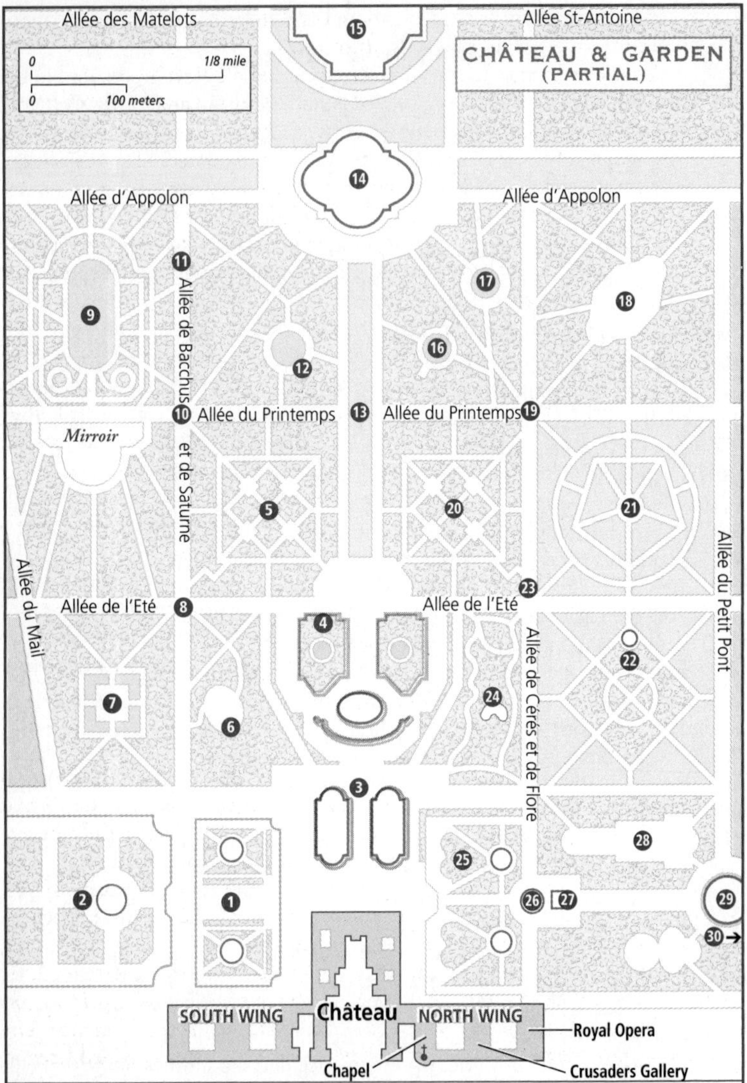

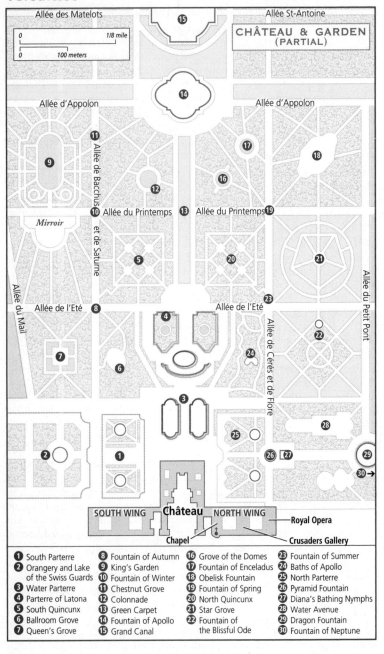

Allée des Matelots
Allée St-Antoine
CHÂTEAU & GARDEN (PARTIAL)
0 1/8 mile
0 100 meters
Allée d'Appolon
Allée d'Appolon
Allée de Bacchus et de Saturne
Allée du Printemps
Allée du Printemps
Mirroir
Allée du Mail
Allée de l'Eté
Allée de l'Eté
Allée de Cérés et de Flore
Allée du Petit Pont
SOUTH WING
Château
NORTH WING
Royal Opera
Chapel
Crusaders Gallery

1. South Parterre
2. Orangery and Lake of the Swiss Guards
3. Water Parterre
4. Parterre of Latona
5. South Quincunx
6. Ballroom Grove
7. Queen's Grove
8. Fountain of Autumn
9. King's Garden
10. Fountain of Winter
11. Chestnut Grove
12. Colonnade
13. Green Carpet
14. Fountain of Apollo
15. Grand Canal
16. Grove of the Domes
17. Fountain of Enceladus
18. Obelisk Fountain
19. Fountain of Spring
20. North Quincunx
21. Star Grove
22. Fountain of the Blissful Ode
23. Fountain of Summer
24. Baths of Apollo
25. North Parterre
26. Pyramid Fountain
27. Diana's Bathing Nymphs
28. Water Avenue
29. Dragon Fountain
30. Fountain of Neptune

thousand engravings on this hallowed ground, and that's not including the thousands of exceptional art objects and furniture items.

Perhaps inevitably, the palace was ransacked during the Revolution, and in the years after it fell far from its original state of grace. Napoleon and Louis XVIII did what they could to bring the sleeping giant back to life, but by the early 1800s, during the reign of Louis-Philippe, the castle was slated for demolition. Fortunately for us, this forward-thinking king decided to invest his own money to save Versailles for future generations, and in 1837 the vast structure was made into a national museum. Little by little, precious furniture and art objects were retrieved or re-created; paintings, wall decorations, and ceilings were restored. Not surprisingly, restoration is ongoing; in 2003 a massive renovation and reorganization project that will take place in stages over 17 years and cost close to 400 million euros was unveiled. This is great news for Versailles, but it also means that tourists will have to put up with periodic closings of different parts of the château and grounds while work is being done—so be prepared for the unexpected when you arrive. Even if a few areas are closed, the place is so huge that should you feel so inclined, you can still tour yourself into a 17th-century stupor.

Depending on which rooms are being renovated and how, certain rooms (but usually not star attractions, like the Grand Apartments or the Galerie des Glaces) can only be visited with a guide; others are just more interesting seen through the eyes of an expert. To get on a **guided tour,** simply ask what's on that day at the information desk or at the ticket booth (the tour schedule changes daily), and pull out your wallet: A 2-hour tour costs 7.50€ if you have either a Passport or Chateau ticket, 15€ if you don't. If you don't speak French, there are also daily tours in English.

TOURING THE PALACE

The rooms in the "envelope," or the newer part of the building, were designed to impress, which they do. They include a series of rooms called the Grand Apartments, used primarily for ceremonial events (which were a daily occurrence), The Queen's Apartments, and the Galerie des Glaces. These, along with the King's Apartments, and the Chapel, are the must-sees of the palace. If you have time and fortitude, a visit to the royal family's private apartments, in particular the King's, offers a more intimate look at castle life.

Each room in the **Grand Apartments** ★★★ is dedicated to a different planet (that circles around the sun, as in Sun King), and each has a fabulous painting on the ceiling depicting the god or goddess associated with said heavenly sphere. The first and probably the most staggering, painting-wise, was actually added later, in 1710. Called the **Salon d'Hercule** ★★, it holds an enormous canvas by Paolo Veronese, *Christ at Supper with Simon,* as well as a splendid, divinity-bedecked ceiling portraying Hercules being welcomed by the gods of Olympus by Antoine Lemoyne. At 480 sq. m (5,166 sq. ft), it is one of the largest paintings in France. The **Salon d'Apollon** ★, not surprisingly, was the throne room, where the Sun-King would receive ambassadors and other heads of state.

The ornate **Salon de Guerre** ★ and **Salon de Paix** bookend the most famous room in the place, the **Galerie des Glaces (the Hall of Mirrors)** ★★★. Louis XIV commanded his painter-in-chief, Charles Le Brun, to paint the 12m-high (40-ft.) ceiling of this 73m-long (240-ft.) gallery with representations of his

Reducing Stress While Buying a Ticket & Getting into the Chateau

Because the castle is undergoing a vast reorganization, including lots of renovations (see below), the ticketing schemes change often and can be, to put it mildly, confusing. Recently, efforts have been made to clarify things, and at press time, the system was pretty straightforward—let's hope it stays that way. If you want to spend the day and see as much as you can, invest in a 1-day Passport (20€ weekdays, 25€ weekends and holidays), which gives you access to everything: the castle, the gardens, the Domaine de Marie Antoinette, you name it, plus the use of an audioguide. "But," you protest, "I don't have the time/energy/cash needed to see the whole thing. Isn't there another way?" Yes there is. Just ask for the Billet Château (or Palace Ticket, 14€, 10€ after 3pm), which offers access to all the highlights of the castle, including the King's and Queen's apartments, the Hall of Mirrors, and the apartments of the Dauphin and the Mesdames, and comes with an audioguide. After seeing all that, you might not want to do much else besides stroll around in the garden, which is free.

Here is the run-down on ticket prices:

◆ **1-day Passport** (20€ during the week, 25€ weekends and holidays) offers access to the château, the grounds, the gardens, the Grand Trianon, the Domaine de Marie Antoinette, the Grandes Eaux Musicales (high season weekends only) as well as a free audioguide.

accomplishments. This masterwork is illuminated by light from the 17 windows that overlook the garden, which are matched on the opposite wall by 17 mirrored panels. Add to that a few enormous crystal chandeliers, and the effect is dazzling. It must have been even more so back in the day, when it was furnished with solid silver tables, lamps, and urns (holding orange trees). In 2008, the hall was entirely reopened after a long restoration, and the result is breathtaking. This splendid setting was the scene of a historic event in a more recent century: In 1919, World War I officially ended when the Treaty of Versailles was signed here.

The **Queen's Apartments** ✿✿ maintains more than a little of the decorating style of its most famous inhabitant, Marie Antoinette. In fact, the gorgeous bedroom with its silk hangings printed with lilacs and peacock feathers looks exactly as it did in 1789, when the Queen was forced to flee revolutionary mobs through a secret door, which is barely visible in the wall near her bed. The **King's Apartments** ✿✿✿ are even more splendiferous, though in a very different style: Here the ceilings have been left blank white, which brings out the elaborate white and gold decoration on the walls. The **King's bedroom** ✿✿✿, hung from top to bottom with gold brocade, is fitted with a sort of banister that separated the King from the 100 or so people that would come to watch him wake up in the morning. It was in this room that Louis XIV died from a gangrenous leg in 1715.

♦ **"Billet Château" (Palace Ticket** 14€, after 3pm 10€) includes access to the château and gardens plus an audioguide.

♦ **"Billet Domaine de Marie Antoinette"** (9€, after 5pm 5€) includes the Grand and Petit Trianons, the Chapel, the Hamlet, the Queen's Theater, and other gardens and pavilions.

All the above prices are for visitors over 18; entrance is free for 17 and under.

Another unfortunate aspect of the renovations is that various parts of the castle might be closed when you visit. To be sure of what's open, consult the website (www.chateauversailles.fr/en/570_Temporary_closures.php; there's a link on the opening hours page). But by far the biggest renovations-related ordeal is getting into the chateau. Unless you arrive at opening time (or early mornings during the week), you are bound to be confronted with huge lines. You can limit your waiting time by buying tickets in advance at **Fnac stores** (www.fnac.fr, ☎ 08 92 68 36 22, .34€ per minute), which I heartily recommend. You can also buy a combination 1-day Passport plus train ticket at any SNCF or RER station (see "How to Get There," below). Once you have your ticket, you'll still have to wait in the line to get in, which moves at a mysteriously slow pace. To avoid the crowds, if at all possible, visit during the week, early in the morning. Not only will your wait in line be shorter, but you also won't have to elbow your way through hoards of tour groups once you get inside.

You'll have to take a guided tour to see the **King's private apartment** ★★, furnished in the rococo style of Louis XV. The successors to the Sun King, Louis XV and XVI, lived in these more intimate lodgings with their families, rising early to run over to the official King's bedroom to "awaken" in public. The most magnificent work in this section is the **Astronomical Clock** ★★★ in the Cabinet de la Pendule, which dates from 1754. The fruit of 12 years labor on the part of a gifted engineer and a top clockmaker, this extraordinary clock shows not only the time, but the date, the phases of the moon, and the position of the planets (illustrated by the movement of crystal spheres on top of the clock). There is also a superb **inlaid roll-top desk** ★★ that belonged to Louis XV in the King's inner office.

You should also make sure to see the **Chapel** ★★★, a masterpiece of light and harmony by Jules Hardouin Mansart, where the kings attended mass. This lofty space (the ceiling is over 25m/82 ft. high) reflects both Gothic and Baroque styles, combining a vaulted roof, stained glass, and gargoyles with columns and balustrades typical of the early 18th century. One of the most striking features is the whiteness of the interior; the painted stone and marble surfaces are all intricately carved with religious motifs. At press time, you couldn't actually enter the chapel, which is being restored, but you could get a good look from the entrance.

TOURING THE GARDENS & PARK

Even before you've actually entered the gardens, one thing will be instantly evident: The entire 800-hectare (2,000-acre) park is laid out according to a precise, symmetrical plan. From the terrace behind the castle, there is an astounding **view** ✹✹✹ that runs past two parterres, down a central lawn (the Tapis Vert), down the **Grand Canal** ✹✹ and seemingly on into infinity. Le Nôtre's masterpiece is the ultimate example of French-style gardens; geometric, logical, and in perfect harmony—a reflection of the divine order of the cosmos. The star of this particular cosmos, of course, was the Sun King, and a solar theme is reflected in the statues and fountains along the main axis of the perspective: At the bottom of the formal gardens, just before the canal, is the **Apollo Fountain** ✹✹ where the sun god emerges from the waves at dawn on his chariot. Closer to the castle, Apollo's mother is honored in the **Latona fountain,** a three-tiered wedding-cake-like structure. The cycle once came to a close at Thesis' grotto, but the construction of the North wing sealed the god's hideout for eternity. On the sides of the main axis, near the castle, are a set of six groves, or **bosquets** ✹, leafy minigardens that are hidden by walls of shrubbery; some were used as small outdoor ballrooms for festivities, others for intimate rendezvous out of reach of the prying eyes of the court. The buildings near the Grand Canal are what are left of the Petite Venise, where imported Venetian sailors would sail their gondolas and miniature sailing ships down the canal for festivals, promenades, and musical events. Today, more commonplace festivities take place next to the canal; here is one of the many areas west of the Apollo Fountain where you can picnic, bike ride (bikes can be rented next to the restaurant), or even row a boat on a sunny day.

Northwest of the fountain lies an area now referred to as the **Domaine de Marie Antoinette** ✹✹. It was here that the young queen sought refuge from the strict protocol and infighting at the castle. Her husband gave her the **Petit Trianon,** a small manor that Louis XV used for his trysts, which she transformed into a stylish haven. Recently restored, only the first floor of the Petit Trianon is open to visitors; the upper floor can be visited on a guided tour. When the queen had finished decorating the manor in the latest fashions, she set to work creating an entire world around it, including a splendid **English garden** ✹, several lovely pavilions, a **theater,** and even a small **hamlet** ✹✹, complete with a working farm and a dairy, where she and her friends would play cards and gossip, or just go for a stroll in the "country." Too bad they never stopped to think about the dreadful living conditions of the real country folk who lived only a few kilometers away— a stellar example of the complete disconnect that existed between the aristocracy and the working classes; one of the main causes of the explosion that became the French Revolution. Although the **Grand Trianon** ✹ is not really linked to the story of Marie Antoinette, it is in this neighborhood, and worth a visit. Built by Louis XIV as a retreat for him and his family, this small marble palace consists of two large wings connected by an open columned terrace from which there is a delightful **view** ✹ of the gardens. The furniture and decor dates from the Napoleonic era; Charles de Gaulle used one wing for visits from heads of state (Nixon spent a night here).

How to get there: Take the **RER C** (that's the suburban commuter train, part of the Transilien network; ☎ 08 91 36 20 20, .24€ per minute; www.transilien.fr; 30 min. from the Champs de Mars station; one-way fare 2.90€ adults, 1.45€

4–10, free under 4) to Versailles Rive Gauche–Château de Versailles. *Important:* Make sure the final destination for your train is Versailles Rive Gauche–Château de Versailles and *not* Versailles Chantier, which will leave you on the other end of town, a long walk from the Château. Even worse, the Versailles Chantier trains actually run in the opposite direction, touring all around Paris before arriving at Versailles, which will add an hour or so to your journey. Assuming you've taken the right train, it's about a 5-minute walk from the Versailles Rive Gauche train station to the château—don't worry, you can't miss it.

You can buy a ticket from any Métro or RER station; the fare includes a free transfer to the Métro. You can save a few euros and avoid waiting in at least one line if you buy a combined train fare–château entry ticket, available at any SNCF (train) or Transilien (RER) station. This package, or *forfait* (for-*fay*) costs 22€ weekdays and 26€ weekends and includes round-trip train fare and 1-day Passport, a good deal when you consider that the Passport alone can cost you 20€ to 25€.

Tourist information: Versailles Tourist Office (2 bis ave. de Paris, Versailles; ☎ 01 39 24 88 88; www.versailles-tourisme.com).

CHARTRES

Considered by many to represent the most perfect expression of Gothic architecture, the **Cathedral of Chartres** ✪✪✪ (place de la Cathédral, Chartres; ☎ 02 37 21 75 02; www.diocese-chartres.com; free admission; 8:30am–7:30pm) with its carved portals and three-tiered flying buttresses, would be a stunning sight even without its legendary **stained-glass windows**—though the world would be a drearier place. For these ancient glass panels are truly glorious; a kaleidoscope of colors so deep, so rich, and so bright, it's hard to believe they are some 700 years old. Meant as teaching devices more than artwork, the windows functioned as a sort of enormous cartoon, telling the story of Christ through pictures to a mostly illiterate populace. From its beginnings, this was a place of pilgrimage, which accounts at least in part for the superhuman dimensions of the church. Pilgrims came from far and near to see a piece of cloth that believers say was worn by the Virgin Mary during Christ's birth. The relic is still here, but these days it's primarily a different sort of pilgrim that is drawn to Chartres: Over 1.5 million tourists come here every year from around the globe to admire the artistry that went into the creation of this magnificent edifice.

A Romanesque church stood on this spot until 1194, when a fire burnt it virtually to the ground. All that remained were the towers, the Royal Portal, and a few remnants of stained glass. The locals were so horrified that they sprung to action; money started pouring in from princes and petty bourgeois to pay for a new cathedral, while poorer souls volunteered to help build it. In a matter of only 3 decades the new cathedral was erected, which accounts for its remarkably unified Gothic architecture; in those low-tech times, large churches could take a century or so to build, which is why so many of them are a hodgepodge of styles. The name of the architect who designed the structure has been lost, but he

> ❝ If it were a person, it would be a woman, a very dignified old lady. She is beautiful. She is royal. She has kept her charms. ❞
>
> –Malcolm Miller, Chartres Cathedral

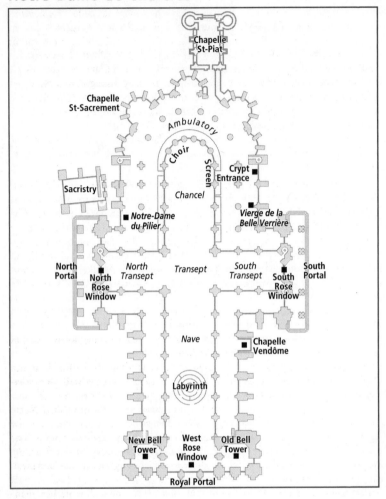

was clearly a great innovator—and one of the first to use flying buttresses as a building support. The buttresses allowed him to build his walls at twice the height of the standard Romanesque cathedrals, which made space for these masterful windows. The new cathedral was dedicated in 1260 and has miraculously survived the centuries with relatively little damage. The French Revolution somehow spared the cathedral; during World War I and World War II, the precious windows were carefully dismounted piece by piece and stored in a safe place in the countryside. The only serious brush with disaster happened in 1836, when a fire destroyed the wooden framework in the roof (this has been replaced with a metal one).

Before you enter the church, take in the **facade** ✰✰, which is a remarkable assemblage of religious art and architecture. The base of the two towers dates from

Tours, Guided & Otherwise

There are **guided tours** of the cathedral in English Monday through Saturday at noon and 2:45pm (10€ adults, 5€ students, no reservations needed). A 1½-hour tour in French is offered Tuesday through Saturday at 10:30am and daily at 3pm from April through October, and at 2:30pm daily from November through March for 6.20€. Another option, in both French and English, are the **audioguides,** which rent for 6.20€.

the early 12th century (before the fire). The tower to your right (the **Old Tower,** or South Tower) is topped by its original sober Romanesque spire; that on your left (**New Tower,** or North Tower) was blessed with an elaborate Gothic spire by Jehan de Beauce in the early 1500s, when the original burned down. Below is the **Royal Portal** ✮✮✮, a masterpiece of Romanesque art. Swarming with kings, queens, prophets, and priests, this sculpted entryway tells the story of the life of Christ. The rigid bodies of the figures contrast with their lifelike faces; it is said that Rodin spent hours here contemplating this stonework spectacle. You can **climb to the top of the New Tower** (☎ 02 37 21 22 07; 7€ adult; 4.50€ 18–25; free under 18 accompanied by adult; Sept–Apr Mon–Sat 9:30am–noon and 2–4:30pm, Sun 2–4:30pm; May–Aug Mon–Sat 9:30am–noon, 2–5:30pm, Sun 2–5:30pm) to take in the **view** ✮; just remember to wear rubber-soled shoes, as the 300 steps are a little slippery after all these centuries.

Once inside the cathedral, you'll really understand what all the fuss is about. The gloomy atmosphere is pierced by the radiant colors of the **stained-glass windows** ✮✮✮, which shine down from all sides. Three windows on the west side of the building, as well as the beautiful rose window to the south called **Notre Dame de la Belle Verière** ✮ date from the earlier 12th-century structure; the rest, with the exception of a few modern panels, are of 13th-century origins. The scenes depicted in glass, read from bottom to top and recount stories from the Bible as well as the lives of the saints. There are 176 windows in the cathedral, each one filled with dozens of scenes and portraits. You will soon find yourself wondering how in the world medieval artists, with such low-tech materials, managed to create such vivid colors; the blues, in particular, seem to be divinely inspired. In fact, scientists have finally pierced at least part of the mystery: The blue was made with sodium and silica compounds that made the color stand up to the centuries better than glass made with other colors.

Another indoor marvel is the **chancel enclosure** ✮✮, which separates the chancel (the area behind the altar) from the ambulatory (the walkway that runs around the outer chapels). Started in 1514 by Jehan de Beauce, this intricately sculpted wall depicts dozens of saints and other religious superstars in yet another recounting of the lives of the Virgin and Christ. Back in the ambulatory is the Chapel of the Martyrs, where the cathedral's cherished **relic** resides: a piece of cloth that the Virgin Mary apparently wore at the birth of Christ, which was a gift of Charles the Bald in 876.

When to Visit & When Not To

Though the cathedral is open daily from 8:30am to 7:30pm, the staff asks that you not wander around during religious services, which are generally held in the late morning and early evening. You are welcome to sit in on services, of course.

Chartres also harbors a rare **labyrinth** ✪, which is traced on the floor of the cathedral near the nave. A large circle, divided into four parts, is entirely filled by a winding path that leads to the center. In the Middle Ages, these labyrinths represented the symbolic path that one must follow to get from Earth to God; pilgrims would follow the path while praying, as if they were making a pilgrimage to Jerusalem.

Downstairs is an eerie **crypt** (guided visits only; 2.70€ adults, 2.10€ students and over 60, free under 7; Nov–Mar Mon–Sat 11am and 4:15pm; Apr–Oct Mon–Sat 11am, 2:15pm; 3:30pm, and 4:30pm; June 22–July 22 there is additional tour at 5:15pm), which dates from the earlier Romanesque construction and includes a series of chapels. In one of these, the chapel of Notre Dame de Sous-Terre, or Our Lady of the Underground, is a copy of an 11th-century statue of the Virgin.

Once you've left the church, give yourself at least a little time to wander around the **town.** The ancient streets, many of which boast half-timbered houses, wind up the hill; stone bridges cross the narrow Eure river down below.

How to get there: Trains (SNCF; 3635, 34€ per min.; www.voyages-sncf.com; 55 min.–1¼ hr., depending on how many stops the train makes; once or twice an hour; 13€ one-way) leave from the Gare Montparnasse station in Paris and let you off in the center of Chartres, about a 5-minute walk from the cathedral.

Tourist information: Chartres Tourist Office (place de la Cathédral; ☎ 02 37 18 26 26; www.chartres-tourisme.com).

VAUX LE VICOMTE

The rise and fall of Nicolas Fouquet, the original owner of the **Château de Vaux le Vicomte** (Maincy; ☎ 01 64 14 41 90; www.vaux-le-vicomte.com; 13€ adult, 10€ students, free under 6; candlelight evenings 16€ adults, 14€ students, free under 6; audioguide [in English] 2.50€; mid-Mar to mid-Nov and Dec 20–Jan 4 (except Christmas day and New Years day) Mon–Fri 10am–1pm and 2–6pm, Sat–Sun 10am–6pm; candlelight evenings May to mid-Sept 8pm–midnight) reads like a Hollywood screenplay. This brilliant finance minister and lover of both arts and leisure was the toast of Paris in the early 1700s; his penchant for pleasure and beauty drew France's top artists and intellectuals to his lovely home in the country. Unfortunately, Fouquet underestimated the jealousy of his superiors, in particular the young king, Louis XIV. A messy financial scandal presented his enemies with an excellent excuse to topple the much-admired finance minister (in fact, Fouquet was more or less innocent of any wrongdoing); his fortunes took a precipitous fall on the evening of August 17, 1661. Oblivious to the fact that Louis XIV was already fed up with his penchant for stealing the spotlight, when the King

When to Visit & When Not To

The castle of Vaux le Vicomte is only open from the third week of March to mid-November. The rest of the year only the gardens are open to visitors.

expressed a desire to stop by and see the latest improvements on the castle, Fouquet organized a stupendous party his honor. He pulled out all the stops: There was a sumptuous meal, a play written and performed by Molière, and a fireworks display—no one had seen anything like it. Three weeks later, Fouquet was arrested by the King's fabled musketeer d'Artagnan. Though writers like Madame de Sévigné and La Fontaine wrote in Fouquet's behalf to the King, the once untouchable financial minister spent the rest of his life in prison.

Though his reaction was extreme (and unfair), Louis XIV's jealousy was not too hard to understand. Not only was Fouquet getting too powerful for the King's taste, but his castle and its gardens were the epitome of 17th-century artistry and elegance. Once Fouquet was out of the picture, Louis XIV seized the castle, confiscating a number of artistic treasures. The palace then passed on to various dukes and nobles, who eventually grew tired of it and more or less abandoned it at the end of the 19th century. In 1875 a certain Alfred Sommier bought Vaux le Vicomte at a public auction. The buildings were in a sorry state: The château was virtually empty and some of the outbuildings were in ruins. Slowly but surely, Sommier restored the castle, which has since passed down to his descendants, who still hold the reins. The castle is now entirely restored and filled with splendid tapestries, carpets, and art objects.

One of its most impressive rooms was actually never finished: the oval **Grand Salon** ✪✪, which Fouquet never got a chance to paint or furnish. Here, you actually don't miss all the decorative trimmings; the bare white pilasters and detailed carvings have a classical beauty that stands on its own. For something more ornate, there is the **King's bedroom** ✪✪; this lavish ensemble of chandeliers, brocade, and painted ceiling (by Le Brun) was a model for the King's Apartments in Versailles. The **Salon des Muses** ✪ also gets a fabulous ceiling by Le Brun, as well as several fine tapestries covering its walls. To help imagine what Fouquet's dinner parties were like, take a stroll through the elaborately decorated **Salle à Manger** ✪ (dining room), where a table is set with stacks of rare fruits and gold candlesticks, and a sideboard displays a set of extraordinary majolica. You can see life on the other side of the banquet table downstairs in the **kitchen,** with its more humble servants' dining area.

The **gardens** ✪✪✪ are almost as spectacular as the château. The carefully calculated geometry of the flowerbeds and alleyways makes this a study in harmony, even if you couldn't call them exactly natural. Nature is lurking close by, however—the entire ensemble is surrounded by seemingly endless kilometers of trees. Just behind the castle are two enormous semirectangular blocks filled with boxwood that has been trimmed into elaborate designs; Le Nôtre took his inspiration from the patterns in Turkish carpets. In fact, looking down from the castle, the garden looks like an abstract tapestry: The curls and swirls of the boxwood stand out in a frame

Vaux le Vicomte

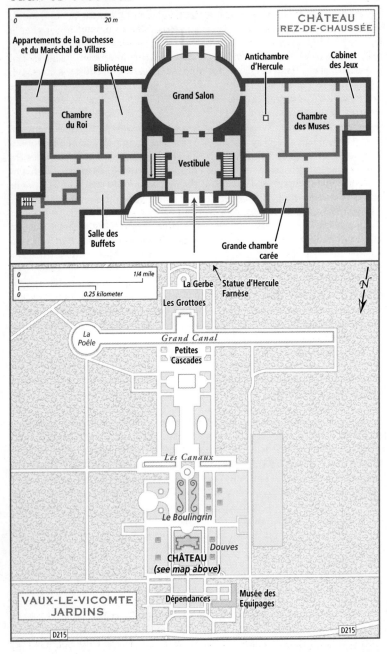

CHÂTEAU
REZ-DE-CHAUSSÉE

0   20 m

Appartements de la Duchesse
et du Maréchal de Villars

Bibliothèque

Antichambre
d'Hercule

Cabinet
des Jeux

Grand Salon

Chambre
du Roi

Chambre
des Muses

Vestibule

Salle des
Buffets

Grande chambre
carée

0   1/4 mile
0   0.25 kilometer

N

La Gerbe
Statue d'Hercule
Farnèse

Les Grottoes

La
Poêle

Grand Canal

Petites
Cascades

Les Canaux

Le Boulingrin

Douves

CHÂTEAU
(see map above)

VAUX-LE-VICOMTE
JARDINS

Dépendances

Musée des
Equipages

D215   D215

of greenery, while the square parterres and round basins fill out the background. If you'll look into the distance you'll see what seems to be an uninterrupted vista of alleyways and fountains—in fact, the far end of the gardens is crossed by a large **canal**, which you don't even see until you are just about on top of it. At the far end of the gardens lies a series of grottos, each sheltering a statue of a different river god.

Finally, from the last basin, turn around and take in the lovely **view** ✶ of the gardens with the château rising in the background. The château is visible from every part of the garden and this is no accident: Le Nôtre skillfully used perspective and optical illusion to make the château dominate the grounds as a symbol of the power of the master of the house. The **fountains** play on the second and last Saturday of every month (that the château is open) from 3 to 6pm. You can't picnic in the gardens, which is a pity, because the castle closes between 1 and 2pm and your only other choice for lunch is the overpriced cafeteria. Though not as scenic, there's a small **picnic area** next to the parking lot.

By the way, if you notice that the castle has some of the same elements as Versailles, that's no coincidence. Some years after Fouquet's fateful party, the Sun King hired the same talented team who created Vaux—painter Charles Le Brun, architect Louis Le Vau, and landscape artist André Le Nôtre—to build his new palace. Versailles might be grander and it certainly is larger, but in some ways, Vaux is more esthetically pleasing. Part of it is its dimensions; though it is definitely a castle, it's on a human scale. Then there's the architectural harmony and symmetry; the edifice is perfectly framed by its gardens and surrounding forest. Most of it, though, probably has to do with the refined tastes of its original proprietor, the much-abused Nicolas Fouquet.

How to get there: Trains (Transilien; ☎ 08 91 36 20 20, .24€ per minute; www.transilien.fr; 24 min., every hour or 2; 7.15€ adults, 3.55€ ages 4–10 one-way) run from Gare de Lyon to Melun, the closest large town. You could also take the suburban commuter train, the **RER D** (Transilien; ☎ 08 91 36 20 20, .24€ per minute; www.transilien.fr; 52 min.; 2 or 3 per hour; 7.15€ adults, 3.55€ ages 4–10 one-way). The two advantages to this choice, which takes twice as long, is that there are more trains per hour, particularly during the morning rush hour (during the evening rush hour there are more regular trains), and you can take it from either Gare du Nord, Châtelet or Gare de Lyon. Once you get to the station

Vaux by Candlelight

To give you just an inkling of what Vaux looked like on the evening of the famous party Fouquet threw for Louis XIV back in 1661, from May to mid-October, on certain nights, the castle and gardens are illuminated by candlelight. Some 2,000 candles burn on Saturday nights between 8pm to midnight (Fri nights as well, in July and Aug), when the grounds are open to the public. You can visit the interior of the castle or just stroll in the gardens, where classical music plays and a champagne bar is open. To top off your evening, rent a deck chair near the musicians and close your eyes and luxuriate in this remarkable 17th-century atmosphere.

at Melun, take the **Châteaubus shuttle** (20 min.; 3.50€ one-way; buy your ticket on board), which you'll find in front of the cafe next to the station. There are two to five shuttles per day; see the castle's website for a schedule. Otherwise, a **taxi** for up to four people costs around 16€ to 17€ during the day Monday through Saturday and around 20€ evenings and Sun. You can reserve ahead if you like at ☎ 01 64 52 51 50, or else simply head for the taxi stand next to the station.

Tourist Information: Château de Vaux le Vicomte (Maincy; ☎ 01 64 14 41 90; www.vaux-le-vicomte.com).

FONTAINEBLEAU

Napoleon called it "the house of the centuries; the true home of kings," and few could argue with his logic. After all, **Château de Fontainebleau** ✫✫✫ (Fontainebleau; ☎ 01 60 71 50 70; www.musee-chateau-fontainebleau.fr; Grands Appartements circuit 8€ adults, 6€ ages 18–25, free under 18 and for all the first Sun of each month; chateau entry plus 1 guided tour 13€ adults, 11€ ages 18–25, free under 18; Grands Appartements circuit plus 2 guided tours 19€ adults, 16€ ages 18–25, free under 18; Oct–Mar Wed–Mon 9:30am–5pm, Apr–Sept Wed–Mon 9:30–6pm) was a royal residence for over 700 years. Though the castle existed before, the first hard evidence of a royal inhabitant is a charter signed here in 1137 by Louis XVII. Philippe August and Saint Louis (Louis IX) both spent a good deal of time at the castle; 13th-century sovereign Philippe le Bel was born and died here.

Though the original castle was nothing to sniff at, it was during the Renaissance that Fontainebleau really took on its regal allure. In 1528, inveterate castle-builder King François I decided to completely rebuild Fontainebleau and make it into a palace that would rival the marvels of Rome. He tore down the medieval castle, saving only the *donjon* (the central core) of the building, and hired an army of architects and artisans to construct a new one around it. He also brought in two renowned Italian artists, Il Rosso, a student of Andrea del Sarto, and Primaticcio, a disciple of Giulio Romano, to decorate his new home. Their style of work came to be known as the School of Fontainebleau, which was characterized by the use of stucco (moldings and picture frames) and frescos that depicted various allegories and myths. This school was highly influenced by the Mannerist style of Michelangelo, Raphael, and Parmigianino.

François I was also an art collector: His vast accumulation of Renaissance treasures included Da Vinci's *Mona Lisa* and *The Virgin of the Rock,* both of which once hung here. After François' death, his descendents continued work on the castle, but it wasn't until the 17th century and the arrival of Henri IV on the scene that there were any major transformations. Henri added several wings and a courtyard (le Cour des Offices), and also made major changes to the decor, inviting a new clutch of artists, who established a second School of Fontainebleau. This time, the artists were of French and Flemish origins (Ambrose Dubois, Martin Fréminet, and others), and used oil paint and canvas instead of frescos. Louis XIV, preferring Versailles, didn't bother much with Fontainebleau, but Louis XV and Louis XVI found the palace very much to their liking and added their own decorative and architectural flourishes. Napoleon was also very fond of this palace and made a lasting imprint on the castle's interior. No doubt,

Fontainebleau made an imprint on the Emperor as well: On April 20, 1814, he abdicated here, before being sent off to exile on the island of Elba.

TOURING THE CHATEAU

The outside of this castle is almost as impressive as its interior; give yourself time to walk around and appreciate this majestic conglomeration of architectural styles.

Your first encounter with the château will take place in the **Cour du Cheval Blanc** ✹✹ at the entrance to the palace. It was in this grand square, which is surrounded by wings of the castle on three sides, that Napoleon said adieu to his faithful imperial guards. "Continue to serve France," he pleaded, "Her welfare was my only concern."

The main building before you dates from François I's era; the sumptuous **horseshoe staircase** ✹ was added by Henri II. On the left, as you enter, is the **Chapelle de la Trinité** ✹. When he was 7, Louis XIII climbed up the scaffolding to watch Martin Fréminet, his art instructor, paint the glorious ceiling. This is where Louis XV married Polish princess Marie Leczinska; the future Napoleon III was baptized here as well. Linking the chapel with the royal apartments is the **Gallery of François I** ✹✹✹, a stunning example of Renaissance art and decoration. Overseen by Il Rossi, a team of highly skilled artists covered the walls with exceptional frescos, moldings, and *boisseries* (carved woodwork). The paintings, which are full of mythological figures, pay tribute to the glory of the monarchy and the wisdom of the King's rule. Throughout the gallery (and elsewhere in the castle) you will see the salamander, François' official symbol.

The other major must-see is the **Salle de Bal** ✹✹✹. This 30m (98-ft.) long ballroom is a feast of light and color; the frescos by Primaticcio and Nicolo dell'Abate have been completely restored, and their rich hues radiate like they were painted yesterday. Huge windows let in light from both sides of this long room; the monumental fireplace at the far end was designed by 16th-century architect Philibert Delorme.

You'll also want to visit the **Royal Apartments** ✹✹, which have been decorated and redecorated by successive monarchs. Louis XIII was born in the **Salon Louis XIII** ✹, a fact that is symbolized in the ceiling mural showing Love riding a dolphin. Though several different queens slept in the **Chambre de**

Tours, Guided & Otherwise

You can visit most of the castle's highlights on the Grands Appartements circuit, which includes the royal apartments, the pope's apartments, and the Galerie de Diane. For this circuit, you can wander about on your own or with an English-language **audioguide** (included in ticket, 1€ if you are under 18 and get in free), but there are other parts, like the Musée Napoléon and the Petits Appartements, that you can only access via a guided tour. You can buy a combined entry to the chateau and one or two tours (see prices above); ask at the information desk when you arrive what tours are available, as the schedule changes daily.

Fontainebleau

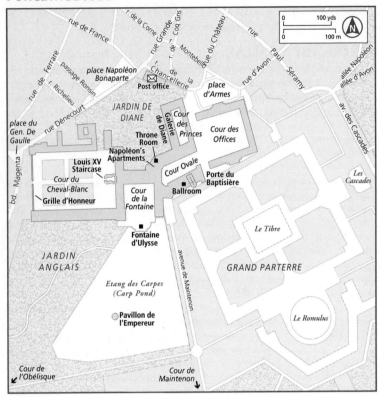

l'Impératrice ★★, its current set-up reflects the epoch of Empress Josephine (Napoleon's first wife). The sumptuous bed, crowned in gilded walnut and covered in embroidered silk, was made for Marie Antoinette in 1787. The queen would never see it; the Revolution exploded before she could arrange a royal visit to the château. Napoleon transformed the Kings' bedroom into the **Salle du Trône** ★, or Throne Room. Since several centuries worth of kings, from Henri IV to Louis XVI slept here, the decor is a mix of styles: The throne and other furnishings are Empire, the folding chairs are Louis XVI, and the ceiling murals date from the 17th and 18th centuries.

You can learn more about the Emperor at the **Musée Napoléon 1er** ★, located in the Louis XV wing (guided visits only), where you'll see historic memorabilia and artwork relating to his reign, like the tent he slept in during military campaigns, and a remarkable mechanical desk. The **Petits Appartements,** Napoleon's private apartments can also be visited, but only on a guided tour (see box).

TOURING THE GARDENS

It is not the large spaces, but the small ones that are the most interesting in this vast garden and park. The formal gardens, with their classic, geometric perspective, must have been beautiful when André Le Nôtre put his hand to them in the 17th

---

When to Visit & When Not To

The gardens are only open from April through October; the flowers are at their most colorful in the spring. The irises are in bloom in May and June, which is when the crowds are the thickest, but the garden is beautiful throughout the season, so for a more serene visit, try to go in summer or fall. Also, it is best avoid weekends, when the gardens get a double dose of both foreign and local tourists.

---

century, but today, though well-kempt, they have been denuded of their elaborate boxwood designs and bowers and look somewhat arid. On the other hand, the additional green spaces to the north and west of the palace are quite lovely. The **Garden of Diane** ✹, a quiet spot of green on the north side of the castle, was created during the time of François I, and centers around a statue of the goddess surrounded by four dogs. Back in the day, it was filled with bronze copies of Roman sculptures, which today can be seen in the Galerie des Cerfs. The **English Garden** ✹, complete with an artificial stream and lush groves of tall trees, was added by Napoleon. The vast **Carp Pond** ✹, which extends directly from the south side of the **Cour de la Fontaine,** has a small island in the center with a small pavilion where an afternoon snack would be served to the royal residents. Surrounding the gardens and its park is the enormous **Fontainebleau Forest** ✹✹, which, if you have the wherewithal, is definitely worth the visit. You can rent bikes at the tourist office (see below) or **A La Petite Reine** (32 rue des Sablons, Fontainebleau; ☎ 01 60 74 57 57; www.alapetitereine.com); there are both paved and unpaved bike trails throughout.

How to get there: Trains (Transilien; ☎ 08 91 36 20 20, .24€ per minute; www.transilien.fr; 35–42 min.; 7.80€ adults, 3.90€ ages 4–10 one-way) will get you from Gare de Bercy (right next to Gare de Lyon) to the Fontainebleau Avon station (there is about one train an hour, except during rush hour, when there are several), from which you will need to take a short **bus** ride (line 1, direction "Château"; 1.60€). You can save about 5€ and some time by buying a *forfait* (for-*fay*) or package ticket at any SNCF train station or Transilien RER station, which includes train and bus fare and the entry fee for the Grands Appartements circuit at the château. The package costs 23€ for adults, 17€ for youths 10 to 17, and 8.10€ for kids 4 to 9 (under 4 rides free).

Visitor information: Fontainebleau Tourist Office (4 rue Royale, Fontainebleau; ☎ 01 60 74 99 99; www.fontainebleau-tourisme.com).

GIVERNY

In 1883, Claude Monet and his family moved to a tiny town north of Paris called Giverny, where they rented a house that came with almost 1 hectare (2½ acres) of land. He didn't know it then, but he would spend the rest of his life there, painting scenes from the fabulous garden that he would create out of the grassy slope behind his house. Today, the **Fondation Claude Monet à Giverny** ✹✹ (84 rue Claude Monet, Giverny; ☎ 02 32 51 28 21; www.fondation-monet.com; 5.50€

adults, 4€ students 12–25, 3€ ages 7–12, free under 7; Apr–Oct Tues–Sun 9:30am–6pm) is open to the public, and for a small fee, you too can wander in and out of the brilliant flower beds, lush bowers, and shady arbors that inspired this impressionist master. What you'll quickly realize is that Monet wasn't just a painter, he was also a gifted gardener. His dual talents complemented each other completely; by the end of his life, the garden was just as much a work of art as the paintings, or perhaps they were the paintings. If you have already visited the Orangerie in Paris, and seen his magical Nympheas, or water lilies, spread across huge canvases in two oval-shaped rooms, in a way, you have already visited this garden; they were painted here, with the aim of faithfully re-creating the feeling you would have if you were looking at the same flowers at Giverny.

There are actually two gardens here: The first and closest to the house is the **Clos Normand** ✪✪, a French-style garden that is resolutely orderly and geometric, despite the riot of colors. Gladioli, larkspur, phlox, daisies, and asters, among other flowers, clamor for your attention; irises and oriental poppies brighten the western lawn. Monet painted here, but his most famous paintings, the endless water lily series, were born in the **Water Garden** ✪✪✪, farther down the slope. Monet bought this piece of property in 1893 with the intention of building a garden that resembled those in the Japanese prints he collected. It was a long process: Just getting permission to dig the ponds took a year or so, but by 1895, he had built the ornate **Japanese bridge** ✪ that figures prominently in several of his canvases. Today the garden looks much as it did when Monet was immortalizing it. Willows weep quietly into the ponds, heather, ferns, azaleas, and rhododendrons carpet the banks. The garden is thick with plant life, including several Japanese species and a large stand of bamboo. This garden was a sanctuary for the painter, who came here to contemplate and explore one of his favorite subjects: the complex interplay of water and light. His other favorite subject, of course, was the flowers themselves, which star in so many of his works.

In 1966, the house and gardens was bequeathed to France's Académie des Beaux-Arts by Monet's son Michel and has been undergoing restorations ever since. **Monet's house** ✪ is now open to visitors who view the artist's living spaces as well as his Japanese print collection. The studio where he created the huge canvases in the Orangerie now houses the boutique.

The only downside to visiting this fascinating spot is that it will be virtually impossible to experience the gardens as Monet did—more or less alone. This is an extremely popular outing for both individuals and tour groups, and in the spring, if you don't arrive right at the opening or just before closing, the ambience will be less than tranquil, to put it mildly (see the "When to Visit & When Not To" box, above). Not surprisingly, picnics are not allowed in the gardens, so you'll have to take yours elsewhere, or eat in the small restaurant (Les Nympheas) right next to the foundation.

How to get there: Trains (SNCF; ☎ 3635, .34€ per minute; www.voyages-sncf.com; 47–52 min.; 12€ one-way) leave two or three times per hour from the Gare St-Lazare train station to Vernon, the closest stop to Giverny, which is about 5km (3 miles) away. From Vernon you can either take a shuttle bus (3€ round-trip), or just walk along the Seine on the marked path.

Visitor information: Fondation Claude Monet à Giverny (84 rue Claude Monet, Giverny; ☎ 02 32 51 28 21; www.fondation-monet.com).

DISNEYLAND PARIS

It isn't particularly French, but there's no denying that **Disneyland Paris** ✰ (Marne-la-Vallée; ☎ 08 25 808 500, .15€ per minute; www.disneylandparis.com; hours vary, but generally Disneyland Park daily from 9am/10am to 7–10pm, Disney Studios daily 10am–7pm, call or see website for latest schedule) is a fun place to visit. To be honest, if I'd traveled many leagues to come to France, I would be hard-pressed to spend part of my precious vacation in such an utterly American environment. On the other hand, Disneyland comes in handy as a sightseeing tradeoff for reluctant kid travelers. Once there, even curmudgeons like myself cannot resist getting swept up by the fun rides and the good cheer; in spite of yourself, you're bound to have a good time, even if you'd secretly rather be reading a book in a Parisian cafe.

In the U.S., there is Disneyland and Disney World; in France, you could call it Disney Universe. There are two parks in this giant resort, the classic Disneyland, complete with the Matterhorn and Space Mountain, and Disney Studios, where you can try your hand at cinematography or delve into the world of cartoons. But the parks are just the beginning of your excellent adventure in Marne-la-Vallée: There are also seven, count 'em seven, hotels, a golf course, a spa, tennis courts, and an ice skating rink, not to mention Disney Village, with its boutiques, restaurants, discotheque, cinema, and IMAX theater. For the purposes of this guide, we'll just stick with parks. In general, Disneyland is a better choice for the under-7 crowd; though even the little ones will still get a kick out of the cartoon attractions at Disney Studios.

DISNEYLAND PARK

Isn't it comforting that some things never change? Here you are in France, and yet there is Frontierland, Adventureland, and Fantasyland, just the way you remember them back home. Okay, not exactly perhaps, for one thing, everyone's speaking French. And Japanese. And Bulgarian, Hindi, and Farsi. The success of this resort is its international appeal; finally, you don't have to come to North America to experience the Disney magic. When you enter the park, you'll step right into **Main Street USA,** that utopian rendition of early-20th-century America, complete with horse and buggies and barber-shop quartets. Here you'll find the **information center** as well as a train, which leaves from Main Street Station. The train, which does a circuit around the park, will whisk you off to **Frontierland,** where you'll find a paddle-wheel steamboat, a petting zoo, and the Lucky Nugget saloon, among other things. Next, you'll chug through **Adventureland,** with old favorites like the Swiss Family Robinson treehouse and the Pirates of the Caribbean, as well as newer attractions like Aladdin's Oriental Palace. Onward towards **Fantasyland** with Sleeping Beauty's Castle (Le Château de Belle au Bois Dormant), whizzing teacups, flying Dumbos, and "It's a Small World." Last stop is **Discoveryland,** home of Space Mountain and the submarine Nautilus, as well as "Buzz Lightyear's Lazer Blast." There are parades virtually every day at 4pm on Main Street, and various shows like a reduced version of The Lion King, or the energetic Tarzan Encounter, run throughout the day.

Tickets & Passes

Ticket prices depend on how old you are, how much you want to do, and how long you want to stay at the resort. A **1-Day/1-Park** pass (49€ adults and children over 11, 41€ ages 3–11, free under 3) gives you access to all attractions at either Disneyland or Disney Studios for the entire day. A **1-Day "Park Hopper"** pass (59€ adults and children over 11, 51€ ages 3–11, free under 3) lets you wander in and out of both parks for the entire day. If you want to spread out your visit, opt for the **2-Day "Park Hopper"** pass (108€ adults and children over 11, 92€ ages 3–11, free under 3) or the **3-Day "Park Hopper"** pass (134€ adults and children over 11, 114€ ages 3–11, free under 3). Be sure to check the website for **seasonal promotions and discounts,** which can lop 10% to 20% off your costs. There are also a variety of hotel/park packages to choose from, should you want to spend a couple of days with Disney.

DISNEY STUDIOS

Though the primary draw here, of course, is Disneyland Park, Disney Studios makes an interesting alternative for older kids who have already done Disney and are up for something different. Along with films, stunt shows, and parades, the park offers an introduction to the wonders of movie making at Disney Animation Studios and Disney Studio 1. Naturally, there are fun rides here too, like the Tower of Terror (based on the *Twilight Zone* TV show), and the Rock 'n Rollercoaster (featuring Aerosmith tunes).

As mentioned above, there are scads of hotels here—some of the hotels are attractions in themselves. If you have the time/patience/money, give yourself a break and spend the night here, rather than slogging back to Paris late at night after one too many cotton candies.

How to get there: You could arrive by **TGV** (the French railways high-speed train), but a less spectacular and less complicated option is to simply climb on the **RER A** (Transilien; ☎ 08 91 36 20 20, .24€ per minute; www.transilien.fr; 40 min.; 6.45€ adults, 3.20€ ages 4–10 one-way) and take it all the way to its terminus at Marne-la-Vallée–Chessy (just make sure that this is the terminus—the RER A has multiple destinations). When you get out, you'll be about a 5-minute walk from the entrance.

Visitor information: Disneyland Paris Guest Relations (Disneyland Paris, Marne-la-Vallée; ☎ 08 25 808 500, .15€ per minute; www.disneylandparis.com).

12 The Essentials of Planning

NOW WE GET TO THE TOUGH PART: PLANNING YOUR TRIP. DON'T BE frightened, planning a trip to Paris is a snap (if you read this chapter!). Below I supply all the nitty-gritty details you need to have a comfortable, safe and affordable stay in Paris, including websites, phone numbers, and other contact information. First I cover the pretrip planning—when to go, how to book, passport and visa issues for foreign nationals, insurance, advance reading—and then I move on to the essential things you need to know once you've landed at the airport and are ready to take to the streets. At the end of this section, I give a rundown of the basics for travelers with special interests and needs: parents with young children, senior citizens, persons with disabilities, and gay and lesbian travelers.

A good place to start your information quest is at the **Paris Tourist Office** (25 rue des Pyramides, 1st arrond.; ☎ 08 92 68 30 00, 34€ per minute; www.paris info.com; Métro: Pyramides). There's always a multilingual person on the other end of the line when you call (if you'd prefer not to spring for an international call, surf to their comprehensive website). The address listed above is the main office; the phone number and website is the same for all six of their Welcome Centers:

> **Gare de Lyon** (20 blvd. Diderot, 12th arrond.; Métro: Gare de Lyon; closed Sun)
>
> **Gare du Nord** (18 rue Dunkerque, 10th arrond; Métro: Gare du Nord)
>
> **Anvers** (on the median strip facing 72 blvd. Rochechouart, 18th arrond.; Métro: Anvers)
>
> **Paris Expo/Porte de Versailles** (1 place de la Porte de Versailles; 15th arrond; Métro: Porte de Versailles; open only during trade fairs)
>
> **Carrousel du Louvre** (99 rue de Rivoli, beneath the glass pyramid in the courtyard of the Louvre, 1st arrond.; Métro: Palais Royale–Musée du Louvre; also stocks information on the Ile de France region)
>
> **Montmartre Tourist Office** (21 place du Tertre, 18th arrond.; Métro: Abbesses or Anvers)

WHEN TO VISIT

Depending on your outlook, any time can be a good time to visit. If you're an inward type, fond of long walks in the rain and moping about the fate of the world, there's no better backdrop than the wet, gray Paris of wintertime. If you're an optimist, and believe in song lyrics, come in the spring, but bring an umbrella—your smile alone will not keep you dry during the periodic deluges of March and April. If you prefer warmer temperatures, head to the French Riviera; even summer can be turtleneck weather, occasional heat waves notwithstanding.

Are you getting the picture yet? One of the best-kept secrets about Paris is that its weather is almost as bad as London's. In almost any season, you're bound to encounter a good dose of gray skies and at least a little rain. That said, there is one other secret about Parisian weather: The best time to come, weather-wise, is in September and October. I can personally testify that in recent years this period was just lovely—a string of warm, sunny days with a few cool breezes. Makes you wonder why there aren't any famous songs that go "I love Paris in the autumn . . ."

The good news is that it is rarely freezing here, or boiling hot for that matter. In recent years, however, there have been a couple of nasty heat waves; in particular the dreadful canicule of August 2003, which caught everyone by surprise. The city was simply not set up for heat wave conditions; the lack of air-conditioning in hospitals and retirement homes, coupled with a high concentration of older people living on their own, resulted in over 10,000 deaths nationwide, primarily among the elderly. Today, everyone is prepared. The minute the temperature passes 80°F (30°C), public service announcements are everywhere, and the ambulances are at the ready. To reassure tourists, hoteliers all over the city have almost all installed air conditioning by now. Due to the restrictions on altering historic buildings, and the high costs of installation, some hotels simply can't put in a cooling system. But before you cross a hotel off your list because it doesn't have any, just remember that the chances of your being here during another heat wave are slim. If you're visiting in summer, and your hotel is sans A/C, ask for room on a lower floor (remember, heat rises) and/or facing the courtyard so you can open your windows at night, if necessary.

> " The American goes to Paris, always has, and comes back and tells his neighbor, always does, how exorbitant and inhospitable it is, how rapacious and selfish and unaccommodating and unresponsive it is, how dirty and noisy it is—and the next summer his neighbor goes to Paris. "
>
> —Milton Mayer, "Paris as a State of Mind," *New York Times*

Below is a chart that will give a general idea of Parisian temperatures. As you can see, they are generally pretty mild, despite the rain.

	Jan	Feb	Mar	Apr	May	June	July	Aug	Sept	Oct	Nov	Dec
Temp. °F	43/	45/	52/	57/	64/	70/	75/	75/	70/	59/	48/	45/
(Max & Min)	34	34	37	43	48	54	57	57	52	46	39	36
Temp. °C	6/	7/	11/	14/	18/	21/	24/	24/	21/	15/	9/	7/
(Max & Min)	1	1	3	6	9	12	14	14	11	8	4	2
Days of Precipitation	10	9	10	9	10	9	8	7	9	10	10	11

Culturally, Paris seethes with excitement from September through May, when theaters, concert halls, and nightspots bubble and brew. By June, things start to slow down significantly though, and in July and August, the scene comes to a crashing halt as millions of tired Parisians, fed up with gray skies, head south to storm the Mediterranean beaches. Despite the exodus, however, summertime is a great time for music festivals in parks and gardens around town; see the events calendar below for a few of the highlights.

So what it boils down to is this: There are things to do in Paris year-round, but if you're planning on spending time outdoors, avoid chilly winter and early spring (and bring your umbrella at any other time of year). Despite the unpredictable weather, summer can be a nice time to visit—but the city will be pretty dead, top restaurants shuttered, and many of the people on the streets will be fellow tourists. The upside to a summer visit is that many hotels are 20% to 40% less expensive (except those in the major tourist areas). Prices stay pretty even the rest of the year, though rates in some hotels shoot up when the trade shows come to town.

Paris's Visit-Worthy Annual Events

Being both the largest French city and the capital of the country, Paris boasts an end-less stream of festivals, concerts, and other cultural happenings throughout the year. It may not be a number-one priority, but when planning your visit, you might want to take into consideration some of these annual events. Below is just a sampling of what's on offer; for a full range, stop by a kiosk and pick either of the two weekly listings magazines, l'Officiel des Spectacles or Pariscope, or invest in a copy of Télérama, which comes with a pull-out listings section. All three magazines come out on Wednesdays. The Paris Tourist Office website (www.parisinfo.com) also has a good listing, if you'd like to plan ahead.

January

New Year's Eve: Like Christmas, New Year's in Paris is mostly about eating—as in the best of the best. Oysters, foie gras, caviar, lobster, and champagne figure prominently on menus; restaurants all over town pull out all the stops, offering special prix-fixe gourmet pig-outs. For a good list of this year's riches (and even some menus), visit the tourist office's website: www.parisinfo.com and click on the "What's On" submenu.

La Fête des Rois (Epiphany): Every year for the entire month, bakeries all around town offer the scrumptious galette des rois, an airy cake filled with almond paste. A fève, a small piece of ceramic (often in the form of a person) is hidden inside, so watch your teeth—the one who finds it gets to wear a paper crown that comes with the cake. There are tiny two-person cakes available.

February

Salon de l'Agriculture: In a country where agriculture is a major source of revenue, the annual agricultural fair is a big event. Farmers and food producers from small dairy operations to huge multina-tional conglomerates converge on the Parc des Expositions at the Port de Versailles to show their wares; visitors can taste samples and see prize livestock. Politicos of all stripes make a pilgrimage here to demonstrate their loyalty to the agricultural community—even President Nicolas Sarkozy shows up to have his photo snapped with prize-winning heifers. The fair usually falls during the last week of February. Details and entry fees at www.salon-agriculture.com.

April

Grandes Eaux Musicales: The magnificent fountains of Versailles play to the music of Jean-Baptiste Lully (Louis XIV's pet composer) in choreographed displays, "performed" several times a day starting in April and running through October. For a schedule and details of other concerts and light shows in the gardens during this period, visit www.chateauversailles-spectacles.fr.

The Paris Marathon: Around 35,000 run-ners gathered on the Champs Elysées for the 2008 edition of this international sporting event, which winds around the city's major monuments. The race generally happens on the first or second Sunday of April; enrollment starts September 1, see the website, www.parismarathon.com, for info.

Foire de Paris: This ain't no ordinary fair. This is a monster home, travel, and leisure show with 30 hectares (74 acres) of exposition space and over 700,000 visitors, all looking to buy the perfect couch, chimney, swimming pool, home cinema, motor home, trekking vacation . . . you get the idea. An annual pilgrimage for most Parisians, an interesting visit for vacationers. The 2009 Foire is set for April 29 to May 10; surf the official website for details and ticketing information: www.foiredeparis.fr.

May–June

The French Open: The French refer to this annual international tennis tournament simply as Roland-Garros, the name of the stadium on edge of the 16th arrondissement (in the Bois de Boulogne) where the matches take place. It's considered by some to be the world's greatest clay court tennis tournament. The 2009 Open is scheduled for May 24 to June 7; tickets go on sale in November. Visit the website (www.fft.fr/rolandgarros) and see p. 227 for more details.

Foire St-Germain: An eclectic mix of antiques, poetry, and literature, as well as theater and music, this 31-year-old event invades place St-Sulpice and the surrounding neighborhood with events as diverse as a book market, poetry market, an antiques fair, plays, art expos, and workshops—all free of charge. The festival generally gets going at the end of May and lasts through June. Details at www.foiresaintgermain.org.

June

Fête de la Musique: The entire nation explodes in music on June 21, the summer solstice. Concerts of every imaginable type of music run all day (and all night)

all over the city. They include everything from rock bands in crowded bars, to classical music concerts in landmark churches. All concerts are free; be prepared for huge crowds. For a more or less complete schedule, visit the website: http://fetedelamusique.culture.fr.

La Goutte d'Or en Fête: A multicultural collage of music, dance, theater, and art held during the last week in June in La Goutte d'Or in the 18th arrondissement—one of Paris's most culturally diverse neighborhoods. All events are free. www.gouttedorenfete.org.

Gay Pride Parade (Marche des Fiertés): Fantastic floats and fabulous drag queens accompany some 800,000 marchers, many sporting spectacular costumes. The route changes every year, consult the website at http://marche.inter-lgbt.org for a map. The big day is usually at the end of June; balls and parties abound during parade week—see listings on www.legayparis.com.

June–July

Paris Jazz Festival: Starting around the second week of June and lasting through most of July, there are free concerts in the Parc Floral (you must pay the park entry, 5€), a lovely garden in the Bois de Vincennes. Big names play here; find the complete program at www.paris.fr.

Festival Chopin: Outdoor concert series organized by the Chopin Society, held in one of the city's most beautiful gardens: the Parc de Bagatelle in the Bois de Boulogne. The festival generally runs from mid-June to mid July; www.frederic-chopin.com.

July

Bastille Day: On July 14, 1789, Parisians stormed the Bastille, setting off the French Revolution. Join the festivities, which start on the 13th with balls and parties in fire stations all over town, then arrive early the next day on the Champs Elysées for the parade (which starts at

10am). Top off the evening with a fabulous fireworks display in front of (and on) the Eiffel Tower. There are huge crowds, and you won't see most of the fireworks unless you're either on the Champs de Mars or at Trocadéro, but if you can find yourself a good view of the tower from a less popular spot, you'll still get a good dose of excellent pyrotechnics.

Tour de France: By the time this legendary bicycle race makes it to Paris, everyone usually knows who is going to win, but who cares? This is a chance to see history in the making—and hundreds of world-class cyclists racing around the city's major monuments. The race finishes on the Champs Elysées. The details and route maps can be found at www.letour.fr; also see p. 227 for more info.

July–August

Paris Quartier d'Eté: Since 1989 the city has hosted this citywide fiesta of mostly outdoor events in gardens, parks, and monuments like the Tuileries Garden and the Grand Palais. Contemporary music, theater, and dance are on offer, as well as storytelling, art installations, films, and workshops. Details of this year's program (which runs from mid-July to mid-Aug) are available at www.quartierdete.com.

Les Etés de la Danse: The central hall of the Grand Palais is so impressive you could almost forget that you're here to watch a performance. This new dance fest, which runs for 2 weeks at the end of July and the beginning of August, highlights an invited company—in 2008 it was Les Grands Ballets Canadiens. www.lesetesde ladanse.com.

Paris Plage: Tons of sand are barged in to create a miniresort on the riverbank of the Seine, complete with a beach, lounge chairs, palm trees, and suntanned bodies. Since its inception in 2002 this faux beach has been an enormous success; in 2008 there were actually three beaches: one at the Bassin de la Villette, on the Quai de la Gare in front of the Bibliotheque François

Mitterand, and the original on the quays between the Ile St-Louis and the Louvre. Each year new features are added (cafes, concerts, movies, fitness areas, and so on). Expect huge crowds on the weekends.

August

Cinéma au Clair de Lune: During most of the month of August, films are shown outdoors in various parks and squares in Paris (Butte Montmartre, Parc André Citroën, place des Vosges, among others) at around 9:30pm. For this year's program, visit http://clairdelune.forumdesimages.fr.

August–September

Classique au Vert: Held in the Parc Floral in the Parc de Vincennes, this classical music festival serves up free concerts every weekend from the beginning of September to the end of August (park entrance 5€). More info at www.paris.fr.

September

Jazz à La Villette: One of the city's best jazz festivals, held at the Parc de la Villette way out in the 19th arrondissement during the first 2 weeks of September. The 2008 festival included several dance/jazz collaborations between choreographers and jazz artists like Archie Shep and Joshua Redman. See the program at www.jazzalavillette.com.

Journées Européennes du Patrimoine: During one weekend in mid-September, dozens of historic monuments that are usually closed to the public open their doors to one and all. That means fabulous mansions like the Hôtel de Sully, the Hôtel de Ville (city hall), La Sorbonne, and the like are open. Visit the website for a detailed program—www.journeesdu patrimoine.culture.fr, or keep an eye on local news-papers and listings magazines.

October

Nuit Blanche: The name of this newish event (another brainchild of mayor Bertrand Delanoë), loosely translates as "all-nighter," which is exactly what it is. A mega-street party that runs from dusk until dawn, Nuit Blanche celebrates contemporary art and music in multiple venues (museums, galleries, gardens, monuments) around the city. It usually falls during the first weekend in October; see the program for exact dates at www.paris.fr.

Fête des Vendanges de Montmartre: There are still a couple of vineyards in Montmartre, and every year the beginning of the annual grape-picking season is celebrated with a ceremony and followed by a parade, a concert, and fireworks above the Sacré Coeur. Food stands also set up in the place du Tertre for sampling regional specialties. For dates and program, visit www.fetedesvendangesde montmartre.com.

Paris Motor Show: A major international auto show, with hundreds of brands and hundreds of thousands of visitors. A premiere platform for automobile makers to unveil their latest models, concept cars, and media campaigns, it is held in the exposition halls at the Porte de Versailles. Details and dates at www.mondial-automobile.com.

December

Festival d'Art Sacré de la Ville de Paris: Annual sacred music festival in churches and other venues throughout the month around Paris. Works by composers such as Handel, Mendelssohn, Poulenc, and Messaien are performed at sites like St-Roch and St-Eustache and the Musée d'Art et d'Histoire de Judaïsme. All tickets are 10€; more details at www.festivaldart sacre.new.fr.

Christmas Illuminations: The Champs Elysées glimmers and glitters with lighting displays all up and down the avenue; the Grands Magasins (Printemps and Galeries Lafayette) compete to see who can come up with the most amazing Christmas light designs on the sides of their buildings; Au Bon Marché goes all out with animated dolls and puppets in its windows.

FINDING A GOOD AIRFARE TO PARIS

At press time, the rising price of oil had sent airline ticket prices skyward, with rates fluctuating according to the current cost per barrel. In addition, airline companies had taken to tacking on extra charges (fuel surcharges, in particular) to make up for their loss of revenue. The important thing to remember is that despite the dismal economic facts of life, if you look hard enough, you are bound to find promotional pricing or discounts that will take some of the pressure off your pocketbook. Your strategy for finding the airfare of your dreams should include the following steps:

1. **Book early.** Airlines have a desperate need to know if their planes are filled and reward passengers who sign up in advance with special promotional prices. The cheap seats come in limited quantities, so in this case, the early bird definitely gets the worm. That said, there is such a thing as too early; if you book more than 4 months in advance, you may actually pay more (except for peak dates).

2. **Search online.** The biggest search stars on the Web these days—**Expedia, Orbitz,** and **Travelocity**—are sturdy and reliable ways of finding good fares, but they don't cover some discount carriers. To make sure you haven't missed a good deal, try some of the alternate search engines like **Sidestep.com, Kayak.com,** or **Mobissimo.com,** all of which search airline websites directly, don't add service charges, and often find fares that the larger websites miss.

(Consider also checking a "consolidator" website; see point #6, below.) U.S. carriers like **American Airlines** (☎ 800/433-7300; www.aa.com), **Delta Air Lines** (☎ 800 241-4141; www.delta.com), **United Airlines** (☎ 800/538-2929; www.united.com), and **Continental Airlines** (☎ 800/231-0856; www.continental.com) all have direct flights to Paris from U.S. cities, as do **Air France, British Airways** (☎ 800/247-9297; www.ba.com), and **Air India** (☎ 800/223-7776; www.airindia.com). **Air Canada** (☎ 888/247-2262; www.aircanada.com) has direct flights from Toronto and Montreal. **Travelers from the U.K.** have it better, not only because the flight is not as long, but also because of the discount carriers that fly from multiple British destinations to Paris (see below). Students can get great deals through student travel agency websites like **Student Universe** (www.studentuniverse.com) and **STA Travel** (www.statravel.com). Some intrepid travelers are flexible enough with their itinerary to use alternative booking websites, such Skyauction.com, an eBay-like site where you can bid for tickets.

3. **Consider discount carriers to get to an international hub.** While low-cost airlines like Southwest and Ryanair have flourished in the U.S. and many European countries, there isn't a single one based in France, and at press time, there weren't any North American discount carriers that make transcontinental flights to Paris. If you're flying from Britain, however, you can choose from several low-cost carriers with Paris connections like **Ryanair** (www.ryanair.com), **EasyJet** (www.easyjet.com), and **bmibaby** (www.bmibaby.com). North Americans who are considering flying to London to take advantage of these airlines (not a bad strategy, as London remains the cheapest European gateway from the U.S.) should factor in the time and energy it will take. Hopping the pond and then the channel may require that you change planes and possibly airports. A wiser use of low-cost airlines might be to get yourself to the closest international airport hub to your hometown. In general, the least expensive flights from the U.S. to Paris depart from the New York City area. You'll sometimes find discounted rates out of Atlanta, Boston, Los Angeles (via Air Tahiti Nui, in particular), Miami, and Chicago as well. Check airlines like **JetBlue** (☎ 800/JETBLUE; www.jetblue.com), **Southwest** (☎ 800/435-9792; www.southwest.com), **USA3000** (☎ 877/872-3000; www.usa3000.com), and **AirTran** (☎ 800/247-8726; www.airtran.com) for a fare deal near you to one of these more attractive cities.

4. **Fly when others don't.** Rates are generally cheaper for midweek flights, especially if you stay over a Saturday night. If possible, try to book your trip in low season (approximately Oct–Mar) when airfares can be as much as half of what they would cost during spring and summer.

5. **Book at the right time.** It sounds strange, but you can often save money by booking your flight at 3am. That's because unpaid reservations are flushed out of the system at midnight, and since airfares are based on supply and demand, often prices sink when the system becomes aware of an increase in supply. As well, consider booking on a Wednesday, the day when the airfare sales that popped on Monday and Tuesday are being matched by other carriers. Be sure to watch travel websites like Frommers.com and SmarterTravel.com, which highlight fare sales.

Package Deals vs. Booking Independently

There area some great hotel-airfare packages out there, but you need to know where to look. For more information on this tantalizing subject, see our accommodations chapter, p. 22. *And remember:* Packages really only work for couples. Solo travelers will be charged "single supplements" which inevitably erase any savings.

---

6. **Try booking through a consolidator.** These companies buy tickets in bulk passing along the savings to their customers. Start by looking in the Sunday newspaper travel sections; U.S. travelers might look at the *New York Times,* the *Los Angeles Times,* and the *Miami Herald.* Some of the larger U.S. consolidator websites are **Cheapflights.com** and **Airlineconsolidator.com;** Canadian travelers can visit **Airticketsdirect.com.** If you reside in Europe, one of the best ways to find a consolidator that services your area is to go to the British **Cheapflights** website (www.cheapflights.co.uk), which serves as a clearinghouse for consolidators both large and small. Be careful though: Some charge outrageous change fees, so read the fine print before you book.

ENTRY REQUIREMENTS

One of the less tantalizing—but essential—parts of any traveler's life is official paperwork. Mastering, or at least semi-understanding passport, visa, and customs regulations will help speed you through those long lines at the airport, and get you on the plane. Below are the bare essentials; for more detailed information, call or visit the websites of the agencies listed in each section.

VISAS

VISITORS WHO ARE CITIZENS OR HAVE PERMANENT STATUS IN THE EUROPEAN UNION If you are a legal resident of a country that is in the European Union, in theory you don't even need to bring your passport, just a national ID card (in reality, U.K. citizens should bring theirs to make sure they can get back home).

As of this writing, citizens of the United States, Australia, Canada, and New Zealand with a valid passport are allowed to stay in France for up to 90 days without a visa. This is also true for most other non–E.U. nations in Europe. For specifics, visit the **French Foreign Ministry** website (www.diplomatie.gouv.fr/en; click on "Going to France"), or visit a French Consulate website before you leave home. U.S. residents can visit www.ambafrance-us.org; Canadians can go to www.ambafrance-ca.org; Australians can visit www.ambafrance-au.org; and British citizens, www.ambafrance-uk.org. If you do need a visa (because you're staying long-term in France), apply as soon as possible; French bureaucracy is infamous for its red tape and lethargic pace.

MEDICAL REQUIREMENTS

No inoculations or vaccinations are required to enter France, unless you're arriving from an area that's suffering from an epidemic (cholera or yellow fever, for example). A valid, signed prescription is required for those travelers in need of medical treatment that involves **narcotics,** and it's a good idea to bring one for any prescription medicine you need to use while you are traveling. Those travelers in need of **syringe-administered medications** should contact the French Consulate to determine if they need a special permit. It is extremely important to obtain the correct documentation in these cases as illegal possession of each carries significant penalties in France.

CUSTOMS: WHAT YOU CAN BRING IN & WHAT YOU CAN TAKE HOME

Strict regulations govern what can be brought into and taken out of France (for details on French customs, visit www.douane.gouv.fr). Keep in mind that these regulations extend to food products and plants, most of which are prohibited—but don't worry, most countries will let you take back a box of chocolates to Aunt Maude. Below is a chart showing certain items non-E.U. visitors may bring into and take out of France (in essence, citizens of E.U. countries can bring home what

Customs Limits

	What You Can Bring into France	What You Can Take out of France
Currency	No limit, but if you bring in more than 10,000€, you must file a report with the French customs office	No limit, but if you take out more than 10,000€, you must file a report with the French customs office
Tobacco	200 cigarettes, or 100 cigarillos, or 50 cigars, or 250 grams of loose tobacco	*US citizens:* 200 cigarettes and 50 cigars *Canadian citizens:* 200 cigarettes and 50 cigars or cigarillos and 200g of tobacco and 200 tobacco sticks *Australian citizens:* 250 cigarettes or 250g of tobacco products *New Zealand citizens:* 200 cigarettes, 50 cigars, or 250g of tobacco; or a mix of all three weighing no more than 250g
Alcoholic Beverages	2 liters of wine or under 22-proof liquor, or 1 liter of over 22-proof liquor	*US citizens:* 1 liter of wine or 1 liter of liquor *Canadian citizens:* 1.14 liters of liquor or 1.5 liters of wine *Australian citizens:* 2.25 liters of alcoholic beverage *New Zealand citizens:* 4.5 liters of wine or beer and 3 bottles of no more than 1.125 liters liquor spirits
Other goods (gifts)	Over 15, 175€ worth of goods; under 15, 90€	*US citizens:* $800 worth of goods *Canadian citizens:* C$750 worth of goods *Australian citizens:* over 18, A$900 worth of goods, under 18, A$450 *New Zealand citizens:* NZ$700 worth of goods

they want as long it is for their personal use, and they have already paid all taxes and duty; U.K. citizens may be required to show proof that their goods are for personal use if they bring in large quantities). If you want to be absolutely sure of what you can bring home without getting your goodies confiscated at the airport (or slapped with a duty charge), check with your home country's customs office. In the U.S., the **U.S. Customs Service** has a helpful brochure on its website (www.customs.gov) called "Know Before You Go." For a summary of Canadian rules, the **Canadian Border Services Agency** has a website (go to www.cbsa-asfc.gc.ca and click on "Travellers"); look for "I Declare." The **Australian Customs Service** (www.customs.gov.au) also has a brochure, as does the **New Zealand Customs Service** (www.customs.govt.nz).

TRAVELING FROM PARIS TO OTHER PARTS OF FRANCE

BY AIR

If you're really strapped for time, you can fly to other parts of the country, but this can get very expensive if you go with a major carrier. Fortunately, the boom in discount airlines in Europe has intra-France flying way more attractive. So attractive, in fact, that **Air France** now is competing with deep discounts on its French website. Go to www.airfrance.fr and click on "promotions"; you can find some excellent deals here, but you'll have to navigate in French. Next, compare those prices with the rates you'll find at www.wegolo.com which tracks such airlines as **Ryanair** and **Easyjet.** At press time, those were the only two low-cost carriers with flights within France, but low-cost routes and airlines change frequently, so check around for others.

BY TRAIN

Your best bet for traveling in France is the train. France has an excellent railway system. The speediest and most comfortable network is the **TGV** *(train à grande vitesse),* high-speed trains that will whoosh you to your destination in half the time it would take you to drive. Regional trains can be a little hit and miss—if you're lucky you'll get a shiny new number, but wagons on some of the less popular lines can be pretty old. In general, trains do run on schedule and offer a low-stress mode of transportation, particularly if you have young kids who hate being in the car.

If you anticipate doing a lot of train travel, a **train pass** is a good option, but be sure to buy it before you leave your home country. For more information on Eurail and other train passes, visit **Eurail** (www.eurail.com) or **Rail Europe** (www.raileurope.com).

You don't have to have a pass, though. Unless you're traveling during a national holiday, train tickets are easily reserved and purchased, even a few days ahead of time, at any office of the **French National Railway** (the **SNCF,** which has ticket windows at any of Paris's half dozen train stations), or on their website: www.voyages-sncf.com, which also posts terrific discounts. Trips to popular destinations tend to be more expensive, especially on weekends and holidays; in general the earlier you reserve, the better price you'll get. If you have children, and you'll be making more than two train trips in France, consider buying a **Carte Enfant**

Plus (www.enfantplus-sncf.com), which gives a 25% to 50% discount for up to four adults traveling with the child in question (the child rides free up to 4 years old, 50% 4–12). It costs 70€ for the year, but it could pay for itself in one or two trips. *Note:* 50% discount seats are limited in number and nonexistent during peak holiday periods; reserve ahead to get the best rates. Two other cards, the **Carte 12–25** (www.12-25-sncf.com, for ages 12–25, 49€) and **Carte Senior** (www. seniorsncf.com, for the over-60 set, 56€) operate on the same principal, though there is no discount for companions. You can use the last two cards for reductions on travel to other European countries as well.

BY CAR

I wouldn't recommend driving in Paris to my worst enemy, but renting a car and driving around France can be a lovely way to see the country. All of the major car-rental companies have offices here (see below), but you'll often get better deals if you reserve before you leave home. **AutoEurope** (www.autoeurope.com) is an excellent source for discounted rentals. Check its prices against:

> **Avis:** ☎ 08 20 05 05 05; www.avis.com
> **Budget:** ☎ 08 25 00 35 64; www.budget.com
> **Europcar:** ☎ 08 25 358 358; www.europcar.com
> **Hertz:** ☎ 08 25 861 861; www.hertz.com
> **Rent-a-Car:** ☎ 08 91 700 200; www.rentacar.fr
> **Thrifty:** ☎ 01 45 60 00 21; www.thrifty.com

Before you step on the gas, at the very least, try to get a hold of a list of international road signs; your rental agency should have one. Driving in France is not substantially different from driving in most English-speaking countries (though British travelers will have to get used to driving on the "wrong" side of the road); you'll mainly have to get used to French drivers, who tend to zoom around with what the more timid among us would call reckless abandon. Truthfully, since the installation of radars a year or so ago, drivers have become much more well-behaved; you too should pay attention to speed limits or risk a steep fine. The two biggest driving differences: *priorité à droite,* which means priority is always given to vehicles approaching from the right at intersections, unless otherwise indicated; and the fondness for roundabouts. Rule number one for these tricky roads: The person getting into the roundabout does *not* have priority. Rule number two: Be sure to take a look at the sign posted before the roundabout that indicates which exit goes in what direction so that you'll be prepared when its time to get off. The good news is that if you miss your turnoff, you can just circle around until you figure out where it is.

TRAVELING FROM PARIS TO OTHER PARTS OF EUROPE

BY AIR

If you can, by all means take advantage of the ongoing low-cost airline revolution. Even though French attempts at discount airlines have crashed and burned, other European discount carriers fly from Paris, including **Air Berlin** (www.airberlin. com), **Air Europa** (www.aireuropa.com), and **Sky Europe** (www.skyeurope.com).

For a more complete list, search the helpful **Independent Traveler** website (www.independenttraveler.com). The leader in low-cost airlines in Europe is the U.K.; **Ryanair** (www.ryanair.com) not only has ridiculously cheap flights from the U.K. to Paris but also from Paris to Rome, Stockholm, and Madrid, among other destinations. **EasyJet** (www.easyjet.com), which also offers great fares to and from the U.K., also flies from Paris to Berlin, Milan, and Athens, among other cities. Other discount travel booking websites you may want to visit include: **Anyway.com** (www.anyway.com), **Nouvelles Frontieres** (www.nouvelles-frontieres. com), and the French version of **Lastminute.com** (www.lastminute.fr). A few travel search websites also specialize in low-cost carriers, including **Skyscanner.net, wegolo.com, Travelsupermarket.com**, and **Whichbudget.com.**

BY TRAIN

Trains are also a feasible option. The French train network (the SNCF, see above) connects to those of all neighboring countries, including the U.K. The **Eurostar** (www.eurostar.com), which passes under the channel for a nerve-wracking 20 minutes, will get you from the Gare du Nord to Saint Pancras Station, London in just 2½ hours, which when you factor in getting to and from the airports, is the same or less than by plane. If London is your destination, know that even though the regular ticket price is high (231€ one-way!), there are scads of discounts available—at press time there was a special deal with a round-trip for 77€. Staying on the continent is easier on the budget: Only an hour and a quarter away by high speed train, Brussels, for example, is only 82€ and discounts go down to 25€ if you book online. Visit the **Thalys** site (www.thalys.com) for high-speed trains to Brussels, Amsterdam, and Cologne. Once the distances get longer, well, the trip gets longer. You can get a train to Rome for 150€ one-way, but it will take you over 14 hours to get there. In general, there's no need to pay extra for first class, as second class is quite comfortable, although it makes sense to check what reductions are available on the day you're traveling—sometimes there are discounts in first class that are comparable to a regular second-class ticket.

BY BUS

Cheapest of all, and the most time consuming, is the bus. For travel within Europe, contact **Eurolines** (☎ 08 92 89 90 91; www.eurolines.com) a consortium of 32 different bus lines with routes that span the continent and then some (Casablanca to Moscow, anyone?). All buses in the group are modern, have toilets, and are non-smoking. They also offer multi-country passes. For travel to Germany or Eastern Europe, try **Gullivers** (☎ 49 30 311 02110, in Berlin; www.gullivers.fr), a German bus company affiliated with Eurolines; and for trips to Britain, **Eurobus Express** (☎ 01 78 02 01 85; www.eurobusexpress.net), which has a round-trip to London for 38€ if you are willing to go back and forth in 1 day.

TRAVEL INSURANCE—DO YOU NEED IT?

Before you even attempt to answer this question, find out what insurance you already have. Between your credit card, your personal medical insurance, and home insurance, you might already be covered for anything that might befall you during your Parisian stay. Emergency health coverage, repatriation, valuables, and travel costs are often part of your personal insurance package.

Pauline Frommer Says:

When purchasing a big-ticket travel item—a guided tour, a cruise, a safari—it's essential to buy travel insurance. Many unforeseen circumstances can interrupt or cause you to cancel a trip and with these types of trips that could spell a large financial loss. But do you need it for your trip to Paris? Not necessarily. If you're purchasing the insurance to cover lost luggage, or cancelled airfare, you may already be covered by your home-owner's insurance, if you're an American citizen. And hotel stays should never be insured as most hotels usually allow you to cancel 24 hours in advance with no penalty.

So what may you want to insure? If you've booked **an apartment stay** and have had to put down a large deposit, that should be insured as should **pricey airline tickets,** and **any valuables you may be carrying with you** (since the airline will only pay up to $2,500 for lost luggage domestically, less for foreign travel). Check first to see whether your home-owners insurance covers valuables, however.

A note about health insurance: Doctors' visits are so much cheaper in France than in the U.S. (around 28€ as opposed to upwards of $100) that Americans may decide to come here to get their next check up. France has an excellent (highly subsidized) health care system, generally acknowledged to be the best in Europe. So minor fixes and pharmaceuticals will generally not be a problem, nor will they take a bite out of your budget. The first step in deciding whether or not you need health insurance is to find out what your insurance at home covers when you are traveling overseas. If it covers emergencies, and you don't have any major ongoing healthcare concerns, you probably don't need it.

If you do decide to buy insurance, you can easily scan the different policies available by visiting the website **InsureMyTrip.com,** which compares the policies of all of the major companies. Or contact one of the following reputable companies directly:

- **Access America:** (☎ 800/284-8300; www.accessamerica.com)
- **AIG Travel Guard:** (☎ 800/826 4919; www.travelguard.com)
- **CSA Travel Protection:** (☎ 800/873-9855; www.csatravelprotection.com)

HOW DO I GET TO THE AIRPORT?

Thankfully, getting to and from the Paris airports isn't too difficult. You can take advantage of several different transit options relatively easily, provided you aren't bringing along umpteen suitcases. Long distance international flights almost always arrive at **Charles de Gaulle (CDG;** which is in the outlying town of Roissy, north of the city), shorter European flights and flights within France arrive at **Orly** (south of the city). Information for both airports can be had at ☎ 3950 (.34€ per minute; if you are calling from outside France, dial ☎ 01 70 36 39 50) or on their more or less comprehensive website: www.aeroportsdeparis.fr, which includes transit information as well as flight arrival and departure times.

BY TRAIN   If your hotel is on the central north–south access of Paris, and you don't have too much luggage, the cheapest way to get **CDG** is to take the **RER B,** the suburban metro line (☎ 08 91 36 20 20, .23€ per minute; www.transilien. com). It runs every 10 to 15 minutes from around 5:30am to midnight, and the trip takes 30 minutes from the Gare du Nord station and 35 minutes from Châtelet–Les Halles. Buy a **combined ticket** (8.40€ adults, 5.90 children 4–10) in any metro or RER station that will cover the RER and any Métro connection you need to make. *Important:* Be sure to figure out which terminal (1, 2, or 3) that your flight is departing from before you get on the train, as you will need to get off at "Aéroport Charles-de-Gaulle 1" for Terminals 1 and 3, and at "Aéroport Charles-de-Gaulle 2–TGV" for Terminal 2 (are you still with me?). There's usually, but not always, a list of which airlines are at which terminal on the train, in case you forget. Even if you mess up, the new airport shuttle, called the *navette* CDGVAL, will make your life easier once you arrive at the airport. This electric minitrain make stops at all three terminals and connects with both RER stops (though it still helps to get off at the right stop), as well as the bus. The shuttle runs ever 4 minutes from 4:30am to 1:30am, otherwise they pass every 20 minutes in the wee hours of the morning. *Note:* Terminals are sometimes referred to as *aérogares.*

To get to **Orly Airport,** you can take the **RER B** south to the Antony stop and change to the Orlyval minimetro, which will scoot you over to the airport (Orlyval runs every 4–10 min. 6am–11pm). Depending on which terminal your flight is leaving from, get off at either Orly Sud or Orly Ouest. A **combined RER/Orlyval ticket** is 9.60€ for adults, 4.80€ for children 4 to 10. The total trip from the Châtelet–Les Halles RER station to Orly Airport should take 30 minutes. If you are closer to a RER C stop, you can also get to Orly by taking the RER C to Pont du Rungis and taking the shuttle (marked "Paris Par Le Train") to Orly Sud or Orly Ouest. The combined trip takes around 35 minutes from Gare d'Austerlitz, 40 minutes from St-Michel–Notre Dame, and 45 minutes from Invalides; adults pay 6.10€ and children 4 to 10 pay 4.30€.

BY BUS   The two bus companies that serve **CDG** might be a little more expensive, but if the stops are near your hotel, they're a little more direct, though you should factor in time for traffic. The first, **Roissybus** (☎ 3246, .34€ per minute; www.ratp.fr; Métro: Opéra), which is run by the public transit authority and runs to all three terminals, departs from the corner of rue Scribe and rue Auber on the west side of the **Palais Garnier** opera house (otherwise known as the **Opéra**). The ride takes 45 to 60 minutes, buses run every 15 to 20 minutes from 5:45am to 11pm, and a one-way ticket costs 8.90€ (buy your ticket on the bus). The second, **Les Cars Air France** (☎ 08 92 35 08 20, .34€ per minute; www.cars-airfrance.com), run by the airline of the same name (you don't have to be flying Air France to use the service), has two different lines that go to Terminals 1 and 2 at CDG. **Line 2** leaves from 1 av. Carnot, just off the place Charles de Gaulle (at the center of which is the **Arc de Triomphe**) and makes a stop to pick up more passengers at blvd. Gouvion St-Cyr, on the east side of the convention center

(Palais de Congrés) at **Porte Maillot.** This line takes around 50 minutes; buses run every 30 minutes from 5:45am to 11pm. A one-way ticket costs 14€ one-way for an adult (22€ round-trip); children 2 to 11 pay 7€, and those under 2 ride for free. **Line 4** leaves from rue du Comandant Mouchotte, on the east side of **Gare Montparnasse,** and makes a stop to pick up passengers on boulevard Diderot in front of the **Gare de Lyon.** This line takes around 50 minutes; buses run every 30 minutes from 7am to 9pm. A one-way ticket on this line costs 15€ for an adult (round-trip 24€), 7.50€ for children 2 to 11, free under 2. Buy your ticket for either line on the bus or at any Air France ticket office (no credit cards accepted on the bus).

The same companies can bus you to **Orly Airport.** The transit authority runs **Orlybus** (☎ 3246, .34€ per minute; www.ratp.fr; Métro: Denfert-Rochereau), which leaves from **place Denfert-Rochereau** (between ave. René Coty and blvd. St-Jacques) and makes stops at both Orly Ouest and Orly Sud terminals. The trip takes about 30 minutes; buses run every 15 to 20 minutes from around 5:30am to 11:00pm, and one-way tickets are 6.30€. **Les Cars Air France** (☎ 08 92 35 08 20, .34€ per minute; www.cars-airfrance.com) **Line 1** leaves from the *aérogare* at Les Invalides (2 rue Robert Esnault Pelterie), makes a stop at Gare Montparnasse, and then makes stops at Orly Ouest and Orly Sud terminals. The trip takes 45 minutes, buses run ever 30 minutes from 6am to 11pm. There is a new line, called Line 1* that leaves from Etoile, makes a stop at Gare Montparnasse, and then heads on to Orly Ouest and Orly Sud; the trip takes about 50 minutes. One-way tickets for either of these lines is 10€ for adults (16€ round-trip), 5€ for children 2 to 11, free under 2. Like the other lines on this bus service, you can buy your tickets either on the bus or at any Air France ticket office.

BY TAXI   Certainly this is the easiest way to get the airport, but also the most expensive. Trips take anywhere from 50 to 60 minutes, depending on traffic, and your total fare to **CDG** will run around 50€ to 55€ from 7am to 7pm, not including the 1.25€ supplement for each piece of baggage. To Orly the trip will take around 30 minutes (without traffic) and cost between 35€ and 40€. Rates at all other times are 15% higher. It won't cost extra to reserve ahead, which will spare you the trouble of finding a taxi stand; some of the larger taxi companies include **Taxis G7** (☎ 01 47 39 47 39), **Taxis 7000** (☎ 01 42 70 00 42), and **Taxis Bleus** (☎ 08 91 70 10 10, .23€ per minute).

BY SHARED SHUTTLE   Several shared shuttle bus companies will pick you up from your hotel or apartment and deliver you directly to your airline terminal at a per-person price that is generally way lower than that of a taxi. The only problem is, they will need to stop in several places along the journey to pick up other customers, which will make your trip at least a half-hour longer than if you took other transit options (60–90 min.). This method makes the most sense for solo or duo travelers; if you're traveling in a party of three or more, a taxi will cost about the same and will take less time. **ParisShuttle** (☎ 01 53 39 18 18; www.parishuttle. com) charges 27€ for one person, 20€ per person for groups of 2 to 4, and 17€ per person for groups of 5 to 8 for shuttles to either CDG or Orly. **Paris Blue Airport Shuttle** (☎ 01 30 11 13 00; www.paris-blue-airport-shuttle.com) charges 26€ to 29€ for one person, 36€ to 38€ for two, 48€ to 51€ for three, and 62€

to 66€ for four, depending on the time of day; this shuttle only makes sense for CDG as rates to Orly are comparable (or higher than) a taxi. Both of these services require advance reservations.

WHAT TO PACK

I know everyone wants to be comfortable when they travel, but unless you don't mind sticking out like a sore thumb, in Paris you need to make at least a little effort to dress well. Many travelers seem to be under the impression that they're invisible, and thus dress in ways they would never dare if they were visiting people they didn't know at home. Actually, the opposite is true: By wearing loose, floppy outfits and jogging suits, you might as well be carrying an enormous banner that says, "Hey everybody! I'm a tourist!" It's not that people here walk around in Chanel suits, but they do put a good deal of thought into how they look, even if it's just a pair of jeans with a nice top. Actually, I still haven't figured out how French people manage to look so stylish wearing a pair of jeans and a nice top—I think it has to do with accessories and a certain look in their eye—but I can say that both men and women here make dressing well a priority, and you'll get pitying looks, along the lines of "poor dear, she's let herself go" if you dress sloppy. I should know—I've been guilty of it on a regular basis. Outfit choices intensify after sundown; depending on where you're going and what you're up to, evening wear can range from an even more accessorized jeans ensemble to styles straight out of a high-fashion magazine. Incidentally, women need not worry about wearing something that's too form fitting—circulation-restricting clothing is par for the course here.

Style issues aside, you should definitely bring comfortable walking shoes (just ignore those French women who work long hours in service trades in high heels—you've got to draw the line somewhere). Obviously, you should take the weather into consideration. Although Parisian seasons rarely veer towards the extremes, this is not a Mediterranean climate. From October to at least March is definitely sweater weather, though you should pack one just in case even if you visit in August. Layering is always a good idea for unpredictable weather; that way you can be prepared for climate changes without having to stuff your suitcase with bulky winter wear. You should also bring an umbrella and some sort or rain-resistant outerwear no matter when you come. Whatever you do, don't pack too much. You're not traveling to the wilds of Borneo; if you realize that you forgot something essential, you can always buy it here.

MONEY MATTERS

No one believed it would ever happen, but since 2002 Europe has indeed had a common currency, the euro. Not all countries have signed up yet—the United Kingdom, for example, stubbornly refuses to give up its pounds—but most countries in the European Union have converted, including France. Whatever the inconveniences have been for the people living here, the euro is good news for tourists, in that there is no more need to change money when going from one euro-zone country to another. The bad news is that while in 2002 the euro was very close in value to the US dollar, at press time, the exchange rate had sunk to new, depressing lows: 1€ was equal to about US$1.60, which means that things are expensive here. Even for French people, it's no party—between merchants taking advantage of the euro to up their prices and the rising price of oil, prices have risen dramatically here over the last few years.

Euros come in 5€, 10€, 20€, 50€, 100€, 200€, and 500€ bills, which grow in size according to their value. .01€, .02€, and .05€ coins also increase in size and are copper colored (be sure not to mix up the .02€ and .05€, which is easy to do), then the color changes with the .10€, .20€, and .50€ coins, which are all gold and also increase in size according to value. A 1€ coin has a silver center and a gold outer ring; a 2€ has the same look but is larger.

GETTING CASH

The days of travelers' checks are numbered, now you can get a low-fee cash withdraw at **automated teller machines.** ATMs are all over Paris, and most are part of the larger networks like Cirrus and Plus. This means that instead of going through the hassle of buying travelers' checks before you leave, and then trying to find someone who will change them once you get here, you can simply belly up to the nearest ATM, put in your home bank card, and out will pop your requested number of euros. What's more, French banks will almost never charge a fee for withdrawing from an ATM, although your bank will. But even if your bank charges a fee for foreign transactions, you'll still get a much better exchange rate than you will with traveler's checks (check with your bank before you leave to see exactly how much they charge per withdrawal). *Important note:* French ATMs will only accept a four-digit PIN; call your bank before you leave if your code has more or less.

If my comments in the paragraph above have not dissuaded you and you simply can't leave home without a wad of **travelers' checks,** try to exchange them at a bank or at the **American Express Office** (11 rue Scribe, 9th arrond; ☎ 01 53 30 99 00; www.americanexpress.fr; Métro: Opéra) to get the best rate. *Note:* Don't try to use American Express's new check cards here; merchants are not familiar with them, and even the staff at the main Amex office is unsure of how to use them.

If your American Express travelers' checks are lost or stolen, contact their offices at ☎ 0800 908 600.

If you insist on bringing cash from home and changing your money at a money exchange, you'll not only have a hard time finding one (many went out of business with the changeover to the euro), but once you do, you usually get a lousy rate. You'll get a better rate at a bank, if you can find one that still offers an exchange window; most have stopped this service since the conversion to the euro. Below are a couple of money exchanges that are still in business:

- **Comptoir de Change Opéra** (9 rue Scribe, 9th arrond.; ☎ 01 47 42 20 96; Métro: Opéra, RER: Auber)
- **Exchange Corporation France** (140 ave. Champs Elysées; ☎ 01 40 75 00 49; Métro: George V)

To sum up: You'll get the best exchange rates using your ATM card (though your bank may charge high fees). Credit cards (once again, high fees notwithstanding), offer the second best rates, and traveler's checks and money exchanges offer the worst. However you end up changing or getting your money, don't overdo it. It's foolhardy to carry large amounts of cash on your person anywhere in the world, and Paris is no exception.

Does That Include Tax?

Taxes are always included in the price of anything you purchase, including restaurants meals, with the exception of hotel bills, to which a small per person, per night sum (around 1€) is added. This means your bill is usually nice and round, and there are no unpleasant surprises at the cash register.

CREDIT CARDS

Credit cards can be very handy on your Paris vacation—not only do they dispense with the need to change money or carry a lot of cash around, but in general, you'll get a very good rate of exchange when it comes time to pay your bill. However— and this is a big "however"—you should check with your credit card company to see what kind of extra fees they charge for foreign transactions. Some banks, like credit unions, are very generous in this respect and don't attach extra fees, others make a killing this way. Whatever you do, don't withdraw cash on your credit card, unless you can't do it on your bank card. You'll not only pay high fees, but you'll pay interest from the minute the ATM spits out your bills.

MasterCard and Visa are accepted in most places; many merchants don't accept American Express because of the high fees attached, and Diner's Club takers are rare. Discover cards remain undiscovered in France, so you may as well leave it at home. Most merchants have a 10€ to 15€ minimum for credit card purchases.

French credit cards, called Carte Bleu, are all equipped with a security chip; merchants plug the card into a reader and ask the card holder to punch in a secret code (no signature required). Before the addled clerk tries to shove your card in to the machine, tell them that you have a foreign card (*carte étrangère,* cart ay-trahn-*zhere*) without a chip (*sans puce,* sahns poose), and they'll usually know that it needs to be swiped (there's usually a slot on the machine). In small shops that don't get a lot of tourists, this is sometimes a problem, so be prepared to pay cash (or run out to a machine) when shopping in these types of establishments.

If your card gets lost or stolen, contact your card issuer, or call one of the following toll-free telephone numbers:

Visa: ☎ 0 800 90 20 33
Diner's Club: ☎ 0 800 22 20 73
Eurocard–Mastercard: ☎ 0 800 90 23 90
American Express (USA): ☎ 0 800 900 888;
  (other countries) ☎ 01 47 77 72 00

TIPPING

In France, **waiters and waitresses,** even in cafes, are paid a living wage and get health benefits and vacations like any other working stiff (unlike in certain countries in North America), and thus don't rely on tips for their income. Therefore, they do not expect tips, although they certainly won't be insulted if you want to leave one. If you want to show your appreciation, it's customary (but not obligatory) to leave a little something (say .20€ for a coffee, or a euro or two for two full meals). **Taxi drivers** expect tips—a euro or two should suffice. For attendants at **public toilets,** there's usually a basket for tips (.20€–.50€ will do here). **Ushers** in theaters get a tip of .50€ to 1€. Tip **porters** 1€ per suitcase.

SAFETY & HEALTH

Despite the bad press the city got in 2006, when there were car-burnings and riots in the outer suburbs, Paris is basically a safe city—you can roam the streets of most neighborhoods at any hour of night or day without worrying about your health or welfare. If you want trouble, you generally have to go looking for it. Most neighborhoods within the city limits are safe, especially those in the city center, though it's best to avoid the area around Les Halles late at night (especially the gardens). Other neighborhoods that get a little rough in the evening hours include the non-Montmartre parts of the 18th arrondissement, and the area around place Pigalle, Paris's famous red-light district. Most of the city's parks and gardens are closed at night, with the exception of the Bois de Vincennes and the Bois de Boulogne, where it is not recommended to go for a late-night stroll. In fact, don't be surprised if you're in the Bois de Boulogne around sundown and start to see exotic-looking "women" who could be characters from an Aldomovar movie; the Bois is known as a nighttime gathering spot for transvestite prostitutes.

That's about it for the dark side of Paris. However, as with any big city, if you are unfamiliar with the territory, purse snatchers and other bad guys are likely to pick up on it, and you'll be a more likely target than an in-the-know local. There's no need to be paranoid, but you do need to keep your wits about you.

- **Beware of pickpockets, particularly in tourist areas and in the Métro:** Don't keep wallets in your back trouser pocket, keep your purse and other bags closed, and try not to display your expensive camera too prominently. Avoid "fanny packs" which are easily removed by pickpockets and mark you as a tourist.
- In general, the French are a shy people; if someone **approaches you and aggressively offers their services,** be extremely wary and graciously decline the offer.
- **Be aware of what's going on around you when using ATMs** (cash machines), particularly at night. If anything feels fishy, find another machine elsewhere.
- **Keep passports and valuables in your hotel's safe,** rather than walking around town with them. Make a photocopy of your passport to have on your person just in case you need to identify yourself, or if your real passport gets lost or stolen. If you do lose your passport, contact your embassy or consulate as soon as possible (see contact information in the ABCs section, later in this chapter).
- **In an emergency, you can contact the police from any phone by dialing 17.**

By the way, if you see the word "Vigipirate" being bandied about, it has nothing to do with swashbuckling sea captains, but the city's anti-terrorism plan, which is put into effect when there is any kind of threat. This includes asking citizens to report any abandoned luggage (don't leave your own lying around public

What Will My Vacation Cost?

The little things in Paris are generally not outrageously expensive, although with the exchange rate being what it is, they can add up. Here are some prices for a few everyday items:

Métro or bus ride	1.60€
Taxi ride, Eiffel Tower to place de la Bastille	10€
Tube of toothpaste	2.30€
Box of 24 regular tampons	3.90€
Package of 38 disposable diapers (Pampers)	12€
A 355 ml bottle of contact lens solution	13€
Croissant	1€
Cup of espresso (depending on how chic the café is)	1.50€–4€
Café au lait	2.50€–4.50€
Sandwich in a *boulangerie*	3€–5€
Croque-monsieur	6€–7€
Continental breakfast in a café	6€–12€
Restaurant lunch (cheap restaurant)	9€–14€
(moderate–expensive restaurant)	15€–30€
Restaurant dinner (cheap restaurant)	11€–17€
(moderate–expensive restaurant)	18€–50€
Glass of wine in a cafe	2€–4€
Glass of soda in a cafe	3€–5€
Cocktail in a bar	5€–12€
Bottle of water in a grocery store	.25€–.70€
Bottle of water in a café	2.50€–5€
Average museum entrance fee	9€
Average ticket at a well-known theater	25€
Ticket to see chanson legend Juliette Greco	60€
Movie ticket	9€
Souvenir T-shirt	19€

places or it's likely to be confiscated and possibly blown up), sealing all trash cans (that's why most public trash cans you'll see are clear plastic bag holders), and the closing of any left-luggage services in train stations and airports.

STAYING HEALTHY IN PARIS

If you get sick or need a doctor for any reason, relax, you're in good hands in Paris. The French are blessed with one of the best health care systems in Europe, which is almost entirely paid for by the government, which means you'll not only get good care, but you'll get it at a low cost. Doctor visits are a fraction of what you would pay in the U.S., as are pharmaceuticals—in fact, you might want to consider bringing along a prescription or two to get filled at a French pharmacy.

Speaking of **pharmacies,** if you're just mildly sick and just need some good advice and over-the-counter medicine, these are the places to seek out. Pharmacists have a high social standing in this nation of hypochondriacs, and with good reason—they're highly trained and are repositories of a wealth of medical knowledge. Pharmacies are all over the place, just look for the green cross (usually in neon) hanging outside of their doors.

If you're sick enough that you want to see a **doctor,** the U.S. Embassy has a list of English-speaking ones; call the **Office of American Services:** ☎ 01 43 12 22 22. If you're so sick that the idea of getting up and going to the doctor's office is too much to deal with, or if you have an urgent problem but are not ready to call an ambulance you can get a doctor to come to you (in your hotel, apartment, or wherever) at any time of day or night by calling **SOS Medecins** at ☎ 01 47 07 77 77 (they'll try to send an English speaking doctor if at all possible). If you need **emergency assistance,** call the **SAMU** (the French emergency services); just dial 15 from any telephone.

SPECIAL TYPES OF TRAVELERS

Of course everyone's special, but some travelers have particular needs that won't always be met by standard tourist infrastructure. Here are a few leads for finding ways to make your trip even more enjoyable.

ADVICE FOR TRAVELING FAMILIES

On the surface, Paris doesn't look like a family-friendly place. There are too many museums, too many historical sites, and too many rainy days keeping the kids inside. Start digging a little deeper and you'll find that there's plenty of kid stuff—but you'll have to do some looking.

Children's activities. Is it raining outside? Fear not, the city's listing magazines are filled with puppet shows, children's theater, circuses, and other activities for children. The very grown-up newspaper *Liberation* publishes an entire pullout supplement filled with kids' activities every other month called *Paris Mômes* (*môme* is slang for "kid"); offerings include everything from philosophy discussions for 10-year-olds, to Italian cooking classes for 5-year-olds, to painting workshops at the Musée d'Orsay for 5- to 11-year-olds. *Télérama* magazine has a good summary of children's theater productions around town, as do the old standbys, *l'Officiel des Spectacles* and *Pariscope,* which also give the lowdown on where to find puppet shows. The only downside to this wealth of activities is that most of it requires a certain level of proficiency in French. But not all. The doings at a traditional **Guignol puppet show** are usually so archetypal that language is not a barrier (see "Guignol, the Puppet Show Hero" box, p. 222). The shows and **activities for truly tiny tots** (say 3 and under) aren't really language-dependent either. Neither are **circuses,** which come to Paris on a regular basis. Many circus troupes are of the modern, avant-garde variety, so be sure that the one you choose is appropriate for children. For **outdoor activities** in the city's many parks and gardens, see our "Paris Outdoors" chapter. If your kids are museum age, you'll be happy to know that most museums let the under 5 crowd in for free, and often the under 18 crowd as well. There are tons of children's activities (guided tours, art workshops, and so forth) at Parisian museums, but almost all of them require French language skills.

Family accommodations. Lodging is a bigger challenge: Since most affordable (and even the unaffordable) hotels have small rooms, you'll often end up paying for two to accommodate your gang—here is where renting an apartment makes terrific financial and practical sense. You'll not only have more room, but you'll have a kitchen, as well as a heck of a lot more privacy. For tips on how to find a short-term rental, see our accommodations chapter.

Babysitting. If you do end up in a hotel, the good news is that many of them can hook you up with a good babysitter service, if you're aching to get out at night without the kids. If you need to find someone on your own, try:

- **BabyChou Services** (31 rue du Moulin de la Pointe, 13th arrond.; ☎ 01 43 13 33 23; www.babychou.com) often works with hotels and has English-speaking sitters on request (reserve a week in advance to be sure that an Anglophone sitter is available). You'll pay a 16€ agency fee, plus 8€ per hour for one child (9€ for two, and 10€ for three) with a 3-hour minimum; after 11pm add another 10€ for a taxi for the babysitter to get home.

- **Au Paradis des Petits** (21 rue Raymond du Temple, Vincennes; ☎ 01 43 65 58 58; www.auparadisdespetits.com). In business for 16 years, this agency uses primarily university students, most of whom speak at least some English. Rates run 7.20€ per hour for one or two children (2-hr. minimum), agency fee is 10€, and there is an 8€ fee to help pay for the taxi if you come back after 11pm. This agency is closed from mid-July to mid-August.

Need more tips? There are some useful websites out there that offer family-specific travel advice, like the **Family Travel Network** (www.familytravelnetwork.com), which offers tips on everything from pre-teen passports to family tour packages, and **Family Travel Forum** (www.familytravelforum.com), which has several articles for Paris en famille.

ADVICE FOR TRAVELERS WITH DISABILITIES

I guess you could blame it on the age of the city, but there's really no excuse for the lack of accessibility in Paris. Tortuous sidewalks, minimal or nonexistent ramps at public facilities, endless stairways in Métro stations—it isn't a pretty picture. Slowly, very slowly, the municipality has become aware of the problem, and they're taking steps to improve the situation; in 2001 they launched an awareness campaign and a label "Tourisme & Handicaps" (www.tourisme-handicaps.org) which is awarded to hotels and other facilities that have disabled access. This distinction is divided into four categories: physical, mental, hearing, and visual disabilities; there's a chart on the Paris Tourist Office website (www.parisinfo.com) that details which sites and establishments have been awarded which type of label. So far, the list isn't particularly long—for the moment, Paris is still a challenge.

Hotels: Most of the small family-run hotels, which make up a great percentage of affordable Parisian lodging, are not accessible to disabled travelers, due to the age of the buildings and the difficulty in altering historic edifices. However, many modern chain hotels do have facilities, in particular, the reasonably priced and omnipresent **Ibis** chain (www.ibis.com, see our accommodations chapter for details). The Paris Tourist Office website has a good listing of accessible lodgings (www.parisinfo.com), as do some of the disabled persons associations (see "Associations," below).

Restaurants: Restaurants with wheelchair access are few and far between; many restaurants are too small and too crowded to accommodate them. On the other hand, several offer sidewalk seating where space is not as big of a question. Your best bet is to call ahead to check. A few accessible restaurants have received the Tourisme & Handicap label (see above).

Museums: Here is where some significant progress has been made. Several of the larger museums, like the **Louvre** and the new **Musée du Quai Branly,** are wheelchair accessible. The **Pompidou Center** has access throughout the building as well as free wheelchairs at the entrance. The **Musée d'Orsay** offers tours in sign language, as well as free entry for disabled people and one companion. The full list is on the Tourisme & Handicaps page at the Paris Tourist Office website.

Transportation: The **Métro** is daunting, and with the exception of the newish No. 14 line, and a few other with-it stations, fairly impossible to manage. They're working on it, however: Consult the RATP website (www.ratp.fr) for a list of accessible stations. The **bus** is a much better option. Almost all buses now have an extendable ramp for wheelchair access, as well as reserved places in the bus. If you are heading for another town or country, certain long-distance **trains** are now equipped for persons with disabilities, though you must reserve in advance; visit the SNCF website (www.voyages-sncf.com) for more information.

Associations: Specialized organizations are a gold mine for travel and access tips. One of the largest associations for disabled people in France is the **Association des Paralysées de France** (13 place de Rungis, 13th arrond.; ☎ 01 53 80 92 97; www.apf.asso.fr). Despite the name, they cover all disabilities, and are an invaluable storehouse of information, including lists of accessible hotels, restaurants, museums, cinemas, and monuments (call or write and they'll mail you brochures). Another great resource, a website called **J'accede** (www.jaccede.com), lists accessible cafes, restaurants, nightspots, hotels, and even spas and hair salons. The **Groupement pour l'Insertion des Personnes Handicapées Physiques** (GIHP; 505 place des Champs Elysées, Courcouronne; ☎ 01 60 77 20 20; www.gihpidf.asso.fr), offers assistance getting to and from the airports, for a price: 60€ to 80€ one-way; reserve at least 1 week in advance). The London-based Access Project, publishes a helpful guide called **Access in Paris** (www.accessinparis.org); the latest one came out in 2008; there are downloadable chapters available on the website.

ADVICE FOR GAY & LESBIAN TRAVELERS

The French have a refreshingly "live and let live" attitude towards people's personal lives, which is reflected in the fact that there's little discrimination against gay people, particularly in the capital. The best example of the level of tolerance here is the mayor, Bertrand Delanoë, who's openly gay. Not only was it not an issue during the electoral campaign, but 7 years into his mandate, no one seems to care; they're much more interested in what he has been doing for the city (which is a lot). On the other hand, loudly declaring your sexual preferences is frowned upon; as with religion, private matters are supposed to stay private. And despite the tolerant attitude, it's still illegal for gay people to adopt children, and marriage is out of the question (though gay couples can get legal partnership status).

Paris has the country's largest gay population, and the most visibly gay neighborhood is the Marais. To find out about parties, nightspots, and other events, pick up a copy of *Illico* or *2X* (both free at bars and bookstores).

The city's largest gay bookstore is **Les Mots à la Bouche** (6 rue Ste Croix de la Bretonnerie, 4th arrond.; ☎ 01 42 78 88 30; www.motsbouche.com; Métro: St-Paul). A good to place to find out about gay associations and events, as well as the political picture, is the **Centre Lesbien, Gai, Bi et Trans** (63 rue Beaubourg; ☎ 01 43 57 21 47; www.cglparis.org; Métro: Bastille), an advocacy group that offers support and information to the gay community. Another good resource is the **France Queer Resources Directory** (www.france.qrd.org), which has classified ads, events, and a good Internet directory. All of these websites are in French; if you're looking for an English-language group, try the **Gay International Circle of Paris** (☎ 06 31 86 31 40; www.gaipar-asso.com), which organizes get-togethers for foreigners just arriving in or passing through Paris every third Thursday of the month at **Bar Duplex** (25 rue Michel-le-Comte, 3rd arrond.; ☎ 01 42 72 80 86; Métro: Rambuteau).

ADVICE FOR SENIOR TRAVELERS

I think it's safe to say that there is less "age-ism" in France than in some other countries. There's no automatic assumption that you're less attractive/intelligent/praiseworthy just because you happened to have lived over 50 or 60 years. If you're a woman, it's really refreshing to still be considered beautiful, and even sexy, at a post-box office age—some of the hottest female news anchors here are "women of a certain age." France is still a relatively traditional country, and elders tend to be treated with respect. That said, if you have mobility concerns, Paris is not an easy place to get around (see "Advice for Travelers with Disabilities," above). Being over 60 often will get you into museums and other monuments for free or a reduced price; be sure to tell them you are a Senior, pronounced *see-nyore*, when at the ticket window. Older people do not, however, get discounts on mass transit (unless they live in Paris full-time and have the card to prove it), but they do on long-distance trains; if you're going out of town, make sure you get the 25% to 50% discount (see www.voyages-sncf.com, or the "Traveling from Paris to Other Parts of France" section, earlier in this chapter, for details).

Joining **AARP** (American Association of Retired Persons, 601 E St. NW, Washington, DC, 20049; ☎ 888/687-2277; www.aarp.org) before you leave home is a good idea (if you're over 50) because it can get you discounts on hotels, airfare, and car rentals. The well-respected **Elderhostel** (☎ 800/454-5768; www.elderhostel.org) organizes 2-week trips around a particular theme (history, literature, food, and so forth); some trips stay more or less in Paris, others also include other destinations. You might barge down the Seine to the D-Day beaches in Normandy, for example, or continue on to the chateaux of the Loire Valley.

STAYING WIRED WHILE YOU'RE AWAY

France was a little late getting on the information superhighway and took a few wrong turns once they did, but today, most French people are connected in some way to the Internet (at least the younger ones). Most hotels (even the little bitty ones) offer some sort of Internet access, and there's a growing number of cyber-cafes around town. Wi-Fi (pronounced wee-fee around these parts) is increasingly popular, but Paris is by no means a Wi-Fi zone.

Outside your hotel, it's best to look for a cybercafe for Internet access; library facilities are for card holders only, and the strange looking cyber-stands at the post office are expensive and inconvenient. *Note:* French keyboards are just different enough to be extremely irritating when you're trying to type fast (some keys are in places that they ordinarily aren't). If you're in a hurry, ask if English keyboards are available. Cybercafes come and go with astounding rapidity so I recommend hitting the yellow pages (www.pagesjaunes.fr) and searching "cybercafe"; at least that way you'll get the ones that are still in business. Below are four well-estab-lished cyber outfits that, at least at press time, seemed to be here to stay.

Cyber Cube (5 rue Mignon, 6th arrond.; ☎ 01 53 10 30 50; www.cybercube.fr; .15€ per minute, 30€ for 5 hr., 40€ for 10 hr.; Métro: Odéon or St-Michel) has three comfortable locations in Paris: In addition to the above address, you can go to **Cyber Cube Bastille** (12 rue Daval, 11th arrond.; ☎ 01 49 29 67 67; Métro: Bastille) or **Cyber Cube Montparnasse** (9 rue d'Odessa, 14th arrond.; ☎ 01 56 80 08 08; Métro: Montparnasse or Edgar Quinet).

Cybersquare (1 place de la République, 3rd arrond.; ☎ 01 48 87 82 36; www.cybersquare-paris.com; 2.30€ for 15 min.; Métro: République). The decor is basic, but the equipment is good.

Luxembourg Micro (81 blvd. St-Michel, 5th arrond.; ☎ 01 46 33 27 98; www.luxembourg-micro.com; 1€ for 15 min., 2€ for 30 min., and 2.80€ for 1 hr.; RER: Luxembourg). In the heart of the Latin Quarter, a friendly, reliable cyber-spot.

Milk (31 blvd. Sebastapol, 1st arrond.; ☎ 08 20 00 10 00; www.milkinternet hall.com; Métro: Les Halles) has seven locations and is one of the brightest spots on the cybercafe scene. Open 24/7, rates start at 3€ for 30 min and get cheaper the longer you stay; after 10pm rates go way down.

RECOMMENDED BOOKS & FILMS ABOUT THE CITY

Where to begin? You could fill a library with all the books that have been written about Paris; the very mention of the name seems to make writers dive for their fountain pens. Novels, while not necessarily historically accurate, are a wonderful way to get a feel for the atmosphere of the city. A few timeless literary classics:

- *Les Miserables* and the *Hunchback of Notre-Dame,* by Victor Hugo
- *Père Goriot,* by Honoré de Balzac
- *Nana,* by Emile Zola
- *A Tale of Two Cities,* by Charles Dickens

Paris was a very fertile stomping ground for dozens of expatriate writers in the '20s, '30s, and '40s. For a more bohemian view of the city, try:

- *The Rosy Crucifixion* trilogy *(Sexus, Nexus, and Plexus)* by Henry Miller
- *The Alice B. Toklas Cookbook,* by Alice B. Toklas
- *A Movable Feast,* by Ernest Hemingway
- *Down and Out in Paris and London,* by George Orwell

346 Chapter 12   The Essentials of Planning

A great way to get a taste of Parisian-focused literature across the last century or so without lugging around several weighty tomes is to pick up a copy of *Paris Tales* (edited and translated by Helen Constantine), a collection of short stories about the city by French authors as varied as Colette and Zola to modern literary stars like Frédéric Beigbeder and Anna Galvada.

For a more historical look at the city, take a peek at:

* *Paris: Biography of a City*, by Colin Jones
* *Paris in the Sixties*, a photo collection edited by George Perry
* *Citizens: A Chronicle of the French Revolution*, by Simon Schama

and for a look under the city:

* *City of Light, City of Dark: Exploring Paris Below*, by Valerie Broadwell

And don't forget the memoirs:

* *Selected Letters*, by Mme de Sévigny
* *Paris France, Personal Recollections*, by Gertrude Stein
* *Memoirs of a Dutiful Daughter*, by Simone de Beauvoir

As far as films go, it's impossible to do a thorough listing here, but there are a few must-sees with excellent views of the city at different periods of its life. You could start with François Truffaut's *400 Blows*, an autobiographical story about a young boy who gets involved with petty crime in the 1950s, and then move on to Jean-Luc Godard's, quirky thriller/romance *Breathless*, for a look at Paris in the black and white 1960s. For Paris in the New Wave 1980s, try *Diva*, Jean-Jacques Beineix's topsy-turvy mystery involving a mail courier and an opera star. Another Truffaut film, *The Last Métro* (filmed in the 1980s), takes on Paris during the Nazi occupation, while Krzysztof Kieslowski's *Blue*, a half-disturbing, half-hopeful look at a woman who loses her husband and child in a car crash, shows the heroine trying to restart her life in a more or less contemporary Paris in the 1990s. The most successful recent love affair between a director and the city, in my humble opinion, is Jean-Pierre Jeunet's *Amélie*, a delightful, dizzying spin through Montmartre in its most ideal state; it's virtually impossible not to feel like jumping on the next plane to Paris after watching this modern fairy tale. Paris has "appeared" in dozens of other classic films—like *Les Enfants du Paradis*, *Casablanca*, and *An American in Paris*—that were mostly shot on studio lots, but even if liberty was taken with the scenery, you still feel the city's mythic presence.

The ABCs of Paris

Area Codes All French phone numbers must be preceded by a "0" if you are calling within the country, followed by the regional area code, which in Paris is "1," which is why phone numbers look so long (10 digits!). Cellphones all get their own prefix "06," followed by eight other numbers. To call France from outside the country, you must start with the country code (33), then drop the "0" and dial the remaining 9 numbers. So, for example, the phone number 01 42 00 00 00 would become 011/33 1 42 00 00 00 if you were dialing from the U.S., for example. To dial another country from France, dial "00" plus the country code and then the number. Numbers beginning with 08 00 are toll free, however many other numbers starting with 08 are toll calls; the merchants using these numbers are supposed to let you know what the rate is (which can be anywhere from the price of a local call to 1.20€ per minute), but in case they don't, either keep your conversation short, or look up the rates in a phone book.

ATMs & Currency Exchange See "Money Matters," earlier in this chapter.

Business Hours Most stores are open Monday through Saturday from 9am or 10am to 7pm. Many larger ones now have "nocturnes" once a week when they stay open to 9pm. Many smaller stores still close between noon and 2pm, but this tradition is increasingly rare in Paris (though it still is strong in the provinces). Almost all stores are closed on Sunday, and some take Monday off as well. Banks are usually open weekdays from 9am to 1pm and 2 to 5pm; many are also open on Saturdays (with similar hours).

Drinking Laws The legal age for the purchase and consumption of alcohol is 16. You'll rarely be carded, but it's a good idea to have ID on you. Interestingly, in spite of—or perhaps because of—this lax attitude, young French people do not tend to abuse alcohol, and when they go to bars, the major motivation is to talk and flirt, not to drink. Drunken rowdiness is definitely frowned upon, and you might have a close encounter with the police if things get out of hand. Authorities are very strict about drunk driving. If convicted, you face a high fine and a possible prison term.

Electricity France uses the European standard of 220 to 240 volts AC (50 cycles), as compared to the 110 to 120 volts AC (60 cycles) standard in the U.S. If you bring electrical appliances that use 110 to 120 volts, be sure to have both an adaptor (for the plug size, which is different in France) and a voltage converter, or whatever you plug in will be sure to blow out. Most computers and digital cameras are set up for both voltages, but make absolutely sure before you plug anything in without a converter. Bring your adaptors and converters from home, as they are hard to find in Paris.

Embassies & Consulates If you have a passport, immigration, legal, or other problem, contact your consulate. Call or visit their website before you go; they often keep strange hours and honor both French and home-country holidays. Contact information is as follows:

Australian Embassy (4 rue Jean Rey, 15th arrond.; ☎ 01 40 59 33 00; www. france.embassy.gov.au; Métro: Bir Hakeim)

British Consulate-General (18 bis rue d'Anjou, 8th arrond.; ☎ 01 44 51 31 02; www.amb-grandebretagne.fr; Métro: Madeleine)

Canadian Embassy (35 ave. Montaigne, 8th arrond.; ☎ 01 44 43 29 00; www.amb-canada.fr; Métro: Franklin Delano Roosevelt)

New Zealand Embassy (7 ter rue Léonard de Vinci, 16th arrond.; ☎ 01 45 01 43 43; www.nzembassy.com; Métro: Victor Hugo)

United States Embassy (Office of American Services, 2 rue St-Florentin, 8th arrond.; ☎ 01 43 12 22 22; http:// france.usembassy.gov; Métro: Concorde)

Emergencies Dial 17 for the police, 18 for the Fire Department, and 15 for the SAMU emergency services, who will send an ambulance. If you don't want to call an ambulance, but you need to get to a hospital and you want to get there on your own, see "Hospitals" below for a list of addresses. You can also call a private "ambulance" service, which is basically a taxi that specializes in getting people to the hospital. Remember, if you want someone to call a medically equipped ambulance, tell them to call the SAMU. If you think you have been poisoned, call the **24-hour anti-poison line:** ☎ 01 40 05 48 48.

Holidays The following days are national holidays when all government offices, banks, and pretty much everything else is closed. January 1 (New Year's), the Monday after Easter (Easter Monday), May 1 (Labor Day), May 8 (End of WWII), May 20 (Ascension), July 14 (Bastille Day),

August 15 (Assumption), November 1 (All Saints' Day), November 11· (Armistice 1918), December 25 (Christmas). As you may have noticed, May is a long string of long weekends. Museums stay open on some holidays; check ahead before you go on these days.

Hospitals French hospitals have very high standards and offer good care. Most have 24-hour emergency rooms; here are a few of the larger facilities:

Hôpital Hôtel Dieu (1 place du Parvis Notre Dame, 4th arrond.; ☎ 01 42 34 82 34; www.aphp.fr; Métro: Cité)

Hôpital Européen Georges Pompidou (20 rue Leblanc, 15th arrond.; ☎ 01 56 09 20 00; www.aphp.fr; Métro: Balard, RER: Pont du Garigliano)

Hôpital Bichat (46 rue Henri-Huchard, 18th arrond.; ☎ 01 40 25 80 80; www.aphp.fr; Métro: Porte de St-Ouen)

Hôpital Necker (**Children's Hospital;** 149 rue de Sèvres, 15th arrond.; ☎ 01 44 49 40 00; www.hopital-necker.aphp.fr; Métro: Duroc or Sèvres-Lecourbe)

Hôpital St-Antoine (184 rue du Faubourg St-Antoine, 12th arrond.; ☎ 01 49 28 20 00; www.aphp.fr; Métro: Reuilly-Diderot or Faidherbe-Chaligny)

If you really want a fully English-speaking hospital like back home, there is the **American Hospital of Paris** (63 blvd. Victor Hugo, Neuilly; ☎ 01 46 41 25 25; www.american-hospital.org; Métro: Pont de Levallois,10–15 min. walk from station), which is private and very expensive, and the **Hertford British Hospital** (3 rue Barbès, Levallois Perret; ☎ 01 46 39 22 22; www.british-hospital.org; Métro: Louise Michel or Anatole France), which is also private but integrated into the French health care system.

Libraries Public libraries are sprinkled throughout the city, and they often have some books in English (though you won't be able to check any out if you aren't a resident). For a complete list of branches, visit the municipal website at www.paris.fr and look for "bibliothèques."

There are a few English-language libraries in town, but they are all private and require stiff membership fees.

Mail At press time, domestic postage rates were .55€ for postcards and letters that weigh up to 20 grams (.7 oz). For international mail, a first-class letter or postcard to another country in the European Union and Switzerland is .65€ for up to 20 grams, the same weight letter or postcard to anywhere else in the rest of the world is .85€. For more rates, branch addresses, and then some, visit the website of **La Poste,** the French national post office, at www.laposte.fr. In case you're wondering why the lines are so long at the post office, La Poste is also a bank, so people are fiddling with their finances while you're waiting to buy stamps. A stamps-only window or machine is usually somewhere on the premises; you can also find stamps at a "tabac," a counter selling cigarettes which is usually found in cafés (indicated by the red diamond sign outside).

If you want to receive mail and you aren't sure where you'll be staying in Paris, you can have mail sent to you general delivery, which is called "Poste Restante" in French. Simply have the sender write your name, "Poste Restante," and then the postal code and the name of the branch of a Parisian post office where you'd like to pick up your mail (see the website for codes and branch addresses), and then "Paris, France." You'll need to pick up your mail in person and have official ID (a passport or national identity card) at the ready. Most post offices are open Monday through Friday 8am to 7pm, Saturday 8am to noon.

Newspapers The major newspapers in France are national, even if they are published in Paris. *Le Monde* is the leading paper, and the easiest for foreigners to read; the weekend edition includes a small section in English, with articles from the *New York Times. Liberation* has a heavily left-wing slant, and *Le Figaro* leans a bit to the right. *Le Parisien* has more local, Paris-oriented news. Though it isn't as intellectual as the national papers, it has a lot of good information on what's going on in town. The **International Herald Tribune** is the leading English-language newspaper; owned by the **New York Times,** it focuses primarily on French and international news and seems to be geared towards businessmen these days. Many newsstands carry international papers, in particular, British papers are widely available. The Sunday **New York Times** can be found at a few English-language bookstores, but you'll pay through the nose for it (around 15€).

Pharmacies They are everywhere—you'll know you're in the vicinity when you see a green cross (like a plus sign) hanging in front of a store. The French consume the most medicine of all of Europe, and pharmacies are an essential element of life here. You'll need to go to a pharmacy to get just about any over-the-counter drug, including aspirin, and these are not self-serve affairs; you'll need to wait at the counter to be served (unless you're looking for cosmetics). Most are open Monday to Saturday from 9am to 7pm, and they're almost all closed on Sunday. If you are desperate, there should be a "pharmacie de garde" open on Sunday in each arrondissement. The trick is finding out which one is open, as they take turns; they should be listed in the newspaper "Le Parisien," or you can try the website www.paris.pref.gouv.fr/garde2007/index.html. There are a very few 24-hour pharmacies, including:

Pharmacie Européene (6 place de Clichy, 9th arrond.; ☎ 01 48 74 65 18; Métro: place de Clichy)

Grande Pharmacie Daumesnil (6 place Félix Eboué, 12th arrond.; ☎ 01 43 43 19 03; Métro: Reuilly-Diderot)

Pharmacie Les Champs (84 ave. des Champs Elysées, 8th arrond.; ☎ 01 45 62 02 41; Métro: George V)

Smoking At press time, strict nonsmoking laws were being put in place by the French government. Smoking will be prohibited in all indoor public places, but it is not yet clear if this will include all bars and restaurants, as the owners of small cafes and *tabacs* were up in arms about this possible blow to their income. Check to make sure before you light up.

Taxes The hefty 19.6% Value Added Tax (which goes by the initials TVA in France) is included in the price of everything you buy here, so you don't need to worry about extra charges at the cash register. This tax is also included in restaurant and hotel rates, though you will pay an additional (around 1€ per person, per night) tax at hotels.

Telephone Calling out from your hotel room can be a very expensive affair; you'll be better off buying a **prepaid phone card** *(carte téléphonique)* at a smokeshop, *tabac* (which can be in a bar—just look for the red diamond-shaped sign outside), or a newsstand. There are two kinds of cards: the kind that can only be used in a telephone booth and has a chip in it *(carte à puce),* and the kind that can be used from any phone and has a code *(carte à code).* The second is far more practical, as well as cheaper; you can usually get several hours worth of international calling on a 7.50€ card. Remember to ask for an international card and to mention which country it is you want to mainly be calling; you can always use these cards for calls within France as well. These cards are much, much cheaper than using your credit card or using one of the cards or codes that your home phone company (like AT&T) will try to sell you.

Telephone booths, if you can find them, don't take coins and require a special pre-paid card with a chip in it (see above) that you can find at any *tabac* or newsstand. You simply plug the card into the phone and dial; you'll see your time tick away on a small display. You can also use the carte à code in a phone booth (don't try to stick it in the slot, just dial your code!).

Most American or other non-GSM standard cell phones will not work very well in France, or if they do, they will cost you a fortune to use. If you have a quad or triband phone that can use GSM, you can buy a temporary SIM card from a mobile-phone store for about 10€, and then buy a pay-as-you-go phone recharge card. This still won't be cheap, but at least you'll be paying local rates, as opposed to outrageous international roaming charges. If you have a GSM phone, you shouldn't have too much trouble using it, though you'll probably pay higher charges for calls than you would if you were at home. Contact your cell phone service before leaving home to find out if your phone needs to be "unlocked," or you could find yourself phone-less overseas.

To **call home collect** (called PCV), dial 3006 and then the number that will be footing the bill (remember to precede the country code with "00"). For an **AT&T operator,** dial ☎ 08 00 99 00 11; for MCI Worldwide Access: ☎ 08 00 99 00 19).

Directory assistance has become a nightmare since the powers that be decided to privatize this service. There are at least a half a dozen different, unmemorizable six-digit numbers that you can call, each with different fees. You may as well just dial old reliable France Telecom, at 118 712, which charges 1.12€ for the privilege. It's an expensive operation; your best bet is ask for the **Yellow Pages** *(Pages Jaunes)* at your hotel, or to look up phone numbers on the Internet at www.pagesjaunes.fr.

Time France is 1 hour ahead of Greenwich Mean Time (GMT) in Britain and 6 hours ahead of Eastern Standard Time in the U.S. So when it's noon in Paris, it's 11am in London, and 6am in New York. France uses a 24-hour clock, so don't be surprised to see that a museum reopens at 14:00 (2pm).

Tipping Please see p. 338, earlier in this chapter.

Toilets There are free high-tech public toilets in cylindrical booths on the street. You go in, close the door, do your thing, close the door again, and the interior of the entire booth gets squirted with high pressure jets and disinfectant, which means the next person has a spotless toilet at their disposal. Sounds great, but I have to confess, I've never had the nerve to try one, due to a slight case of claustrophobia and fantasies that the door will get stuck and I'll be the one who gets squirted. Really, there's no danger here, but parents should accompany small children. Your other options are rather limited to toilets in large department stores, but if you aren't near one about the only thing you can do is go into a cafe and plead, or if you don't have the courage to do that, buy a coffee at the counter (where it's cheaper) and make use of the facilities.

Water Parisian water is safe to drink, but it's not particularly tasty. If you have a sensitive stomach, or just prefer to drink fresh tasting water, buy bottled water at a minimarket or supermarket—it's a fraction of the price you'll pay at a snack bar or drink stand.

13 A Closer Look

BEFORE THERE WAS PARIS, THERE WAS THE SEINE. MUCH WIDER THAN IT is today, the river looped and curved through the region, and at one point, split into two branches. One branch eventually dried up, leaving a wide band of marshlands to the north, the other, sprinkled with islands, would one day become the lifeline of the future French capital. At first sight, this swampy bog offered little indication that it had potential for urban grandeur. But it did have two things going for it: a river that led all the way to the Atlantic and those strategically placed islands, which offered both protection and shelter. The largest one, the core of what would one day become the Ile de la Cité, attracted the attention of a tribe of Celtic people called the Parisii, who fished and traded along its banks somewhere around the 3rd century B.C. Though they weren't the first Parisians (traces of human habitations have been found that date back to Neolithic times), they were the first to firmly implant themselves in the area, and they made ample use of the river not only as a source of food, but as a trade link. Their island had the good fortune of being on the "Pewter Route," a trade route that stretched from the British Isles to the Mediterranean. As a consequence, the Parisii's wealth was such that by the 1st century B.C., they were minting their own gold coins.

ROMAN RULE
(1ST CENTURY B.C.–2ND CENTURY A.D.)

There is no recorded history of Paris before the Romans showed up in 52 B.C., but when Caesar and his boys marched in, the Parisii numbered several thousand and the island bustled with activity. Soon thereafter, however, the Parisii's main activity would be trying to get rid of the Romans. Though they fought valiantly, after a ferocious battle they were massacred by Caesar's troops, and a new Roman town was built both on the island and on the Left Bank, on the slopes of the Montagne St-Genvieve (where the Panthéon, p. 183, now stands). The new town, for reasons that remain unclear, was baptized Lutécia, and ran along a ramrod-straight north-south axis; the line of this road survives in today's rue St-Jacques. (The Parisii would eventually get their due, however, as the city would be renamed Civitas Parisiorum in the 4th century, which eventually was whittled down to Paris.) Though there were only around 8,000 inhabitants, by the 2nd century the town boasted three Gallo-Roman baths (you can see the ruins of the largest of these at the corner of blvd. St-Michel and blvd. St-Germain) and a vast amphitheater (a piece of which can be seen at the Arènes de Lutèce, p. 186).

BARBARIAN INVASIONS
(3RD–5TH CENTURIES)

By the 3rd century, the city was subject to waves of barbarian invasions. Most of the population took refuge on the Ile de la Cité, which was then encircled by ramparts. Somewhere around this time, St-Denis was decapitated when he was martyred up on a nearby hill, which in time would be dubbed **Montmartre** (p. 245). Legend has it that the saint picked up his severed head and walked with it for several kilometers, preaching all the while; the basilica of St-Denis (just north of Paris) was built on the place where he finally dropped. Where the legend ends and the truth begins is unclear, but the event, which supposedly happened around 250, coincides with Christianity's first appearance on the Parisian scene. Another particularly pious Christian, a young nun named Geneviève, was credited with turning Atilla the Hun away from Paris in 451. Alerted that the barbarians were approaching, the citizenry was in a state of panic; Geneviève reassured them, telling them that God was with them and urging them to resist the invaders. In the end, the Huns didn't march on Paris, but on Orléans; the grateful population, convinced it was Geneviève's doing, made her into the city's patron saint. A church was raised in her honor on the hill that's now known as the Montagne-Ste-Geneviève; it was pulled down and replaced by a magnificent new one, commissioned by Louis XV in the 18th century, which was subsequently turned into a national mausoleum after the Revolution and renamed the **Panthéon** (p. 183).

MEROVINGIAN & CAROLINGIAN DYNASTIES
(6TH–10TH CENTURIES)

At the end of the 5th century, the Franks (a Germanic people) invaded and established the Merovingian dynasty of kings; the first, Clovis, made Paris the capital of his new kingdom in 508. The Merovingians were ardent Catholics; under their rule the city sprouted dozens of churches, convents, and monasteries. Childebert I, the son of Clovis, inaugurated a small basilica that would soon be dubbed St-Germain-des-Prés after the saint was buried there in 576. Over time, this church would grow into a powerful abbey and intellectual center that would dominate much of the Left Bank up until the Revolution. Even after the abbey was dismantled, and many of its buildings burned, the church lived on, as did the name of the neighborhood. Though the city enjoyed a certain amount of prosperity during this time, it was short-lived; the Merovingians, who were known as the "do-nothing" kings, were eventually toppled, and by the 8th century, a new dynasty, the Carolingians, had replaced them.

The most famous member of this clan was Charlemagne, who went on to conquer Italy and was crowned emperor by the Pope in 800. Arts and letters thrived during this period, and the city began to build up on the Right Bank, around the church of St-Gervais–St-Protais, and the Port du Grève, where the **Hôtel de Ville** (p. 182) now stands. Starting in the mid–9th century, the city was periodically ravaged by Normans and Vikings, who would sack Paris on their way to plundering Burgundy. The Normans were particularly persistent; after a barricade was erected on the Seine to keep their boats from passing in 885, they laid siege to the city for an entire year. It was only after King Charles the Simple signed a treaty in

911 giving the Normans Normandy that life returned to normal; but by then Paris was in ruins. The age of the Carolingians was drawing quickly to a close.

THE FOUNDING OF THE CAPETIAN DYNASTY (11TH CENTURY)

In 987, Hugues Capet, the Count of Paris, was crowned king of France; his direct descendents ruled the country for $3^1/_2$ centuries, and two branches of the Capetian dynasty, the Valois and Bourbons, would continue to rule (with a brief pause during the Revolution) until 1792. With the Capetians came stability, and Paris rebuilt and grew, particularly on the Ile de la Cité and the Right Bank. The Left Bank, flattened by the Normans, was left as it was; little by little it was covered with fields and vineyards. The 12th century was a period of economic growth—it saw the birth of **Les Halles** (p. 253), the city's sprawling central market, around which a new commercial quarter developed. In 1163, bishop Maurice de Sully decided that Paris deserved a new cathedral, and ground was broken on the **Cathédral de Notre-Dame de Paris** (p. 129); it took 200 years to finish, but it was, and remains, one of the world's most exquisite examples of medieval architecture.

It was around this time that that mushy, marshy strip of land on the Right Bank, known as the Marais (or swamp), was partially drained and carpeted with farms. Philippe Auguste, before taking off on a crusade, had a sturdy rampart built around the newly extended city limits; fragments of this wall can still be seen today (see "Walkabouts," p. 229). Philippe's grandson, Louis IX (St-Louis), added another architectural jewel to the cityscape: the **Sainte Chapelle** (p. 133), a small church whose upper-story walls are almost entirely made of brilliantly colored stained glass. Louis had it built to house a treasure he bought from the debt-ridden Byzantine emperor: Christ's crown of thorns and some fragments of the holy cross (the relics are now in Notre-Dame).

MEDIEVAL GLORY & GORE (12TH–14TH CENTURIES)

By the 12th century, Paris was coming into its own. The city boasted a population of around 200,000, much larger than other European capitals, as well as a burgeoning reputation as an economic as well as intellectual center. High-quality fabrics, leather goods, and metalwork were produced in the city, as well as art objects like sculptures, paintings, and illuminated manuscripts. The University of Paris was slowly coming into being, and colleges were popping up all over the left bank; in 1257, Robert de Sorbon established a small theological college that would eventually grow into the Sorbonne. The city seemed unstoppable.

But the 14th century, would, in fact, put an end to this fruitful period. When the last Capetian king, Charles IV, died in 1328, the succession to the throne was disputed, in part because the closest descendent was Edward III, king of England, who also presided over a chunk of southwestern France. This, and many other gripes exploded into the Hundred Years War, which devastated France for over a century. Expansion in Paris came to an abrupt halt, the endless wars and riots wore down the populace, and in 1348 the Black Plague killed tens of thousands. In the early 1400s Paris was hit by famine and a string of extremely cold winters:

between one disaster and another, the city lost about half of its population during this period. In 1420, the English occupied Paris; despite the efforts of Joan of Arc and Charles VII, who laid siege to the city in 1429, troops loyal to the Duke of Bedford (the English Regent) didn't leave until 1437. This same duke was responsible for having Joan burned at the stake in Rouen in 1431.

RENAISSANCE RENEWAL (16TH CENTURY)

Slowly, the city came to life again. The population increased, as did commercial and intellectual activity. The invention of the printing press spread new ideas all over Europe; the primary trend, Humanism, would find a home in Paris. Great thinkers were drawn to city's universities, such as Pic de la Mirandole, Erasmus, and John Calvin. More colleges emerged from the academic landscape: in 1530, François I established a school that would become the prestigious College de France, and in 1570 the Académie Française was founded by Charles IX. If the Renaissance made its mark on the intellectual life of the city, it had little impact on its architectural legacy. The Renaissance kings liked Paris but lived and did their building elsewhere. François I, the most construction-happy among them, was responsible for bringing some of the greatest masters of the Italian Renaissance, like Leonardo da Vinci and Benvenuto Cellini, to France, but their genius was mostly displayed in François' châteaux on the Loire and at **Fontainebleau** (p. 314), not in the capital. The king's primary contribution to the cityscape was the remodeling of the **Louvre** (p. 138) and construction of the **Hôtel de Ville** (p. 182), designed by the Italian architect Boccador. The latter building was unfortunately burned down in 1871 during the fall of the Paris Commune; the existing edifice is a fairly faithful copy erected in 1873. Two glorious churches, **St-Etienne du Mont** (p. 189), and **St-Eustache** (p. 186) were also built during this period; their decoration attests to the jubilant spirit of the times.

War interfered once again with the city's development in 1557 when the bloody struggle between the country's Protestants and Catholics morphed into the Wars of Religion. Even the marriage of the future king, Henri of Navarre, a Protestant, to Marguerite de Valois, a Catholic, did not diffuse the conflict: a week after their wedding, August 24, 1572, the bells of **St-Germain l'Auxerrois** (p. 187) signaled the beginning of the St-Bartholomew's Day massacre, which resulted in the deaths of between 2,000 and 4,000 Parisian Protestants. When in 1589, Henri was declared King of France (as Henri IV), Parisians would not let the Protestant monarch enter the city. After 4 month's of siege, during which the city was periodically bombarded, the starving citizens relented and in the end, to show his good will, the King converted, famously declaring that "Paris is worth a mass."

Henri IV lived on to be an enormously popular king, whose structural improvements left a lasting mark on the city. He was the force behind the **Pont Neuf** (p. 188), which straddles the Right and Left Banks, as well as the Ile de la Cité. To create the bridge, two small islets off the western tip of the Ile de la Cité were filled in and made part of the larger island; the tranquil **place Dauphine** (p. 235) was also created during this time. Henri also conceived the strikingly harmonious place Royale (now called place des Vosges, p. 147). The King would not live to see it finished; in 1610, when the royal carriage got stuck in a traffic jam on rue de la Ferronerie, he was stabbed by Ravaillac, a deranged Catholic who was convinced that Henri was waging war against the Pope.

THE AGE OF LOUIS XIV (17TH CENTURY)

There was a building frenzy amongst the aristocracy of the 17th century. Marie de Médicis built the Italian-style Palais du Luxembourg in 1615, around the same time that the **Marais** (p. 188) was inundated with splendid palaces and *hôtels particuliers,* or mansions. The new **Ile St-Louis** (p. 230), made from the joining of two previously uninhabited islets to the east of the Ile de la Cité, was filled with stately mansions that only the rich could afford. After Marguerite de Valois moved in to the neighborhood, the St-Germain quarter also became a place to see and be seen. Finally, in 1632 the powerful Cardinal Richelieu built a huge palace, now called the **Palais Royal** (p. 180), near the Louvre, which encouraged yet another new neighborhood to develop.

In 1643, a 5-year-old boy named Louis XIV acceded to the French throne, where he would stay for the next 72 years. One of the most influential figures in French history, Louis XIV's early years were spent in Paris, under the protection of his mother, Anne of Austria. It was not a happy time: the city was writhing under a nasty rebellion called La Fronde, instigated by cranky nobles trying to wrest control back from the powerful prime minister, Cardinal Mazarin, and the young monarch and his mother were chased from one royal residence to the next. When he grew up and things calmed down, he settled into the Louvre, commanding his team of architects, led by Le Vau, to finish up the Cour Carée and other unfinished parts of the palace. The spectacular colonnade on the eastern facade dates from this period. Louis eventually decided to build his own castle, however; one that was far enough from the noise and filth of the capital, and big enough to house his entire court—the better to keep a close eye on their political intrigues. The result was the **Château of Versailles** (p. 299), a testament to the genius of Le Vau, as well as master landscape architect André Le Nôtre.

Even if Louis XIV didn't live in the city, he certainly added to its architectural heritage. He was responsible for construction of **Les Invalides** (p. 155), a massive military hospital, as well as two grand squares, place des Victoires and place Louis-le-Grand, which today is known as **place Vendôme** (p. 149). Two gigantic entry-ways, celebrating Louis' military victories, were built at the city gates; the Porte St-Denis and the Porte St-Martin. Both of these triumphal archways still hover over parts of the 10th arrondissement, looking somewhat out of place in this working-class district.

FROM ENLIGHTENMENT TO REVOLUTION

Paris continued to grow, and the population density continued to increase. At the turn of the 18th century, there were 500,000 Parisians crammed into a vast network of narrow, mostly unpaved streets. Sewers were nonexistent and clean drinking water a luxury. While life in the rarified atmosphere of the aristocratic salons of the Marais was brimming with art, literature, and deep thought, down on the ground it was filled with misery. Poverty and want were the constant companions of the vast majority of Parisians. On an intellectual level, the city was soaring— under the reign of Louis XV, Paris became a standard-bearer for the Enlightenment, a school of thought that championed reason and logic and helped construct the intellectual framework of both the American and French Revolutions. Salons—regular meetings of artists and thinkers in aristocratic homes—flourished, as did cafes; drawn in by the wildly popular new drink called coffee, they were the ideal meeting place for philosophers, writers, and artists, as well as a new breed of politicians with some revolutionary ideas. Political debates were particularly passionate in the cafes in the galleries of the **Palais Royal** (p. 180), which had been filled with shops and opened to the public by Duke Louis Philippe d'Orléans.

Meanwhile, back in Versailles, the court of Louis XVI seemed to be utterly oblivious of the mounting discontent in the capital. As the price of bread skyrocketed and more and more Parisians found themselves on the street (there were over 100,000 homeless people in the city in 1789, out of an overall population of between 600,000 and 700,000), the disconnect between the aristocracy and the common man threatened to rupture into a bloody conflict. Amazingly, Louis XVI and his wife Marie Antoinette continued to live their lives as if the civil unrest in the capital didn't concern them. A financial crisis in the royal treasury prompted a meeting of the Estates-General in Versailles in May, 1789, a representative body that had not been convened since 1616. The assembly began demanding a more democratic system of taxation, and better representation of the Third Estate (the people). When the King tried to close down the proceedings, the group, which had renamed itself the National Assembly, dug in its heels and wrote a constitution. The royals kept dithering and trying to break up the assembly, until finally, the Revolution erupted on July 14, 1789, when an angry mob stormed the Bastille prison. There were only 7 prisoners in the fortress, but no matter—the genie was out of the bottle, and the pent-up anger of the populace was unleashed.

Not only was the royal family imprisoned and beheaded, but after the initial euphoria faded and the high ideals were set down on paper, the leaders of the Revolution began to squabble between themselves, and the factional skirmishes became increasingly deadly. The events of the Revolution are too many to relate here, but within a few years, not only were aristocrats being sent off to the guillotine, but just about anyone who disagreed with the ruling powers, including many of the leaders who wrote the rules. Finally, Robespierre, who directed the most bloody phase of the Revolution, known as "the Terror," had his turn at the guillotine, and a new government was set up. Called the Directory, this unsuccessful attempt at representational government met its end when a general named Napoleon Bonaparte staged a coup in 1799.

THE EMPIRE

Under Napoleon, Paris slowly put itself back together. The economy restarted, and the Emperor turned his attentions to upgrading the city's infrastructure, including building bridges (**Pont St-Louis, Pont des Arts, Pont d'Iéna,** and **Pont d'Austerlitz**), improving access to water (the Canal de l'Ourcq), and creating new cemeteries, like **Père Lachaise** (p. 152) because the old ones were so crowded that they had become public health hazards. Napoleon was also responsible for the rue de Rivoli, a wide east-west boulevard that was the first of several that would be laid down later on in the 19th century. The collection of the **Louvre** was greatly enhanced by all the booty the Emperor acquired during his many military campaigns. Napoleon's love of war would eventually be his undoing; after his defeat by the English at Waterloo he was exiled to the island of Ste-Helena, where he died in

1821. Paris sports some huge monuments to his memory—in particular, the **Arc de Triomphe** (p. 131), which honors the Imperial Army.

THE RESTORATION & URBAN RENEWAL

Incredibly, after all the blood that was spilled in the name of the Republic, Louis XVI's brother (Louis XVIII) became King of France in 1814. What's more, another brother, Charles X, became king after Louis XVIII's death. What both brothers had in common is that they tried to bring back the old days of absolute monarchy, while the citizenry had become accustomed to the reforms of the Revolution and the relatively benign rule of Napoleon. This, coupled with the continuing poverty of many Parisians resulted in two serious uprisings, *"Les Trois Glorieuses,"* the three "glorious" days in July of 1830, and the Revolution of 1848. In fact, it is these two uprisings, and not the Revolution itself, that are honored on the column in the **place de la Bastille** (p. 182), the site of the infamous prison. After Charles, a republic was declared, and Napoleon's nephew, Louis-Napoleon, ran for and won the presidency. He liked being president so much that he didn't want to give up power at the end of his term, so he staged a coup and declared the birth of the Second Empire, calling himself Napoleon III.

Under Charles X, the unhygienic state of the city center started to cause serious alarm, particularly after a cholera epidemic in 1832 devastated the population. Anyone who could was fleeing to the outer limits of the city, away from the insalubrious and overcrowded poor quarters where the filthy streets were often completely clogged with traffic. City administrators began to draft plans for new boulevards, in particular the prefect, Rambuteau, who went ahead and started laying down wide boulevards, like the one named after him.

But it was Napoleon III who really changed the face of Paris, when he gave urban planner Baron Haussmann free rein to "modernize" the city. Not only did Haussmann lay down wide boulevards that eased congestion and opened up vistas, he cleverly arranged them so that if ever there was yet another popular uprising, they would facilitate military maneuvers and make it tough for citizens to set up barricades. Over half of the city was ripped up and rebuilt; Haussmann instituted strict regulations for the height of the new buildings and the style of their facades. The result was the elegant buildings and boulevards you see today. On the plus side, the city finally got a decent sewage system and water access, and the squalid slums were knocked down. Several parks were created, such as **Buttes Chaumont** (p. 217) and the **Bois de Boulogne** (p. 219) as well as grand plazas like the **place de la République** and **place du Trocadéro.** On the other hand, the character of the city was completely changed, and much of its social fabric was pulled down with the houses. Working-class Paris has been slowly disappearing ever since.

FROM THE COMMUNE TO THE BELLE EPOQUE

The boulevards were put to the test during the Paris Commune of 1870, a brief, but bloody episode that was yet another attempt of the French people to construct a democratic republic. The boulevards did their job: the rebellion was crushed and at least 20,000 communards were executed. When the smoke cleared, a new government was formed, and to everyone's surprise it was a republic. The National Assembly had intended to form a constitutional monarchy, but the heir to the throne had no interest in the word "constitutional." As a stop-gap measure, a temporary republic was set up—little did anyone know that it would last for 60 years.

There must have been an audible sigh of relief from Parisians, who would finally enjoy a little peace and harmony—or at least enough of a break from war and woe to have a good time. And so they did. During the "Belle Epoque," the years at the end of the 19th century and the beginning of the 20th, the arts bloomed in Paris. Ground-breaking art expositions introducing new movements like Impressionism (around 1874) and Fauvism (around 1905) changed people's ways of seeing painting. Up in Montmartre, an entire colony of artists and writers (Picasso, Braque, Apollonaire, and others) were filling cafes and cabarets in their off hours. The Lumière brothers and Léon Gaumont showed their newly hatched films in the city's first movie theaters. The city hosted a number of World's Fairs including that of 1889, which created the **Eiffel Tower** (p. 128), and 1900, which left behind the **Pont Alexandre III bridge,** as well as the **Grand and Petit Palais** (p. 170 and 168). Another great moment in 1900 was the inauguration of the Paris Métro's first underground line.

THE WORLD WARS

The fun came to an abrupt halt in 1914 with the outbreak of World War I, which killed 8.4 million Frenchmen. Calling all Parisians to arms, General Galiéni and his troops fought off the approaching German army (the Battle of the Marne) and saved Paris from occupation. The city did get bombarded however; on Good Friday, 1918, the church of **St-Gervais–St-Protais** took a direct hit and over 100 people died. The city rebounded after the war, both economically and culturally, especially during the 1920s, "*Les Années Folles*" (The Crazy Years). Paris became a magnet for artists and writers from all over. Americans, in particular, came in droves—F. Scott Fitzgerald, Henry Miller, Ernest Hemingway, and Gertrude Stein were some of the better-known names. They and other European expats like Marc Chagall, James Joyce, and George Orwell gathered in **Montparnasse** cafes like **Le Dôme, Le Select,** and **La Coupole.**

The 1930s brought economic depression and social unrest—a dreary backdrop for the approaching war. The Germans were re-arming, and Hitler was rising to power; in May 1940 Germany invaded the Netherlands, Luxembourg, and Belgium and broke through France's defensive Maginot line. The Germans occupied Paris on June 14, and for 4 years the city would know hunger, curfews, and suspicion. The Vichy government, led by Marchal Pétain, in theory governed unoccupied France, but in fact, collaborated with the Germans. One of the darkest moments of the occupation was in July of 1942, when for 2 days the French police rounded up 13,152 Parisian Jews, including 4,115 children, and parked them in a velodrome before sending them off to Auschwitz; only 30 survived. General Charles de Gaulle became the leader of the Free French and organizer of the Resistance; after the Allies landed in Normandy in 1944, Paris was liberated and de Gaulle victoriously strode down the **Champs Elysées** before a wildly cheering crowd. He would later become president of the country (1958–1969).

POST-WAR PARIS

Writers and artists filtered back to the cafes once the war was over (some had never left), and the **Café de Flore** (p. 121) and **Les Deux Magots** (p. 121) were headquarters for existential all-stars like Jean-Paul Sartre and Simone de Beauvoir. But the late 1940s was also the beginning of the end of French colonial rule, which was punctuated by violent clashes, including a revolt in Madagascar and a war in Indochina that would eventually entangle the United States. In North Africa, Morocco and Tunisia won their independence relatively peacefully, but France would not let go of Algeria without a long and bloody fight, with repercussions that are still being felt today. The war in Algeria led to the collapse of the French government; de Gaulle was asked to start a new one in 1958. Thousands of Algerian refugees flooded France, with many settling in the Paris region; Algeria finally gained its independence in 1962.

The writer André Malraux was de Gaulle's minister of cultural affairs from 1958 to 1969 and was responsible for protecting and restoring many endangered historic districts like the Marais. Elsewhere, modern architects were putting their own questionable stamp on the city, like the doughnut shaped **Maison de Radio France** in the 16th arrondissement, and the vaguely "Y"-shaped Maison de UNESCO in the 15th. The late 1960s also marked Paris in less concrete ways. In May 1968, students, hoping to reform the university system, joined a general workers strike that was in the process of paralyzing the nation. The police invaded **La Sorbonne** to calm the protests, and more students and sympathizers took to the streets. The confrontations became violent, with students attacking police with cobblestones—**boulevard St-Michel** was subsequently paved with asphalt. This was a period of profound social change; those who participated still proudly refer to themselves as *soixante-huitards* (68ers).

The 1970s was a period of architectural awkwardness—horrified by the idea of becoming a "museum city," then-president Georges Pompidou decided to modernize. One of his ideas that, thankfully, never came to fruition was to pave over the Canal St-Martin to make way for a freeway that would cut through the center of the city. The dismal **Tour Montparnasse** dates from this period, as does the destruction of the old Les Halles marketplace, which was replaced with an unpleasant underground shopping mall (**Forum des Halles**). Pompidou's one "success" is the nearby **Centre Pompidou** (p. 150), whose strange, inside-out design provoked howls of outrage when it was built but now has been accepted as part of the Parisian landscape. When François Mitterrand became president in 1981, he too wanted to leave an architectural legacy, and the list of his grands projets ("big projects") is lengthy. Fortunately, most were considerably more palatable than his predecessor's. It is to Mitterrand that we owe the **Musée d'Orsay,** the **pyramid** (and underground shopping complex) at the Louvre, and the ultramodern **Bibliothèque National François Mitterrand,** as well as the **Institute du Monde Arabe** (p. 156) and the **Opéra Bastille** (p. 278), among other projects. By the time Jacques Chirac became president, there was nothing left to build—though he was the force behind the excellent new **Musée du Quai Branly** (p. 147), which opened in 2006.

In the last decade or so, life has been relatively calm in Paris, with the notable exception of the terrorist attacks on Métro stations in 1995, a year that also brought paralyzing transportation strikes. Tourism has become one of the city's major sources of wealth—the attacks on the World Trade Center in 2001 and the subsequent reticence of travelers, particularly Americans (the city's most frequent visitors), to take trips overseas was a severe blow to the industry. Slowly but surely—to the extreme relief of hotel and restaurant owners—tourists have been coming back, and even the painfully high dollar/euro exchange rate has not kept visitors from continuing their on-going love-affair with the city. Paris has been looking slicker and cleaner in the last few years; renovation of historic buildings is ongoing, and a vigorous anti-dog doo campaign has even made inroads on cleaning up the notoriously poopy sidewalks. This cautious sense of optimism (Parisians are always cautious about being optimistic—excessive displays of enthusiasm make them nervous) reached a peak in 2005, when all signs pointed to Paris winning the bid for the 2012 Olympics. City administrators were all set to pop the corks on hundreds of champagne bottles, when the bad news came that London won the prize. Perhaps they were wise to be cautious after all.

Though many were disappointed, life has gone on and the city has continued to evolve, sometimes in surprising ways. While "cycling" and "Paris" are not words you would usually associate, the advent of the **Velib' bike program** in 2007 (p. 12) is slowly transforming the city into a bike-friendly place. Mayor Bertrand Delanoë, who backed the program, has also pushed through other "green" measures, like bus lanes and bike paths, which may have snarled traffic, but definitely cut down the duration of your average bus trip. Elected in 2007, the new French President Nicolas Sarkozy has yet to make his mark on the capital—though his energetic love life has definitely made a splash in the local papers and his new wife's (ex-model Carla Bruni) fashion sense has impacted the wardrobe of many a Parisienne.

If Paris has lost some of its former glory, if it is no longer at the forefront of culture and the arts as it was back in the days before World War II, it is certainly none the worse for wear; it has managed to carefully conserve its architectural heritage while making a serious effort to enter the modern world. Although many complain that the city has turned into a museum, there is ample evidence to the contrary; Paris is, after all, the capital of France, one of the major players in the European Union, and a certain dynamism comes with the territory, even if it is framed in Belle Epoque swirls and Mansart roofs. And maybe it is exactly that gentle aesthetic that makes the city a one-of-a-kind. Even if Paris does not run at the same lighting speed as say, New York, or Tokyo, it is undoubtedly one of the great capitals of the world. It has managed to stay that way without entirely giving up one of its most valuable assets—a unique way of life, rooted in a history that stretches back centuries. It is rare in today's turbulent world to find a city that so harmoniously mixes tradition and modernity, without enslaving itself to either one or the other.

If the pulse of life in the capital ticks faster than it once did, it still ticks slow enough that Parisians still take time to eat their lunch or go to the park for a Sunday stroll. It still allows for aimless intellectual discussions in cafes, or just rooting for the home team at a soccer game. And it still beats hard enough to produce excellent dance and theater productions that don't have to rely on box office revenues for their future, and contemporary and classic music festivals that are world renowned. As Humphrey Bogart put it in the film *Casablanca*, "we'll always have Paris." Heaven willing, we always will.

14 French Words & Phrases

IT IS OFTEN AMAZING HOW A WORD OR TWO OF HALTING FRENCH WILL change your hosts' disposition in their home country. At the very least, try to learn a few numbers, basic greetings, and—above all—the life-raft phrase, *Parlez-vous anglais?* (Do you speak English?). As it turns out, many people do speak passable English and will use it liberally if you demonstrate the basic courtesy of greeting them in their language. Go out, try our glossary, and don't be bashful. *Bonne chance!*

THE BASIC COURTESIES

ENGLISH	FRENCH	PRONUNCIATION
Yes/No	**Oui/Non**	Wee/Noh
Okay	**D'accord**	*Dah*-core
Please	**S'il vous plaît**	Seel voo *play*
Thank you	**Merci**	*Mair*-see
You're welcome	**De rien**	Duh ree-*ehn*
Hello (during daylight)	**Bonjour**	Bohn-*jhoor*
Good evening	**Bonsoir**	Bohn-*swahr*
Goodbye	**Au revoir**	O ruh-*vwahr*
What's your name?	**Comment vous appellez-vous?**	Kuh-*mahn* voo za-pell-ay-*voo*?
My name is	**Je m'appelle**	*Jhuh* ma-pell
How are you?	**Comment allez-vous?**	Kuh-*mahn* tahl-ay-voo?
So-so	**Comme ci, comme ça**	Kum-*see*, kum-*sah*
I'm sorry/excuse me	**Pardon**	Pahr-*dohn*

GETTING AROUND & STREET SMARTS

ENGLISH	FRENCH	PRONUNCIATION
Do you speak English?	**Parlez-vous anglais?**	Par-lay-voo zahn-*glay*?
I don't speak French	**Je ne parle pas français**	Jhuh ne parl pah frahn-*say*
I don't understand	**Je ne comprends pas**	Jhuh ne kohm-*prahn* pah
Could you speak more loudly/more slowly?	**Pouvez-vous parler plus fort/plus lentement?**	Poo-*vay* voo par-lay ploo for/ploo lan-te-*ment*?
What is it?	**Qu'est-ce que c'est?**	Kess kuh *say*?
What time is it?	**Qu'elle heure est-il?**	Kel uhr eh-*teel*?
What?	**Quoi?**	Kwah?
How? or What did	**Comment?**	Ko-*mahn*? you say?
When?	**Quand?**	Kahn?
Where is?	**Où est?**	Ooh eh?

ENGLISH	FRENCH	PRONUNCIATION
Who?	**Qui?**	Kee?
Why?	**Pourquoi?**	Poor-*kwah*?
here/there	**ici/là**	ee-*see*/lah
left/right	**à gauche/à droite**	a goash/a drwaht
straight ahead	**tout droit**	too drwah
Fill the tank	**Le plein,**	Luh plan,
(of a car), please	**s'il vous plaît**	seel-voo-play
I want to get off at	**Je voudrais descendre à**	Jhe voo-*dray* day-son drah-ah
airport	**l'aéroport**	lair-o-*por*
bank	**la banque**	lah bahnk
bridge	**le pont**	luh pohn
bus station	**la gare routière**	lah gar roo-tee-*air*
bus stop	**l'arrêt de bus**	lah-*ray* duh boohss
by means of a car	**en voiture**	ahn vwa-*toor*
cashier	**la caisse**	lah *kess*
cathedral	**la cathédrale**	lah ka-tay-*dral*
church	**l'église**	lay-*gleez*
driver's license	**permis de conduire**	per-*mee* duh con-*dweer*
elevator	**l'ascenseur**	lah-sahn-*seuhr*
entrance (to a	**une porte**	ewn port building or a city)
exit (from a building	**une sortie**	ewn sor-*tee*
or a freeway)		
gasoline	**du pétrol/de l'essence**	duh pay-*trol*/de lay-*sahns*
hospital	**l'hôpital**	low-pee-*tahl*
luggage storage	**la consigne**	lah kohn-*seen*-yuh
museum	**le musée**	luh mew-*zay*
no smoking	**défense de fumer**	day-*fahns* de fu-may
one-day pass	**ticket journalier**	tee-kay jhoor-nall-ee-*ay*
one-way ticket	**aller simple**	ah-*lay* sam-pluh
police	**la police**	lah po-lees
round-trip ticket	**aller-retour**	ah-lay re-*toor*
second floor	**premier étage**	prem-ee-*ehr* ay-*taj*
slow down	**ralentir**	rah-lahn-*teer*
store	**le magasin**	luh ma-ga-*zehn*
street	**rue**	roo
ticket	**un billet**	uh *bee*-yay
toilets	**les toilettes/les WC**	lay twa-*lets*/les vay-*say*

NECESSITIES

ENGLISH	FRENCH	PRONUNCIATION
I'd like	**Je voudrais**	Jhe voo-*dray*
a room	**une chambre**	ewn *shahm*-bruh
the key	**la clé (la clef)**	la clay
How much does	**C'est combien?/**	Say comb-bee-*ehn*?/
it cost?	**Ça coûte combien?**	Sah coot comb-bee-*ehn*?
That's expensive	**C'est cher/chère**	Say share

ENGLISH	FRENCH	PRONUNCIATION
Do you take	**Est-ce que vous**	Es-kuh voo
credit cards?	**acceptez les cartes**	zaksep-*tay* lay kart
	de credit?	duh creh-*dee*?
I'd like to buy	**Je voudrais acheter**	Jhe voo-dray ahsh-*tay*
aspirin	**des aspirines/**	deyz ahs-peer-*een*/
	des aspros	deyz ahs-*proh*
condoms	**des préservatifs**	day pray-ser-va-*teef*
dress	**une robe**	ewn robe
gift	**un cadeau**	uh kah-*doe*
hat	**un chapeau**	uh shah-*poh*
map of the city	**un plan de ville**	uh plahn de *veel*
newspaper	**un journal**	uh zhoor-*nahl*
phone card	**une carte téléphonique**	ewn cart tay-lay-fone-*eek*
postcard	**une carte postale**	ewn carte pos-*tahl*
purse	**un sac**	uh sahk
road map	**une carte routière**	ewn cart roo-tee-*air*
shoes	**des chaussures**	day show-*suhr*
soap	**du savon**	dew sah-*vohn*
stamp	**un timbre**	uh *tam*-bruh

NUMBERS & ORDINALS

ENGLISH	FRENCH	PRONUNCIATION
zero	**zéro**	*zare*-oh
one	**un**	oon
two	**deux**	duh
three	**trois**	twah
four	**quatre**	kaht-ruh
five	**cinq**	sank
six	**six**	seess
seven	**sept**	set
eight	**huit**	wheat
nine	**neuf**	noof
ten	**dix**	deess
eleven	**onze**	ohnz
twelve	**douze**	dooz
thirteen	**treize**	trehz
fourteen	**quatorze**	kah-*torz*
fifteen	**quinze**	kanz
sixteen	**seize**	sez
seventeen	**dix-sept**	deez-*set*
eighteen	**dix-huit**	deez-*wheat*
nineteen	**dix-neuf**	deez-*noof*
twenty	**vingt**	vehn
thirty	**trente**	trahnt
forty	**quarante**	ka-*rahnt*
fifty	**cinquante**	sang-kahnt

ENGLISH	FRENCH	PRONUNCIATION
one hundred	**cent**	sahn
one thousand	**mille**	meel
first	**premier**	preh-mee-ay
second	**deuxième**	*duhz*-zee-em
third	**troisième**	*twa*-zee-em
fourth	**quatrième**	*kaht*-ree-em
fifth	**cinquième**	sank-ee-em
sixth	**sixième**	*sees*-ee-em
seventh	**septième**	*set*-ee-em
eighth	**huitième**	*wheat*-ee-em
ninth	**neuvième**	*neuv*-ee-em
tenth	**dixième**	*dees*-ee-em

Index

See also Accommodations and Restaurant indexes, below.

GENERAL INDEX